THIRD EDITION

MANAGING SPORT FACILITIES

Gil Fried, JD
University of New Haven

Human Kinetics

Library of Congress Cataloging-in-Publication Data

Fried, Gil, 1965- author.
Managing sport facilities / Gil Fried. -- Third edition.
p. ; cm.
Includes bibliographical references and index.
I. Title.
[DNLM: 1. Fitness Centers--organization & administration. 2. Health Facility Administration--methods. QT 256]
GV401
725'.8043--dc23

2014023074

ISBN: 978-1-4504-6811-4 (print)

The web addresses cited in this text were current as of January 2015, unless otherwise noted.

Acquisitions Editor: Myles Schrag
Developmental Editor: Judy Park
Managing Editor: Anne E. Mrozek
Copyeditor: Amanda M. Eastin-Allen
Indexer: Susan Danzi Hernandez
Permissions Manager: Dalene Reeder
Graphic Designer: Joe Buck
Cover Designer: Keith Blomberg
Photograph (cover): AP Photo/Paul Spinelli
Photographs (interior): © Gil Fried, unless otherwise noted.
Photo Asset Manager: Laura Fitch
Photo Production Manager: Jason Allen
Art Manager: Kelly Hendren
Associate Art Manager: Alan L. Wilborn
Illustrations: ©Human Kinetics, unless otherwise noted.
Printer: Edwards Brothers Malloy

Printed in the United States of America

10 9 8 7 6 5 4 3 2 1

The paper in this book is certified under a sustainable forestry program.

Human Kinetics
Website: www.HumanKinetics.com

United States: Human Kinetics
P.O. Box 5076
Champaign, IL 61825-5076
800-747-4457
e-mail: humank@hkusa.com

Canada: Human Kinetics
475 Devonshire Road Unit 100
Windsor, ON N8Y 2L5
800-465-7301 (in Canada only)
e-mail: info@hkcanada.com

Europe: Human Kinetics
107 Bradford Road
Stanningley
Leeds LS28 6AT, United Kingdom
+44 (0) 113 255 5665
e-mail: hk@hkeurope.com

Australia: Human Kinetics
57A Price Avenue
Lower Mitcham, South Australia 5062
08 8372 0999
e-mail: info@hkaustralia.com

New Zealand: Human Kinetics
P.O. Box 80
Torrens Park, South Australia 5062
0800 222 062
e-mail: info@hknewzealand.com

E6112

To all the men and women who keep our public assembly facilities running. They are the unsung heroes who keep facilities safe and ensure an enjoyable experience for everyone involved.

Contents

Preface

Almost all of us have fond memories of a sport-related experience. The experience might entail our first game as a spectator, our first request for a ballplayer's autograph, or even eating our first hot dog at the ballpark. We may look back at having wonderful seats to watch a game, catching a foul ball in the stands, or attending a game with a special promotional giveaway. Whatever the experience, more than likely a sport facility was involved.

For some people, attending an event at a sport facility that was in the past only an image on the television screen might feel similar to a religious experience. Many travelers put visiting a famous sport facility on the top of their to-do list, and many sport facilities offer tours where loyal fans can step foot on the field or visit the locker room used by their idols. Others might focus on how to navigate through crowds and traffic in the shortest possible amount of time or think about the sights, sounds, and smells that made an event memorable. For smaller facilities such as health clubs, people might think about convenience and the breadth of services available. For others, attending a favorite fitness facility embodies the quest for excellence or athletic glory. Regardless of the reason, sport facilities play an important role in people's lives.

The facility experience is vastly different for those managing sport facilities. Very few people realize what an enormous undertaking it is to develop and operate these facilities. For example, how much toilet paper needs to be ordered for 1,000 bathroom stalls? How many hot dogs need to be ordered if 70,000 fans will be attending a game? What happens when the facility's water pressure is interrupted? What if a power outage occurs during a sporting event, as happened during the 2013 Super Bowl? What if a storm or environmental disaster damages or destroys the playing field? How do you promote a rock concert one day and a monster truck pull the next? How do you change over a facility from an ice hockey surface to a basketball surface in just 3 hours without ruining the ice? How do you handle disorderly or rowdy fans and customers? How do you hire and manage a part-time staff of possibly 600 ushers, concessionaires, ticket takers, and security personnel? What happens when a facility runs into financial hardships? These are just some of the questions that a facility manager faces on a daily basis.

THE PURPOSE OF THIS BOOK

This book addresses how to effectively manage a sport facility. Although the text focuses on sport facilities, much of the subject matter is also applicable to any number of public assembly facilities, including music theaters, auditoriums, convention centers, and high school and college arenas and stadiums. Public facilities can also include bowling alleys, health clubs, sportsplexes, park and recreation facilities, and numerous other natural and man-made environments.

Written for students in sport and facility management (FM) as well as professionals already working in the field, the text provides a comprehensive knowledge base. An introductory-level discussion is provided for those who have never before studied sport FM. Thus, after reading this book, beginning students will have the knowledge base necessary for applying the fundamental skills in FM. In-depth explanation, real-world examples, and detailed assessment of various FM issues are also provided to expand understanding and spur knowledge application for industry professionals. Some of the FM concerns discussed in this text include preventive maintenance, facility planning, event administration, box office management, house and grounds management, systems management, marketing, finance, and personnel administration. Readers will get a feel for how complicated the field is and why, even though facility managers work very long hours, it is one of the most enjoyable jobs in the sport—and any other—industry.

Every facility (and its management structure) is different. Some facilities rely on an owner to make all decisions, from designing the building and obtaining funds to removing the trash every day. In other facilities, primarily larger ones, multiple people serve in different capacities: A financial consultant might develop the funding strategy, a construction manager might work during construction, a facility manager might handle bookings, and an outside contracting company might provide security and concession services.

Most other FM texts focus solely on safety, marketing, construction, or event management. They fail to combine these important disciplines into one comprehensive text and rarely cover important topics such as the history of sport facilities, the types of systems within a building, and the ways in which buildings are actually built and managed. This text covers sport FM in a comprehensive manner that includes both educational perspectives through extensive research and professional industry insight on what happens behind the scenes at sport facilities.

Over the past several years, the push to build large, high-tech sport facilities that are more complex to operate and manage than those in the past has highlighted the need for a comprehensive sport FM text. Similarly, fitness, recreation, and sport facilities have fueled significant career opportunities that present unique issues such as how to develop a facility business plan, which finance vehicle is most effective for raising necessary capital, how to control costs through preventive maintenance, how to schedule and book event dates, how to make facilities as environmentally friendly as possible, and how to market luxury and premium seating to maximize revenue. After reading this text, current or future sport facility managers will be in a better position to respond effectively to new challenges.

HOW THIS TEXT IS ORGANIZED

After presenting an overview of sport facilities through the ages, the text focuses on what is involved in FM and also on the manager's primary responsibility: getting employees at the facility to accomplish their jobs. The text walks the reader through the basics of developing and running a facility. It then turns to issues involved in running programs and managing personnel. Finally, it examines what is required to produce a high-quality event at a sport facility.

The text is organized into five parts. Part I introduces the sport facility industry. It provides a brief historical perspective that highlights how sport facilities have evolved over the years. It then addresses the role of facility managers and the various concerns they face. Because facility managers must accomplish goals primarily through employees, the last component of Part I deals with the art of effective managerial communication and leadership.

Part II analyzes the complex process of building and financing a facility and discusses such topics as the validity of feasibility studies, how to select a site, and how to handle environmental impact issues. Part II continues with an in-depth analysis of the initial process of planning a facility, a discussion of how to obtain financial and political support, and an examination of the various types of facilities and fields that can be built. It then highlights the process of building a facility and includes an analysis of how to develop a site plan that maximizes the available resources. Part II ends with a thorough analysis of the construction process.

After a facility is built, it has to be operated. Part III covers the operations side—both internal and external—of facilities and such topics as maintenance and housekeeping. Part III covers systems management, emphasizing major systems such as facility infrastructure; heating, ventilation, and air conditioning; energy management; waste management; and all exterior systems. Most FM texts overlook these topics; however, this text gives special attention to some of the more intricate systems that are essential to sport, such as building and maintaining a grass field. Part III ends with a review of green strategies that sport facilities are undertaking.

Part IV looks at some of the critical administrative areas that a facility manager supervises, such as marketing, finance, legal issues, risk management, and how a facility is actually run. Managers need to know how to market their facility effectively, comply with a budget, meet legal obligations, and manage the entire facility to meet the desired outcomes set forth in the facility's mission or vision statement. Facility managers have significant responsibilities and this section covers some of those key areas by which they will be judged.

Part V includes step-by-step details on how to attract and put on events and examines the process of actually running a sport facility during these events. It is not just the pre-event preparation as management needs to be active during and after an event as well.

HOW TO USE THIS TEXT

The text is organized to clearly convey concepts using several special elements. Each chapter includes a list of specific objectives, a chapter overview, a chapter summary, and discussion questions and activities. Also included are Facility Focus sections, which provide the facts about particular facilities and discuss their strategies for success, and Behind the Scenes sections, which present unique concerns and strategies that can make a facility manager more successful. All of these elements weave the material into a full, coherent picture of facility management.

UPDATES TO THIS EDITION

I was very touched by the support I received after writing the first two editions of this text. Possibly the best response was from facility managers themselves, who told me that the text was the first book they had read that captured the essence of what it means to be a facility manager. When asked how I could improve on a text used at more than 100 universities and translated into several languages, I had to think outside the proverbial box. When I teach sport FM, I normally teach half the class from the textbook and the remainder of class time is spent working on projects, listening to guest speakers, and visiting facilities. Because it is impossible to visit a facility in a textbook, I did the next best thing by bringing the facilities to the reader. The Facility Focus sections have been expanded to include several major facilities that have been built since the second edition of this text, such as the new Yankee Stadium and AT&T Stadium. Also, each chapter begins with an introduction from an industry executive that highlights how the material in the chapter fits into what he or she does on a daily basis. These introductions, which include a sport architect discussing how he plans to build a facility and a major facility executive explaining how she motivates her employees, highlight the value of the text for those working in the industry. They also encourage the reader to think about how theory can be applied in the workplace. Finally, I am especially happy about the addition of a chapter on green sport facilities. Although the trend for greening sport facilities has been going on for around 10 years, it has picked up steam over the past 4 or 5 years and merits its own chapter.

One of the key benefits of this third edition are the instructor ancillaries presented by both the author and publisher. The new versions of these ancillary materials, available to all textbook adopters, are enhanced with PowerPoint slides for each chapter; a 20-minute video highlighting the building of a sport facility; video interviews with employees and senior executives at major sport facilities; an Instructor Guide that provides innovative teaching options; and a large test bank of true-or-false, multiple-choice, and essay exam questions. These ancillary materials are available at www.HumanKinetics.com/ManagingSportFacilities.

eBook
available at
HumanKinetics.com

NOTE TO STUDENTS

In the fall of 2010, I started my undergraduate studies at the University of New Haven. As classes began, I quickly learned that there is much to the sport industry that most fans never see or experience. I was introduced to many areas in the sport industry, but the one that stood out to me was facility management.

In my sophomore year I enrolled in the sport facility management course and Professor Fried's sport law course. Taking both of these courses simultaneously truly opened my eyes to what it takes to run a facility. We were asked questions such as how to design a state-of-the-art stadium while keeping potential liabilities

Photo courtesy of Kaitlyn Ragaisis

in mind and how to maintain crowd control while still bringing in thousands of spectators. These questions allowed us to see how much work is involved in running an event and maintaining sport facilities.

Every semester, Professor Fried posts internships and employment opportunities for students. One day I noticed a posting for an operations intern at Rentschler Field. Home to the University of Connecticut football program, the stadium was built in 2003 and seats 30,000 spectators. Located just outside of Hartford, Connecticut, it's a popular location for both sporting and entertainment events year round. I secured the internship with them for the summer of 2012 and quickly learned how much planning preparing the facility for events requires. My days were long, but they were full of tasks that included stadium maintenance, event setup, crowd management, and more. As my internship progressed, I enhanced my leadership, communication, and organizational skills while showing my determination to do well in the field. The support I received from the University of New Haven and Rentschler allowed me to excel.

My senior year I won an academic scholarship from the Stadium Managers Association and interned for them during their annual conference. As a scholarship winner, I served as an ex officio member of the board and helped generate new ideas and coordinate events for more than 400 attendees. Attending the conference and knowing I helped in organizing it was an exciting experience that helped expand my skills and allowed me to network with many industry leaders.

Because I had taken the facility management course before I started interning, I was able to apply what I learned in the classroom to real life. The textbook assigned to us was *Managing Sport Facilities, Second Edition,* by Gil Fried. Between the wealth of knowledge in the textbook and my professor's teaching, I had a solid foundation that allowed me to easily understand my supervisor's discussions and gave me the ability to contribute to meetings with clients when I began working.

Managing Sport Facilities takes students through every aspect of the sport facility industry and helps them learn or better comprehend the subject of facility management. The chapters on facility design, finance, crowd management, and event management enabled me to truly grasp the concept of facility management and see the buildings beyond the mind of an average fan. The information in these chapters in particular gave me an upper hand in my internships and even in other course work. This intriguing, insightful book made everything finally come to life for me.

I hope you gain as much knowledge and understanding from this edition as I did from *Managing Sport Facilities, Second Edition.* In addition to being incredibly well known in this industry, Professor Fried is someone the entire student body truly looks up to. He takes great pride in his teaching and has a tremendous work ethic, which has rubbed off on my fellow classmates and me. I congratulate you, Professor Fried, on the continued success of this book and wish you the best in all your future endeavors.

—*Kathryn Ragaisis, 2014 BS in sport management, University of New Haven*

Acknowledgments

I thank my wife and kids for their time and for the patience they have shown over the past couple years as this third edition was being completed. Writing a book takes a lot of effort, and those around me had to understand and appreciate the long hours and the time away from family. My parents were always there to listen to my thoughts and ideas, and I love them and appreciate everything they have done for me over the years.

I extend a special thank you to the entire College of Business at the University of New Haven for their assistance throughout the project. Special accolades go to my close colleagues, mentors, and friends, including Dr. Allen Sack, Dr. Kimberly Mahoney, and Dr. Ceyda Mumcu. A special thanks goes to Daniel Kmiechick, my graduate assistant during the 2013-2014 year, who did significant work on the text and some of the ancillary materials.

I also extend a special thank you to all the wonderful folks with the International Association of Venue Managers (IAVM) and the Stadium Managers Association (SMA) for all their educational help and support over the years. In addition, a special thank you has to be extended to some of my dearest friends in the industry, who have been teaching me for years. I can safely say that I would not have the knowledge I am able to share in this text without them: Bill Squires, Frank Russo, Leah Becki, Nancy Freedman, Don Aeslin, Tom Beebe, Tom Saunders, Don Westfall, Michael Schneider, Joe Abernathy, Kimberly Mahoney, Duke Diaz, Kenneth Wajda, Kathryn Ragaisis, Carla Varialle, Shane Beardsley, and Steve Zito.

The entire Human Kinetics staff has been phenomenal through both the good times and the bad. Myles Schrag and Judy Park provided valuable advice and assistance in getting the book finished. Numerous additional professionals at Human Kinetics, including Amanda Eastin-Allen, Anne Mrozek, Dalene Reeder, and the rest of the HK team, made the book the ideal text I hoped to produce. The entire production staff at Human Kinetics was instrumental in this process, and I really appreciate their help.

PART I

Introduction to Sport Facility Management

What is sport facility management? Many people might say it involves putting on a great event. Others might claim it involves producing a safe event or running a facility under budget. Still others might say it involves building a new facility or maintaining an old facility. Although there is no one correct definition of sport facility management, from a facility management perspective, the key to success is having no problems or issues associated with the facility. It is impossible to control what happens on the field; however, a negative experience with the facility, restrooms, concessions, parking, Wi-Fi, or other facility elements can forever harm a customer relationship.

Every facility can be well run, regardless of the team's win–loss record or how much money the city council gives the facility manager for operations. Chapter 1 covers the first step in this process of determining how to effectively run a facility. To effectively run a modern facility, all facility personnel need to understand and appreciate how facilities have evolved and what others have done in the past. By examining how the Greeks and Romans managed their facilities, a facility manager can learn skills such as crowd management or facility changeovers. A facility manager should learn from both the successes of well-run facilities and the past failures of others.

Chapter 2 focuses on the hands-on skills needed to effectively manage a facility. The chapter starts by analyzing the myriad responsibilities of facility managers and the significant responsibilities they face on a daily basis. The chapter then examines the people a manager needs to work with to accomplish the job. Finally, it discusses the managerial functions of planning, organizing, implementing, and controlling.

Chapter 3 focuses on the tasks a manager undertakes when working with others. The chapter starts by examining theories that have guided managers for years; these theories are put to the test when a facility manager becomes a leader. The chapter then discusses how leaders and managers can leverage technology to help them run a facility more effectively. It also discusses outsourcing—the practice of hiring experts to help accomplish critical jobs. The last part of chapter 3 focuses on the various employees working in a facility. A manager needs to know who is working at the facility, how to hire the right people, and how to both promote and terminate employees.

History and Future of Sport and Public Assembly Facilities

Chapter Objectives

- Understand how the Greeks and Romans used sport facilities for political and cultural ends.

- Have a historical understanding of how sport facilities have changed to accommodate changes in sport and spectating demands.

- Identify how sport facilities have evolved from multiuse to single-use facilities.

- Appreciate the history behind several major sport facilities.

- Understand how facility trends have evolved over the years in the United States and internationally.

- Understand how and why politics, especially the Olympic movement, will continue to influence sport facilities in the future.

How many sport facilities exist in the world? This is a difficult question. The answer depends on your definition of a **sport facility**. Arenas, stadiums, YMCAs, school gyms, fitness facilities, and bowling alleys can all be classified as sport facilities. Typically excluded from the definition of a sport facility are natural areas, such as lakefront property where people might engage in water-related sports, and open recreation areas, such as golf courses. While a golf course is a self-contained sport facility, some might categorize it as a recreation facility that can be torn down quickly to be replaced by a business park. Thus, permanency could be a factor in defining a sport facility. However, any facility can be torn down and replaced by a business park. Over the past 20 years, numerous stadiums and arenas have been torn down and turned into parking lots. In fact, the parking lots at Citi Field and Turner Field include outlines of the former playing fields and markers where the bases once stood. Therefore, permanency might not be as important as other factors, such as being enclosed, being able to control conduct in the facility, or having room for participants and spectators. For purposes of this text, a sport facility is defined as any enclosed facility built, installed, or established as a location where sports are played. The enclosure can be either natural or man-made. However, the enclosure has to be complete so that the facility is self-contained. The two sport facilities most frequently analyzed are stadiums and arenas. Stadiums are often defined as venues that contain a playing surface surrounded by spectator seating and are used primarily for outdoor sport events. Arenas are enclosed indoor structures with a large open space surrounded by tier seating areas. Since the seating area is tiered, the playing surface is located at the lowest point to provide for the best line of sight.

Another equally important term is *public assembly facility* (**PAF**). PAFs include sport facilities as well as other entertainment or nonentertainment facilities where large groups of people can gather. Typical examples of PAFs are arenas, stadiums, theaters, and convention centers. All these types of facilities can host sport-related events. This text uses the term *PAF* as well as the term *sport facility*. No matter which term is used, sport

The Yankee Store in Times Square, New York, sells merchandise and tickets that benefit a stadium and team, but it is not classified as a sport facility.

facilities can be very fluid and change quickly. For example, over the past several years we have seen football and baseball stadiums transformed into outdoor hockey rinks to host record crowds, and a women's professional basketball game was held at a major tennis stadium. Such conversions show that facilities can be craftily manipulated to meet the needs of the facility users.

From ancient times to the present, sport facilities have been the hallmark or focal point of many cultures. Sport facilities have changed, but the changes are not as dramatic as they might seem. Table 1.1 highlights the timeline of facilities over several centuries.

The ancient Greeks and Romans used their sport facilities to entertain the masses so they would not revolt and to train athletes, entertain fans, and achieve political agendas. Present-day Olympic stadiums serve the same purpose. This

Russo: Changes are a constant in business

Photo courtesy of Frank Russo.

My name is Frank Russo, and I am the senior vice president for business development and client services for Global Spectrum, a company that manages more than 115 facilities (including 47 sport arenas) throughout the world. Our clients consist primarily of city, county, and state government entities that are looking to book more events and to improve their bottom line and therefore have decided to privatize their facilities. Our clients rely on Global Spectrum to make their facilities more competitive by introducing sound business practices, because—make no mistake—sport facilities are businesses.

I began my career as an assistant city manager in Hartford, Connecticut. This led to an opportunity to manage the Hartford Civic Center, home to the WHA and ultimately the National Hockey League (NHL) Hartford Whalers, University of Connecticut basketball, a Boston Celtics six-game home-away-from-home series (1975-1982), and countless other sporting and entertainment events. My career in providing private management of public assembly facilities began in 1988 when I joined Ogden Entertainment of New York City. During my tenure with Ogden I served for 1 year as the general manager of the Target Center in Minneapolis, home of the National Basketball Association (NBA) Timberwolves.

During my experience at the Hartford Civic Center and the Target Center, as well as my involvement in the development of several major and minor league sport facilities, I witnessed a number of changes that have become the reality of sport facility management. These include the following:

- Sports have become big business, and the cost of access is out of reach for many.

- Teams and facilities rely heavily on lucrative television contracts, as well as corporate advertisers, sponsors, and ticket buyers, for financial viability.

- Modern sport facilities cannot survive economically without building (at significant expense) premium seating and corporate dining and entertainment amenities such as suites, club seats, loge boxes, lounges, and fine dining and catering capabilities.

- Traditional forms of advertising and marketing such as billboards, fliers, mailers, and television/radio advertising are no longer the best and most direct way to reach potential ticket buyers. Traditional advertising now supports interactive marketing (e.g., data collection, e-mail, Internet, social media). Social media tools, coupled with the appropriate strategy, effectively support and enhance traditional marketing campaigns.

- Because of the increasing number of competitive facilities in several U.S. markets, **customer** service has become critical to success at all levels—because when there is more than one choice, people go where they are treated best! This adds significantly to the cost of constructing a new facility because facilities need to be built with all the latest technology and comfort to attract fans.

- Sport facilities and sports in general are no longer necessarily recession proof. It has become increasingly difficult to book viable events, sell tickets, and maximize event revenue from sources such as food and beverages, merchandise, and parking.

- One developing trend is the implementation of entertainment zones inside and immediately around sport facilities. These zones offer interesting and fun things to do both before and after an event and are meant to capture a larger portion of the market for longer periods of time by turning the facility into an exciting destination. Examples include L.A. Live at the Staples Center and Xfinity at the Wells Fargo Center.

In summary, my job is to help clients design, develop, manage, market, and operate their facilities in the most competitive and successful manner possible. Their success—and ours—depends on it!

This bowling alley in Times Square, New York, shows how fancy even a smaller sport facility can be.

chapter presents information on ancient through modern facilities, focusing on how facilities have evolved, what might have led to this evolution, and what the future holds for such facilities. Facilities were initially publicly funded to provide entertainment and promote religious and political goals. In brief, facilities have gone through a transformation process such that they still often focus on entertainment but also promote financial objectives as much as political goals. The Greeks and Romans mastered the art of the **multiuse facility**—facilities used for numerous types of events from chariot races to mock naval battles. Similar facilities were built in the 1960s and 1970s to host baseball and football games, but these facilities became extinct with the boom of single-use outdoor facilities in the 1990s. Indoor arenas, however, still host multiple events and can

switch from a setup for one event to a completely different setup in just a couple of hours.

After outlining how facilities have changed over time, this chapter examines several professional and collegiate facilities to show the variety of facilities that exist today. Discussion then turns to future trends such as international facility issues, the growth of Olympic facilities, and the ways in which politics will continue to affect sport facilities in the future.

FACILITIES IN ANCIENT TIMES

To appreciate current and future issues involved in sport facility management, it is critical to understand how far the industry has progressed since ancient times. However, a review of some facts associated with Greek and Roman sport facilities suggests that we are still using some of the ancient strategies.

Greece

In ancient Greece, sports were a form of worship. Olympia, one of the oldest religious centers in the Greek world, was a natural site for the origin of the Olympic Games. The Games were part spectacle and part religious ceremony. The Greeks undertook a major religious festival honoring Zeus, and the festival held at Olympia was the biggest event in the world at that time ("Real Story," 2002).

Original Olympic Facilities

The first known Olympic Games were held in 776 BC. They were subsequently held at the base of Mt. Olympus every 4 years for almost 1,000 years. The original Games consisted of only one event: a 200-yard foot race called the stadion. The first winner was a cook named Koroibos. Although many believe that the Greeks competed nude, they actually wore shorts in the early Games. In 720 BC, one athlete stripped off his trunks in an attempt to run faster. It worked, and others stripped off their clothes thereafter.

The Olympics also hosted the first Mixed Martial Arts (MMA) event. Called pankration, the event featured wrestling, boxing, and martial arts in which arm twisting, punching, kicking, breaking bones, and even strangulation were allowed.

Table 1.1 Facility Timeline

Period	Key years	Key facilities	Special features
Beginning of recorded history	Between 8500 and 7000 BC	No enclosed facilities	Self-sufficiency, rather than building complex structures, was primary focus
Neolithic period	8000 BC	Houses and villages	Utilized mud-brick construction
Classical antiquity	776 BC	Stadiums	The first known sport complex
Ancient Greece	331 BC	Olympic stadium	Represents the grandfather of modern facilities
Ancient Rome	6 BC	Circus Maximus	Used for chariot races and other major events
Ancient period	Before Middle Ages	No real sport facilities in Europe- primarily churches and castles, Mayan/Aztec ball courts in Central/South America	Showed tension between the divine and mortal worlds
Late Middle Ages	1300s-1800s	Religious and military facilities with some facilities built for jousting and other royal games	Larger facilities used primarily for religious festivals
Early modern era	1862	Union Grounds	The first ballpark built in the United States
Mid modern era	1896	Panathinaiko	The host facility of the Games of the I Olympiad
Late modern era	1912-1930	Yale Stadium Fenway Park Yankee Stadium	Development of collegiate sport facilities, including the first football-only college stadium Major baseball stadiums being built
Contemporary era	1960s-1970s	Multiuse facilities	Became trendy after World War II as a way to save money
Late contemporary era	1980s-2000	Single-use and intimate stadiums	More focus on luxury seating, personal seat licenses (PSLs), naming rights, and high-end concessions
Current era	2001-present	Gillette Stadium/Patriot Place AT&T Stadium Barclays Center Nationals Park*	Green trend integrated with cutting-edge technology for spectators Development of destination locations

*In 2008, Nationals Park became the first official green ballpark in the United States (Environmental News Service, 2008).

The Games were not safe for spectators, either. Hats were banned because they could block others' views, so sunburn and heatstroke were common. Rain sometimes helped cool off fans, but food and drink were better hydration options. Concession items included sausages, stale bread, and old cheese. If spectators needed to use the restroom, they had to go outside the stadium and use a dry river bed.

People came from near and far to participate in and watch the games at Olympia. The throngs of people needed a place to gather—in other words, they needed a PAF. The original Olympic stadium, built in Olympia in 776 BC, was an extension of an already existing religious sanctuary dedicated to Zeus. Combining the sanctuary and other buildings added over time, the facility formed the first known **sport complex**, complete with altars, a hostel for visitors (built in the fourth century BC), training facilities for wrestlers and boxers, a gymnasium with a covered running track, and the facility called the Stadia, where the actual events took place ("Real Story," 2002).

The Stadia was shaped like a U built into the hillside, with massive sloping embankments on each side of the U that served as seating. On the fourth side, the natural slope of the hill was also used for seating. Athletes and umpires came into the Stadia through their own entrance. There were multiple vaulted entrances for spectators. The chief judges and a priestess sat in special stone seats. According to some, all women except for the priestess were banned as spectators. Others believe that only unmarried women were welcome to enter the stadium ("Real Story," 2002).

Inside the Stadia, the track was about 230 yards (210 m) long and 35 yards (32 m) wide. It was separated from the sloping embankments by a low stone parapet, beside which ran an open stone water channel with basins at intervals. There was enough space for 20 people to run at one time. There was also enough space for cart races and chariot races ("Real Story," 2002). Sources show some discrepancy about what events were held in the Olympic stadium and when they were held. Some evidence suggests that Olympic Games date back to a time before the actual stadium was built. In fact, various open fields and areas were used for religious sanctuaries. It seems logical that games were held in these places as part of the religious ceremonies.

Some historians argue that a foot race of one stadium length was initially the only competition held in the new stadium at Olympia. Others say that even in the beginning the Olympic competitions consisted of a wide variety of sports that are still represented in modern-day Olympic competitions. There is widespread agreement that by classical times, 18 contests were held, including boxing, wrestling, horse races, the pentathlon, and other running events.

In addition to athletic events there were religious ceremonies that included sacrifices, speeches by well-known philosophers, poetry recitals, singers, parades, banquets, and victory celebrations. Merchants, craftsmen, and food vendors sold their wares. And, of course, no large gathering would be complete without gamblers, con men, prostitutes, and pimps ("Real Story," 2002). Though considered large even by today's standards, the original Olympic stadium could not have begun to accommodate current numbers of athletes and spectators. The Atlanta Olympic Games in 1996 attracted 10,700 athletes from 197 countries. There were more than 2 million live spectators and as many as 3.5 billion television viewers ("Context," 2002). These numbers will probably continue to increase in future Olympics. An all-time participation record was set when 202 countries and 11,099 athletes participated in 28 sports and 296 events in the 2004 Olympics in Greece ("Athens 2004," 2004). The 2008 Olympics in Beijing hosted 204 countries, 10,500 athletes, and 302 events. It is estimated that the Chinese government spent more than $42 billion on new facilities; facility renovations; and infrastructure development such as roads, subways, airports, and other needed public projects. The 2012 Olympics in London, England, involved 204 countries and 10,500 athletes and cost £8.77 billion. Some additional facts from the 2012 Games show the scale of the event:

- More than 21,000 accredited media communicated the Games to a potential worldwide audience of 4 billion.

- A total of 2,961 technical officials and 5,770 team officials worked the Games.

- A total workforce of around 200,000 people, including more than 6,000 staff, 70,000 volunteers, and 100,000 contractors, were involved in the Games.

- London Organising Committee of the Olympic and Paralympic Games (LOCOG) sourced more than 1 million pieces of sport equipment for the Games, including 510 adjustable hurdles, 600 basketballs, 2,700 footballs, and 356 pairs of boxing gloves.

- During the Games, 20 million spectator journeys were made to London, including 3 million on the busiest day of the Games.

- Approximately 14 million meals were served at the Games, including 45,000 meals per day in the Olympic Village ("London 2012," 2013).

Information on basic comfort and hygiene in ancient facilities is difficult to come by, which may indicate that there were no restrooms. However, 50,000 to 60,000 visitors slept outside the stadium, under the stars, so there must have been some accommodations. Wealthy people and members of official delegations erected elaborate tents and pavilions. Water was carted from springs a half-mile (1 km) away. Water was critical and probably fostered the first concession sales because the stadium was uncomfortable, dusty, and hot.

Similar to Madison Square Garden (see the Facility Focus section later in this chapter), the stadium at Olympia did not remain in its original location. Around the middle of the fourth century BC, the stadium was moved 90 yards (82 m) east and a little to the north of its original location. Although it moved, it retained its connection to the sanctuary via the Krypte, a covered entrance that ran through the embankment. This was the entrance through which athletes and officials entered the stadium. Just as it is today, location was important in the choice of a stadium site. Olympia was convenient to reach by ship. Athletes and spectators traveled from Greek colonies as far away as modern-day Spain, the Black Sea, and Egypt.

The stadium at Olympia was not the only stadium in Greece. The Olympic Stadium in Athens was built in 331 BC and held 50,000 spectators. Like many older modern facilities it has gone through major renovations, beginning with a reconstruction in AD 160. However, it lay dormant for centuries, beginning in AD 393 when Emperor Theodosius abolished the Games for being "too pagan" ("History," 2004a). This facility was used to host the 1896 Olympic Games.

Hippodromes and Theaters

Other PAFs developed by the Greeks included theaters and hippodromes. Greek theaters had three main parts. The scene, or skene, was a painted backdrop. The orchestra was a circular area in front of the scene. The actors performed on a narrow raised platform, called the logeion, in front of the scene. Last, there was the koilon for seating. The koilon, which was originally built from wood and later from stone, was semicircular and built around the orchestra. The koilon was divided into two sections, called diazoma, which included upper and lower seating tiers. Special seats were reserved for officials and priests. Examples of Greek stadiums can be seen in Epidaurus (where the stadium was built around 330 BC), Argos, and Delphi. These theaters seated 14,000; 20,000; and 5,000; respectively ("Epidauro," 2002).

Many hippodromes were built around Greece. These facilities were for horse races as well as chariot races. They were originally open fields lined with raised banks of earth. There was no seating—spectators stood for the races. Eventually these rudimentary facilities evolved into huge stone facilities seating tens or even hundreds of thousands of spectators. The hippodrome in Olympia lay south of the stadium in the open valley of the Alpheus. No trace of it has been found.

Rome

The Roman Empire followed the Greek Empire as the dominant culture of its time. During the ancient Roman era, young people participated in sports such as wrestling, boxing, racing, and jumping. The Romans loved their sports, and the leaders leveraged this interest into a means to control their subjects for days on end. Some events lasted for several days, with spectators eating and drinking themselves beyond traditional limits. It was hoped that the excited and tired subjects who had spent all their money would eventually return to their homes and not complain about the leadership because they had experienced such a wonderful event. To help effectuate these plans and meet the demands of those sports, the leaders needed large facilities such as the Roman Coliseum and Circus Maximus.

Roman Coliseum

As Roman civilization rose, the need for PAFs rose with it. Most notable was the Roman Coliseum with its spectacles and gladiators (Blickstein, 1995). The Romans built their stadiums based on past Greek structures. In some cases, as with the amphitheaters, Rome simply renovated or rebuilt old Greek structures.

The Roman Coliseum was originally named the Flavian Amphitheater after the emperors who built it: Vespasian and Titus, both of the Flavian family. Construction began around AD 70 and took about 10 years to complete. When it was done, the coliseum stood 160 feet (48 m) high with four stories of windows, arches, and columns. Each of the three exterior floors consisted of 80 arches ("History of the Colosseum," 2002). Visitors climbed sloping ramps to their seats and were seated according to sex and social class. Women, slaves, and the poor stood or sat on wooden benches in the fourth tier of seating. The reserved luxury seats were marble, and their bases

The Roman Empire stretched far and wide and contributed to the building of hippodromes as far away as Caesarea along the Mediterranean coast of modern-day Israel.

were inscribed with the names of the senators and knights who occupied them. Vestal virgins, religious officials, soldiers, civilians, and boys with their tutors had special seating sections. A place of honor was given to the editor, who organized and paid for the games. The emperor, who often paid for the games, had a special box (similar to sky boxes today) for himself and his family.

It is estimated that 50,000 people could enter the arena and be seated in about 15 minutes, owing to the ticketing system developed by the Romans. Before an event a spectator would pick up a ticket, often made from pottery shards. Each ticket had a number that corresponded to one of the 78 entrance archways, which all had numbers above them. Tickets also had levels and seat numbers. Similar ticketing systems are used to this day ("History of the Colosseum," 2002).

The Roman Coliseum incorporated much of the technology of its time. Enormous colored awnings made of canvas could be stretched overhead to prevent the hot sun from making spectators uncomfortable. These awnings, called velarium, were attached to rigs operated by sailors who were hired solely for this purpose. The wooden floor contained lifts, pulleys, and at least

24 giant trap doors. The coliseum also had subterranean chambers where the gladiators, as well as the animals, were kept before performances. A hand-operated elevator was used to raise animals from the basement up to the arena floor. The underground chambers could be flooded with water and the stadium then used to stage mock naval battles. Over time this activity damaged the flooring and was thus discontinued ("History of the Colosseum," 2002).

The lower level of the Coliseum, called the hypogeum (Greek for "underground"), was two stories (6 meters) tall, 250 feet (76.2 m) long, and 145 feet (44 m) wide and was located under the stadium floor. Over the years the area was filled with dirt, rubble, gardens, feed storage, and even animal droppings. The amphitheater above was used for numerous purposes, including businesses for cobblers, blacksmiths, priests, glue makers, and money changers. In the late 16th century Pope Sixtus V, who built Renaissance Rome, tried to turn the Coliseum into a wool factory, but the cost proved too much and the plan was abandoned. That led to what the Coliseum was most known for over several hundred years: a wondrous garden that more than 330 different species of plants called home (Mueller, 2011). By the 19th century the hypogeum was covered by 40 feet (12 m) of dirt. In removing all the debris, archeologists uncovered some interesting facts about the hypogeum's nearly 400 years of continuous use. For example, they found 60 manual elevators called capstans, each of which was two stories tall and turned by four men on each level. Forty of these capstans were for raising animals such as lions and tigers, whereas the remaining 20 were used for moving scenery. The archaeologists also found canals that helped empty the flooded arena floor and scenery platforms that were operated through a system of cables, ramps, hoists, and counterweights.

The events normally started with a major morning procession called the pompa. During this event the editor's standard bearers, trumpeters, performers, fighters, priests, nobles, and carriages bore effigies of the gods. After the pompa was the morning's main event: the venatio, or wild beast hunt. There could have been a parade of beasts to show the variety of animals that soldiers were able to catch to actual hunts and battles between unusual beasts. Some emperors offered between 9,000 and 11,000 animals to be slaughtered. The hypogeum was critical for these hunts because it allowed those putting on the event to bring different animals to the floor at different times and to change the environment in a couple of minutes. In some of the hunting events the audience was encouraged to participate and was allowed to use spears or bows and arrows to help shoot the animals.

After the hunt was the intermission, called the intermezzos, during which the crowd was treated to handsome stewards carrying trays of cakes, pastries, dates, sweetmeats, and wine. Similar to today's games, various promotional events were held during which prizes, such as tokens, money, or even the title to an apartment, were distributed. As would be expected, a mad scramble ensued to obtain such prizes.

At the midday games (ludi meridiani), criminals, barbarians, prisoners, and other captives (called condemned, or damnati) were executed. No credible evidence exists that Christians were killed in the Coliseum for their faith. After these killings, the main event, involving gladiators, was held. The event managers were always on guard to make sure that the event ran smoothly. It was not unusual for an event manager who made a mistake to be the next person thrown into the arena for the next fight. This kept all the event workers on their toes.

Although the Roman Coliseum was a major focus of the world at the time, the world was changing. In AD 392 Christianity was becoming the official religion of the Roman Empire, but the transition was slow. In the year 404, a Christian monk named Telemachus jumped into the ring to break up a fight and was stoned to death. Emperor Honorius banned the Games the following year. There was a saying that if the Roman Coliseum fell, Rome would fall. Sure enough, in the year 410 the Visigoths sacked Rome. The Coliseum as it stands today appears to have been destroyed by an earthquake. However, the building fell apart because builders looking for supplies would take stones from the Coliseum. Many of the stones were used to build St. Peter's Basilica. The only thing truly holding the Coliseum together today is gravity. The stones are starting to vibrate and shift due to the rumbling of passing traffic.

Circus Maximus

In addition to the Roman Coliseum and other Roman amphitheaters, the Romans had the circus. The circus was the Roman version of a racetrack. It was the setting for chariot races and other events, both equestrian and nonequestrian. The most famous Roman circus was the Circus Maximus, built to emulate the Greek hippodrome and considered one of the architectural wonders of the ancient world. Constructed of wood in the sixth century BC, it was destroyed by fire twice and was subject to flooding. On at least two occasions the stands collapsed, killing many people. Eventually the Circus Maximus was rebuilt of stone and masonry ("Amphitheater," 2002).

Historians have estimated the seating capacity of the Circus as ranging from 150,000 to more than 300,000. It is assumed that the number of spectators surpassed seating capacity and that many observers stood for the duration of the events. Unlike other Roman PAFs, men and women could sit together at the Circus. The Circus also had skyboxes and reserved seating for the emperor, senators, knights, judges, a prize-awarding jury, and financial backers for the various races ("Circus Maximus," 2002). The track was one-third of a mile (0.5 km) long and 150 yards (137 m) wide. It was covered with earth and then a layer of sand. The sand allowed chariots to hold the track. It also protected the horses from injury and allowed water to drain off. Like today's racetracks, the track was a large oval.

Admission to the Circus Maximus was free; however, it was still a revenue center. Concession stands sold fast food and snacks. Spectators could rent a seat cushion if they did not bring their own from home. In his book *Roman People*, Robert B. Kebric describes the Circus as a four-story facility with a maze of shops, rooms, stairways, and arcades. Thousands of people moved about the large corridors throughout the facility. There was also a plethora of prostitutes, gamblers, pickpockets, girl watchers, and drunks (Kebric, 2000).

FACILITIES FROM THE MIDDLE AGES TO THE 1800s

Most sports and games of medieval times were less organized than today's sports. The sports also involved more "folksy" types of activities that highlighted the skills of the local citizenry. One of the popular sports during this time was folk football, which was a wild and rough attempt at the organized attacking of other people. The more common events included such activities as hunting, falconry, and tracking with hunting dogs. These events did not require a set facility and often were conducted on hunting grounds or in forests.

Medieval events that were most suited to such settings included jousting and archery matches. Jousting was probably the best-known sport of the times, especially for the upper class. The common folk were more accustomed to archery matches, which often pitted one town against another. The lower class was allowed to participate in other simultaneous events (separate from the matches involving royalty and knights) such as running, jumping, cudgeling, and wrestling. These matches often involved large feasts, which included a large amount of alcohol. The abundance of alcohol and lewd conduct was one reason the Church stepped in and tried to stop these events. In fact, religion played a major role in sport for many years.

In addition to the Greeks and Romans, the Chinese, Japanese, indigenous natives of North, Central, and South America, and other groups developed various sports around religion. For example, cuju is an ancient code of soccer that originated in China between 206 BC and AD 220 that was also played in Korea, Japan, and Vietnam. Every culture had informal or organized sport in some manner, even if the facilities were rudimentary. Although organized sport was not frequently documented, a greater amount of information is available concerning military training and how sports have been used to strengthen and discipline soldiers. For example, military training in ancient China included all kinds of sports, such as wrestling, pugilism (boxing), fencing, tripod lifting, horse racing, stone throwing, hunting, and swimming.

The Christian emperor Theodosius stopped the Olympic Games because he thought they were pagan rites. However, in the Middle Ages the Church supported horse races and tournaments as long as the events honored the Virgin Mary (Aurandt, 2002). The Church and the government sometimes encouraged and at other times banned sport. In fact, in England during the 14th century, working people who were caught playing football or tennis (played with a pig's bladder or leather stuffed with rags) were imprisoned for up to 6 years. The upper class and clergy were not subject to such punishment (Aurandt, 2002).

Because of the lack of support from the clergy and government, the Middle Ages were not the high point for PAFs. In fact, PAFs went into decline at the end of the Roman Empire when the Church outlawed theaters. However, it was the Church that kept theater alive through seasonal festivals, which took on a dramatic form to help better illustrate the religious connotations to illiterate congregants. Because the authorities were concerned about touring companies carrying the plague or about civil unrest caused by drunken spectators, theaters did not prosper ("Greek Theater," 2002). Although theaters eventually thrived after the Roman and Greek periods, sport facilities were hard to find. In fact, research has shown very few sport facilities except for informal areas established for such events as horse races, hunts, and other outdoor, open-air events that did not necessarily require any fixed seating areas. Thus, although cricket and tennis were to become popular in the United States, there is no record of any public facilities for these sports until the end of the 19th century (Manchester, 1931).

In the 19th century, most restrictions against sport were lifted, and one of the first facilities built in the United States was Union Course, constructed in New York in 1825. The horse racing facility included stands, a clubhouse, and a balcony. It was very popular—more than 60,000 spectators attended one race (Manchester, 1931). Baseball started gaining popularity in the 1850s, and facility management rules were initially developed in the 1870s. The first three major rules for the National League had to do with banning alcohol from the parks, removing the betting booths from the field entrances, and removing gamblers from the stands (Manchester, 1931).

FACILITY MANAGEMENT FROM ANCIENT TO MODERN TIMES

Although facilities have changed significantly over the years, management and operation of facilities have remained somewhat stable. Just as there were different classes of seating in the Roman Coliseum, amphitheaters, and Circus Maximus, we have different classes of seating today. Just as important people had reserved seats in advantageous positions in earlier eras, we have club seats and luxury suites today.

The behind-the-scenes workings of an event are often beyond the knowledge of average facility patrons. Security, stagehands, and medical services are just a few examples of behind-the-scenes support services. In ancient times there were also staff members whose job it was to keep things running smoothly. At the Coliseum, sailors were employed to work the enormous colored awnings used to shelter spectators from the hot sun. Archers took stations on catwalks above the crowd in order to shoot rowdy fans, resistant participants, or animals that presented a threat to the audience.

Regardless of the type of entertainment offered by large public venues, many of the managerial concerns have stayed the same. Some of the considerations that have remained consistent over the centuries include the following:

- Controlling and moving large numbers of people
- Managing rowdy or violent crowds
- Maintaining flexibility in multiuse venues (e.g., gladiators and mock naval battles; basketball and ice shows)
- Providing security and protection for very important people (VIPs)
- Controlling the petty crimes that are inherent with large gatherings of people
- Keeping facilities clean and operational
- Navigating the politics associated with getting appropriate funding for publicly owned facilities

Of course, changes have occurred in the PAF industry over the years. A few modern-day concerns that did not trouble managers in ancient times are these:

- Providing amenities for the press, such as interview rooms and press boxes with Internet access
- Setting up television camera platforms and cable hookups
- Selling advertising space and naming rights
- Providing batting cages and other practice areas
- Providing athletic training rooms
- Utilizing heating, ventilation, and air conditioning (HVAC) systems
- Anticipating parking concerns for thousands of cars and buses
- Complying with environmental, zoning, accessibility, and other legal issues

These differences have evolved over many years, led by the change in sport facility owners and providers. Initially the government and churches were behind PAFs. As facilities evolved, they focused more on generating profits. Such an evolution required a new way of thinking about, building, and running sport facilities. One example is the shift of concession sales from peanuts and Cracker Jack to sushi and five-star cuisine.

EVOLUTION OF PROFESSIONAL AND COLLEGIATE FACILITIES

The modern era for sport facilities started in the late 1860s. Baseball was one of the driving forces for larger sport facilities, especially when it came to generating revenue from fans. The first game with paid admission—a three-game series pitting the best from New York City against the best from Brooklyn—was held at Fashion Race Course on Long Island in July 1858. Admission was 50 cents. This game showed that people would pay to watch baseball. In 1862, Union Grounds—the first enclosed ballpark—opened in Brooklyn.

Facilities Trivia

History is replete with leaders who banned ball games for various reasons, including the following:

- England's Edward II banned football (soccer) in 1314, due in part to the noise caused by those playing the game. Violators could face imprisonment.
- England's Edward II outlawed even more games in 1365, including casting the stone (shot put) and bandy ball (the forerunner to field hockey).
- France's Charles VI prohibited an early version of a ball game in 1369.
- Scotland outlawed futeball (soccer) in 1427. Other similar laws were passed in Scotland in 1457, 1471, and 1491.
- The Republic of Venice banned the sport of bocce in 1576. Players who were caught were subject to a fine and imprisonment.
- The British Highway Act of 1835 prohibited playing soccer on public highways.
- In the United States, lawn bowling was banned in Boston in 1898 because heavy drinking and gambling were associated with the sport.
- Paintball was banned in New Jersey until 1988 because the guns were considered firearms.
- In December 2009, Rio de Janeiro banned the soccer ball-based game altinho on 54 miles (87 km) of beaches due to the danger and injury it caused to women and children (Chetwynd, 2011).

Because the facility was enclosed, everyone who wanted to watch had to pay. Union Grounds and other ballparks of that time were generally made of wood and often did not have outfield fences; instead there was a barrier at the end of the property to prevent freeloaders (Schlossberg, 1983). Horse-drawn carriages and, later, cars were allowed to pull into the outfield so that paying fans could watch the game from their vehicles. Other spectators were allowed to sit on backless planks of wood. The Philadelphia Nationals built the Baker Bowl in 1887 and opened the season to an attendance of 14,500 fans. The Bowl cost $80,000 to build, which 90 years later was the average yearly salary for a Major League Baseball player (Schlossberg, 1983). Thus, the initial drive for larger stadiums was simple: monetary gain.

These early facilities started the trend for building new facilities, which included some of the current staples such as reserved seats, luxury boxes, press boxes, and ladies' days. These innovations were quickly lost, though, primarily through fires that destroyed a number of ballparks from 1871 (Union Base-Ball Grounds in Chicago was destroyed in the great Chicago fire) until parks were built with steel. A number of stadiums also experienced bleacher collapses. These tragedies led to the Golden Era of ballparks (1909-1923). The first fireproof baseball stadiums built of concrete and steel opened in 1909, with Philadelphia's Shibe Park and Pittsburgh's Forbes Field (Blickstein, 1995). The last game to be played in a wood stadium before concrete and steel stadiums became the norm took place at Robison Field in St. Louis, Missouri, on June 6, 1920.

Skeptics thought that Forbes Field would be a disaster because it was built 3 miles (4.8 km) from downtown Pittsburgh, but the stadium's success showed that fans were willing to travel to watch a game. This era was followed by the cookie-cutter era (1960-1980), during which 18 new stadiums—many looking like each other—were built. These stadiums include Atlanta–Fulton County Stadium, Riverfront Stadium (Cincinnati), Three Rivers Stadium (Pittsburgh), and Veterans Stadium (Philadelphia). This era morphed into the dome era around the same time frame during which the Astrodome (Houston), the Kingdome (Seattle), the Metrodome (Minneapolis), and the SkyDome (Toronto) were built. That era was

Although concession stands can sell almost anything, a portable stand that is not vented or that does not have a sink cannot sell many cooked foods, which limits its offering to packaged food, pretzels, and possibly hot dogs.

followed by the retro era starting in the 1990s, during which ballparks such as Camden Yards (Baltimore) and Coors Field (Denver) harkened to older stadiums with a more aesthetic feel which focused on quality, design, and comfort rather than sheer large volume of seats.

Intercollegiate sport also helped further the development of sport facilities in the United States. In 1912-14, Yale was the first university to build a large football-only stadium. This facility had wood planks that sat 18,000; in 1916 it was expanded to seat 33,000 fans. Yale's perennial nemesis, Harvard, had jumped on the bandwagon earlier in 1904 when it built the first steel- and concrete-reinforced stadium in America, which seated 23,000 fans. In response, Yale spent $235,000 building a steel and concrete stadium that could seat 50,000 fans (Blickstein, 1995). Yale also built one of the oldest active baseball stadiums, which is used by the university's baseball team and has been used by several minor league professional baseball teams.

As mentioned previously, the big push for stadiums—often called "cookie-cutter stadiums" because they all looked alike, sprang up in the 1960s and 1970s. Examples of the cookie-cutter multiuse stadiums include those in Atlanta (51,500 capacity, opened in 1966, cost $18 mil-

lion), Cincinnati (51,744 capacity, opened in 1970, cost $45 million), Philadelphia (55,371 capacity, opened in 1971, cost $52 million), Pittsburgh (50,500 capacity, opened in 1970, cost $36 million), and St. Louis (49,275 capacity, opened in 1966, cost $26 million). This growth was not fueled by revenue or attendance demands but rather by federal funds. The federal government was throwing money at cities for urban renewal projects, and people wanted stadiums rather than housing projects (Joyner and Copeland, 2008). The Detroit Tigers built their new $300 million stadium in 2000 not far from the original Tiger Stadium that was built in 1912. The old stadium, sitting empty, became a financial drain, and the city had to pay between $200,000 and $400,000 annually for security and ground maintenance (Antonen, 2006). In 2006, the city council announced plans to tear down the original stadium in 2007 and to build in its place a retail store, apartments, a museum, and a youth baseball field. The first stage of the process was to hold an online sale of ballpark memorabilia, which sold numerous items to dedicated fans. Fans bought unusual items such as urinals, a batter's box stencil, cement-encased base pegs, and football down markers. One of the more historically significant items sold was Al Kaline's locker. Auction sales were anticipated to reach into the hundreds of thousands of dollars (Brown, 2007).

Auctions of old stadium and arena memorabilia are a growing trend. In 2000, the Pittsburgh Sports and Exhibition Authority earned more than $1 million by selling Pittsburgh Steelers and Pirates memorabilia from Three Rivers Stadium before it was demolished. A similar auction in 2004 of items from Philadelphia's Veterans Stadium yielded around $700,000. A 2005 auction of relics, including Albert Pujols' locker, from the old Busch Stadium in St. Louis garnered several million dollars (Brown, 2007).

Although some baseball teams have played for numerous years at the same facility (e.g., Fenway Park, built in 1912, and Wrigley Field, built in 1914), only two expansion teams—the Tampa Bay Rays and the Arizona Diamondbacks—have been in the same stadium since their inception. Sometimes the facility journey undertaken by a team is as significant as the way the team has evolved, as in the case of the Cincinnati Reds. Table 1.2 highlights the various names the team has used and the facilities they have played in over the years. Note that Crosley Field in Cincinnati hosted the first lighted night baseball game in the majors in 1935.

Although professional baseball teams have moved over the years, moving is usually not an option for college and university teams and facilities. Most colleges, especially well-established colleges that are housed on large campuses, do not move. These schools often have had facilities for numerous years on campus and have continually expanded the facilities to meet attendance demands. Table 1.3 lists the opening dates and seating capacities of football stadiums in the Big Ten Conference.

As shown in table 1.3, teams that have traditionally been national powerhouses (i.e., Penn State, Michigan, Ohio State University) have the highest seating capacities to maximize their revenue potential. These facilities have often undergone significant renovations to expand their seating bowls over the years. In contrast, teams that have traditionally not been as strong (e.g., Northwestern) have not expanded their facilities because the market demand for tickets has not dictated such an expansion (even if tickets are scarce in the years when the school does very well). Such a decision can affect opposing teams since gate receipts are usually shared, and if the venue is too small, this will eventually hurt other teams playing there.

Although collegiate facilities have remained relatively constant with some updating, professional sport facilities have changed significantly. The 1960s saw a trend of building multiuse facilities to save money. However, in the 1990s there was a push for single-use and more intimate stadiums

Table 1.2   Cincinnati Reds' Stadium Odyssey

Year	Stadium	Team name
1876-1879	Avenue Grounds	Cincinnati Red Stockings
1880	Bank Street Grounds	Same
1881	Did not play	
1882-1883	Bank Street Grounds	Same
1884-1889	League Park	Same
1890-1901	League Park	Cincinnati Reds
1902-1911	Palace of the Fans	Same
1912-1933	Redland Field	Same
1934-1952	Crosley Field	Same
1953-1958	Crosley Field	Cincinnati Redlegs
1959-1970	Crosley Field	Cincinnati Reds
1970-1996	Riverfront Stadium	Same
1997-2002	Cynergy Field (name changed)	Same
2003-present	Great American Ball Park	Same

Table 1.3 Big Ten Football Stadium Opening Dates and Seating Capacities

Facility, university	Opened	Capacity
Camp Randall Stadium, Wisconsin	1917	76,129
Ohio Stadium, Ohio State	1922	101,568
Memorial Stadium, Illinois	1923	70,904
Memorial Stadium, Nebraska	1923	87,091
Ross-Ade Stadium, Purdue	1924	67,861
Ryan Field, Northwestern	1926	49,256
Michigan Stadium, Michigan	1927	107,501
Kinnick Stadium, Iowa	1929	70,397
Spartan Stadium, Michigan State	1957	72,027
Memorial Stadium, Indiana	1960	52,354
Beaver Stadium, Penn State	1960	106,537
TCF Bank Stadium, Minnesota	2009	50,805
High Point Solutions Stadium, Rutgers	1938 Original/1993 New	52,454
Capital One Field at Byrd Stadium, Maryland	1950	51,802

as well as larger arenas with more luxury seating options. During the building boom between 1987 and 2002, 84 new stadiums and arenas were built, often under the threat of current teams moving to a new city if a facility was not built. Between 2002 and 2014, 12 major new stadiums or arenas opened in the United States. The building of new facilities is often fueled by teams moving from one city to another. Six National Football League (NFL) teams switched cities between 1980 and 2002, three NBA teams switched between 2000 and 2008, and three NHL teams moved in the 1990s (Ellis, 2002). Table 1.4 shows the various major professional leagues in the United States, the number of teams in the leagues, the number of new facilities built, and the number of facilities planned as of 2014.

While the threat of a team leaving a given city can help fuel a push to build a new facility, other factors include strong economic trends (as witnessed in the 1990s), new marketing trends such as the luxury suite and naming right trends of the 1990s, special event needs such as the Olympics or the World Cup, and technological innovations such as retractable roofs or domed stadiums. For example, the first domed stadium ever built was the Astrodome in Houston, completed in 1965. Nine additional domes were built in the 1970s, including the Silverdome, Kingdome, and Superdome. In the 1980s only 7 domes were built. In the 1990s, 12 domes were built ("Domed Stadiums," 2002). Between 2000 and 2002, 7 domed stadiums were constructed, and 4 new dome stadiums were built after 2002. These numbers indicate that

Table 1.4 New Stadium and Arena Construction Since the 1980s

League	Number of teams	Number of new facilities	Number of proposed facilities
Major League Baseball	30	26	1
National Basketball Association	30	27	1
National Football League	32	22	2
National Hockey League	30	26	0

Additionally, four National Football League stadiums underwent major renovations after 1980.

Adapted from Ballparks.com 2004.

domes are still being designed to help eliminate one of the biggest marketing disasters that can befall a facility—inclement weather.

The 2013 season Super Bowl was held in New Jersey, and the cold weather was the biggest fear for years leading up to the game. The stadium has no dome and the weather is unpredictable, which created significant unrest for facility personnel for weeks leading up to the game. (However, the temperature turned out to be slightly below average, it did not snow, and the game went off without a glitch.) The drive to minimize uncertainty and address most potential issues, from weather to Wi-Fi, has significantly increased the price tag for new stadiums.

The NFL stadiums most recently built include Lucas Oil Stadium (completed in 2008, cost $720 million), AT&T Stadium (completed in 2009, estimated cost $1.15 billion to $1.6 billion), and MetLife Stadium (completed in 2010, cost $1.5 billion). On the Major League Baseball side the costs are not as high because the stadiums often have half as many seats, but the three highest-cost stadiums built over the past several years include Nationals Park (cost $611 million, completed in 2008), Citi Field (cost $900 million, completed in 2009), and the new Yankee Stadium (cost $1.5 billion, completed in 2009). In contrast, Marlins Park cost only $515 million, but the complicated financing plan (under investigation by the Securities and Exchange Commission) will end up costing the public $2.4 billion over 40 years (Cohen, 2012). The newest stadium—the $1.2 billion Levi's Stadium for the San Francisco 49ers in Santa Clara, California—opened in 2014 with 68,500 seats, 165 suites, and a green rooftop with solar panels and a garden for growing herbs for cooking in the facility. Price is not the only thing increasing with these facilities—their size is, too. Gillette Stadium was built with 1.3 million square feet (120,773 sq m) of space, the Dallas Cowboy's AT&T Stadium was built with 2.7 million square feet (250,838 sq m) of space, and MetLife Stadium has around 2 million square feet (185,806 sq m) of space. The more space available, the more opportunities the facility has to earn money. The recently completed Levi's Stadium has only 1.85 million square feet (171,871 sq m) of space partly due to the very high real estate costs in California (Cohen, 2012).

One of the biggest advances over the past 40 years has been the transition to more privately financed and built facilities. Government entities are the most common owners and operators of sport facilities. In socialized countries such as Great Britain and Canada, numerous sport facilities are owned and managed by government entities. More than 80,000 athletic and sport facilities are registered in Sport England's Active Places system as of 2014, including 895 field hockey fields, 1,060 swimming pools, 79 weightlifting clubs, 47 ice rinks, 5,059 artificial grass fields, 69,120 grass fields, 29,616 school-based facilities, 11,218 tennis courts, and a host of other facilities.

A significant number of government facilities also exist in the United States. There are 98,905 public schools in the United States, and almost everyone has a multipurpose room, gymnasium, or playing field (or more than one of these). In addition, there are thousands of park and recreation departments, most having several facilities and fields. Although there is no definitive number of park and recreation facilities in the United States, most of the 35,000 towns or cities in the United States have at least one park or recreational facility, and larger cities possibly have many facilities. The National Recreation and Park Association has more than 40,000 members.

During the 1990s, as is typical in strong economic periods, government-owned sport facilities were being built across the United States. This does not usually represent a problem. However, just building a facility does not end the financial and managerial responsibility of operating the facility. When the economic environment soured in the 2000s, state and local government units began to get strapped for cash. To reduce budget problems, government facilities started to reduce staff, cut maintenance budgets, or reduce hours—or they closed outright.

Many elections are held each year throughout the United States to determine whether a sport, recreation, or educational institution should be built and whether public funds should be used to build a facility. Numerous stadium and arena projects have ended up in court for a determination about whether political expediency excluded voters from the funding process. For example, residents in Arizona hosted a mock Boston Tea

Party protest after their elected supervisors approved a countywide quarter-cent sales tax hike to help finance the Bank One Ballpark. The citizens were not necessarily opposed to the stadium or to allocating more taxes to the project; they just wanted a say in the process (Pitzl, 1996). In 2014, the Securities and Exchange Commission of the federal government was still investigating a possible pay-to-play scheme in which elected Miami officials allegedly received compensation for their vote in favor of the stadium (see chapter 12).

The political fight is not just over government subsidies; it is also over whether a facility should be built. For example, more than 90 civic organizations ganged up against the Washington Redskins' planned new stadium in Landover, Maryland. The group sued to overturn a zoning change that would have allowed the team to build the stadium at the preferred site ("Stadium Suit," 1996). The stadium was eventually built at another location.

Government officials have a fiduciary obligation (obligation to act truthfully and honestly) to protect their constituents, the people who voted them into power. A conflict arises when a politician promotes building a facility that might benefit some individuals but can cause harm to others. This concern has reared its ugly head on numerous occasions. For example, a San Diego council member was forced to resign her seat and pled guilty to two misdemeanors for allegedly taking gifts from the San Diego Padres ownership. Although the gifts were legal, the council member did not report the gifts as required and did not excuse herself from council votes regarding the Padres' ballpark ("Padres' Park," 2001).

Before the 1990s, very few large privately owned facilities existed. The most well-known private facilities are Lambeau Field for the Green Bay Packers and Dodger Stadium in Los Angeles. The next wave of privately owned facilities was ushered in by Joe Robbie, who built Dolphin Stadium in Miami for the Dolphins. (The stadium's name has changed seven times since its construction. In 2009 it was for a short period renamed Land Shark Stadium for a beer promotion, but it is now named Sun Life Stadium). Since the 1990s a number of privately financed facilities have been built, and an even larger number of facilities have been built, or are scheduled to be built, with a blend of public and private funds. Some of the premiere privately financed stadiums include San Francisco's AT&T Park, FedExField, the Dallas Cowboys' AT&T Stadium, and the New England Patriots' Gillette Stadium and the surrounding Patriot Place.

People who privately finance and manage sport facilities often do so as a profit-generating business enterprise. Thus, while a government-owned facility might focus more on providing a service than on generating revenue, a private facility does not have that luxury. Any money saved at a private facility results in greater profits. Thus, the managerial perspective required to run a private facility is significantly different from that required to run a public facility.

FACILITY FOCUS

This section highlights some of the premiere public and private facilities in the United States and Canada, along with a relatively smaller arena and one of the largest multiuse sport facilities in the world. These sample facilities were chosen because of their name recognition or because they were recently constructed, renovated, or closed and provide an opportunity to explore current trends. In each of the remaining chapters of this book, other noteworthy facilities are featured in "Facility Focus" sections throughout this book. This is an opportunity to get a glimpse of the wide variety of facilities that exist, their unique features, and the multitude of functions and issues that their managers must handle.

The first example highlights a newer arena that has been around for more than 10 years and discusses some of the challenges faced by a facility in a smaller market, the second example explores a newer facility that was built with student input, and the last two examples highlight facilities with rich histories that have moved or been replaced.

Webster Bank Arena

Webster Bank Arena (formerly the Arena at Harbor Yard), completed in the fall of 2001, is home to the American Hockey League's Bridgeport Sound Tigers—an affiliate of the NHL's New York Islanders and the Metro Atlantic Athletic Conference's

Fairfield University men's and women's basketball teams. The arena took 721 days to construct and is equipped to accommodate 8,500 people for hockey games and 9,000 people for basketball games. The facility has five locker rooms, seven permanent concession stands, 13 loge suites, 20 portable kiosks, 14 women's and 13 men's rooms, 33 executive suites, 1,300 club seats, 40,000 light bulbs, 10,600 gallons of water (needed to create the ice rink), 6,000 pieces of structural steel, and 4,754 cubic yards (3,635 cu m) of concrete (Elsberry, 2001). Table 1.5 breaks down the construction costs for the project. Based on the 196,300 square feet (18,200 sq m) in the facility,

the cost per square foot was $262.26, and the final construction price was $56,278,684. The original schematic budget was just under $37 million, and the estimated construction price was slightly more than $39 million (Kasper Group, 2001).

Players have their own entrance to the building, giving them privacy and the ability to enter and exit without disrupting or being disrupted by other events. The arena also has an exclusive fitness center for players and five locker rooms that allow scheduling of men's and women's doubleheaders. Members of the media are also treated to state-of-the-art facilities, including a fully equipped media area, interview room, and green room.

Table 1.5 Webster Bank Arena Construction Costs

Category	Cost ($)	Cost/ft² ($)	% of total cost
General insurance and bond issuance costs	3,379,423	15.75	6.77
Additional general requirements	408,057	1.90	0.82
Site work	4,322,600	20.15	8.66
Concrete	4,855,785	22.63	9.72
Masonry	3,238,681	15.09	6.49
Metals	6,949,401	32.39	13.92
Wood and plastics	586,766	2.73	1.18
Thermal and moisture protection	2,260,087	10.53	4.53
Doors and windows	1,194,967	5.57	2.39
Finishes (paint, carpeting, etc.)	3,721,601	17.34	7.45
Equipment	15,175	0.07	0.03
Furnishings including retractable seating	1,640,662	7.65	3.29
Conveying systems (elevators, escalators)	350,445	1.63	0.70
Fire protection	815,850	3.80	1.63
Plumbing	2,623,075	12.22	5.25
Heating, ventilation, and air conditioning	6,911,690	32.21	13.84
Refrigeration	771,925	3.60	1.55
Electrical	5,885,993	27.43	11.79
Construction management fee	2,410,383	11.23	4.83*
Construction contingency	(1,777,304)	(8.28)	–3.56*
Owner's contingency	408,422	1.90	0.82*
Furniture, fixtures, and equipment allowance	5,305,000	24.72	10.62*
Total cost	**56,278,684**	**262.26**	

Adapted from Kasper Group 2001.

*The last four categories show rough percentages of the combined total construction costs displayed in other categories.

Webster Bank Arena was constructed with the potential to host an Arena Football League (AFL) team, but when no deal was reached after around ten years, a center-hung scoreboard was installed, thus making the facility less usable for AFL teams in the future.

The arena features an open ceiling plan, which allows events such as the circus to raise numerous pieces of equipment to the rafters with a very strong rigging system. The rigging capacity can hold up to 118,000 pounds (53,524 kg) to suspend items such as nets, curtains, trapezes, and other equipment from the rafters. Rigging capacity is critical for attracting large circus events and concerts where big stages need to be erected. Some large concerts require numerous trailers of gear that must be hoisted for the stage, video boards, and sound wall. The arena's rigging capacity was originally not affected by a center-hung scoreboard. When the arena was being designed, the facility management was trying to attract an Arena Football League (AFL) team and decided to hang scoreboards on the wall so the middle of the field would be unobstructed. No AFL team ended up playing at the arena. This shows that a facility might plan for certain options but that those options might not materialize. About 10 years later, without any hope of landing an AFL team, the arena installed a center-hung scoreboard. When the arena was being proposed there was significant talk about attracting major concerts to the facility. Although some major acts such as Barbra Streisand, Elton John, Nickelback, the Jonas Brothers, and Fleetwood Mac have performed at the arena, most major touring groups (which produce the large paydays) such as the Rolling Stones, Bruce Springsteen, and U2 play at other venues in neighboring states.

Connecticut is a small state with a population of around 3 million citizens. The state lies between New York and Boston, which both have significant public assembly venues that can be reached in less than 2 hours from most places in Connecticut. Thus, a significant number of facilities are vying for patrons' entertainment dollars. Instead of performing at one of the smaller venues in Connecticut, many acts pass the state by to play at facilities in Boston, New York, and New Jersey. Even within the state, Webster Bank Arena has to compete with several large outdoor concert facilities (Chevrolet Theatre and New England Dodge Music Center), larger university facilities (Yale and University of Connecticut), public arenas (XL Center), and concert venues at two large casinos (Foxwoods and Mohegan Sun).

University of New Haven's David A. Beckerman Recreation Center

I distinctly remember the request from the president at the University of New Haven for me to serve as the chair of the Programming, Space Planning, and Site Selection Committee to build a student recreation center on campus. On average, facility managers might help build one facility during their careers, and I did not know if I would ever get another opportunity, so I jumped at the offer. Although there was a small weight room and a gym on North Campus, these facilities were primarily used by athletes, and there was nothing near the dorms to engage a large number of students. Thus, the committee was charged with trying to design the most appropriate facility to meet the needs of all potential constituents.

The committee was assisted by Sasaki Associates Incorporated (which later helped design the Olympic Village for the 2008 Beijing Olympics) and Petra Construction Company. Architects from Sasaki designed the facility, and Petra built the facility. The committee involved a number of on-campus constituents, from faculty members and students to administrators and staff members.

The first step in the process was to determine how much money was available for the project (initially $12.5 million) and where the facility should be built. If the money would not allow building certain types of facilities or if the campus could not find space, then numerous options would not be viable. The committee conducted a student survey, which was completed by more than 250 students. The majority of survey respondents lived on campus. Only 13% of the survey respondents were involved in athletics or sport clubs, and 31% had used some type of campus recreation facility. Almost 72% of the respondents indicated that if there were a student recreation center, they would use it at least twice a week. The survey asked what activities the students wanted in the gym, and the most frequently cited activities were basketball, cardio, and weightlifting. Swimming, which is often an available option in a recreation center (although a pool is one of the most expensive elements to add to a facility), was the least-cited activity in the survey.

The survey results helped develop a baseline for what to include in the facility. However, Sasaki went one step further by developing an interactive communication process with the students. Large poster boards were placed in the student center, with pictures of various recreation center elements. Students were encouraged over several days to post their thoughts and to talk directly with the architects. This hands-on process helped excite the students about the project and allowed the architects to hear firsthand what the students wanted. The architects also looked at all locations on campus and contacted relevant parties to access potential locations. For example, the local mayor had to be consulted to see what he would support or which location might raise concerns for the city. With all this information, the committee created a vision statement, of which the first paragraph is as follows:

Building Vision Statement

The Fitness and Recreation Center (the Center) for the University of New Haven (UNH) shall be located within the heart of the campus to strengthen the collegiate experience for both residential and commuter students. The facility shall be a new "signature" building for the campus, projecting an enhanced image of the school and thereby serving as a significant recruitment and retention asset. The Center should be the starting point for campus tours. Aesthetically, the building should be forward-looking but fit in with the character of existing campus structures and materials. At night as well as during the day, this new Center should announce its presence as well as contribute to one's first impression upon arrival at the campus. The Center should be a magnet, attracting maximum use by students as well as by all other members of the UNH community (faculty, staff, administration).

The committee finalized a location on a major roadway next to campus. The architects built an elevated track with glass walls so those driving on the major road would be able to see activity and students to help highlight activities on campus. The final price tag for the 56,500-square-foot

(5,249 sq m) building was $15.5 million. The final building, which opened in 2008, has two full-size basketball courts, a multiactivity court, a 6,000-square-foot (558 sq m) fitness facility, a juice bar, locker rooms, a fitness room, a spinning room, and two racquetball courts.

Some unique components of the Center include the floor choices and room sizes. The weight room has a Nora rubber flooring system that is 3.5 millimeters thick. The 3,800-square-foot (353 sq m) cardio center has a Mondo rubber flooring system. The two basketball courts, which have a total area of 21,475 square feet (1,995 sq m), have a floor made of Aacer Chanel wood. The multiactivity court has an area of 16,000 square feet (1,486.5 sq m) and features an Indoor Bounceback high-impact copolymer suspended court surface and mechanically operated retractable backboards. The suspended court is made of individual tiles (12 inches by 12 inches and 0.75 inch thick, or 30.5 cm by 30.5 cm and 1.9 cm thick) that weigh 18 ounces (510.3 g) each. The individual tiles are tested to meet various industry specifications and safety criteria. This is especially important when sports such as inline hockey are played on the floor.

The locker rooms are small for a facility of this size because the center is across the parking lot from the dorms. Both the men's and women's locker rooms have 4 showers and 46 lockers (30 for rental and 16 for daily use) and are each less than 400 square feet (37.2 sq m) in size. The facility also has approximately 2,000 square feet (185.8 sq m) of storage and 1,000 square feet (92.9 sq m) of office space.

Project Timeline

Committee appointment and meetings	October 2005
Sasaki Associates hired as the architect	October 2005

Communication with stakeholders before developing the University of New Haven's David A. Beckerman Recreation Center led to the construction of a facility that had a glass facade facing a major street to help promote the city of West Haven as a vibrant location

Ground breaking	September 20, 2006
Soft opening	December 11, 2007
Grand opening	February 11, 2008
Dedication	April 12, 2008

Madison Square Garden

Madison Square Garden in New York, known as "the world's most famous arena," includes a 5,600-seat theater, a 20,000-seat arena, a 40,000-square-foot (3,716 sq m) expo center, two restaurants, and 89 club suites. The facility is often called MSG or the Garden. This enormous facility had its humble beginnings as an abandoned railroad shed. P.T. Barnum purchased the shed in 1874 and replaced it with a roofless structure that he named Barnum's Monster Classical and Geological Hippodrome. Some of the early events featured were chariot races, waltzing elephants, and fire eaters ("New York Landmarks," 2002). The earliest incarnation of the Garden was a 10,000-seat velodrome for races. The name Madison Square Garden was derived from the fact that the first two versions of the Garden were built at Madison Avenue and 26th Street. Between 1890 and 1925, the Garden was an indoor arena that could seat 8,000 fans; it cost $2 million to construct. Between 1925 and 1968, the Garden was located at 50th Street and 8th Avenue and could seat 18,000 fans. The current Madison Square Garden is located directly above Pennsylvania Station on 34th Street. Construction of the new facility began in 1963; its concrete foundation was poured in 1964. The building cost $116 million to construct ("New York Landmarks," 2002).

The current version was built on top of the railroad terminal used by the Pennsylvania Railroad. The joint venture was very beneficial because the railroad still had its major hub in New York and was able to strike a deal with a developer willing to develop a large-scale commercial and entertainment center. The relationship was very beneficial for the Garden as fans could take the subway or train from near and far and simply walk up several flights of stairs to get to their entertainment venue. This proximity eliminated the need for significant parking space, which is not available in most of New York City. The Garden became a destination location before the term came into vogue. The Garden allowed people to take in a show, go to a fancy dinner, shop at upscale stores, and spend a nice day and a lot of money in one of the busiest cities in the world.

Here are a few interesting facts about Madison Square Garden:

- The facility has more than 1,000,000 square feet (92,900 sq m) of space.
- It hosts more than 600 events each year.
- It hosts more than 4 million visitors each year.
- The roof is 404 feet (123 m) wide and 64 feet (19.5 m) high (Schoenberg, 2001).

Over the years the arena has hosted dogs and cats, elephants and athletes, award shows, musical artists, superstars, and even Big Bird. Currently it is the home of the New York Knicks, the Rangers, and the Liberty. The Westminster Kennel Club Dog Show, the National Horse Show, and Ringling Bros. and Barnum and Bailey Circus are regular events. One of the famous fights between Muhammad Ali and Joe Frazier took place at the Garden in 1971. Paul Simon, the Grateful Dead, and Elton John

© giovanni mereghetti/age fotostock

Despite recent renovations totaling nearly one billion dollars, Madison Square Garden's lease of the original Penn Station facility will expire in 2023.

are just a few of the musical acts that have passed through the Garden's doors over the years. Madison Square Garden is a prime example of a successful multipurpose PAF (Schoenberg, 2001). Thus, the Garden is not just a building but also a piece of New York, United States, sport, and entertainment history.

MSG was considering a move two blocks away, but in 2008 a decision was made to renovate the Garden once again in time for the New York Rangers' 2011-2012 season. The $1 billion, full-scale renovation focused on the interior of the building and used the Garden's current footprint. Some of the renovations undertaken include the following:

- Dramatically redesigned 7th Avenue entrance
- New, more comfortable seats with better sight lines
- Wider and more spacious public concourses with significant views of the city skyline
- State-of-the-art lighting, sound, and video systems
- New food and beverage options
- New bar areas that open directly to the arena bowl
- 68 new midlevel suites that are 50% larger than the former suites and closer to the playing surface
- 20 new floor-level suites
- Improved dressing rooms, locker rooms, green rooms, and production offices

- A new upper level with a fan and group-sales party deck that replaced the older upper suites
- Additional new restrooms (Madison Square Garden, 2008)

The initial renovations were expected to cost $500 million but grew to about $1 billion. Such expenditure was questioned by many, not just because of the large cost but because MSG's lease over Pennsylvania Station was supposed to expire. Just after renovations were completed, the New York City Council voted in 2013 to terminate the facility's lease in 2023 ("MSG's Lease," 2013).

Maple Leaf Gardens

In 1931 Conn Smythe, then manager of the Toronto Maple Leafs, built Maple Leaf Gardens in Toronto. This 16,000-seat multipurpose facility was to host the Maple Leafs for the next 68 years. During that time it also hosted a wide variety of concerts by such performers as Duke Ellington, Elvis Presley, the Beatles, Pearl Jam, and Rush.

The following are interesting facts about Maple Leaf Gardens:

- It took 1,200 construction workers 5 months and 12 days to build the yellow brick-faced structure.
- The facility was built for $1.5 million.
- It had 16,000 seats and 85 box seats.
- The building materials included 750,000 bricks, 77,500 bags of cement, and 70 tons of sand.
- The 350- by 282-foot (106 by 86 m) building extended 13 stories (44 yd or 40 m) above street level.
- Opening-night seat prices ranged from $0.95 to $2.75 ("Maple Leaf Gardens," 2002).

The Gardens was financed in a unique manner. The land was purchased for $350,000 from a major backer. To help reduce construction costs, Smythe entered into an agreement with the unions stipulating that those working on the project would receive Gardens stock in exchange for a wage reduction of 20% ("Maple Leaf Gardens," 2002). Since the facility was built during the Depression, material costs were between 20% and 30% lower than pre-Depression costs because of low demand.

In an attempt to provide a sport complex, the Gardens originally included a six-lane bowling alley, a billiards room, and a gymnasium. These areas were transformed over the years into carpenter and electrician workshops and storage areas. The ice surface was 85 by 200 feet (26 by 61 m), and it remained in place from late August to the end of the hockey season. During nonhockey events, sheets of plywood covered the ice, and the staging and chairs were placed on top.

In 1999 the Maple Leafs hockey team left Maple Leaf Gardens and moved five blocks away to the state-of-the-art, $265 million Air Canada Centre. Concert promoters cleared out of the Gardens shortly thereafter. Faced with a future of minor concert and sport bookings such as lacrosse and junior hockey games, Maple Leaf Sports and Entertainment Ltd. put the facility up for sale. In 2004, Maple Leaf Gardens was sold to Canada's largest food retailer, Loblaw Companies, for $12 million. A condition of the purchase was that the facility could not be used for sporting or concert events that would compete with the Maple Leafs' new facility. Loblaw turned the historic venue into a megamarket that opened in 2011. After receiving some funds from the Canadian government, a university athletic facility was also added to the historic building.

The Gardens was a venerable facility with a rich tradition. The trick for the new facility was to embrace the past but launch a new future for the city and the teams that play there. The Air Canada Centre was built on the site of the original Canada Post Delivery Building. Thus, the architects combined the historic east and south walls of the building into the new arena's design. The roof was built with a flat design to help with acoustics and to minimize the building's impact on the surrounding skyline. The architects developed the new arena with a 140,000-square-foot (13,000 sq m), 12-story office tower, which is called the Air Canada Tower. Air Canada, which purchased the naming rights to the arena ($2 million a year for 20 years), occupies the top six floors of the tower.

The Air Canada Centre was built just south of the GO train tracks, with the Galleria connecting the train station with the Centre. The Galleria is a covered, climate-controlled throughway where people can walk by ticket offices, food courts, and retail establishments. Thus, whereas Madison

Square Garden has numerous amenities under one roof, the replacement for the Canadian version of the Garden is more spread out. The Toronto Maple Leafs' owners also completed a $500 million expansion that included building towers with more than 800 condos, a mini hotel, and retail and office space next to the Air Canada Centre (Munsey and Suppes, 2009). The new arena highlights how a city can transition from a beloved older facility to a new facility and not miss a beat. In fact, attendance at the Air Canada Centre is hovering near 100% of capacity, and the arena is an economic engine that in its first 10 years is supposed to generate $2.4 billion in economic benefit (Munsey and Suppes, 2009).

THE FUTURE OF SPORT FACILITIES

As noted earlier in the chapter, Greek and Roman facilities were the precursors of modern PAFs. However, other civilizations, from the Far East to South America, also contributed to the spread of sport facilities. For example, the Mayans (AD 300-AD 1200) and the Aztecs (AD 1200-AD 1500) played ball games in stone courts; nobles could sit inside to observe the competition, and all other spectators had to listen to the event from the outside (Leonard, 1974).

From ancient times to the present, the basic structure of such facilities remained essentially unchanged until the past 50 years. Tremendous changes over the past 50 years include such innovations as domed stadiums, stadiums with retractable roofs, and structures that can rotate on tracks to change a large arena into an intimate performing arts stage. Although the United States has been the leader in terms of the breadth and diversity of new stadiums and arenas in the past 40 years, the facility construction boom that hit North America in the 1990s spread internationally, and that is where many building innovations are now occurring. The greatest growth at the start of the 21st century occurred in Japan and Greece. Japan went on a massive binge of building soccer stadiums to cohost the 2002 World Cup with Korea. The largest of the stadiums is International Stadium in Yokohama, which can seat 71,416 and cost $526.32 million to build. A total of 20 facilities were built at a cost of $4.64 billion ("Kick-off for 2002," 2001). It is estimated that Korea spent an additional $1.7 billion on facilities, while France spent $1.5 billion on facilities for the 1998 World Cup. These numbers highlight the magnitude of international facility growth and show how expensive stadiums are to build and how prices have escalated because of the desire for domed or adjustable facilities and other expensive innovations.

Numerous large, well-run sport facilities exist all over the world. Some of the largest stadiums are used for soccer, especially in the five primary leagues: Premier League in England, Ligue 1 in France, Bundesliga in Germany, Serie A TIM in Italy, and Liga BBVA in Spain. In each region, teams and stadiums generate different amounts of match-day revenue. The highest amounts of revenue are generated in Scotland (48%), Switzerland (39%), Greece (32%), and Spain (31%). The average for the "big five" leagues is 21% of revenue from match day; 46% of revenue comes from broadcasting, and the remaining 33% comes from other operating revenue (Sartori, 2011).

Such revenue is generated even though a number of stadiums are very old. The average age of stadiums in Scotland is 80 years, followed by 71 years in England, 66 years in Sweden, and 65 years in Italy. Thus, the major professional teams in Europe are playing in much older stadiums compared to the relatively new major stadiums in the United States. These stadiums are often upgraded; however, in Scotland the average time since the last major upgrade is 15 years. Newer facilities can be examined in terms of the cost per seat. Two of the most expensive international facilities built are Wembley Stadium and Emirates Stadium, both in London. Wembley Stadium opened in 2007 and replaced a stadium built in 1923. The 90,000-seat stadium cost €912 million (about $705.6 million US) to develop, which results in a cost of €10,137 ($7,800 US) per seat. Emirates Stadium opened in 2006 and can seat 60,335 fans. The development cost was €440 million (about $363.5 million US), which results in a cost of €7,292 ($6,000 US) per seat (Sartori, 2011).

A 2012 survey of 2,000 sport fans in England examined what the public wants to see in future sport facilities. The top answers include the following:

More comfortable and spacious seating	49%
Better transportation options	32%
Better crowd modeling to help crowd movement	32%
Better technology to show replays and different angles	30%
Safety-designed standing room (European soccer)	27%

Other upgrades requested by fans include better mobile reception, better parking and transportation options, heated seats, greater access to referee commentary and match analysis, electronic access for ease of entry, and a blocking system that blocks phone calls during a game. These fans also felt that a facility's design can make it iconic (62%) and that the length of lines for the restrooms has the most negative effect on a fan's experience (41%) ("What Fans Want," 2012).

Major soccer stadiums are not the only facilities being renovated or rebuilt to save money. This cost aspect is also seen in Olympic Games facilities. Athens mounted a tremendous construction effort to prepare for the 2004 Olympic Games. The Olympic Stadium had to be refurbished and renovated. A couple years before the Games, a large percentage of the 23 facilities required to host the Games had yet to be built ("Athens' Challenge," 2001). The International Olympic Committee was concerned about the completion of the facilities and voiced a strong warning to Greece to hasten their construction efforts. In fact, construction was not completed until hours before the Games began. The Games budget was estimated to be $1.7 billion, with a large percentage of these funds dedicated to sport facilities, but it grew to more than $11.6 billion (Varouhakis, 2004). In contrast, constructing all the facilities necessary for the Australian Olympic Games in 2000 cost more than $3 billion. The required buildings included the 110,000-seat Stadium Australia; the 20,000-seat Sydney SuperDome; the Sydney International Athletic Centre; and several other aquatic, sailing, and shooting facilities (Jackson

and Menser, 2000).

Beijing, China, hosted the 2008 Olympic Games. It was estimated that 37 stadiums and arenas would be either built or renovated for the Games. The expected cost of completing all the required facilities was $3.4 billion. In addition, another $1.94 billion was supposed to be spent on ancillary facilities such as the Olympic Village, press center, and broadcasting center ("Beijing to Spend," 2002). The costs kept growing throughout the construction process and ended at around $42 billion. The Winter Olympics in Sochi are estimated to cost around $51 billion; much of the money was reportedly wasted on government corruption (Yaffa, 2014). The stunning costs to host the Games spooked at least five large cities from moving forward with bids for the 2022 Games. Candidates who pulled out included Oslo, Norway; Switzerland; Stockholm, Sweden; and Munich, Germany.

One of the issues for these Games (and all past and future Olympics) is how to utilize the facilities after the Olympics have ended. Nobody wants the facilities to become "white elephants," but there are significant financial issues associated with running facilities. For example, the Calgary Olympics in 1988 generated a $150 million profit, but the lasting legacy has been the facilities, which are still actively utilized. The Olympic Oval is one of the fastest speed skating tracks in the world and is used as a training center (Sibold, 2002). The Calgary facilities have fared well because they were close to downtown and there was a need for the facilities. The facilities developed for the Vancouver Games in 2010 were also designed or renovated to help save costs. The main ice hockey rink, Rogers Arena, was a pre-existing hockey rink used by the Vancouver Canucks. It was a narrower, NHL-sized ice rink, measuring 200 by 85 feet (61 by 26 m), which was 4 meters narrower than traditional Olympic hockey facilities. Because it didn't have to expand the ice, the facility could be used again for its intended purpose and saved more than $10 million in renovation costs. Other past Olympic sites have not been as lucky. In fact, most of the facilities utilized for the Athens Olympic Games have fallen into disuse, and some have become encampments for traveling gypsies (Rogers, 2008).

One year after the Beijing Olympic Games, the iconic Bird's Nest Stadium served no real purpose. It has no home team but has held several concerts. A number of visitors pay 50 yuan (around $7.00) to picnic in the stands and take pictures. An amusement park was added to one corner (Meyer, 2009). The stadium generated $38 million in revenue during the first year and a half after the Games (70% of those funds came from tourists), but by December 2009 the number of tourists declined from a high of 50,000 per day to around 10,000 per day (Brown, 2010). The goal of the Beijing Olympic Games was to prove to the world that China could host the Games. They did, and were successful. Project 119 was named for the number of gold medals that the Chinese wanted to win when the Games came to China. China somewhat succeeded on this ambitious front as well: They won 100 medals, including 51 gold medals. Yet for all the accolades, the citizens of Beijing cannot drink the tap water or even exercise in clean air.

However, even with all these issues, China was able to save money and valuable real estate. Eight of the 31 venues were temporary. Thus, the baseball diamond is now a mall construction site. Greece might wish they had built more temporary facilities. Some of the facilities have fallen into complete disrepair and other elements are trash dumps. Even though it is in horrible shape, the Greek government has reportedly spent close to $1 billion to maintain facilities that are basically unused.

Heeding these lessons, the facilities for the London Olympics were built to be later reduced to a more manageable scale. The 80,000-seat Olympic stadium was reduced to a 54,000-seat home for West Ham United Football Club. The basketball arena was a temporary structure that was torn down after the Games (basketball is not as popular in England), and the dismantled building and flooring were on the market for $3.3 million. The 3,000 units of the Athletes' Village were built without kitchens because food was provided to the athletes; this allowed more athletes to sleep in each unit. After the Games, kitchens were added to each unit, which were then sold to create the new neighborhood known as East Village. Last, the 17,500-seat aquatic center was reduced to a more manageable 2,500-seat swimming facility.

These Olympic examples highlight a major initiative for sport facilities in the future, as these facilities need to be built assuming that they will not be utilized effectively or will lose money. Although there will always be a demand for health clubs and school and community sport facilities, most countries or communities cannot afford to spend hundreds of millions of dollars for new, state-of-the-art facilities. Thus, older facilities that might be condemned in richer countries need to be kept open in poorer countries. Even wealthier countries have a mix of old and new facilities. A typical sport facility is designed to last 50 years. It is possible for 50-year-old facilities to be in great shape and for those that are only 10 years old to be in poor shape. Political, financial, equipment, personnel, and other factors can help explain why some facilities are in good shape and others are not. There can also be a blend of facilities, such as on a college campus (e.g., Yale University) that has some very old and some modern facilities.

Sometimes an emergency facilitates building a new facility. For example, Brazil hosted the 2014 World Cup. The facilities were surveyed before the games, and one facility that was highly criticized was Estádio Fonte Nova in Salvador, voted the worst of the 29 major stadiums in the country. In 2007 a portion of the stands collapsed during victory celebrations after a soccer game, injuring at least 50 people and killing 8 (Astor, 2007). This and other stadiums needed to be repaired or replaced to host the World Cup games. The initial budget of $2.3 billion for facility construction ended up increasing to around $3.5 billion. It is hoped that a number of the stadiums will be used for the Olympics in 2016. However, the 71,000-seat Estádio Nacional de Brasilia, which cost around $600 million, will not have a tenant after the World Cup (Panja, 2013).

Although poorer countries may not be able to afford to build new PAFs, richer countries must carefully evaluate any efforts to modify or build facilities. Any new construction effort may necessitate compliance with requirements that can significantly affect building budgets and even the ability to build or renovate. One of the key concerns with building Olympic dream facilities is accessibility. In Greek and Roman times, disabled persons who could not enter a facility would be out of luck; now a disabled person can sue to get into a facility. Immediately after the Olympic Games, the Paralympics are held. These Games for the disabled use the same facilities as the Olympics, which must accommodate the needs of the disabled. Thus, handicapped access and other services need to be considered in construction. This concern was evidenced in the Atlanta Olympic Games in 1996, 6 years after the Americans with Disabilities Act (ADA) was passed. The ADA requires facilities and programs to accommodate the needs of the disabled whenever practicable. All new construction projects in the United States are required to comply with this law, which is one reason the Atlanta Olympics were viewed as the most accessible Games held to date (Beasley, 1997).

TRENDS THAT WILL AFFECT FUTURE FACILITIES

As noted earlier, political and religious concerns helped foster construction of the Roman Coliseum and Circus Maximus. The idea was that if citizens were busy enjoying sport and other events, they might be more content and would not try to overthrow the government. Modern facilities are often built with the same political goals in mind. Most voters would be hard-pressed to find an elected official who wants to be known as the politician that lost a professional team. Elected officials often go out of their way to provide any assistance possible to attract or retain a professional team. Debacles involving poor political planning are numerous. Examples from the past twenty years include the following:

- Cincinnati officials did not reveal the true cost of their new stadiums until after the election ended; they then raised the estimated price for the football and baseball stadiums approximately $100 million each, just 1 day after the voters approved the construction (Fried, Deshriver, and Mondello 2013).

- Tampa officials bought the argument raised by the Tampa Bay Buccaneers' owner that he needed a new stadium because he was losing money in his old facility, but they never checked to confirm the veracity of his statement (Fried, Deshriver, and Mondello 2013).

- Texas officials negotiated a contract with the Texas Motor Speedway that exempted the Speedway from property tax requirements, which cost the local school district more than $21 million a year and prompted the schools to sue (Fried, Deshriver, and Mondello 2013).

BUILDING A TEMPORARY SPORT FACILITY

Have you ever thought about building a temporary sport facility and where would you put it? The Winter Classic is an outdoor hockey event that pits a variety of lower-level hockey teams (such as local clubs, high school, college, and semi-professional teams) against each other; the headline is an NHL game. This event has been played outdoors at various stadiums, including Wrigley Field, Fenway Park, Heinz Field, and Citizens Bank Park, since 2008. A temporary structure is built for the event and includes a large refrigerated truck to keep the ice cold. This was especially critical for the 2014 game at Dodger Stadium, where it took 4 days to build the ice. Special solar blankets were used to reflect the sun so that the ice would not melt during the game, which was played on a sunny, warm day. Around 56,000 fans watched the hockey game outdoors, whereas only around 18,000 fans can watch a game at Staples Center.

Basketball games have also been moved to unique venues, including a game played on the USS Carl Vinson in 2011. The competitors were Michigan State and North Carolina, who played each other in the previous year's National Collegiate Athletic Association championship game. The attendees included crew members, wounded warriors, and their families. A 150-person crew had 9 days to set up the bleachers for 7,000 fans, tents, locker rooms, souvenir stores, and so on, and it took 4 days to tear down after the event. A secondary court (in case of rainouts) was built on the hanger deck. To help accommodate the culinary needs of the fans, the civilian caterers ordered 4,550 hot dogs, 3,000 bags of chips, and 12,000 bottles of soda and water (Murphy, 2011).

■ Houston voters agreed to build a downtown baseball stadium even though an advisory group recommended a different site. Elected officials along with a wealthy businessman and his company, which hoped to cash in on a downtown site, spearheaded the site change. The businessman was Kenneth Lay, and the company was the now-bankrupt Enron.

Since these scandals, numerous voter-associated groups have aggressively advocated for better voter knowledge about the financial benefits, or possible lack thereof, for various proposed facility referendums. The recent economic turmoil has voters rallying against spending their tax dollars on sport facilities, so any new referendums for the next several years will face significant voter scrutiny and a demand for more accountability. For example, the shenanigans associated with government funding for the Miami Marlins' stadium that opened in 2012, including a public-funding plan that could eventually cost Miami–Dade County $2.4 billion, led to significant litigation, contributed to the ouster of several local politicians, and triggered a Securities and Exchange Commission investigation.

These examples highlight why there have been significant battles after almost every vote to build a stadium or arena for the primary benefit of a private business owner. Although some facilities are financed entirely with private funds, most are built with a majority of public funds. Public funds are utilized because of the perceived benefit that a stadium (and its major tenant team) will provide the city or region. The true benefit is hard to quantify, but arguments on both sides are possible regarding whether a stadium or arena provides a benefit or whether people are willing to invest several dollars a month in extra taxes in order to be able to talk about the local team around the water cooler at work. Although public funding was a popular trend in the 1990s, a poor economy at the start of the 21st century curtailed some projects. Other projects have faced the voters' wrath. Some projects, such as the newer stadium for the New York Jets and Giants, included a significant private contribution to the total proposed construction cost. The teams initially indicated they would contribute a total of $800 million toward the $1.5 billion price tag for the stadium (Heyman,

2003). However, as construction progressed, each team contributed $650 million to the new stadium (Kaplan, 2007).

Chapter 4 provides a more detailed analysis of political issues. However, it is necessary to acknowledge the political issue here because PAFs have for centuries been closely tied with politics. Any effort to analyze PAFs without examining the political influences associated with how facilities are built, funded, and maintained fails to recognize the historical social significance these facilities have had. Political entities do not build facilities just to placate the masses. Every issue, from bond issuance and tax abatements through safety inspection and zoning or nuisance debates, intertwines the facility and various government entities. These and other overlaps are discussed throughout this book. It is important to understand from the beginning that without government support (or we could say the support of "the public"), sport facilities as we have them today would not exist.

Other trends besides political shifts include technological and sport-related changes. Technological innovations range from new rigging systems (to support large weights such as scoreboards) to stadium fields on rollers (to allow the use of natural grass in a domed stadium; in favorable weather conditions the grass can be rolled outside). One of the most important current trends in technology involves applications (apps) that get fans more involved with the event. If stadiums and arenas didn't have the latest technology, fans would stay home to watch games on their large-screen televisions and have access to all their gadgets. The Major League Soccer franchise Sporting Kansas City opened a new soccer stadium in 2011. Of the $200 million construction cost, $6 million went toward a high-density wireless network that has 220 miles (354 km) of fiber (seven times the norm for a stadium of its size). The high-tech environment allows almost 25% of fans (compared with an average of 10% at most NFL stadiums) to use the team's supplied app, called Uphoria. The app allows fans to customize their watching experience and engage with other fans electronically (Wiedeman, 2013).

Sport-related changes can be seen with new sports. Extreme sports are changing numerous sport and recreation facilities. Skateboard and paintball parks were being built in record numbers through the mid 2000s to help keep kids off city buildings and out of dangerous locations, but similar to other facility fads a good number of these facilities have closed. Other facilities that are not traditionally considered sport facilities, such as bridges, can become havens for base jumpers and other extreme sport enthusiasts; such usage can generate significant liability and safety trends that facility managers need to carefully consider and act on.

Summary

Sport facilities have undergone significant changes over time, especially over the past two centuries. The Greeks and Romans intertwined politics and religion to build large PAFs to placate the masses. These types of facilities have evolved over the years into architectural and mechanical marvels. Today's PAFs serve as economic catalysts for growth to promote economic, geopolitical, and local political ends. Although this chapter gives more attention to larger facilities, smaller facilities have also undergone changes that have made them more marketable and economically viable. This growth will undoubtedly continue in the future, and the same trends seen in the growth of facilities in the United States will feature more prominently around the world. In fact, recent Olympic and World Cup facilities show that the world has caught up with the United States in producing the best facilities for the needs of current teams and fans.

Discussion Questions and Activities

1. What do you think current facility managers have learned from their predecessors?

2. What similarities and differences can you see between Madison Square Garden and Maple Leaf Gardens?

3. Take a tour of your university athletic fields and athletic facilities. What similarities and differences can you see between your facilities and the facilities at the University of New Haven?

4. Why did the Romans build stadiums?

5. Why did modern universities build major sport and recreation complexes on campuses?

6. Why do cities build stadiums and arenas for professional sport teams with public money?

7. Is building new Olympic stadiums and facilities a good investment? Why or why not?

8. Which recent Olympic venue do you think is the best for its intended and future use?

9. If you were charged with building a new Olympic facility (or other major venue), what high-tech bells and whistles would you add and why?

2

Facility Management

Chapter Objectives

- Understand what facility management is and what the facility manager's role is.
- Appreciate the complex blend of duties required when managing a facility.
- Appreciate the consumer orientation required to effectively run a facility.
- Appreciate the effect that external entities (i.e., stakeholders) have on a facility.

Facility management involves significant dedication on the part of the facility manager to present events that have value and to present these events in the most attractive, most convenient, and safest environment possible. Facilities have so many components requiring management that the failure of any one can spell disaster. Imagine a fire sprinkler system turning on in an arena and flooding the floor. Imagine 20,000 people in an arena without any air conditioning. Imagine half of the stadium lights going out in the middle of an internationally televised Super Bowl game. Patrons would be irate and the facility would suffer significant negative publicity and economic damages. Thus, the responsibility of making sure that a facility is operating correctly rests on a facility manager's shoulders.

This chapter starts with a critical analysis of facility management and the role that the facility manager plays in achieving the facility's goals and objectives. The facility manager has numerous duties that are significantly affected by the facility size and ownership structure. The chapter also introduces facility and personnel management issues.

Facility managers do not operate in a vacuum. They are influenced by numerous parties, from the lead tenants to government entities or private companies. A facility manager's most important **constituents** are the customers and employees. In addition, facility managers must report to numerous other **stakeholders.** Stakeholders range from the politicians who authorized funds to help build the facility to the independent parties who provide facility management outsourcing services. Fans and teams are some of the most important stakeholders. The last part of this chapter highlights managerial functions, specifically planning, organizing, implementing, and controlling the facility and those working in the facility.

WHAT IS FACILITY MANAGEMENT?

Managing sport and public assembly facilities (PAFs) is often referred to as facility management, and the people who perform the duties are called facility managers. Facility management can also refer to managing any other type of facility, from an office building to a hospital or an entire university with hundreds of buildings. **Facility management** entails a broad array of disciplines including, but not limited to, planning, designing, leasing, space planning; project management; capital management; construction management; property management; facility marketing, building and operation management, and real estate acquisition, planning, and disposal (Teicholz and Noferi, 2002). Facility managers for larger facilities often have to spend more time marketing, developing ancillary income streams (concessions, catering, merchandising), and booking and scheduling events, especially if there is no anchor tenant. Differences between sport facilities may be due to size or ownership structure. That is, a high school or college sport facility may not have to make money every day the facility is open, but a stadium or arena will normally not open on a given day unless there is an event that will generate enough revenue to cover all costs.

A significant focus for facility management is to make sure an existing facility runs smoothly and is safe for its intended purpose. Facility management often focuses on the hardware required for smooth operation of the facility. Are parking lots ready for 10,000 cars? Are the bleachers, walkways, elevators, escalators, and other facility components operating safely? Managers have to coordinate maintenance and renovation schedules to make sure that existing facilities do not deteriorate from abuse or from failure to properly maintain them. However, facility management can also apply to building a new facility. A university might call on a facility manager to help design a new gymnasium and manage the construction process. Facility managers cannot do everything, so they need to work with others, including architects, designers, contractors, governme nt officials, and numerous other parties, to accomplish the required goals and objectives. Working with others is one of the most important tasks a manager undertakes.

Managers may have to design and launch a new facility, but this process may occur only once in a manager's professional career. Thus, a facility manager needs to focus more on actual building operations to meet the facility's service-oriented goals. The facility's goals often focus on filling

Becki: Building relationships

Photo courtesy of Leah Becki.

My name is Leah Becki and I am the general manager of the Ryan Center and Boss Ice Arena at the University of Rhode Island. I am honored to write this introduction and dedicate this chapter to Terry Butler, my former boss, mentor, and friend. Terry was an expert in facility management. He was a master at building relationships and had experience managing numerous university venues, including the Mackenzie Arena at the University of Tennessee at Chattanooga, the Mitchell Center at the University of South Alabama, and the Ryan Center and Boss Ice Arena at the University of Rhode Island. Terry wrote this introduction for the second edition of *Managing Sport Facilities*.

I had the great privilege of working with Terry in his role as the general manager of the Ryan Center and Boss Ice Arena. Terry first ventured into the world of private facility management when he was hired by Global Spectrum to manage the facilities for the state university. Terry's ability to build relationships was the key to creating a successful environment where both state and private entities could work together to achieve a common goal. Terry opened both buildings in the summer of 2002 and managed both facilities until his passing in 2011. The Ryan Center, a 7,800-seat arena, and the Boss Ice Arena, a 2,500-seat ice rink, prospered under Terry's management. He made these building what they are today, and, although it was heart wrenching, I was honored to take over Terry's role as general manager after his passing and to continue running the wonderful facility he had built.

As mentioned in this chapter, facilities serve three main constituents: customers, internal relations, and external relations. As you read through this chapter you will understand that everything facility managers do is about building relationships, whether with employees, customers, clients, vendors, or others. One of the many things I learned from Terry is the importance of the relationships between facility managers and their employees. As managers, we need our employees to be experts in their areas but also to wear many hats or take on new roles at any given time. The team is responsible for making the business a success. We must respect our employees' decisions, honor them, rely on them, give them opportunities to grow, and—most importantly—give them our time. This is the starting point for success in facility management because when the team is positive and happy, it trickles down to great customer service, content vendors, and clients who are well taken care of.

the facility's time and space opportunities and conducting events in a safe and client-oriented fashion. Facility management also entails the art of coordinating the physical workplace with the people and entities that will use the workplace. In essence, facility management blends a wide variety of disciplines, including architecture, engineering, business, and behavioral science, to optimize how a facility and its users interact and optimize the use of the facility. In summary, facility management entails every aspect of making sure a building is operating efficiently in terms of safety, revenue production, tenant satisfaction, and preventive maintenance.

Facility management is not an easy job. With diverse responsibilities and obligations, a facility manager must have many highly specific skills. Facility managers also need a significant amount of time to complete their tasks. The facility manager is often the first person to arrive on the job each day and the last to leave. In many facilities, the facility manager has to be present on game nights and may be present on weekends. But although the job may at times seem thankless and unusually time consuming, putting on well-received events in the facility can be a tremendous reward. Most facility managers would say that their job affects their family life and that they miss a number of major life events, but these same managers would say that they have tremendous job satisfaction, in part because of the variety of activities that make every day unique.

THE FACILITY MANAGER

A facility manager is the person responsible for coordinating all the employees and entities involved in the facility to ensure that they work on behalf of the facility and help meet its short- and long-term goals and objectives. Many people are in fact facility managers in their daily lives and do not realize it. The person who is the head of a household is really a facility manager. That person needs to purchase the house, pay the mortgage, paint the rooms, install new equipment such as air conditioners, maintain existing systems such as the roof, manage facility "subletting" (as in determining who is going to get which room), interact with government entities to pay taxes, and employ tradespeople such as plumbers and electricians.

The term *facility manager* is often used in the context of general facilities such as office buildings, but most of the same duties and responsibilities also apply to sport facility managers. Facility managers for big and small buildings face the same daily concerns. A facility manager's role is affected by the facility size and the workforce available to the manager. In a small facility, the facility owner may be the manager and can be responsible for opening and closing the facility as well as painting the walls and cleaning the restrooms. A facility

FACILITY FOCUS

CANDLESTICK PARK

Candlestick Park (more recently known as 3Com Park) is a well-known sport facility in San Francisco. San Francisco is a major earthquake area, and the facility is not far from the San Andreas fault. San Francisco has had a number of large earthquakes, including a major one in 1909 that destroyed a large part of the city. In a historic incident, an earthquake interrupted a 1989 World Series game between the San Francisco Giants and the Oakland A's. When the quake struck, the power was lost in large portions of the San Francisco area, including Candlestick Park, where the game was being played. The game was being nationally televised, and the chaos in the stands was shown across the country. Executives rushed to turn on the emergency generator, but it was out of gas. Furthermore, the public address system was not even connected to the generator. To communicate to the fans in the stands, police cars with loudspeakers were brought onto the field. However, the speakers were able to reach only the first several sections, and word of mouth was required to convey directions to those farther up in the stands.

Photo by Rich Pilling/Getty Images

manager for a large facility may have several dozen full-time and possibly hundreds to thousands of part-time employees handling everything, from cleanup crews to ushers and ticket takers. Because of the diverse duties each facility manager faces, facility management can be considered both an art and a science.

Specific duties need to be undertaken to ensure that a building can be opened for a planned event. From making sure there are enough hot dogs to monitoring indoor air quality, facility management has many facets. Managing all these tasks can appear to be onerous. Smaller facilities often rely on one individual to undertake all facility management activities. In many instances, a smaller facility has only one person who serves as the owner, manager, custodian, and secretary. The manager of a small health club has to find an appropriate location to build or must lease an existing structure (chapter 4). Part of the location identification process focuses on choosing the proper area (chapter 5), sales and marketing opportunities in the area (chapter 11), and financing options (chapter 12). Managers must work with outside vendors and government entities to secure necessary permits and complete any needed construction or renovations. The facility manager may have to design the facility, choose appropriate color and material schemes, and purchase and install all necessary fitness and office equipment (chapters 5-8). Once the facility is completed the manager will need to maintain it (chapter 9), consider strategies for addressing sustainability and environmental concerns (chapter 10), make sure the facility is operating within the law and in accordance with contracts (chapter 13), and then focus on planning for future needs and marketing to increase income streams. Smaller facilities that start to grow will often need to add employees, and then the facility manager must apply basic human resource skills (chapter 3) to appropriately manage the employees. The job is even more difficult when the facility needs constant attention, forcing the manager to spend time on keeping the facility clean and running rather than on generating revenue.

Larger facilities may have several different crews responsible for different functions such as ticketing, marketing, game operations, mechanicals, and janitorial responsibilities. Thus, facility management for larger facilities involves orchestrating the work of employees and volunteers to help accomplish the facility's goals. Because a PAF is dedicated to attracting events that will generate income or indirect economic activity (ripple effect; see chapter 4), PAF managers must always examine the facility's best use and determine what events will produce the most positive outcome to the bottom line consistent with the facility's mission. A manager for a larger facility has some duties similar to those of a small-facility manager, such as marketing and financial management. The general manager of a minor league baseball team may have to sell tickets, groom the field, move furniture, and undertake tasks involving both team and facility management because the budget typically does not allow the hiring of others. In contrast, a manager for a large facility typically has a staff that can undertake marketing, maintenance, renovations, and numerous other functions. This gives the manager the opportunity to work on broader issues such as long-term planning, developing strong constituent relations, and making sure the right employees are doing the various jobs.

Even though the duties undertaken in facility management may be fluid and can change according to the facility size, a facility manager has some well-defined expectations. According to the International Facility Management Association (IFMA), facility managers are critical for implementing any facility management plan and need to understand and appreciate several distinct functions. The latest study conducted by the IFMA (International Facility Management Association, 2007) highlights that the future competency of facility managers should entail the following:

- Operations and management
- Facility function
- Real estate
- Finance
- Human and environmental factors
- Quality assessment and innovation
- Planning and project management
- Communication
- Technology

Furthermore, to prepare properly for the future, facility managers should develop their skill sets in regard to some of the following major current concerns:

- Linking facility management to strategy
- Emergency preparedness
- Change management
- Sustainability
- Emerging technology
- Globalization
- Broadening diversity in the workforce
- Aging buildings

Numerous activities occupy a facility manager's time:

- The facility manager needs to plan all facility activities, control schedules, manage contracts, develop work standards, and evaluate both employees and external contractors.
- Managers need to hire and organize all personnel, develop work schedules, and implement appropriate policies and procedures.
- Facility managers need to develop short-, intermediate-, and long-term plans, with a strong focus on financial ramifications for each option.
- The facility manager needs to develop an inventory of available space and manage that space by allocating it as needed and obtaining additional space for future growth.
- A facility manager needs to have a strong appreciation and understanding of building design and planning, architectural design, engineering design, code and zoning compliance, construction costs, and building systems and their maintenance needs.
- Workplace planning and design entail procuring and managing furniture and equipment for such areas as concessions, locker rooms, and press box.
- Facility managers need to focus significant effort on budgeting, accounting, and economic forecasting.
- Managers need to be involved in managing construction projects or moving from one area or facility to another.

- A facility manager will need to spend significant time on operations, maintenance, and repairs. These activities can include exterior maintenance of the building and aspects such as trash and pest control.
- Since 9/11, facility managers have been forced to deal with security and life safety concerns to a much greater extent than ever before.
- Last, managers have to supervise general administrative departments such as food service or a mail room (Cotts and Lee, 1992).

Although these functions are numerous, the primary function and the overriding concern for any facility manager should be employee and patron safety. After safety, legality is the next most important concern for facility managers (Cotts and Lee, 1992). When surveyed in 1988 about the most frequent managerial activities, facility managers indicated that maintenance absorbed the greatest amount of their time (17%), followed by space management (14%), interior design (11%), and budgeting and forecasting (9%) (Cotts and Lee, 1992). It could be assumed that managing people and human resources and administrative responsibilities consumed a large portion of the remaining 49%. A more recent survey would probably show that facility managers are now spending more time on security, air quality, compliance with laws such as the Americans with Disabilities Act, and workplace violence issues.

Not every manager is an expert in each area. However, working with competent employees, receiving training from good mentors, working with management teams, and getting direction from an educated advisory board can help managers effectively balance their various roles.

The various highlighted roles show that managers first and foremost must manage the various stakeholders associated with the facility. This means that before a manager can open a facility's doors, or even plan to build a new facility, she must understand who will use the facility. Constituent analysis helps define who the manager must interact with to positively affect the facility's long-term success.

TOP MANAGEMENT SKILLS

What are some of the top skills a facility manager needs to master? The following list highlights some of the skills that will help a facility manager meet the most important objective—ensuring the highest degree of customer service.

- *Infuse pride in everyone in your organization.* If all the employees have pride in what they are doing, they will work and provide services at a much higher level.
- *Delegate to others.* It is sometimes very difficult for a manager to delegate to others, but to be successful a manager needs to empower those around him and then give them meaningful assignments.
- *Understand what the fans want.* A manager needs to know what the customers want and how to deliver the best fan experience.
- *Communicate with a sense of purpose.* A manager needs to develop a vision and then communicate that vision to everyone around her.
- *Track and measure success.* A manager needs to judge those around him, and if a known and identifiable measurement standard is developed and utilized, employees will know what they need to accomplish and how the manager will evaluate them.
- Give unique rewards that people will remember. To be effective the reward needs to be given immediately in a public manner and needs to be personalized. A reward can be a trophy, bonus, pay increase, or a favorable parking spot, among other things. Some of the most effective rewards are not monetary and can include two close colleagues being able to share an experience (e.g., traveling to a conference together), a sincere "thank you," or a donation to a favorite charity.
- Understand what organizational structure will be the most effective. Organizations have shifted from traditional organization charts, which have a top down structure similar to a pyramid with the manager at the top, to more of a matrix structure in which an employee may be accountable to two or more functional areas or departments. Thus, in the past a custodian might report to the director of custodial services.

Today, a custodian might report to the director of operations and vice president of facility management and be shuttled between the two departments based on need. This can cause significant friction, which requires more managerial oversight.

Management is not all about directing others. Employees want to be led and look for guidance from a true leader. Some of the key traits employees look for in their manager include the following:

- Decisiveness. The manager makes quick decisions and does not waver afterward.
- Understanding. The manager remembers how he felt when he was managed by others and shows understanding for employee needs and concerns.
- Consistency. The manager is consistent in how he deals with issues and employees. He treats everyone the same and does not play favorites.
- Trust. The manager shows true trust in his employees.
- Happiness. The manager allows employees to be happy by giving them time to exercise or meditate during the day, write a positive workplace journal, or post a happy message to their social support network.
- The manager and the employees both give their best effort. The manager asks employees on a regular basis if they have the opportunity to do what they do best on the job.

It is often easier for people to claim they can manage, but what does management mean? Management is the art of getting things done through using people and equipment (as highlighted in chapter 3). Management entails developing appropriate strategies to help accomplish desired goals. This often entails putting best practices into action. If a best practice already exists, it is often wiser and easier to attempt what has been done before rather than to try something that has not been attempted. The following is a 10-step process for putting best practices into action.

1. Review current business practices and develop appropriate benchmarks both from inside a facility and from industry sources (e.g., publications, associations, mentors).

(continued)

TOP MANAGEMENT SKILLS *(continued)*

2. Connect with other facility managers to study their best practices, share ideas, and help garner different opinions.

3. Identify one task that needs improvement. Start small, but make sure it is a visible project so that, if successful, the improvement can be promoted throughout the facility.

4. Examine how the task is currently being completed and determine ways in which it could possibly be improved.

5. Decide who in the organization should follow the best practices (hopefully everyone).

6. Establish a team for final review and approval so that others have a say in the process.

7. Decide how you will implement and evaluate the change. Will there be flexibility if roadblocks are encountered and the solution needs to be tweaked?

8. Ensure that the procedure chosen is accessible and is recorded in a way that lets others know what to do and how to do it. Some organizations videotape everything from meetings to job interviews to the decision making process. This serves as a training aid for employees.

9. Verify the success of the best practice. Numbers, such as cost reductions or increased efficiency, provide a tangible measurement.

10. Start all over again with a new task (Garris, 2006).

The second step in this list might be the most important part of the process. The industry of sport facility management is very small, and those in the industry are often willing to share what they are doing, discuss what has or has not worked, and provide guidance to other managers that can help them do their job more effectively. Managers must realize that managing is not simply a random bunch of actions but rather a process that involves numerous stakeholders. A manager could be likened to a conductor who needs numerous instruments (stakeholders) in order to create music.

STAKEHOLDERS

Many people put their trust in a manager. Employees come to work assuming that the facility will not be dangerous and that they will be paid a reasonable wage. Customers attend an event assuming that the event will go on as scheduled, will be safe, and will provide an enjoyable entertainment experience. Companies may be willing to put their names on a building for millions of dollars, assuming that the facility management team will not undertake any action that will diminish the sponsorship value. Government entities may allow the facility's doors to open for an event because they trust that the facility managers will follow all applicable laws. Because a large number of people rely on each other to ensure that a facility is run successfully, a facility manager needs to constantly balance his interests with the interests of all other constituents. This balancing act can be difficult. Furthermore, it is impossible to develop a facility's goals, objectives, and mission without understanding the constituents who affect the facility.

Constituents, now commonly referred to as stakeholders, come in all forms. Workers are often seen as primary stakeholders, but unions might fall off the radar for some. Union carpenters and contractors took out a full-page advertisement in a New York daily paper to remind the world about their contribution in building Citi Field in New York City. The ad included a quote from Mets third baseman David Wright thanking the union members for their work and the quality of their craftsmanship. The ad made sure that everyone knew about the numerous union workers who helped build the stadium, including carpenters, millworkers, dock builders, timbermen, cabinet makers, and floor coverers. The advertisement also encouraged fans to log into their website at www.builditunion.com to receive a free Citi Field pin.

No matter whom the stakeholders are, every facility needs to meaningfully engage them by involving the intended users in the evaluation and planning processes. These intended users could be individuals or organizations that are invested in the program, are interested in the result of the evaluation, and have a stake in the project. These individuals and organizations should be involved in the entire process (Walinski, 2012).

Some researchers identify three major stakeholder groups:

- Group 1: Those served or affected by the facility, including clients and guests, advocacy groups, community members, and elected officials. They are often classified as external constituents.

- Group 2: Those involved in the facility, such as staff, management, sponsors, and funding partners. These are often referred to as internal constituents.

- Group 3: Users of any evaluation reports or studies, such as banks, government agencies, investors, taxpayers, and any others who might be affected by the facility.

Individuals who need to be involved in the planning process for a facility could include the following:

- Concessionaires
- Operations personnel
- Promoters
- Booking agents
- Police or fire marshals
- Disabled-needs groups
- Meeting planners
- Engineers
- Architects
- Environmental officials
- Disaster planners
- Performers
- Athletes
- Local transportation authorities
- City officials
- Chambers of commerce
- News media
- Religious and civic groups
- Focus groups
- Suite owners
- Fans/patrons
- Sponsors

With all these representatives at the table, the facility developer can cover topics such as amenities, atmosphere, cleanliness, concessions, group sales, crowd management, parking, traffic patterns, noise concerns, lighting concerns, ticket sales, signage, marketing, merchandising, potential tenants, potential events, funding issues, and any other issues that might affect the relationship between the facility and the stakeholders.

Recently there has been a push for joint facilities. For example, a parks and recreation department might work with a school to build a joint facility, or a small college that does not have the resources to build a recreation center can partner with a YMCA to build a joint facility. Although such a solution might work great, it can raise a number of sticky issues (e.g., who has priority in scheduling, what color scheme works best) that need to be resolved before major disputes arise. The organizations would have to also consider their own stakeholders, such as students or YMCA members, and what these stakeholders might want or require.

The primary responsibility of a facility manager is to make sure that people can attend events at the facility in a safe and secure manner. Customers, fans, and ticket buyers can be demanding. Customers want the food they want, the way they like it, at the best location, and at the lowest price. It is impossible to deliver exactly what each customer wants when there are thousands of customers. A VIP may receive personal attention in a luxury box because that is one of the amenities the facility manager can ensure for a box. It is more difficult to provide such a high level of service to a section seating several hundred people. However, one of the critical skills for a manager is providing the highest level of service possible given the strengths and weaknesses inherent in the facility and its personnel. If a manager makes every effort to provide quality service, one hopes that the customers will see the effort and be happier even though they are not getting everything they want. Note that 90% of customer service problems are linked to managerial issues—this means that customers are upset or disappointed not because the facility is bad but because employees might not be well trained or do not execute their assignments. Thus, if a patron is upset that a facility is not clean, it is not the facility's fault. Rather, the problem represents a breakdown in communication between management and employees about why the facility is not being cleaned according to schedule.

Promoters want a facility to be clean and ready for setting up a show. If a facility regularly opens late, is in poor condition, provides unsatisfactory employees, and lacks amenities such as loading docks and storage areas, promoters will shy away from working with the facility, which will then affect its reputation. The facility management industry is small enough that a poor reputation will make it impossible for such a facility to meet its goals, objectives, and mission.

One of the most important stakeholders is the tenant. If a municipality owns an arena, the professional basketball and hockey teams that play in the arena would be the key tenants. The key to tenant relations is developing and preserving a first-rate relationship; this can be accomplished through getting to know the tenants and meeting their needs. Tenants define the value and quality of a relationship, so understanding their point of view is critical. Regular face-to-face meetings where both sides lay out their expectations and needs can help create a strong relationship. While the location and quality of a building are important, the key to a relationship is service. Service can include resolving problems, accommodating special requests, following through on commitments, professionalism, consistency, courtesy, and accessibility. When a manager shows such service to a tenant, the tenant normally will be happy. A happy tenant, all other issues aside, would prefer to stay at a good facility that is well managed. For a building owner, it is much easier and cheaper to maintain a relationship with an existing tenant than to search for a new tenant. Many big cities have burned their bridges with a professional team tenant and then spent large amounts of time and money trying to find new tenants.

It is important for prospective facilities to carefully differentiate the stakeholders because each group and subgroup can have very unique needs. One example is a proposed $100 million fitness facility for the University of Connecticut in Storrs. The new facility was designed to replace the existing fitness facilities, which were aging and cramped. The university planned to build the facility using no state funds, which means that the university would issue bonds and then repay those bonds through student fees. Undergraduates were expected to pay $500 in additional student fees per year to help fund the facility. Although a large percentage of undergraduates supported the new fee, graduate students, who often pay their own way through college, were upset that they would be charged $400 per year to help defray the costs. Although these fees were only proposed, the resulting negative publicity drew significant criticism from graduate students (Megan, 2013).

State lawmakers can affect what events might be held in a given facility or whether state resources can be used for a particular purpose. For example, state boxing commissions can license a fighter or deny the fighter's application. Even if a facility wants to host a fight, that boxer cannot compete if the state revokes or does not grant a license. Some events are also specifically barred. In 2013 a number of facilities in Connecticut petitioned the state legislature to allow mixed martial arts fights in the state. At the time, Connecticut and New York were the only two states that did not allow any professional mixed martial arts events. Later in 2013, Connecticut passed legislation allowing mixed martial arts events to be held in Native American-run casinos in the state.

Besides government-based constituents, numerous external vendors can affect a facility. A facility manager needs to establish cordial relationships with a number of external people or companies that may be able to provide a benefit in the future. A private company can become a ticket purchaser in the future. A private company can also provide items such as office supplies, toilet paper, and concession items. A facility manager needs to develop harmonious relationships with these providers to ensure the consistent flow of needed supplies, especially when thousands of hot dogs, hamburgers, and bottles of beer, for example, are sold at every event, and new deliveries will be needed for another event several hours later.

Another example of knowing one's stakeholders involves historic Wrigley Field in Chicago. In 2013 the owners of the Chicago Cubs proposed a $500 million upgrade to the facility, which included a 6,000-square-foot (557.4 sq m) video board in left field and a 1,000-square-foot (92.9 sq m) advertising sign in right field. The proposed upgrades also included a hotel and a 20,000-square-foot

(1,858 sq m) shopping center. The projected $500 million cost was to be paid by the team's owner. Through the planning process and hearing before the Commission on Chicago Landmarks the video board sign was reduced to 4,000-square feet (371.61 sq m) and the right field was modified to have several advertisements and another large scoreboard. Although fans and the city were not in opposition, neighbors were fighting these changes. The 16 members of the Wrigleyville Rooftop Association were upset because they have developed viewing grandstands, bars, and restaurants where fans can watch games on top of their buildings. These properties have liquor licenses and catered buffets, and the revenue from their seats have propelled the market value for these properties to more than $60 million. Thus, they felt that the proposed changes would negatively affect their revenue and the value of their buildings. In 2004 the building owners signed a 20-year agreement with the team that provides the Cubs with 17% of their gross sales (estimated

FACILITY FOCUS

MANAGING A FACILITY WITH MULTIPLE TENANTS

MetLife Stadium is unique in that it is the only National Football League (NFL) stadium with two NFL tenants: the New York Giants and the New York Jets. Managing one NFL team is hard enough, but the situation can become chaotic when the same facility is used by two teams with competing interests and demands. The new facility was designed from the start to benefit both teams on their own terms. Both team owners utilized a consultant (Bill Squires, who wrote the introduction for chapter 3) to coordinate logistics and planning. Everything, from team flags to seat colors to the team store, had to be carefully coordinated. For example, the 4,800 square feet (445.9 sq m) of artificial turf in each end zone is sectioned into 40 precut, prepainted panels, each weighing about 1,500 pounds (680.4 kg) when wet. Forklift operators have to pry up the blue-and-red Giants end zone one panel at a time to make room for green-and-white Jets tiles. The tiles are stored in compartments built into the bottom of the stands. The entire process of switching an end zone takes between 8 and 10 hours (Henig, 2010).

The team store was recognized with several retail design awards for features that allow it to become exclusive space for either the Jets or the Giants on game days. The 9,600-square-foot (891.9 sq m) flagship store features customized lighting and a white design finish that can be illuminated in either Giants blue or Jets green. A large light-emitting diode video wall and illuminated projections of either Jets or Giants players add a customized feel, while revolving perimeter display panels allow for an easy switch of merchandise for game days. Approximately 25 employees help change the store over from one team to another after a game. These employees strip the Giants shirts from mannequins and dress them in Jets gear; restock 300 T-shirts, 300 sweatshirts, and 500 caps; and switch the store lighting from blue to green. An additional 30 merchandise kiosks around the stadium have to be flipped by about 70 additional workers, who wheel most of the Giants gear into the warehouse behind the store or stash it in drawers under the display stands. The jerseys have a special hiding spot behind sections of the store's walls that spin with the tap of a foot lever (Henig, 2010).

The end zones and stores are just two components of hundreds that needed to be negotiated and finalized to the satisfaction of both partners in the stadium. By having all stakeholders at the table, solutions that could benefit everyone involved were found.

at just over $4 million in 2012). However, these seats also represent a drain because tickets for the rooftop bleachers compete with in-stadium seats (Nightengale, 2013). The team (which also owns the stadium) and the building owners are at times working together and at times competing against each other.

The drama is also affected by Chicago's unique brand of nostalgia-driven politics where politicians are often loath to change traditions. Wrigley Field was the last major league ballpark to install lights for night games. The lights finally came on in 1988 after a 6-year battle with the city council and a group of activists who were opposed to lights—and after the team threatened to relocate to the suburbs (Suddath, 2013). Wrigley Field also has a hand-operated scoreboard and a wooden roof that is not up to fire code, and part of the upper deck is wrapped in netting to prevent cement from falling on fans. Obtaining approval for any modifications can be tough, and politics can play a major role in this challenge. The Wrigleyville Rooftop Association has donated more than $171,000 to a local alderman who consistently supports them and encourages other council members to reject the Cubs' proposals (Suddath, 2013).

MANAGERIAL FUNCTIONS

What is management? Management is not necessarily an art, and neither is it a science. Management is a process of utilizing appropriate personnel to help achieve predetermined goals and objectives. Management entails several specific tasks or functions that help the company or organization reach its goals and objectives. According to the most well-regarded model, there are four primary functions of management: planning, organizing, implementing, and controlling (Bridges and Roquemore, 1996). Others categorize the primary functions of management as planning, organizing, leading, and evaluating (Chelladurai, 1985). Within each of these functions are numerous subcategories. For example, under planning, a typical manager may engage in activities such as scheduling, evaluating, hiring, problem solving, auditing, interpreting, budgeting, and communicating.

Before addressing the four primary functions, it is important to consider the facility's **mission** (see "Sample Mission Statement for a University Intramural Facility"). It is impossible to plan without knowing what the facility is trying to accomplish. The mission statement states the end result envisioned by the facility's owner and encompasses the overall goals and objectives critical for the facility's success. The mission statement provides the roadmap for the facility. If the mission statement indicates that the facility should be open for free use by the public, then the goals will center on attracting users, and the manager will plan strategies to accomplish that goal. Every facility will have a different mission statement to guide its path, and that mission statement can change every couple of years based on internal or external variables. Traditionally, the people at the highest level of a facility—whether owners, elected officials, or board members—help determine the facility's mission with some input from stakeholders such as the public, management, and employees.

Innumerable mission statements have been written for sport teams, organizations, leagues, and so on, but very few such statements focus on or even mention the facility and how the facility needs to be managed. The reason is that a facility is often not the main focus of any sport business. At the same time, though, without the facility there could not be a sport business. A health club, for example, may have as its mission statement the need to provide quality service to members to help them live a happy and healthy life. This mission statement will hopefully help the health club become successful, but there is no mention of the facility. However, without a clean and attractive facility, it will be impossible to attract and retain members. To highlight the facility and its importance, managers need to specifically mention the facility in the mission statement. Thus, the mission statement serves as a planning tool that helps a facility manager accomplish the other managerial functions.

Some facilities use a vision statement as an aspirational tool to describe what they want to be, and the mission statement supports their vision statement. Other facilities and businesses also have a value statement that explains what is

> ## SAMPLE MISSION STATEMENT FOR A UNIVERSITY INTRAMURAL FACILITY
>
> The Intramural and Sports Club Program (ISCP) joins in a partnership with the university to improve the quality of student life on campus and to provide valuable recreational opportunities for students, faculty, staff, their families, and the greater community. The ISCP will utilize the following principles to help fulfill its mission:
>
> - Provide diversity in programs to meet the constantly changing needs and interests of users
>
> - Maintain safe and clean facilities to enhance the user experience
> - Adhere to green building technology and principles to help conserve energy and avoid waste
> - Provide adequate facility access to ensure an opportunity for everyone to participate in desired activities

important to the organization. For a large arena the various statements could be as follows:

Vision Statement- To be the leading arena in the tri-state region for hosting professional sport events and major concerts.

Mission Statement- To serve as the home court for both an NBA and NHL team and supplement any open dates with concerts and family shows to host over 250 events a year.

Value Statement- To not cost taxpayers any money beyond debt service and to produce several free events every year for the local community.

Whatever the term used, the key of any type of statement is that it provides a direction that helps guide the facility in the planning process. The rest of this chapter highlights the four primary functions of management used in this text.

Planning

Planning focuses on setting goals and objectives and then developing the plan to reach those goals and objectives. Planning involves developing both short- and long-term goals and is a constant challenge produced by changing circumstances. In essence, planning can be summarized as deciding in advance what to do, when to do it, and how to do it. Another way to phrase this is that planning is a blueprint for the future. Planning forces those who control a facility to examine the internal and external environment as a means to hold events that will maximize the goals set for the facility.

Planning is difficult because it is associated with change. Most people do not like a lot of change in their lives. Through planning, a manager may determine that little change is needed if the goals and objectives stay the same. Nevertheless, planning needs to be conducted on a regular basis since internal and external conditions change and goals and objectives can quickly become obsolete. Planning is also beneficial in that it can reduce organizational conflict since all those involved will know what they are working to achieve. Planning can also help eliminate overlapping or wasteful activities. If a manager plans effectively, she may be able to identify areas where employees are overlapping work and be able to assign employees to more productive activities (Davis, 1994). It should be noted that poor planning is often the primary cause for failure, whether in the classroom or the board room.

Although the facility leaders develop the mission statement, managers often have the flexibility to develop plans that help the facility accomplish its mission. Planning can be broken down into categories such as strategic, operational, single-use operational, standing operational, and functional. **Strategic plans** are designed to help achieve the highest-level goals and objectives for the facility; that is why they are often called master plans. **Operational plans** are more detailed and are used to help carry out the strategic plans. Operational plans can include single-use operational plans that may apply to a one-time event such as hosting the Olympics. In contrast, standing operational plans are set plans for doing everything from ordering paper to issuing a refund to a patron.

Facilities Trivia

In the 2013 National League Championship Series (NLCS), a stare-off between Cardinals pitcher Joe Kelly and Dodgers outfielder Scott Van Slyke following the national anthem lasted 12 minutes and caused a delay in the first pitch of the game. Play started when the umpire finally motioned for the players to exit the field. Kelly moved first, rendering Scott Van Slyke the winner of the first and only stare-off in NLCS history. From a managerial perspective, how could a facility manager avoid such a situation, which might be humorous but could delay a broadcast, cost a lot of money in overtime, or affect when the game ends?

Functional plans focus on what operational plans are designed to accomplish; marketing plans and safety plans are examples (Bridges and Roquemore, 1996). Another type of plan is a contingency plan that can be used if one of the other plans fails and the facility has to pursue another strategy.

Plans are often synthesized into organizational guidelines. Guidelines are often referred to as "red tape," but they represent how any activity needs to be accomplished so the plan can work. For example, a facility may have a standing operational plan for ordering chairs. If a chair breaks, an employee is required to report the break to a maintenance employee. That employee decides whether or not the chair can be fixed; if not, he may need to complete a damage report and then a requisition form to purchase another chair. Some think of this type of process as a headache, but the guidelines are in place to prevent overspending on new equipment and to allow for repairing equipment if at all possible. The guidelines help save money and provide specific steps to help accomplish the facility's goals.

Goals and Objectives

What is a goal? We have often heard that a coach wants to have a winning season. Is a winning season a goal? The answer for some people is yes. For others, the goal may be to have a good time. While the mission statement focuses on the overall direction a facility wants to pursue, the goals are more refined. A facility's goal could be to have 20 sellouts or to host 10 major conferences a year. It is impossible to list all potential goals, since all facilities and all stakeholders associated with the facility will have their own goals. This does not mean that the goals are inconsistent. An employee may have a goal to sell 100 beers a game. A customer may have a goal to enjoy the event, and part of that process includes drinking beer. If the customer buys a beer, then both the customer and the employee are working to reach their respective goals.

Sample goals for a health club could include the following:

- Maintain a 95% retention rate for current members.
- Attract 100 new members every year.
- Minimize the number of customer complaints to five per week.

Sample goals for a campus intramural facility might include the following:

- Offer five new classes each year.
- Have 40% of on-campus students participating in at least one intramural event each semester.
- Offer one tournament for each sport each year.
- Hire only students to officiate games and work in the equipment room.

The main difference between the two sets of potential goals is that a health club will focus its goals primarily on high-quality service and revenue, whereas an intramural program will focus its goals primarily on reaching out to students. This does not mean that an intramural program should not meet its budget, but an intramural program is not designed to generate a profit, whereas a private health club will close if it does not generate a profit.

Each of the goals is measurable, which is critical for analysis. If a club has a goal to have happy customers, then there must be a means to measure that happiness or the club will never know whether it reached the goal. Thus, many facilities conduct yearly surveys to see what the patrons think. If a patron's feelings can be expressed as a number, then patron reaction can be evaluated and used to develop future goals.

Some commentators believe there is very little difference between goals and objectives (Bridges and Roquemore, 1996). I disagree, noting that the emphasis should be on the level of detail. **Strategic** goals are set by the highest-level managers and are introduced to affect and empower the overall facility for the long run. Strategic goals often focus on broader aspects such as market share, profitability, industry leader position, or changes in the facility. **Tactical goals** are often introduced by midlevel managers and focus on what needs to be accomplished to reach the strategic goal. Operational goals are set by low-level managers and are more short term, referring, for example, to what can be done to reach the tactical goals (Bridges and Roquemore, 1996). To incorporate these concepts into an example, a health club may have a strategic goal to become the largest health club in the market. The tactical goals could be to increase membership by 10% each year and to minimize nonrenewals by 50%. The operational goals could be to attract new members by introducing new programs such as discount packages or new workout opportunities.

Many students learn about goals through the mnemonic device of SMART goals:

- **S**pecific- goals need to be specific rather than vague statements.
- **M**easurable- goals need to have a specific measurable element to evaluate whether the goal was reached.
- **A**chievable- goals should stretch employees to do better, but still need to be achievable.
- **R**esult-focused- while some measure activities, goals should measure results achieved.
- **T**ime bound- goals needs to be based on a specific time frame to be completed.

The operational goals are often more accurately referred to by some as **objectives**. Whereas the goal is a specific directive, an objective focuses on how to reach a goal. In our example of the employee and the customer regarding the beer transaction, the employee's objectives could be to carry the best-tasting beer, have the coldest beer possible, and sell at the lowest possible price to reach the goal of selling 100 beers. The tactical component that would help the employee sell the beer would include stocking the beer, loading her carrying case, obtaining small change to help facilitate transactions, and other steps that need to be taken to develop and close the transactions. Goals will never be reached if there are no concrete means to reach them. I believe that objectives are more closely aligned with what are often called tactical goals. Then, operational goals would be closer to tactics required to help reach the objectives. Regardless of the nomenclature used, the key is

A TACTICAL PLAN FOR REACHING OBJECTIVES AND GOALS

Assume that a professional baseball team wants to have a successful year. They examine their direction and come up with the following plan. It entails trying to generate several sellout games so that they can help reach their team's mission.

- *Mission statement:* The New Haven Flounders are dedicated to providing wholesome family entertainment at a reasonable price.
- *Strategic goals:* The team will sell out at least 10 home games. (This is measurable and concrete.)
- *Objectives:* Develop 20 theme nights designed to attract key constituents to the games. (It is hoped that 10 of these games will result in the sellouts being sought in the strategic goals. The objectives are also concrete and measurable, but they provide some flexibility so managers can be more creative.)

- *Tactics:* Contact local church groups, develop several ethnic themes (e.g., Hispanic Day, Kosher Night), hire a fireworks company, schedule giveaway nights, develop attractive ticket-pricing packages for 5 of the 20 key games, and so on. (Tactics are the simplest steps to be completed in order to help accomplish the objectives.)

As this example highlights, managers need to make sure employees know why they are undertaking tactics, that tactics help reach objectives, that objectives help reach goals, and that the goals help fulfill the team's mission. Once everyone knows why what they are doing is important and that their work leads to the overall success of the team, they are often more motivated and empowered.

to have a process in which strategic planning can identify the specific steps needed to meet goals and further a facility's mission (see "A Tactical Plan for Reaching Objectives and Goals").

Although managers can develop objectives, the most effective technique is to get employees involved in the process. Noted management guru Peter Drucker coined the term *management by objective* (MBO) in 1954; the MBO theory focuses on management developing realistic, achievable, and motivating objectives with employee input (Davis, 1994). This process turns facility goals and objectives into group and individual goals and objectives. Objectives should not be developed in a vacuum and are more effective when there is institutional buy-in.

It is worthwhile noting that although goals and objectives are well known, some businesses do not use them and instead use policies and procedures. Policies are the most general guidelines; they should be flexible and give basic direction to managers and employees. Procedures are a series of job tasks or steps that employees need to take in a pre-established manner to achieve the end results. For example, a policy might be that each new customer has to pay at least $40 a month for gym membership. The procedures might indicate what an employee can say to a prospective customer to avoid making fraudulent statements or getting the customer upset.

Short-Term Planning

A facility manager plans every day. Who will be using the facility? Does the facility have insurance? What type of crowd will be there? Are all the systems operating? Are there enough employees to work the event? Will the weather affect either the facility or the event? These are all questions that may not be answered until the event day. However, through proper planning the manager will know what options exist depending on the circumstances that develop.

Short-term plans typically cover less than 1 year and focus on activities that may have a sense of emergency. A facility may have a short-term plan that a given event be sold out to help accomplish the facility's mission. Besides short-term plans, intermediate-term plans that may extend for several years can be used. These plans need to be flexible enough to respond to environmental changes and at the same time concrete enough to provide directions to employees who are charged with implementing the plan.

Long-Term Planning

The facility manager, or a designated employee, needs to focus on the future and determine what events or services will maximize revenue generation and the facility's long-term goals. Often a facility books events several years in the future. For example, if a facility manager knows that a competing facility is being built 40 miles away, she may enter into long-term contracts with several traveling shows and circuses to prevent them from going to the new arena for a number of years.

Long-term plans are particularly important for older facilities. Most facilities are built to last 50 years at most. This does not mean that a facility cannot be overhauled and last much longer, but after around 50 years the cost to keep such a facility open becomes prohibitive or technology makes the facility obsolete. When a facility enters its 40th year, investing time and resources in creating a long-term plan for the future of the facility becomes critical.

Business Plans

Besides short- and long-term plans, **business plans** need to be developed. The business plan examines the product, marketing, legal, financial, and general business outlook for a facility. Every facility needs to develop a business plan that may cover individual events through yearly business cycles. Each event can face financial hardship if patrons do not show or if too much is spent on marketing. That is why a budget (e.g., a pro forma budget) is a critical part of any business plan. Business plans for building facilities are covered in chapter 4, and those for hosting events at a facility are discussed in chapter 15.

Business plans rely on forecasting what can happen when business decisions are made. Forecasting, a critical component in planning, can be accomplished only with good information. This is why it is imperative for a manager to acquire reliable information from whatever sources are available. Colleagues, employees, friends, newspapers, television stations, magazines, and other sources are essential elements in effective planning because they all provide input that can help influence the decision-making process. Information can be critical when planning an event for a facility. Necessary information may include data on facility availability, competing events and facilities, weather conditions, **building load capacity**, current economic conditions, demographic breakdown of expected fans, and numerous other variables specific to a facility or event. The recent focus on "big data" is based on the ease with which data can be found and the high-powered computers that can process the numbers. However, numbers can be misleading and are often analyzed by people who have biases or prejudices that can easily skew data. A manager therefore needs to carefully acquire the right data, process it correctly, and then review it correctly to help make the right decision for the future of the facility. This is not an easy task.

Organizing

Organizing, the second function of facility managers, refers to a blend of human resource management and leadership. This element is sometimes referred to as staffing. One of the most difficult tasks for a manager is to assign the right person with the right skills and interests to a given job. The fact that someone's job description specifies certain tasks does not make that individual the best person to do a particular job. A manager must recognize this and understand the skills that each employee brings to the facility. If this process is not undertaken, either other employees or the manager will be forced to carry the extra load created because an employee performs inadequate or incorrect work. If it is necessary to rotate jobs or change job descriptions, then the manager must be able to do so even if this means that employees might not support their new roles. Although some employees might learn to like or appreciate their

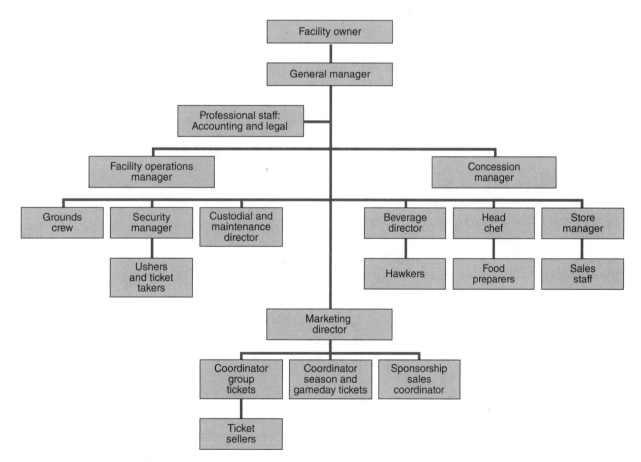

Figure 2.1 Sport facility organizational flowchart.

new positions, others might forever complain about the changes.

In addition to assigning the right person to a task, managers need to ensure that proper resources are provided to employees. Talented employees have little value if they are not given the proper tools and resources. Someone who is a great ticket seller cannot sell tickets if she cannot check a computer system to see what tickets are available. Often a manager's most important role is to hire the right employees, give them the resources they need, empower them to do their jobs effectively, and then get out of the way.

Besides creating specific job descriptions, defining job qualifications, providing resources, and identifying appropriate responsibilities, a manager must specify and adhere to organizational relationships. Every business has a set of organizational relationships, often depicted in an **organizational flowchart** (see figure 2.1). The flowchart shows who reports to whom and what the lines of managerial and supervisory responsibility are. But although the organizational chart may place one employee above another, thus giving the upper-level employee the right to manage the lower-level employee, there still may not be a leadership relationship. In other words, the organizational chart does not guarantee a following or dedication; it merely represents a hierarchical order of responsibility and obligations.

Organizational charts have taken a significant beating over the past decade. Companies are eliminating numerous positions that were previously classified as middle manager. This has created flatter organizational charts where a manager might supervise more workers than in the past. Technology has helped in this renaissance through being able to track employees more effectively and to utilize telecommuting and teleconferencing to reduce personnel needs and expenses. Organizational charts are also influenced by team-related organizations where individuals are pulled from various units within a company to work together in a multidisciplinary approach. In the past those from finance and marketing departments would rarely interact (except for their supervisors possibly interacting at the highest managerial level), but now individuals from these departments might work together on specific projects to leverage their respective skills and knowledge.

Implementing

Implementing, the third managerial function, refers to executing goals and objectives with the appropriate personnel. Plans have no value in the absence of a structured system for executing them. In implementing, the manager is in some ways like the conductor of an orchestra. Available to the conductor are people, money, constituents, legal opportunities, and other resources for meeting the facility's mission. However, all these elements cannot simply be thrown into a blender to create "success soup." Each element needs to be carefully measured and added with the proper motivation to direct the facility.

One of the keys for implementing managerial plans is ensuring that all employees know the various goals, objectives, and tactics and that the right people are in place. Thus, if a manager is interested in accomplishing a goal of selling out 10 games, the implementation process could entail authorizing employees to contract with bands or firework providers or reassigning employees to focus more time on selling tickets for specific games.

Implementing is where managers often face their stiffest challenge. It is sometimes easier to develop a plan and put the right pieces together, but if the execution backfires the entire process fails. This example can be seen in numerous professional teams where they have a plan to win the championship, they recruit and bring aboard the best talent, and then the team stinks on the field. That is the execution part. Management then needs to determine what happened in order to change things for the following year.

Controlling

The last managerial function is controlling. Controlling involves evaluating the work of people who report to the manager and providing appropriate feedback, whether positive or negative. Controlling is a monitoring process that ensures that the facility is accomplishing its mission and goals. At the same time, the manager needs to monitor whether employees are following their job descrip-

A DAY IN THE LIFE OF A FACILITY MANAGER

The job description of every facility manager is different. Facility managers of indoor facilities have some unique concerns such as lighting, air conditioning and heating systems, locker rooms, and flooring systems. Facility managers for outdoor facilities have unique concerns such as the effect of weather, water, and animals as well as access-control concerns. Even with the various differences between all the facilities, most facility managers have the same basic concerns on a day-to-day basis.

Some managers might have 30 years of experience while others might be thrust into the role of a facility manager their first day on the job. Although every manager is different, they all have the same basic responsibilities. They have to manage all the equipment and personnel that are in or need to be in the facility. Most facility managers will have two typical workdays—one a nonevent date and one an event date. The following might be considered a typical manager's schedule:

Nonevent Date

Time	Activity
8:00 a.m.	Walk to office using different routes each day to check for any problems such as graffiti or broken windows
8:30 a.m.	Review phone messages and return calls; check with night supervisor to determine status of evening changeover and cleaning; review write-up about the facility and coming acts online; follow up with budget projections
10:00 a.m.	Weekly staff meeting to discuss pre- and postevent information with representatives from all departments
11:00 a.m.	Advance the show (discuss the specific event times and dates, ticket prices, seating manifest, staffing needs, security needs, and so on) with future game or team promoters with a focus on maintaining the integrity of the event and the facility. (These discussions are then written down into production notes that are discussed with staff members and become the event's "bible," which is often referred to as a script.)
1:00 p.m.	Lunch
2:00 p.m.	Weekly meeting with facility tenants to analyze complaints or problems; issues covered in such meetings focus on financial consolidation, capital projects, business outlook, tenant concerns, cleanliness, and so on
3:00 p.m.	Call promoters and facilities in other states to analyze potential events that could generate additional revenue for the facility and negotiate potential contracts; look for ways to reduce expenses such as talking with new vendors
6:00 p.m.	If lucky, get to go home

Event Date (Night Event)

Time	Activity
5:00 a.m.	Arrive with the trucks to set up the facility and help the back-of-the-house crew examine rigging, stage, sound system, and so on; often need to meet with a representative of the event to make sure everyone knows their roles and complies with the contract
8 a.m.–2:00 p.m.	After the facility is set, shower and get dressed in a suit to work with the front-of-the-house staff on customer relations, ticket sales, the media, and so on
12:00 p.m.–6:00 p.m.	Do a typical day's work and address any issues that arise before the event
6:00 p.m.	Security meeting to discuss specific procedures with all ushers, managers, and emergency personnel (police, fire responders, emergency medical technicians)
6:30 p.m.	Open doors to allow for security searches; work with those in the back of the house (e.g., stagehands, facility workers, caterers, and custodians) to make sure the work is being done correctly and safely; walk the facility to spot any concerns and talk with patrons to make sure they know what is going on and that the facility has a visible face
8:00–9:00 p.m.	During the event, head to the administrative offices to sit in on the settlement process (paying the bills and totaling the revenue to help resolve any issues with the stage hand bill or staffing costs)
10:00–11:00 p.m.	Work with the night crew to get the load out (set removal) started, which can take several hours, and then prepare the facility for the next day
2:00 a.m.	Hopefully go home, though many promoters want the facility manager there from the beginning of an event to the end

tions and reaching their individual employee goals. The process is designed to either strengthen good conduct or correct inappropriate conduct. Correction is easier to accomplish when the evaluation criteria are objective. Problems often occur in the employee evaluation process when subjectivity enters into the analysis. Will an employee be reprimanded because he failed to meet one of 10 goals or because of some interpersonal factor?

Going back to the ticket sales example, the controlling function would examine whether 10 games were sold out, what games were sold out, why the games were sold out, which employees did their jobs correctly, and what tactics and objectives worked. Once management knows what works and what does not work, it becomes easier to plan for the future based on solid information.

Summary

Facility management is hard to define. Many aspects of managing focus on the facility and on making sure that the facility is safe and is well designed, constructed, and maintained. Among other issues that face a facility are legal, finance, marketing, and human resource concerns. Last, facility management entails working with various people and groups to ensure that all the elements fit together. A facility in optimal condition will not be a good facility if employees do not take pride in working there and making sure the facility is running correctly. In contrast, a facility in poor condition can still attract people if management makes a strong enough effort.

Through working with both internal and external stakeholders, facility managers can develop a platform from which they can run a facility. This is the plan—whether short term or long term—that forms the basis for managing the people and the facility. Stakeholders help management determine the appropriate goals, objectives, and mission so that the facility can plan for the future. The plan becomes a blueprint for organizing and implementing successful strategies that lead to positive results.

Discussion Questions and Activities

1. What is planning, and how would you go about planning for a new or existing facility?

2. If you were hired as the new manager of a public fitness facility in a small community, what are some of the goals and objectives you would develop? What would the goals and objectives be if you were the facility manager of a large stadium used by a professional baseball team?

3. Analyze the voting results from several stadium elections to see what issues affected the vote. Identify how those issues can affect planning.

4. Read a management book or article and critique its application to the facility management area. What can you take from the book or article to apply in the facility management context?

5. Develop a list of all the possible stakeholders for a YMCA, a small college athletic program, a large college recreation facility, or a minor league baseball team.

6. If you were to create goals for building a new sport facility, what goals would you include and why?

7. If you were asked to develop a way to more effectively manage and motivate low-paid custodians, what would you recommend and why?

3

Management Theory and Human Resources

Chapter Objectives

- Understand how facility management differs from personnel management.

- Identify and apply appropriate managerial and leadership strategies.

- Appreciate the need for ethical facility management.

- Understand how important communication is for managers and how lack of communication can sometimes be the cause of managerial failures.

- Appreciate how outsourcing can help a facility run more efficiently.

- Characterize various types of employees a facility manager may have to supervise.

- Understand the basics of hiring, promoting, and terminating employees.

- Know the basics of how to properly classify independent contractors to avoid litigation.

- Understand some of the essentials of evaluating and training employees to maximize their contribution to the facility.

- Appreciate the legal challenges that arise from managing employees.

Chapter 2 deals with the diverse duties a facility manager faces. From finance and marketing concerns one day to maintenance and legal concerns the next, a manager has to work around numerous obstacles. It also highlights some of the key skills a manager needs to use and how to plan for the future with various stakeholders. A manager for a small facility needs to wear many hats and often has little help in the process unless he hires new employees or brings in external contractors. However, a manager for a larger facility such as a stadium or arena needs to work with and through numerous employees.

Facility management focuses on managing equipment and structures to make sure they are working correctly, but it also involves a totally different type of task—managing people. Equipment that needs to be repaired is fixed and will hopefully run smoothly in the future or will be replaced. In contrast, employees have emotions, feelings, moods, desires, and complex personalities. It is fairly straightforward to manage a piece of equipment and make sure it operates effectively. Managing a staff that may number in the hundreds is much more difficult. Thus, facility managers need to focus on their most important skill, which is using management theory and practice to help a facility reach its goals and objectives. As noted in chapter 2, a manager can be compared to an orchestra conductor. A manager who focuses only on facility systems and infrastructure can be likened to a conductor who makes sure all the musical instruments are in good shape. However, the musical instruments cannot play themselves; playing requires musicians. Managers need to conduct not only the instruments but also the musicians.

Facility managers have a specific role in making sure all their employees perform their work in an appropriate manner. This chapter explores various management-related theories, strategies, and leadership concerns associated with a manager's effectiveness and provides specific strategies to help manage the people in a facility. Special attention is given to working with employees and contractors and the particular leadership concerns that arise in working with these groups. Facility managers cannot manage without employees. A typical professional football game at a major stadium may require 500 to 700 ushers and security personnel, 200 to 300 concessionaires, and numerous other people doing everything from restroom cleaning to field maintenance to parking management. Even small facilities need employees and contractors to manage the heating, ventilation, and air conditioning (HVAC) systems, clean the facility, market the facility, and perform countless other tasks.

Facility managers spent a significant amount of time and energy dealing with personnel-related issues and must consider numerous issues when working with employees. Important questions include the following:

- What types of employees are needed?
- What is the proper training for sport facility employees?
- Should the facility hire part-time or full-time employees?
- What should happen when employees do not show up for work?
- How should employers deal with workplace violence and sexual harassment?

These questions represent just some of the issues associated with hiring, managing, and terminating employees. This chapter covers basic human resource issues, including employment options and legal issues. The chapter starts with an overview of management theory, the decision of hiring an employee versus outsourcing the work, the types of jobs in sport facility management, and the hiring process. The next sections cover the processes of motivating and evaluating employees as well as training and termination. The final section deals with the various legal issues that arise in the context of employment.

MANAGEMENT THEORY

Management is defined as the achievement of predetermined objectives (based on goals or missions) while working through others such as employees and contractors (Bridges and Roquemore, 2004). The difference between facility management and personnel management is that facility management involves the use of equipment or buildings to help achieve the facility's

Squires: Leading one team with one mission

Photo courtesy of Bill Squires.

My name is Bill Squires, and I have been working in the sport facility management industry since 1987. During that time, I have managed the following facilities:

- Yankee Stadium, Director of Stadium Operations (1987-1990)

- Giants Stadium, Assistant General Manager of Stadium Operations (1990-1996)

- Disney's Wide World of Sports, General Manager (1996-1999)

- Cleveland Browns Stadium, Stadium Manager (1999-2000)

- Giants Stadium, Vice President and General Manager (2000-2002)

Currently, I have my own sport facility consulting company, The Right Stuff Consulting Inc. In addition, I was a member of the board of directors of the Stadium Managers Association from 1999 to 2008 and the president of the association from 2007 to 2008.

Before entering the world of sport facility management, I was a pilot in the United States Navy. My leadership and management philosophies were developed during the 4 years I attended the United States Naval Academy and the 12 years of active duty that I proudly served this great country. I retired as a commander after serving another 16 years in the Naval Reserves.

I have always believed that leaders are only as successful as their staff or teams will allow them to be. As a result, every leader needs to develop trust within the team and motivate them to do their best. Although I am a hands-on leader, I will allow my staff to manage their areas of responsibility once they have earned my trust and confidence. I understand that people will make mistakes, but I don't expect them to make the same mistake twice. I view the team of employees who work at a sport facility, both full-time and part-time staff, just as I did the officers and enlisted personnel in the squadrons I served in. We are one team with one mission,

and if everyone understands their roles and responsibilities and performs to the best of their abilities, then the mission will be accomplished.

In any business, ethics, integrity, and character are extremely important. If you are an honest, hardworking, and motivated person, good things will come your way. I have been extremely fortunate during my career to have had several terrific people work for me who are now leaders in various facilities, and I fully expect them to continue to grow within the industry. I think it is very important to groom your staff and provide direction since these people are the future of the sport facility management industry. When I retire from the sport management facility business, if I ever do, I want to be judged on the success and the accomplishments of those who worked with me in this business, not on my personal accomplishments.

An effective leader will seek out good performance and make sure that those who are exceeding expectations are recognized and complimented. A leader who focuses on and addresses only poor performance is, in my opinion, not doing all that he or she can to build a strong team. I also believe that an effective leader will have an excellent working knowledge of the organization's mission and vision statements. These statements are the core beliefs of the organization, and every member of the team should fully understand them.

Finally, the following are some helpful tips that an effective leader should follow and encourage:

- Don't tolerate tardiness. Encourage staff to be on time, all the time.

- Work the different job functions (e.g., usher, concession stand worker) during an event to fully understand the job function and the issues that event staff encounters. This will not only provide a good education but will earn the respect of the event staff as well.

- Follow the six Ps: Proper prior planning prevents poor performance.

- Ensuring the safety and security of the facility, staff, and ticket holders is your most important job function.

mission, whereas personnel management focuses on how people can help reach the facility's goals. Thus, the fact that someone is an expert in HVAC systems or in negotiating stadium lease agreements does not mean that the person can manage people. But while facility management and personnel management are significantly different, in fact they are integrated because equipment in a facility cannot operate without people. Even a computer maintenance management system (see chapter 9) cannot run a facility's maintenance process because it requires a computer operator, programmer, technician, and people to do repair work. Management theory helps a manager determine how to efficiently synthesize equipment and people.

Management trends are constantly evolving and changing. They also are contingent on other variables such as economic conditions. A facility manager has more difficulty finding employees and providing appropriate motivational strategies during good economic times than during tougher times since employees have many other work options. In contrast, during hard economic times, people may be scouring for jobs and take whatever is available. Employee management is one of the most difficult components of a facility manager's job. The dynamics imposed by dead-end positions, inadequate budgets, hiring freezes, union disputes, the requirement to use student employees (in effect at certain college facilities), and the burdens of working with full-time employees who may have wholly contradictory motivational issues and crazy work schedules makes human resource management a major headache. Concerns related to human resources are highlighted later in this chapter. Having to work with existing employees who may not be motivated gives managers one of their biggest challenges and opportunities. That is why motivation and leadership are so important in implementing any management theory. Nevertheless, although a manager needs to learn how to motivate people, being able to motivate does not turn a manager into a leader. A leader is a manager who has the ability to motivate with fewer tricks or gimmicks.

Motivation is just one component in the management process and comprises three basic elements:

- Motivating the person
- The job as a motivator
- The environment as a motivating force

By understanding the interrelationships among these elements, a manager can better succeed at getting the most out of employees. For example, it is important to know what has motivated someone to work as a janitor for a facility for 10 years when the job is not exciting or rewarding. Is the reason that the employee has no other employment option? If that is the case, fear may be a motivator because the person will not want to lose the job—but this type of motivator could also result in leadership problems in the future. In contrast, if the janitor likes the people he works with, the manager could throw more staff parties or allow coworkers to take their breaks at the same time. These strategies represent just some options that might motivate the employee. Some employees are so enthralled with working in the sport industry that the job is the key motivator. A person who works for a perennial top-level team might want to keep working for low pay in order to say they work for the team. Last, some workplaces are so exciting that employees love going to work, even if they have to work long hours. Being around sports is so important to some employees that they are motivated just because they are working in the industry they want to be in.

Getting the most out of employees becomes more critical in a technological era. For example, computers are changing the way people perform their work. Tasks that used to take a great deal of time may take seconds with new technologies. Instead of the need to take manual temperature and humidity readings for a gym, for example, a computer associated with an energy management system can take the readings and automatically adjust all the HVAC equipment to maintain the most cost-efficient and comfortable levels. But although computers can provide significant value, they can also represent a management dilemma. Some employees may refuse to work with computers, or a union can fight automation efforts that may save money but cost union jobs. Thus, one of the important motivational tasks focuses on helping employees embrace computer technology. This is an even greater task for new managers in the field who have grown up with computers and now have to manage people who have been doing their jobs for 20 years without computers. Technology is also allowing more people to be creative with their schedules. Some industries allow employees to telecommute as a workplace incentive. However, the sport facility business requires hands-on attention, which precludes telecommuting and some other strategies utilized in other industries.

MANAGEMENT RESEARCH FAILURE

Management has had a rough history over the years with numerous strategies and theories coming into vogue and then often being disproved just as quickly. Numerous researchers and pundits who have become management legends through their research have turned out to be data manipulators, finding ways to legitimize consulting projects, careers, or agendas. Fredrick Taylor's scientific management research has been shown to be based on data that were intentionally manipulated to prove a point. For example, he used the strongest workers he could find, observed them for a short period, and then extrapolated the results over a full day (Stewart, 2009). Elton Mayo's famous Hawthorne Studies, discussed in most management courses, have likewise been shown to support what the researchers were trying to promote versus what the data actually proved. There are numerous theories on how best to manage people, but many of these concepts do not work or have been proven to be fraudulent. The best way to manage is to treat people with respect, provide appropriate rewards, and give employees the opportunity to develop the skills they need to be successful.

Managers try to solve problems or issues using various strategies. If no money for raises is available, conventional wisdom and research has suggested giving something of value such as a title, preferential parking, or days off of work. However, communication (both listening and talking with someone) and related soft skills can be the best approach to possibly avoid a managerial failure. Because not every employee responds well to the same approach, managers need to

Facilities Trivia

Managers are known for having a bad name. The following punch lines to the joke "How many managers does it take to change a light bulb?" illustrate just how despised some managers are.

- A roomful—they have to hold a meeting to discuss all the ramifications of the change.
- None—they like to keep employees in the dark.
- None—they form a task force to study the problem of why light bulbs burn out and then try to figure out what management can do to make the bulbs work smarter, not harder.
- None—they will ask for a memo about the issue to be delivered to them the next morning.
- None—they complain to upper management that there is not a policy on changing light bulbs.
- Three—two to find out whether it really needs to be changed and one to tell another employee to change it.

know their employees rather than simply know the latest general theories. A manager who can track employee successes and failures will be better prepared to help employees succeed; as a result, the manager succeeds and moves up the corporate ladder. Managers who destroy employees on the way up will fail. In contrast, managers who make their employees better grow together with such employees.

Thus, most early research touted that treating employees better and paying attention to them motivates them to work harder and produce more. This started a trend of humanizing employee management and focusing on making employees feel good. Although this is a noble and ethically correct strategy, the results of these early studies were skewed to disprove what really motivated employees to work more: money. When the employees were paid more, they produced more (Stewart, 2009). Thus, managers need soft skills to really connect with employees, but when push comes to shove, if they cannot pay employees an appropriate salary it will be hard to get the most out of them. This is especially true with low-paid employees such as parking lot attendants, ticket takers, and food workers.

COMMUNICATION

Management tasks cannot be accomplished without talking, writing, or communicating in some way. A manager needs to communicate effectively, whether through a policy and procedure manual, an employee handbook, staff meetings, one-on-one meetings, or hundreds of daily emails, phone calls, and texts. No one correct way to communicate exists, and every manager has a unique style. Some managers do not need to say a lot and still get everything done. Others might be micromanagers who need to personally get involved in everything and are constantly communicating with everyone out of fear of being misunderstood. Such an approach might turn off some employees who want freedom and want a manager to respect their ability to do their job, whereas others might need that kind of hand holding. Managers usually customize their communication approach based on the person with whom they are working.

A manager should not sit in an office waiting for information to come to her; rather, she should proactively go out looking for information. By walking around a facility and talking with everyone she meets, a manager can learn about the people who work at and visit the facility and get to know them on their own turf. A manager who goes into employees' offices and talks with them changes the managerial dynamics: Employees are normally more laid back if they can communicate with the manager in spaces other than the manager's office.

Computers are an integral component of any manager's communication strategy. Managers can communicate instantaneously through e-mails, texts, and other types of technology. However, the same tools that can make a manager more effective can also hinder managers and employees. Managers who rely on crunched numbers from a computer program might lose out on great opportunities not reflected in those numbers. The numbers, for example, might not reflect a hunch that a manager might have that a certain color scheme might be liked by fans, even if the numbers showed a different color scheme would do better. Also, managers can be bogged down with numerous e-mails when employees prefer using an impersonal mode of communication rather than directly talking with a manager.

A pre-event briefing with all employees, such as this one before a Rush concert at the Webster Bank Arena, can ensure that everyone is on the same page for an event.

COMPUTER-AIDED FACILITY MANAGEMENT

Facility management has evolved significantly over the years because now almost every aspect of facility management can be undertaken with or through computers. **Computer-aided facility management** (CAFM) originated in the 1970s, but at that time it referred to space and asset management systems that also contained a rough **computer-aided drafting** (CAD) component (Teicholz and Noferi, 2002). CAD systems, which are utilized in the design of facilities, allow facility architect/designer to plan a facility and move it around on the screen without having to make a new set of blueprints each time an element is changed. Over the years, CAFM has developed to include any technology platform that assists a facility manager in running a facility. CAFM and the systems integrated in it, such as HVAC systems, are covered in greater detail in chapter 7. There are six primary areas in which CAFM has been applied (Teicholz and Noferi, 2002).

1. Space and asset management focuses on occupancy information, space planning, asset management, and move management. Asset management focuses on how to use the real estate, buildings, and equipment in the most effective manner, along with the need to buy, repair, or sell current and future assets. In space planning, the manager examines how much additional space may be required. If the current occupant utilizes 100 square feet (9.3 sq m) per employee and there are 100 employees, then the utilized facility space is 10,000 square feet (930 sq m) (100 square feet × 100 employees). If it is anticipated that the workforce will grow 10% in the next year, the occupant will need 11,000 square feet (1,022 sq m) to house the current employees and the anticipated 10 additional employees. This information can be useful for ensuring that each employee has sufficient space, which will help in motivation.

2. A CAD system is used to plan and design the floor plan for the facility to optimize flow and function. For example, if inventory can be moved to a more accessible location, this might save employee time and potential wear and tear on a facility. The CAD system does not deal with numbers or strategies but rather with drawings such as floor plans.

3. **Capital planning** and facility condition assessment track the condition of the facility and equipment to improve operation, maintenance, and management. Employees utilizing such a system are able to make sure that the workplace is safe by quickly tracking hazardous and other conditions that may need to be addressed. Employees may be more highly motivated if they have a say in how the workplace will evolve to meet their needs for safety and future growth.

4. Maintenance and operation, through computerized maintenance management systems, tracks any asset or equipment that needs to be fixed or any situation in which maintenance personnel need to be more effectively utilized.

5. Real estate and property management helps track all the space and how it is being purchased, leased, managed, and disposed of. While asset management programs may cover these issues, some programs separate these areas if the facility is part of a very large bundle of properties and there are large numbers of acres and buildings.

6. Catch-all application is used to streamline the entire facility management process or integrate some of the previously listed components. However, the larger the system, the more difficulty some employees may have in operating it.

The CAFM system is just one example of the changing dynamics of facility management and its effect on employees. Older employees who might have been at the facility for several decades might resist change, whether related to computers, new ticketing procedures, new ground maintenance procedures, or any other unfamiliar method for accomplishing work-related tasks. That is why managers need to learn how to motivate and encourage employees to embrace change, even if this is difficult at first.

SIMPLE MANAGERIAL STRATEGIES

There is no one best way to manage a facility, but certain strategies and techniques have helped managers over the years. Such strategies represent fundamental management trends that have been utilized over time and are as appropriate today as they were when first identified.

It is often the little things a manager does on a day-to-day basis that represent great strategies for motivating others or represent leadership in its truest sense. For example, some managers achieve success through being friendly. Not merely superficially nice, they show genuine compassion and understanding. These managers may know the name of every person in the facility and address each employee personally. Other similar behaviors include writing personalized thank-you notes, remembering administrative assistants on their birthdays and Administrative Professionals' Day, always being on time and prepared for meetings, and showing compassion when someone is sick or injured. Although these strategies may not represent structured managerial theories, they are concrete steps a manager can take to get employees to work well. Managers need to be careful that they do not simply adopt the latest managerial fad. Countless management and leadership books touting the greatest managerial breakthroughs and ways to increase productivity are published yearly. The truth is that no magic pill exists and that managing takes time, effort, and trial by error. They key is to find what works for each manager and his colleagues. One point that everyone agrees with is that managers never seem to have enough time in their workday, making time management a fundamental ability of a successful team leader.

Time Management

Time management is a very important skill for a manager. Some managers seem to be always putting out fires while rushing from one concern to another. Executives are known to arrive early in the morning and leave late at night. Facility managers must make sure the facility is ready for each day it is open, and a facility manager can easily work 60 to 80 hours a week if the building is heavily used. Thus, any strategy that can help save time means more time to do other activities or accomplish additional work. Computers, tablets, smartphones, and day planners can all be used to remember key tasks, times, and dates. One of the most important time management strategies entails streamlining meetings.

Meetings

No matter what strategy or technique is used, facility managers spend much of their time in meetings. Meetings are held daily to discuss everything from budgets to upcoming events and security issues. Many managers would also say that meetings are often ineffective. Thus, it becomes important to know how to make meetings more productive.

Meetings should be held on a consistent date each month or week, should be held at the same time (preferably early in the morning before the regular workday begins), and should be held earlier in the week rather than later (Conrad, 2000). The following are additional meeting pointers:

- Always be on time.
- Start and end meetings at specified times.
- Control the meeting; do not allow interruptions (e.g., ask attendees to turn off cell phones and similar electronic devices).
- Create a meeting agenda and distribute it to all the attendees before the meeting.
- Insist that attendees come prepared.
- Before a meeting, talk to those who try to control meetings to let them know how the meeting will work and that it is important for them to comply with the agenda and with time restrictions.
- Encourage quiet people to participate. For example, ask for each person's opinion.
- Get everyone's feedback before making a final decision (this will prevent "yes" men and women from simply agreeing with the decision).
- Give specific assignments and dates they are due.
- Keep meetings friendly by bringing food or small gifts.
- Before a meeting, develop a strategy to determine what needs to be accomplished during the meeting.
- Create the proper environment. A well-placed joke, story, or video can help set the mood before a meeting.
- Frame issues as questions and solicit solutions. Every meeting can be titled around a question (such as "How will we market the event on November 3rd?"); invite everyone who might have answers to attend.
- Keep all meetings on a tight schedule, and do not hold too many meetings.
- Use walls and other surfaces to post various critical pieces of information.
- Require all those in attendance to contribute something to the meeting.
- After brainstorming ideas, obtain consensus on the ideal direction and then move forward.
- Do not overuse PowerPoint. People will lose interest and tune out the speaker and the message.
- Brainstorming can often be controlled by one or two people. A more effective way to brainstorm is to have everyone anonymously write down ideas on index cards, shuffle the cards, and post the cards on a wall. When the top ideas are finalized, hold a blind vote; write each person's vote on a piece of paper so the results are anonymous.
- Once in a while, invite a guest speaker (e.g., for specific training, motivation).

Through effectively running meetings, a manager can develop a reputation as an efficient person. Employees are more motivated when managers give them a clear and concise charge. Whether through gestures such as calling employees by their names, through established managerial strategies, or through meetings, managers have numerous options not just for getting the job done but also for leading employees. Each facility takes on the management style of the facility manager. Each facility also takes on the characteristics of the facility leader, who may or may not be the facility manager.

LEADERSHIP

Celebrated business leaders in recent history include Estée Lauder, Henry Ford, Steve Jobs, and Indra Nooyi. What makes a good leader? Every leader has had his or her own unique style and technique. The leader needs to be an activist for the facility and needs to be the voice for quality, safety, ethics, consistency, collaboration, and compassion. In other words, the facility manager's leadership style is the spark that can make the facility succeed or fail. A facility manager can get employees to be more effective by using motivational tools such as more money. This does not necessarily make the manager a good leader. A good leader may be able to motivate employees through means other than more money or other techniques of buying respect and compliance—through devotion or a sense of respect, for example. Thus, one can view leadership as a way of properly motivating employees through a combination of traditional or nontraditional techniques.

Almost every facility has a veteran employee who has been there for more than 20 years. This person may be a manager, but even if she does not intend to become a leader, the person may possess leadership authority based on years of experience or technical expertise. However, the longtime employee can also be someone without any ambition who criticizes the facility management at every turn but does nothing to make the facility better. Leaders are traditionally good at speaking and communicating and are cost conscious, decisive, good at multitasking, very outgoing, action oriented, and able to deal with all types of people and problems with a level head (Cotts and Lee, 1992).

Leaders also have one critically important skill that sets them apart from others: Leaders hire well. This means that a leader can see potential in less experienced employees and can tell when they have the capabilities to become great. Besides hiring well, a leader can groom others well and train them to be future leaders. In fact, some leaders believe their best legacy is to train others to lead. Thus, leaders spend a lot of time searching for the right people to help make their team stronger. A good nonsport example is the process a newly elected president goes through while putting together his cabinet and staff positions. By properly vetting each person and looking at individual potential, the president can be surrounded with the best talent; that talent then helps the president look better and produce better decisions. A leader should be good at working on a team and should not be afraid to delegate; however, a leader also needs to know when to step back and let others succeed or fail.

There is no right way to become an effective leader. However, the tools required of a good leader include being able to identify and communicate a shared value with others, developing and embracing a team concept, choosing the right players on the team to assume key roles that maximize their skills and potential inputs, motivating team members with appropriate incentives, working with team members to achieve their predetermined goals, and being willing to work with team members to share risks as well as rewards. Other key skills include being accessible (e.g., having an open-door policy), customizing how to approach each issue or person, motivating underperformers, publicly recognizing success by others, being a great listener, being able to convey a vision to others, leading by example, and being ethical at all times.

Successfully Leading

The leader and the manager can be the same person. Some managers have gained leadership positions through years of service, and new leaders can also become great managers. There is a significant distinction between a leader or manager who has been established for a long time and someone who was recently hired from the outside. It is more difficult for a leader to delegate duties when she does not know the employees well. A new leader must prove her abilities, even if she was an internationally acclaimed facility leader in a prior position. Steps that a new leader should take include the following:

- Immediately assess the facility through an internal and external SWOT (strengths, weaknesses, opportunities, and threats) analysis. The SWOT analysis is covered in greater detail in chapter 4.

- Implement change by starting small and then expanding as time progresses.

- Explain all changes to the staff.

- Take charge and make a change if something does not work.

- Make a major decision with definite cost reductions and then publicize the results. This will show an intention to make the facility better. Another way to follow this strategy is to allow employees to recommend changes and share in the cost reductions.

- Undertake very visible projects such as repainting restrooms and concession areas; this shows a desire to make the work environment better.

- Take a lead in developing appropriate short- and long-term budgets and plans.

- Review and manage all existing service and supply contracts to see whether services are at a high standard. If they are not acceptable, facilitate change; this will show employees a willingness to make changes (Cotts and Lee, 1992).

If these strategies are successful, employees may embrace the changes and the leader who implemented them. Even a poor decision can make a manager a great leader if the manager takes personal responsibility for the decision while identifying and correcting the problem.

Being a successful business person or manager does not make a person a good leader. Almost everyone has worked for a boss who was a great manager but a poor leader. A manager may be able to motivate employees to reach sales goals, but it may be that not every employee in that department will respect or consider the manager her leader. The employees reach their goals because they want to keep their jobs, but they may not strive to reach a higher level because they do not believe they are being led to greater success. Conversely, many people have worked with great leaders who were poor bosses. Employees may love a manager who leads them, but if the manager cannot properly plan or organize resources so that employees can reach their goals, she is not an effective manager. For example, a good leader can inspire employees to make numerous cold calls to sell tickets, but if the leader does not provide employees with proper ticketing equipment and supplies they will not be able to finalize the sales and achieve their goals.

Leadership by Example

Leaders can be effective managers, and vice versa, by doing employees' jobs just as well as the employees do. If a facility manager has worked up from the janitorial ranks to the position of crew chief and finally to the position of assistant manager, most employees will respect the person because of his work "in the trenches." If someone fresh out of college obtains the same managerial position, lower-level workers may perceive the person differently. Until the manager has proven himself and shown the requisite knowledge for performing the job, he will be eyed with suspicion.

If the manager has had prior experience and can gain the trust of lower-level employees by pitching in to clean toilets, working a changeover shift, or selling hot dogs, then she can lead by example. Leading by example also focuses on ethical behavior.

Ethics

Every facility manager has to have the ethical underpinnings to be honest in all his dealings. Some booking agents are sleazy and unscrupulous. This does not mean that a facility manager needs to stoop to that level. A reputation is one of the most valuable assets a person will ever have. If another party is not acting ethically, the manager can rise above the mediocrity and act in an impeccable manner.

Ethical behavior means identifying what conduct is right and wrong and then choosing to take the right path. The question becomes, What is right? The fact that the law allows a manager to act in a certain way does not mean that the action is ethically correct. For example, a facility manager has to comply with the Americans With Disabilities Act (ADA) requiring facilities to provide reasonable accommodations to the disabled (see chapter 13). It is possible for a facility manager to comply with the law but for a disabled patron to still be unable to enjoy the event. Is it ethical to take the position that the manager has acted within the law, or should the manager go beyond the letter of the law to make sure that the patron can in fact equally enjoy all benefits other patrons receive? This example suggests that ethical conduct requires a blending of legal and moral obligations.

As another example, suppose that a boxing match is scheduled at a facility. The match is secured by a contract. If one of the parties does not show, he is breaching the contract and the facility can recover damages. But should the facility be allowed to sue if the fight is canceled and the facility loses money? Would the answer change if the boxer had lost a very close family member and wanted to attend the funeral, or if the event was canceled because of a snowstorm? Under each option, the manager knows that others will be looking at the decision that is made and at its future effect. Numerous issues will come before a manager, and the actions taken will help determine what type of leader the person may be.

Because of the large number of people who rely on each other to ensure a successful facility, facility managers need to constantly balance their interests and ethical underpinnings against the interests of all other constituents. This balancing act can be very difficult but also represents an opportunity to utilize integrity to advance while still protecting constituents. At times, managers may determine that the best answer to a problem is to bring in an expert who can more effectively complete the desired work.

OUTSOURCING

Good leaders and managers know what they can and cannot accomplish. Managers cannot do everything, and if there is an area they are not strong in or if they want to focus on their key competencies, they can outsource their work. Thus, some facility owners do not want to manage

---

BEHIND THE SCENES

LEADERSHIP BALANCE OF ETHICS, UNIONS, AND SAFETY

There is no right way to manage any part of a business. The same holds true for facility management. Assume that you are the manager of a large stadium that has a unionized workforce. One of your janitors cannot read. Although this may not appear to be a problem, the employee works with some hazardous materials and needs to be able to read the material safety data sheets mandated by the Occupational Safety and Health Administration. The employee admits he cannot read but says he has been doing fine for more than 20 years and will not change now. He also brings the union into the dispute. The union raises concerns under the collective bargaining agreement, which prevents you from punishing a person without just cause, and raises the potential of an ADA violation. How would you resolve such a dispute? What steps do you need to take to protect patrons, other employees, this particular employee, the facility, the union, and all other affected parties?

As it turned out when a situation similar to this actually occurred, the facility manager worked with the union to provide a remedial reading program for the employee. The employee was able to take the classes during normal work hours while he was still on the clock and getting paid. Everyone agreed that if he were able to correct his reading problem and thus provide for his own safety and the safety of others, he could return to his position without any difficulty. However, management and the union also agreed that if he did not improve his reading he could be terminated because then he would represent a threat of harm to himself and others, including other union members. This example shows how facility managers need to resolve conflicts and generate unique solutions for various problems. It also suggests that legal and ethical issues come into play every day. The manager could have terminated the worker and then fought with the union over various grievances before possibly proceeding to a court battle. This ethical decision helped save all parties headaches and costs.

the facility at all but only want to run events in the facility. They may outsource all facility management operations to a company specialized in facility management.

Many management companies provide services to both private and public facilities. These for-profit companies attempt to provide optimal services at a reasonable price to maximize revenue. The owner of a facility, whether private or public, may hire a third company to run the facility as a way to reduce costs or a means of allowing the facility management to focus on their key responsibility—producing successful events in the facility—rather than worry about the HVAC system, for example. Managers can also hire outside companies to complete very specific tasks such as janitorial services, brewing fresh coffee, or photocopying. The facility management services offered by an **outsourcing** company can include

- facility analysis and assessment to make sure the facility is running smoothly and tenants are satisfied,
- energy usage analysis to determine where energy conservation measures can be taken to reduce costs,
- HVAC and energy management to more effectively maintain and operate HVAC equipment,
- construction and renovation management so the owner does not have to hire contractors and tradespeople,
- preventive maintenance through developing corrective maintenance plans or installing a computerized maintenance management system,
- budget and pro forma analysis to make sure the facility is operating within a budget and not spending too much money, and
- housekeeping and environmental services to ensure that the facility is clean and to prevent illegal waste dumping or the use of environmentally unfriendly cleaning agents.

Private management companies are generally more focused on the bottom line compared with facility managers. Some contracts require a management company to reduce costs. Outsourcing is often obtained through a competitive bidding process, which means that various companies are competing against one another to win a contract.

This in turn means that the competitors are trying to win the contract by offering their services at the lowest price while still trying to maintain the highest level of safety and cleanliness. Management companies typically offer the following advantages:

- Increased operating efficiency through buying in bulk or having one expert who can focus on reducing costs
- Increased continuity, since a management company often keeps tenants happier, which reduces the loss of tenants who may leave if dissatisfied
- Fast reaction time in response to problems and opportunities, as outsourcing firms often utilize CAFM systems to make a facility more efficient, which can help solve problems or reduce costs
- Professional marketing and group sales support
- Performance-based compensation for key management employees, which is negotiated in the contract so that the facility will know the long-term goals of the management company
- A more efficient procurement process for goods and services, since a management company can not only negotiate the best price but can also establish distribution systems to quickly deliver goods and services
- Ability to take risks using past experience at other facilities as a guide to help change facilities
- Ability to invest in a facility, as outsourcing contracts often require the management company to install new equipment and help upgrade the facility

Pros of Outsourcing

Cities, counties, universities, and other facility owners hire privatized facility management for numerous reasons such as the following:

- A network of managed facilities creates event booking leverage (i.e., more events, better deals). If a management company runs 10 facilities in a given state, it can significantly increase its bargaining power to attract events because it can package the tour at multiple facilities. If each facility negotiated its own contract, some events might not be scheduled because there are not enough facilities interested in meeting the demand or schedule.

- Increased corporate support (professional staff) results in more comprehensive management, oversight, and on-site assistance. Professional facility managers who often manage outsourced facilities have greater access to facility experts in their companies and do not need to chase after tradespeople such as plumbers, technicians, and electricians.

- Reduced stress, time, and budget implications for other governmental or university departments since they can focus on their key strengths rather than on running a facility. For example, a physical education department may have to teach classes and manage a facility. With someone else managing the facility, the instructors can focus on their teaching.

- A private management company is often the most effective means for a city, county, or university to balance competing departmental interests, since all facilities are treated the same and athletics will not receive preferential treatment over the science or math building.

- More effective negotiation and renegotiation of labor agreements through the ability to focus workers on their specialty and to give them specific responsibilities that can be negotiated into their labor contracts.

- Facility staff will have greater opportunities for professional growth since staff can focus on their expertise instead of trying to wear multiple hats, which often occurs when budgets are tight.

- Increased contacts and knowledge, resulting in more ideas and better problem solving.

- Shared database and industry research.

Cons of Outsourcing

Although there are numerous advantages to outsourcing facility management, some facility owners and managers are not so receptive to private management. Some facility owners want to be hands-on and want their own employees to manage the facility. In fact, this is typically the case for smaller facilities. It is primarily the largest facilities or larger groups of buildings that are outsourced. Outsourcing has disadvantages, including the following:

- Expense: Expenses include an obligation to pay a fixed monthly management fee plus incentives.

- Control: In some cases, facility owners are better off relying on their own management expertise.

- Loyalty: Some facility owners fear a turnover of loyalty to the private management company if employees are ever fired or reassigned or if tenants are forced to leave.

- Responsibility: Private management companies are sometimes put in the position of aggressively pursuing the bottom line at the expense of the owner's goals, objectives, desires, and external responsibilities.

- Incentive fee-driven cost cutting that would lead to long-term cost increases: If a management company is forced to lower costs, it may spend less on service, which in the long run will damage equipment and create more expensive problems in the future.

- Excessive turnover of the general manager due to opportunities at other network facilities: If a management company installs a general manager for the property, that person can develop a great reputation and save money but may be switched by the management company to a different property that needs managerial help.

As the pros and cons of outsourcing suggest, a manager can use external assistance to help solve problems, and as some problems are solved, other problems can arise. In general, though, the outsourcing of services has been a very positive step in facility management since it allows owners and managers to focus on their key competencies and lets professional facility managers take charge of the facility and reach certain service and quality levels.

Global Spectrum won a competitive bid in 2013 to manage the XL Center in Hartford, Connecticut. To win the contract, Global Services was willing to spend $2.75 million immediately for capital improvements and then spend $1 million a year thereafter to improve the aging facility. Such expenditure would have cost the state more than

$20 million if they had to issue bonds to cover the expenses. The state is also going to reinvest $2 million (to be taken from XL Center operations) in the facility. Such expenditures will eventually help cover the estimated $16 million in improvements needed to sustain the facility's operations. Global Spectrum is to be paid a management fee for running the facility. The fee is estimated to be around $721,000 a year, but that rate could go up or down every year depending on revenue targets (Gosselin, 2013).

Outsourcing is often broken down based on the service being outsourced. Some companies such as Global Spectrum and Anschutz Entertainment Group (AEG) manage only facility operations; others might provide security or janitorial services. Services offered by a large company could include custodial services, operations and maintenance, groundskeeping and landscaping, facility setup services and conversion, green certification, environmental stewardship programs, leasing management, new building commissioning, and energy management. In the sport realm, there are several key players in concessions. The majority of the concession food market is broken down based on stadium and arena and then further broken down into general food and the much more lucrative and expensive premium concessions (often seen in suites and luxury seating areas). A 2013 survey of the 123 big-league venues that outsource concessions listed the following as the top providers of stadium general concessions ("Carving Up," 2013):

Aramark	27%
Sportservice	24.3%
Centerplate	21.6%
Levy	14.9%
Legends Hospitality	4.1%

Although outsourcing has significant benefits, hiring the wrong company can lead to disaster. In 2013, the cities of Hartford and East Hartford in Connecticut had several issues with a company, MDM Golf Enterprises that was hired to manage several municipal golf courses. The golf courses were in significant disrepair and had areas of mud and fungus, among other problems. A city audit in Hartford found that MDM (which had signed a 5-year contract in 2009 to manage two public courses) failed to make hundreds of thousands of dollars in capital improvements, allowed the courses to fall into disrepair, and cut down trees without proper permission. After receiving numerous complaints, the city exercised a clause and cancelled the contract (Carlson, 2013).

Ancillary Service Providers

The number of companies that provide services to facilities is almost endless. It would be impossible to list all the companies that provide services apart from facility management. These companies deal with food products, fire suppression, crowd management, concession management, architectural design, engineering design, insurance, uniforms, cleaning, janitorial, and countless other services. A manager needs to select these companies, monitor them, and terminate relationships with them when necessary. A security company can provide several hundred people to work a stadium event. Facility managers do not necessarily need to manage these employees, as the security company is responsible for hiring, training, managing, and firing the security personnel. However, the facility manager needs to monitor and track the security service provider to make sure the personnel are doing their jobs, the contract is not being violated, and patrons are happy with the service.

Besides for-profit businesses, several associations provide guidance and direction for facility managers, including the Stadium Managers Association, the International Association of Venue Managers, and the International Facility Management Association. These and other organizations offer several specialized conferences each year on topics such as stadium management and crowd management. Students can also become members of these organizations.

If a manager cannot outsource or hire an outside service provider, he needs to hire employees. The rest of this chapter examines some of the key issues associated with hiring and managing employees.

FACILITY FOCUS

STAPLES CENTER

The Staples Center is one of the crown jewels in Phil Anschutz's sport empire. Mr. Anschutz has quickly become one of the most powerful sport moguls by owning several Major League Soccer teams, a stake in the Staples Center, interests in the Los Angeles Lakers and Kings, and interests in several European hockey teams and facilities. He also built the Home Depot Field. These entities are structured under AEG, which has significant development plans for the Los Angeles market. AEG is proposing a large-scale entertainment center near Staples Center with a 1,500-room hotel, a smaller luxury hotel, and a 7,000-seat arena that could serve as the home for the Emmy Awards. The development is a continuation of the $7 billion growth in investment in Los Angeles spurred on by the Staples Center. The development called LA Live, which is the national headquarters for Herbalife and AEG, also houses a 14-screen movie theater, ESPN Zone and studios, the Grammy Museum, and numerous restaurants ("Nokia Theater," 2009).

The following facts give a picture of the Staples Center in Los Angeles, which is home to two National Basketball Association (NBA) teams and one National Hockey League (NHL) team ("Staples Center," 2000):

- Built: 1997-1999 (total construction time was 18 months, and a penalty in the contract provided for a $50,000 fine for every day the project went past the 18-month timeline)
- Cost: $375 million
- Basketball seating: 20,000
- Hockey seating: 18,118
- Luxury suites: 160
- Party suites: 32
- Club seats: 2,500
- Concession stands: 23
- Total square footage: 900,000 (83,610 sq m)
- Elevators: 10
- Escalators: 11

- Restrooms: 55
- Locker rooms: 12
- Watts of audio amplification: 125,500
- Feet of fiber-optic cable: 148,000 (45,110 m)
- Tons of structural steel: 2,500
- Cubic yards of concrete: 73,000 (55,810 cu m)
- Miles of data and telephone cables: 14 (22.5 km)
- Square yards of carpeting: 32,500 (27,175 sq m)
- Square feet of terrazzo tile: 81,000 (7,525 sq m)
- Square feet of drywall: 2,865,000 (266,170 sq m)
- Feet of broadcast production cable: 3,800,000 (1,158,240 m)

© Picture Alliance/Photoshot

AEG's success has also led the company into the facility management market. AEG has managed or worked with more than 60 facilities since it was formed. Some of the facilities managed by AEG Facilities in 2014 include Prudential Center (Newark, New Jersey), Sprint Center (Kansas City, Missouri), the Rose Garden (Portland, Oregon), WaMu Theater (Seattle, Washington), Target Center (Minneapolis, Minnesota), and O.Co Coliseum (Oakland, California); it also manages four large stadiums in Brazil, two in Sweden, and one in Russia.

SPORT FACILITY JOBS

To appropriately manage employees at a sport facility, a manager needs to know the types of jobs available there. There are numerous jobs associated with a sport facility, but every sport facility is different. A small health club in a strip mall may have very few facility management concerns and may not need any employees to work in facility management. A larger facility may have hundreds of employees. The need for specialized employees is magnified even more when the facility is unionized and employees are limited in what jobs they pursue. In some facilities, a unionized tradesperson may make more money than the facility manager. For example, if the **collective bargaining agreement (CBA)** requires a union member to replace any glass over dasher boards at a hockey rink, a union member must be at hockey games from start to finish. Typically the union member earns overtime wages for those hours. Some of the functions facility employees undertake include the following:

- Facility manager
- Box office managers and ticket takers
- Security
- Parking
- Architecture and engineering
- Maintenance
- Scoreboard operator
- Audiovisual coordination
- Press box administrators
- Locker room attendants
- Grounds grew
- Garbage removal
- Customer relations
- Finance and human resources
- Concessions
- Sponsorship sales

This is by no means an exhaustive list. At a large arena, for example, in the concession area alone different people are responsible for inventorying and ordering the food, delivering the food, preparing and cleaning the cooking areas, preparing the food, packaging the food, selling the food, and cleaning debris. In smaller facilities, the person in charge of the locker room may also be responsible for the equipment room and laundry facilities. Indeed, most employees at small facilities are trained to assume multiple responsibilities and duties as might be required by the event or circumstances. A manager of a small health club may have to assume numerous duties while a manager of a larger facility might have 15 to 25 full-time employees and possibly several hundred part-time employees.

There are so many types of jobs in facility management that it would be impossible to cover them all. The following sections cover several facility-related positions and their typical duties.

Concessions Manager

Food and souvenirs are among the highest profit centers for a facility. A soda may cost 15 cents to serve but can generate $3.00 in revenue. Even after all the costs are paid, there is the potential for a nice return on investment. For this reason a concession manager needs to constantly monitor concession operations so that they generate the greatest revenue possible while costs are kept down. The concession manager spends a significant amount of time on human resource issues (hiring, training, scheduling, and terminating employees) and inventory management (ordering, pricing, tracking, and disposing of supplies and products).

Box Office Manager

The box office manager is the critical link to selling tickets, from coordinating season tickets to managing the will-call window and game-day ticket sales. Box office managers work all year long, even if they are working for a football stadium where there may be only 10 home games a year. When a season ends, box office managers start working on the next year. They must develop marketing campaigns, ticket packages, customer mailers, and training for new salespeople and must coordinate external sales policies and procedures with companies such as Ticketmaster.

Facilities Engineer

The heart and soul of a building are housed in the inner workings such as plumbing, electrical, and sound and lighting systems. Without these back-house systems, the facility would not be able to operate. In a large arena there are miles of electrical wires and plumbing. These systems can be very complex, with electrical, phone, visual, and data systems intertwined. Because of this complexity, most facilities have several tradespeople who work exclusively in particular areas, such as an electrician, a plumber, or a computer network engineer. These people are all managed by the facilities engineer, who coordinates their work schedules, filters work orders, assigns repair and maintenance jobs, follows budgetary guidelines, and makes sure the facility is operating correctly before, during, and after an event.

Turf Manager

Although a number of positions are critical for both indoor and outdoor facilities, the position of turf manager, or head groundskeeper, is very specialized—one that might be appreciated by those who love to work outdoors. The key to the position is learning how to use pesticides to ensure the quality of grass fields. People may be accustomed to applying various weed killers at home, but the chemicals used on commercial fields are very strong and involve significant environmental concerns. Therefore, the government (both local and national) regulates pesticide applications. People wishing to apply these chemicals need to obtain a license, which requires both significant learning and training. Because of what it takes to obtain a license, those with a license are in great demand among employers, from golf courses to park and recreation departments to colleges with a large number of fields.

A turf manager, besides having to know how to properly spray the grounds, must know about soil composition, operation of heavy land-moving machinery, growing seasons, types of grass that work best on given fields, the effects of weather conditions, and ways to repair fields after a rainstorm. It is also necessary to have a strong underpinning in human resources to work with and manage assistants as well as the ability to work with external contractors who may be utilized to apply chemicals or install a new drainage system. A typical job description for a turf manager is presented later in the chapter.

EMPLOYMENT OPTIONS

One of the first questions for any facility is whether the facility will need to hire any employees. The facility owner, a third-party contractor, interns,

---

HOW MUCH CAN YOU EARN?

One of questions asked most frequently by students interested in studying facility management is how much they can earn working in the field. In general, the salaries for many facility management positions are higher than those for individuals working for professional sport teams. Here is a breakdown of some salaries as published by the International Association of Venue Managers in 2013 (VenueDataSource, 2013).

Position	Average Salary
Sales or booking manager	$41,484
Senior event manager	$45,457
Chief of security	$49,737
Box office or ticketing manager	$50,724
Director of guest services	$60,081
Vice president or director of operations	$70,641
Vice president or director of sales	$83,608
Deputy senior executive	$89,452
Senior executive	$118,179

The following are approximate hourly rates for game-day staff working an event. Note that rates vary based on experience, union settings, and geographic regions.

Position	Average Hourly Rate
Box office manager	$18.00
Ticket seller	$11.00
Head usher	$12.00
Usher	$10.00
Ticket taker	$10.00
T-shirt security or door guard	$15.00
Police	$28.00
Fire	$28.00
Emergency medical technician	$28.00
Overnight police	$32.00
Custodian	$10.00
Forklift driver	$15.00

A typical game with thousands of employees can generate several hundreds of thousands of dollars in wage expenses.

volunteers, family members, or independent contractors can help run a facility. However, each category raises unique issues and concerns. Interns, for example, may need to be paid even if they are receiving university credit. If an intern is replacing an employee and is not receiving valuable skills as part of the career education process, the Fair Labor Standards Act requires that the intern be paid at least the minimum wage and possibly overtime (Fried and Miller, 1998).

The basic employment options include employees, volunteers, interns, and independent contractors. **Independent contractors** are covered earlier in this chapter in terms of outsourcing and ancillary service providers. Although some facilities contract with an entire outsourcing company, some facilities might hire a single external contractor to do a specialized task such as plumbing or window washing. This section focuses on people hired or retained in the traditional employment or volunteer relationship.

An employee is someone hired directly by the facility to perform a specific set of tasks. An employee can be full time, working 40 or more hours per week. If the employee works overtime (anything over 40 hours per week) and is not an exempt managerial-level employee (either on salary or having managerial responsibilities), the facility must pay the employee time and a half for all time over 40 hours. Because sport facilities are open long hours, overtime pay is a key concern.

Employees can also be classified as part time. These employees often have other jobs but work nights or weekends for a facility. Since they are not full-time employees, the facility does not usually have to worry about overtime compensation or benefits such as health care.

Employees can be either unionized or non-unionized. As discussed later in this chapter, unions were formed to protect employee rights and ensure safe working conditions. However, from a management perspective, the insertion of unions in the workplace can sometimes lead to a more difficult communication process between managers and employees.

Volunteers are often brought in to help run events such as a college football game. The alumni office may coordinate 200 alumni to help work as ushers. Although this free labor is a great money saver, the facility still needs to provide appropriate training and support for these people. A facility manager needs to determine whether the volunteers will be covered by workers' compensation insurance if they are injured. The facility can also be held liable for a volunteer's negligence, so all volunteers need to be properly trained. A simple decision to save money by having volunteers work a game can backfire if the volunteers are negligent and expose the facility to liability.

HIRING PROCESS

If outsourcing, interns, or independent contractors are not used or are not sufficient to fulfill the employment needs, the facility will need to hire one or more people. The hiring process typically starts with a detailed analysis of the activities involved in the proposed job. A **job analysis** highlights the basic activities that are necessary to perform a specific job. A facility manager first needs to determine what activities need to be accomplished to reach the specific job goals. The job analysis for a ticket salesperson might include the following elements: phone skills, communication skills, ticketing options, accounts receivable, long job hours, and possibly other tasks. The job analysis leads to the **job description.**

Through carefully analyzing what is involved in a job, a manager can then develop a detailed job description highlighting all the skills, abilities, and training needed to effectively perform the job. The job description focuses on skills required to reach the job goals and includes the required job responsibilities along with the nature of the job, such as whether someone will need to manage or supervise (see "Sample Job Description for a Collegiate Box Office Manager" for an example). All duties and responsibilities identified in the job description should be essential for the job and listed in the advertisement to avoid any claim of discrimination. If the job does not require a college education, asking for only college graduates could be construed as an intent to discriminate.

Job descriptions must indicate the exact training required and any degrees or certification that may be necessary. For people who will be using pesticides, for example, do they have the training and skills necessary to work with those chemicals as well as knowledge of any applicable statutes? Some positions in the facility management industry are certified. For example, the Ontario Recreation Facilities Association has developed the designation of certified ice technician for those in the industry who complete a 90-hour program including theory and hands-on training in such areas as basic refrigeration, ice making, ice painting, ice maintenance, and equipment operations ("Certified Ice Technician," 2001). Many positions require specific training such as first aid and CPR.

The hiring process varies in complexity according to what positions need to be filled. Low-level entry positions such as parking attendant or concession sales may be easier to fill since a larger number of people are qualified for such positions compared with a job as an HVAC specialist, which may require licensure. Other variables affecting the hiring process include such issues as the region in the country, economic conditions, prevailing wage rate, and available benefits. High-end positions may require recruiting activities other than advertising in the local newspaper or using job placement agencies. However, because there are always many people seeking employment opportunities in the sport industry, normally a large number of people are regularly submitting resumes to work with teams or facilities.

Advertising a Position

The job description can be used as a basis for writing an advertisement. But while this strategy works well with a flier that can be posted on a bulletin board, most advertisements use a limited space. Publications often charge for ads by the word or line. Thus, some facilities merely ask those interested in a position to visit the facility's website. In other cases, ads mention only the very basics associated with the position. This strategy may save money, but in the long run it can also create the need to process many applications from people who are not qualified, so the idea of saving a few dollars can in fact cost the facility much more in processing time and resources. Applicants are normally obtained through many avenues, from newspaper and Internet advertising to college placement offices and executive recruiters. The tendency in the sport industry is to produce a large number of applicants for almost every position. The Internet has increased this trend. Although it is critical to advertise a position in different media outlets, the most beneficial advertising media are word of mouth and personal referrals. The sport facility industry is a very small community, and a personal recommendation of a candidate goes much further than an unsolicited resume.

SAMPLE JOB DESCRIPTION FOR A COLLEGIATE BOX OFFICE MANAGER

The XYZ Center, a 10,000-seat arena, and the GFH Stadium, a 25,000-seat stadium, on the campus of PDQ University are seeking a box office manager.

Responsibilities: The manager is responsible for ticket sales at the arena and at all other facilities on campus, such as the ABC Theater. Ticketing responsibilities include ticketing for all intercollegiate events on campus. The position supervises a full-time staff of three and several student employees. Other responsibilities include daily deposits, sales reports, postevent settlements, and event creation for ticketing sales growth. The manager will also be responsible for working with event promoters to develop event setups in all the various venues and to provide daily ticket sales and cash accounting.

Qualifications: Strong knowledge base of box office management and operations, including a high degree of independent judgment making and responsibility. Additional skills include a high-level command of ticketing procedures and applying ticketing policies to various situations as well as the ability to contribute to the university's administration of its venues. Because of the nature of the position, the candidate will need to have a flexible schedule, including evenings and weekends. The position requires at least 5 years of progressively responsible experience, working your way up from sales person to box office manager, preferably with a Division I-A school. The ideal candidate will have experience working with multiple venues and a thorough knowledge of Word, Access, Excel, and contemporary ticket software application.

Salary range: $38,818 to $48,920.

CLASSIFIED ADVERTISEMENT FOR A FACILITIES ENGINEER

The FGH Field, located in downtown New Haven, is seeking a facilities engineer. The facilities engineer will report directly to the facility general manager. This position is responsible for energy and power plant management, HVAC, electrical, plumbing, mechanical equipment, artificial turf, and all preventive and regular facility maintenance. The qualified candidate should have experience in hiring, training, and supervising a maintenance staff; have a proven track record in energy and maintenance management; have worked with large professional sport facilities; and have at least 5 years of experience as well as either a bachelor's degree in engineering or an additional 3 years of hands-on electrical or systems experience.

CLASSIFIED ADVERTISEMENT FOR A TURF MANAGER

The town of Sportsville is searching for a leader to direct the operations of the park and recreation department's turf and grounds maintenance program. Responsibilities include all care and maintenance of athletic fields, other lawn areas, and shrub, recreation, and school areas. Requirements include a bachelor's degree in agronomy, landscape design, or turf management plus 5 years of experience in turf and ground management, including at least 3 years of supervisory experience. Applicants must possess the CT Custom Grounds applicator's supervisory license or equivalent. The salary range for this position is $45,000 to $68,000.

Screening Applicants

Management must process all the applicants and then interview enough people to be able to make a decision. It may be necessary to hire more employees than are actually needed in order to have a pool of people who are available and have been prescreened. For example, if 200 security staffers are needed for an event, it would probably be prudent to have 500 prequalified individuals who can be called on to fill the needs for any given event. The extra candidates could be essential for some positions requiring background checks and formal training. Having a surplus is also more important for stadiums and arenas; because the work is often considered seasonal, a large percentage of those who would work in the facility have other jobs and need to coordinate their schedules.

Once employees are hired, they need to be eased into the job rather than simply thrown in. They need to be trained so they can accomplish their specific tasks. Maintenance personnel who worked for 5 years at one facility may be lost at a different facility; for example, pipes may not be marked, electrical outlets may not be live, or it may not be obvious which storage areas contain hazardous materials. Here are some strategies for helping employees better integrate into an organization:

- Give new hires access to financial, product, strategy, and facility information as early as possible.
- Give new employees a comprehensive tour and a map of the facility.
- Introduce the new employee to all constituents with whom they will work.
- Talk with new employees after their first week and month on the job to make sure they are properly oriented.
- Make sure employees know what their role in the organization is and why that role is so important.
- Make sure the employee is adapting to the facility's culture, or find a solution if a problem exists.

EMPLOYEE MANAGEMENT

Once an adequate number of employees are hired, the next phase of the employment process—employee management—begins. The greatest expense for any facility is not the construction expense but rather the salaries and expenses associated with employees. All employees need to be properly coordinated and managed to maximize their effectiveness. That is where innovative motivational techniques need to be implemented.

Management needs to examine what techniques can help motivate an employee who is underperforming. For example, according to **Maslow's hierarchy of needs**, people at the bottom of the pyramid will not be as motivated by some strategies, such as a new title or a bigger office, as they may be by more vacation time or a higher salary. Once management knows what will motivate an employee, it is much easier to manage the employee's movement up the pyramid based on concrete strategies rather than mere guessing. (See "Strategies for Motivating Employees" for more ideas.)

There is no one correct method of managing employees. What works at one facility will not necessarily work at another. However, it is not enough to utilize different ideas or campaigns to motivate people. Constant monitoring is also necessary. At times facility managers who may appear to be simply relaxing and walking around may actually be evaluating employees. Managers sometimes conduct tests themselves or through the use of secret shoppers. Secret shoppers are hired by the facility to act like regular customers and evaluate their service experience. A manager or secret shopper might see a dirty napkin on the floor and observe whether any employee stops to pick it up. He can also observe how employees interact with customers to see whether they are friendly and courteous. These and other similar techniques help demonstrate whether managerial strategies, leadership skills, and various benefits actually succeed in changing behavior.

Regardless of the managerial techniques used, evaluation of employees is necessary in that it provides valuable information to managers on whether employees are achieving the predetermined goals.

Employee Evaluation

Evaluations are used in every facility. Marketing efforts are regularly evaluated for their effectiveness. Benchmarking standards are used to evaluate the effectiveness of everything from maintenance efforts to the HVAC system. Just as all the mechanical and administrative efforts of a facility are evaluated, the human capital must be evaluated. If an employee is not living up to the expectations specified in the job description, the employee needs to be motivated, retrained, or terminated.

STRATEGIES FOR MOTIVATING EMPLOYEES

- Hang a plaque in the main hallway to recognize employees of the month.
- Give meaningful awards to employees in the front office, those working concessions, ushers, and so on.
- Recognize employees by featuring their names and pictures in game programs or on the scoreboard or by letting them throw out a game ball.
- Let employees exchange jobs for a day with another employee or with a manager.
- Empower employees to make decisions.
- Give employees a specific amount of money to spend any way they want during the year to make customers happy (such as buying an unhappy fan a drink or ticket upgrade).
- Provide a cash benefit for recruiting new employees.
- Allow employees to engage in job rotation or job modifications such as flexible hours.
- Provide employees with better benefit options.
- Allow employees to bring their families to games, and let them enjoy the game from the best seats in the facility with free food.

Employee evaluation can take various forms, from on-the-job analysis to goal attainment. A ticket sales executive could be given the goal of selling 10,000 tickets in a specific price category in a given season. Selling 10,000 tickets means the person has met the goal. Selling more means she is entitled to additional benefits. If the person sells fewer than 10,000 tickets, she could be reprimanded, terminated, retrained, or managed differently. Other employees are often harder to evaluate since there may not be clear-cut criteria for evaluation. An usher would face a significantly different evaluation process than a ticket salesperson. Since an usher's job is not contingent on the number of people seated but rather the quality of service, the evaluation standard is subjective rather than objective. Ushers could be evaluated based on their efficiency, the number of compliments and complaints received, the quality of work performed, and related standards. Because the process can be highly subjective, it is imperative to perform such evaluations in an unbiased manner to prevent claims of discrimination or wrongful termination.

Management must take numerous factors into consideration when examining evaluation programs. If an employee is being evaluated based on criteria outside his control, the evaluation system will be perceived as biased and unfair. This could lead to significant distrust. One way to avoid such a problem is to determine the criteria for evaluation and job retention when an employee is hired. If concession workers know they will need to sell 100 sodas each game over a season, the variability of external factors can be somewhat reduced. Some games may be rained out; others will occur in hot weather, which will produce increased sales. Thus, sales could be averaged. However, if the team is losing every game, the evaluation criteria should be adjusted or the facility will lose all its employees because they do not meet preseason goals. The key concern in this example involves communication. The goals for employees must be clearly communicated; all employees should know what they are expected to accomplish and how each person's success will complement the work of other employees.

If a manager wants to improve the workplace and the employees therein, it is critical to evaluate whether any skill deficiencies exist. A manager is not doing her job if she does not monitor employees and make sure they have the skills and training required to effectively do their jobs. If with additional training an employee can complete a job in 2 hours rather than 4 hours, the training will save the facility significant time and money. To start this process, a manager determines what skill deficiencies exist by using work audits (which can be triggered by a complaint or poor evaluation), customer surveys, performance appraisals, and peer reviews. A combination of all these will result in a full review by all those who interact with and are affected by the employee. Such an evaluation process should also examine whether the employee's work is proactive versus reactive or planned versus emergency as well as the employee's work quality, attitude, frequency of returned calls, and so on. Some of these issues are inherent in the job and cannot be controlled by the employee; others might be the result of employee conduct. A manager must focus a deficiency analysis on what is within an employee's control. At the same time, if an employee is hampered by the organization, then policies and procedures should be evaluated to determine whether they are the cause of any deficiencies. The reviews then result in action steps, including training, retraining, purchasing required equipment, reassigning employees, designating teams, or even possible termination.

Termination

Employees who are not productive either can be terminated or may leave if they are not sufficiently motivated to do the job. Employees leave their jobs for a number of reasons, including personal reasons such as moving to a new area or opportunities to obtain a better job. Employees stay when they feel appreciated, when they get along with coworkers and managers, when management supports them, and when they believe they contribute to the facility's overall mission (Shenker, 2002). Specific reasons for losing employees include poor supervision, frequent supervisory changes, unclear or unreasonable expectations, lack of feedback, lack of rewards for quality work, poor pay, lack of advancement opportunities, company culture clash, and a host of others. The key for a facility manager is to communicate with employees to see what they are thinking so that management can create a better work environment that may entice some disgruntled employees to stay. Communication is the key, since the lack of communication can often lead to employee unrest and ultimately the loss of good employees.

Although some employees need to be retained, others need to be cut. Turnover can be a good means of bringing in fresh ideas and new approaches. Any change will cost money. These costs include hiring, retraining, severance pay, unemployment pay, position advertising, recruiting costs, applicant testing, background checks, signing bonuses, relocation fees, and possibly higher salaries. Indirect costs include lost business, staff time, lost productivity, delay as the new employee reaches an acceptable productivity level, and possibly a negative aura in the workplace from "bad vibes" or hurt feelings (Shenker, 2002).

One of the processes associated with evaluation is the grievance process. Most employees at sport facilities are employees at will, which means they can be terminated for any reason or no reason whatsoever. This is true except in the case of union employees covered by a CBA. Thus, if the manager does not like the clothes an employee wears one day, she can technically terminate the employee. However, most employers utilize a grievance system to help maintain morale or to comply with a union's CBA. The typical grievance process involves several stages such as an initial warning, subsequent written warnings, and then potentially a termination. This process is called the **progressive disciplinary approach.** If a manager fails to provide an employee with a progressive process, the terminated employee can file a wrongful termination or discrimination suit. The chance that the former employee will win in such a suit is significantly decreased if the progressive disciplinary process was used and all the misdeeds were documented.

The heart and soul of the management process entails appropriate motivation and employee training. Employees are hired because they presumably have the appropriate and necessary skills and talent to perform the job. If they are not doing the job as well as expected, something needs to change. The employee may not live up to expectations because he does not care. In this case the only option is to terminate. For employees who are willing to work to improve their performance, two primary options can be used singly or in combination: appropriate motivation so that the employee can achieve a higher level of success, and training to reach a higher skill level.

LEGAL CONCERNS

In addition to hiring, motivating, and terminating employees, the entire process of managing human resources requires close supervision to adhere to legal requirements. For example, reducing employee conflict seems to be a noble idea to make the workplace more harmonious. However, it is just as important for preventing future legal concerns as it is for enhancing the workplace. If two employees have a strong dislike for each other, this makes for more than just a hostile environment. It can lead to workplace violence, discrimination claims, and even harassment claims, all of which can generate significant legal costs.

A multitude of federal regulations, such as the **Civil Rights Act of 1964** and the ADA, apply if an employer has more than 15 employees. If a facility employs only five people, most civil rights and antidiscrimination laws are inapplicable. However, some laws, such as workers' compensation insurance coverage and Fair Labor Standards Act reporting requirements for minimum wage and overtime work apply even if there is only one employee.

Biased assignments for training programs can raise legal concerns such as discrimination claims. Such a claim represents just one of the many legal matters involved in the employment process. Throughout the hiring process there are countless other legal traps. The following is a list of some basic legal issues that can arise during the employment process.

- Inappropriate application forms or questions
- Poor or inappropriate interview questions
- Improper classification of employees as at-will employees
- Lack of standardized documents
- Failure to review and update employment policies

FACILITY FOCUS

CONNECTICUT SPORTSPLEX

The Connecticut Sportsplex is New England's largest sport complex. Its five-field outdoor facility hosts baseball and softball tournaments every weekend (national, state, and sectional tournaments) in addition to weekday leagues. The sportsplex includes a 75,000-square-foot (6,965 sq m) indoor dome facility that offers four multisport fields and a state-of-the-art artificial turf surface for indoor soccer, softball, field hockey, flag football, and other activities. In 2014 several outdoor full length artificial turf soccer fields were added. It also includes a 25,000-square-foot (2,320 sq m) field house that houses a 40-seat pub-style restaurant, an arcade, virtual golf simulators, batting cages, pool tables, air hockey tables, a basketball court, a jungle gym, a moon walk, a party area, and an area for cheerleading and gymnastics. With all these amenities, the Connecticut Sportsplex needs a large number of employees to operate effectively. It also needs a flexible workforce—during downtimes only 3 or 4 employees may be needed to run the facilities, whereas more than 20 employees may be required to work a tournament.

Some of the specific employment-related concerns faced by the facility include the following:

■ Having employees who are old enough to serve alcohol at the bar

■ Finding enough employees to work nights and weekends, when the facility is the busiest

■ Finding employees who can work with mechanical equipment such as lawn mowers

■ Preventing employee theft from the concession area

■ Retaining independent contractors such as umpires to work games

■ Terminating employees who fail to meet predetermined goals

■ Interviewing and mentoring interns to work at the facility

■ Failure to monitor, evaluate, and secure personnel files

■ Failure to evaluate employees in a timely, honest, and tactful manner

■ Failure to have appropriate evaluation criteria

■ Failure to properly document evaluations and all other employment decisions

■ Failure to provide a proper grievance process to try to resolve disputes

■ Failure to provide proper notice for discipline and the opportunity to be heard

■ Failure to act promptly to terminate an employee who has engaged in egregious or violent conduct

■ Failure to review each termination and to make sure appropriate records are maintained

■ Failure to consider all applicable local, state, and federal laws

In the United States, a potpourri of federal and state laws affect the employment law landscape. One of the most relevant laws is the **Fair Labor Standards Act (FLSA)**, which covers everything from minimum wage and overtime to teenage workers. Young employees are a major concern for sport facilities. As reported by the Department of Labor in 1997, 51% of all the teen workers in the United States work in the retail industry, and the US service industry (e.g., YMCAs, swimming pools, parks and recreation centers, ball parks, and amusement parks) also employs 34% of the remaining teen workers (Fried and Miller, 1998). By 2013 the numbers had shifted a bit. For example, people might think that teens are the largest demographic of workers in the fast-food industry. However, in 2013 less than 30% of those working in fast food were teens; more than 36% were over age 20 and had children. The increased number of parents working in the service industry helped increase the call for raising the minimum wage to benefit these older workers (Perkins, 2013). While fast food employment numbers have changed, service industry numbers showed an increase in teen employees even in a poor economy since 2008: Two-thirds of all teens currently work in the retail or service industries. Ignorance of the law is the most frequent reason for failure to comply with the FLSA. Numerous employers post the required FLSA poster, but employees fail to read or follow the information. In addition to prescribing hours that teens can work, the FLSA prohibits teenagers from 18 specified jobs. Facility managers should check with the experts before placing teen employees on lawn mowers or having them build or mend fences, work late at night, or operate mechanical amusement rides. Knowing and complying with the law also benefits an employer via increased employee morale, improved public relations, decreased insurance expenses, and a safer work environment.

In addition to FLSA, the **Occupational Safety and Health Administration (OSHA)** is a major legislative framework that affects sport facility managers. OSHA requires specific conduct to be undertaken to ensure a safe work environment. Safety steps are required, for example, to secure people to a building whenever they are working at elevations, such as on the rigging inside an arena. Thus, employees who may work in such positions need to be given safety harnesses and be trained in how to use them. OSHA also covers a host of other workplace-related safety concerns, from the noise level at concerts to wiping down countertops and benches to avoid contact with bloodborne pathogens.

Besides concerns listed earlier, numerous other legal concerns present unique challenges to sport facilities. Among the most significant of these concerns are unionization, ADA compliance, workers' compensation, and sexual harassment. Additional legal concerns are highlighted in chapter 13.

Unions

Those studying employee motivation and management often overlook unionization. Sometimes students who are prospective managers think that if they are properly motivated and are best friends with their employees, they may be able to leverage that relationship to receive the most from employees. However, the realities of the workplace are very different. Many publicly owned, school, and college facilities have unionized workforces.

The primary function of a union is to negotiate and administer the CBA with the employer, which covers the conditions of employment for the union members. Unions have a significant effect on the employment environment. They reduce a manager's authority, control over personnel policies, and prerogative to make certain decisions without union involvement. At the same time, unions represent a significant benefit for employees through providing a unified voice, psychological satisfaction, strength in numbers, and economic benefits for its members (Fried and Miller, 1998). Although it may appear that employees have a one-sided weapon against employers through unions, specific federal legislation provides both sides with tangible benefits.

There are both national and local unions. National unions establish rules under which local unions may be chartered and permitted to retain their membership in the national union. Such rules cover dues collection, initiation fees, union funds administration, and new member admission criteria. Local unions represent the direct interest of their constituency by monitoring management activities and making sure the CBA is being followed. In addition, local unions help members rectify any unjust treatment or sponsor grievances claimed by local members.

Local unions operate through a business representative who negotiates the CBA and administers the agreement. When a union member has problems, she brings the problems to the attention of the union steward, who represents the union member's interest in her relations with immediate supervisors and other managers. Some stewards are paid by the employer solely to reconcile disputes involving union members in reference to work-related disputes. This creates several bureaucratic levels that can often make the employment process more difficult. For example, a manager may not be able to ask a union employee to clean a restroom if that activity is not in the employee's job description. Thus, the manager may have to find a busy janitor to clean the restroom while the other employee sits doing absolutely nothing except wait for work detailed in the job description. In some facilities it is difficult to ask an employee to do anything, even when it is in the person's job description, without going through a union supervisor.

Besides national and local, unions can be further classified as closed shops and open shops. Closed shops operate under a CBA wherein all employees as a condition of employment need to be union members. In open shops, both union and nonunion employees can work for the employer even if the employer has a CBA with a union.

Both unions and employers are forbidden to require union membership. However, unions can secure from each employee a financial contribution to help pay for representation costs, and this contribution is typically the same as union dues paid by union members. In approximately 24 U.S. states, though, "right to work" laws forbid unions from seeking financial contributions from nonunion employees (Fried and Miller, 1998).

The laws related to unionization, union activities, retaliation, antitrust violations, and associated issues are very complex. It is critical for a unionized facility to hire a talented labor law specialist. A potential union will not undertake formation efforts without competent counsel. To face trained labor organizers without proper assistance is tantamount to committing business suicide. Many businesses fight to avoid unions by providing strong benefits. Happy employees often do not want unions since they do not want to lose these benefits. However, if an employer does not treat employees well, the employees may unionize to gain bargaining strength in numbers. Employees often unionize to obtain safer working conditions or other specific concessions. By addressing employee concerns, management can often avoid dealing with unions and thus avoid significant cost increases and a reduced ability to work with employees.

Ancillary facilities, such as the Ice Den practice facility in Scottsdale, Arizona, served as workout venues for NHL players that were locked out of their main facilities during the 2012 strike.

Americans With Disabilities Act

Although facility access is a major concern under the ADA, the act can affect everything from advertising a position to terminating an employee. For example, it is illegal to ask someone whether he has a disability. A facility manager can ask whether someone can carry 50 pounds (22.7 kg), if the job requires carrying 50 pounds, but cannot ask whether the person has any back problems. This does not mean that every potentially disabled person needs to be hired. Rather, it means that the employer cannot dismiss disabled applicants who can do the job simply because they are disabled. On the other hand, the fact that a disabled applicant can do the job does not mean the employer must hire that person. Another applicant who is more personable or better at establishing rapport can be hired instead. Thus, the ADA is very clearly designed to provide a level playing field for all potential employees. The ADA is covered in greater detail in chapter 13.

Workers' Compensation

Some work environments produce significant and sometimes serious injuries. Construction, work with hazardous chemicals, firefighting, security, and punch press machine operation are among the activities that produce either frequent or in some cases life-threatening injuries. Typically, 6,000 to 7,000 people in the United States die in the workplace each year, and another 11 to 15 million are hurt in work-related accidents. That translates to 18 deaths and 36,000 injuries every day (Fried and Miller, 1998). In 2007 the top two industry segments in the United States with the highest percentage of injuries were the skiing facilities (33,500 employees with an injury rate of 16.5%) and sport teams and clubs (64,900 employees with an injury rate of 16.2%) ("Table: SNR01," 2008). In 2013 the number of workers injured in the workplace was still a major issue. More than 3 million employees were injured in 2012. Two employees died during construction efforts at Levi's Stadium before it opened in 2014.. The most common workplace injuries in 2014 were slip-and-fall injuries, injuries from being hit by or against an object, and strains. The most common causes of workplace deaths in the sport industry are motor vehicle accidents (e.g., a golf cart turning over or a truck crashing) and work-place violence. These losses cannot be completely avoided, but they can be reduced through safety education and equipment.

The purpose behind **workers' compensation insurance** is to have a no-fault safety net for every employer and employee. The no-fault system means that coverage begins immediately after the employee is injured and that the coverage is complete. In exchange for prompt and complete payment of claims, the injured employee waives her right to sue the facility unless the facility management engaged in wrongful conduct such as failing to eliminate a known hazard.

Workers' compensation premiums are based on past claims associated with a given career and the prospect for injuries. Some facility-related jobs are highly dangerous, and the workers' compensation insurance premium may be 50% of every dollar paid in salary. That would mean that if a construction or rigging worker earned $50,000 a year, the facility would have to pay $25,000 to purchase workers' compensation insurance just for that employee. The high price of workers' compensation insurance reflects the high claims totals for those injured in the industry. It should be noted that injury claims and deaths are much more common in hazardous industries such as mining, construction, and manufacturing.

One of the biggest traps for unsuspecting employers is the failure to purchase workers' compensation insurance. Workers' compensation insurance needs to be purchased for employees and interns but not for independent contractors. In California, failure to purchase workers' compensation insurance can lead to a misdemeanor charge (6 months in jail and a $1,000 fine), criminal prosecution, and even an order suspending the use of employees.

Besides having workers' compensation insurance, facility management should organize a safety committee comprising managers and various lower-level employees who consistently work in environments with hazardous conditions such as pools, food service, maintenance, weight rooms, and related program areas. The safety committee can be empowered to

- analyze safety concerns,
- provide suggestions for facility modifications or alterations,
- suggest potential safety precautions,
- help develop a safety manual and educational aids,
- help update the safety manual,
- help train other employees, and
- assume overall responsibility associated with safety matters.

Besides being an effective risk management tool, a facility may be required by state law to have a safety committee. In states with such laws, facility managers must do more than establish a safety committee; they are also required to act on the committee's recommendations. Safety committees should

- meet at least once a month to discuss current issues,

- prepare minutes from all meetings,
- make periodic site inspections,
- review all incident and injury reports,
- review any safety complaints, and
- process any safety suggestions and recommendations (Fried and Miller, 1998).

Although safety committees appear to be a win–win proposition for employees and employers, the primary concerns are the potential inadvertent formation of a union and the possibility that evidence can be generated that can undercut an employer at a future trial.

Sexual Harassment

There are two types of sexual harassment. Quid pro quo refers to the situation in which an employer (supervisor, boss, or anyone with a position of authority over the employee) requires sexual activity or conduct as a condition of employment, future employment, future job advancement, or future salary increases. Many employees, managers, and employers understand that it is inappropriate to directly utilize sex as a vehicle for job advancement, but this still occurs. Examples still exist of employees, from administrative assistants to senior managers, who are forced to compromise their principles for their careers. This difficult choice is the reason sexual harassment is such an important issue. Employees should not have to choose between their dignity and their jobs (Fried and Miller, 1998).

Title VII of the Civil Rights Act of 1964 is violated by the second type of sexual harassment—conduct that creates a **hostile or offensive work environment**. The same law also covers other forms of discrimination based on race, religion, nationality, and sexual orientation. A different law, the Age Discrimination in Employment Act,

covers age-based discrimination. The Supreme Court has concluded that not all conduct that may appear to be sexual harassment is in fact sexual harassment. The conduct must be sufficiently severe or pervasive to alter the condition of the victim's employment and create an abusive or hostile working environment. Some courts have held that creation of a hostile work environment does not occur in instances in which an employer, upon learning of harassing conduct against an employee, takes prompt remedial action against the offending employee (Fried and Miller, 1998).

Although sexual harassment is clearly a big problem, there are solutions. The key solution is to develop a sexual harassment education and compliance program. Such a program is contingent on adopting a sexual harassment policy that is signed and followed by all employees. Besides developing a less hostile environment, a facility manager needs to develop a process for responding when sexual harassment occurs or is alleged. The facility manager needs to designate a representative who will be in charge of handling all sexual harassment claims. That person must be sympathetic and listen to any complaints. The representative then must investigate the claim, being mindful of personal and possibly civil rights, especially if the accused turns out to be innocent. If the accused has engaged in inappropriate conduct, the person must be disciplined according to the severity of the conduct, whether through a warning or immediate termination or various other options in between. The entire process must be documented, and all employees must understand that there cannot be retaliation against anyone involved in the process. The representative should also follow up with the alleged victim, government entities, and insurance companies as appropriate to make sure the matter is resolved and to minimize the possibility of similar incidents occurring again.

REDUCING THE RISK OF SEXUAL HARASSMENT

Examples of sexual harassment or potential sexual harassment due to a hostile work environment can be found in many sport facilities. In one case, 25 women worked as cleaning and janitorial staff members at a large stadium. Imagine that you are a foreign worker and your supervisor threatens to deport you or hurt your chance of staying in the country if you do not do what you are told. You are not asked to clean the supervisor's car or perform other tasks that are inappropriate; rather, you must perform sexual favors to keep your job or avoid deportation. At this sport facility, the cleaning supervisor grabbed the women, tried to take off their clothes, attempted to have sex with them, and threatened them with termination if they did not cooperate. The women filed a claim with the Equal Employment Opportunity Commission (EEOC). The EEOC and Astrodome USA worked out a settlement of more than $500,000 to settle the claims (Fried and Miller, 1998).

Some people think that sexual harassment entails only physical contact or very inappropriate conduct. However, the scope of activities that can constitute potential sexual harassment is very broad. The following are examples of inappropriate conduct that reach the level of sexual harassment.

■ Behavioral acts: ogling, leering, staring, making gestures, mooning, flashing

■ Verbal acts: requests for dates, personal questions, lewd comments, dirty or sexual jokes, whistling, catcalling, obscene calls, sexual comments, rumors

■ Written or visual acts: love letters or poems; obscene letters, cards, notes, posters, pictures, cartoons, or graphics

■ Touching: violating personal space, patting, rubbing, pinching, bra snapping, caressing, blocking movement, kissing, groping, grabbing, tackling, hazing

■ Power acts: retaliation, using position to request dates or suggest sexual favors, gender-directed favoritism, disparate treatment, hazing rituals, bullying, intimidation, condescending or patronizing behavior

■ Threats: quid pro quo demands, basing evaluation or references on sexual favors, retaliating for refusal to comply with requests

■ Force: attempted rape or assault, rape, assault, pantsing, stripping, extreme forms of hazing, stalking, sexual abuse, physical abuse, vandalism

Inappropriate conduct cannot always be eliminated, but managers can significantly reduce the chances that sexual harassment will occur by both educating employees on what constitutes inappropriate conduct and empowering employees who feel harassed to communicate with their supervisor or the facility manager. Role playing, preventing retaliation, having an open-door policy, and related strategies that allow free communication with a manager may minimize the chance that an employee will be harassed. Further, these approaches should make clear the manager's stance on the behavior so that an employee who is harassed has no reason not to notify the manager of the alleged inappropriate conduct.

Summary

Facility managers must manage facilities and the people who are in them. Although facilities cannot be motivated or fired, employees can, and that is why facility managers have to spend a significant amount of time managing employees.

Besides managing employees, facility managers have to become leaders or retain leaders who can motivate personnel to provide the highest level of service quality. Leadership entails making tough decisions, and one of the more difficult decisions may be whether to use an outsourcing company rather than existing personnel.

Managing people is an art and an acquired skill. Not everyone is comfortable with managing others. However, leaders need to be found in every facility to take charge and ensure that work is done, whether by employees, volunteers, interns, or independent contractors. By combining current employees and industry professionals, along with using information from industry associations, a manager can increase his skills and comfort level in managing and leading others, and the result will be a better facility and work environment for everyone.

A facility manager is often called on to be a referee in disputes involving other administrators, employees, patrons, external contractors, government officials, the media, and many others who can affect those working in a facility. Besides mediating disputes and helping to resolve conflicts, a manager has to serve as a mentor and psychologist at different times. The other major element that necessitates significant managerial oversight comprises all the legal requirements related to hiring, training, promoting, and terminating employees. Issues from unionization to sexual harassment take a significant amount of a manager's time, and there is never downtime when it comes to legal concerns.

Discussion Questions and Activities

1. Define management and then leadership, and then explain the difference between the two.

2. How would you motivate employees if they do not respect you as a leader?

3. Do you have the managerial strength to fire a friend who has not performed up to expectations but has not done anything wrong?

4. Read a management book and critique it for application to the facility management area. What can you take from the book to apply in the facility management context?

5. Why would a facility want to hire a facility management company?

6. What would you include in the job analysis and description for an usher, a concessionaire, and a facility manager?

7. Under what circumstances would it be advisable to outsource facility management functions?

8. How would you handle a sexual harassment complaint in a sport facility?

9. Develop specific policies and procedures you believe would be important to include in an employee manual.

10. Interview at least one facility manager and two to three subordinates at a sport facility. Explore the lines of communication and whether any miscommunication occurs between the various parties. Write a memo about any possible communication concerns and what solutions could help resolve those concerns.

PART II

Facility Development

Although it is critical to know how to run a building, the first item to address is having a building. Part II examines the process of creating and building a sport facility. Because numerous types of sport facilities exist, it is impossible to examine each and every kind. Thus, the chapters in this part provide an overall view to acquaint the reader with the general steps in planning, designing, and then building a facility.

Chapter 4 highlights the facility planning process. Imagine preparing for a wedding but failing to contact a caterer, a hall, or a photographer. The event would be a disaster. Similarly, a comprehensive planning process is crucial to making sure the right facility is built with all the right components. This chapter discusses what issues to examine during the planning process, suggests strategies for garnering community support, identifies the possible constituents who should be involved in the decision to build a facility, shows how to conduct a needs assessment, describes the types of facilities that can be built, and concludes with an analysis of feasibility studies.

Chapter 5 highlights how to choose the best potential site for building a new facility. The adage "location, location, location" is very appropriate, as a facility built in the wrong location can never be perfect. Fans want to go to a game or event and travel the best route and be in the best area. Once a facility is built, it usually cannot be moved, so location is critical. This chapter also covers analyzing potential sites, the strengths of and concerns with various sites, and the costs associated with various sites. Finally, the chapter discusses facility design issues.

Chapter 6 examines how to build the facility. The building process, from deciding who will build the facility and at what cost to obtaining the occupancy permits, can be very stressful and involve many hurdles. This chapter covers various construction elements, from the materials used to build facilities to specific components in sport facilities, such as fields and locker rooms. The chapter ends with an analysis of the cost involved in building a facility and what is required to finalize a facility before it can be used.

Most facility managers might be involved in a single construction project during their careers. This section is not intended to provide a comprehensive overview of the construction process. Rather, it gives the reader a basic understanding of what issues to expect and familiarizes the reader with industry jargon commonly used during the process of building a facility.

4

Facility Planning

Chapter Objectives

- Understand the principles of planning a facility.

- Appreciate the need to continually plan for existing facilities.

- Develop a thorough understanding of how to plan for a new facility.

- Compare the various types of sport facilities to help familiarize a planning committee with possible facility components and design elements.

- Appreciate that some of the data utilized to justify building new facilities will be uncertain or biased, and try to verify all data.

- Develop an understanding of the entire facility business plan process and the components necessary to gain appropriate approval.

Planning is the process of determining a facility's future direction. Facility management is not conducted using a fortune teller gazing into a crystal ball; rather, it occurs through proper planning and then execution of the plan. This chapter deals with the planning process and its importance for facility managers.

As discussed in chapter 2, planning is a fundamental skill required of all managers. Managers must plan for capital improvements, staffing needs, crowd dynamics, emergencies, and booking and scheduling (including breaks for scheduled and unscheduled maintenance). Whether developing goals and objectives or planning new marketing techniques, any facility manager finds that planning occupies a significant amount of time. The planning process is most evident in facility management, which involves planning for each event, all repairs, ticket-selling strategies, financial decision making, facility renovations, and all new construction. Thus, planning can originate as a result of short-term needs or a long-term vision. There are numerous planning demands for a large stadium or arena and different issues for a high school facility. Since these demands are so different, it would be impossible to cover all issues for each facility. Thus, this chapter covers general planning issues, including the steps involved in the planning process. Special attention focuses on the steps involved in the planning process for a new facility. We examine the types of facilities that exist, how to conduct a feasibility study, how to determine the best site selection, and how to develop an appropriate facility plan that can be used to convince the voters or lenders to support the project. A critical component of this plan is the financing element. How will the new facility be financed, and where will the money come from for continued operations and maintenance?

FUNDAMENTALS OF PLANNING

Planning can help make an otherwise unworkable deal work. For example, Clark College in Vancouver needed some extra classroom space for sports medicine and sport management classes so they worked out a deal to help construct a 5,000-seat baseball stadium to be shared with a professional baseball team. Both entities would receive something of value through looking outside the box to solve a problem (Hewitt, 1998). Planning needs to examine unique solutions that accommodate the needs of multiple parties. Robert Kraft, owner of the New England Patriots, is another example. To generate additional profits, Kraft wanted to develop a comprehensive entertainment establishment for his team. He initially promoted moving the team to the Hartford, Connecticut, area; this helped him receive some very valuable financial support from the state government of Massachusetts for infrastructure work in Massachusetts. Although Boston was the ideal choice, he had to move outside of Boston due to the amount of land he needed for his concept. Through aggressive land acquisitions, he purchased a large amount of land and built Gillette Stadium. He then built adjacent to the stadium Patriot Place, which features numerous stores, restaurants, and entertainment venues.

There is no one correct method in planning. Nevertheless, a facility cannot exist without planning. Some facilities lie vacant because of incorrect planning, while other facilities have too many events and demands on facility time because of poor planning. For example, stadiums have remained empty after several past Olympic Games, and empty stadiums is often one of the biggest concerns examined in any current Olympic bid. Numerous sport stadiums in China are dramatically underused or are not used at all, and the government loses a significant amount of money by keeping them open without scheduling events that generate revenue. Large new stadiums and arenas have been torn down in China over the past several years because they were not used or were inappropriately planned. Thus, **planning** is the process of determining the appropriate allocation of precious resources to ensure facility success. The failure to properly plan will not necessarily lead to failure of a facility. However, it can lead to significant hardship that may take years to overcome or may never be overcome.

The adage "If you will build it, they will come" is a fantasy. The thought is that once the facility is built, people will come and the money will follow. However, fortunes have been dashed when

Aselin: Planning for facility success

Photo courtesy of Don Aselin.

My Name is Don Aselin, and I am the former owner and operations manager for Sportspark of New York in Rochester. My first job after graduating with a degree in accounting was as a sales account executive for a national music company promoter. After working in that capacity for 10 years I decided to change venues in my life—do something I loved—and became an event administrator for the local county parks department programs. My daily responsibilities included

- managing 300-plus softball teams, from youth to adult leagues,

- directing the scheduling and special events of these countywide leagues, and

- coordinating all equipment needs and field maintenance.

After working in that job for 3 years I decided to take on a partner and build a 40-acre multisport facility in New York called Sportspark of New York. At the complex, I worked my way up from facility manager to operations manager as I learned the specific needs of the sport industry. The most difficult part of my job was handling the facilities planning, budgetary process, large-scale scheduling, various team scheduling conflicts, food service trends, field and court maintenance, staffing advertising, and promotion of the amateur sports we were involved in. In the 1970s there were no national amateur sport facility support groups to help find the answers to our operations questions. Our needs included, but were not limited to, the following:

- Exchanging ideas with other parties around the country that were doing basically the same thing we were

- Establishing high standards among amateur sport facilities to promote growth of all our programs and facilities

- Setting up a bulk purchase pool to help defray costs and maintain the integrity of our facility budgets

- Coordinating the construction standards to improve facility designs to best accommodate multiple amateur sports for complete multiuse of facilities

- Working as a liaison with the national amateur sport sanctioning bodies to help promote the sports and events for our facility

- Establishing and coordinating standards in hiring and training staff for a multisport facility

In 1981 a group of amateur sport facility owners and operators and park and recreation directors started a national nonprofit organization called Sportsplex Operators and Developers Association (SODA) to resolve and work on some of these problems on a national level. I am happy to have worked my way up to become its executive director in 1997. SODA works hand in hand with the governing bodies of national amateur sports to help set standards for safe and efficient playing environments for all amateur athletic facilities. At SODA, some of the biggest mistakes we see developers run into most often are as follows:

- Overplanning on a scale that is not attainable with local market demographics or conditions and not allowing enough green space for future development

- Limiting a facility to a single sport instead of multiple sports as needed to survive swings in popularity in amateur sports

- Not developing sport facilities in stages (at least three) to preserve cash flow and help pay for portions of future expansion

- Not limiting debt service where possible

- Not finding the appropriate and adequate financing to carry out the proper development of a major sport facility (most facilities built in the past 10 years ran out of money before the projects were completed)

Publications such as this one are a must in maintaining the integrity of the amateur sport industry and in giving guidance to those who wish to develop it, promote it, and make it a viable national business. Had such resources been available to me some 42 years ago, my life would have been much easier in the area of facilities planning and management.

someone plans or builds a facility expecting that everyone will use it. The problem is that although many people might like a facility, not everyone will visit it more than once or pay money to use it. Thus, the most important planning questions for a revenue-supported facility under consideration is whether enough traffic exists on an annual basis (not just in several key months) to support the facility and what the right price point is. These questions help stress the point that a sport facility is not in the sport business but rather the facility utilization business and that money is lost any time the facility is not used (Brown, 2009a). Part of understanding this point is understanding the famous 80–20 rule. A developer for a proposed facility should not listen to the 80% of members who use the facility infrequently (once or twice a month) but rather should listen closely to the 20% of members who use the facility the most (four or more times a week) because the frequent users will spend the greatest amounts of time and money at the facility.

The facility planning process is just that—a process. The process centers on collaboration. Some facilities use a top-down approach where plans are dictated from above and the end users have very little say in what is built. In contrast, the most successful facilities utilize a multidisciplinary, collaborative process in which every department creates specific goals for development and input is provided at every level until an almost-complete plan reaches the upper administration. This ground-up approach ensures institutional buy in. The owners become the users and the most vocal advocates for the project because they were involved in the planning process. Note that external constituents are heavily involved throughout this process as well. Long-term part-

The Montreal Biodome languished for years of underuse after it was originally built as a velodrome for the 1976 Olympics. In 1992 it was converted into the Biodome and is now a popular tourist attraction.

nerships can be developed with architectural, design, and construction firms, who can all be on the same page and help reduce overall costs.

Two types of planning are critical for facilities: planning for existing facilities and planning for future facilities.

PLANNING FOR EXISTING FACILITIES

A manager may be hired to help develop a facility from the beginning conceptual stages, since a manager may be able to identify concerns or opportunities during the planning process. Some facility managers specifically take a job managing a yet-to-be-built facility because they want the challenge or the opportunity to be part of something new and exciting—and it can be very exciting to work on a building from the design phase all the way through to obtaining the **occupancy permit**. But while most facility managers never plan for more than one new facility during their careers, managers of an existing facility always need to plan for the next day, month, and year.

Planning for an existing facility entails examining the current uses and future potential uses. For some facilities this process can be fairly simple.

FACILITIES FOR ONE-TIME INTERNATIONAL SPORTING EVENTS

The latest trend is designing and building facilities for large sporting events, such as the Olympics or the World Cup, that can be repurposed or redesigned after the event is held. The Olympic Village in Vancouver was planned and built with both sustainability (e.g., a biofriendly sewage system, efforts to conserve water) and conversion in mind. The facilities built for the London Olympic Games were similarly planned to enhance the surrounding neighborhoods and give back to the community once the games ended. Such planning required significant input from local organizations, including civic groups, churches, political entities, and even local teams hoping to use a facility once the Games ended.

South Africa spent more than $1.3 billion on 10 stadiums for the 2010 World Cup. Although these stadiums were ideal for soccer, they were too small for cricket and were not built with suites neces-sary for rugby, the two primary spectator sports in South Africa. A lack of communication was one of the biggest problems in designing the facilities for success in years to come. The president of the South African Rugby Union told members of parliament that Durban city official and rugby officials never met before a $400 million, 70,000-capacity stadium was built. Before the stadium-building boom, the president wrote a letter to the minister of sports highlighting some of the problems associated with not being able to use the stadiums after the games. Unfortunately, the president said, "We were all taken up by the soccer World Cup and in the hype we forgot we should have been talking to each other" (Imray, 2010). Another concern cited was that some of the facilities were in remote parts of the country that many spectators couldn't reach and that had very few major sport teams nearby.

Managers of a single-use facility such as an ice rink know what events will be held in the future and how to plan for those events. Such planning includes coordinating maintenance schedules and personnel; monitoring electricity usage to keep the ice frozen; scheduling daily events, special events, and games; coordinating concession purchases and sales; and dealing with numerous other concerns associated with various facets of the facility and its ancillary areas (bathrooms, parking lots, and so on). Fiscal planning is often the most important planning concern. In an ice rink, a breakdown of the Zamboni can generate five-figure expenses within minutes. If the facility has only $5,000 in the bank and no credit, how can it handle such emergencies? Through planning, the facility can analyze existing systems and maintenance needs to project future capital requirements.

Money, Personnel, and Scheduling

Facility-related costs are frequently an after-thought. It is not uncommon to walk into a gymnasium and see nonfunctioning lights. Is the school waiting for more lights to go out so that it is worthwhile bringing in a hoisting unit, or does the school simply lack funds to replace the lights? Thus, a critical planning question is whether enough money will be available in the future to operate the facility. Many facilities rely on government assistance, but what if that government assistance ends? This is a major concern for many municipally owned facilities, including schools, park and recreation facilities, and some major sport facilities. For some facilities that were built during good financial times, the coffers were bled dry by other priorities once the economy changed and the debt needed to be repaid. For example, in 2005 the city of Stockton, California, completed as part of a downtown redevelopment project a 10,000-seat arena, a 5,000-seat minor league stadium, and a waterfront area. The effort was launched when housing prices were going up and more people were moving to the midsize city. The new facilities increased the city's debt service to $977 million. Almost a billion dollars in debt, the city was unable to cover its total debt obligations. The initial construction plan was supposed to cost around $114 million but grew to $145 million (Vekshin, 2012). The city pursued the project even though a perfect economic environment would be required for the project to succeed, but that environment did not materialize. When the economic downturn occurred, the city fell into significant financial distress and eventually filed for bankruptcy protection in 2012—the largest city bankruptcy in United States history.

Personnel is another major concern in planning for existing facilities. Are there enough employees to operate the facility? The hours that the facility will be open and the events that will be held help dictate the number of people that will be required for facility operation. The planning process will also help determine where employees may be needed and what skills will be needed.

Another major issue in the planning process is facility scheduling. If the facility has 20 events scheduled for a week, how will all the events work together without causing problems? Scheduling may also raise equity issues. Will all the basketball games be played at night? If so, is this fair to the minor sports such as volleyball or badminton? Could such a schedule be seen as discriminatory, particularly if the volleyball players are all women? Furthermore, would it matter what participant numbers are expected for each event? These types of questions require careful consideration.

These examples suggest how important planning is for an existing facility. The planning processes required for the future of an existing facility are similar to planning for a new facility. Background data (internal and external) need to be obtained and compared with facility policies and procedures. All this information is crafted into a document—the plan—that helps drive the facility into the future.

Space Management

Space management refers to current and future space needs and the proper allocation of time and space for bookings, which are the best means to maximize revenue generation. A facility may be large enough to support current needs, but what if new activities are added and there is no additional room? Management might need to lease (rent) additional space so there will be enough space for all activities. Space management applies to all spaces. Numerous managers spend their time examining office space, moving people between offices to help facilitate smoother workflow or relocating offices for political and ego reasons. **Move management** may require analyzing where in a building people or equipment can be moved to free up space. However, space planning requires a more significant effort to provide for the future. The failure to plan can result in unnecessary moves and relocating expenses, the need to rent additional space, underutilization of existing space, and related situations that not only waste money but can also demoralize those who must pay the price for poor space management.

Facility managers normally plan based on standard allocations such as the square footage required for each staff member multiplied by the number of staff members. If each marketing employee requires 100 square feet (9.3 sq m) and there are currently 10 marketing employees, then the office space for marketing, not including corridors or other commons areas, needs to be at least 1,000 square feet (93 sq m). If the office area is only 1,000 square feet, what would happen if a new employee was hired? Another 100 square feet would be needed. Through space planning, a facility manager creates space for future growth through such means as redesigning existing space or leasing additional space with the idea that personnel can grow into a facility.

Other space planning concerns include swing space and growth space. **Swing space** is any space that is available during renovations, alterations, or realignment. A corner of the gym used to store equipment during renovation of a room is an example of swing space. **Growth space** is space contiguous to currently utilized space that allows a business to expand without undertaking any additional construction or leasing (Cotts and Lee, 1992). Large businesses require 2% to 3% growth space, and smaller businesses require 5% to 7% growth space. Growth space is based on historical growth data, or anticipated future growth if new programs or activities are planned. Thus, growth space planning requires significant managerial input.

Facilities often face problems when administrators plan for growth and do not tell the facility managers about the plans. In one facility, the school administrators planned for a nature trail with a crushed-gravel walkway. The facility administrator was not asked about facility-related concerns and was not consulted during the entire process until the construction began. At this point he rushed to raise concerns such as the lack of toilets to service the area, the lack of electricity, the need to ensure compliance with the Americans with Disabilities Act, and other problems relating to the growth space. These last-minute concerns cost the school a significant amount of time and money. This situation probably could have been avoided through proper planning. In summary, space issues that should be examined include the amount and type of space available, the overall condition of the facility, architectural limitations, and any other space limitations.

PLANNING FOR FUTURE FACILITIES

Future facilities raise numerous concerns such as where to build, what to build, and how to pay for the facility. Only through effective planning can a facility be developed that meets the greatest current needs, anticipates future needs, and causes the least amount of harm. For example, facilities today need to be planned with an eye toward media exposure, demographics, property size, planned events, being environmentally friendly (Leadership in Energy and Environmental Design, or LEED, certified), and the sellability of commercial rights such as naming rights and personal seat licenses. "Typical Planning Questions for a New Sport Facility" lists planning questions that one should ask when considering the construction of a new sport facility.

This planning process starts with an analysis of existing internal and external constituents (stakeholders). The **internal constituents** are the people who will use the facility, such as athletes, students, or spectators. The **external constituents** are stakeholders outside the facility such as government leaders, alumni, donors, and others who have an interest in the facility but are outside the traditional facility planning process. A politician may approve funds that can help construct the facility, and she may eventually use the facility. However, this person is still considered an external constituent since she is not a primary user.

People who are potential internal constituents because they might at one time use the facility are distinguished from people for whom the facility is planned and who may use the facility every week.

How should a group, whether public or private, plan for a new facility? Steps include the following:

- Conducting a feasibility study
- Developing a potential budget
- Organizing various planning committees
- Setting realistic goals and objectives
- Researching the political and financial marketplace
- Trying to bring aboard the right people before the project even starts
- Garnering community support
- Conducting a needs assessment
- Identifying comparable facilities

When planning a facility, many architects and facility owners hope to receive some type of certification, which is regarded as a badge of honor. Although every facility needs to meet minimum safety requirements and pass inspection before receiving an occupancy permit, many facility owners look for a way to proclaim to the world that their facility is better than the rest. Each certification can be classified based on complexity, thoroughness, green standard, costs to build the facility, and a variety of other criteria. The difference between each certification type might rest with the organization offering the certification. Some government and nonprofit organizations offer certification, and some for-profit entities have entered into the business. Some certifications take years to receive and are very complex, whereas others might require the completion of a simple survey focused on what the facility is doing. The cost of certification can range from yearly fees to more than $50,000 for elite certifications.

Some common certifications include the following:

- Leadership in Energy and Environmental Design (LEED) is a voluntary, consensus-based program that provides third-party verification of green buildings. Developed by the nonprofit U.S. Green Building Council, LEED provides building owners and operators a framework for identifying and implementing practical and measurable green building design, construction, operations, and maintenance solutions. More than 7,000 buildings have gone through the certification process. Based on the number of points received, a facility can be certified as silver, gold, or platinum. The first National Football League stadium to receive LEED certification was Soldier Field (existing building) in 2012. The first Major League Baseball stadium to be certified was Nationals Park (new construction) in 2008. Several National Basketball Association and National Hockey League arenas underwent modification and received LEED certification in 2009, including Philips Arena, Moda Center, Bell Centre, and American Airlines Center. Although the fee for certification is less than $0.10 per square foot (roughly $20,000-$60,000 per project, plus other soft costs that can be in the thousands), the bigger costs is in the construction, renovation, and operation phases, where strategies need to be followed to earn the necessary points. These costs typically are reclaimed over time through energy efficiency and reduced operating costs.

■ Green Globes is an online auditing tool that guides the integration of environmental performance in primarily new construction projects and assesses the design of green buildings against best practices and standards. Green Globes is used primarily in Canada, where it was adopted by the Building Owners and Managers Association of Canada in 2004.

■ Society of Environmentally Responsible Facilities (SERF) was founded in 2010 to provide a cheaper and faster alternative to LEED. Facility owners can choose a prescriptive or performance-based criterion evaluated by a third-party architect or engineer. The process costs between $4,000 and $12,000 and evaluates components such as energy or water efficiency, occupancy health, waste reduction, and innovative practices.

■ EarthCraft is a 400-point evaluation program that requires energy data for 12 months, a design review, a preconstruction meeting, two predrywall visits, and a final visit upon completion of the project. The review costs $6,000 for up to 3,000 square feet (278.7 sq m) and then $0.50 for every additional square foot.

Why should a facility, whether existing or new, explore certification? Certification provides a seal of approval from an independent organization. In addition, certified building are more cost effective, are better for the environment, and last longer with fewer issues over the life of the building.

Community Support

If any public funds will be used, the planning process requires community involvement in order to generate community buy-in. Any effort to reach out to the public requires the facility planners to be honest. People should not be invited to meetings if they will not be allowed to provide meaningful input that will be used. If people attend the meetings and are ignored, the process will generate more negativity than would be the case if it had never been undertaken. Although the community meeting should be very formal, it must also be fun and engaging to help bring people to meetings in the future. Numerous community boards fail because the meetings are not productive, are boring, and are a waste of everyone's time. This process can also be enhanced if the board members are focused on the public good rather than individual agendas.

Often the most important part of gaining community support is convincing the public about the need for the facility. Through utilizing common sense and allies, facility planners can win some opponents over. Some opponents may need incentives, which can be identified through negotiations. Others will always be opponents. But planners should never burn bridges, even if there is posturing. People who are major opponents today may change their tune years down the road (e.g., when they have grandchildren who want to use the facility). Thus it is important to take care when dealing with opponents in the planning process.

Some opponents will use the strategy known as NIMBY ("not in my backyard"). According to this position, the facility is worthwhile and is needed, but it should be built someplace else. For example, citizens frequently are in favor of jails but do not want one built in their town. And although some die-hard sport fans would love to see a stadium within walking distance of their homes, other fans do not want the traffic and noise associated

TYPICAL PLANNING QUESTIONS FOR A NEW SPORT FACILITY

- Will the facility be an integral part of the organization?
- Does the facility take into account current and future needs?
- Is the facility planned for maximum usage?
- Is the facility centrally located, and are there existing transportation routes such as roads?
- Is adequate parking available?
- Are utilities available such as electricity, sewage, water, and gas?
- Will the facility comply with all local, state, and national standards?
- Has the soil been tested for any contamination?
- Has the title been searched to make sure there are no claims against the property such as liens?
- Will the facility be constructed with cost reduction, environmental concerns, and reduced maintenance costs as top priorities?
- Can the space be maximized—for example, can the rooftop be used for additional recreational activities?
- Has safety been highlighted throughout the planning process?
- Has system engineering been analyzed to reduce electrical and maintenance costs?
- Are locker rooms planned with sloped floors so water can drain effectively?
- Have surface choices been analyzed to lower maintenance costs and reduce the threat of dust, allergens, and other airborne material?
- Is the facility planned with adequate buffer room between activity areas?
- Will the ceiling height be sufficient to support all intended uses?

- Is the facility designed with enough usable storage areas?
- Will the facility meet all lighting, sound, and related usage standards?
- Will the facility utilize security systems such as closed-circuit television, card scanners, or special locks?
- Have broadcasting issues been taken into consideration if there may be broadcasts in the future?
- Are the needs of the media, such as a press box, being considered?
- Are scorekeeping and timekeeping needs being considered?
- Will the facility need specialized equipment such as backboard systems, floor plates, wall hangers, ceiling attachments, and other specialty items?
- Will specialized rooms be needed for such activities as ticket sales or laundry?
- Will personal transportation (vertical, horizontal) be installed?
- Will the facility accommodate the needs of the disabled, and how will it accomplish this goal?
- Will the facility utilize general or reserved admissions, and what type of seating options will be available?
- What risk management steps have been taken to avoid both minor and serious threats?
- How many bathrooms will be available, and will there be options for men, women, children, and families?
- Is there enough room for people to mingle?
- How many concession stands will be built, and where will they be positioned?

Based on *Details, details* 1985.

with having a stadium in their "backyards." At the extreme ends of the spectrum are supporters who want the facility no matter where it is built and their opposites, the BANANA ("build absolutely nothing anywhere near anything") opponents. These people oppose building a facility because of a reluctance to spend public funds, a dislike of sport, or countless other reasons. Regardless of the reason for support or opposition, a facility planner needs to understand and appreciate opponents and respect their right to disagree.

For example, a minor league baseball stadium was built in 1996 in New Britain, Connecticut, on land formerly used as high school baseball and softball fields. This caused some conflict with the high school, which eventually moved to another field at the park. Neighbors were supportive of some elements of the stadium but not other elements; this led to a lawsuit and city council hearings in 2002 after the team held fireworks shows after a number of Friday-night games. Some neighbors complained that the fireworks broke windows, disturbed their sleep, upset their pets, and even caused structural damage. The team countered that not a single neighbor complained or requested compensation for damaged property. The fireworks were not an issue in previous years because they occurred between 9:00 and 9:45 p.m. and lasted around 15 minutes. However, in 2002 a game was delayed due to a high school graduation ceremony next door and then ran 15 innings; therefore, the fireworks did not go off until around 11 p.m. and lasted 8 minutes. The late-night disturbance galvanized the residents. The city council adopted a 10:30 p.m. limit for fireworks and formed a committee made up of all involved parties, but the neighbors were not satisfied and sued to prevent the fireworks promotions, which sometimes involved a schedule of 15 fireworks shows a season. The suit filed in 2005 asked the court for an injunction limiting the number of fireworks shows and for monetary damages. The court issued an injunction, limited the team to only one fireworks show a month, and awarded the neighbors who sued $100 each. The neighbors won in court and were able to prevent the regular fireworks displays. Many of the neighbors regularly go to the games so some of the biggest detractors were also supporters of the team, but wanted their voices heard (Esposito v. New Britain Baseball Club, Inc., 2005).

It is also crucial for planners to be forthright from the very beginning. If those involved in the planning process believe that they have been heard and that their concerns have been addressed, they will be more likely to be supporters rather than detractors. Fairfield University in Connecticut was sued by four neighbors over playing fields equipped with lights. The neighbors claimed that the sound was too loud and that lights from the fields allowed them to read the newspaper in their houses at night without any of their own lights on (Tepfer, 1999). If these neighbors had been involved in the planning process and had been informed about the systems being installed and the times they would be used, the lawsuit could possibly have been averted. At the same time, though, it is important to note that even if everyone is involved in the planning process and every view has been raised, there will always be disgruntled people who will challenge the plans for a facility.

Some community facility planning boards travel to visit other facilities to compare and contrast various features. This is an active planning component that can generate enthusiasm among participants because they learn more about their purposes and the importance of their analysis in shaping the facility. However, voters and supporters may be resentful if too many trips are taken or if the trips are used as political payoff. Special care should be taken to choose committee members who will represent their constituents in an honest and forthright manner.

Planning Committee

It may seem relatively easy to create a committee to help plan for the future facility; the difficulty lies in determining who should be on the committee. The appointment process is often very political, and leaving out key constituents can lead to significant trouble for a planned facility. The process is designed to elicit critical assistance, not develop enemies. A typical committee to plan for a college recreation center might include the following representatives (Greusel, 1992):

- Administration (student life, development, finance, provost, student activities, public relations, and even the president)
- Athletic department (administration, coaches, trainers, student-athletes, alumni athletes)
- Faculty (faculty users, faculty senate, physical education faculty, staff members)
- Recreation staff (intramural staff, club sport staff, student participants)
- Students (traditional, dorm residents, commuters, evening, undergraduate, graduate, international, minority, and disabled students along with student government)

NAVIGATING COMMUNITY SUPPORT

Members of the public should always be involved in hearings that might affect them and others around a sport facility. At one high school in Connecticut the football field had no lights, so the school had to hold all games during daylight hours. To increase school spirit, the athletic department wanted to bring in portable lights and host several evening events. The athletic director sent a letter to all nearby residents explaining what the school was interested in doing and that they were submitting an application to the town's planning and zoning commission. The following is an excerpt from the letter encouraging neighbors to support the effort (Remigino-Knapp, 2008).

I am proposing a limited number of night games to be held at Hall Stadium this fall, each of which would require temporary additional outdoor lighting. On Friday, September 19, 2008, the Hall football team would play a game beginning at 7:00 p.m. and ending at approximately 9:30 p.m. On Saturday, September 20, we would play a double-header, with a girls' field hockey game from 5:00 p.m. to 6:00 p.m. followed by a girls' soccer game from 7:00 p.m. to 9:00 p.m. I would anticipate that approximately 400 to 500 fans would attend the football game and 250 to 300 fans would be at the field hockey and soccer games.

Based upon our experience with the night football game this past fall (at another high school in town), we would need to use 17 portable lights to illuminate the playing field and the surrounding area for each of the proposed evenings. The lights are powered by diesel fuel and have a maximum extension of 30 feet. The lights will be positioned on each sideline on the track surrounding the stadium field. A picture of the proposed lighting arrangement is attached to the letter.

Hall High School is hopeful that you will support this proposal for temporary lighting to be used at the Hall Stadium field on a limited basis this fall. Please note that these lights are not permanent, and the school administration has no plans to request permanent lights or to play night games on a more consistent basis. Our proposal is merely intended to provide each of our teams with a night game experience.

The language of this letter clearly shows that the school was trying to inform neighbors, prevent confusion or rumors, and focus on the key beneficiaries—the students. Student-athletes also went door to door with the letter so that potential detractors could see the faces of those who would benefit. This strategy worked, and the zoning commission allowed the lights to be used. The neighbors might not have been as supportive if the school wanted to install permanent lights. There already were tennis court lights on school property (right next to the football field)

that ran until 11:00 p.m., so additional lights could be a major concern for neighbors.

The student-athletes really enjoyed the experience even though the lights were used only a handful of times over a couple years. In 2013 school supporters made a push to install permanent lights at the high school field. Although some might have considered the initial effort for temporary lights to have been deceptive, the school had not had light for years and the growth of high school sports necessitated the addition of field lighting.

Detractors formed an organization called "Save Our Neighborhoods." They argued that the lights would increase noise from game announcers and crowds, that traffic would spill over onto adjacent streets, that there would be traffic pollution, that people attending the evening events would generate trash, that local property values would decline, and that security issues would increase. Although these are standard arguments often raised for any new project, no proof existed that these issues would actually materialize. Proponents argued that the lights would result in youths being together in a supervised, safe, and constructive environment, which could help keep them off the street and out of trouble. They also cited the potential for hosting tournaments and playoff games, which could generate additional local business revenue and increase ticket and concession sales. Proponents also proposed using environmentally friendly and efficient lighting with hoods to help light only the athletic field. The lights were expected to cost around $250,000; half of those funds would come from the state and the rest would come from fundraising efforts, so local tax dollars would not be used.

The zoning board approved the proposal to install the lights. About 10 evening events were held in the year after the lights were installed, and no significant effects on local traffic or housing values were reported.

The high school posted signs encouraging donations to help defray the cost of lights.

- Off-campus constituents (alumni, booster clubs, university foundation members, local government officials, neighbors, local nonprofit organizations, high schools, athletic organizations)

Part of establishing a planning committee is choosing one or more leaders to lead the meetings. Leaders must get everyone to cooperate and work toward the same goals. Part of this task requires the leader to focus the participants on ideas rather than personalities. Sometimes people have great ideas, but the ideas are not heard over personality clashes or turf and ego battles.

One of the leader's responsibilities is to foster compromise. Areas in which compromise can be successful include space, time, programs, and quality (Greusel, 1992). For example, marble may be the material of choice for part of a facility, but it is expensive. A compromise is to use a special finish that looks like marble but costs significantly less. Compromises take place throughout the planning process. However, it should be noted that those who can override the planning process also shepherd in numerous changes. Thus, the committee might decide on a particular material only to have the mayor override the decision. This happens commonly and can lead to exasperation of the board members.

Even with significant planning and compromise, there is no guarantee that elements from the planning process cannot go wrong. For example, the mayor of Bridgeport, Connecticut, was convicted of numerous racketeering and corruption charges, some of them stemming from deals regarding the design and construction of a baseball park and arena ("Ganim Goes to Trial," 2003). Even though the facilities are operating well and were running fine before the convictions, the convictions created a negative perception of the facility and of the integrity of the planning process.

These types of concerns should be examined throughout the planning process, as biased people can disrupt or destroy the project by trying to advance their own agendas or poor choices. Thus, leaders need to exercise strong managerial skills to prevent the committee from being hijacked. Direction can be provided by assigning subcommittees very specific tasks, called charges, such as researching sites. Having been organized and given its charge, the committee must critically analyze what type of facility is needed.

Needs Assessment

The planning process for a new facility always starts with a needs assessment made by the planning committee. The assessment might show that professional sports are a major benefit to the community and economy. This is especially true if a city is trying not to lose a professional sport franchise. The **needs assessment** can be based on internal demand as highlighted by future facility users or by industry-driven needs. Industry-driven needs can be based on various factors, from competing institutions to market forces.

The market-driven needs assessment can be based on industry data showing whether or not a current facility meets industry standards. A 1999 survey examined college fitness centers and determined the average types, size, and amenities. The survey results showed, for example, that the average college fitness center had increased 10% to 20% between 1994 and 1999. Furthermore, during the same period, the number of recreation directors reporting that they needed to share facilities with athletics or physical education decreased from 80% to 56%. This research showed that more collegiate fitness centers were being built across the United States and were often being dedicated exclusively to student fitness needs (Patton, 1999). Since that survey, college fitness facilities have grown in average cost from $14.2 million in 2004 to $19.4 million in 2009 (Bogar, 2008). It is not uncommon to see a new student recreation center being built on a large college campus for more than $50 million. These facilities have developed some new trends such as more space for small workout rooms, more rooftop usage, more environmentally friendly facilities, and a return to mixed-use facilities to prevent wasting floor space. This type of information can be critical in the needs assessment area if one of the primary concerns for a fitness facility is to help recruit more students. If prospective students are comparing various colleges, one of the considerations that may tip the scale is the availability of a recreation center. If a college wanted to stay competitive, it would need to build such a facility. One problem with this "me too" approach is that some older facilities might have climbing walls, whereas the recent trend has been away from climbing walls because the market demand for students using climbing walls has significantly decreased.

Demographics-based market-driven concerns can focus on age, nationality, religion, race, and gender. Some facilities have thrived by catering to specific clientele. Some churches are building health clubs for their current and future members as a way to distinguish themselves and recruit individuals looking for a more wholesome workout environment. Curves for women and other health clubs reach a particular market segment in need of such facilities.

Facility users' gender is an important consideration. If a college is 75% female, more equipment or program space should be set aside for women's activities versus male-oriented equipment or activities chosen strictly on the basis of their overall popularity. Table 4.1 lists preferred fitness equipment based on a gender survey. Such data are crucial for determining space needs and proposed activities for a given facility. On the basis of these data, and unless internal surveys suggest otherwise, a new fitness center that expects to serve equal numbers of men and women would probably emphasize treadmills and bikes to please the largest number of users. Knowing what the internal and external constituents want helps to identify the type of facility to be built. The latest trends also need to be examined. For example, kettlebell workouts and CrossFit classes are popping up in smaller facilities around the United States.

Types of Facilities

There are countless types of sport facilities, from empty fields to billion-dollar stadiums. Some sport facilities are easy to distinguish. Stadiums and arenas are obviously sport facilities if their primary tenants are professional teams. Other facilities, such as civic centers and multipurpose venues, are blended-use facilities in that they are used for sport but also for numerous other types of events. Another category includes facilities that are used primarily for other activities but also sometimes for sport. Recreation areas such as open fields or beaches may not traditionally be considered sport facilities but at various times serve as such. Knowledge of the broad array of facility types can help planners determine the best facility (or facilities) to serve the constituents.

Stadiums

Stadiums are large facilities that house certain field sports such as football, baseball, soccer, lacrosse, rugby, and track and field. Stadiums may seat fewer than 100 spectators or more than 100,000. Professional baseball stadiums often hold between 40,000 and 50,000 people; football stadiums often hold between 65,000 and 90,000. All stadiums need a relatively flat surface for play. Almost all fields are built with a crown to assist in water runoff. The crown, a raised section in the middle of the field that a person at ground level can see at the end of a gradual incline, helps reduce the accumulation of water on the field through the use of gravity. Sport stadiums also have additional commonalities such as spectator seating, locker rooms, parking lots, concession stands, press boxes, and television and audio

Table 4.1 Preferred Equipment by Gender

Choice	Men	Women
1st	Free weights	Treadmills
2nd	Bikes	Steppers
3rd	Treadmills	Elliptical trainers
4th	Steppers	Bikes

Note: Women are generally more inclined to try new fitness options such as yoga and Pilates. Women are also generally more flexible than men and are more interested in toning than in building muscle mass.

From Patton 1999.

STAKEHOLDER NEEDS AND COSTS

Two facilities on opposite sides of the Atlantic help highlight the differences between building types and the elements that various stakeholders might want in each facility. Every facility is different and will have different costs and construction elements that need to be clearly communicated to relevant stakeholders. When information is missing or not communicated, stakeholders have a harder time supporting a proposed facility.

Corby International Pool

Corby, East Midlands, England spent £18 million (approximately $30 million U.S., which calculates to £2,970 per square meter, or approximately US$1,545 per square foot) to build the Corby International Pool. The design of the facility incorporated a shell shape to reduce the visual impact on the surrounding ancient woodlands. The facility includes a number of fitness components and a 50-meter swimming pool. The pool was built with submersible booms and movable floors that allow the water depth to be adjusted for various uses, including junior international diving. The facility also has a 20-meter training pool and a leisure pool with a flume ride. The architects designed the facility with large areas of natural daylight, natural ventilation, and a system that uses reclaimed waste pool water to flush toilets (Sport England, 2010).

The building was made with the following elements:

- Frame: Steel frame with integrated glulam (laminated wood pieces that can be as strong as steel; sometimes called laminated stock) structure
- Cladding (exterior facade): Timber (wood) cladding and curtain walling (often made of aluminum and glass, but due to the light weight of wall it is not a load-bearing wall that can support the roof)
- Roofing: Standing seam roof constructed out of lightweight sheets of metal that feature an outer layer of the corrosion-resistant material zinc (considered one of the most durable roofs)
- Internal walls: Lightweight concrete blockwork and stud-based portioning in the dry areas
- Wall finishes: Painted plaster in dry areas and render (can include stucco, cement, and other finishes) in wet areas

- Swimming pool: Reinforced concrete tank with nitrogen monoxide. submersible booms and moving floors
- Lighting: The pool hall uses metal halide floodlights with a lux level of 500 (1 foot-candle = 10 lux, so this is equivalent to 50 foot-candles); the fitness suite uses metal pendant fitting with a lux level of 300; and the changing rooms, offices, and café use recessed fluorescent downlights and spotlights with a lux level ranging from 300 to 500.

TD Bank Sports Center at Quinnipiac University

The facility is comprised of twin arenas for hockey and basketball that share a common foyer and concession area. The 180,350-square-foot (16,755 sq m) Connecticut facility cost $52 million (approximately $288 per square foot) to build over 2 years and opened January 27, 2007. The hockey arena can seat 3,286 and the basketball arena can seat 3,570. The facility houses five concession stands and two merchandise shops. There are 10 locker rooms (four home locker rooms and six visitor locker rooms) and eight public restrooms (five for women and three for men). Each arena has one center-hung scoreboard and two auxiliary scoreboards. To increase viewing enjoyment, there are 299 lights in the hockey arena and 190 lights in the basketball arena.

The 240-acre (1 sq km) site was designed by Centerbrook Architects (Centerbrook, Connecticut) and built under the general contractor Dimeo Construction (Providence, Rhode Island). During construction, 62 subcontractors and 58 materials suppliers were used. An average of 83 people worked on the building every day, with a high of 173 workers on one day. The arena was built on a mountain, which needed to be leveled before construction could begin. More than 410,000 cubic yards (313,467.5 cu m) of rock and earth needed to be moved. To move this material the mountain needed to be partially demolished, which required around 300,000 pounds (136,078 kg) of explosives. According to environmental regulations, none of the rock and dirt could be removed from the site, so it all had to be redistributed across the site. Some other big numbers include the following (Quinnipiac University, n.d.):

- 12 miles (19.3 km) of piping under the ice hockey surface

- 16 miles (25.7 km) of plumbing and mechanical piping
- 166 miles (267.2 km) of electrical wiring (not including phone and data wiring)
- 602 tons of steel reinforced with concrete
- 1,875 fire protection sprinklers
- 2,470 tons of steel
- 2,510 gallons (9,501 L) of paint

- 9,774 cubic yards (7,472.8 cu m) of concrete
- 13,300 square feet (1,235.6 sq m) of glass
- 80,115 bricks
- 120,110 concrete blocks
- 130,300 square feet (12,105 sq m) of roof
- 346,680 labor hours
- 2,178,309 fasteners

sound rooms. These areas vary based on facility size. Thus, a small high school football stadium may have a stand on top of the press box for filming a game, whereas a college or professional stadium may have several rooms for the same purpose.

Structurally, stadiums are now built exclusively with steel and concrete. In the 1900s, the first stadiums were built with wood and often burned down. Chapter 1 includes discussion of the stone coliseums—they are still around today, although they may not be in the best shape. Today, stadiums are primarily built for safety and fan convenience.

Arenas

Arenas differ from stadiums in that they have the capacity to host more types of events and they are protected from the elements. Arenas are fixed-seating facilities that can hold from several hundred to more than 30,000 spectators. Professional sport arenas typically hold between 12,000 and 22,000 fans. Similar to stadiums, larger arenas typically have locker rooms, storage areas, press boxes, and concession stands. One of the key elements of an arena is an open floor plan for basketball or hockey. This means that various techniques need to be used in the design process to support the weight of a roof and possibly a scoreboard without any middle support columns.

An arena can host sport events, concerts, circuses, family shows, conventions, and a multitude of other events to increase profits. In fact, most economists argue that a single-use stadium such as a football-only stadium has very limited financial return. A lot of money can be made during the 10 to 15 event days at a stadium, but the low number of event days puts a limit on total profitability. In contrast, an arena may generate 200-plus event days a year, which provides opportunities to earn more total revenue per year than is the case for stadiums.

Arenas can be constructed with an ice surface for skating or hockey. These systems are very

Facilities Trivia

Some interesting tidbits about New York baseball stadiums include the following:

- The site of the old Shea Stadium was once a landfill. Similarly, Fenway Park was also built as part of a land deal to cover a swamp (called a "fen" in Irish, thus the name Fenway Park).
- Yankee Stadium was built on an old lumber yard purchased for $600,000 by Yankees owner William Waldorf Astor.
- Although Yankee Stadium was built on time in 11 months (185 working days), Shea stadium took 29 months to build. Because of the delays, the Mets had to play two seasons at The Polo Grounds.
- Shea Stadium cost between $25 and 28 million, whereas Yankee Stadium cost $2.5 million.
- Shea Stadium was originally designed to allow for an expansion up to 90,000 seats.
- Because New York officials choose the site for Shea Stadium in the winter, when flights into LaGuardia Airport take a different route, they never anticipated that so many planes would fly over spring and summer baseball games.
- In 1975, Shea Stadium became the busiest stadium of all time when the Yankees, Mets, Jets, and Giants all shared the stadium when Yankee Stadium and Giants Stadium were under construction.
- Yankee Stadium had the first warning track in baseball.

complex and beyond the scope of this text. Ice floors require miles of piping and wires to transfer brine or other solutions to the floor subsurface. Numerous layers of water are sprayed and frozen to build an appropriate surface. The efforts required to prepare an ice surface are detailed and complex. Significant planning is needed when designing such an arena. For example, most arenas require a large number of mounting plates in the floor to help hoist the tons of equipment needed for events. Circuses can use more than 100 tons of hanging equipment, and the mounting plates help lift all this weight and serve as tie-down spots. The plates need to be installed before installing an ice-making system since drilling any holes can rupture underlying pipes.

Gyms

Some gyms are health clubs that have floor space for aerobics. Other gyms are mini arenas with a complete basketball court and space for other indoor activities. Today, more than ever, gyms are sprouting up all over the country because of their adaptability. A gym can be used for basketball, volleyball, badminton, dancing, aerobics, floor exercises, indoor games, and other activities. Being multipurpose is the key to the modern gym. Through technical innovations, improvements in floor surfacing, and other modern amenities, gyms can now be quickly converted from basketball to volleyball and badminton and then to indoor soccer, lacrosse, or dance classes. Gyms are often equipped with multipurpose activity courts; there are currently several hundred such facilities in the United States at various levels (Popke, 2001). The multipurpose activity court surfaces often include hardwood, synthetic sheet goods, poured urethane, interlocking plastic tiles, and similar flooring elements that can be used for various sports. These types of courts have been installed in facilities measuring 65 by 165 feet (20 by 50 m) as well as in facilities as large as the 104-by 185-foot (32 by 56 m) facility at the University of California at Santa Barbara (Popke, 2001). Similar to gyms are small recreation centers that might focus on quick workouts, such as Curves, or on a specific sport, such as martial arts centers.

Community Sport Centers

Community sport facilities can be anything from a pool to a health club, a bowling alley, or an enclosed field. Public parks and schools are the most frequently built and managed community facilities. Other community facilities include YMCAs, community recreation centers, and sport facilities built by homeowner associations. Pools are often a major component in community-based sport facilities. As with ice skating and hockey surfaces, pools are highly complex and beyond the scope of this text. Pool construction itself may be simple, but the heating, pumping, and chemical filtration systems are not. Many people and companies are experts in these systems and are able to help develop and manage pools.

Sportsplexes

A **sportsplex** is a multisport facility that may include indoor or outdoor spaces or a combination of the two. Sportsplexes can be owned by a public entity or a private entity, partnership, or corporation. Typically, sportsplexes have softball fields, soccer fields (both indoor and outdoor), roller-hockey rinks, basketball courts, volleyball courts, and various other recreation facilities or a combination of these.

According to the Sportsplex Operators and Developers Association (SODA) site newsletter, the average sportsplex lies on 47.9 acres (0.2 sq km) of land (SODA, 1993). About 43% of these facilities have 25 to 35 acres (0.10-0.14 sq km), the most popular size range. The average sportsplex has 6.5 softball fields, and the majority of the fields have lights. The average facility is in operation 9 months of the year and has been in existence for 8 years. Volleyball is the second most popular sport played at SODA facilities, and soccer is gaining in popularity at these facilities (SODA, 1993).

Domes

Domed stadiums have had a major effect on sport facility development since the 1960s. The Astrodome, which was built in 1964, was the first domed stadium. The Astrodome ushered in the building of other domed facilities in cities such as New Orleans, Seattle, Minneapolis, Indianapolis, Atlanta, and Detroit.

One of the major reasons for creating domed stadiums was to ensure that games would take place. Cities with unfavorable climates could remove the weather factor by playing indoors.

NEW HAVEN CITY-WIDE FIELD HOUSE

The New Haven City-Wide Field House is a large gym with an indoor track, a weight room, space for a portable full-size basketball court, concession areas, locker rooms, and other amenities to serve several public high schools in New Haven, Connecticut. Some interesting facts about this facility include the following:

■ The 219-yard (200 m) indoor track is housed in a 360- by 160-foot (110 by 50 m) building frame.

■ The precast wall systems were built in Quebec, Canada, and trucked to New Haven.

■ There are 58,900 square feet (5,472 sq m) of sport surfaces.

■ The entire facility is 102,000 square feet (9,476 sq m).

■ The school district considered a Mondo system (rolls of synthetic surfacing) but utilized a liquid applied surface costing $350,000 that has no seams but is harder to clean.

■ Approximately $4.5 million was spent on steel, with 160-foot-long (50 m) trusses, weighing 45 tons, having to be cut in half to be transported and then welded back together in New Haven.

■ The total construction costs were estimated at between $250 and $260 per square foot.

■ The heating, ventilation, and air conditioning system utilizes two air-handling systems the size of trucks that are mounted on the roof. When the heat index reaches 100 (39 C) and the air cannot be cooled, participants need to be sent home; the participants are also sent home if the outside temperature is at 0 °F (–18 °C) and no heat is available.

■ The seating capacity is 2,500 and includes both fixed and portable seating. The portable seating is rolled out with hydraulic lifts that are transported on movable surfaces so the weight of the lift and seats does not harm the floor.

The field house was initially managed by an external management company, using unionized custodial staff under a collective bargaining agreement with the New Haven public schools. After several years the public schools brought the management in-house to maximize their potential revenue and more effectively control scheduling and maintenance. Scheduling is more complicated for the facility compared with many other facilities. Although the field house is attached to Hillhouse High School, the facility is designed to be used by all 12 public high schools in the city.

The planning process was complicated by the political battles associated with a citywide field being attached to one of the key athletic-oriented high schools in the region. Many believed that Hillhouse High School would have an unfair advantage because the school would be able to use the facility during class time (which they do) and would have preference when scheduling events. When developing a rotation schedule, management had to carefully decide when each high school would use the facility. Management has had to deal with a variety of political battles when making these hard choices, but such battles were not unexpected when the facility was being planned. Thus, the same political battles that raged before the facility was built are still being fought to this day.

Ticket holders would not need to worry about whether the game would go on. Also, bad weather could deter fans from attending games, hurting ticket sales. Another important reason for building a dome was the ability to hold a variety of events year-round. Domes can host numerous events—the Superdome in Louisiana, for example, hosts New Orleans Saints football games, Tulane University football games, the Nokia Sugar Bowl, and the Bayou Classic and has been the scene of five Super Bowls and three National Collegiate Athletic Association Final Fours. However, with the development of retractable-roof stadiums, the fixed-domed stadium has decreased in popularity.

One of the major disadvantages of domed stadiums is that they do not work perfectly for every event. The Seattle Kingdome had a configuration that was not optimal for either football or baseball. For baseball, 50% of the seats were in the outfield. Also, when the weather was nice, fans were not able to enjoy the game with Mother Nature. This concern helped foster retractable-roof stadiums in the 1990s. The Toronto SkyDome, which opened in 1989, was the first stadium capable of opening and closing its roof. Since then, retractable-roof stadiums have been built in cities such as

Houston, Seattle, and Milwaukee. Their popularity has increased because many teams no longer wish to share facilities and want a stadium built for their specific sport. The Astrodome, which now has no professional sport team tenant, can still hold events and create revenue in other areas. Across the street from the Astrodome is NRG Stadium, home of the Houston Texans, which has a retractable-roof system. The Arizona Cardinals' stadium (University of Phoenix Stadium) opened in 2006 with a rolling field that can be positioned outside the facility to optimize sun and water absorption and then brought into the domed stadium so fans can enjoy games indoors on the best possible grass surface.

Domes are being built more frequently for facilities other than stadiums, such as pools, tennis courts, and synthetic fields. More facilities are utilizing fabric domes to increase their revenues and operating seasons. Domes fall into four categories:

- Solid construction involving glass, metal, or wood and sometimes built on movable tracks

- Air-supported structures in which fabric is kept in place by air blowers and possibly cables

- Frame-supported structures in which fabric is stretched over an aluminum or steel frame (the frame can be either permanent or removable)

- Construction involving tensile membrane fabric stretched over masts, similar to the construction of circus tents (Cohen, 2001)

Fabric structures are inexpensive compared with solid structures. A typical frame-supported structure can cost about 30% to 50% less than a conventional solid structure; an air-supported structure can be built for as little as 10% of the cost for a solid structure (Cohen, 2001). Thus, with about a $1 million investment, a dome can be raised where a conventional building would have cost $10 million. However, although the construction costs are lower, the operating costs (e.g., air conditioning and heating) are significantly greater. Extra expense is also required to remove snow, prevent deflations during storms, and provide adequate lighting. Thus, fabric-based domes are not necessarily the right solution if the facility is meant to last 20 to 30 years. However,

if the facility is designed to provide a large field without any support beams, an air-supported structure may be the best solution.

The various designs discussed here need to be considered in the planning process to help determine appropriate design issues. Although geographic issues with proposed sites will affect a facility's design, a rough design needs to be considered based on similar projects. An experienced architect can help design a practical and economical building. However, care should clearly be taken to make sure the designer has developed similar facilities in the past.

Movable Facilities

The world of sport facilities is constantly changing. The Floating Pool Lady—a decommissioned cargo barge with a 4-foot-deep (1.2 m), 25-meter pool that can hold 175 swimmers—docked outside several industrial piers in New York Harbor. This floating pool, launched in 2007, represents an evolution in ideas and managerial needs. To solve the issues associated with the ever-evolving needs of facilities and management, in 2012 *Popular Science* published an article on how facilities can revolutionize sport. The article examined the possibility of floating venues that could be brought into a major port. Using modular seating sections, the venue could be transformed to meet various configuration needs. The barge-based facility could use plastics such as ethylene tetrafluoroethylene to create a translucent, lightweight roof; utilize elevated stands to improve sight lines when needed; and have a self-contained barge attached for bathroom facilities (Carey, 2012). The article examined the creativity that managers in the future will use to think way outside the box and solve facility-related concerns.

Another example of a moveable facility comes from the 2008 Olympic swimming trials, held in Omaha, Nebraska. After the trials the pool was moved to a 54,000-square-foot (5,017 sq m) indoor aquatic facility in Richmond, Virginia. The movable pool was purchased after the trials for $1 million, which is about one-half the cost of a new pool. Such savings also helped sell the two pools used for the 2012 Olympic Trials before the event was even held. Seven of the nine pools used in the 2012 Olympic Games were movable pools, and all seven were sold to municipalities in the United Kingdom to serve communities after the games ended (Popke, 2012b). The fact that pools no longer need to be in the ground shows that any facility can undergo a major transformation.

Other Facilities

There are countless types of facilities that can be used for recreational purposes. Often facilities were not intended for sport-related purposes but have evolved into such facilities. For example, wilderness areas can be used for fishing, hunting, backpacking, camping, and other recreational purposes. The front facade of a courthouse can become the best local skateboarding hangout. Other facilities are specifically designed for sport-related activities. These facilities can range from golf courses to water parks.

Some communities prefer to package recreation and sport needs in one location. A community sport complex can be very large and can include an anchor facility (arena or stadium) as well as ancillary facilities such as golf courses, playing fields, pools, playgrounds, and other sport and recreation amenities. Such facilities can often take advantage of a common parking area or common concession stands. Sport complexes are gaining popularity as a means to leverage a location, parking, or other amenities while offering the greatest variety of sport facilities. Numerous youth sport complexes exist that may have several baseball fields, soccer fields, or a combination of various sport fields. These facilities are often similar to sportsplexes but may be connected with schools or park and recreation facilities.

Urban sport environments present unique challenges since it is harder in cities to find usable space. This has helped spawn unique facility types such as rooftop facilities. Several universities have built tennis courts and fields on top of parking decks and other structures to reduce the need for additional space. Green roofing refers to planting grass, shrubs, and trees on rooftops to help absorb heat and water while producing attractive areas for birds and for humans to relax. Another benefit of green roofs is the opportunity to play golf. Some green roofs on company buildings include putting greens for use by employees at lunchtime. This setup is similar to that of facilities such as Chelsea

Piers in New York, a 30-acre (0.12 sq km) sport village, which is an entire recreation center built on top of a water treatment plant. A roof-based system consists of a waterproof membrane, vapor barriers, thermal insulation, flashings, and a system to both retain and drain water ("Miniature Golf," 2002).

No matter what type of facility is being considered, it is essential to develop a facility plan and determine its viability through a feasibility study.

Feasibility Studies

No matter which facility is considered, when the needs assessment has been completed, the next step in the process is typically a **feasibility study** to see if the needs can be met and at what cost. The feasibility study is not developed simply to raise funds but rather to identify strengths and weaknesses in the planning process. Questions typically asked are what legal challenges exist, whether the right administrative team is in place, what the facility will be used for during dead time periods, how future expenses will be covered after the facility is completed, and what site options are the best.

The purpose of the feasibility study is to answer the following questions and provide research information about the project to help make a financial decision:

- Can the project be accomplished?
- Will the project be suitable and successful?
- Is the project logical? (Farmer, Mulrooney, and Ammon, 1996)

The feasibility study focuses on various concerns, from demographic makeup to competitors in the marketplace. A traditional strengths, weaknesses, opportunities, and threats (SWOT) analysis is often a cornerstone of a feasibility study. A **SWOT analysis** attempts to weigh the various positive and negative factors that can affect the proposed plan. Strengths can include inexpensive land, favorable borrowing terms, and strong community support. Weaknesses could include contaminated land, high property taxes, and poor managerial foresight. Opportunities could include new leagues, a young and active population, and new technologies or fads. Threats

INPUT REQUIRED FOR A FEASIBILITY STUDY

1. Prospective owner's financial data
   - Balance sheet or statement of net worth
   - Business experience
   - Present cash position
   - Any sport-related experience (e.g., have any managers previously owned a club or managed a team)
2. Prospective site locations
   - Type of ownership to be obtained and present status of selected site
   - General topography of selected site
   - Present improvements, including utilities
   - Current zoning of site
   - Population within 20-minute drive of site
   - Proximity to other sport facilities
   - Neighboring businesses or residences
   - Metropolitan map and demographics
3. Present local competition
   - Present number of facilities and teams, by sport, in the largest adjacent sport programs
   - Cost breakdown of all neighboring programs
   - Number of competitors that have opened or closed in the past couple of years and the reasons why
   - Name, address, and phone numbers of directors of all sport-related teams, facilities, leagues, and organizations
   - Number and description of all similar facilities within a 20-minute drive
   - Listing of typical services and amenities offered by sport facilities in the general area of the proposed site, including officials, awards programs, team incentives, and the like
   - Breakdown of percentage of youth versus adult programs by sport currently in area and any other relevant demographic breakdowns that can highlight market potential

could include significant competition, a lack of trained leaders, and economic downturns. If there are major threats such as a competitor opening a facility at the same time, such information needs to be analyzed or else the facility may be doomed because of poor research and planning.

A key component of any feasibility study is the financing section. Voters, constituents, proponents, and opponents want to know how much public money will be spent on a project and where those funds will come from. It may be that a public recreation area is built by the citizenry, a major donor has given the land, and a foundation has paid for the renovations and construction. However, the public coffers may be tapped for the operational and maintenance costs. In contrast, a private fitness center needs to specify all the anticipated revenue sources and expenses in the business plan and pro forma statements.

Table 4.2 indicates where potential financing sources can be found to finance a stadium or arena. It is important to separate preopen-ing expenses and postoccupancy revenue and expenses since some revenues and expenses are a one-time occurrence while other expenses reoccur annually. Also, some facilities sell their contractually obligated revenue, such as naming rights contracts and luxury suite leases, to generate immediate funds to help build a facility. The problem with such an approach is that it can deplete the facility of future operating revenue that will be needed to pay for operating expenses such as maintenance.

Throughout the planning process, data are gathered on the feasibility of a given plan, site, or facility. The data must be unbiased and must address legitimate issues. Simply having numbers will not seal a deal. On the other hand, having appropriate numbers that answer critical questions can help diffuse numerous attacks. Thus, data need to be reliable. Although some feasibility studies make wild assumptions not backed by hard facts, effective planning requires the use of accurate data.

OUTPUT OBTAINED FROM A FEASIBILITY STUDY

1. General industry conditions that are favorable and unfavorable for the proposed facility
2. Statistical and systemic experience of three to five other similar facilities, including critical analysis of the strengths and weaknesses of these facilities as compared with the proposed facility
3. The recommended facility size and scope
4. How many employees will be needed to operate the facility
5. The development costs
6. The operating costs for the first 5 years
7. The projected revenues for the first 5 years
8. How the facility will affect the local community
9. Components of the local community that will positively and negatively affect the facility
10. The main facility users and what additional users the facility could attract
11. Data that can help the facility obtain necessary financing
12. Specific indications of what data were not obtained and why they were not obtained so the study can be qualified (Day, 1992)

Preliminary Phase

Determining the feasibility of a major project is normally a two-phase process comprising a preliminary phase and an expanded phase. The purpose of the preliminary feasibility study is to summarize the initial findings. Frequently the study is based on one visit to the proposed site, a cursory review of background materials, and preliminary financial and building program examples provided by the owners.

Additional information may become necessary depending on the scope of the study. For example, in the case of a new arena, the first phase of the study may include previously discussed elements as well as a preliminary market demand analysis for potential events, preliminary testing of potential demand for premium seating (private suites and club seating) and sponsorships, and a rough estimate of operating expenses to determine if there is sufficient economic merit to pursue the project.

As with any major building project, the size and comprehensiveness of the feasibility study

Table 4.2 Preconstruction and Ongoing Operating Revenue

Revenue source	Preconstruction revenue	Ongoing operating revenue
Owner	Direct contribution	Direct contribution
Users	Personal seat licenses Ticket deposits Club and suite leases Parking outsourcing contracts Concession outsourcing contracts Naming rights details Taxes (e.g., sales, ticket surcharge)	Personal seat licenses Ticket deposits Club and suite leases Parking revenue Concession revenue Naming rights revenue Ongoing taxes (e.g., sales, ticket surcharge)
Targeted public	Targeted sales taxes Car rental taxes Hotel taxes Sin taxes (liquor and cigarettes)	Sales taxes Car rental taxes Hotel taxes Sin taxes (liquor and cigarettes)
General public	General sales taxes Property taxes Utility taxes General public obligations	General taxes for road and other improvements

From Harris County Sports Facility Public Advisory Committee 1996.

depend on the size and scope of the project. There are no set requirements for the size or depth of the analysis. Studies may range from a few pages to several hundred pages.

Regardless of the proposed sport facility's size, essentials of a preliminary feasibility study are as follows:

- Site feasibility (based on a preliminary visit)
- User-usage feasibility (based on brief background provided by owners)
- Design feasibility (based on conceptual design and plans)
- Financial feasibility (based on preliminary financial information provided by owners)

Much like the size and depth of the study, the cost and time requirements vary. The cost of a preliminary study can range from several thousand to more than a million dollars. A full feasibility study could costs millions, especially if a high-powered national accounting firm undertakes the study.

Expanded Phase

After the feasibility study comes the all-important (and often all political) economic impact analysis. The political reality of both feasibility and economic impact analyses is that they are usually undertaken to justify a position that either a sport organization or elected officials have adopted or are proposing (Howard and Crompton, 1995). Frequently the goal of independent studies is not to find the truth but rather to legitimize the project that the sponsoring group wants to develop; these studies can seldom be more than position papers for proponents or opponents of a particular project.

Economic impact is defined as the net economic change in a host community that results from spending attributed to a sport event or facility (Howard and Crompton, 1995). Economic impact studies typically examine direct impact (the effect of the first round of spending), indirect impact (the ripple effect of additional rounds of spending), and induced impact (further ripple effect resulting from spending by employees of affected businesses).

What is the economic impact of a sport facility? For a large stadium or arena with a professional sport team, the impact is felt through direct spending, indirect beneficiaries, and increased salaries for those only tangentially related to the facility. Thus, every event and facility generates some impact, ranging from customers' spending on tickets to the facility's buying hot dogs from a local distributor.

The following is a sample of results from an economic impact report for an event at a motor speedway. The economic impact was based on several assumptions, including the following:

- Projected attendance was 130,000 fans.
- Approximately 45% of the fans were to travel from more than 150 miles (240 km) away and stay overnight, while the remaining 55% were local or regional fans.
- Approximately 80% of the overnight stays were to be double occupancy.
- The estimated travel expenditures were based on a U.S. travel data study.

Based on these assumptions the projected economic impact was $8,881,700 and was calculated as follows:

- Local fans: 36,000 spending $22 each = $792,000
- Regional fans: 40,000 spending $44 each = $1,760,000
- Double-occupancy main guests: 23,400 × $151 each = $3,533,400
- Secondary guests: 23,400 × $44 each = $1,029,600
- Single-occupancy guests: 11,700 × $151 each = $1,766,700
- **Total $8,881,700**

From Charlotte Motor Speedway 1994.

All economic impact studies include a **ripple effect**. The ripple effect represents the spread of money through the economy. Assume a pebble is dropped in the water. The pebble will create a ripple of expanding waves in the water. Similarly, one dollar spent at a sport facility will create a ripple effect throughout the community as parts of that dollar pay wages, buy products, cover expenses, and so on, which helps redistribute the money throughout the community. This concept of a ripple effect in an economy is termed a multiplier by economists (Andelman, 1992). Commonly used multipliers are sales, income, and employment. The multipliers are derived from input–output tables that disaggregate an economy into industries and examine the flow of goods and services among the affected industries.

These data need to be carefully scrutinized for accuracy. Sometimes additional expenditures are left out of the equation, such as media expenditures when a large number of press members are attending an event. On the other hand, economic impact studies often overstate simple issues such as how many people who may be staying overnight are in fact sharing a room. For some events, it is not uncommon for four or more people to occupy a room designed for two. If this fact is not considered in the initial estimate, the estimate will be overinflated. This is one reason a number of studies have concluded that large sport facilities do not produce the economic benefits projected in the economic impact studies (Johnson and Sack, 1996).

Other concerns regarding economic impact studies include **redirected spending**, which refers to money that would have been spent on other entertainment in the same area, such as spending at a local movie theater rather than at the ballpark; **displacement**, which refers to a portion of hotel rooms that would have been full regardless of whether the event took place (e.g., conference in town); and **induced effects**, which refer to the multiplier effect and visitor spending being recirculated in the community (Schumacher, 2001). These concerns are not necessarily bad, but they need to be analyzed in the feasibility study in order for the study to be taken seriously. It should also be noted that in some cases the data are not as important as in others. For example, even if the economic impact section of the feasibility study shows very little prospect for return, a city may still pursue building a large stadium or arena to achieve "major league" status, revitalize a city, develop a positive image, or serve political agendas (or achieve a combination of these) (Schumacher, 2001). Thus, ego and civic pride rather than significant economic impact often are the driving forces behind building a new facility (Day, 1992).

Other areas examined in the expanded feasibility study include, but are not limited to, the following:

- Private financing (equity, corporate bonds, letters of credit, limited partnerships, public offerings, leasing versus purchasing)
- Government financing (government obligation bonds, revenue bonds, special districts, certificates of participation, grants, redevelopment districts)
- Hybrid financing (private equity/government bonds, public land/private improvements)
- Operating assumptions (income, expense, payroll, general and administrative, per cap estimates, usage estimates, break-even analysis, stabilized levels, normal capacity)
- Business plan (preopening, opening, and executive summary)

Site Planning

Site selection and design are covered in detail in chapter 5. However, site selection needs to be critically addressed in the planning process because of the impact that a site may have on the success of a project. Most feasibility studies examine at least one site for a proposed facility. It is important to examine site issues at this point in the process because a plan will be worthless if the land is too expensive, for example, and if the economic assumptions will not work.

A site also needs to be analyzed for legal and governmental concerns. For example, if a stadium is planned for a parcel near an airport, federal officials may need to be contacted to make sure the facility will not interfere with the line or height of flight to and from the airport. Environmental issues are another concern.

Some states have specific guidelines for sport facilities that can affect the sites to be potentially presented to the public. Massachusetts has specific school standards requiring that a school with more than 12 classrooms have a separate gymnasium with at least two teaching stations, each measuring a minimum of 3,000 square feet (280 sq m). Gymnasiums at the secondary level require two stations, and each station must be 6,200 to 7,500 square feet (576-700 sq m) ("Education Laws," 2002).

Besides local and governmental concerns, a potential site can involve significant community concerns. The NIMBY argument can doom a

BEHIND THE SCENES

ECONOMIC IMPACT ANALYSIS

The following represents the type of comprehensive economic analysis that is undertaken for an event that will attract a large number of out-of-state spectators. The example assumes the event will attract 10,000 spectators from another state and totals the direct expenditures attributed to these fans. It should be noted that the per person per day expenditure is derived through interviewing a representative sampling of event attendees and extrapolating from those results what a typical out-of-state fan would spend.

This chart highlights that the average out-of-state fan will spend $54.50 a day at the event, which generates a total direct infusion into the community of $545,000.

Category	Per person per day expenditure	Total direct expenditure
Food and beverages	$15.00	$150,000
Night clubs and bars	$2.00	$20,000
Retail shopping	$15.00	$150,000
Lodging	$20.00	$200,000
Miscellaneous expenses	$2.50	$25,000
Total	**$54.50**	**$545,000**

project even if the project satisfies all the feasibility concerns and promises to be very successful. If the facility is to replace an existing facility loved by the local population, the plan may be sunk if the citizens go to the federal government and obtain historical designation, which would prevent tearing down the old facility. This is only one option. The citizens can also petition for reconsideration, start a letter-writing campaign, hold fund-raisers to buy the property and preserve it, or use a host of other strategies. That is why it is critical to develop a selling plan to generate support and hopefully avoid detractors. It is impossible to get rid of all detractors; they will be present in every project. However, it is possible to dampen their influence or even win over a large percentage to support the facility.

When examining potential sites, numerous sources of information can be useful. Data can come from the following sources:

- Federal and state agencies such as the U.S. Geological Survey, Army Corps of Engineers, and regional land-planning studies
- Information from city and county authorities, such as zoning maps, property tax records, and planning abstracts
- Public records such as mortgage histories, liens, leases, and easements

- Site-specific issues such as blueprints or building permits
- Interviews with current or former owners, real estate appraisers, and planning consultants (Cotts and Lee, 1992)

Developing and Selling the Future Plan

All the data obtained through numerous studies will not necessarily influence the right people. Those who are in support of the proposed facility will not necessarily require convincing. However, additional data can reinforce their decision and provide them with information to buttress their positions. Those opposed to the facility may be willing to change their minds if the right data are presented to address their needs or concerns. The information is most important for those who are sitting on the fence and can be convinced that the project is in fact worthwhile. Those who need convincing can range from voters and politicians to people who will be asked to underwrite the bonds used to finance the stadium or arena. Smaller facilities can also utilize the data to support or reject initial notions about the success of a given facility.

Selling the plan for a proposed facility can take many forms. Conventional campaigns such as advertising on billboards and in the newspapers are traditionally undertaken. However, support can also be generated through word of mouth, letter-writing campaigns, social media campaigns, asking individuals to serve on committees or assume honorary posts, holding public meetings, and bringing athletes to community events to generate support. Gathering support is a very sensitive process. Some people may be willing to vocally support a new facility, but normally the opponents are much louder than the proponents. It is critical to examine means to interest people in the project without alienating opponents. Chapter 5 discusses this fine line in greater detail.

Attempts to approve new stadium deals often come under attack. For example, supporters of a referendum in Wilmington, North Carolina, raised an estimated $112,000 to help promote the vote for a proposed $37 million minor league baseball stadium. Approximately 78% of the $112,000 was raised by five individuals and entities who stood to directly benefit from the property tax increase and sale of land for the stadium. In contrast, Americans for Prosperity, which advocates for limited government, raised 85% of the funds to oppose the referendum. Even though the "vote yes" campaign spent three times more than the "vote no" campaign, less than 30% of voters supported the referendum ("The Score," 2012).

Business Plan for a Facility

If economic impact numbers are simply plugged into a press release, most readers do not know how to interpret them. If the data are properly presented through the business plan for a facility or through a similar document, the planning process is often more successful than when the feasibility report is utilized by itself. Similarly, if no feasibility study is used, the business plan may be the only comprehensive planning tool that a prospective facility manager undertakes.

Once the basic background information is gathered, an initial business plan for a facility needs to be developed. This process is designed to solidify the entire facility planning process from theoretical, practical, financial, and managerial perspectives. By acquiring additional information on the site and on construction and operations costs, management can develop a more detailed business plan that will be required by anyone considering funding the facility. Thus, even though elements not yet discussed in this book are required for a business plan, it is important to consider business plans as part of the planning process. The business plan is the roadmap that incorporates ideas for the facility into a formal document for others to examine.

The business plan serves multiple purposes such as helping allocate resources and setting realistic goals and objectives. It also establishes standards for measuring feasibility and operates as a benchmark for future activity. Whenever a facility veers from its course, the plan can help the manager make decisions to get the facility back on the right track. Of course, no matter how well the business plan is prepared, it cannot guarantee reaching the destination safely (see "Major Construction Project Pitfalls").

Starting a facility without a well-thought-out business plan is like traveling into unknown territory without a map. If prepared with care, the business plan or roadmap will not only indicate the route to follow to reach goals but will also highlight hurdles that may be encountered along the way. Creating an effective business plan involves seven steps:

1. Determine and define the business opportunity. A facility is a living entity that will grow and change. Therefore, people starting a sport facility need to take the time to determine exactly what type of facility they want and what they want the facility to become as an extension of themselves.

2. Make an operational plan. This covers geographic location, facilities and their improvement, production, layout, and key strategies and planning plus certain areas of administration, depending on the facility. The operational plan highlights how the facility will be managed. It specifies, for example, when grass will be planted, what type of grass it will be, how it will be watered, how the soil will be compacted, what type of crowning will be used, what aeration technique will be used, and what fertilizer will be used.

3. Create a marketing plan. For good reason, market analysis is often considered the most important activity an entrepreneur can engage in before a business start-up. This analysis teaches the person not only a great deal about the marketplace and prospective competitors but also much about the prospects for success. The marketing plan specifies how the facility will be marketed toward teams, events, tournaments, and other revenue-producing activities, from arcade games to concession items. It is as critical to properly budget for the marketing of a facility as it is to budget for building the facility. Failing to develop a sufficient budget and marketing plan will doom even the best-designed building. The days of "If you build it, they will come" are long gone given the multitude of events and other activities competing for our time and resources.

4. Develop a business structure. Will the business operate as a sole proprietorship, with a partner or partners, or under the corporate/LLC (limited liability corporation) form? Each of these forms has certain advantages and disadvantages. This part of the business plan specifies who is involved in the planning process or if a management team is being formed that will help launch the facility and then remain in place. Frequently people reach this step and only then receive

legal advice that the project cannot be completed because of zoning or other legal restrictions. That is why it is advisable to have an attorney and an accountant on the management team during the organizational planning step. A developer needs to obtain input from others before progressing and must heed their advice.

5. Define your resources. This part of the plan focuses on resources that will be used, ranging from political ties to financial resources. The impact of any recent legislation affecting the facility needs to be noted.

6. Work up a financial plan. The financial plan will also serve as an operating plan for the financial management of the facility. This will be the final test of the viability of the overall business plan. Whereas the budget helps track the future direction of the facility, the financial plan dictates whether the budget is realistic, what steps will be needed to obtain funding, and exactly how much money will be needed.

7. Complete the business plan. After all the preceding elements have been completed and if

MAJOR CONSTRUCTION PROJECT MISTAKES

- Failing to involve all the stakeholders in developing the facility's mission and both long-term and short-term goals
- Failing to develop and then follow a well-defined process, such as how long the development process will take
- Not giving enough time to develop and complete the project; most projects take about 3 years to complete (2-3 months to assemble the project team; 3-4 months for the feasibility study; 2-3 months to bring a public project to a vote; 6-8 months to design; 12-18 months to construct; and 12-18 months to prepare for a facility's opening) (Ballard and King, 2002)
- Failing to find and acquire all the necessary support—both political and financial—for a project
- Both not listening to all the stakeholders and spending too much time trying to please each and every potential constituent

- Not building at the right location and not having enough land for future expansion needs
- Focusing on building a perfect facility rather than trying to make the best possible facility while considering its various constraints
- Failing to set aside enough money for emergencies and for an operating fund to run the building once it is opened
- Failing to critically review the qualifications and track record of the architect and builders (this includes failing to monitor their work)
- Trying to do some things cheaply, such as spending less on certain critical items for the facility (e.g., a roof) and spending more on items that are not as critical

the decision is to go forward with the facility, then all the plans need to be coordinated and reviewed for fine-tuning purposes. Nevertheless, simply completing the business plan does not finish the job because the business plan is worthless unless it is acted on.

Financing the Facility

Chapter 12 discusses financing in greater detail. Still, it is imperative that the planning process include analysis and confirmation of the financial viability of a proposed facility. The facility planner needs to determine whether to purchase, build, or lease. This analysis examines the cost of capital, lease terms, purchase price, the cost and political ramifications associated with borrowing money, and any political ramifications associated with owning versus leasing. Although a project may not make sound economic sense, some facilities are built to accomplish political goals. If a busi-

ness or municipality builds a facility to appear progressive, obtain a competitive advantage, or meet some other ulterior objective, the fact that the facility is a loss leader may not be as big a concern for the politicians. If a facility has been built for purely political motives, the planning process most likely failed to critically examine costs and expenses. If the facility has not been properly planned, political opponents can attack the financing scheme or revenue sources. Thus, financial planning is critical even in politically motivated projects.

The financial ramifications also affect final selection of the site and the design. Chapter 5 addresses various site-related issues, from political ramifications to hostile neighbors. It is imperative to base any decision about a facility being built on a combination of variables, and among these the financial concerns should be the most carefully analyzed.

Summary

Planning for a new facility is the process of examining what type of facility will meet a given need or objective and working out the justification for building or leasing the facility. The types of facilities that can be built are limited by people's imaginations, the laws of physics (e.g., whether or not a design can hold the weight of the roof), political constraints, laws and regulations, and the amount of money available.

Besides determining what facility to build or lease, a facility planner needs to justify the need for the facility. Not many buildings are built in the absence of some need. The planning process for a specific facility should examine the rationale for building the facility based on solid empirical numbers rather than hunches. If the financial numbers from a feasibility study indicate that a project is not viable, then the project should not be undertaken. However, if the planning process indicates success, then the next step is to finalize the site selection and facility design.

Discussion Questions and Activities

1. Why is planning important for an existing facility?

2. Why is planning essential for a future facility?

3. What can go wrong if you do not plan well?

4. Who should be involved in the planning process for building a major college stadium?

5. Who should be involved in the planning process for building a YMCA?

6. Research a recently built stadium or arena. What planning was undertaken and how long did the planning process take?

7. Design a business plan for a martial arts studio to be built or leased in your town.

8. Develop a strategic plan for facilities on your campus to help them grow over the next 2 years and then over the next 5 years.

9. Create a checklist of the steps one needs to take (who needs to be informed, what needs to be done for financing, what planning needs to be done, and so on) before building a facility near your campus.

5

Facility Site and Design

Chapter Objectives

- Understand the importance of location in choosing the proper site.
- Analyze the various components that need to be considered when choosing a sport facility site.
- Analyze the various external issues affecting a proposed facility site.
- Understand specific components in a facility such as locker rooms and concession areas.
- Appreciate the layout needed for an effective floor plan.

Sport facilities are traditionally designed to last 50 years. The design process takes into consideration elements such as regional temperature, average snowfall totals, water concerns (humidity, sea salt, mist), seismic movement, wind-related concerns, and other environmental issues. The process also considers human issues (e.g., fan movement, fan experiences, and parking lot movement) as well as the aesthetics and artistry of the building, which is an expression of the owner, team, city, and architect. The planning process requires a critical analysis of all these elements to help determine the most appropriate type of facility to build.

Although a number of technical characteristics (i.e. which sports will be played there, number of seats required, type of HVAC system, etc. are involved in deciding what type of facility to construct, the process offers numerous opportunities for creativity. A gym does not need to be a rectangular cement building. Planners can choose colors that brighten the facility, blend with other buildings, or blend into the surrounding landscape. Tile, glass, wood, and other materials can be chosen that enhance a given design or form a type of facility that has never been attempted before. Various roofing systems can be added to help reduce costs and provide optimal lighting. Facilities are limited by three basic constraints: money, site configuration, and the creativity of everyone involved in the planning process.

Chapter 4 discusses the steps in facility planning, which includes completing a needs assessment and feasibility study. The next steps are determining the site and designing the facility. The first part of this chapter examines some of the broader concerns regarding site location and its effect on the proposed facility. The chapter concludes with an analysis of site selection and design, including the various facility components that must be designed and their effect on the decision to build a given facility.

SITE LOCATION

Site location is one of the most important considerations when planning a sport facility. .Even a high-quality complex cannot succeed if the population for which it is designed does not use it, does not know where it is located, or refuses to travel to the site. Deciding on the right site requires analyzing numerous issues (see figure 5.1). Acquisition methods, cost considerations, and environmental constraints are just some of the factors. There are also political, community, and accessibility issues.

Private organizations that are considering building will have different goals from the entities involved in a public facility. A private facility is normally built to generate a profit. In contrast, a publicly funded facility is normally built to meet community needs. All facilities must be revenue generators to survive, but the private facility must generate a profit. Public ownership can have many drawbacks, such as limited funds, bureaucratic management, and the need to obtain voter approval on new funding initiatives. Other problems include the need to utilize the competitive bidding process, which can lead to the least expensive but not necessarily the most qualified contractor. Political agendas and conflicting egos of political leaders can also hamper negotiations and make the process almost unbearable (Chapin, 1997). Even with these problems, the ability to tap public land and public coffers is a tremendous benefit and can be a great opportunity.

Private entities may want to work with government entities because of the eminent domain power held by government units. **Eminent domain** allows a government entity to seize private property and use it for the public good after compensating the owner for its fair market value. If a private facility developer wants a piece of land but cannot convince the landowner to sell, the facility has to be canceled or has to be built around the unobtainable lot. A facility can also be held hostage to a landowner who demands a huge payoff. The situation is different if a government entity is involved or if the private entity enlists governmental help. In this case it may be possible to seize the property for the public good and then use it for the facility.

Site Planning

Whether a public or a private facility is to be built, site planning begins with the appointment of a site committee or an individual to find the right site. Typically a site committee is organized and then meets to discuss the goals of the facility. Although

Freedman: Insights on critical design decisions

Photo courtesy of Nancy Freedman.

My name is Nancy Freedman, and with more than 25 years of experience as an architect at Sasaki Associates, specializing in the design of collegiate sport facilities for the past 10, I have led more than a dozen project design teams in the process of site and facility design for recreation and athletic sport venues.

Sasaki Associates is a large interdisciplinary design firm that places a very high value on integration of site and building design. The firm began more than 50 years ago as a landscape architecture and planning practice and has evolved into a world-renowned design firm with equal acclaim for its campus and urban planning (2008 Beijing Olympics), landscape architecture, interior design, site design, eco-technologies (sustainable design), and campus architecture of all building types. The unique history of Sasaki has yielded a sport design practice that is particularly focused on the importance of site selection, site design, and building design and the sensitive integration of all three.

As a principal and project manager, part of my job is to guide clients (college and university presidents, facility directors, recreation directors, athletic directors) through the process of site selection. Most sport facilities for college campuses are large buildings—often they have the largest footprint of any building on the campus. Typically they take up large volumes of space and have high roofs and few windows. If handled poorly, these buildings can become eyesores, since they can be out of scale with the majority of other campus buildings. Also, they require large sites and often large parking areas in close proximity. Choosing an appropriate site is the first critical task facing the client and design team. A great building cannot overcome a poor site choice if the building is located in the wrong part of campus or if the site is encumbered with zoning restrictions, poor soils, steep slopes, wetlands, utilities that must be relocated, unreceptive neighbors, and so on. Usually there is no ideal site, so the process is one of understanding each site's pros and cons and the costs associated with necessary improvements.

The sport projects I lead often include outdoor fields. Planning and design of these fields involve a detailed understanding of a plethora of factors: size required for each sport, preferred playing surface (natural grass or synthetic turf), types of synthetic turf, drainage requirements, maintenance requirements and institutional capability, solar orientation preferences, spectator requirements, ancillary buildings (equipment, dugout, toilets, maintenance vehicles), lighting, broadcast, acoustic impact, and trash collection and removal. A basic understanding of costs is also critical, since many owners will have to analyze the trade-offs of each amenity against the project budget.

As an architect, most of my time is spent managing the process of designing the buildings. The basis of the building design is the program—a detailed description of each space that should be included in the building. For each space, the program lists the size, function, desired adjacencies, architectural features (walls, floors, ceilings, dimensions, acoustics, lighting), and building systems (temperature, humidity, electrical requirements). Once the program is agreed on, the design work begins. Design typically evolves through phases (schematic design, design development, construction documents), with the product for each successive stage getting more detailed and specific. The final documents are actually the basis for the contract with the builder, setting out the design intent in sufficient detail such that the builder can implement the design.

This chapter describes the critical fundamental design decisions that are made early in a project, ideally before the start of schematic design. Understanding the factors that go into making these decisions is key, since they are complex and have far-reaching repercussions for a future facility.

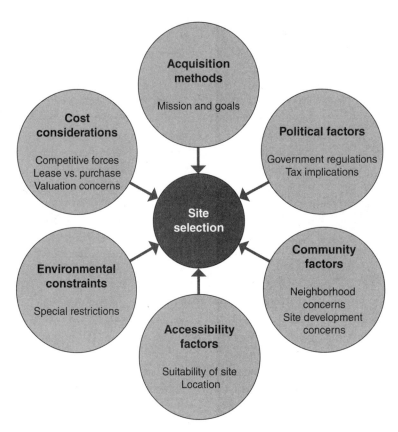

Figure 5.1 Issues that affect site selection.

one person can certainly find a site, an individual will not likely appreciate every concern or issue that might arise. That said, some very successful facilities have been built with one person spearheading the entire process.

Next, committee members develop a site mission statement. The mission statement will drive the options available for the most appropriate sites. The mission statement might focus on choosing a site that minimizes the negative impact on natural resources or that leverages the relationships between various government and nongovernment entities. After writing the mission statement, the site committee develops goals and objectives. The goal, for example, might be to purchase a facility within a half mile of a major freeway. A site objective might be to purchase a site with more than 3 acres (12,140 sq m) for less than $300,000. Appropriate tactics for realizing this objective might be driving around the area and determining which properties have at least 3 acres, contacting the assessor's office to find out the assessed value, and contacting property owners to see if they are interested in selling. Other tactics might include

contacting a real estate broker or determining which property owners are in default on their mortgages or property taxes. The goals and objectives will affect various site options. For example, if the facility will need an external water source for irrigation, then being located near a water source such as a lake or river might be an important goal or priority. Analysis of the proposed facility leads to a better understanding of site needs. Although it is preferable to have the mission statement, goals, and objectives in writing, many facilities have been developed without these tools. The problem with not recording this process in writing is that different parties might have different understandings of possible goals and objectives.

In site planning, a SWOT analysis can be particularly helpful. As detailed in chapter 4, the SWOT analysis encompasses strengths, weaknesses, opportunities, and threats. A hypothetical SWOT analysis for a sportsplex with several softball fields is shown next. The SWOT analysis, coupled with the strategies and objectives, is synthesized into an action plan, which will help determine how much land is needed.

HYPOTHETICAL SWOT ANALYSIS FOR A SPORTSPLEX

1. Strengths
   - Convenient location
   - Cheap land
   - City willing to work with owners
   - Strong local support
2. Weaknesses
   - Rough neighborhood surrounding the property
   - Needs extensive infrastructure repair
   - Limited funds from the city and state
3. Opportunities
   - Many softball players in the area are not being served
   - Local schools may want to use facility
   - Parks department needs more space
4. Threats
   - Parks department wants to build its own fields
   - A competing facility 20 miles (32 km) away is starting to advertise in the area
   - The popularity of the softball is decreasing throughout the country

Size

There is no formula for determining the size of the parcel required. Whatever type of analysis is used, extra room needs to be considered for future growth and for handling problems that might arise in the construction process. If there is not enough room and the construction process uncovers problems, the land may not be usable. The appropriate site size is contingent on the sports that will be played in the location. Table 5.1 provides dimensions for the playing areas for fields and gyms.

Once the specifics of a site are determined, a search committee is formed to look for an area that meets the land size requirements, keeping in mind the facility's goals and objectives as well as preliminary design concerns. All potential sites should be reviewed closely with respect to the following questions:

- What are the surrounding businesses?
- What is the residential neighborhood status within a 5-mile (8 km) radius?
- Will resident neighbors and the community welcome or object to the facility?
- How can the area benefit from the intended facility?
- Are the proper utilities (gas, electric, sewer, water, phone) in place?
- What, if any, are the zoning restrictions?
- How will nighttime lighting and noise influence the surrounding area?
- Is extra parking already in place?
- Will the sale of alcohol be met with resistance?

How the committee answers these and similar questions will influence the final site chosen for the facility. One important decision is whether to communicate potential site locations before the land is purchased. Any leaked information concerning a potential site can have a significant effect on the land's potential price. Thus, until the land has been purchased, the plan should be communicated to only a small audience.

Potential Sites

After locating several sites, the facility developer must determine which route to take to acquire the site. In any real estate investment, the purchaser should always have more than one prospective location. If the first choice is inadequate for whatever reason, the developer will have another option. Another reason to have more than one property in mind is leverage. If the facility developer can make the seller think he is competing with another potential landowner, the seller may be more willing to negotiate a more favorable price.

When examining potential sites, a facility developer needs to sell the project. Although

Table 5.1 Playing Field Dimensions

Activity	Indoor/Outdoor	PLAY AREA Width	PLAY AREA Length	SAFETY SPACE Width	SAFETY SPACE Length	TOTAL AREA Width	TOTAL AREA Length
Badminton	Indoor	20.0	44.0	6.0	8.0	32.0	60.0
Basketball							
Junior high instructional	Indoor	42.0	74.0	6.0	8.0	54.0	90.0
Junior high interscholastic	Indoor	50.0	84.0	6.0	8.0	62.0	100.0
Senior high instructional	Indoor	45.0	74.0	6.0	8.0	57.0	90.0
Senior high interscholastic	Indoor	50.0	84.0	6.0	8.0	62.0	100.0
Neighborhood elementary school	Indoor	42.0	74.0	6.0	8.0	54.0	90.0
Community junior high school	Indoor	50.0	84.0	6.0	8.0	62.0	100.0
Community senior high school	Indoor	50.0	84.0	6.0	8.0	62.0	100.0
Boccie	Indoor	18.0	62.0	3.0	9.0	24.0	80.0
Fencing							
Competitive	Indoor	6.0	40.0	3.0	6.0	12.0	52.0
Instructional	Indoor	3.0	30.0	2.0	6.0	7.0	42.0
Field hockey	Outdoor	180.0	300.0	15.0	15.0	210.0	330.0
Football	Outdoor	160.0	330.0	15.0	30.0	190.0	390.0
Lacrosse							
Boys	Outdoor	180.0	330.0	18.0	15.0	216.0	360.0
Girls	Outdoor	210.0	300.0	13.0	30.0	236.0	360.0
Air rifle	Indoor	5.0	50.0	6.0	20.0	17.0	90.0
Shuffleboard	Indoor	6.0	52.0	6.0	2.0	18.0	56.0
Soccer							
Outdoor*	Outdoor	225.0	360.0	5.0	–	235.0	360.0
Indoor*	Indoor	82.0	137.8	–	–	82.0	137.8
Squash							
Singles, hard ball	Indoor	18.5	32.0	–	–	18.5	32.0
Doubles, hard ball	Indoor	25.0	45.0	–	–	25.0	45.0
Tennis							
Deck (doubles)	Indoor	18.0	40.0	4.0	5.0	26.0	50.0
Hand	Indoor	16.0	40.0	4.5	10.0	25.0	60.0
Lawn (singles)	Indoor	27.0	78.0	12.0	21.0	51.0	120.0
Lawn (doubles)	Indoor	36.0	78.0	12.0	21.0	60.0	120.0
Paddle (singles)	Indoor	16.0	44.0	6.0	8.0	28.0	60.0
Paddle (doubles)	Indoor	20.0	44.0	6.0	8.0	32.0	60.0
Table	Indoor	9.0	31.0	–	–	9.0	31.0
Volleyball							
Competitive and adult	Indoor	30.0	60.0	6.0	6.0	42.0	72.0
Junior high school	Indoor	30.0	50.0	6.0	6.0	42.0	62.0
Water polo	Indoor	65.6	98.4	–	–	65.6	98.4
Wrestling	Indoor	28.0 diameter		5.0 diameter		33.0 diameter	

Note: All dimensions are shown in feet.

*Represents the dimensions of the largest recommended playing field; some fields, given limited space and resources, can be smaller in size.

National Federation of State High School Associations (2014). *Court and Field Diagram Guide.* Indianapolis: National Federation of State High School Associations.

it is important to have several locations under consideration, a developer will eventually have to focus on one primary site in order to obtain necessary approval and support. Even for small facilities, surrounding businesses or residents can become the greatest supporters or opponents of a proposed site, and their response can either help finalize a site or doom the site before the facility can be built.

Promoting the Positive

Communicating the plan includes letting the surrounding businesses know exactly how the facility will enhance the area. The idea of attracting customers to an area may greatly influence local business owners but can possibly anger residents. The local government authorities should be informed if they are not already part of the committee. It is important to get the support of local leaders to increase perception of the site's positive aspects. Government officials welcome the opportunity to say they were part of a new facility. Getting positive government officials involved early will only enhance the facility's success.

The community will also need to be informed about the project and about how the facility will improve the area. Surrounding neighborhoods and organizations will want only what is in their best interest, not necessarily what is best for the community as a whole. Showing the community the positive aspects of the project and getting the community's support are critical. The following are examples of positive community influences:

- Increasing property values
- Lowering crime rates among youth groups by keeping kids off the streets
- Allowing the community better access to recreational events
- Additional tax revenues from out-of-town teams competing in tournaments
- Additional spending in surrounding areas resulting from increased traffic
- Increasing civic pride of the neighborhood around the facility
- Enhancing the city's reputation to help attract new businesses and residents

Although such positive influences are possible with any project, a facility can also reduce property values, increase crime rates, and reduce recreational choices. Every facility project needs to be critically examined to determine what true positive and negative effects may occur over time. A nice new facility can be an economic engine or can become an unused eyesore. The facility developer needs to accentuate the positive over the entire time period of the project. Initial interest might be positive, but the positive feelings can wear thin after months of torn-up roads, noise, and other construction issues.

Once communities, politicians, and others are notified, the next step is getting their input. Local leaders such as church officials, neighborhood board of directors, and other community leaders will want to have input into the new facility during the entire process. Careful attention needs to be paid to the information provided by the community leaders. Including these people on the organization committee or on an advisory board can alleviate some concerns. The public will probably wish to have major input in the facility's design (e.g., the exterior color or the size). However, some people can also be troublemakers who can make the process more difficult. Such people may demand numerous modifications that could make a proposed facility impractical.

Handling Opposition

Once the public knows about the proposed site, opposition to the project is bound to arise. Normally, the opposition is much more vocal and organized than is the support for a project. After the opposition has been identified, their concerns should be addressed quickly and thoroughly. The more rapidly the facility developer can help influence the opposition, the better chance the project will have of being realized. Restating the positive influences mentioned earlier and emphasizing how the opposition can benefit will hopefully change the opinions of some. Being able to change the opinion of any member of the opposition will greatly enhance the facility's creditability. The opposition's arguments will also bring up issues not initially considered. Thus, having an open forum to discuss a proposed site or facility can produce valuable benefits.

Opponents should not be ignored or scorned, as they can be a positive tool for facility growth. Addressing their concerns can be the most challenging part of site selection. For example, if religious leaders are doubtful about game scheduling on Sundays, the committee might inform them that all Sunday games will be played after 2:00 p.m. This will allow participants to go to church in the morning. A site close to a church can be chosen to reduce travel time for possible church goers wanting to use the facility, or the facility can be opened for church league participants.

Finally, several managerial issues should be considered when sites are being explored. Secrecy is a major concern from a political, financial, and competitive perspective. Political squabbling can follow any potential site, and such squabbles can be minimized if no specific site is identified until the very end. On the flip side, if homeowners or businesses are affected, they can rebel if they have not been part of the process from the very beginning. Financially, if landowners know that a facility is being planned and that their land is being considered, they will try to raise the selling price. Last, competitors who know that a new facility is being planned may purchase the land to stifle competition.

The analysis discussed so far is appropriate for private facilities. However, most public sport or recreation facilities are built on public land that is already owned or is being acquired through eminent domain. Since such land may be in unique areas, sport facilities are often customized or adapted to fit the surroundings. Public land that lies in a flood plain might still be used for sport fields most of the year. Nevertheless, although site selection issues may be minimized if the public owns the land, they do not disappear. Some issues can be resolved quickly—zoning issues, for example, since the government can modify the zoning for the public benefit. However, irate neighbors can still pose a problem. If the lights from a new field will spill over into a neighborhood, the residents will be up in arms regardless of whether the facility is public or private. Thus, for public facilities, significant effort still needs to be expended to avoid the same problems that befall private facilities.

Site Considerations

Every potential site must be analyzed for unique concerns, from cost to environmental factors. For example, will the landowner be unwilling to sell the land no matter how much the facility developer is willing to pay? On the other hand, if the public is involved, what political ramifications might there be if the city took the property through eminent domain, even if it paid the prevailing market value?

Other important criteria to examine about potential sites are applicable laws or jurisdictional regulations. Even if price is not an object, if the site is not properly zoned or if the municipality does not allow certain structures, the site will not be an option unless the laws change. For example, state laws may dictate what size facility is required for a school. Thus, even if price or zoning were not issues, the ability of the site to accommodate the required building size would need to be determined before proceeding.

Alaska, for example, has specific regulations governing school pools. The regulations allow state reimbursement for building expenses if the pool is used for an instructional program or as an emergency water storage facility within a fire suppression system. However, funding is not available to combine the two features, even though such a strategy would not be difficult to accommodate. The regulations cover details such as competitive pool size, which must be at least 75 by 30 feet (23 by 9 m) in order to handle 30 students per class and 720 students per year in swim-related classes. Beginning swimmers, under the guidelines, must have at least 100 square feet (9.3 sq m) each, and intermediate and advanced swimmers must have at least 120 square feet (11 sq m) each ("Swimming Pool Guidelines," 1997). Other examples of regulations include the required number of parking spaces and how far the entrance of a facility that serves alcohol can be from a church or school.

To successfully plan and describe a multipurpose facility, the committee must include a detailed plan of what the facility will entail, what sports will be offered, what amenities will be offered, and what the community can expect from the new facility. Some issues include the following:

- Area size and availability (both funds to purchase and willingness to sell)

- Appropriate historical information records showing, for example, whether the land was used as a Native American burial ground or used for storing chemicals

- Legal issues such as accessibility, convenience, parking, safety, and adaptability

- Orientation of the playing fields

- Government (federal, state, and local) regulations

- Time allotted for development (Farmer, Mulrooney, and Ammon, 1996)

Location, zoning and other regulations, user needs, community impact, and land features are also important site considerations. These are discussed next.

Location

The facility developers must ensure that the location is suitable for the type of facility or business being planned. For example, someone who is planning to build a large recreation complex should probably not look into investing in a piece of land that is a wildlife sanctuary, a wetland, or a flood plain. Choosing a site entails doing some intense research but also requires common sense. A developer who plans a facility that will cover 4 acres should not buy 4.5 acres, as there will not be enough room for parking or expansion. It is always important to allow room for adequate parking, and it might be important to purchase additional land for future expansion. It is key to a successful investment to locate an area that generates proper exposure, has good vehicular access, comes at a reasonable cost for site development, and meets government restrictions or zoning laws.

One option for maximizing space is to build sport fields on top of parking garages or other flat structures, such as an underground parking garage with a roof that is even with the ground, an elevated field, or a partially elevated field if the facility is built into the side of a hill. An example of such a facility is Union City High School in Union City, New Jersey. The architects transformed the site of an old football stadium into a new high school with playing fields on the roof. One concern was whether water would leak through the turf into the building. After installing a significant waterproofing system, sloping the structure (putting a crown in the center of the field), using five waterproofing layers under the synthetic turf, and installing an electric field vector mapping system to pinpoint possible leaks, the concerns with leaking were addressed. The $175 million project is solid due in part to the 10-foot-wide (3 m) trusses used to support the roof. The 366,550-square-foot (34,054 sq m) rooftop athletic complex opened in 2009 and allowed up to 4,500 people to watch football and other sports while also enjoying views of Manhattan (Drexel, 2008).

Zoning and Other Regulations

Zoning is the regulation by local government of the use of real property. It restricts a particular territory to residential, commercial, industrial, or other uses. A site should be zoned so that commercial recreation is a compatible use. This saves the additional step of changing the zoning or acquiring a **variance**. Since *recreation* is a broad term as used in zoning regulations, it is often possible to "slip the project through" in many zoning classifications. Industrial and manufacturing zoning usually accommodates commercial recreation. Business and commercial zoning is generally too expensive for consideration. Residential zoning is not recommended because of the fights that can erupt with neighbors. There is a split regarding open space and agricultural zoning that can be resolved only on a case-by-case basis. Zoning issues can also affect liquor-related policies and procedures.

Lighting and noise from a potential site can also raise zoning concerns. The most important aspect related to lighting and noise is the effect on the neighborhoods around the facility. Most cities and neighborhoods have restrictions against intrusive lighting and disturbing noise. Light and noise issues could relate to the type of events that will be held in the facility, the time of day and days of the week events will be held, and the type of crowd that will be attending the various events. A number of complex and thorny issues that can revolve around zoning regulations are in place to promote quality of life for those living in a given community. Although some issues can be resolved through negotiations with neighbors, in the end zoning and variances are changed by elected or appointed officials on land commissions or other bodies. Zoning concerns, however, are not the only regulatory issues that may affect a site.

Apart from local or regional guidelines, laws such as the Americans with Disabilities Act (ADA) pose further restrictions for a proposed site. Critical consideration of ADA issues needs to be part of the design process (chapter 13 deals with the ADA in detail). If participants or spectators will need to travel over rough terrain to get to the facility, it may be inaccessible and thus possibly violate the law. One last concern might be a historical building. If a building has been designated as a national historic site or any similar protected designation, then a potential builder might not be able to tear down or renovate the building. In some contentious projects, opponents have petitioned to obtain protection of older buildings as a way to stop a proposed development.

User Needs

After the analysis of government regulations, the next step is to analyze the potential users. The first question to ask is who the typical facility users will be and what their needs are. Future facility users typically want to know the following:

- Size of facility
- Proximity to major transportation routes
- Hours of operations
- What events will be held
- The cost of building and using the facility

The second question is what groups will be able to effectively utilize the facility. It may be envisioned that local community organizations, charity groups, service organizations, schools, and professional teams will be permitted to use a facility, but what if people in these groups cannot reach the site? If a facility is planned for use by a school, will children be able to walk there, or will a bus be used? Who will have priority for use? Will schools always have first priority, or will the facility be reserved on a first-come, first-served basis?

The third question has to do with what the community wants from the site. If the site has historical value or is part of a natural habitat, the community may fight vigorously to prevent its use. That is why it is so important to appreciate and address user needs when deciding on a potential site.

Community Impact

Another important consideration is the facility's potential economic impact. Specifically, are there intangible benefits or cultural benefits associated with the site? The economic effect of a new facility could include new enterprises in the area and increased local land values because of increased traffic flow (i.e., local businesses will increase tax revenue and offer more employment opportunities). Negative aspects of the site may include lights, noise, or traffic in residential areas. Indeed, the failure to properly consider these factors is often the most costly blunder from a public relations and legal perspective.

Land and Environmental Considerations

So far the site considerations have centered on external issues, from government concerns to community impact. But the focus will always come back to the land. If the land option is not appropriate, whether because of location or geographic limitations, the site should not be pursued. Other features to review regarding the site may include the following:

- Detailed geography (soil, subsoil, vegetation)
- Demographics of area
- Constituency representation (political clout)
- Flood areas (drainage, runoff)
- Climate, precipitation, winds, natural disasters (e.g., hurricanes, tornadoes, earthquakes, floods)
- Capital improvement plan maps (illustrating current and planned projects by council district)
- Enterprise zone ownership and land use maps
- Acreage (adequacy for buildings, parking, picnic areas, and so on)
- Additional acreage for expansion
- Shape (acute angles or odd shapes are possible wasted space)

- Topography (level terrain, steep slopes)
- Zoning regulations (e.g., permit requirements, parking, setbacks)
- Access (from principal roads and local streets; truck or bus access)
- Security considerations

It is very difficult to obtain approval for all environmental and off-site challenges without having outside cooperation. Facility developers must do their homework by checking and rechecking all issues when considering each site option. No single site will meet all the requirements for any facility developer. However, once all the affected parties are contacted and all the requirements finalized, it is much easier to select the best site options.

Several impact studies are required for every potential site. These studies must be completed before any work begins. The developer must find out if the land contains any hallowed grounds (e.g., Native American burial grounds). Other types of sensitive sites include cemeteries and sites of archeological finds or digs. Some sensitive sites can be uncovered through a review of old newspaper articles or interviews of local residents. Contamination is another potential issue. If there was a gas station or a manufacturing plant on the site in the past, then it is likely that the site was contaminated.

Soil Testing

When surveying the land, soil testing is important because it will reveal what is beneath the soil. **Soil testing** helps determine whether the land has been polluted or used as a waste dump. In one example, a wealthy philanthropist offered to give a private school some land for new school grounds. The land was located next to old railroad tracks and had been used for dumping over the years. The school conducted soil testing to see if there were any potential hazards to which the children could be exposed. Because of this heightened duty to protect children, the school

When land is scarce, gyms may be built up rather than out. One such example is the Payne Whitney Gym at Yale University. The expensive exterior renovation took so long that the university had to eventually buy the external scaffolding that they had been renting for years.

paid more than $140,000 to test the soil and then had a second test conducted when some results were inconclusive. In the end the land was shown to be contaminated with everything from heavy metals to cyanide and oil. The costs to clean the soil were potentially so high that the school gave the land back to the donor.

Another issue related to soil testing is what surface will be best suited for the facility. If the surface will be grass, for example, the ground needs to be tested to ensure that it can support grass. In many instances the type of grass used (see chapter 8) can be adapted to the present soil. However, some facilities look to use a specific type of grass. In these cases the soil must be examined for compatibility with that type of grass or the facility will have to budget for bringing in appropriate soil.

Finally, soil treatment may also be a major concern. If the playing surface requires chemicals to help the grass grow effectively and to protect from weeds and bugs (e.g., football, baseball, and soccer fields), the chemicals need to be tested for effectiveness in various climates as well as for environmental friendliness. The primary con-cern is any kind of runoff into rivers or drainage into other properties. If there is a potential for chemical runoff from the proposed site to another property, this could mean potential litigation or future cleanup concerns.

Core Drilling

It is important to understand the kind of foundation the facility will be built on; therefore, an engineering firm is needed to conduct **core drilling** to test whether the foundation is sand, clay, dirt, or rock. New technology allows the rock and soil density of a site to be examined using ground penetrating radar. A rock foundation will raise the excavation costs significantly because of blasting or other major work. Clay varies in consistency and is affected by wetness. Clay can be very sticky, messy, and difficult to work with in constructing a building or developing a field. Another important consideration is whether or not the land is at sea level. Water may become a problem if the foundation has to be set deep in the ground. The ground around and under the foundation can be saturated and therefore difficult and expensive to work with. In this situation, equipment must be brought in to pump out the water, adding to the cost. Thus, what may have seemed a good deal on cheap land could turn into a major expense. Common sense suggests that if the price is too good, there might be a reason for the low value.

Grading

Every site needs to be graded, or leveled and prepared for construction. This can include removing dirt, rocks, trees, and other vegetation. **Grading** can also include disposing of wood, concrete, metal, or other building materials left on the site. Additional grading may be necessary if the site is located along a river or other body of water. Most grading involves moving dirt. The type of soil and the amount being moved determine most grading costs.

Because grading can be costly, the facility builder needs to get bids. Prices vary depending on the type and quantity of material being moved. Soil is easier to move than other types of material such as rocks or trees. Grading costs are determined by the cubic yard. The cost to move (and possibly replace) dirt, plus equipment, labor,

Facilities Trivia

There are two types of construction: horizontal and vertical. Horizontal buildings need to be built from the back of the property to the front so that equipment can be easily removed when the exterior is completed. A field house that covers an entire football field is an example of a horizontal building. With a vertical facility, one floor needs to be built and completed before the next can be added. A typical example of vertical construction is a skyscraper. Historical facts associated with skyscrapers include the following:

1855: Sir Henry Bessemer patents a method for mass producing steel, which provides the framework for all future skyscrapers.

1857: Elisha Otis designs the first safe passenger elevator for the 5-story E.V. Haughwout department store in New York City.

1903: The 15-story Ingalls Building—the first reinforced-concrete skyscraper—is built. It is still standing today.

1931: The Empire State Building in New York City is completed in 410 days. It is the tallest building in the world until 1972.

1972: The World Trade Center in New York City is completed and becomes the tallest building in the world.

1973: The Sears Towers in Chicago is the world's tallest building at 1,451 feet (442.3 m).

1998: The 1,483-foot-high (452 m) Petronas Twin Towers in Malaysia are completed with a sky bridge that can retract during high winds.

2004: Taiwan erects the 1,670-foot-tall (509 m) Taipei 101. The elevator ascends at a speed of 37.7 miles (60.7 km) per hour.

2010: The 2,722-foot-tall (829.7 m) Burj Khalifa is completed in Dubai.

2013: Work begins on the 2,749-foot-tall (837.9 m) Sky City One in Changsha, China (Green, 2013).

and trucks, can exceed $25 per cubic yard (0.76 cu m), but the cost does not necessarily end there. A survey team is needed because the area to be graded needs to be precisely measured. If significant grading costs are anticipated or additional expenses are involved, the site could turn out to be too expensive.

Wetlands and Endangered Species

With any construction project, there will be consultation with and approval from federal and state governments. The site must not be on any protected land. Some wetlands are federally or state protected, as are some trees, especially older trees. Animals that have been placed on the endangered species list can also pose a problem. Thus, if there are protected oak trees that also serve as the nesting grounds for protected owls, there is almost no chance that a variance will be given to remove the trees. However, if the proposed facility poses at the most a minimal threat to an endangered species or to protected land, the government will probably give a variance. As part of the site analysis process, the facility developer must retain an environmentalist to examine the site and determine what wildlife will be affected. The time of year when the site is examined has an effect on protected migratory animals that may use the site in certain seasons and not others. If the habitat survey is conducted at different times during different seasons, any potential effect on migratory animals can be minimized.

Accessibility

Does the prospective site have access roads to handle the future traffic? If yes, will it be able to handle the traffic flow? Can the current roads handle the exiting traffic without causing major delays for other motorists? Will the facility be located next to a highway, or will people need to travel on back roads to get to the facility? Will access roads go through neighborhoods where parking and noise could become major issues? Will stop signs or stop lights need to be installed, and if so, how far apart will they be placed? Can public transportation alleviate some of the traffic- and parking-related concerns? Regardless of the answers to such questions, the next question is who will build the needed roadways and how

much they will cost. The state department of transportation will probably be involved in significant road analysis and construction issues. Thus, it is important to get local officials, residents, and state officials involved in any thoroughfare planning process. Although infrastructure issues are covered in the accessibility analysis, there may be a number of noninfrastructure concerns such as the need for police and traffic patrols for any new roads. Such elements can be significant because a facility may have to pay thousands of dollars for off-duty police to help with traffic flow and pedestrian crossing.

Road access is not the only access-related factor. Buses may need to reach the facility, and large trucks need to deliver items and remove trash. Such vehicles may be able to travel only on certain roads. Parking areas need to be developed for these vehicles, and entry and exit bays may need to be built to allow vehicles to load and unload. Some facilities also have a helicopter pad to allow for arriving dignitaries and emergency transportation flights.

With any new construction or renovation project, the state needs to be involved in the process from the very beginning. One major concern for the state could be the facility's effect on traffic. The state transportation department might require a certain number of entryways and exits from the parking area to make sure vehicles can exit in case of an emergency and that exiting traffic would not pose a hardship to the existing traffic flow.

Utilities

Site utilities are another concern, as the cost of bringing utilities to a remote site may be prohibitive. Where the sewage waste will go and where the utilities will come from are just two of the issues that need to be addressed. Water usage must be considered for sprinklers, fire protection, and building use (e.g., restrooms). Storm drainage, energy sources, telephone lines, and solid waste disposal are also factors. Economic factors such as acquisition costs, taxes, financing, and development costs should also be considered for all utilities (Farmer, Mulrooney, and Ammon, 1996). The primary utility concerns include gas and electricity, phone, and cable or satellite service.

With respect to electricity and gas, if the

complex is built in an open area, as the Houston Astrodome was more than 50 years ago, supply lines will need to be run to the site. Facility developers who will be relying on city or municipal services should make sure that the city is able to generate the amount of power needed, or that the extra energy can be purchased on the open market or produced through options such as solar cells, fuel cells, or wind-powered devices. If the site does not have enough capacity in the area for the proposed facility's needs, the facility and utility company might need to build generators or a substation.

Issues of capacity and load capabilities also apply to telephone and cable systems. Will new phone lines be added? If so, will they be above ground or possibly fiber-optic cables buried underground? Cable may be very expensive if it has to go through rock. With the growth of cellular service and data delivery, one of the biggest new expenses for a facility is outfitting it for all the data needs of the business and possibly 100,000 fans. Such data transmission and reception systems can cost millions of dollars, and the site's location can significantly affect this cost.

Water, Drainage, and Sewer

When working with water and sewer provisions, it is extremely important to know if a city has the capacity to serve the facility's needs. The following factors must be considered:

- Is there water on the site?
- Is there an existing well?
- Will water be brought in and removed through city or municipal delivery systems?
- Will the facility need to build its own water and sewer systems (e.g., septic system, drain fields)?
- How big are the current sewer lines and will they need to be enlarged?

If water will be transported or additional delivery lines need to be built, the project will become more expensive. That is why some facilities build their own sewer tank and wastewater treatment plants on-site or utilize recycled water (gray water). Water concerns also are prominent when it comes to irrigation or a sprinkler system for the playing surface.

Where will the water come from? How much will it cost? These questions help determine if a site is suitable and which grass type should be used. The $455 million University of Phoenix Stadium for the Arizona Cardinals was built with a field tray (retractable field) so the field can be removed from the stadium to obtain more rain and sunshine and to allow the facility to be more versatile. It is the first retractable field in North America, and the green revolution might encourage other stadiums interested in grass fields to follow the same strategy of increasing the number of hours grass is outside the facility to obtain more water.

Besides water delivery, a site must be able to deal with water drainage and retention. The site slope must be just right to allow the proper drainage so that water does not remain standing, and when the water leaves the area it should collect in an either man-made or natural basin. The next problem is how to get the water out of the basin. Some water will evaporate, and some will soak into the ground. The remaining water will need to be pumped out and placed elsewhere. This is extremely important in areas that get an abundant amount of rain. Water that does not get moved away from the facility can become a breeding ground for mosquitoes.

After examining all the potential land and environmental concerns, the facility developer is almost ready to make some final decisions. The following suggestions can help narrow the list of potential sites:

- Physical examination of proposed sites
- Feasibility studies (see chapter 4) specifically developed for the potential sites (facts including development trends, conditions, and populations)
- Site information, including site surveys, soil testing, erosion analysis, surface water resources, wetland issues, groundwater, precipitation, climate, open areas, utilities, existing buildings and roads, projected roads, residential areas, commercial and industrial developments, easements, rights-of-way, and zoning restrictions
- Meetings with local leaders, citizen committees, and other groups
- Analysis of recreational, aesthetic, and engineering features

- Most important, the cost of each option and what the facility developer can afford

SITE COST

Obviously, care needs to be taken in buying and developing land to ensure the best possible deal for the amount of money spent. If facility developers cannot afford a piece of land, they cannot buy it. Three important questions are involved in cost consideration: how much the land will cost, who will pay for it, and how much money will be left over to build and start operating the facility. If the public owns the land, then the decision may not be as difficult, even for a private facility developer. Many facilities, from professional baseball stadiums to local gyms, are built with a blend of public and private cooperation, land, and perhaps financial assistance.

No matter who pays for the land, there needs to be enough money available to keep the facility operating. Facility operations can assist in paying off a facility's debt service, but this is not advisable. For a successful project, there needs to be enough money for both building and operation. If all operational revenue goes to debt service rather than maintenance and growth, the facility will fail.

Affordability

The most important question facility developers can ask themselves is "What can I afford?" When it comes to determining land value, there are three valuation methods: the cost approach, the direct sales comparison approach, and the income approach. The cost approach determines value by adding the value of any improvements to the value of the vacant land when purchased. If the land was purchased for $1 million and $500,000 in improvements will be made, then the land should be valued at $1.5 million.

The direct sales comparison approach analyzes similar properties in the area that have sold recently. If three properties in the area sold for $20,000 an acre, then the property in question should be worth around $20,000 an acre. However, such an approach works only when land is being compared. When buildings are being compared analyzing can become tricky if a building has limited uses or few similar facilities. Thus, this approach is very difficult for sport facilities since there rarely are multiple sport facilities for sale in the same area.

In the income approach, land value is based on the present value of future benefits of property-generated income (Fisher and Martin, 1994). This approach requires analyzing future income streams and then determining the present value of those streams. Thus, a city might be able to project that a stadium can generate $20 million a year in the future. Based on this revenue stream, the land can be given a specific value based on what will be built on the site and how much money the site can generate.

After determining the property's value, developers must decide if the price is within their limits. It is not wise to settle for a tract that is cheaper because of its size. It is normally better to give up some of the location benefits in order to obtain the right amount of land. At the same time, though, it is important to once again remember "location, location, location": If the large parcel is too far away from customers, it may not be the ideal choice. A recent trend has been to create a destination location. Such a location combines a sport venue with ancillary retail, lodging, and entertainment options. Although some of these destination locations are downtown, such as Staples Center in Los Angeles, others are being built outside city limits, such as Gillette Stadium (including Patriot Place) in Foxborough, Massachusetts, and AT&T Stadium in Dallas.

Taxes

If a private developer is buying land, he must also consider what taxes will have to be paid. Taxes are charged based on a percentage of the property's assessed value. Government agencies have created incentives through the granting of tax credits, depreciation deductions, and property tax reductions to encourage developing and rehabilitating certain properties. The value of such incentives is deemed nonrealty interest (Fisher and Martin, 1994). Negotiating with government officials before buying a property is crucial to lowering property taxes. If government leaders really want a facility, they may waive significant tax obligations, and this can make a project economically feasible. Such an approach can also anger local residents, who might be called on to cover any tax shortfalls, especially to help support schools, police, and fire departments.

Other Fees

Other fees may include land-clearing costs and even surveying costs. These costs are incurred in all projects, but their extent varies. For example, a site may include swampland or a high water table, requiring drainage, as well as forest land that needs to be cleared. These costs can be significant. However, every challenge can also represent a potential opportunity. One way to ease the financial burden of land clearing is to have a logging company come in and clear-cut the land for timber. Of course, this would be an option only with heavily wooded property and if a logging company is interested in buying the trees. Thus, good lumber tress can be an asset for a given site.

Buying Versus Leasing

Facility developers often stretch their financial resources to purchase a site, clear the land, lay a foundation, build a shell, complete the interior, equip the facility, and then open the facility for business. This is clearly a long process with numerous expenses. The only means to avoid these start-up costs is to renovate and utilize an existing facility instead of building a new facility. An existing facility often has appropriate government approval (zoning); parking areas; heating, ventilation, and air conditioning (HVAC) equipment; and other options that significantly reduce the price in comparison with the price of a new building. Although the developer loses some of the glamour associated with building a new facility and the flexibility to build exactly what is needed, the cost savings can be substantial. Some eager landlords are willing to help sponsor a facility's renovation in exchange for obtaining a long-term lease from the new tenant. However, although an existing facility might be cheaper to start with, the renovation costs for some projects are so large that it is often more worthwhile to build a customized new facility.

To help make a sound financial decision, it is important to perform a buy–lease analysis. In this approach, the net present value of the cash outflow associated with the lease option is compared with the cost for buying the property. All else being the same, the option with the lower present value is preferred (Cotts and Lee, 1992). This means that the current value of the cost of building is compared with the cost of leasing a facility, and the project that costs less from the beginning (assuming all other factors are the same) is chosen. The following two options highlight the analysis required to compare projects:

■ *Option 1*: signing a 5-year lease, with payment of $5 million each year, for a facility that can be occupied with only minor modifications. The minor modifications are not covered by the landlord, but all other maintenance and facility expenses are covered by the landlord.

■ *Option 2*: buying a building for $25 million and spending another $10 million modifying the building, which after 5 years would have a salvage value of $20 million. Operating and maintenance for the facility will be $1 million a year.

Yearly projections for the two options are shown in tables 5.2 and 5.3.

Leasing the facility would cost the facility developer $11.03 million over 5 years after taxes. In contrast, purchasing, renovating, and then selling the building (salvaging) after 5 years would cost $8.86 million. Thus, in this example, option 2 would make the best sense if the project was evaluated just on the basis of which project would make the most financial sense. There is a risk when buying in that the price of the property (salvage value) could decrease or increase significantly. On the other hand, when leasing it may be difficult to find another viable facility option after 5 years, or the new lease obligations may be significantly higher. These issues need to be explored when trying to determine whether to purchase or lease. One of the key benefits associated with leasing the facility is that the lease payments are deductible as a business expense. This results in the tax shield reducing the overall cost for leasing the facility.

For a first-time facility developer, leasing may be the only option because of capital restraints. Yet even major corporations utilize leasing methods to tackle expansion and short-term needs. Leases can have the drawback that the owner may limit

Table 5.2 Yearly Projections for Option 1

Action				YEAR		
	0	1	2	3	4	5
Lease obligation	−5	−5	−5	−5	−5	
Minor maintenance	0.4	0.4	0.4	0.4	0.4	
Tax shield	2.9	2.9	2.9	2.9	2.9	
Net cash flow	−2.5	−2.5	−2.5	−2.5	−2.5	
Discounted cash flow	−2.5	−2.38	−2.18	−2.05	−1.92	
Cumulative facility cost	−2.5	−4.88	−7.06	−9.11	−11.03	−11.03

Shown in millions ($).

Table 5.3 Yearly Projections for Option 2

Action				YEAR		
	0	1	2	3	4	5
Purchase of building	−25					
Renovations	−10					
Depreciation	−4.5	−4.5	−4.5	−4.5	−4.5	−4.5
Operations and maintenance	1	1	1	1	1	1
Tax shield	1.94	1.94	1.94	1.94	1.94	1.94
Salvage value						20
Net cash flow	−29.56	0.94	0.94	0.94	0.94	0.94
Discounted cash flow	−29.56	0.89	0.85	0.81	0.79	17.36
Cumulative facility costs	−29.56	−28.67	−27.82	−27.01	−26.2	−8.86

Shown in millions ($).

renovations or uses of the building. Ultimately, if a leased project fails, developers may lose more money than if they owned the land outright. This happens since the developer might have lease payment obligations that can continue for years (many leases are for 10-20 years) and will have no assets when the lease period ends.

A lease allows predictability of rental costs and the ability to deduct rental costs as a business expense, but only minimal control. The landlord controls issues such as renting adjoining space to competing businesses and can prevent certain activities not expressly covered in the lease. These policies can make the facility less attractive for the facility developer. To avoid such problems, a lease agreement needs to cover the concerns that could potentially arise during the lease term. The following are some of the key clauses that should be included in a lease:

- The parties to the lease and what the facility will be used for
- Description of the leased property
- Commencement date and length of time of the lease
- Payment amount or method of calculating rent
- Responsibility for expenses: property taxes, insurance, utilities, janitorial and maintenance, and management
- Method of handling delinquent payments
- Alteration or improvement restrictions
- Restrictions on the operation of the tenant's business or on subsequent assignment or subleasing
- Use of common areas and facilities
- Indemnification of landlord and insurance requirements

- Remedies in the event of total or partial destruction
- Rights in the event of condemnation
- Right of entry
- Early-termination penalties
- Arbitration provisions for resolving disputes
- Statement that the lease represents the entire agreement
- Future options in the lease
- Subordination and partial invalidity of the lease
- Compensation if the government takes the land (eminent domain) (Fisher and Martin, 1994)

The other option when it comes to obtaining a location is buying the land. One major advantage of purchasing the land is that if all else fails, the developer can walk away from the project with land that could be sold.

SITE SELECTION

As explained so far in this chapter, before a final site can be chosen a committee must look at all variables. Once the potential sites have been narrowed to a manageable final list, each site must be inspected one last time. Various factors go into making a final decision:

- Review of feasibility studies (economic and political impact) as covered in chapter 4
- Permits (lease, license, or letter) and whether they can be obtained
- Site information (from environmental issues to historical concerns such as burial grounds)
- Regulations (building codes, health ordinances, and other concerns that may make a proposed site unusable)
- Community involvement—is there a significant amount of opposition?
- Affordability and decision whether the facility should be purchased or leased
- Easements—will the neighbors have the right to go across the property?
- Zoning (cluster, flood plain, open space) issues and whether the facility can be classified as business use only or as commercial and residential
- Restrictive covenants that may limit who can purchase the land or use it for certain purposes
- Aesthetic value of the site and whether there are any beautiful views, trees, or waterways that may affect the site's use
- Recreational opportunities such as whether the site can be used for indoor and outdoor facilities

No single variable makes one site better than another. A good analogy has to do with the purchase of a residence. Although one spouse may want more space in a house, the other may want a nice neighborhood or beautifully manicured lawns. One family member may want a certain type of restroom, while others may want energy-efficient appliances. With so many variables, it is difficult to develop a consensus that forces a lot of people to compromise on their final choice. The factors on the preceding list are some of the compromise elements that those on the planning committee may have to consider.

Finally, the benefits and costs for each site are compared and the final site is selected. Often site selection comes down to a "gut" decision. Site selection can be finalized because of a hunch or just a feeling, but only after a thorough review. If a developer has done all the analysis before making this gut decision, then there is no problem with using this technique: There may be two equally attractive options, and a final decision will need to be made on instinct or intuition.

FACILITY DESIGN

Once a site has been selected, facility design is the next step. The design may incorporate elements of the site; Camden Yards in Baltimore, for example, incorporated brick warehouses as part of the design. A recent phenomenon has been to design open-air stadiums to incorporate a view; stadiums in Denver and Pittsburgh have views of the downtown skyline. Although every design and every facility is different, every facility will face numerous planning considerations, such as the following:

DALLAS MAVERICKS' FAILED PROPOSAL

The entire planning and construction process is obviously complex. This example is from a planned, but failed, initiative to build an arena in Lewiston, Texas, for the Dallas Mavericks and Stars. Before American Airlines Center was built in Dallas, the Mavericks and the Stars were looking for a new home. They looked both in and outside Dallas. One proposal was the city of Lewiston in an adjoining county. The voters in Lewiston narrowly defeated a bill that would have authorized the selling of bonds to build the proposed arena. The initiative involved more than 87 steps—primarily related to financing and feasibility but also to construction issues—before the facility would even open its doors (City of Lewiston, 1995). The vote failed for one simple reason: Those who were in favor were mildly in favor and did not come out in big numbers to vote. In contrast, those against the effort were galvanized and came out in large numbers. The key to any such vote is bringing out the best supporters in large numbers.

1. Do financial and political groundwork for creating new state law necessary to levy taxes.

2-3. Call and hold election for half-cent sales tax.

4. Hold half-cent bond closing with the release of bond proceeds.

5-6. Hire political consulting and public relations firms.

7-8. Call and hold general obligation bond (GOB) election for county residents.

9. Release GOB bond proceeds.

10. Develop complete financing package.

11-12. Negotiate and determine the arena ownership structure and contract.

13. Develop memorandum of understanding highlighting key contractual terms.

14. Develop terms and conditions for three categories: anchor tenant, concessions, and sponsorship.

15. Develop terms under which the anchor tenant will be bound to stay in the facility.

16. Research and finalize potential sponsors.

17. Research and finalize agreement with concessionaire if food service is being outsourced.

18. Retain consultants to help in securing additional sponsors.

19. Research and finalize list of potential facility management providers.

20. Retain consultants to research potential facility management companies.

21. Research luxury marketing and suites sales, including having staggered expiration dates to maximize revenue.

22-23. Analyze potential purchasers of luxury suites and obtain commitment for 75% of luxury suites before progressing further with project.

24-25. Analyze potential purchasers of premium seating and obtain commitment for 75% of premium seats before progressing further with project.

26. Analyze various companies that will be asked to provide long-term services to the arena.

27. Research all necessary equipment and fixtures such as concession stands.

28. Send request for financing to commercial banks and institutional investors.

29. Obtain binding letters of financing that provide the terms for borrowing money.

30-31. Test the debt instruments and potential equity instruments to determine and gauge interest.

32. Obtain bond opinion letter from attorney indicating that conditions of bond indenture comply with all applicable laws.

33. Escrow closing of bonds and release funds to start construction.

34-35. Examine site needs and undertake a detailed survey of all potential final sites.

36-37. Conduct geotechnical engineering of subsurface and environmental and wetlands analysis at final site(s).

38. Conduct phase I feasibility study to determine market demand for events, sponsorship, and so on.

39. Conduct phase II feasibility study examining premium seating market.

40. Conduct phase II feasibility study examining financial projections.

41. Undertake an economic impact report for the direct, indirect, and induced spending impact of the new arena.

42. Undertake a traffic study to see what impact the arena will have on local and regional traffic.

43. Close on the site and purchase the land.

44-58. Undertake various steps with the state legislature and department of transportation to build a highway bypass for the arena.

59. Conduct design phase involving architectural, structural, mechanical, electrical, interiors, acoustic, civil, planning, landscaping, codes compliance, elevators, lighting, roofing, rigging, and related professional services.

60. Use order of magnitude package to clarify the project's scope—a preliminary pricing tool.

61. Receive estimates from initial engineering analysis followed by the first round of value engineering.

62-63. Architect prepares schematic design, then developers undertake value engineering to reduce costs.

64-65. Architect prepares design documents, then developers undertake value engineering to reduce costs.

(continued)

BEHIND THE SCENES *(continued)*

66-67. Architect prepares construction documents, then developers undertake value engineering to reduce costs.

68. Build suite mock-ups to simulate how the suites will look and help sell suites.

69. Work with architect to hire appropriate consultants such as construction managers.

70. Hire a graphic designer to prepare signs and graphic images of the new facility.

71. Ensure that the architect works with the developer throughout the construction process.

72-73. Solicit bids for construction, award the contract to the best builder or contractor, and begin physical construction.

74. Undertake site preparation such as clearing and grubbing.

75. Set foundation and slab-on-grade such as drilled piers.

76. Pour concrete structures such as columns and decks.

77. Install precast seating such as precast stair treads and risers.

78. Build roof structure.

79. Build enclosures such as masonry and glass.

80. Build interior partitions with masonry and drywall.

81. Install finishes such as carpentry, painting, and floor coverings.

82. Place fixed and movable seating.

83. Finish all suites.

84. Finish concession fit-outs for all cooking and service equipment.

85. Finish building parking garage.

86. Reach substantial completion of project, and complete punch list.

87. Obtain occupancy permit.

- Off-site variables (e.g., rivers, sewage treatment plants, industries)
- Safety factors (roads, buffer zones, sight lines, emergency access)
- Proper drainage for turf and hard-surface areas (flood zone area)
- Fencing and planting to serve as separation of areas
- Placement of service building for safety, control, and supervision (access for vehicles)
- Layout of walkways for safe and efficient circulation (must meet ADA requirements)
- Lighting of fields, courts, and general areas
- Cost of maintenance (preventive and corrective)
- Provision of first aid facilities, equipment, and supplies
- Taking advantage of existing topographic features, trees, and vegetation
- Accessibility and use of the site for the aging and disabled
- Use of durable and vandal-proof materials and equipment

The facility developer will also have to determine how all the building elements will fit together in the facility. This part of the design process allows for significant creativity—within the budget. A facility planning committee can develop numerous ideas and communicate these ideas to the architects and engineers. However, at some point the words need to be transformed into drawings that will hopefully adequately portray the desired results. Architects can help highlight the possible results through scale models and blueprints. A **scale model** is a miniature version of what the facility will look like. Construction documents, which include **blueprints** and written specifications, also show how the facility will look.

The facility design begins with a **site plan** that includes a number of separate drawings—the master site plan, grading plan, irrigation plan, landscape plan, traffic flow plan, and fencing plan. Additional plans include the building plan; floor plan; construction drawing; lighting plan; and specifications for all irrigation, lighting, fencing, recreation area (playground) equipment, buildings, and regular facility equipment.

The master site plan gives an overall view of how the finished facility will look on the site. The grading plan shows how the site will be leveled, where dirt will be moved, and what trees or natural areas will not be touched. The irrigation plan shows where sprinkler systems will be placed. The landscaping plan shows where shrubs, flowers, artwork, and even man-made streams may be located and how they may be incorporated into an overall landscaping strategy. The traffic flow plan indicates where cars will park and how roads will be designed to ease congestion and speed entry to and exit from the facility. The fencing plan indicates how natural boundaries and man-made fences will be incorporated to secure the property in the most aesthetic manner possible. The other plans show how different elements of the facility will fit together to produce the best design for accomplishing the facility's objectives safely and cost-effectively. An architect can help analyze numerous concerns during the design process to help maximize the building's value. For example, although it might be nice to build a very high ceiling, if more space can be created by expanding the building (length- or widthwise versus heightwise), a larger facility could possibly be built for the same cost. The architect can examine not just the design but also how much it will cost to operate a facility since a bigger facility requires possibly more janitorial costs compared with a tall building that might require more energy to circulate air.

Building Systems

Components in any facility include exterior enclosures from walls to roofs, windows, doors, and other elements such as skylights. The interior can include **vertical space dividers** such as walls and partitions, **horizontal space dividers** such as floors and ceilings, plumbing systems, HVAC systems, fire protection subsystems, electrical networks, communication systems, security systems, and **furniture, fixtures, and equipment (FEE)**. The numerous systems in a sport facility are covered in greater detail in chapter 7. However, it is important to note here that buildings, especially the technology-driven buildings of today, are not just a collection of walls. They are often as complex as the human body. There are miles of cables running throughout a building along with wood, steel, ductwork, and glasswork, among many other components. All these materials present design and construction challenges (construction is covered in chapter 6) that need to be analyzed during the planning process. For example, a glass wall may appear attractive, but the potential energy loss and cleaning costs may make such an option less attractive than a brick wall that requires very little maintenance and conserves a significant amount of energy.

In 2013, *Athletic Management* published a list of the top 25 innovations in indoor facilities (Read, 2013). Some of the top innovations according to this list include the following:

- Video in scoreboards to enhance the viewing and communication experience
- Bleacher seats that have full backs, cushions, cup holders, and so on
- Synthetic gym floors that are almost indistinguishable from wood floors
- Automated delivery of pool chemicals to help remove the chore of manually adjusting pool chemicals
- Energy-efficient lights, including high-efficiency fluorescent lamps and light-emitting diodes (LED)
- Antimicrobial locker rooms that help prevent methicillin-resistant *Staphylococcus aureus* (staph infections)
- Floor and wall graphics that can be stuck on almost any surface

Numerous other innovations have changed facility construction and facility management efforts. These changes often first appear in homes and then spread to larger facilities. Some of these innovations include the following:

- Ikea has developed modular homes (BoKlok) that are less than 800 square feet (74.3 sq m) and cost less than half that of traditional homes.
- Smart houses are being built where all the systems, such as sprinklers, water leak detection, thermostats, and variable lighting options, can be controlled through the Internet
- Flexible concrete that comes in sheets can help solve the issue of builders having to pour cement in place. The sheets are made with concrete powder sandwiched between two fabric surfaces linked by connected fibers. Once exposed to water, the sheets harden into concrete. The fibers provide reinforcement when the concrete dries.
- A complete new green city (Songdo, South Korea, which has more than 25,000 residents

so far) has a 100-acre central green space that requires no external water supply, and water taxis that run on saltwater canals are part of the public transportation system. Waste is removed through pneumatic tubes in all buildings, streets, and parks, and 95% of parking spaces are underground (Arndt, 2013).

Ancillary Facilities

One of the important considerations in the design process involves ancillary facilities. It is one thing to say that a gym will be built but another to specify what ancillary rooms or areas will be built around the gym. Those involved in the planning process will undoubtedly generate numerous ideas and, if the budget allows, many ideas will be incorporated when the facility is being designed since it is cheaper to build in the extra areas than to add them at a later date. Some of these adjacent areas could include locker rooms, coaches' offices, training rooms, exercise areas, media rooms, restrooms, storage areas, and equipment rooms.

One of the key factors in accurately determining the price for a structure is the details of the elements in the structure. For example, what size should the locker rooms be? How many lockers should be installed? How many toilets and shower stalls should be included? Each element costs money and needs to be examined before the construction process starts. The design process also affects the price (e.g., tile walls vs. marble walls).

There is no one correct calculation for proper facility construction standards or requirements. However, through significant research some organizations have developed guidelines to help in the facility design and planning process. One such association is the National Intramural-Recreational Sports Association, which published their research findings in *Space Planning Guidelines for Campus Recreational Sport Facilities* (Brown and Haines, 2009). The study highlights numerous potential guidelines. For example, a college campus building an indoor sport facility should have 228 assignable square feet (ASF) of locker room space for every 1,000 students on campuses with 3,000 to 9,999 students. Using this figure, a campus of 5,000 students building a new indoor facility would utilize approximately 1,140 ASF [5 (5,000 students divided by 1,000 since the number

is based on 1,000 students) × 228] for men's and women's locker rooms. Thus, the proposed new facility should have around 1,140 square feet (106 sq m) of locker room space equally divided between the men's and women's locker rooms (570 ASF each).

Some significant ancillary facility elements that present interesting design challenges include restrooms, roofs, and concession areas. The following examples of specific facility components show the types of issues and challenges that need to be considered when designing a facility.

Restrooms

People often do not think about what they really want in a restroom until they are sitting in a restroom. Maybe they would want the toilet paper dispenser to be closer to the toilet, or maybe they would like stall doors that actually lock. Restrooms and locker rooms have undergone significant transformation over the years. The number of people using lockers to store items has decreased. The number of stalls needed in women's restrooms has increased as the number of women attending events has increased. Industry formulas are used to help determine the optimal number of restroom stalls, sinks, drying stations, and so on to create the most efficient restroom and reduce cleaning time.

Users now demand better amenities and want green and family-friendly options. For example, baby changing stations have become an important addition to many restrooms. These changing stations cannot simply be pieces of wood; rather, they need to

- be equipped with full-length steel on steel hinges with 11-guage mounting supports,
- comply with any applicable regulations and be confirmed with third-party testing,
- have a smooth, concave surface without any pinch points,
- be constructed of high-density polyethylene with antimicrobial technology built in to prevent spread of disease or accumulation of bacteria, and
- have a built-in dispenser for sanitary bed liners.

Weight Rooms

Weight rooms have been transformed into warm and inviting places that include open areas, glass that lets large amounts of light in, equipment with monitors or televisions, and central attractions such as climbing walls. Some gyms, such as Anytime Fitness, have even replaced some employees with video monitoring from a central location that allows users to come in when they want rather than only during open hours. Although most owners cannot create large facilities without significant cash outlay, they can usually improve the environment in the space that already exists by making some simple renovations.

For example, flooring comes in a variety of colors and patterns and can be used to create unique designs in the weight room. A way to do this is to use one color for workout stations and another color for pathways (Sherman, 1997). The walls can also be painted various colors to generate a more relaxed atmosphere. However, too many colors can become overwhelming, confusing, and "noisy" and can decrease lighting effectiveness. Indirect lighting, or up-lighting, can help create a better and brighter environment. The downside of this approach is that more light fixtures are needed, compared with fluorescent lighting, to adequately light the room.

Repainting and replacing old padding on machines can give equipment a renewed look. The old paint must be sandblasted off the machine; then the machine is repainted and new padding is added. Using nontraditional or school colors when repainting the machines can give the room a personal feel (Sherman, 1997).

Noise-reduction decor can not only decrease the noise generated by clanking weights or loud music but also enhance the feel or look of an area. The concept of function over form does not mean that innovative approaches cannot be taken while designing a visually appealing environment for all users.

Roofs

Roofs are often viewed as a topper and are given little consideration. However, large sport facilities need large trusses that span the playing and seating areas. That is why roofs can cost up to 40% of the entire cost of a facility. Sometimes the roof works great. The retractable roof in Toronto's Rogers Centre was a construction miracle back in the 1980s and still runs without many problems. Other times a roof can generate more issues than expected. For example, during a tornado the roof of the Dallas Cowboys' practice facility collapsed, killing one coach and gravely injuring another. In another example, when the new Yankee Stadium opened the wind came off the roof line in such a strong manner that it interfered with high fly balls and generated a lot of home runs. Various strategies were considered to help decrease the rash of home runs that occurred right after the facility opened.

A roof can also pose a hazard to a facility during heavy winds. A strong gust can cause a roof to buckle and destroy the facility's structure. Designers of the 37,000-seat Marlins Park in Miami needed to build a retractable roof that would survive a hurricane. The roof was constructed with 8,000 tons of high-strength steel and consisted of three roof panels on rails. These panels are more than 530 feet (161.5 m) long and are moved on two horizontal concrete track beams that are 548 feet (167 m) apart and 750 feet (228.6 m) long. The roof can go from fully closed to fully open in 13 minutes. The roof panels remain slightly open during storms so the air pressure can dissipate. Designed to withstand a wind speed of more than 146 miles (235 km) per hour, the panels have four 3-yard (2.7 m) gaps that allow the air to flow in and out; these gaps help reduce the wind pressure by 25%. The gaps also helped the designers save $4 million in construction costs and an additional 1,000 tons of steel, which would have been required if there were no gaps in the roof ("A Smarter Roof," 2013).

Concessions

Concessions are a major revenue generator, so concession areas need to be built with money in mind. A sink placed too far away from a preparation area could be a health code violation, but it also would mean that employees need to spend more time preparing food, which means lost income. Similarly, concession areas need to be designed to help sell the most items possible in the shortest time period. Thus, concession areas often have a large number of point-of-purchase

AMERICAN AIRLINES CENTER

American Airlines Center, home of the National Hockey League Dallas Stars and the National Basketball Association Dallas Mavericks, is a fan-friendly complex utilizing the very latest technology. It was built after the failed attempt to get voter approval for an arena in Lewiston (highlighted earlier in this chapter). David M. Schwarz Architectural Services of Washington, D.C., was the primary entity responsible for creating the arena. Mr. Schwarz designed the center to evoke deco-tinged civic buildings from the 1920s and 1930s, complete with soaring arches, vaulted roofs, and square pilasters with streamlined concrete capitals (Dillon, 2002). The arena was built with four lobbies, one for each side of the facility. Although the design has no specific source, a person might see similarities to everything from a train station to an airline hangar.

The center was meant to be the heart of a new urban commercial area (called Victory Park) designed to reinvigorate the city of Dallas. Victory Park is a $3 billion, 75-acre (0.3 sq km), mixed-use development with more than 4,000 residences and 4 million square feet (371,600 sq m) of commercial and retail space (Victory Park, 2009). It's initial phase was built by Hillwood Development Company, a large company owned by Texas billionaire Ross Perot and his family and more buildings are under construction. Since the development is just a stone's throw away from downtown Dallas, the project needed to serve as a continuation of downtown. The location is between Interstate 35, Dallas North Tollway, and the Woodall Rodgers Freeway. Thus, it is conveniently located and next to an arts district. The site was part of a destination location and will continue to be an economic engine for downtown Dallas.

American Airlines Center revolutionized sport building systems, especially in terms of new technologies. Wrightson, Johnson, Haddon, and Williams was responsible for acoustics and noise control recommendations, design of the building's sound reinforcement system, design of all video systems including distributed television, the broadcast cable system, design of the low-voltage cable system, and the scoreboard and replay systems. The ceiling of the center is lined with acoustical tiles, nylon swags, and large flat-plane surfaces. Nylon swags absorb sound during concerts, and the planes direct fan noise back to the playing surface for sporting events. The ceilings and walls are covered with perforated vinyl and metal, giving sound a place to escape.

Video was also pushed to new levels. In January 2001, American Airlines Center awarded a $7.9 million digital signage package to Daktronics. The deal, which was one of the largest and most sophisticated in the world for a sport venue, provided an integrated scoring, video, and information display system. The unique scoreboard, which hangs 35 feet (10.7 m) above the playing surface, has eight sides and is 25 feet tall by 49 feet wide by 49 feet deep (7.6 by 15 by 15 m). It weighs 80,000 pounds (36,300 kg) and took eight cables to raise. Daktronics ProStar VideoPlus LED technology is incorporated in the scoreboard, which is a 68-billion-pixel color display system capable of showing video, animation, and graphics. Additional displays are located throughout the facility, including one continuous ring of full-color digital advertising technology that circles the entire inside of the arena on the platinum-level facade. American Airlines Center is the first venue to use high-definition wide-screen televisions throughout. The facility is also the first building to incorporate three major displays: the scoreboard, the end zone displays, and the 360° ring around the club level.

"The technology allows us to sell every item to every seat," said Martin Woodall, the Mavericks' representative on arena issues. "No other building does this" (Wrightson, Johnson, Haddon, and Williams, 2004).

Here are some key facts about American Airlines Center (Mooradian, 2001):

- 19,200 seating capacity for basketball
- 18,500 seating capacity for hockey
- 20,021 seating capacity for concerts
- 1,600 club seats
- 2,000 platinum seats
- More than 500 accessible seats
- 142 suites ranging in price from $150,000 to $300,000 per season
- 840,000 square feet (78,038 sq m)
- 24 ticket windows
- 12 escalators and 10 elevators
- 550 televisions throughout the facility
- 280 men's room urinals and 96 stalls
- 337 women's room stalls

In 2008 *Forbes* ranked American Airlines Center the fourth most lucrative arena in the United States. *Forbes* has not published an updated listing, but based on the total number of events held at American Airlines Center, the only two arenas in the world that could possibly top it are Madison Square Garden and Staples Center.

Photo courtesy of American Airlines Center

locations so orders can be processed quickly and lines are minimal. The optimal number of purchase processing locations can be calculated using a formula based on the latest industry research that examines how many people can purchase drinks in a given period. Chapter 15 covers the concession area in greater detail.

Other Areas

Calculations similar to those for restroom stalls and concession stands can be made for other facility components. One industry consultant recommends 8.5 to 10.5 gross square feet (0.8-1.0 sq m) per student as a base number for a recreation center. This number can be higher in small residential colleges where the students will use the center more frequently than on large urban campuses, where students may be members of other clubs. More space needs to be added to the base number for employees (1-1.5 gross square feet [0.09-0.14 sq m] per employee) and alumni and community members (5-7.5 gross square feet [0.46-0.70 sq m] per alumnus or community member) (Brailsford and Noyes, 2000).

Space concerns are also important in the design of office space, as people do not like small offices that may be hard to move around in. However, some offices can be built into gym walls that have glass windows so that employees who supervise the gym can see into the gym. In fact, many facilities have unique internal areas. At Ohio State University, among several other places, dorms have been built into the football stadium to maximize space usage.

Sport facilities also have numerous attributes not found in typical office buildings, such as family restrooms, luxury suites, bleachers, and audiovisual rooms. Some of the often overlooked adjacent areas that need to be planned in a sport facility are shipping and receiving (loading docks, storage, access to dumpsters, proximity to users and freight elevators), security (operations center, guard post, access to storage equipment), a mail distribution room, and food service (access to refrigeration and cooking equipment, vending locations, loading docks) (Cotts and Lee, 1992).

Layout

Regardless of the amenities or rooms being considered, all ideas need to be highlighted in the initial layout. Ancillary areas need to be included in the initial drafts since structural issues may be associated with these areas that can affect the facility. For example, the wiring, soundproofing, and viewing perch of a sound booth need to be developed with careful foresight. Architects often try to identify all the usable areas for the facility and then develop a way to link all these areas. They frequently use **common space** such as a foyer or an atrium from which usable spaces can be accessed. Areas can be linked by hallways, which are also a common space. Some areas in the facility will be dedicated to specific uses such as stairways, elevators, janitor closets, and storage closets.

Some of the additional concerns that architects analyze are as follows (Walker and Stotlar, 1997):

- Path of travel and distance an athlete would have to walk from one area to another, such as from a locker room or training room to the competitive area
- Noise from one area that can affect another area
- Security concerns between different areas
- The availability of storage rooms and janitorial closets
- Government regulations, such as Occupational Safety and Health Administration requirements that may affect placement
- Environmental surround concerns, such as rooms requiring windows or a view

No one correct layout exists. The key for layout is functionality. A design layout that maximizes movement (e.g., large concourses), provides the best viewing lines in the seating bowl, or functional placement of cardio machines in a fitness facility, for example, will represent appropriate layouts for those facilities

Blueprints

No matter what elements are eventually decided on by the facility developer, these concepts, elements, thoughts, and concerns will eventually need to be documented. It is best for an architect to have been involved with the facility planning process from the beginning. If not, all the ideas need to be boiled down to a written description showing how all the elements fit together. During

FACILITY FOCUS

THE NEW YANKEE STADIUM

Although the new Yankee Stadium in New York is beautiful, the $1.5 billion facility (the most expensive Major League Baseball stadium built to date) is right across the street from the old stadium and has identical dimensions. However, within days of opening, the complaints began pouring in. People were complaining about more than just the high cost of tickets behind home plate, which were selling for more than $2,000 a game. What was the biggest complaint? The wind. According to Yankees general manager Brian Cashman, "We're dealing with some phenomenon that we don't have our hands wrapped around" (Antonen, 2009). Within the first 23 home games, 87 home runs had been hit, making the park the favorite for long-ball batters throughout the league.

The culprit named by many is a jet stream to right field. Wind patterns are a critical element during the design phase, similar to sun movement patterns, rain, and other natural elements. The Yankees even conducted several wind analysis studies during the design phase and hired a specialized engineering firm to look at the issue before opening the stadium. Since public funds, along with private funds, were used in the construction process, opponents of the project started attacking the construction of a "bad stadium" (Antonen, 2009). After studying the stadium for several years, various "experts" concluded that the culprit was not wind but rather the height and shape of the right field wall. Wind can affect not only home runs but also the patrons' experience; fans do not like to watch baseball in swirling winds, under a scorching sun, or while wearing coats because of the cold weather. Fans for years braved the summer winds at Candlestick Park in San Francisco, where pins were given away in the 1990s to fans who were able to survive the cold temperatures and wind during extra-inning night games. The Yankees could possibly change the stadium's roof slope, add material to the roof to move the wind, or raise the outfield walls. In 1994, after the Texas Rangers opened their new stadium, they added a mesh windscreen to the roof to alter the wind. In Philadelphia and Houston, the teams had to increase the height of the outfield wall in response to the wind's effect on the number of home runs hit when the new ballparks were opened.

The Yankee Stadium example highlights how architects and builders can overlook or underestimate design issues even in the most expensive stadiums. Only when a facility is actually used will some of these flaws come to light.

The new Yankee Stadium has 52,325 seats (including some standing seats), which is 4,561 fewer seats than the old Yankee Stadium. In the old Yankee Stadium seats ranged from 19 to 22 inches (48.2-55.8 cm) wide, whereas seats in the new facility range from 19 to 24 inches (48.2-60.9 cm) wide, giving some fans more room to relax and enjoy the game (Dodd, 2009). When the stadium was unveiled the most expensive seats cost $2,625 per game. The lowest-priced tickets are $5 obstructed-view seats. Approximately 80% of the nonpremium seats sold for less than $100 per game. The Yankees sold all 52 of their full-season suites, generating revenue of between $600,000 and $850,000 per year.

The Yankees received $1.2 billion in tax-exempt bonds and $136 million in taxable bonds. Although the team paid for construction, the city owns the stadium. The Yankees deal was estimated to cost the city $362 million, but the financing structure allowed the Yankees to save $787 million over 40 years. Opponents estimated the cost to the public (including foregone property taxes) to be around $4 billion.

© Eco Images/UIG/age fotostock

this process, ideas may be scrapped or modified, and a site may even be ruled unfeasible because of design constraints. This process often entails multiple rounds in which changes and more changes are tinkered with to reach a final decision. It is best to have any changes identified and incorporated at this point in the process to reduce costly alterations when construction begins. When this review process is completed, a final set of drawings called the blueprints will emerge. Blueprints are increasingly created on computers to reduce paper waste and increase ease of access.

Blueprints are so named because the diagrams were initially made with white lines on a blue background. (Today the diagrams are made with blue or black lines on off-white paper, making it easier to write comments and notations.) Many diagrams are drawn for any given project, from broad depictions showing the building envelope to detailed mechanical drawings showing where all the plumbing components will be located. The plan view is a bird's-eye view from the top down of how the facility will look. In contrast, an elevated view is a view from street level showing what the outside walls will look like. The detail view drawings show internal elements such as individual rooms or stairways in detail. A sectional view is a detailed view of how a horizontal or vertical element will look when cut in half. This could be a drawing of metalwork or insulation inserted into a wall to provide appropriate reinforcement. This cutaway view in the sectional prints is used by the construction crews to construct building units pursuant to necessary strength or building code requirements. The mechanical view highlights the mechanical and electrical systems in the planned building. Last, the plot and survey lines show the boundaries of the property on which the building will be constructed (Borsenik and Stutts, 1997).

Summary

This chapter focuses on identifying the best possible site for building a sport facility. Although it is impossible to have a perfect location, a number of locations might be very good for an intended project. Each site needs to be evaluated based on variables such as size, cost, location, zoning concerns, and community impact.

With very strict state and federal laws affecting land use, some facility sites may not be appropriate because of environmental concerns. Soil tests are administered in the hope of finding a site with minimal cleanup needs. Sites can also be chosen based on the expense of elements needed to make the site usable, such as access to water, roads, and utilities, which can be expensive additions to any proposed site. After these variables are considered, each site needs to be evaluated based on the anticipated cost for completing the project on that particular site. After this analysis has been completed, a site is chosen and a facility is designed. Chapter 6 covers how the facility is actually built.

Discussion Questions and Activities

1. What would make the best facility site for a stadium?

2. What would make the best facility site for an arena? Is it different from a site that would be great for a stadium?

3. What concerns arise with government entities and proposed facility sites?

4. Examine a newly built facility and research issues that arose in choosing that site. What political, legal, and financial hurdles may have been encountered?

5. What are some arguments to make to convince local businesses and residents to support a planned arena or stadium in their community?

6. What design elements would you like to see in a community swimming or recreation center?

7. What do you think are the best design elements in an existing professional sport arena or stadium?

8. Create a search committee to find a prospective site in your area for a new all-purpose gym. Who would be on the committee, why, and where would you ultimately suggest building the facility?

9. Look for a parcel of land in your city that would be a good location for a new stadium or arena. What makes the choice of land favorable? What are some possible negative aspects of the choice?

6

Facility Construction

Chapter Objectives

- Appreciate how plans for building a structure are finalized.
- Understand the public bidding process often used to construct new facilities.
- Appreciate the elements involved in the construction process.
- Understand how to calculate construction costs.
- Know how to complete the construction process.

There are two primary ways to build a sport facility. The first is to determine how much money might be available for the project and then to fit the facility into the budget. Thus, if a school bond issue raises $2 million for a gymnasium, the school will have to make sure that the facility is constructed for less than this figure because it will still be necessary to purchase furnishings (chairs; special bleachers; basketball hoops; and other furniture, fixtures, and equipment). If the school does not have any other funds to dedicate to the construction process, then the options are very limited.

The other option, referred to as the **planned approach**, entails examining what is specifically needed and then developing an ideal facility within rough cost constraints. After a basic analysis has been completed, a detailed cost estimate can be developed. When all the component prices are roughly established, a facility developer can start eliminating items that have a low priority or are not feasible economically in order to fall within the potential budgetary constraints. This process is often referred to as value-based engineering. Unlike other approaches that are more reactionary and often produce a facility that is less than desired, the planned approach strives to utilize management prioritizations to allocate funds in a rational manner. This text emphasizes the planned approach of researching potential options and then developing a comprehensive building plan.

Although budgeting should have been analyzed in both the planning and design processes, costs are still a major issue in the construction process. Change orders, material discrepancies, union disputes, delays in material delivery, budget overruns—there are thousands of cost concerns that can cause price fluctuation. For example, the cost of metals such as steel and iron increased significantly from the late 1990s until 2007 due to an international building boom. However, the economic downturn reduced demand, and prices have fallen significantly. Thus, demand increased construction prices, and reduced demand reduced costs. A facility developer needs to appreciate these variables since prices can fluctuate significantly before, during, and after a construction project.

Assuming a reasonably stable budget, this chapter focuses on the process of building a sport facility. The chapter starts by analyzing site preparation procedures through the construction planning and preconstruction phases and then moves on to the foundation, frame, and roofing. The last sections cover project costs and completing the facility.

The facility construction process involves various elements decided through the planning and site selection processes. No one builds anything, whether a bookcase or a house, without detailed advanced planning, deciding on the right size, and obtaining the right materials. The following phases help put the construction process in the proper context with issues previously discussed and those covered later in the text:

Programming Phase

- Deciding what to build
- Examining space, cost, and other criteria
- Deciding what events will be held at the facility, including capacity and amenities issues
- Deciding the number and location of food and beverage preparation and sales areas
- Finalizing support areas that will be needed

Design Phase

- Designing the facility with architects
- Preparing schematic drawings and cost estimates
- Developing the design and adding details such as heating, ventilation, and air conditioning (HVAC) systems
- Reviewing and verifying the documents
- Reviewing operations to ensure that systems will operate as intended
- Preparing construction, legal, and bidding documents

Construction Phase

- Awarding the contract after checking references and qualifications of all parties
- Developing the construction schedule through substantial completion of the facility
- Completing the construction process and change orders
- Going through the inspection process

Beebe: Collaborating for Success in Facility Construction

Photo courtesy of Thomas Beebe

My name is Thomas Beebe, and I have been involved in facility planning, facility management, program management, and construction for more than 35 years. I am currently the senior program manager for Arcadis U.S. Incorporated, a large facility design, planning, and facility consultancy company. Before joining Arcadis I was the director of business development for Petra Construction Corporation, which assisted the University of New Haven in more than 35 projects that ranged from cost estimation and program management to construction of the David A. Beckerman Recreation Center. At the time, this was the single largest construction project in the university's history at 56,504 total square feet (5,249 sq m), providing fitness and recreation space for students, staff, and faculty. The highly visible project exceeded all expectations and is the focal point on campus.

We were intimately involved in the project from inception, translating to a higher-quality process and product. It is critical for the owner, design professionals, and construction manager to collaborate as soon as possible to identify a clear scope of work, budget, and schedule.

It is equally important to effectively lead the process, especially since there are a multitude of ongoing issues and decisions that require a very organized and structured approach. Team leadership can be from the owner or in this case the program manager. In simple terms, the ongoing challenges can be characterized as follows:

- Clearly define the issue.
- Identify and evaluate the options.
- Make informed decisions as they affect quality, cost, and schedule.

The recreation center presented some unique challenges. The soil was not stable enough to support the massive building, and the best solution was to install more than 250 aggregate piers (holes drilled in the soil and filled with compacted rock). Surplus soil was reused elsewhere on campus at a substantial cost savings. Input from students, staff, and faculty was critical. University representatives from voice, data, security, and audiovisual departments provided key input early in the design phase to ensure appropriate design and cost analysis. As the design progressed, Petra and the design professionals evaluated the most cost-effective structural steel and glass systems for this application.

At the end of each design phase, a detailed soft cost analysis was completed by the program manager, while the construction manager completed construction cost estimates based on input from subcontractors. This important process provided the owner with an accurate snapshot of the anticipated total project costs and schedule.

The project was initially over budget. The university was presented with specific options to either eliminate some program elements from the building (jogging track and racquetball courts) or increase the budget. The budget was increased because the program elements were considered very important to the use of the building.

The project team met twice a week throughout the project to analyze constructability and identify cost reduction opportunities. It is important to recognize the use of durable materials and quality workmanship in the building, particularly with respect to operating expenses. Facility management should collaborate with the project team to offer their perspective on materials and maintenance. The large lighting fixtures over the three courts were designed to be switched at three different light levels to conserve energy. The mechanical systems were fine-tuned for maximum value, and the local utility company participated in project team meetings to advise the team on available rebates.

The world of design and construction is undergoing a major evolution. The design professionals and the builder must be the appropriate fit for the project, and the process must be based on collaboration, trust, and synergy. It is critical to implement teams and processes that will result in the best buildings at the highest possible value to the owner. To accomplish these objectives, the owner must be very clear about the program and must make timely and informed decisions, all while actively engaged as a focused and informed member of the project team.

Occupancy Phase

- Finishing, including completing punch lists
- Obtaining the occupancy permit
- Doing facility maintenance and renovations

CONSTRUCTION PLANNING

Chapter 4 covers some of the planning issues that affect the facility. However, once the facility design, style, and site are chosen, several steps still need to be taken before construction actually begins. During the construction planning phase, the first question is who is going to build the facility. There are several issues to examine when deciding on the final builder, such as reputation, the final cost, and the construction contract.

Builders

Every project, including public facilities, has an owner. Owners can build the facility themselves if they have the resources. A government entity that has a public works department may have all the construction personnel already on the payroll to build a facility. This can save time and money compared with the situation in which owners must hire each trade group needed. Private owners may have a designated builder that has worked with them in the past and is willing to build the sport facility. However, the primary step to be taken by a facility owner is to interview several builders, obtain several price quotes, and then select the builder. Owners who do not want to be involved in the process can hire a consultant, construction manager, or contractor to manage the building process. An **owner's representative** is the middle person between the owner and those who will build the facility, such as the architects, construction managers, and contractors. No one approach is best. The approach taken depends on variables such as the owner's intended involvement, budget size, and time frame, among others.

Public projects are significantly different from owner-constructed facilities. In the latter case, the owners can choose whomever they wish to design and build the facility. Almost all public projects must go through the bidding process. The bidding process may come into play in the planning process as various architectural, consulting, or design companies are examined.

Project Bids

One of the first elements in the bidding process is the **request for qualifications** (RFQ). The RFQ helps determine which companies meet the minimum requirements for building the facility. This does not mean that a given company will construct the building; rather, it determines which companies will move on to the next round, in which financial and other variables are analyzed. Most states require by law that professional services be procured based on qualifications, not necessarily price. Normally, RFQs determine the best company to assist with tasks such as developing the master plan; consulting projects such as feasibility studies or soil testing; architectural, engineering, or design services; construction management; or facility management.

RFQs are typically published in the legal sections of the newspaper to provide appropriate public notice. The RFQs may contain written descriptions mailed to past contractors with the municipality; these letters contain a project summary, a detailed analysis of services being requested, detailed explanation of the expected deliverables, and possible submission requirements or selection criteria. Potentially interested companies are often invited to attend a walk-through in which they can examine a potential facility or site.

Besides the cost to advertise an RFQ, the bid package itself can be expensive. It can cost $300 to print the documents (specifications and drawings) for a typical bid set. Bidders are often asked to put down a deposit that covers the printing costs; they will obtain a refund after a winner is chosen. Regardless of what process is used, the expense needs to be considered, and a reprographic business needs to be consulted to make copies for any potential bidders. The bidder may have to pick up other costs with no guarantee of ever getting any contracts. It is not uncommon for a company to submit numerous bids and qualifications during a year and receive only a limited number of actual projects, if any.

In addition to RFQs, there are **requests for proposals** (RFP) and **requests for bids** (RFB), which are basically the same. Both request particular action; for example, an RFP can ask a company how it would propose solving a problem or what

BUILDER CRITERIA

Although there is no one correct list of expected experience or skills for any company responding to an RFQ, RFP, or RFB, the following are some basic concerns:

- Length of company existence (to determine staying power if something goes wrong)
- Relevant project experience (have they built something similar in the past)
- Expertise and experience of engineering staff
- Experience with other companies already working with the facility planners

- Past experience working for the municipality
- Staff experience on similar projects
- State or other required licensure (both firm and personal licenses) .
- Existence of required elements such as insurance or local office
- Technical competence
- Letters of recommendation
- Past record of coming within budget
- Past experience with problems and how they were resolved

price it would charge to build the facility. Sometimes an RFQ produces a list of several qualified companies, and those qualified companies receive an RFB and are asked to bid on a project. "Builder Criteria" lists criteria for determining who might get the bid.

The bidding process requires significant give and take. The owner or management team must know what other major projects are going up for bid, must give potential bidders enough time to submit a bid, should not set a submission date before major holidays, and should require a bid bond that would prevent the winning bidder from backing out (Kocher, 2007). Not providing enough time for bids can cause inaccuracies in bids, which can result in increased future costs. An owner needs to know what other projects a builder is engaged in to determine whether the builder is stretched too thin to complete the work.

A bid is often the starting point for negotiations and developing a contract. However, the bid can be modified and redeveloped during the construction process as issues or concerns arise.

Contracts

The person or business that wins the bid or is awarded the contract normally meets with the facility developer to finalize a contract and all the associated terms. Each entity involved has to understand its role in the construction process.

Facility developers often feel entitled to do whatever they want with the facility when it is being built. However, any efforts on their part to change the facility design during the construction process often result in large time delays and increased costs.

To help deal with this concern, specific contractual relationships need to be developed. The options available are listed next. The advantages and disadvantages of some of the options are outlined in table 6.1.

- Pay a lump sum for the construction so the total costs are known at the start. If costs rise, however, the quality might have to decline.

- Pay a set cost plus a fixed fee to the contractor as his profit. The contractor knows he will earn his profit, so he will try to build the facility under budget and try to avoid cutting corners.

- Hire a construction manager or general contractor to serve on the developer's behalf, and give that person the financial authority to complete a project. The construction manager handles all the details and is an advocate for the developer, so he works to reduce costs and save as much money as possible through value engineering and getting multiple bids from subcontractors.

- Hire a construction company to complete the project for a guaranteed maximum price.

■ Enter into a **turnkey contract** in which a construction company builds the facility with very little input from the future owner; when the construction is completed, the construction company turns the keys of the new building over to the new owner.

■ Enter into a **design–build contract**, which is similar to the turnkey process with the exception that the owner rather than the builder provides the land and may control the schedule and budget (Bentil, 1989).

A conventional design–bid–build system uses a designer and a general contractor, and numerous subcontractors help complete the project. A design–build system consists of two parties: the owner and the design–build firm that works with the owners from the construction phase through completion of the project.

Each system has pros and cons depending on the owner's needs, budget, and capabilities. The choice of which system to use is affected by factors such as how the owner will pay, the proposed completion date, the terms that parties are willing to agree to in a contract, the contract incentives that parties demand, and how pricing issues are handled. Most parties try to reach a middle ground that benefits everyone. Thus, an architect will not propose expensive external elements that might look nice but are out of the project's budget. This is where value engineering and related strategies come into play.

If a construction manager/general contractor (CM/GC) is used, he or she needs to be involved in the very earliest phases of the construction process—most frequently, in a private facility, during the planning process. As the party responsible for final construction and for hiring the subcontractors, the CM/GC can collaborate more effectively with all other parties, including the developer and architect. The CM/GC can also help with reducing budgeting and scheduling restraints since he or she is involved from the beginning and represents the developer. The CM/GC is also a facilitator to ensure that the design, schedule, cost, and "buildability" issues are working smoothly.

One of the requirements of starting the construction process is often some form of guarantee that the work will be completed. Although contracts provide some form of protection, they

Table 6.1 Advantages and Disadvantages of Various Construction Options

Construction option	Advantages	Disadvantages
Lump sum	• Fixed price • Owner in control of quality and of operation and management (O&M) • A single responsible contractor	• Lengthy process • Numerous revisions over time • Effect of cost escalation most severe • Contractor and owner or designer not necessarily working together
Construction management	• Effect of price escalation reduced • Construction management works as owner's agent • Owner in control of quality and of O&M • Design construction time reduced	• Total cost not known until construction started • Extra costs when modifications made
Guaranteed maximum price	• Complete plans can be finished later • Maximum price known from start • Owner in control of quality and of O&M • Design construction time reduced	• Any changes increase costs • Contractor and owner or designer not necessarily working together • High contractor's profit margin
Turnkey	• Complete plans not necessary • Price fixed at start • Design construction time reduced	• Hard for owner to make changes • Contractor and owner or designer not necessarily working together • Less say on quality and O&M • High contractor's profit margin

Modified from Cotts and Lee 1992.

are worthless if the construction company goes out of business or has multiple shell companies to hide its money. One step that can be taken to avoid this problem is to have construction bonds or insurance that pays the facility owner if the builder or general contractor fails to perform. In one example in Connecticut, a city hired a pool builder to build the city pool. As part of the construction bid requirement, the builder was required to post a $950,000 bond. The project faced significant delays and cost increases. The contractor blamed the delays and cost increases on the rocks found on the site. On the basis of the delays, the town council voted that the contractor was in default. Such a step was required in order to start the process of collecting on the performance bond (Gannon, 2002).

PRECONSTRUCTION PHASE

Besides finalizing the builder and any contractual issues such as construction bonds or liquidated damages clauses to penalize a builder that does not finish construction on time, several additional steps need to be taken before actual construction begins. For example, preconstruction meetings are held to make sure the architect or engineer, owner representative, contractors, and other parties are all on the same page. Does each party have all necessary resources and personnel to complete its tasks, especially if these may be needed in a sequential manner? No project runs without glitches. However, some glitches are more expensive than others. If a roofing crew is supposed to begin installing the roof starting on July 1 but the trusses are not completed on that date, the crew could be waiting around for the trusses to be completed, all having to be paid. The workers must be available because if they move to a different job, there is no guarantee they will be available when the trusses are finally up—delaying the project even more and incurring even more expenses. Thus, all the parties (including project managers, superintendents, engineers, architects, laborers, carpenters, subcontractors, material suppliers, equipment suppliers, consultants such as surveyors, professionals such as lawyers, and even city or municipal building inspectors) need to work together on a set schedule. Even with a set schedule, there will always be delays caused by workers not showing up on time, inclement weather, materials not arriving, or inspectors being on vacation. That is one reason why builders and owners need to set aside contingent schedules and funds for any and all potential delays.

Documentation

Also important in this phase is making sure that all the proper documentation is available to all parties. The preconstruction documents that are needed, in addition to the construction contract, include what are commonly referred to as contract drawings. Among these are the following:

- Site drawings, which provide information on the geographic location, how the project contours to the land, any roads and parking lots, and where current and future utilities will be placed
- Architectural drawings, which show the floor plans from the lowest to the highest floor
- Structural drawings, which depict all the supporting systems such as foundations, columns, floor systems, roof systems, and other elements in great detail (e.g., where pieces should be welded together and how)
- Plumbing drawings, which depict the water distribution system from piping to fixtures
- Mechanical drawings, which provide information about the HVAC system (e.g., the location of ductwork and where heating and air conditioning units will be placed)
- Electrical drawings, which show the electrical and electronic demands for the building and placement of electrical and electronic fixtures (Bentil, 1989)

Once all the documents and parties are ready, the construction process can begin. The first step is site preparation.

Site Preparation

Building contractors cannot just start building on a site. They first need to establish a field office and then build an access road for equipment and materials to reach the site. Next, the rough grade of the site needs to be evaluated. This may entail removing existing buildings, utilities, vegetation, and other impediments to construction. The process of removing tree stumps, bushes, and other

CONSTRUCTING AND MAINTAINING A BASEBALL OR SOFTBALL FIELD

It is important to hire an experienced general contractor and architect. Any contractor who has ever moved dirt says that she is capable of following a grading plan and constructing fields. Potential architects will also claim that a field is a minor project for them. However, there are many nuances to the grading plan, irrigation system, and other systems that directly affect the facility's quality for years to come. Anyone interested in building a baseball or softball field should ask potential general contractors and architects for references concerning fields they have actually built and then question the maintenance person who takes care of those fields to ensure that the fields are functioning properly.

Various Field Layouts

What is a great infield? The standard and accepted softball infield is a "skinned" surface which is a flat dirt infield. A dirt surface is easier to maintain than a grass surface and holds up better under the extensive use a field receives. The actual mix of dirt used depends on the facility's location. Various clays and mixes can be purchased, but over the long term the field will end up with indigenous materials of some sort, such as clay if clay is commonly found in that region. The facility developer should choose material that is free from rocks and small pebbles and then properly apply and maintain it. A properly maintained clay and sand mix will result in a first-class infield.

The infield cannot be too hard or too dry. Players' cleats should be able to penetrate the surface and leave an imprint without displacing a lot of soil. The quality of the infield dirt is based on the infield mix (sand, silt, and clay) used and how it is maintained (water usage, dragging, grooming, and using soil conditioners). A properly constructed and managed infield contains 60% to 80% sand, 20% to 30% silt, a smaller amount of clay, and a very small amount of gravel. The skin surface should be 4 to 6 inches (10.2-15.2 cm) deep. Heavily used areas, such as batter's boxes and the pitcher's mound, use soil that is heavier in clay or use unfired clay bricks that are at least 35% clay because regular infield sand is not stable or durable enough. Fields in rainy climates normally use more sand and thus have around 19% silt and clay; this allows water to drain more quickly. In contrast, dry regions require more silt and clay to help the water drain more slowly. Some field builders recommend using up to 20% clay to go along with 20% silt and 60% sand. The more clay used, the more likely that the infield mix will compact and get hard.

No matter what percentages of different elements are used in the infield mix, the field needs to be constructed with a grade to help water run off and away from the field. The typical field should have a 0.5% to 1.5% slope away from the center of the infield similar to a crown on a football or soccer field.

The infield will change throughout the year. A well-maintained field requires watering, scarifying and dragging, leveling, lip removal, and conditioning. How frequently these maintenance procedures are performed will depend on the infield mix used, particle size, dryness, weather, and field usage. Water is the most important element. More water is needed to soften fields with high silt and clay content, whereas less water is used on coarse, textured mixes that contain more sand.

The top of the infield mixture is a loose layer, about 0.25-inch (0.6 cm) thick, called the cap. This area requires the most grooming and care—including periodic scarification, leveling, and smoothing of the skin surface—because any imperfections or disruptions in the cap can cause a ball to bounce the wrong way. A weighted item (e.g., a wood board) with nails in it is dragged across the skin to loosen the top 0.25 to 0.5 inch (0.6-1.3 cm) of the infield mix. This broken-up material is then leveled to help prevent puddles and increase drainage. After leveling, a steel drag, or cocoa mat, is then dragged across the cap to groom the surface for play. Such a thorough process improves drainage, safety, and playability and helps prevents lips (mounds or ridges of dirt between the infield and the turf). To prevent lips, the 1-foot (30 cm) area on either side of the turf needs to be groomed by hand. Stiff-bristle brooms are used to move infield mixture from the turf back into the infield. This practice can also be undertaken with leaf blowers, irrigation hoses, or power washers.

Conditioners are materials that are spread on top of the skin surface to help improve playability and address weather conditions. One of the most common conditioners is calcined clay, which is heated to 1,200 °F to form granules of clay that remain hard even when exposed to water. Finer calcined clay is often spread on the skin surface during wet weather to help absorb water on the infield. After a game the clay can be swept up, dried, and reused.

Drainage is a major consideration in the construction of infields. The infield must be crowned to induce drainage, but more important is a regular schedule of infield dragging patterns so that material is not constantly being dragged off the infield. There is no one set pattern, but the dragging should try to evenly distribute the infield material rather than pushing the infield material to the lip of the outfield grass. The problem areas around home plate and the bases should also be properly maintained and dragged in a pattern that is consistent with the rest of the infield.

A second issue that is rarely addressed is the cut of the infield dirt. The cut is the distance of the radius around the pitcher's rubber at which the outfield grass starts. Baseball and softball have gone to a livelier ball, that is; a ball with a core allowing more pop when it is hit, and the bases have been moved back. Although some baseball sanctioning bodies now recommend a 65-foot (20 m) radius for the grass cut, some facility developers recommend a minimum of a 75-foot (23 m) cut. This solves some of the grass maintenance problem, as it decreases the size and cost of the irrigation system and maintenance, and provides some additional flexibility for women's events.

The turf in the infield and outfield is another concern. Due to the numerous concerns associated with grass fields, artificial turf has grown in popularity. More than 1,000 synthetic turf fields are built every year. The primary benefits of synthetic turf fields are the savings in money and time. A grass field requires around 700,000 gallons (2,649,788 L) of water each year for irrigation and 15 to 20 pounds (6.8-9 kg) of fertilizer per 1,000 square feet (92.9 sq m), plus herbicides, pesticides, and hours spent on mowing and maintenance. In contrast, synthetic turf contains a significant amount of oil-based products, and some product opponents claim the infill contains hazardous chemicals and are volatile when exposed to heat. Around 25 million used tires help produce the infill material used on synthetic fields ("Athletic Fields," 2009). A typical grass field can be used for around 15 years before needing to be replaced, whereas a synthetic turf field usually lasts around 10 years.

A second consideration when constructing the outfield is warning tracks to warn players they are getting close to the wall or fence. Lawsuits have been filed against complexes without warning tracks after players have run into fences. Warning tracks also have some practical, cost-saving effects: They cut down on the cost of the irrigation system and maintenance of turf, provide access for the occasional vehicle that must cut across the field, are easily maintained, and add prestige to the complex. The material used on the warning tracks does not need to be scrutinized as closely as that used in the infield. A crushed-rock mix that absorbs water is most appropriate. The critical concern is keeping the warning track and infield substances separate so that the infield is not contaminated with the substance from the warning track. Warning tracks are generally constructed using the same material as dirt parking lots and walkways because this option is inexpensive.

Maintenance and Irrigation

After a field is built, it needs to be maintained or it will deteriorate very quickly. Holistic integrated pest management can reduce costs and exposure to toxic chemicals. Water the lawn no more than three times a week. Overseed in the fall and use weed killers in the spring; weeds cannot emerge through thick, healthy grass. Using native and other climate-friendly grasses can help the field resist droughts and can reduce water use by up to 50%.

Steps that can be taken to improve a turf field include the following:

1. Test the soil on a regular basis using 20 to 30 core samples from all over the field to ensure that the right fertilizers are used.

2. Fertilize the turf. Fertilization is often the most important component of healthy turf and can help produce a dense, dark-green turf that resists pests and environmental stresses.

3. Mow two to three times a week to keep the grass around 2 inches (5 cm) tall. Keep the mower blades sharpened.

4. Aerate the field twice a year. Aeration is the process of disturbing the soil to relieve compaction, which inhibits air, water, and nutrients that are essential to grass root growth.

5. Utilize topdressing (the addition of sand or soil to the surface of the turfgrass to help improve soil quality) to improve the seedbed for future grass seeds, and level the playing surface.

6. Overseed in the late winter, early spring, or early fall. Seeds need to be in contact with the soil and have space to germinate. Perennial ryegrass is often the best seed for overseeding because it can germinate quickly.

7. Make the playing surface as flat as possible to prevent puddles.

8. Take special care with transition areas (e.g., where the grass meets the infield, where players run on and off the field) to ensure that they do not have lips, dips, or other safety hazards.

Effective turf maintenance requires proper watering, fertilizing, aerating, and mowing. Of these elements, water is the most critical. The type of irrigation system is determined by the facility's climate; however, all facilities require some sort of automatic irrigation system. The sprinkler systems with smaller heads are safer and better suited for the playing surface than systems with large heads. Skimping on the irrigation system can be a serious error.

Some options that can be included in the irrigation system are an automatic clock, a computer monitor, and a sensor system. The automatic clock is not really optional as it is an integral part of the irrigation system; any system without a clock is inadequate. The clock should provide watering in the various cycles during the hours the fields are not in use. The size of each station can be determined by the professional who designs the irrigation system. It is of course vital that the complete watering cycle be accomplished within 8 to 12 hours so it does not interfere with games.

A sensor system is very cost-effective in areas where irrigating can be expensive. A sensor system shuts off a station when it determines that the root system has received adequate water. These systems can cost around $3,000 per field and result in a highly efficient use of water. A sensor-based system can produce a 30% to 50% reduction in water consumption. It also eliminates overwatering and the accompanying maintenance problems.

A final consideration for the irrigation system is to install couplers within the dirt portion of the infields, located so hoses can water down the dirt in the infield and then be removed for play. The most common maintenance problem

(continued)

in the dirt areas is lack of water. Couplers or faucets allow the field maintenance staff to bring a hose to the center of the field and water the infield.

One new development throughout baseball and softball are fields that use turf rather than dirt infields. The Cal Ripken Experience (Myrtle Beach, South Carolina), Baseball Heaven (Yaphank, New York), Kean University, Emerson College, and even some high schools have all adopted completely turf field designs. One turf, at Salisbury University, has mixed a turf infield with a real grass outfield.

---

undergrowth is called **grubbing** and is normally accomplished fairly quickly with a bulldozer. Existing buildings can be more complicated. Tearing down some old stadiums has required a significant amount of explosives. Other facilities may have asbestos or other hazardous components that may require care, money, and time to abate.

Soil boring is then undertaken to determine if the soil is suitable for the proposed foundation. Core drilling, covered in chapter 5, can include testing of the subsoil strength. Testing for contaminants or rocks often does not go as deep as strength testing to determine how deeply cement pylons may have to be sunk to ensure a strong support. Through the boring process, a contractor can determine the presence of rock, organic materials, or a water table that can affect the foundation. After the clear surface for the site is exposed, earthwork operations begin. Earthwork includes stripping the existing topsoil, mass excavation or filling (site grading), building excavation, and backfill (Bentil, 1989). Typically, the first 4 to 6 inches (10-15 cm) of a site is removed, unless a facility existed on the same site in the past, because it is not a suitable base on which to build a foundation. The area that needs to be cleared is the **building area**, which is defined as 5 feet (1.5 m) beyond the limits of the proposed structure.

Normally the ground is not flat but has dips, valleys, hills, mounds, and other irregularities. A topographic survey of the site will show all these contours and help the contractor determine what areas need to be lowered or filled so that the site will be properly graded for supporting the foundation. The grading plan was discussed in chapter 5. Rough grading is the initial movement of clay, earth, gravel, or sand; fine grading is the smoothing of the site to a finished surface.

If a hole needs to be dug to support the foundation, or for a basement, garage, elevator shaft, or substories for a structure, the contractor will need to excavate the site. This process often entails using earth-moving equipment and hauling the materials off site.

The contractor can utilize machine excavation (trenching machines, bulldozers, and excavators) or hand excavation. During the excavation process the contractor may run into water and then will need to engage in dewatering, or extracting water. Water can be removed through pumping the water out directly, pumping the water from one pit to another, draining the water to a lower elevation, or installing a permanent pumping system (Bentil, 1989).

After the site is at the appropriate level, the soil is chemically treated to prevent insects such as termites. Utilities are also added at this point, and some of the basic landscaping may be completed at this time.

CONSTRUCTION ELEMENTS

Building a facility is similar to putting together a jigsaw puzzle. Most people put a puzzle together by looking at the picture on the box to see what the puzzle should look like. They then sort the pieces with edges and put the frame together. After the frame is in place the inside can be completed. Similarly, the construction process for a public assembly facility typically starts with examining the plans, building a foundation for a solid structure, creating the external shell, and then completing the interior. The construction process must include examination of the material used for the facility's base, the exterior components, and then the interior elements.

In the future, stadiums might be built in weeks rather than years. New construction methods allow main boards to be built at a factory and installed at the site. The boards come with everything—water pipes, ventilation shafts, floor tiles, lights, and even toilets—already assembled. A 30-story building was recently built in China using this technology, and there was no need for welding, water, or dust at the construction site. More impressively, the building was put together on site in less than 360 hours (15 days). This process cuts construction site waste down by almost 99%. The buildings are more energy efficient because they have preinstalled thermal insulation and use four-pane windows, and they have much better air quality.

Foundation Materials

Before examining the foundation, it is important to understand the basic construction material that will be used throughout the construction process. Wood is one of the materials most commonly used since it can be easily shaped or cut to size. Wood is typically used for joists, columns, posts, beams, and trusses. If the wood is laminated, which provides greater strength, it can also be used for rigid frames, arches, vaults, and other areas requiring significant strength. Most lumber is categorized by size—for example, 2 by 4 inches (5 by 10 cm) and 4 by 4 inches (10 by 10 cm)—and grade, which refers to its quality.

Concrete is one of the most frequently seen construction materials because it is not flammable, is highly versatile, and is relatively inexpensive. Cement (or Portland cement) is made of silica, lime, slag, flute dust, and alumina. These ingredients are mixed, heated, cooled, and pulverized, and then the powder is sold either in bulk or in bags. Combining cement with water, sand, gravel, crushed stone, and other inert items makes concrete. Concrete is rated by its strength after it has been allowed to cure (harden) for a 28-day period. Concrete that will be exposed to freezing elements, such as in sidewalks, needs to have a strength of about 4,000 pounds per square inch (psi). Stronger concrete can reach a strength of 19,000 psi (Bentil, 1989). Since concrete can suffer from tension and shear, reinforced steel is often placed in designated locations to strengthen it. Concrete can be cast in place (poured on the spot) or precast (formed at a different location and then trucked to the spot where it will be erected), or it can take the form of masonry such as concrete blocks, which are used for load-bearing walls. Precast concrete is high quality due to the controlled manufacturing conditions in the factory, and it allows workers to very rapidly erect and construct elements on site. Entire buildings—including walls, floors, beams, and so on—can be precast.

In addition to concrete, walls can be made of bricks, stones, rocks, and other inert hard compounds. Concrete pavement is commonly seen in sidewalks, but, as shown in table 6.2, not all pavements are the same. The initial cost and life expectancy of building materials are critical factors to consider in both the design and construction phases.

Structural steel is often used to frame a building. Steel can lose strength over time because of corrosion or when exposed to severe heat, as evidenced in the 9/11 tragedy. Steel is produced from three basic materials: iron, ore, and limestone.

Table 6.2 Comparative Cost and Longevity of Different Pavement Types

Pavement type	Approximate installed cost ($/ft^2)	Estimated service life (yr)
Asphalt (conventional)	0.10-1.50	7-20
Concrete (conventional)	0.30-4.50	15-35
Porous asphalt (water penetrable)	2.00-2.50	7-10
Pervious concrete (water penetrable)	5.00-6.25	15-20
Paving blocks	5.00-10.00	20+
Grass/gravel paving	1.50-5.75	10+

Adapted from Gregerson 2010

Steel is often used to help carry the vertical and horizontal loads of the structure to the foundation. Steel columns can support elevated concrete slabs on higher floors because of the strength that steel possesses.

Just because a facade can comprise almost any solid material does not mean that even the strongest material works well. The facade of Barclays Center was built with weathered steel panels that were attached using bolts. This task was made more difficult because each steel panel was individually fabricated. Iron workers had to replace hundreds of bolts that anchored the panels to the building's structure because the bolts initially used were too weak. After examining every joint, engineers determined that 8% (1,768) of the 23,351 weaker bolts needed to be replaced. The fabricator had incorrectly sent 0.625-inch (1.6 cm) bolts that were half as strong as the bolts that had been ordered (Bagli, 2013).

These examples show the breadth of construction materials that can be used. New materials are constantly being developed, and the growth in energy-efficient materials will continue to expand the types of materials available. For example, building blocks made of plastics or other recycled products can have as much strength as concrete blocks.

Substructure and Load

Once the types of materials are known, it is easier to appreciate the various elements that make up the structure's lowest levels. The level at and below ground level is called the **substructure**. The substructure helps transfer the **structural load** from a building into soil or rocks for the safest base possible. The substructure is typically made of a slab-on-grade and a foundation. (The process is called slab-on-grade if a concrete floor placed directly on the ground can support the structure.) The slab of concrete is poured over a polyethylene sheet (commonly called Visqueen), which is laid over crushed gravel or stone to prevent moisture from penetrating the concrete and getting into the structure. The slab is usually reinforced with steel-wire mesh to provide additional strength.

The foundation transfers the building weight (load) to the earth below. Several types of load need to be carried. Dead load refers to the total weight of the entire building including frame, walls, floors, roof, and foundation. Live load includes all the people, furnishings, equipment, and elements such as rain or snow on the roof. The live and dead loads are carried down to the foundation through columns. The columns can be set in either a shallow or a deep foundation. A shallow foundation utilizes "footers" to transfer the load to the earth below the foundation. However, if the earth below the foundation is not strong enough, a deep foundation may be used. A deep foundation transfers the load deep into the ground to bedrock if the subgrade surface is not strong enough. This deep transfer is completed utilizing piles sunk into the ground; the piles are made of timber, concrete, or steel (Bentil, 1989). To ensure that the piles provide a stronger base, they are often driven into the ground in clusters and then capped.

Superstructure

The previous element deals with the ground level and everything underneath that supports the structure. The **superstructure** is everything above the substructure and includes the framing, columns, beams, and trusses. Framing can be made with steel, concrete, wood, or masonry. The various materials can be formed at another location and then set, bolted, welded, or connected on site. Concrete is often poured in liquid form to be cured and finalized in place. Cast-in-place concrete requires significant planning for formwork, which consists of creating the molds used to contain the poured concrete. Formwork is the critical component for holding poured concrete in its intended shape and can amount to about one-third of the cost of the overall concrete work. Table 6.3 lists the cost percentage breakdown of various components in a complete concrete-framed building.

Exterior Components

In addition to the frame, the **support** is an integral component of the construction process. The support is also referred to as the exterior closure, building skin, or envelope. This element, which is often the most expensive, not only serves as an external barrier to the elements but can also serve as a structural element such as a load-bearing wall.

Table 6.3 Cost Percentage Breakdown of a Concrete-Framed Building

Component	Percentage
Form labor to make the concrete mold	28
Concrete	24
Reinforcing steel materials	19
Placing labor	11
Reinforced steel labor	11
Form material	7

From Bentil 1989.

The exterior can be made of wood, cement, metal, or other materials, often covered first by a waterproofing material and then with an external material that can be seen from outside the facility. This outside "skin" of a building is frequently called the exterior fascia or external facing. The exterior fascia can be made of glass, brick, steel, plastic, masonry, wood, or other elements. These elements, or combinations thereof, are held in place with a metal frame. The frame can be precast or built on the spot; fascia can be built around a frame or can be hoisted into place from precast segments. No matter what method or material is used, all fascia needs to be weatherproof and must provide some degree of insulation to minimize energy usage. Other exterior components that must be built include the roof, turf, and watering system.

Roofing

A roof is not as expensive as might be assumed. However, a problem with a roof, such as a leak, can cause extensive damage to the building and items within the building. There are three types of roof: pitched, flat, and dome. A pitched roof is built at a slope to facilitate drainage and the melting of snow. A flat roof has a minimal slope [a drop of 0.125-0.5 inch (0.32-1.3 cm) per foot of run] to drains. A dome can be used to provide greater clearance for internal activities while also ideally allowing water and snow to drain more effectively. However, a number of sport domes and traditional roofs have collapsed because of wind, the weight of excess snow, or both. Roofing is covered in greater detail in chapter 7 as one of the primary building systems.

A roof is typically supported through a truss system of wood or steel angles connected together to increase strength. These frames support the roof and serve as a support mechanism for such items as the scoreboard, speakers, lights, and other rigging. These support systems are even more important in basketball and hockey facilities that use a large-span roof since there cannot be any center support beams. In other facilities where a center support column can be used, the weight load potential for the roof can significantly increase. These facilities can often support heavy weights on the roof such as HVAC systems. Such weights cannot be sustained by most open-span roofs.

Internal Construction

At the same time the roofing system is being installed, internal construction can begin. The substructure, superstructure, exterior fascia, and roof need to be mostly completed before internal work begins to prevent weather damage to internal components.

Although most people focus on the visible parts of a facility (e.g., walls, ceilings, lights), the strength of a building lies in its core. This core can include the foundation, electrical wiring in the walls, plumbing in the walls, and similar elements that the facility could not operate without. A facility is not just the walls and ceiling but rather consists of all the systems, both internal and external, that help it run effectively. This is why it takes so long to build a facility correctly.

The facility construction process can be magnified in an effort to develop green buildings. For example, a facility can attempt to capture storm water after the building is completed, but it is much more effective if elements for capturing storm water are incorporated into a building's design during the planning and construction phases. The process of storm water capture prevents a large portion of rain water from entering the municipal storm water system. The two basic approaches include the following:

1. Detention systems manage the water runoff from the building site. A detention basin or reservoir acts as a temporary storage area. The water can then be released slowly from this catch basin so that the city's sewer system is not flooded. Some facilities use a pond or lake as an ingenious way to hide such a system in the open. The key is to determine how slowly or quickly the detention system will fill with water. Before the basin's fill rate can be calculated, the regional average rainfall needs to be calculated. In New York City the 5-year rain total design analysis (the average storm for 5 years compared with the extreme, such as the rare 50- or 100-year storms which supposedly happen once every 50 or 100 years and produce significant rain totals) would show approximately 5.95 inches (15.1 cm) of rain per hour to be anticipated in a catch basin or detention tank. A 30,000-square-foot (2,787 sq m) roof has a flow rate of 4.1 cubic feet (0.1 cu m) per second, or 1,845 gallons (6,984 L) per minute. Thus, a 30,000-gallon (113,562 L) detention tank would fill with the roof's overflow in around 16 minutes. Another detention strategy entails controlling the rate water flows off the roof (Benazzi, 2010).

2. Retention systems utilize the water for other purposes such as irrigation or use in toilets and cooling towers. The same 30,000-square-foot roof in New York would capture a total of 900,000 gallons (3.4 million L) of water a year. One Bryant Park, a 55-story building in New York with an 80,000-square-foot (7,432 sq m) roof, has stormwater tanks that collect 87% of the average rainfall. The tanks [including four 7,000-gallon (26,498 L) tanks in the tower] save 2.3 million gallons (8.7 million L) of potable water annually. Gravity immediately supplies the available water to help flush toilets; this system eliminates the need for pumps to bring water up from the bottom of the building (Benazzi, 2010).

Turf

One of the important decisions for any facility is whether to have natural turf fields or artificial turf, such as AstroTurf or FieldTurf. A new system that reduces rug burn and is softer on ankles is the FieldTurf infill system, which utilizes a loosely laid mixture of recycled rubber granules and sand within a fiber mat consisting of 2.5-inch-long (6.4 cm) polyethylene fiber imitation grass blades. The mat rests on a compacted subgrade of free-draining rock and an underground drainage system (Korcek, 2001). (The subgrade is the surface underneath the mat.) For FieldTurf the underneath structure consists of stones [normally 1-2 inches (2.5-5 cm) in size] compacted down so they do not move but also spaced so that water can filter down to the drainage system. Some claimed that AstroTurf, which traditionally had a subgrade made of cement with padding on top, contributed to ankle sprains (Korcek, 2001). The subgrade is critical for more than just safety reasons. A well-designed subgrade can help drain a field, allowing teams to play even in bad weather conditions. The FieldTurf system can drain 10 inches (25 cm) of rain from a field in an hour.

The FieldTurf system has been increasing in popularity since the late 1990s; the average cost per square foot is $7 using the infill system versus $16.50 for synthetic fields (Korcek, 2001). This price range has stayed consistent for years and represents the installed costs for these types of fields. In one project, Northern Illinois University installed 94,720 square feet (8,800 sq m) of the infill type of synthetic grass in 5-yard-wide (4.5 m) sections. The project also used 370 tons of silica sand and 90 tons of granular rubber, which came from recycled tires (Korcek, 2001). Savings from such systems include time and expense savings because yard marker lines do not have to be painted. Synthetic grass can come already painted and the paint does not wash away, which can save numerous hours of repainting.

The Nexxfield turf system from Montreal, Canada, represents a new approach to dealing with artificial turf and the concerns associated with rubber infill. Instead of infill, this system uses a high-density fiber blend over a high-performance underlayment. The system was adopted by the Montreal Impact of Major League Soccer. One of the benefits of the system is the removal of infill cleaning, moving, and respreading that is required on traditional turfgrass fields.

FIELD RENOVATIONS

In spring 2007, bulldozers started removing the grass turf at the Hall High School field in West Hartford, Connecticut. After examining the cost–benefit analysis for installing an artificial turf field, West Hartford decided to replace both high school grass fields with artificial turf systems. The process began with preparing the area around the field that would not be changed. Protective tarps needed to be installed over a synthetic track to avoid causing the track

harm. Next, all the equipment and supplies were brought in to avoid potential delays. While removing some grass turf, numerous dump trucks carrying stones were brought in to install the underlying drainage system. The following photo sequence highlights some of the steps taken in the process to install the field that cost almost $1 million. The total installation process took approximately 5 months to complete—just in time for the fall football season.

The first step in the process of converting a grass field to an artificial turf field is to remove the grass.

You should not start a building project without having all the necessary supplies. On this project all the drainage piping was stored on the side so that it did not interfere with the construction process.

Once the grass is removed and enough topsoil is removed for drainage preparation, a laser-guided bulldozer will level the field.

In this renovation effort the high school already had a nice track, so the track was covered to protect it from harm and a drainage system was installed on the perimeter of the new field to assist with drainage.

(continued)

BEHIND THE SCENES *(continued)*

Once the field is leveled, a covering is placed over the soil to prevent weeds from coming through. Then, drainage pipes and stones large enough to allow for percolation are added before the final field surface is installed.

Once the artificial turf is installed, the playing surface can look immaculate and the upkeep costs associated with seeding, mowing, watering, fertilizing, and weeding a grass field are eliminated.

HydroChill, a turf-cooling system that reduces turf field surface temperature by 50 °F, was launched in 2013. A special infill coating traps moisture, and the moisture is released as the field is heated by the sun. The chilling effect can last for 2 to 3 days after the turf has been watered and reduces one of the biggest concerns associated with a turf field: how hot it becomes on a hot day.

Watering System

As mentioned in chapter 2, most facility managers who have grass or turf fields need to pay careful attention to weather reports. Rain can be the saving grace for a dry field, but too much rain can lead to puddles and excessively fast drainage with failure of the water to soak into the ground. Too little rain requires the facility manager to spend significant time and money making sure that the surface is watered at the right time. Since it's impossible to know when it might or might not rain, a water delivery system must be installed to supplement the drainage system in each field.

The steps for installing a watering system are as follows:

- Clear the area.
- Grade the area.
- Select the necessary pipes.
- Install the watering system.
- Cover with rocks to ensure proper drainage.
- Cover with appropriate soil and sand.
- Add grass (select type of grass and method of planting according to type of soil, events, and weather conditions).
- Water significantly.
- Maintain the field through proper mowing, aeration, watering, fertilizing, and pest control.

Other External Components

Other external components that should be examined include areas such as parking lots, roads, lights, security cameras, fences, billboards, outdoor restrooms, and a host of external amenities that can be added to a facility. These elements can often be added at the same time. For example, the best time to install electrical lines for lights and closed-circuit television cameras is before the pavement is finished when a parking lot is being constructed. Some facilities have external buildings such as maintenance sheds or garages for storing vehicles. These types of buildings might need water and other utilities, which need

HIGH SCHOOL FOOTBALL FIELDS

High schools are jumping on the artificial turf bandwagon to obtain several specific benefits. The primary benefit is that an artificial turf field can be used almost every day and around the clock. Most grass fields need time off to grow, cannot be played on more than a couple hours a day at most, and require constant maintenance. The cost to maintain a grass field at a high school can be $20,000 to $50,000 a year when mowing, fertilizer, resodding, aeration, pesticides, and general maintenance are taken into account. Thus, many schools are willing to invest possibly a million dollars to install an artificial turf field. In fact, approximately 3,500 such fields have been installed throughout the United States.

In 2004, the Chappaqua Board of Education (New York) passed a resolution to appoint a committee to explore the concept of installing artificial turf on the competition field at Horace Greeley High School. The committee met and examined the cost associated with installing an artificial turf field versus the maintenance cost for a grass field. The costs associated with maintaining a grass field include the following:

Lining fields and minor repairs (12 hours/week × 20 weeks × $25 per hour)	$6,000
Lining materials and equipment costs for all sports	$3,500
Contract grass mowing, trimming, and field aeration	$6,000
Twice-yearly overseeding ($2,500 per application)	$5,000
Sprinkler repairs, including labor and materials	$2,000
Total yearly natural turf costs	**$22,500**

In contrast, the annual cost to maintain an artificial turf field was estimated at $2,500. The cost to install a 90,000-square-foot (8,360 sq m) artificial turf field was estimated as follows:

■ Excavation and base construction costs, including the entire drainage system, were estimated at $2.50 to $3.00 per square foot, or $225,000 to $270,000 for the field.

■ Installation of the artificial grass system would cost $3.85 to $4.30 per square foot, or $346,500 to $387,000 for the field.

■ Underlying padding for the turf (if applicable, as some systems do not require padding) would cost $0.80 per square foot, or $72,000 for the field.

■ Adding lines and logos to the field costs $3,000 for a set of lines, for a total cost of $15,000.

■ Total cost for installing the field was estimated at **$658,500** to **$744,000** (Athletic Field Turf Committee, 2004).

Besides examining cost and maintenance issues, the committee examined 23 brands of available turf. All brands were installed over sand or a sand and rubber mixture. This was important because the committee was looking into safety associated with the artificial turf field. The two primary concerns were shock absorbency and injury prevention. Early in the life cycle of the first AstroTurf fields, the turf was installed over concrete, which resulted in a very hard surface that caused numerous injuries.

Shock absorbency of any field, be it natural grass or artificial turf, is measured by the G-Max level. A field's level of shock absorbency is determined by using a unit of measurement called the G-Max, where one "G" represents a single unit of gravity. An artificial turf field with a high G-Max level has a lower ability to absorb the force of a collision (which places more impact on the athlete). In contrast, a surface with a low G-Max level absorbs more force, which lessens the impact on the athlete. Much of the basic work on shock absorbency in the United States relates to protection from head injury and focuses on trauma from major impacts. According to the U.S. Consumer Product Safety Commission, a playing field on which the G-Max level is 200 or more should be replaced. A G-Max level under 200 is generally considered safe. Following is a list of different surfaces and their approximate G-Max levels (Athletic Field Turf Committee, 2004):

■ Muddy grass: 75

■ Natural grass (dense, good condition): 80

■ Synthetic infill turf with standard padding: 110

■ Packed clay baseball infield: 175

■ Frozen natural grass: 200

This analysis shows that synthetic fields are a little less shock absorbent than natural grass fields, but since the G-Max level is consistent all year round, the artificial turf fields are safer and prevent unstable or quickly changing conditions.

to be installed early in the construction process. External systems are covered in greater detail in chapter 7.

Interior Components

The primary internal components include partitions, millwork, doors and hardware, building systems, and furniture and finishings. Partitions may be either movable or permanent. A locker room may have permanent partitions between the visitors' and home locker rooms. An example of a movable partition is a gym divider that can be raised to create a large gym space or lowered to create distinct playing areas. Partitions can also serve as firewalls or load-bearing walls to support trusses.

Millwork refers to wood, plastic, or metal components with customized finishes. The term originated from the milling process that converted soft woods into such items as molding and trim.

Facilities Trivia

One of the major legacies from artificial turf fields was significant injuries. A study of injuries sustained by California high school football players found higher rates of injury on turf. While there were 13.8 injuries per 100 session hours on turf and only 8.4 injuries per 100 session hours on natural grass, the type of injury matters as some turf related injuries do not arise on natural grass. Players on synthetic turf fields are more prone to injuries such as the following:

- Turf toe
- Turf burn
- Muscle trauma
- Knee injuries

A number of famous National Football League (NFL) players have been sidelined by turf toe, including Matt Ryan, Sterling Sharpe, Steve McNair, Charles Woodson, Jack Lambert, Ray Lewis, and Deion Sanders. A number of additional injuries were due to the abrasive nature of artificial turf. Sliding on artificial turf used to leave a raspberry-type burn; however, softer new technology has helped reduce these injuries. Furthermore, either putting more cushioning under the new artificial turf or embedding it in the turf can also reduce injuries. Additional research has found that rates of injury were higher on outdoor artificial turf fields compared with similar indoor fields. Interestingly, female soccer players had a lower rate of injury on artificial turf compared with natural grass (Boulianne, 2008).

Over the years new processes have been developed to make millwork from other materials. Examples of millwork include door frames, coving, handrails, shelving, and similar components that add a distinctive look and feel to a building.

Doors, frames, and hardware refer to metal or wood doors hung on wood or metal frames using hinges. There are numerous variations, from revolving doors to turnstiles, that affect how people get into and out of a facility. Whether wood or hollow metal, doors typically carry a label with either a letter (A to E) or an hour rating (from 20 minutes to 3 hours), which is the fire rating for the door.

In addition to completion of all internal components, systems must be integrated throughout the building. Systems include HVAC, electrical, communication (sound, computer, telephone), plumbing, and fire suppression (covered in more depth in chapter 7). Each system requires wires, pipes, ducts, and other components that need to be installed before the walls, ceiling, and floors are put in place. Many facilities are built with drop ceilings on each floor. These ceilings are in fact like false closets. They create a space between the ceiling of one floor and the floor above. Within the space a significant amount of wiring and HVAC and water piping can be installed for easy access and changes. Drop ceilings often have a metal grid with light fixtures and fireproof acoustical tile.

Furniture and Finishings

Finishings include such items as paint and wallpaper, ceiling tiles, flooring, and artwork on the walls. Wall finishes include paint and wallpaper and other coverings. Ceilings can also be finished; many facilities use fire-retardant acoustical sprays that both protect against fires and help bounce sounds back to the floor. Flooring can be hardwood, tile, ceramic, or commercial carpeting. Flooring choices are often based on cost and maintenance criteria. However, usage also dictates finishing needs, since areas such as showers require tile or other types of water-resistant surfaces on the walls and floor. Artwork can also be classified as a finishing because it enhances the ambiance of the facility. Sport facilities often have a significant amount of sport memorabilia on the walls that may need protection from deterioration or theft. Finishing also refers to drapes, mirrors, light fixtures, and numerous other elements that make the facility more pleasant.

In older facilities, materials may have stayed the same color as when they were made. For example, concrete areas typically stay gray. Now, the number of options is almost limitless; for example, dyes can be added to cement, and cement adhesion paint can transform dull areas into a bright environment.

The furniture and finishings component of facility construction is often one of the most innovative aspects of building a new facility. There are almost infinite options for everything from stadium seats to chairs or benches in a locker room. Furniture includes all the various items installed in the facility that make it functional. For a locker room, the furniture can range from dressing booths and television sets to entertainment systems and whirlpool tubs.

Furniture, fixtures, and equipment are commonly referred to as FFE in the facility management industry. In a large stadium or arena, FFE could refer to everything from the scoreboard and sound system to photocopiers and Zambonis. Smaller facilities have an equal number of FFE elements, from free-weight machines in a gym to the juice dispenser at the health bar. Typically each item in a facility that is not physically attached to the property or that can easily be removed is put into the category of FFE.

Seating

One thing that needs careful consideration in the design of a facility is the fanny of the customer. Some spectator seating entails wood or metal bleachers, while higher-quality seats are made of formed plastic. Similar to the situation with airline seats over the years, stadium seats have been shrinking as facility designers and managers try to squeeze more people into the stands. In Europe, seats are a minimum of 29.5 inches (75 cm) wide; the recommended minimum is 30 inches (76 cm). The typical seat in the United States is 33 inches (84 cm) wide. However, at some colleges the width per seat is as little as 17 to 19 inches (43-48 cm). Although this may appear too narrow, airlines regularly use 17- to 18-inch (43-46 cm) seats. In the New York subways, width per seat was 16.5 inches (42 cm) in 1907, increased to 17.25 inches (44 cm) in 1927, and settled at 17.6 inches (45 cm) in 1971.

INTERIOR COLOR CHOICES

A component of a new facility that is often overlooked is the color scheme and paint job. Color is an important part of any facility. A dull or bland color presents a completely different atmosphere than bright and coordinated colors do. It has been shown that colorful classrooms with full-spectrum lights help reduce students' blood pressure, produce less off-task behavior, reduce aggressiveness, lower the number of disruptions, and improve academic performance (Johnson and Maki, 2009). Such results were shown in a test where the control classroom was all white and the testing room had three beige walls (which reduced tension) and a blue-gray front wall (to help reduce eyestrain).

Painting entails several steps, including preparing the surface to be painted, using a primer, painting an undercoat, and then painting the finish coat. Four primary coating types exist:

- Alkyd (which is usually vegetable-oil based) is traditionally economical, easy to use, and provides good protection from wear and tear. However, it is not ideal for all surfaces. This slow-drying paint is often used in rural or mild urban environments. Over the years these paints have been used primarily for residential applications.

- Epoxy (two-component coatings and sealers that have incredible resistance to many chemicals) is normally water and chemical resistant, abrasion resistant, and very hard.

- Latex (acrylic paint that is water based) has improved performance, excellent adhesion, and great color options; is easy to apply and clean up; and is safe to use (i.e., volatile organic compound compliant). The paint must be kept from freezing, so winter application is possibly problematic.

- Polyurethane (sealant used on woods) results in a hard, tough, and flexible coating that is chemical resistant and provides good abrasion resistance.

The old seats in the Indiana Pacers' arena were 18 inches (46 cm). However, the newer Conseco Fieldhouse has a minimum seat width of 21 inches (53 cm) (Jorgensen, 2001). The size of seats and benches affects issues such as capacity, aisle width, egress, and emergency evacuations.

Flooring

Flooring can include carpet, resilient flooring (vinyl tiles), composite flooring, wood flooring, and stone. Flooring can make a significant difference in sport facilities. For example, the system used to support the wood floor in a basketball gym can take many forms with different levels of support, or resiliency. The substructure of a high school basketball court is significantly different from that of a professional basketball court based on the weight load and physical demands placed on the floor.

According to the Maple Flooring Manufacturers Association, approximately 70% of all sport floors installed in the United States each year are made with maple (Kronish, 2002). Maple is utilized because it is durable, long lasting, flexible, easy to maintain, and very attractive. A well-maintained maple floor could last 70 to 100 years. The famous parquet floor in the old Boston Gardens exemplified the beauty and durability of wood flooring. However, wood flooring has different degrees of quality. First-grade lumber is almost defect free and the most expensive. Most colleges and professional teams play exclusively on first-grade floors. After first grade is second grade (better grade). Third grade, the least expensive, is the quality grade most frequently used by schools on a tight budget.

One of the most important decisions in installing a wood floor is uniform stability. Uniform stability ensures uniform ball bounce, faster play, and longer durability. This is more important than higher shock-absorbency levels. The floor system should also have a well-engineered subfloor system that does not compromise stability. One method is to use padding underneath the subfloor. In fact, under wood floors there are often several levels of padding and shock-absorbent systems that allow the floor to give. Point-elastic surfaces restrict the impact underfoot to the point of contact, whereas with area-elastic surfaces an impact can be felt up to 20 inches (51 cm) away

(Viklund, 1995). Specific differences in climate and performance expectations can also dictate which wood floor will work best in any given gym.

Synthetic floors are utilized if wood flooring is not the preferred choice for expense reasons or if the facility will have multipurpose uses unsuitable for wood. There are three types of synthetic floors. Poured urethane is embedded with rubber granules to meet resilience needs. The urethane is poured onto a concrete substrate and can last almost 40 years if it is properly maintained (damp mopping and use of some industrial cleaners) and resurfaced every 10 years. The maintenance requirements for such floors are less than for wood floors, which may need to be resurfaced every year if used extensively (Kronish, 2002). Rolled and sheet goods are various types of synthetic surfaces that are purchased in large rolls or sheets and are applied directly on top of cement or other subflooring. These floors typically do not last as long as urethane, but they are simple to clean and come in a variety of colors. The last category of synthetic floors is modular polypropylene tiles. These plastic-based tiles are resistant to water, more difficult to damage, and very easy to install and repair. However, they do not provide the same resiliency and do not have the same look as some of the other synthetic floor systems.

The steps in the floor selection process include the following:

- Determine which room or space the floor will cover.
- Prioritize which sports and activities will use the room.
- Determine whether the floor should be area-elastic or point-elastic.
- Review the performance criteria for the various floor types being considered.
- Test floor options and compare costs.
- Review potential warranties.
- Compare the life-cycle costs for the various floor options.
- Conduct activities on floors installed in other facilities.
- Make the final decision.
- Hire people who have previously installed the type of floor selected (Viklund, 1995).

ISSUES TO CONSIDER WHEN BUYING A HARDWOOD GYM FLOOR

1. What activities will take place on the floor, in addition to basketball and other games? Will there be concerts and food- or drink-based events? Will bleachers or basketball hoops need to be moved across the surface? How?

2. What type of subflooring system should be used? In 2012, 49% of gym and athletic floors in the United States were floating floors and 23% were anchored floors. There has been an uptick in the number of fixed subfloors that incorporate steel and synthetic materials (e.g., pins, channels, or clips). In contrast, in floating floors, evenly spaced 0.75-inch (1.9 cm) rubber pads separate the subfloor from two 0.5-inch-thick (1.3 cm) layers of plywood. Strips of maple wood are stapled to the top piece of plywood.

3. How much moisture will the floor potentially encounter? Maple expands as it takes in moisture and contracts when it dries, thus moving on a regular basis. It requires either small voids on either side of the boards or a 0.125-inch expansion gap every 2 feet (0.6 m) between tongue-and-groove boards.

4. How environmentally conscious will the floor be? Will the floor be made of postconsumer recycled products? Are there any Leadership in Energy and Environmental Design (LEED) requirements?

5. What grade of maple should be used? The highest level of maple flooring is first grade, which has the best color and appearance. At the other end is third grade, which might have pin knots and staining. Second-and-better-grade is nice quality and in between first and third grade wood and is used on 70% to 75% of all gym floors.

6. What finish should be used? Oil-based finishes are not allowed in some states. Although water-based finishes are safer (i.e., no volatile organic compounds are released when the finish dries), they can cause problems with panelization (when moisture causes the water-finished planks to glue together, thus preventing self-adjustment).

7. When should lines and graphics be painted? The best time is during flooring installation. Temporary graphics have gained in popularity, but several major slipping incidents have discouraged their use.

8. How often does the floor need to be maintained? Maintenance needs to be performed on both a scheduled basis and an emergency basis. If a spill occurs or fans are bringing in dirt, then more-frequent cleaning is needed. Otherwise, a routine of daily dust mopping and regular cleaning with a solution recommended by the manufacturer should be followed. The floor should also be screened and recoated once a year and sanded down to the bare wood (followed with resealing, repainting, and refinishing) once every 10 to 15 years.

9. Who should install the floor? The floor needs to be installed by someone who knows what they are doing and has been properly vetted with several reference checks.

10. Can testing prove the value of a floor? Several certifying organizations exist for wood floors. One of the more comprehensive certifications is the Maple Floor Manufacturing Association's Performance and Uniformity Rating system. The five characteristics analyzed include shock absorption, vertical deflection, area of deflection, basketball rebound, and surface friction (Steinbach, 2012).

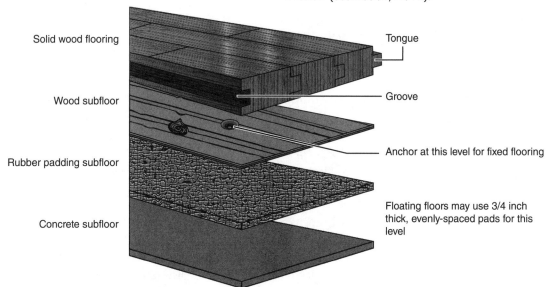

Solid wood flooring

Wood subfloor

Rubber padding subfloor

Concrete subfloor

Tongue

Groove

Anchor at this level for fixed flooring

Floating floors may use 3/4 inch thick, evenly-spaced pads for this level

Figure 6.1 A wood floor is not just wood thrown on top of a cement floor. From shock absorbers to membranes that reduce the risk of water damage, a wood floor is similar to a large sandwich: It has many layers that provide strong playability and reduce the risk of injuries.

One of the keys for a synthetic floor is having an appropriate concrete subfloor in which no curing agents have been used and in which the variation is no more than 0.125 inch (0.32 cm) for every 10 feet (3 m). The slab should have a hard, steel-troweled finish and should be adequately waterproofed ("More Than Just a Gym Floor," n.d.).

Vinyl composite tile is one of the "mistakes" associated with gym floors since they are not appropriate for sport activities. Such tiles are commonly used in school classrooms, hallways, cafeterias, and multipurpose rooms because they are eight times harder than traditional tile or synthetic floors. Vinyl composite tile is also inexpensive: It costs around $1.50 per square foot, whereas modular synthetic tile or poured-in-place surfaces often cost $4 to $6 per square foot (Popke, 2009). However, this kind of tile is inappropriate for use in sport because the ball bounce, the feel of the floor, the sound generated by sports, and the wear on participants' bodies are less than desirable. Therefore, facility owners should not always look at the cheapest option when such options might result in an unsuitable surface.

The issues involving flooring can be complex. From shock absorption and deformation to surface friction or rolling loads, there are many concerns that are typically beyond the scope of knowledge and experience of most beginning facility managers. That is why it is beneficial to use an expert who understands both wood and synthetic floors to help choose the right materials.

Restoration and Renovation

No analysis of the construction process would be complete without consideration of **restoration** and **renovation**. Because of the cost of some sport facilities or their historic importance, the decision may be to renovate rather than build a new facility. Renovations can be almost as expensive as construction, and restorations can cost more than a facility originally cost to build. The renovations and restorations of historic Soldier Field in Chicago cost approximately $606 million. This amount is significantly greater than the initial cost of building the stadium in the 1920s, which was $13 million ("Make No Small Plans," 2003). Renovations are often undertaken on college campuses, where building a new stadium or arena may be cost prohibitive, and the nostalgia evoked by an old facility would make any effort to demolish a stadium futile and politically suicidal in the eyes of alumni and major givers. One concern with renovations is that initial construction may have complied with existing rules and laws, but renovations need to comply with current building codes and laws. The need for renovations to comply with building codes can open a Pandora's box. In fact, some facilities do not undertake any renovations because they may create more problems than solutions. This can occur, for example, when renovations affect asbestos-covered materials and the costs for required asbestos removal (abatement) are more than the total value of the anticipated renovation project.

It may not make sense to spend a lot of money on the outside of a facility when the inside is worthless because of incompatible electrical systems or because insulation or fire protection will be too expensive to modify. Thus, the process of restoring or renovating a facility often requires more planning than that of designing a new facility. The following are some of the issues that need to be covered:

- Is information available on maintaining existing systems?
- Are there health concerns such as asbestos or lead paint?
- What effect will the work have on existing tenants?
- Are parts still available, or will items need to be hand or machine made?
- Is there time available? (Restorations often take longer than building a new facility.)
- Are there qualified workers who can help on the project?
- Is a lot of money available for when things go wrong and unexpected scenarios arise?

Buildings are sometimes built with renovations in mind. This phenomenon has more recently been seen with newer Olympic facilities, which are being built with significant temporary seating that can be removed after the Games so the facilities are easier and cheaper to maintain. Some Olympic facilities undergo significant renovations. Georgia

RENOVATING SOLDIER FIELD

Soldier Field, home of the Chicago Bears of the NFL, opened in 1924. The facility has had a rich tradition, with a panoramic view of Lake Michigan and perimeter columns that made it a landmark in Chicago. However, as an older facility it had problems that were hard to overcome, such as poor sight lines for viewing the game, uncomfortable seats, and not enough restrooms. The stadium underwent numerous renovations, the largest occurring in 1979 when new lights were installed along with artificial turf and upgrades to locker rooms, seats, and sight lines. More restrooms and concession stands were added several years later. Several years after those renovations, the artificial turf was removed and replaced with a natural grass surface. At the same time, 116 skyboxes were installed, increasing the seating capacity to 67,000 fans by the end of the 1980s (Ryan, 2004).

Even with all these changes, the facility was not ideal, and the Bears wanted a new stadium. Thus, in 2001 the decision was made to build a new stadium inside the old stadium. Instead of tearing down the old stadium, as has occurred with many new football and baseball stadiums, Soldier Field's facade was barely touched. The inside received a significant makeover, with the architects creating a sleek metal oval-shaped stadium inside and above the older rectangular stadium. The $606 million project, completed in 2003, has twice as many restrooms and four times as many concession stands as before. The Bears paid $200 million of the renovation costs and covered cost overruns totaling almost $50 million. Surprisingly, the new stadium lost seats and now sits only 61,500 fans, making Soldier Field one of the smallest stadiums in the NFL. There are 133 luxury suites that can sit 16 people each. Below the suites is a 100,000-square-foot (9,300 sq m) club that opens directly into an underground parking lot (Ryan, 2004). The renovations have been a hit, as the facility regularly hosts more than 200 event days each year.

Although every renovation project can present challenges, the renovation of Soldier Field was especially difficult because of the tight time schedule and the amount of work needed to complete the project. The Chicago Park District, which owns the stadium, inserted a clause in the contracts that penalized each contractor $4.5 million for every game the Bears missed because of construction being incomplete. Since the project was supposed to start right after the season ended, the contractors had only several months to complete their work. One of the key areas of the project was replacing a significant amount of cement. The concrete restoration was supposed to start in March 2002. Most of the concrete components were almost 80 years old. The Public Building Commission of Chicago refused to issue a repair permit without an updated condition survey of the concrete. All the concrete surfaces had to be sounded, and deteriorated areas were marked with paint, measured, identified by number, and entered on the plans. The permit was issued after a 2-month delay. This forced National Restoration Systems, the cement repair contractor (working with the primary general contractor, Turner Construction) to start its work 2 months later than planned.

The concrete restoration contractor was faced with a 300% increase over the original contract, an expanded scope of work. Numerous critical locations throughout the structure had to be repaired on second shifts and weekends because of worker congestion and safety concerns. Double shifts, 7 days a week, were scheduled as necessary to complete the concrete repairs. More than 60,000 square feet (5,500 sq m) of concrete repairs were completed on time, and the crew completed the project with a perfect safety record ("ICRI 2005," 2005).

The renovation project was not without controversy. After a year of being open, broadcasters were still making fun of the stadium's new shape, and fans did not appreciate the blend of the old and the new. Although typical renovation projects are not as extensive as the process at Soldier Field, this example helps highlight that facilities may go through many renovations until some point in time when they need to be gutted or torn down to build a new facility.

© FOTOSEARCH RM/age fotostock

Tech University made a $45 million renovation to the site of the 1996 Olympic swimming and diving events. The facility was turned into a campus recreation center with a pool, diving well, water slide, hot tub, and three-story climbing wall. Two floors added above the facility offer six basketball courts, exercise studios, a roller hockey rink, and an elevated jogging track ("Tech Puts $45 Million," 2004).

PROJECT COSTS

Cost-based concerns are numerous, and costs often drive the entire construction process. To help complete a project with the lowest potential costs, facilities often utilize **value-based engineering**. Value-based engineering can be combined with value construction to see where money can be saved. Value-based engineering needs can be addressed at all points during the design and construction processes.

The costs of new buildings or facilities differ based on numerous variables. Generally speaking, there are six standard budget items for a new building:

1. Preliminary costs
   - Acquisition of site
   - Site decontamination
   - Site development
   - Legal fees
   - Cost of bond issue
   - Promotion and publicity
   - Preliminary architect fees for preparation of preliminary plans
   - Consultant fees (legal, tax, bonds, polling, political)
2. Architectural fees
   - Preparation of architectural and engineering plans (working plans)
   - Supervision of construction
   - Engineering requirements
3. Construction costs
   - Building contract and subcontracts
   - Supervision costs
   - Building permits

4. FFE (up to 15% of the total budget)
   - Building
   - Outdoor play areas
5. Insurance costs to pay the facility developer if the construction company fails to complete the project
6. Contingencies (usually 10% of the total cost)—may include more money for paint, new toilet seats not included in the initial budget, and countless other last-minute additions or changes to the original design budget (Gabrielsen and Miles, 1958)

This breakdown of costs associated with the construction process was written more than 50 years ago; however, numerous cost elements have stayed the same over the years. Costs are often examined today in terms of whether they are direct or indirect. This categorization is somewhat misleading because all costs end up being direct costs in that the facility developer will have to pay them. Traditional **direct costs** include labor, materials, equipment, and subcontractor costs. **Indirect costs** typically include builder profits, legal fees, insurance costs, printing costs, and other such expenses. Costs that are often overlooked include strikes by laborers, escalating costs associated with inflation and litigation delays, and weather-related delays.

Cost Variables

When constructing a facility, it is necessary to examine variables that can affect project costs. Every construction project faces changes before and during the construction process. When a facility is being designed, cost considerations can help dictate whether to use tile or marble as flooring. During the construction process, the builders often run into trouble when unexpected issues arise. For example, a chosen window design might no longer be available, so a more expensive alternative is required to complete the project on time. Each change costs money, but some changes can be less expensive if different materials can be used. Cost variables apart from those relating to design and construction include the following:

- Access to market and distribution centers and the cost to penetrate a market

- Cost of transporting and purchasing supplies
- Site-related costs
- Relocation and moving expenses
- Interest expenses on borrowed funds
- Environmental costs
- Prevailing wage rate for laborers and skilled craftsmen
- Costs related to various taxing and permitting authorities that get involved
- Costs related to various government authorities such as building inspectors and their requirements (Cotts and Lee, 1992)

An additional variable affecting cost is quality. The higher the quality of items used, the higher the price. For example, the typical cost for a wood basketball floor is between $8.00 per square foot for a low-quality floor and $18 per square foot for an NBA-quality floor. Between these two extremes, most facilities try to get the best bang for their limited dollars. A typical college basketball court is 94 by 50 feet (29 by 15 m), or 4,700 square feet (436 sq m). At $10 to $15 per square foot, such a floor would cost $47,000 to $70,500 installed.

Quality can be seen in almost every facet of the construction process. Skilled artisans can be brought in to complete the fine woodwork, which can be very attractive—and expensive. Machine-finished woodwork may not be as attractive, but it can be significantly less expensive and still have a high enough quality that it does not enhance the risk of injury or future failure of the item. Paint can also vary based on quality and cost. An interior paint designed to last for 10 years will be cheaper than a paint designed to last for 20 years. Although the initial cost for the cheaper paint may make it an attractive option, the costs of repainting down the road should encourage any facility builder to go with the better paint to avoid higher future maintenance costs. Every possible component can be purchased at various price points. The key is quality, looks, longevity, politics, and price.

Construction and Other Costs

Construction costs can be calculated in several ways. The most accurate cost analysis always occurs after a facility has been built and all the costs have been tabulated. However, this does not help those on a fixed budget. Banks, lenders, and investors need to know the cost of a project before it begins. Several techniques exist for estimating the potential cost for a building. The three primary methods are the **end-product units method**, the **ratio method**, and the **physical dimensions method**.

The end-product units method is used when enough historical data are available to compare the proposed building with previously built facilities. Thus, if other gyms were recently built in a given region for $1.5 to $3.0 million, the builder

TOTAL PROJECT COST ESTIMATION FORM

1. Probable construction cost — $30,000,000 _____

2. Design-related cost
Multiply line 1 by 0.1 — $3,000,000 _____

3. Furniture, fixtures, and equipment
Multiply line 1 by 0.05 (normal), 0.1 (above average), or 0.15 (extensive) — $3,000,000 _____

4. Subtotal
Add lines 1, 2, and 3 — $36,000,000 _____

5. Contingencies
Multiply line 4 by 0.15 — $5,400,000 _____

6. Total project costs
Add lines 4 and 5 (does not include financing, land acquisition, or other special costs) — $41,400,000 _____

COMMON PITFALLS WHEN BUILDING A FACILITY

Given all the construction issues raised in this chapter, many readers might be concerned about building a sport facility. However, building a sport facility can be the highlight of a facility manager's career. From seeing blueprints to seeing a finished building, the process can be very invigorating. Numerous concerns such as the following may occur during the process. However, these challenges are worth the completed product.

- Not contracting with an experienced sport architect or engineering firm

- Not letting the designers know all the facts

- Allowing the architect or engineering firm to interview and hire consultants, which can lead to a loss of control and increased pricing

- Hiring a contractor who has never built a facility in the given market
- Failing to establish a hard budget
- Approving changes before they can be evaluated and costed
- Not monitoring work done by subcontractors
- Failing to have regular planning and progress meetings
- Failing to define requirements for documentation, including punch lists
- Allowing politicians to get involved in the construction process
- Failing to have proper training before taking over the facility
- Failing to budget enough for contingencies

From Cotts and Lee 1992.

could assume that a new gym would fall into the same range.

The ratio method is used for facilities with extensive equipment needs. The equipment costs are so high that their cost is multiplied by a ratio based on historical data to help determine the potential completed cost.

The physical dimensions method examines components being included in the facility and then adds the square foot values of those components to determine a potential price. One service that compiles such data is Means Building Construction Cost Data. Someone building a 20,000-square-foot (1,860 sq m) gym could look at the data and see that similar gyms have been built for $98.80 per square foot, which translates to approximately $2 million as the estimated cost to build the new gym.

Construction-related expenses should include not only the cost for the facility itself but also all FFE. Design and start-up and move-in expenses such as the following should also be estimated:

- Freight, storage, delivery, and setup
- Office supplies, cleaning supplies, and day-to-day materials

- Maintenance supplies
- Advertising and communication costs
- Facility insurance
- A sinking fund for the replacement of building components that wear out

In an analysis of the total construction costs, a worksheet can help determine what the real costs may be for a given facility. "Total Project Cost Estimation Form" highlights a hypothetical $30 million project that quickly escalates to a $41 million project when the design-related costs, FFE, and contingencies are added. This analysis helps highlight how certain projects can quickly get out of hand and why constant financial vigilance is required to avoid cost overruns.

COMPLETION AND ANALYSIS

After the facility is constructed, it is not necessarily finished. Many facilities have opened for an event or game before the facility was complete. Part of the final building process entails cleaning up the spot. Some final completion projects might take several days or weeks. One major concern is when builders leave a lot of trash and debris behind when they leave a site.

A prefinal inspection is conducted with the general contractor, architects or engineers, owner, and possibly others (fire and city inspectors) to examine the quality of the construction. Any deficiencies are recorded on a **punch list.** A punch list can record small matters, such as a gap in a door or window frame or torn carpeting, that need to be addressed before the owner will take ownership of the building. After all these problems are corrected, a final inspection is completed. The architect or engineer accepts the project as final on behalf of the owner, and then the contractor submits a request for final payment. When all the work is completed, the owner or builder needs to apply to the local government authority for an occupancy permit allowing the doors to be opened to the general public.

Thereafter, the project needs to be finalized. This happens when as-built drawings and any operating and maintenance manuals are obtained, along with affidavits showing that all amounts have been paid and there are no builder's liens against the property (Bentil, 1989). This is when the project's overall success and cost can be analyzed. Whether or not a project was successful is largely subjective and is determined by many factors, including intermediate scheduling and completion dates, procedures, accidents or mistakes along the way, and of course the end result.

Cost analysis is much more objective. Actual project costs can be assessed in terms of the budget, industry norms, and comparable facilities. Although no two facilities are the same, some comparisons can be very beneficial. Table 6.3 presents the costs for two sportsplexes. These comparisons show that some facilities can be significantly more expensive than others based on a number of variables. The Illinois facility spent $310,000 more on its design for three fields as compared with the six-field Arizona facility. The Illinois facility was significantly more expensive in terms of shrubs and trees, lighting, site mobilization, snack bars, and development fees. The Arizona facility was more expensive when it came to having to spend $100,000 to drill wells in the desert to help water the fields and for an administrative building.

Table 6.4 Cost Comparisons for Two Sportsplexes

Description	SIX-FIELD COMPLEX IN ARIZONA		THREE-FIELD COMPLEX IN ILLINOIS	
	Actual cost ($)	Average cost per field ($)	Actual cost ($)	Average cost per field ($)
Engineering/architectural plans	40,000	6,666.67	350,000	116,666.67
Site mobilization	140	23.33	122,938	40,979.33
Site grading and prep	65,480	10,913.33	166,367	55,455.67
Storm drains	0	0	71,632	23,877.33
Sewers	19,036	3,172.67	14,860	4,953.33
Water system	45,000	7,500.00	14,894	4,964.67
Underground cable	6,000	1,000.00	10,000	3,333.33
Well costs	100,000	16,667.67	5,000	1,667.67
Topsoil	6,000	1,000.00	24,000	8,000.00
Sod and soil	59,000	9,833.34	139,445	46,481.67
Shrubs/trees	23,230	3,871.67	298,000	99,333.33
Paths/walls	66,100	11,016.67	72,000	24,000.00
Warning tracks	5,015	835.83	12,000	4,000.00
Area lighting	21,201	3,533.50	131,000	43,666.67

(continued)

Table 6.4 (continued)

Description	SIX-FIELD COMPLEX IN ARIZONA		THREE-FIELD COMPLEX IN ILLINOIS	
	Actual cost ($)	Average cost per field ($)	Actual cost ($)	Average cost per field ($)
Sports lighting	185,000	30,833.33	220,000	73,333.33
Parking paving	101,450	16,908.33	100,000	33,333.33
Fencing	57,900	9,650.00	65,000	21,666.67
Scoreboards	15,000	2,500.00	22,000	7,333.33
Batting cages	48,890	8,148.33	63,775	21,258.33
Tot lot	27,785	4,630.83	62,542	20,847.33
Volleyball court	20,403	3,400.50	27,551	9,183.67
Basketball courts	0	0	88,223	29,407.67
Picnic area	11,772	1,962.00	5,000	1,666.67
Entryway	4,000	666.67	10,000	3,333.33
Snack bars	290,150	48,358.33	446,150	148,716.67
Trash enclosures	4,700	783.33	4,000	1,333.33
Maintenance shed	14,215	2,369.17	66,500	22,166.67
Admin building	300,000	50,000.00	13,750	4,583.33
Barbeque area	25,000	4,166.67	3,000	1,000.00
Fees and permits	103	17.17	8,900	2,966.67
General conditions	10,950	1,825.00	109,000	36,333.33
Maintenance equipment	35,000	5,833.33	22,500	7,500.00
Concession equipment	65,000	10,833.33	40,000	13,333.33
Park furnishings	3,000	500.00	8,000	2,666.67
Computers	0	0	10,000	3,333.33
Video security/public address	17,000	2,833.33	6,000	2,000.00
Bleachers	10,600	1,766.67	20,000	6,666.67
Signage	2,900	483.33	6,000	2,000.00
Inventory and supplies	22,000	3,666.67	8,000	2,666.67
Preopening expenses	16,000	2,666.67	20,000	6,666.67
Legal/accounting	8,500	1,416.67	30,000	10,000.00
Feasibility study	3,800	633.33	25,000	8,333.33
Development fees	144,600	24,100.00	225,000	75,000.00
Totals	**$1,901,920**	**$316,986.66**	**$3,168,027**	**$1,056,009**

Reprinted, by permission, from G. Fried, S.J. Shapiro, and T.D. DeShriver, 2003, *Sport finance* (Champaign, IL: Human Kinetics), 110.

Summary

For anyone who has seen a building go up from a flat piece of land, the experience can be moving. The creation process is more intense if someone has invested a significant amount of time and energy in designing the facility and obtaining necessary funding. The construction process is easier when it is possible to simply contact a construction company and have the company build a facility from plans. However, most larger facilities need to follow the bidding process, which should lead to a competitive contract and a lower total price.

After a contract is entered into with a general contractor or another entity responsible for building the facility, the site needs to be prepared. Once the site is cleared, the foundation can be laid, followed by the substructure, superstructure, roof, flooring, FFE, and landscaping. Numerous issues arise throughout the construction process, often focusing on cost and quality. The elements that complete a project—systems that are installed within a facility—are covered in the next chapter.

Discussion Questions and Activities

1. What material would you use to build a facility if you were concerned only with appearance (as opposed to price)?

2. Where can money be saved in construction of a facility?

3. Should a facility be built with a lot of glass windows? What are the pluses and minuses?

4. Travel to a construction site and observe what construction phase the facility is going through. Pay careful attention to the types of equipment and materials being used along with the number of people working at the site.

5. Develop a project completion timeline highlighting all the various steps seen from the time a facility is first conceived until the construction process is completed.

6. How would you reduce waste in the construction process?

7. What green solutions could you develop that are more creative than changing light bulbs or using solar or wind energy?

8. Pick a color scheme for a prospective facility. What mood and tone are you trying to set? Why?

9. Look up a facility that is currently being built nearby. What process of construction are they in (i.e., did they just break ground, are they adding the trusses, or are they pouring the parking lot), what materials have they decided to use (i.e., steel and brick walls, large windows), etc. The key is to show you appreciate the various steps that need to be followed and the types of materials used in construction.

10. Track the construction of a building over the course of a semester. Visit the construction site every week to take a picture, and at the end of the term do a presentation showing how the construction process evolved over time.

PART III

Facility Systems and Operations

Think of a car for a second. Most people would love to have a car with a flashy exterior and a comfortable interior. However, the main function of a car is to travel from one place to another. Thus, no matter how beautiful a car might look or feel, the heart of the car is the engine and all the ancillary systems, such as steering, transmission, and cooling. All these parts need to work well together in order for the car to work properly. Similarly, a facility contains numerous systems, and these systems need to be maintained in order for the facility to operate effectively.

Chapter 7 examines the basic systems contained in any sport facility. No matter its size, every facility needs to have a heating, ventilation, and air conditioning system; energy systems; and lighting, plumbing, fire suppression, and a host of smaller systems. Systems can raise numerous issues, from how to install the systems to energy conservation concerns. The chapter covers internal as well as external systems and gives special attention to some of the often overlooked systems, such as waste management and audiovisual systems.

Chapter 8 moves on to facility operations, which pertains to how a facility is actually run. Some facilities used for only a single event have fewer concerns than do facilities that host a variety of events (e.g., both basketball and hockey games on a single day) and require major changeovers. Special attention is given to unique sport components such as locker rooms, gym floors, and bleachers. The chapter also focuses on grass fields, from starting a field to keeping it healthy and at the proper height. Although fields are often overlooked, they are one of the most important components of any external sport facility.

Chapter 9 focuses on facility maintenance. Cleaning a room might seem like a simple task, but imagine cleaning a facility that has 1 million square feet (92,900 sq. m). The maintenance process starts with developing a plan, setting aside a budget, finding the right staff, supervising the staff, and then evaluating what they have done. Through conducting a comprehensive maintenance audit, a manager can determine what steps to take in maintaining a facility. Furthermore, through benchmarking, a manager can make sure the facility is running efficiently compared with either pre-established standards or industry norms. The chapter ends by offering some specific maintenance steps and some green building initiatives.

Chapter 10, new to the third edition, focuses on the push over the past 10 to 15 years for environmental friendly and energy conserving green buildings. It is not enough to simply build green buildings; they must also be run effectively, reduce waste, conserve energy, and be cleaned in an environmentally friendly manner.. A Leadership in Energy and Environmental Design (LEED)-certified facility will quickly lose its certification if it cannot maintain the green practices identified during the planning and construction process. This chapter gives special attention to the strategies facility managers can undertake to save money while operating a facility to be as green as possible.

7

Facility Systems

Chapter Objectives

- Understand some of the ways in which the systems in a facility interact.
- Appreciate the issues associated with heating, ventilation, and air conditioning systems.
- Understand the importance of air quality and how it is maintained.
- Characterize the energy systems used in a facility.
- Know how the plumbing system delivers and extracts water.
- Appreciate the various internal and external systems that help a facility function.

Chapter 6 covered the building envelope (foundation, walls, and roof) and the process of building a facility, including all the necessary components such as the electrical wiring, fire suppression piping, phone and data lines, plumbing systems, roof, parking lot, and the all-important **heating, ventilation, and air conditioning** (HVAC) system. Buildings radically changed after World War II. For example, more exterior glass, lighter construction, nonopening windows, and an emphasis on interior comforts changed the way facilities were managed (Carlson and DiGiandomenico, 1992). These new buildings required HVAC systems to ensure compliance with new ventilation codes and to provide a comfortable work environment.

This chapter critically examines the systems in a building, how they operate, and strategies for maximizing their effectiveness. The first and foremost system in a building is the HVAC system. The HVAC system cannot operate without all the appropriate ductwork, electrical supply, and associated hardware. But even if all the mechanical elements are present, if the system is too noisy it can interrupt an event. Concert goers listening to an orchestra play a quiet piece in a quiet theater do not appreciate suddenly hearing the air conditioning system come on and begin to rattle.

Other systems covered in this chapter include lighting, plumbing, various internal systems, and various external systems. These systems are the soul of the building, and no building can work unless they are functioning properly. If the plumbing system malfunctions, spectators will be upset about the toilets or the lack of water. If a fire suppression system is not functioning, scores of deaths could be the result. Parking, an external system, can be a source of revenue, but if the parking lot is not operating smoothly or is not properly maintained, fans will be very upset.

Automation has revolutionized the way systems operate. Systems can be programmed to turn on and off based on variables such as light levels, time, or the number of people in a room. Furthermore, security systems based on an identification card, the iris of the eye, the voice, or thumbprints cannot work without a computer to analyze the information and compare it against information in a database. Older systems relied on information cards to track maintenance records. Now computer programs provide records for energy audits, material inventory, maintenance management programs, scheduling software, and numerous other applications. Thus, it is important to remember that the systems discussed in this chapter need to interact with an automated processing system to function effectively and maximize value while minimizing expenses.

Computers are not used simply to monitor HVAC systems or lighting. These systems need to be integrated with the entire facility. Other elements that should be included in an integrated system and can be monitored and adjusted electronically include security alarms, smoke and fire detectors, occupancy sensors, chemical and carbon monoxide detectors, air intakes, water spigots, and equipment. Technology is significantly changing the manner in which systems— and the facility itself—operate.

The drive for new apps has been applied to almost all facets of sport. One such app makes it easier to identify the most appropriate time to go to the restroom during a game. The product, called Tooshlights, is an automated light-emitting diode (LED) lighting system that helps expedite the flow of traffic in public restrooms. The system notifies users when stalls are available. A green light indicates a free regular stall, a blue light signifies a free handicapped stall, and a red light denotes an occupied stall. An upcoming Tooshlights app will allow sport venue patrons to choose their venue and seating section to see where the closest restrooms are and how many stalls are available. This example illustrates how technology is increasingly integrated in the sport facility experience.

HEATING, VENTILATION, AND AIR CONDITIONING

You have probably sat in your dorm room or apartment sweating on a hot summer day. You open the window to let air in, but there is no breeze and the room is still hot. You turn on the air conditioner, which cools the air. The air conditioner is a form of an HVAC system. An HVAC system is needed in every building because buildings keep inside air inside and outside air outside, unless someone

Saunders: The importance of being efficient

Photo courtesy of Tom Saunders.

My name is Tom Saunders. I am the intercollegiate athletic facilities manager for the University of Maryland, College Park. Our facilities include the Comcast Center, Byrd Stadium, and a host of other athletic venues, administrative offices, team locker rooms, and maintenance facilities.

The importance of efficiently operating facility systems and equipment cannot be understated. These systems include but are not limited to heating, ventilation, and air conditioning; plumbing; lighting; audio; data; safety; security; and waste management. Higher energy costs, increased competition, and becoming more sustainable are but a few reasons for implementing a facility systems plan and keeping equipment in working order.

A facility's HVAC system is one of the greatest start-up costs for a building and is one of the largest annual expenses. Without an efficient HVAC system, energy expenses can eat up a building's operating budget. A networked communications system along with automated programs for regulating air temperature, humidity, and air exchange can control when systems are on and off based on the required setting and schedule. Relying on human control to change settings can lead to lost time and money. Keeping systems in good order through regular inspections and changing working parts such as filters and belts will keep the equipment running properly for many years.

Lighting systems are another part of buildings that use a lot of energy. Implementing a system for controlling a lighting system is key to managing costs. Computer-operated lighting systems allow people to turn lights on and off when needed without having to go from one end of the building to the other. Installing sensors and replacing bulbs and ballasts with high-efficiency equipment is also imperative. We recently executed a new lighting control program that resulted in more than $200,000 of energy savings in its first year for Comcast Center alone.

With the high demand for energy and the importance of sustainability, doing everything you can to decrease consumption is a necessity. Many government departments and energy companies have savings programs that help facilities operate while using less energy. They offer rebates and loans on everything from installing energy-efficient lighting and refrigeration upgrades to cash incentives for running a building on a generator during hot summer days when energy demands are high. With the help of our local power company we were able to change over 90% of the light fixtures in Comcast Center to high-efficiency light-emitting diodes. Facility managers can contact an account executive at their local electric company for a full list of programs.

Building operating systems are interconnected and require detailed procedures to keep them running cohesively and efficiently. The implementation and upkeep of these systems is a top priority for any facility operations department.

wants to interchange the air by opening a window or door. Otherwise, buildings are designed to be closed. A building will always have some passive air coming in through walls, windows, open doors, broken seals, or more aggressive means such as attic fans. Although it is nice to keep warm air inside during winter and warm air out during summer, this is difficult because of building structures (e.g., high ceilings that trap heat near the roof) or building materials that do not effectively prevent air and temperature transfer. Thus, electronic systems, from vents to hot-water registers to air conditioners, are used to keep a room or building at the desired temperature, move air around, and regulate the humidity level.

Heating a building once entailed using a fireplace or a wood-burning stove, which limited the size and scope of buildings. In 1861, William Siemens introduced the first electric furnace. In 1901, the first HVAC system was introduced to cool and control the humidity at the New York Stock Exchange. In 1906, the term *air conditioning* was coined. In 1922, Carrier Corporation invented the first centrifugal chiller. A 1938 study showed that the productivity of workers at The Detroit Edison Company increased 51% after comfort cooling was installed. The Clean Air Act was passed in 1990, and by 1995 manufacturers could no longer make chillers that use chlorofluorocarbons because they contribute to ozone depletion. These milestones show how rapidly HVAC systems have evolved and continue to evolve.

Better ventilation does not simply help maintain air quality and set appropriate temperature levels. Increasing ventilation rates (to around 10 L per second per person from the recommended 8.3 L) can reduce sick building symptoms where colds and diseases are spread through air recirculating in a building. Increasing the ventilation rate can reduce sickness in the workplace (500,000 fewer cases per year throughout the United States), and eliminate 9.4 million employee sick days per year, and boost work productivity by 0.3%. Increasing the ventilation rate even more would result in even more savings and benefits ("Better Ventilation," 2012). Bringing in more external air is good for people in a facility and therefore good for facility management.

One of the key disputes in any workplace or sport facility is whether the facility is too hot or too cold. A 2010 study showed that 10% of workers have fought with others over office temperature. Although 54% felt that the temperature in their workplace was just right, 27% described the office temperature as too hot and 19% said it was too cold ("Office Temperature," 2010).

Air needs to be moved in and out of every building. One area that requires significant ventilation is the kitchen. Kitchen appliances such as deep fryers, ovens, and broilers produce a significant amount of heat that needs to be vented out of the area. In a facility, if the venting system can be run underneath seating areas, then some of the radiant heat can help warm the building. Incidentally, if the system is designed correctly, the smells from the kitchen can be pumped through the facility to help generate interest in purchasing food.

The HVAC system can contain numerous components, and each component needs to be critically analyzed to determine if changes or modifications are needed. An HVAC system typically accounts for 20% to 25% of a new facility's cost. Thus, significant time and effort need to be spent on maintaining the system so it operates effectively.

Heating

A building heating system utilizes an energy conversion process to create usable heat and a control system to distribute the heat. If conventional fuels such as coal, oil, or natural gas are used, the facility needs a heat plant to process the fuel into heat. Other heating options, such as city steam, do not require a heat plant. The fuel is transformed through a heat transference system into steam, warm air, or hot water that is pumped through the facility to generate heat.

Once the heat is generated in a heat plant, it is transferred to the building. One option is a warm-air transference system in which the warm air is pumped by means of ductwork through the same distribution system utilized by the air conditioning system. Hot-water transference systems utilize baseboard heaters or convectors, which are like car radiators. When cold air hits the tubes filled with hot water, the cooler air is warmed, thus warming the room. Steam-heating transference

iceSHEFFIELD ARENA

When Sheffield International Venues (SIV) decided to build a two-sheet ice rink, the HVAC system was a major priority, and they wanted to make sure the system was appropriately monitored to run as smoothly as possible. A system was needed to monitor chillers, boilers, domestic hot-water services, air-handling units (featuring humidification and dehumidification plants), and the complete lighting system. SIV contracted with Tridium, a company focused on building system automation, to develop a web-based monitoring system where managers could monitor all aspects of the facility from any online computer anywhere in the world. This accessibility ensures that all supervisory actions such as monitoring, adjustment, data archiving, and equipment maintenance can take place from any personal computer (Tridium, 2009).

Built at a cost of £15.7 million (approximately US$25 million), iceSheffield features two Olympic-size ice rinks and seating for more than 1,500 people in a state-of-the-art sport facility, located next to the English Institute of Sport. The facility has become very involved in energy management. iceSheffield and its parent operating entity (SIV) published their energy efficiency goal and have been active in highlighting the progress they have made to date. Their energy efficiency commitments are highlighted here:

- Reducing CO_2 emissions
- Reducing energy consumption and costs
- Eliminating as much waste as feasibly possible
- Increasing energy efficiency

They plan to achieve these goals through the following methods:

- Increasing monitoring of usage, load management, and tariff negotiation
- Investing in energy-efficient and green energy technologies
- Improving staff awareness and involvement
- Encouraging voluntary initiatives

SIV produces monthly reports that show energy consumption trends, outline any investments made, compare consumption year on year and month on month, show comparisons with targets, and highlight the reasons for any variances. Reports are also published every year for the board and are made available for public perusal on request (iceSheffield, 2009).

---

systems are similar to hot-water systems, but steam is pumped through the pipes rather than hot water. Steam systems utilize radiators that are similar to the convectors for hot water but are exposed directly to the air in the room; convectors are normally covered to prevent burns.

Once the fuel is transferred to heat and the heat is transferred to the proper location, a heat control network dictates where the heat will actually go. The heat control network is usually governed by a thermostat, which measures the temperature and its location and compares these results with predetermined temperature settings. Computers are also utilized to monitor room temperature and provide more efficient heat distribution. Some facilities use a combination of heating systems. Thus, a facility might have radiant heating but will also utilize ceiling fans to help circulate the hot air. In addition, new technologies are now making it easier to heat a room. In-ground heating coils can be installed in cement floors. These coils heat the cement and radiate the heat more effectively than forced air or radiator systems, which can result in more even distribution and reduced heating expenses.

Cooling

The most popular cooling system is a vapor compression system. The heart and soul of this system is the refrigerant, which starts absorbing heat when it boils. Besides a refrigerant, the vapor compression system requires an evaporator, a compressor, a condenser, and an expansion device. These elements are typically integrated into one or two units. However, such a system is classified not as an air conditioning system but as an air chilling system. Other air chilling systems operate similarly to heat radiator systems except that cold water is pumped to radiators and the surrounding hot air is chilled. No matter what system is used, the intent is to reach an ideal air temperature.

Some people prefer a hot environment while others like it cooler. The HVAC system should automatically maintain an appropriate temperature and humidity level. Most people consider 64.4 °F to 77 °F (18 °C-25 °C) a comfortable and pleasant temperature, and 30% to 60% is the preferred humidity level (Immig and Rish, 1997). The ideal range is a warm environment between 65 °F (18.3 °C) and 75 °F (23.9 °C); the American College of Sports Medicine (1992) recommends a temperature range of 68 °F to 72 °F (20 °C-22.2 °C) (Immig and Rish, 1997). These numbers are not standards, but recommendations.

Another major factor that affects air conditioning is humidity. A high relative humidity means that the amount of moisture in the air is high. Humidity is especially important in sport because it affects the amount of heat produced by an athlete and the ability of air to absorb moisture from the body. If the humidity level is more than 80%, the ability of air to absorb moisture from the body is reduced, and an athlete will sweat more. That is why people tend to sweat much more when competing in humid summer air than when they work out at the same intensity in lower humidity. The American College of Sports Medicine recommends a humidity level below 60%, but this level is very hard to achieve, even in some air-conditioned buildings.

Cooling effectiveness is influenced by the occupant **heat load**. The heat load is affected by two factors: the number of people in a facility and their activity. If a large number of people are jumping around and producing heat, the air conditioning system must work harder to compensate for the added heat they are generating. In addition to occupants, appliances such as stoves produce a heat load.

Larger air conditioning systems typically have three major components: high-volume air handlers to move air around, centrifugal chillers to cool water, and cooling towers to help dissipate the heat generated by the chillers. Air handlers are supplied with 45 °F water from the chiller plant. The cold water passes through coils in the air handler and cools the air as it passes. The centrifugal chiller, in turn, transfers to a cooling tower the heat it generates cooling the water. The cooling tower absorbs the heat and then dissipates the heat by evaporation. Figure 7.1 highlights the components in a typical forced-air air conditioning system.

Ventilation

It is estimated that people in industrialized countries on average spend 70% to 90% of their time indoors (Immig and Rish, 1997). Ventilation helps produce better air quality by extracting older air and replacing it with new air. The American College of Sports Medicine recommends 8 to 12 **air exchanges** per hour in a gymnasium, which can be accomplished with several large ceiling fans. Most facilities utilize multiple intake and exhaust locations to circulate the air appropriately. For example, a central ventilation system for a building draws from every corner of a room and possibly returns the air through a center location.

When a fabric roof is put on top of an existing facility, care needs to be exercised to ensure that the HVAC system is working properly. In 2009, a retractable roof was put over Centre Court at Wimbledon. Ten 246-foot (75 m) trusses were installed to support the roof. Mechanical arms and jacks move the trusses apart, which stretches the fabric taut. Every minute, about 4,400 gallons (16,656 L) of chilled water is pumped from nine chillers in a piping system buried under the ground through the coils in the air handlers located in the roof. The total air conditioning capacity of the system is 2,200 tons of air volume. Diffusers direct cooled and dehumidified air toward the spectators. This helps keep fans (and the grass) comfortable. To prevent condensation the air is circulated toward the roof, and a total of 254,000 cubic feet (7,192 cu m) of air is moved per minute. The air is circulated through ductwork around the edges of the building so that it does not interfere with the fabric. Outside air is also brought in to pressurize the building; this helps keep the indoor conditions at 75 °F and 50% relative humidity (Murphy, 2009).

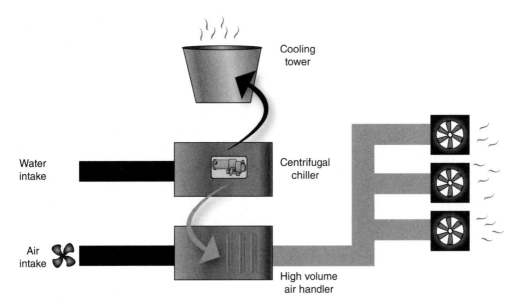

Figure 7.1 Larger air conditioning systems typically have three major components beyond the HVAC ductwork system.

AIR QUALITY

Air quality has various meanings. Some people prefer the broader term *air environment*, which includes air temperature, humidity, and ventilation rate. However, these factors do not necessarily affect air quality. External air quality cannot be managed the same way as indoor air quality. Thus, if a stadium is 1 mile (1.6 km) from a dump, it may be safe on some days, but on windy days the smell may be horrendous. External air quality can be influenced by the following:

- Smells (which can be caused by any of the following)
- Chemicals (volatile organic compounds, pesticides, cigarette smoke, carbon monoxide, and nitrogen dioxide)
- Biological elements (molds, fungi, microorganisms, and dust mites)
- Physical components and pollutants (dust, radiation, radon, respirable particles, electromagnetic fields) (Immig and Rish, 1997)

A variety of factors can also influence indoor air quality (IAQ), which refers to the nature of air that affects the health and well-being of a facility's occupants:

- External variables including climate, water infiltration, and ventilation and infiltration of outdoor air
- Building- and HVAC-related factors such as building design; structural materials; and HVAC design, operations, and materials
- Internal variables such as interior design, building materials (paints, sealants, adhesives, carpets), furnishings, equipment, occupant activities, pest management, cleaning agents, and any internal construction or renovation (Immig and Rish, 1997)

Air quality is such a major issue that the organizing committee for the 2000 Sydney Olympics prepared the document "Environmental Guidelines for the Summer Olympic Games" as part of the city's Olympic bid. All facilities in Sydney were required to comply with the recommendations. Following are some of the IAQ guidelines specified in the document:

- IAQ needs to be considered in all facility design.
- Operating manuals should be developed for all facilities to help maintain good IAQ.
- Facilities should use foliage plants with known capacity to absorb indoor air pollutants.

- Air quality should be managed through selecting building materials that do not emit harmful levels of pollutants; can be easily cleaned with benign cleaners; do not emit harmful levels of radiation; and are resistant to microorganisms such as bacteria, mold, and dust mites.

- Construction should be completed with sufficient time to have the new buildings dissipate any volatile constituents (Immig and Rish, 1997).

Air quality was an even bigger concern at the 2008 Beijing Olympics. Construction efforts produced significant air pollution and waste. This pollution, compounded with the already poor air quality, resulted in some athletes wearing breathing masks and the government banning cars from the road.

One of the greatest concerns about IAQ involves ice arenas. The arenas themselves are not the biggest problem, even though new "airtight" buildings minimize the amount of passive ventilation in a building and temperatures are kept lower to reduce the cooling costs. The problem is with the resurfacers (often called Zambonis). In a study of 19 rinks, those with propane- and gas-powered resurfacers showed a much greater likelihood of having a dangerous level of nitrogen dioxide and carbon monoxide. At one rink the level was 4,000 parts per billion, which was 36 times the recommended maximum exposure ("Breath of Not-So-Fresh Air," 1999). Three states—Massachusetts, Minnesota, and Rhode Island—have standard air quality requirements for ice rinks. Electric resurfacers produce much less nitrogen dioxide but cost about $20,000 more than other resurfacers.

Chemicals in the air are nothing new for sport facilities. Casinos are known for pumping in fresh air or pure oxygen to keep people awake. Some sport facilities take the opposite approach when they anticipate rowdy crowds. Thus, at a monster truck pull or motocross event where the crowd could be rowdy, an arena may slow down the ventilation to keep the carbon monoxide levels high, which makes the fans sleepier and more lethargic and thus lowers the risk of a rowdy crowd. Any such strategies need to be used with caution to avoid violating Occupational Safety and Health Administration or other standards and causing illness. These steps are also affected by laws being passed regarding smoking in public places and the ways in which a facility needs to respond when fans smoke. Thus, ventilation can involve numerous legal and ethical issues. To improve air quality, maximizing air ventilation is more important than maximizing air circulation (Immig and Rish, 1997).

Although there is no magic recipe for improving IAQ, strategies include building with the right materials, removing harmful materials or restricting access to harmful areas, limiting the use of certain pesticides, installing localized exhaust systems, and diluting the environment through more aggressive ventilation (Immig and Rish, 1997).

One way to minimize unpleasant smells and increase IAQ is to use plants, which are one of the world's most efficient air purifiers. Air enters through the soil, is cleaned by the roots, and is then released. Some plants are better air fresheners than others. The 10 plants that freshen air most quickly are the areca palm, corn plant, lady palm, bamboo palm, ficus or weeping fig, Boston fern, English ivy, mum, umbrella tree, and peace lily (Kellogg and Pettigrew, 2008). A large stadium or arena using this approach could require hundreds of plants, each needing a planter, watering, and regular care. Such an approach could cost thousands of dollars every year, plus even more to replace any plants that die.

ENERGY SYSTEMS

Energy, especially electric energy, is indispensable for sport facilities with all their lights, cooking equipment, electronic scoreboards, and so on. Approximately 67% of the energy used in larger office buildings is electrical energy (Carlson and DiGiandomenico, 1992). Large sport facilities typically consume the same percentage of energy during game days through use of all the electronic devices, although they use much less electricity when the facility is not putting on an event. Of the total amount of electricity used in a typical building, 40% is used for the cooling system, 33% for lighting, and 12% for heating. By analyzing where and how energy is utilized, a facility can take specific steps to reduce expenses. For example, alternate

SELLING WITH SCENTS

Most facility managers see an HVAC system as an expense item. Although an HVAC system can provide significant comfort that might increase attendance, such systems have normally not been perceived as profit centers. However, that is all changing. In 2013, the St. Louis Rams worked with ScentAir to inject scents into the HVAC system in an effort to increase concession sales. The team tested 30 smells, and the top three were popcorn, soda, and cotton candy. The team chose cotton candy because the fragrance was long lasting and because it evoked in fans memories of good times. The scents were injected into the HVAC system at both main entrances when fans walked in. The scents helped increase cotton candy sales throughout the stadium and increased concession sales across all other items (Dillow, 2013). Using smells to enhance purchasing is nothing new: Movie theaters for years pumped in the smell of hot popcorn, and Cinnabon pumps out the smell of their delicious treats in malls across the world.

cooling and air movement strategies need to be implemented to reduce HVAC costs. Furthermore, although lighting costs account for 33% of a building's electrical costs, most buildings are unoccupied 72% of the time (Carlson and DiGiandomenico, 1992). Thus, lights need to be shut off when someone is not in a room to help save energy. In addition, new lighting systems are being built using wireless lighting, in which lighting fixtures are connected through a computer program. Instead of turning light switches on and off, a computer monitors the lights and can be programmed to shut them off at specified times. Such a system is a new component of computer-aided facility management.

A watt is a measure of electrical energy used. Higher-wattage appliances utilize more energy than lower-wattage appliances. Electricity is billed in kilowatt-hours (a kilowatt is 1,000 watts), which represents the energy consumption rate. Thus, a room with five 200-watt light fixtures turned on is using 1,000 watt-hours, which equals 1 kilowatt-hour. The cost for electricity (sold in kilowatt-hours) varies based on location and usage. Consumer usage is normally more expensive than industrial or commercial usage. In 2013, the average cost of electricity in the Northeast was 14.52 cents per kilowatt-hour, whereas in the south-central part of the United States the average cost was only 8.74 cents per kilowatt-hour. The most expensive place to purchase electricity was Hawaii, where the average cost was 33 cents per kilowatt-hour.

The biggest concerns with any system are how much it costs to purchase and how much it costs to operate. The lifetime cost associated with an HVAC system is many times more than the initial cost of the HVAC unit and its installation. Electricity costs for common household appliances include the following:

Refrigerator and freezer, 18 cubic feet (0.5 cu m)	$0.56 per day
Oven	$0.25 per hour
Toaster	$0.09 per hour
Central air conditioning, 1,600 square feet (148.6 sq m)	$3.76 per day
Ceiling fan	$0.01 per 2 hours
Washing machine (hot water)	$0.53 per load
Washing machine (cold water)	$0.04 per load
Dryer	$0.25 per load
Vacuum cleaner	$0.07 per hour
Television	$0.02 per hour
Computer	$0.01 per 2 hours

(Davis, 2009).

These prices show how easily a stadium can generate electrical bills in the millions of dollars and how energy reduction strategies can help reduce these expenses. Most stadiums and arenas enter into electrical purchasing contracts to help reduce costs. If such utility bills are not paid, the power is shut off.

Backup generators are critical for life safety systems in a sport facility. With possibly more than 100,000 people in a public assembly facility, what happens if the power goes out? Backup energy is required for lighting and sound systems so exit instructions can be broadcast over loudspeakers or on the scoreboard. A backup generator may also be required to maintain the HVAC systems to keep ventilating the building or remove harmful smoke from certain areas.

Lighting

Imagine trying to read at night without a light. Now imagine trying to see a hockey puck or a baseball coming at you at close to 100 miles an hour (160 km/h) and having poor lighting. In sport, lighting is crucial for seeing the action on the field during a night game, seeing the action on the ice or court in an arena, or seeing weights being lifted. Facility managers need to be concerned with both indoor and outdoor lighting. Before detailing the specific types of lighting at facilities, a general explanation of lighting terminology is in order. **Ambient lighting**, or atmosphere lighting, refers to actual sunlight. Both indoor and outdoor facilities utilize ambient lighting. Indoor facilities utilize free and effective lighting through windows that allow sunlight into a facility. Outdoor facilities typically have light available during daytime hours. However, both indoor and outdoor facilities rely on lights when the sun is blocked or after the sun starts setting. The Houston Astrodome, for example, was originally built with glass panes in the dome to allow sun into the facility to help the grass grow. However, the glare from the sun made it very difficult to field balls, which led management to paint the glass and install AstroTurf.

A lamp refers to any source of light, whether a candle, flashlight, torch, or spotlight. The output produced by any lamp is measured in lumens. A lumen is the amount of light energy that strikes a specific distance from the light source. If 1 lumen falls a distance of 1 foot (0.3 m) from the light source (called a standard candle), the **light intensity** is called 1 foot-candle. The farther one moves away from the light source, the larger the area that the lumens are spread over, so

light intensity decreases. Light intensity is measured by the foot-candles at the playing surface (Borsenik and Stutts, 1997). See "Foot-Candle Requirements at Various Sport Surfaces" for a list of recommended light intensity by sport. These are the recommended numbers when a system is installed; changes can occur as a result of wind movement and burned-out lamps, for example, which requires facility managers to be vigilant with light maintenance. Thus, over several years 100 foot-candles can be reduced to 70 foot-candles and detract from a quality event.

Light levels should be based on the type of activity undertaken at the facility. There are three classes of lighting. Class I lighting is used in facilities that host competitive play in front of a significant number of spectators; the game is possibly broadcast on television. Class II lighting is used in facilities that hold up to 5,000 spectators. Class III lighting—the lowest level—is used in facilities that host small crowds or that are used for recreational purposes. For example, in a baseball facility, class I lighting would be 150 foot-candles in the infield and 100 foot-candles in the outfield, class II lighting would be around 100 foot-candles in the infield and 70 foot-candles in the outfield, and class III lighting would be around 50 foot-candles in the infield and 30 foot-candles in the outfield.

Indoor Lighting

Lighting can be provided by various means, such as windows that let in natural ambient light, gas lanterns, and light bulbs. Light sources can be placed in different locations from the ceiling to the floor. The exact location depends on style and how strong the light needs to be. The optimal light strength and direction also depend on the particular activity. For example, badminton is best played with darker-colored walls to help players see the shuttlecock. However, play can be enhanced either through the use of indirect lights all over the court or through strategic placement of direct lights around the court's outer boundaries to help prevent losing shuttles in the light.

Direct lighting is light that is directed downward from a fixture. **Indirect lighting** from ceiling fixtures focuses the light against the ceiling so that 90% of the light energy is reflected back to the

FOOT-CANDLE REQUIREMENTS AT VARIOUS SPORT SURFACES

These are the recommended numbers when a system is installed. Because of the lighting needs of cameras, a higher foot-candle amount is required for any facility where a broadcast is going to occur.

Baseball	50-150 foot-candles in the infield; 30-100 foot-candles in the outfield
Basketball	30-100 foot-candles
Football	30-100 foot-candles
Hockey	30-80 foot-candles from youth to college competition;
	100+ foot-candles for professional ice hockey
Soccer	30-75 foot-candles
Softball	30-100 foot-candles in the infield; 20-30 foot-candles in the outfield
Swimming	30-180 foot-candles
Tennis	40-125 foot-candles
Track	30-50 foot-candles

From Fried, 1999.

floor from the ceiling. In contrast, **diffuse lighting** reflects only 40% to 60% of the light energy back from the ceiling to the ground, and semidirect lighting reflects 60% to 90% of the light back to the floor. Semi-indirect lighting bounces back only 10% to 40% of the light from the ceiling to the floor, with the remaining percentage being direct light to the ground (Borsenik and Stutts, 1997).

The key to any indoor lighting system is to have the proper light directed at the proper spots and replaced at regular intervals. Table 7.1 shows differences between three types of indoor systems and the effect associated with direct versus indirect lighting.

The fact that a system is cheaper to install does not mean that the system will be less expensive in the long run. Incandescent lamps typically last for 1,000 hours. If such a lamp is in an office and the office light is on 10 hours per day, 4 days a week, for an average of 4.33 weeks per month, the light will be on 173 (10 × 4 × 4.33) hours a month. By dividing the expected life by the hours per month (1,000/173), one can determine that a typical incandescent lamp in that office will last 5.8 months (Borsenik and Stutts, 1997). A fluorescent lamp typically lasts for about 6,000 hours. Knowing the lamp's life expectancy is especially critical for lamps above a gym floor that may be 30 feet (9 m) in the air. To change the lamps the facility must rent or buy an expensive hoist system. The new kids on the block are compact fluorescent lights (CFLs) and LEDs, which are much more energy efficient than traditional light bulbs. CFLs are more expensive than incandescent bulbs and contain mercury, which can cause a disposal issue. LED lights were initially very small but now are being clustered together, and new silicon technology can enhance the lights and reduce the costs. LED lights are long lasting (10 times longer than even CFL bulbs); durable (no filament, so they last longer); cool (generate 95% less heat than incandescent bulbs); and—most important—more energy efficient, as LED lights use one-third the electricity of CFLs and one-thirtieth the electricity of incandescent bulbs ("Energy Efficient Lighting," 2009).

Numerous states have outlawed incandescent bulbs. Metal halide light fixtures have been considered energy hogs for years. In 2012, the War Memorial Arena in Syracuse, New York, switched from metal halide to an LED display specifically designed for sport facilities. The old lights consumed 263,000 kilowatt-hours per year. The new lights reduced the power usage by 87% to 32,000 kilowatt-hours per year. Just as important, lighting increased from 115 foot-candles to 217 foot-candles. The bulbs in exit signs, which normally consume 900 watts of power per year, were replaced with bulbs that use only 150 watts. The arena also saved time by installing the new LED display. To black out the arena for events or player introductions, the old lights had to be covered with blinders; otherwise, it took 30 minutes to turn the lights back on after they had been turned

Table 7.1 Direct Versus Indirect Lighting Systems

Category	Direct	Inverted high bay	Asymmetric indirect
Wattage	400	1,000	1,000
Number of fixtures	40	20	20
Estimated cost to install ($)	13,920	10,600	30,000
Energy use* (kw/yr)	92,160	115,200	115,200
Annual energy cost ($)	3,926	4,907	4,907

*Based on lights being on 16 hours a day, 7 days a week, for 12 months.

From Brooks and Martinez 2002.

off. The new LED lights turn on instantly, which allows the arena to go dark and then back to full light in seconds (Steinbach, 2013).

Rigging

Indoor lighting is normally suspended from the ceiling. Lights, scoreboards, and sound systems cannot merely be attached to the roof or super-structure. The entire system used to suspend items from a facility's roof is called **rigging**. The key variable for rigging is the load capacity. Load capacity refers to how much weight the system can support. For example, a given beam may be able to support 5,000 pounds (2,268 kg) at its center point or 10,000 pounds (4,536 kg) across its whole length. Besides weight loads, riggers need to understand weight limits, forces, geometry, the strength of rigging equipment, safety concerns, and dynamic loading (Donovan, 1994). All these aspects are associated with one overriding concern: safety. Rigging strength can be significantly reduced by age, wear, heat, fatigue, chemical exposure, and the effect force can have on the rigging gear (Donovan, 1994). On the basis of these dynamics, the rigging can help determine what lighting system may be installed in a facility.

External Lighting

In 1883, General Electric installed open-face lights across a minor league field and created what some consider the first night ball game (Steinbach, 2001b). Others claim that the first night game took place in 1924 and that the first professional night game was held in 1935 at Crosley Field in Cincinnati (Lindstrom, 1993). Lighting an athletic facility is not as simple as mounting high-powered lights on towering posts and aiming them at the surface. There are various factors to consider in terms of the actual light, the structures, and the electrical devices needed.

Quantity and Quality The quality of lighting is measured by the uniformity, or evenness, of light on the field. Poor light uniformity poses a threat to player safety and often detracts from spectator enjoyment. Lighting that is uneven makes players appear to change speed when they move from light areas to dark areas, making the action hard to follow (Rogers, 1994).

Besides cost, one of the biggest problems with any external lighting system has to do with light leaving the intended area through glare, trespass, and sky glow (Steinbach, 2001a). **Glare** refers to light that is hard on the viewer's eyes. Glare can also be defined as a point of very bright light. This problem can come from too much light or uneven light on a field. **Trespass** describes light that was intended to go into one area but also enters into another area. Trespass is often referred to as spill (light is spilling from the intended area). **Sky glow** describes light that is directed or reflected upward and is wasted in space. Sky glow can be seen as an orange haze over a city when one is flying in a plane at night. These problems can be minimized with fixed visors, internal louvers, soft lighting systems, and faceted reflectors.

Structural Considerations The two structural components of an outdoor lighting system are the luminaire assemblies and the poles. The luminaire assembly, which consists of the lamps, reflectors, ballast mounting, cross-arm, and mounting hardware, should be engineered as a single integral unit. The unit is installed and positioned by field aiming, which entails creating a grid on the playing surface with strings and flags and then targeting each light fixture to a point on the grid. After all the alignments are completed, light levels are measured and workers lock each light into place.

The poles used for a lighting system can be made of wood, concrete, or steel. Wood poles are the least expensive to purchase and install but have high maintenance costs due to warping and twisting from exposure to the elements. Concrete poles are less expensive than steel poles and can be buried directly in the ground. Concrete poles are often found on the coast, where sea salt can cause extensive damage to steel. Steel poles have a long life, cost little to maintain, and are aesthetically pleasing. New telescoping steel poles are being developed that can be raised and lowered by means of a motorized mechanism. This process can reduce costs by making it cheaper to replace lamps, and the poles can be lowered before a major storm.

Glare associated with lighting is often caused by spill lighting. The solution to this problem often entails mounting offending light fixtures high enough or in the right locations so they can be aimed downward at the correct angle to prevent glare. Through proper angling and using reflectors (which focus the strongest lights in a given area) or blocking devices (which block light to given areas), facility management can cut off direct views of the lamp arc from viewing locations that suffer from glare. Medium-beam fixtures are most commonly used on sport fields to spread the light over a broader area. Narrow-beam distribution are usually confined to lights mounted over 100 feet high when the facility needs very directed lights level at a given spot.

Energy Usage

One of the key elements of managing any system in a facility is tracking usage and expenses. If certain systems cost more to operate than they should, they should be replaced. A refrigerator that runs continuously can cost several hundred dollars more per year than a cycling unit. The largest energy expense for any facility—50% of total energy cost—originates from the kitchen. The greatest single energy use in a kitchen comes from cooking, followed by equipment and lighting (Borsenik and Stutts, 1997).

An **energy audit** examines where energy usage and energy losses are coming from. Assume that a facility uses 1,000 bulbs that are 100 watts each. The energy consumption from these lights will be 100,000 watts (100 × 1,000). The audit can

---

TOP 10 CONSIDERATIONS FOR A SPORT LIGHTING PLAN

1. Identify where and when lighting is needed.

2. To prevent light pollution, choose appropriate fixtures such as shields to properly aim the lights.

3. Pick the best bulb for each application. For example, some bulbs are compatible with motion sensors, whereas other bulbs require additional electrical equipment to work with motion sensors.

4. Analyze energy shut-off controls to help turn lights on and off from a cell phone or from other devices or locations.

5. Consider how high the lights need to be positioned, which can be significantly different in a gym or stadium compared with a fitness facility.

6. Address light trespass by ensuring that the light levels at the property line do not exceed 0.1 foot-candles when the property is adjacent to a business or 0.05 foot-candles when the property is adjacent to residential property.

7. Make sure that the lights produce the correct level of foot-candles for the intended activity and ancillary activities such as broadcasting needs.

8. Bring in a lighting consultant. Lighting is one of the most difficult systems to master. Getting the right people involved from the start can help prevent major problems in the future.

9. After a system is installed, inspect it for compliance with the lighting plan. Regular review can help ensure that the lights stay true to the plan over time.

10. Take care to prevent trespass and glow from indoor lights as well as outdoor lights (Penny, 2012).

help identify the cost associated with such energy usage and then be used to propose acceptable alternatives. If the facility could use 75-watt bulbs in place of the 100-watt bulbs with no appreciable difference in lighting, there could be a significant savings. The 75-watt bulbs would produce 75,000 watts of energy consumption, which is a 25% reduction in energy expenses. Furthermore, it might be feasible to reduce the hours used from 10 to 7 hours per day, which would also represent a significant savings (30%).

After the audit, an energy program needs to be developed. The first phase entails establishing a specific goal. For example, a facility manager could plan to reduce energy consumption 10%. If the facility has a zoned HVAC system (meaning that air is moved only to designated areas), the temperature setting in unoccupied offices could be reduced to 55 °F (12.8 °C) during the heating season and allowed to reach 85 °F (29.4 °C) during the cooling season (Borsenik and Stutts, 1997). Another usage strategy is to limit water consumption by guests. Restrooms in stadiums and arenas often have built-in sensors on toilets, urinals, and faucets to reduce the total amount of water used. Other energy reduction strategies include replacing windows and caulking; installing time clock and motion detection systems to automatically open and close appliances; installing load-cycling systems that monitor electrical usage and turn devices on and off in a cyclical manner to save energy and reduce costs; and using a computer energy control system that can cycle loads, control demand, and reduce total energy consumption. Chapter 10 covers additional strategies for saving energy.

PLUMBING

In a typical office building, restrooms account for 37% of water usage, followed by cooling and heating (28%), landscaping (22%), and kitchen and dishwashing (13%) ("Slash Water Use," 2013). These numbers would be significantly different for sport facilities, where the cooking for a game might be much more significant (such as cooking 20,000 hot dogs) and where thousands of fans use restrooms in a short period of time. Because of the demands surrounding water usage, sport facilities must have a strong, logical, and efficient water movement system.

Plumbing systems help transport water and waste from one area to another; they are critical in sport facilities for restrooms, kitchens, and locker rooms. The first question to raise with plumbing systems concerns the amount of water

BEHIND THE SCENES

PREPARING TO KEEP CALM IN A POWER OUTAGE

Imagine that a light goes out in your house. What do you do? You first check the switch to make sure the light is turned on. You might then check the light bulb. If that does not solve the issue, you might check the breaker box. If that does not work, you might contact an electrician. Now imagine that you are hosting the internationally televised Super Bowl and the lights go out in the middle of the game. That is exactly what happened in 2013. Power to the Mercedes-Benz Superdome in New Orleans is supplied by two 13,800-volt underground feeder cables that connect to the power provider's switchgear vault, located about 0.25 mile (0.4 km) from the facility. The A feeder cable supplies power to the west side of the facility and the B feeder cable supplies power to the east side. When the west side went dark at 7:35 p.m., management knew that the A feeder went down. Seven minutes later there was still no light in the San Francisco 49ers' locker room, and teams were advised to stay on the field to help calm the fans. Eight elevators were stuck—some with people inside.

The facility did not have an automatic transfer switch, so they had to undertake a manual bus tie transfer, which restores designated critical loads to an alternate source when utilities go out of service. In this very complex process, every breaker in the affected area needs to be disconnected and then reconnected in a specific sequence to avoid blowing out the electrical system. The facility had undergone drills just in case a power outage occurred. They were about to complete the bus tie transfer to the B feeder system when the energy company stated that power would be restored to the A feeder shortly. The power was out for a total of 23 minutes. It took another 11 minutes to reboot the operating systems (scoreboards, video screens, headsets, elevators, escalators, and so on) and restore the lights (Sadler, 2013).

pressure necessary to lift water to the highest plumbing fixture. If drinking fountains are on the fifth floor of a stadium, there needs to be enough pressure for the water to rise from below street level to the fifth floor. Otherwise the fixture will not work. If there is not enough water pressure, a water-circulating pump must be used to get the water to reach the fifth floor.

The plumbing system is highly technical. For example, if one pipe is feeding five toilets, 35 gallons per minute (132 L) of water pressure is needed, which would require a 1.5-inch (3.8 cm) feeder pipe. If the facility has 20 toilets all connected to the same pipe, the pipe has to be 2 inches (5 cm) (Borsenik and Stutts, 1997).

Wastewater Systems

Of the miles of plumbing in a large stadium or arena, a large proportion is for water that is going to fixtures for waste removal to the sewer systems. Maintenance concerns include inspections of the traps and vents. A trap is a U-shaped pipe under a fixture that contains a certain amount of water; its purpose is to allow water to drain from the fixture but prevent sewer gases from entering the building. Vents allow air to circulate within the drainage system to prevent waste from coming up through the traps. Besides making sure traps and vents operate effectively, facilities must make every effort to prevent clogging of toilets, which is a major concern and a turnoff for customers. The toilets need to be inspected on a regular basis; maintenance workers should have access to augers, rods, and snakes so that they can unclog a toilet quickly.

Water recycling can also be used to remove wastewater, especially during drought conditions. Thus, it may be possible to recycle shower and sink water for use in watering plants. This process is called gray watering, and water can be taken from numerous sources both inside (sink water) and outside (downspouts) a building. In addition to its uses for drinking, showering, and food preparation, water is required for other systems that may not ever be used, such as fire suppression systems.

Fire Suppression Systems

Although fire suppression systems might not seem to be a major concern, an estimated 364,500 residential fires occurred in 2011, resulting in 2,450 deaths, more than 13,900 injuries, and more than $6.6 billion in damages. An additional 84,500 nonresidential fires caused $2.4 billion in damages. More than 100 people were killed in a fire at The Station, a night club in Rhode Island, in one of the worst public assembly facility fires in U.S. history. The Station did not have any fire sprinklers. In contrast, 3 days earlier a night club in Minneapolis caught fire under similar conditions, but the club's automatic sprinkler system extinguished the fire without any casualties (Monikowski and Victor, 2005). This example highlights the importance of fire suppression systems.

Most people do not think about fire safety as a plumbing issue. However, putting out fires effectively requires more than fire extinguishers and axes. Compounds must be delivered to the fire location, and these compounds are transported through dedicated plumbing systems. The average financial loss in a facility ravaged by fire without a sprinkler system is $2.2 million versus only $0.4 million for buildings with sprinklers ("Understanding the Hazard," 2000). Furthermore, a fire causing more than $1 million in damages occurs every 31 days for facilities without sprinklers versus 152 days for facilities with sprinklers. These numbers are impressive, and the cost to obtain such protection is only $1.5 to $3 per square foot.

There have been a number of sport facility fires over the years; some have killed more than 100 fans (Society of Fire Protection Engineers, 2002). Fire risks have decreased as a result of facility construction techniques. At the turn of the century, numerous baseball stadiums were destroyed by fire since they were made of wood. With modern concrete structures (which are not a fuel for fire), it is harder for a fire to thrive but still possible. In the 9/11 tragedy, the twin towers, primarily made of concrete and steel, were still burning several weeks after the attacks.

The first step in fire prevention entails developing strategies that minimize the potential for fires. Fire prevention involves asking the following questions:

- Does the facility comply with all appropriate codes and industry standards?
- Are the various fire alert and suppression systems adequate?
- Are hazardous chemicals or compounds isolated?
- Are there safe escape routes and exits?
- Are employees trained in responding to various fires?
- Are there annual fire suppression tests?
- Have the fire and carbon monoxide alarms been tested in the past 3 months?

Another step is to determine where there are potential fire hazards. Most fires originate in the kitchen area, from cooked food or hot cooking appliances. Fires can also start in equipment rooms where torches may be used to repair or improve equipment (e.g., waxing hockey sticks) or in places where combustible materials (old boxes) are stored, such as the bottom of stairwells. One of the deadliest fires of all time in a sport stadium occurred when trash that had been accumulating for years caught on fire at a soccer game. On May 11, 1985, at Bradford's soccer stadium in England, 56 fans burned to death and 200 were injured when fire engulfed the grandstands ("Sport Disasters," 2003).

Armed with a good understanding of the potential hazards, facility managers can start the process of developing fire prevention strategies. These strategies can entail facility-related steps such as properly housing flammable liquids and combustible materials and training employees on the proper response to fires. One of the most important steps in fire prevention training is conducting mock drills. If a facility is housing 15,000 for an event, the facility manager needs to conduct large-scale fire simulation exercises to effectively train employees and give local emergency officials the chance to learn about the facility.

The next step is to have proper alarm systems. A fixed-temperature detector identifies when the temperature around the alarm is at a predetermined point and then signals an alarm or triggers a suppression system. A rate-of-temperature-rise detector is triggered when the temperature increases a preset amount in a given time period, such as 15 °F (8 °C) in 30 seconds. Some alarms identify smoke rather than heat. Besides having the proper alarm and detection devices, it is essential that devices be placed in the right areas and then maintained. A typical smoke detector unit covers 900 square feet (84 sq m) and should not be more than 35 feet (10.7 m) from the next detector. Detectors should not be placed in high-humidity areas or where there is excessive air current (Borsenik and Stutts, 1997). Other options include flame-detector alarm systems and manual pull alarms. Regardless of the system used, fire codes require all such devices and control systems (fire panel) to be inspected and tested yearly. Once an audit has been conducted and the proper alarm system developed, a fire suppression system must be installed.

The following are the types of fire suppression systems that can be used in a facility.

- Wet-pipe sprinkler systems are always filled with water that is ready to flow onto a fire when the sprinkler head is triggered.

- Dry-pipe sprinkler systems are used in cold weather where water freezing is a problem. In these systems the pipes are filled with air, which is released when the sprinkler is triggered. The released air triggers a valve that releases water into the pipes.

- Deluge sprinkler systems are similar to dry-pipe systems in that there is no water in any of the pipes. However, all the sprinkler heads are open; if there is a fire, the system triggers a flow of water out of all the sprinklers. These systems can cause significant water damage, since a typical sprinkler set at 15 pounds (6.8 kg) per square inch will distribute 22 gallons (83 L) per minute, which can cover a 16-foot (4.9 m) radius.

- Preaction systems utilize a timed delay to allow putting a fire out with suppression agents before the water flows into the dry-pipe system. This system is used in areas such as computer rooms or accounting offices where water can cause substantial damage.

- Misting and fogging systems suppress a fire by spraying a mist from the sprinklers.

- Standpipe and hose systems are required in addition to sprinkler systems. These large pipes, often seen on the outside of large buildings, are like fire hydrants. A fire department can attach fire hoses to these pipes and start pumping water.

- Chemical systems use carbon dioxide, halon replacements, and dry chemicals instead of water. These systems are critical for handling class B (flammable liquid) and class C (electrical) fires. Dry chemicals can cause significant damage to electrical connectors, so such a system is appropriate around a kitchen but not a computer room (Borsenik and Stutts, 1997).

A last concern about fire is the fact that often the smoke from a fire causes more harm than the fire itself. The building should be designed to funnel smoke outside, and all building codes related to fire suppression must be properly followed (e.g., separation of elevator lobbies from corridors).

Laundry Systems

Every facility produces laundry. High school, college, and professional teams need to wash towels, jerseys, physical education apparel, and other items almost daily. Health clubs that offer towels to their members may have their own laundering system or may outsource to a private company for all laundry work. The proper laundering of athletic apparel depends on having a functional laundry room, maintaining the laundry room, and maintaining the equipment.

The equipment needs for a laundering facility vary depending on the amount of items that require laundering. High schools and small colleges generally require only one or two 50-pound (22.7 kg) washers and 75-pound (34 kg) dryers, while larger universities require as many as 10 of each (Mundt, 1997). Laundry facilities should use microprocessor-controlled washing machines that allow the user to specify fabric-appropriate cycles, spin speed, and water extraction levels. Some facilities forgo having a laundry system by utilizing outsourcing options, such as linen rental services, commercial laundries, or even disposable linens.

Numerous water saving systems are gaining in popularity. One of the most innovative systems is the Washit, developed as a student research project in 2013. The device has a shower on one side and a washing machine on the other side. Between the units are a water heater and a pump that collects, filters, and redistributes water. A typical 15-minute shower uses 40 gallons (151.4 L) of water, and a typical laundry cycle uses 15 gallons (56.8 L). If the water can be filtered and reused from the shower to do the laundry, significant amounts of water could be saved.

A laundry system uses more than just water: Electricity is an expensive component of drying laundry. Dryers account for almost 70% of the energy consumed in a laundry room. Many laundry facilities use equipment with auto-dry options; this can help save costs and reduce inefficiency because humans often get busy with other tasks and let dryers operate for 5 or 10 minutes longer than necessary. Another strategy is to use towels that are less absorbent; terry towels are more difficult and expensive to dry than cloth towels or cotton towels.

INTERIOR SYSTEMS

Interior systems can range from carpeting and floor tiling to video and audio systems. These systems are designed to enhance the overall facility experience. If seats are not comfortable, a fan will not want to come back. If carpeting is not provided between a locker room and a pool, patrons may have to walk on cold and possibly slippery tiles and may not be as comfortable. If the scoreboard or audiovisual equipment is not at the optimal level, fans will not have as good an entertainment experience. This section focuses on some of the important systems in a facility such as audiovisual and sound systems, broadcasting data networks, signage, and personal transportation systems.

Audiovisual Systems

One of the most visible components of any audiovisual system is the scoreboard, and fans would not appreciate going to a game and not being able to see it. Scoreboards started out as manual communication devices with people moving the numbers by hand. The electronic age has produced magnificent scoreboards that cost millions of dollars and provide a plethora of sights and sounds.

The first color display was installed in 1972 at Arrowhead Stadium in Kansas City, Missouri, at a cost of $1 million. In 1986 Sony introduced its Jumbotron. Today's systems utilize LEDs, which have bright colors and can last up to 50,000 hours. New technological advances are expected for displays, including organic LEDs and field-emissive displays, which have excellent resolution and are cheaper to manufacture (Pihos, 2001).

Finding the right sound level in a facility is important. Health club members would not appreciate an aerobics room where the music was too loud. The sound system utilized for large stadiums and arenas has to produce enough sound at an appropriate level of quality with as little noise interference as possible. The sound system at the National Stadium in the National Sports Complex in Malaysia, which was completed in 1998 at a cost of US$220 million, includes 190 amplifiers, 220 loudspeakers, and 700 ceiling speakers (Whelan, 2001). The **front-of-the-house** loudspeakers had to be suspended from the membrane roof, which has only one access point. The distance from the control room to these loudspeakers is almost 1 mile (1.6 km). To improve sound to the lower bowl, 64 additional loudspeakers were installed under the second tier (Whelan, 2001). Eight horns were also installed and attached to eight amplifiers and battery backup units in case of an emergency.

The system is connected through fiber-optic cables to help transmit the converted analog audio signal to the preferable digital form. These cables are fed into the control room, which houses a 16-channel, eight-bus mixing console. Since sound in the stadium changes based on **ambient sound** created by the fans, the system includes automation that keeps the broadcast sound at a predetermined level above the noise created by the fans. As this example highlights, sound systems can be very complex, and a qualified sound technician is critical for ensuring sound quality.

Sound Control

Recreational activity sounds are caused by normal facility use and are unavoidable. Mechanical sounds, on the other hand, are the sounds produced by the machinery on which the facility operates and hence are avoidable; they can be controlled if properly planned for in the design phase. Recreational activity sounds consist of both **airborne sound** and **structure-borne sound**, each with different transmission mechanisms that lead to different control strategies. Airborne sounds are primarily the sounds caused by facility users, such as those from voices, music, whistles, and cheers; structure-borne sounds, or impact sounds, are those caused primarily by direct impact with some part of the facility's structure. A basketball player's foot hitting the floor while the player is cutting to the basket creates both air- and structure-borne sounds. The airborne sound is the screech of the player's sneaker, while the structure-borne sound comes from the direct contact of the player's foot with the floor.

Structure-borne sound is much more difficult to control because it vibrates and is transmitted to the air. Consider a bouncing basketball as an example. The sound caused by the basketball vibrates off the floor and is transmitted to the air, where it spreads in the form of a dull thud. Additional structure-borne sounds can come from mechanical systems, the plumbing system, electromechanical systems (e.g., HVAC), and external factors such as traffic or construction. If a building has single-pane glass windows, external sound will be freely transmitted inside. However, thermal windows will significantly reduce a sound path into the building.

Noise control can be achieved through sound absorption, which involves decreasing echoes and reverberation within a space through the control of airborne sound transmission with doors, ceiling tiles, and so on as well as through the control of impact or structure-borne sounds. Airborne sounds travel through the air with relative ease but are effectively muted by solid barriers. Because airborne sounds travel as compression waves, they will reflect off of hard surfaces such as concrete or wood but can be absorbed by resilient material such as fiberglass insulation or acoustic tile. A solid partition, if it provides complete separation with no "leaks," can also effectively isolate airborne sound (Whitney and Foulkes, 1994). This is especially critical for adjacent areas such as offices next to a gym.

FACILITY FOCUS

SCOREBOARDS AND UPGRADES AT AT&T STADIUM

The Dallas Cowboys' new stadium opened in 2009 and was accompanied by a gigantic four-sided high-definition (HD) scoreboard. Mitsubishi developed the scoreboard using their Diamond Vision technology, which powers the world's largest 1,080-pixel LED displays. The HD screens total nearly 13,000 square feet (1,200 sq m). The $40 million scoreboard is designed in such a way that those sitting on the sidelines can view the two largest screens, and those in the end zone can watch two smaller screens. The following are the key specifics for the scoreboard video screens (Lawler, 2008):

Center-Hung Sideline Displays (2)

Width: 159 feet, 7.625 inches (48.6 m)

Height: 71 feet, 4.75 inches (21.8 m)

Total LEDs: 10,584,064

Screen area: 11,393 square feet (1,058 sq m)

Power consumption: 635 kilowatts

Screen weight: approximately 170,000 pounds (77,000 kg)

Video source: 1,080-pixel HD television

Center-Hung End Zone Displays (2)

Width: 50 feet, 4.75 inches (15.4 m)

Height: 28 feet, 6.75 inches (8.7 m)

Total LEDs: 2,088,960

Screen area: 1,439 square feet (134 sq m)

Power consumption: 80 kilowatts

Screen weight: approximately 25,000 pounds (11,300 kg)

Video source: 1,080-pixel HD television

The scoreboard is suspended 90 feet (27.4 m) over the field. To hold the scoreboard in place, a 72-foot-tall (21.9 m) steel structure that contains a 10-level network of catwalks was created. Steel cables that are 3 inches (7.6 cm) in diameter grip each end of the video board and are tethered to the stadium's large steel box truss arches (Muret, 2009).

The stadium is part of a 3 million-square-foot (278,709 sq m) compound that includes a conference facility, offices, retail establishments, restaurants, a planned museum, parking, and other services.

In 2013 the stadium completed a naming rights deal to be called AT&T Stadium. As part of that agreement, the stadium went through a Wi-Fi network upgrade through Cisco and developed its own distribution antenna system. It replaced the 900 older AT&T access points (for Internet and cell phone usage) with an additional 350 access points in the seating bowl with the ability expand the coverage to the plaza and parking lots outside the stadium. The $10 million upgrade allows up to 30,000 fans to access the system simultaneously. The system was designed to meet future demands and needs, such as the 5-gigahertz spectrum that is entering the market as of this writing. The ultimate goal is to have 1,700 access points (each access point can support 100-200 users) and 100,000 people simultaneously using the system for everything from simple communication to watching videos (Muret, 2013).

© Photoshot

Broadcasting

Although many professional sport teams make money from ticket sales, many also make a large percentage of their revenue from television broadcasts. Most facilities cannot just install a camera and expect to produce images that can be broadcast on national television. A camera is only the beginning of the process. A facility needs to have appropriate lighting that allows athletes to see the action well but at the same time allows those watching at home to see it without numerous shadows or dark areas. For proper placement of a camera, room has to be made on the sidelines and in the stands for mobile camera vehicles as well as overhead for aerial cameras on guide wires attached to scoreboards and goals or baskets. In addition, seats in front of the camera will need to be left empty so fans will not be standing up and blocking the view. Some of the facility requirements for broadcasting an event include the following:

- Place for a mobile control room weighing about 14 tons
- Room for camera vehicles
- Place for a cable tender vehicle
- Room for an electrical generator vehicle
- Space for possible additional vehicles such as aerial antenna trucks
- Location to place possibly several miles of cables
- Location for camera stands that can support up to 600 pounds (272 kg)
- Electrical power source to supply a three-phase 50-hertz, 200- or 300-amp supply
- Rigging or poles to support additional lighting requirements
- Appropriate wall coverings and coloring that provide a suitable broadcast background
- Proper acoustical design of the structure to absorb and reverberate sounds (London Sports Council, 1975)
- Various satellite hook-up trucks to broadcast signals all over the world

One of the often overlooked components of any broadcasting system is space for all the trucks and equipment that come in to broadcast a game. Also, extra security is often needed to protect this equipment, as a typical broadcast group for a National Football League game might be carrying close to $25 million in equipment.

Data Network

The data network is used to deliver data effectively throughout a facility. The data system covers everything from phone lines to the data required to control the scoreboard. With more and more building systems being controlled by computers, a seamless integration of computer systems, ranging from ticketing and security to HVAC and water control systems, must exist. A primary focus is on computer-related data, whether for a ticketing operation or just internal e-mail. Data security is a paramount concern for any data network. Hackers can potentially break into the system and steal the credit card information of season ticket holders or send malicious e-mails to those on the network. Although some safety can be developed through installation of firewall software, designed to prevent hackers from getting into the system, internal controls need to be added since current

FACILITY FOCUS

UPGRADES AT FORD CENTER

Owned by Oklahoma City and managed by SMG, Ford Center has hosted more than 600 events and almost 6 million guests since opening in 2002. On March 4, 2008, Oklahoma City voters approved a temporary one-cent sales tax to fund major upgrades to the Ford Center. Plans included the addition of a grand entrance with a multistory atrium and new restaurants, clubs, concession areas, bunker suites, loge boxes, rooftop gardens, a warm-up basketball court, locker rooms, team offices, and a family fun zone. A scoreboard was also planned for the center as part of the effort to attract a National Basketball Association team. Before the start of the 2008-2009 basketball season, the Seattle Supersonics moved to Oklahoma City and were renamed the Thunder.

Daktronics was chosen in 2009 to design, manufacture, and install an integrated scoring and video display for the Ford Center. The $3.9 million system, weighing 46,000 pounds and measuring 31 feet tall and 35 feet wide (9.5 m x 10.7m), utilizes tilting video panels on the bottom of the center-hung scoreboard which provides high-quality, easy-to-view video and information to fans sitting courtside and in other lower seating areas. The feature was specifically asked for by the team to improve the fans' viewing experience. An LED ring display sits atop the center-hung scoreboard, capable of providing game-in-progress information, statistics, sponsor promotions, cropped video clips, animations, graphics, and advertisements (Daktronics, 2009).

or former employees are often as likely a source of a data attack.

Significant savings can be realized if computer network concerns are addressed during the building of a facility rather than during renovation work. Existing facilities often need to put holes in walls to embed the data lines (fiber or coaxial) so that wires are not exposed. To avoid costly wall repairs, some facilities in special cases have used external wiring that is placed on the ground or near the ceiling and then along the wall. All these headaches and costs can be eliminated when a new facility is designed and provided with appropriate data lines. With the development of wireless systems, facilities can create a complete communication system (Wi-Fi) for all facility employees and patrons at a very reasonable cost. These systems need to be secured to avoid lost and compromised data. The biggest concern now for larger facilities is having enough broadband access for the many fans who want to e-mail photos, post updates, text, and communicate electronically during a game. Facilities are spending hundreds of thousands of dollars on upgrading systems in order to handle the data crunch.

Signage Systems

People like to be in control, and signs give them the opportunity to know where to go. However, signs can be problematic in a number of ways. For example, what if someone is visually impaired or does not understand English? What if signs are posted too high, too low, or are frequently blocked? Which work better: static signs or LED visual boards? Signage supports the people movement plan. Therefore, those creating signage need to think like the facility's guests and consider what will make their visit easier. For example, most societies are biased toward right-handed people. Most people tend to reach right and turn right when they enter a building. Therefore, traffic flow and signage should take such movement into consideration. Another strategy for determining sign placement is to take a picture of a given area to show where all the signs are, remove all the signs from the photograph, and then determine where signs would be most useful. Signs can then be moved to the most appropriate locations. In outdoor facilities, signs are often posted more than 7 feet (2.1 m) above the ground to minimize graffiti and vandalism. Care should be taken to differentiate operational or safety signs from directional or experience signs. This can be accomplished through using different colors, sizes, shapes, icons, and placement.

Personal Transportation Systems

Personal transportation systems include elevators, escalators, and people movers. There are two types of transportation systems: vertical and horizontal. An elevator is a vertical system; a horizontal system moves people across a floor (e.g., people movers or trams at airports). Horizontal systems are not typically found at sport facilities, although some sport complexes with multiple venues install such systems to decrease movement time. In contrast, vertical transportation systems are visible at every sport facility. The Americans with Disabilities Act has forced facilities to make available more vertical transportation systems for persons who are disabled. People who are elderly and other customers may also appreciate vertical transportation systems, and these represent a good customer service option. The former Shea Stadium had 21 escalators to move as many as 56,000 patrons an hour. The Stadium's escalators

Facilities Trivia

The first lighted game took place in 1880 when two department store teams played the first documented night game, sponsored by the Northern Electric Light Company at Oceanside Park in Hull, Massachusetts. However, night games were not a regular fixture in the majors until the 1930s. Many owners were opposed to adding lights to their fields. Philip K. Wrigley, owner of the Chicago Cubs, tried to delay installing lights at Wrigley Field for as long as possible. He finally succumbed to pressure and ordered a light system to be installed starting December 8, 1941. However, on December 7, 1941, Japan bombed Pearl Harbor and set off the United States' involvement in World War II. Wrigley donated 165 tons of steel and 35,000 feet (10.7 km) of copper wire and all associated equipment to the War Department. Wrigley Field did not get lights until 1988, making the Chicago Cubs the last Major League Baseball team to install lights (Leventhal, 2011).

varied from 22 to 48 inches (56-122 cm) wide and were as long as 120 feet (37 m). To help encourage patrons to leave through the stadium's ramps, the escalators were shut off in the seventh inning (Steinbach, 2008).

Whatever the system used, the maintenance of personal transportation systems is very complex. The old Meadowlands sportsplex in New Jersey, which had a stadium, arena, and race track, used an assigned escalator and elevator technician from an outside vendor who worked exclusively with the people movers at the facilities. When something goes wrong with a personal transportation system, it needs to be fixed immediately. That is why many large facilities have a dedicated person on staff or on call to fix personal transportation systems.

EXTERIOR SYSTEMS

Exterior systems provide strength to the building structure and provide ancillary building amenities. Thus, a roof protects the contents of the building and ensures that the building will not face structural problems due to water damage. Other exterior systems covered in this section include landscaping, transportation, and parking. Other external components that need to be regularly inspected and maintained include the building facade, which can deteriorate significantly in urban areas from factors such as car emissions, acid rain, and sea salt. Windows, doors, signs, parking areas, and sidewalks all need to be properly maintained and supervised.

Roofs

There are four basic types of overhead spectator protection, classified according to the amount of coverage they provide. Small sun canopies provide minimal protection as they are not supported by interior columns, which could interfere with the sight lines. These canopies offer protection for the upper rows and are often viewed as more ornamental than functional. Such roofs are often used at sportsplexes to provide some shade.

Full roof canopies, high above the playing surface and crowd, cover most of the facility. These roofs normally have an opening in the middle where sunlight and the elements can enter. One of the biggest problems with this type of system is that as the sun travels across the sky it creates a major headache for televised events. Light areas and shadows tend to change during the course of an event and make photography more difficult. Full roof canopies are often seen at major international soccer venues.

Domes have gained popularity throughout the world in the past 30 years. These roofs cover the entire seating bowl and are supported at the perimeter so that no internal columns are needed. They allow a facility manager to control the temperature and lighting. The major drawback is that many fans and players prefer to have some sun exposure, even in winter conditions.

Retractable roofs have gained in popularity over the past 20 years through innovative designs that allow relatively quick closure. Retractable roofs enable a facility to be open on nice days and can close in about a half hour when inclement weather threatens an event (Mancia, 2003).

For every $1 of damage a roof sustains, an estimated $10 worth of damage occurs in the structure below the roof (Borsenik and Stutts, 1997). There are several roofing systems that can protect a building: overlapping layers of roofing felt, coal tar pitch with gravel, elastomers (which when cured look like vulcanized rubber), thermoplastic roofing that softens when heated and hardens when cooled, fiberglass-reinforced roofing, and steel or aluminum roofing. Each roof has its own benefits and disadvantages. Some roofs work better in cooler weather, and others work best in hot climates. A building designer or architect can help identify the best material to use in the construction of a roof.

Another concern with a roof is the weight that has to be carried. For example, a 1-inch (2.5 cm) puddle of water in a 100-square-foot (9.3 sq m) area on a roof can weigh 520 pounds (236 kg). That weight significantly increases when the water is in the form of snow. Many roofs have collapsed because of excessive snow, metal fatigue, or both. The 2.5-acre (10,117 sq m) roof of the Hartford Civic Center collapsed in 1978 several hours after a University of Connecticut basketball game due to ice and snow accumulation.

As with other systems discussed throughout this chapter, it is imperative not only to install an effective roof system but also to maintain it properly after installation. The roof is one of the most important systems in terms of the need for proper maintenance. One maintenance strategy is to check all downspouts to make sure they are not clogged. Clogged gutters can cause deterioration in wood, and during the winter, frozen water can cause cracks or other problems. Roofs should be inspected on a regular basis, but always at least once in the spring to identify concerns that could be addressed during summertime. A roof requires both an external inspection, to see if parts are falling down or whether there are uneven wear points, and an internal inspection for leaks, rusting, peeling paint, musty odors, discolored ceiling tiles, and warped wood.

Plantscaping at a stadium provides visitors with an attractive area, but it needs to be properly maintained on a regular basis.

Landscaping

One way to address a bland building facade or deteriorating look is to use appropriate plants and art, which can serve as a buffer or visual improvement for the building. This is one reason why landscape systems are so important and why landscaping should not be just random placement of plants.

Most **landscaping** is coordinated with professionals who are experts in soil, climate, water, and horticultural issues to help a facility manager make the right decisions. Although visual appeal is critical, safety is also important. For example, some ornamental plants have prickly leaves. A landscape architect would never plant cactuses or similar prickly plants, for example, in an area where children may play.

But landscaping is for more than just visual appeal. Landscaping can generate cost savings by reducing maintenance-related expenditures. Strategies include the following:

- Utilizing plants that do not grow much after they are planted
- Using plants grown specifically for disease and insect resistance or drought tolerance
- Using perennials in planting beds to minimize grass maintenance
- Planting small shrubs close to each other to minimize the need for weeding
- Installing an automatic irrigation system to reduce water and manpower costs (Borsenik and Stutts, 1997)

When installing landscaping, a facility manager needs to determine the goals and objectives of the landscaping (sometimes called plantscaping) project. For example, how will occupants interact with plants? Will the facility want people to smell the flowers? Do employees and visitors appreciate different plants that are rotated on a regular basis, including some herbs and fragrant plants? Is there enough light to sustain the plants? Should fake plants be used? Is it better to lease plants rather than buy them? Who will be responsible for taking care of the plants (e.g., watering, trimming, bug removal, and so on)? Are plants used to help control traffic?

Transportation Systems

Not every facility has a transportation system. Most facilities have several vehicles for moving items from one location to another. For example, small three-wheel or four-wheel carts similar to golf carts are used by maintenance workers to move from one location to another or for tasks such as trash removal. If any vehicles are in poor shape, the facility may be liable. Thus, if the brakes on a vehicle are poor and are not repaired, the facility may be held liable if as a result an employee is injured or a patron is hit by the vehicle.

Bigger events can require bigger vehicles. The Atlanta Olympics used a large number of buses to transport athletes from events to other events or to the Athletes' Village. However, the entire system was plagued by overworked drivers who did not know routes, were often late, or were even commandeered by irate athletes According to one of the officials, some of the drivers might not have had any training in driving buses (Sullivan, 1996).

Parking Systems

Numerous parking concerns need to be addressed, from drunk drivers to auditing of the parking attendants to avoid fraud. Additional concerns can include handicapped parking spaces, aggressive drivers, rough terrain, managing cars and people parked on multiple levels, and criminal misconduct. Different event goers have different parking habits, as shown in "Parking Habits of Attendees." This type of information may prove useful for determining the appropriate number of parking attendants, identifying crowd management issues, and understanding how to manage and market parking areas more effectively.

Parking Lot Safety

Crime statistics serve notice to facility managers that criminal acts are foreseeable and that facilities can be sued should such acts occur. Fights, assaults, robberies, underage drinking, and illegally scalping tickets are just some of the criminal activities presenting liability challenges. Cases claiming liability on the part of facilities for the criminal acts of third parties often allege such charges as poor lighting, missing or broken light bulbs, weak locks, no access control, poorly trained guards, or poor management policies. One report indicated that approximately 7% to 9% of simple assaults throughout the United States occur in parking facilities or near parking lots. Furthermore, 8% of all violent crimes, 6% of all rapes and other sexual assaults, and 7% of total assaults occur in parking lots or garages (Abbott and Fried, 1998). In 2011, the assault of a San Francisco Giants fan in a Los Angeles Dodgers parking lot raised national attention to the issue of fan safety not just in the stadium but also in the parking lot.

Parking lots and garages are critical for sport facilities, as only 5% of fans attending games utilize public transportation while another 5% take leased buses. Estimates show that football fans are more likely to carpool, averaging 3.5 passengers per vehicle, while baseball fans traditionally travel with 2.5 passengers per vehicle (Abbott and Fried, 1998).

One landmark case concerning liability for conduct that spilled out of a sport facility and led to violence in a parking lot is the Bishop case (Bishop v. Fair Lanes Georgia Bowling, Inc., 1986). According to the case, two groups were using adjoining bowling lanes, and one of the groups engaged in harassing behavior over a significant amount of time. The other group complained to the bowling alley management, which took no action. In fact, the management continued to serve alcohol to the group that was engaging in harassment even though they were

---

PARKING HABITS OF ATTENDEES

- Baseball fans: park, see the game, and leave
- Football fans: make a day of it; park before the game to tailgate (unless the game starts at or before noon)
- Baby boomer concert goers: arrive right before the event

- Country music fans: arrive early, conduct themselves in an orderly fashion, and follow parking rules
- Rock fans: tend to linger after an event; parking problems can persist well after an event

From *Outside the arena, parking is the name of the game* 1997.

RISK MANAGEMENT STRATEGIES FOR ENSURING SAFE PARKING

Because of the potential liability associated with unsafe parking lots, facility managers need to answer the following questions (Abbott and Fried, 1998):

- Are statistics maintained on the frequency and type of criminal activity occurring within a half-mile (0.8 km) of the parking facility?

- Has a thorough security audit been completed, including a review of security policies, and have any findings been acted on?

- Do both security and nonsecurity personnel understand and apply proper security measures?

- What can reasonably be done to prevent criminal behavior?

- Has a long-range goal been established for promoting security and crime prevention?

- Is a public relations program in place to inform patrons and employees about security concerns?

- What does it cost to incorporate additional security versus the harm that may be caused to possible victims?

---

already intoxicated. After the 2:30 a.m. closing, the two groups were the last people to leave the facility. The intoxicated group, which had been the aggressor all evening long, attacked the other group in the parking lot. According to the court's conclusion, a jury could reasonably find that the bowling alley should have been aware of potential physical altercations between the patrons before the altercation occurred and would therefore be negligent for taking no action and failing to make its premises safe for invitees.

Notice is the key requirement for proving that something was foreseeable. In a suit stemming from a brawl during a 1980 AC/DC rock concert, the concert promoter claimed that there had been no notice because no unruly behavior, fighting, or drinking had been observed that would indicate a potential problem. Even though the arena had no prior problems, the court concluded that the promoter was on notice because a police officer had investigated previous tour stops and was informed of various problems. The officer also knew that the band had attracted a rowdy, drunk, and drug-using crowd in past concerts (Comastro v. Village of Rosemont, 1984).

Alcohol management is another key component of a parking security risk management plan. Arrests at sport events often revolve around alcohol abuse or intoxicated behavior (Abbott and Fried, 1998). Risk management strategies designed to reduce alcohol-related injuries include controlling tailgate parties and creating a designated driver program for intoxicated fans (Ammon, 1993). However, designing a safer parking area should be the first step. This can include significant lighting to minimize dark spots and limiting trees or outbuildings that can block parking lot patrols or foster illegal conduct.

Environmental Parking Design

The use of architectural design to provide greater flexibility in protecting patrons is rapidly catching on throughout the world. **Crime prevention through environmental design** (CPTED) is a step that can be taken to reduce criminal activities (Gordon and Brill, 1996). This approach entails design modifications that make a facility safer. For example, concrete stairways in parking facilities are effective hiding places for criminals. Crime prevention through environmental design would change stairwells to include large windows throughout, making it harder for criminals to hide and allowing people on the street to see activity inside the stairwell.

COMBINED INTERIOR AND EXTERIOR SYSTEMS

The various systems highlighted so far in this chapter can often be categorized as interior systems (i.e., bathrooms, weigh rooms, and HVAC systems) and exterior systems (i.e., roofs, parking lots, and landscaping). There are also a number of systems that straddle both indoor and outdoor functions. Examples of such dual systems include security, pest control, and waste management, which are important for ensuring effective utilization and management of the entire facility.

Security Systems

The security system at the Atlanta Olympic Games was considered top of the line. However, before the opening ceremonies, which President Clinton attended, a person was stopped with a gun inside the facility. The intruder had entered the facility using a security company uniform. Even though there were armed guards and an X-ray system to identify hazardous items, the intruder was able to get in. When asked how the intruder had penetrated the elaborate system, a spokesperson replied, "He came early" (Sullivan, 1996). Subsequent Olympic Games faced significant security cost increases such as the approximately $1.5 billion spent at the Greece Games and the estimated £1.85 billion that was spent securing the 2012 London Games. Besides paying for personnel, these funds are spent on numerous technology components such as biometric systems (pupil and fingerprint recognition) and Segway personal transporters (two-wheel balancing vehicles) for quick deployment of personnel. The rise in security costs is a direct result of the post-9/11 environment, and security will continue to be one of the most important systems for all large sport facilities. To help prevent security breaches, a security plan needs to be developed, and to help implement a security plan, security systems are needed. (Chapter 14 discusses security concerns in more detail.)

A security system relies on a number of devices. If a facility is going to be monitored, humans can see only so much even if there are hundreds of guards. To maintain an appropriate monitoring system, a facility may have **closed-circuit television** (CCTV) cameras and a monitoring station. Some sport facilities have more than 100 CCTV cameras scanning both the interior and exterior and recording all images in a digital format that takes up very little data storage space. Some systems are motion activated, while others are integrated with computer systems to monitor crowd activities and signal an alarm if someone is moving the wrong way in a crowd (e.g., sneaking in through an exit).

Alarms fall into two categories: life safety and property protection (Carlson and DiGiandomenico, 1992). Life safety systems, such as a fire alarm, are designed to provide early detection and prompt notification of a hazard. Property protection systems exist in areas housing valuables that may need additional protection. Thus, an athletic facility may have a life safety alarm system in locations where patrons and guests congregate as well as a property protection system in locations where cash or other valuables are stored. Both systems rely on an initiating or a sensing circuit or sensing loop to detect the hazard and then trigger the appropriate alarms.

Every facility has routine security issues, from those involving the loading docks to those related to cash. The ticket office may need additional security to protect tellers or may require a drop safe so that money can be deposited safely every 15 minutes. Each facility needs to undertake a security audit to identify security-related concerns so that appropriate systems can be implemented.

Pest Control

One of the often overlooked facility concerns is pests. Pests represent a health concern. If a facility has a pest infestation and there are cooking or food service areas within the building, there may be health code violations that could lead the health department to shut down the food service. Pests also represent a marketing concern. An unclean facility with bugs can repel facility users and lead to economic loss.

Pests can be a problem in both the interior and exterior systems. Interior pests can include rats, mice, ants, cockroaches, bed bugs, flies, and mosquitoes. Many types of sprays, electronic systems, and even other animals can be used to control pests. For example, the Houston Astrodome utilized cats to keep mice and rats out of the facility. Fans at a game would sometimes have a cat rub against their legs. Astrodome personnel brought the cats to veterinarians each year, and the cats served as a supplemental deterrent. External control is critical for preventing external pests from entering a facility. Solutions can be as simple as fencing or can be more complex, as with ground termite systems. Pest problems can occur in any facility, no matter how clean.

In years past, each annoyance or infestation was handled as it arose. Now the focus is on integrated pest management, which utilizes prevention and environmentally sensitive approaches. Pest-proofing starts with limiting entry points and practicing good sanitation. If pests still come in, a facility can use self-contained bait, natural pesticides, or isolated chemicals directly on pests or as barriers against pest moving around a building. Environmentally friendly methods will not always work; for example, there is no known sustainable method for dealing with termites. In addition, the use of long-term approaches is sometimes inappropriate with pests such as hornets and bees because the risk of allergic reactions is too significant to delay immediate removal. Some of the animal stories from sport can be quite amusing, such as the time a fan who was also a beekeeper had to remove a swarm of bees from right field with a broom and some honey during a Los Angeles Angels game, or when New York Yankees pitcher Joba Chamberlain was attacked by midges (small flying insects) at Cleveland's Progressive Field.

Pest-proofing for larger pests often entails a system of exclusionary devices to keep them out and humane traps to capture those pests already in a facility. Birds can cause health problems, noise, property damage, and slip-and-fall risks. Bird droppings are acidic, so they can stain a building's facade, and—besides being slimy and gross—they carry 60 diseases. Some facilities use reflective solar coatings on windows to conserve energy, reduce heat load in the facility, and show birds that the windows are solid. Some ledges are purposefully angled 45° to make the area inhospitable for birds to land on. Smooth materials such as metal and glass discourage roosting, whereas concrete and masonry encourage roosting.

There has been a movement away from hazardous chemicals to other techniques that do not harm the environment. Some facilities have resorted to natural insect killers or pepper as a deterrent. One technique is to heat the area being treated. A kitchen, for example, could be heated to 120 °F (49 °C) at 25% humidity for 8 to 24 hours to kill all the pests in the kitchen. Care needs to be taken to ensure the fire suppression system will not be triggered by such a treatment and that sensitive equipment is removed from the treated area (Mach, 2005).

Waste Management

One of the often unexpected costs of running a facility is the cost associated with trash removal. A typical stadium or arena can easily spend several hundred thousand dollars on trash removal each year. This amount can be reduced significantly by recycling cardboard boxes, plastic, scraps, bottles, cans, and even cooking oil. Another strategy for minimizing the amount spent on trash removal is buying or renting an industrial trash compactor. Compactors can be purchased for around $10,000. A major restaurant chain experimented with using a $12,500 trash compactor. The restaurant originally had an 8-cubic-yard (6.1 cu m) dumpster that was picked up five times a week at a cost of $2,400 per month. After it started compacting all the trash, it was able to switch to a 4-cubic-yard (3 cu m) dumpster that was picked up once a week at a cost of $1,000 a month. The $12,500 investment paid for itself in less than a year. The restaurant saved an additional $4,300 the first year alone, and the trash compactor would generate savings for years to come (Curtland, 2012).

The unglamorous task of waste management is often contracted out to external trash removal companies. However, these companies often remove the trash only after it has been collected into major receptacles. Most facilities have their own employees or a janitorial service take care of trash. Some facilities utilize volunteers or student groups to help clear trash after a game. Such removal efforts are undertaken either by hand or with equipment such as leaf blowers used to push trash from upper bleachers down to a central collection area. Trash removal from certain areas such as restrooms and kitchens has to be conducted daily to prevent odors and an unpleasant or unsafe environment.

Summary

Discussion of the construction process in chapter 6 highlights how complex the building process can be given the different types of building materials and other construction elements. Among the most important elements in a facility, and often the most expensive on a percentage basis, are the systems built in or added on. Everything from HVAC to energy and plumbing systems need to be installed and maintained in an appropriate manner. A facility cannot be built with a mere collection of systems but rather needs to effectively integrate all the systems to minimize costs and maximize benefits. An HVAC system needs to be connected to the electrical system to monitor air temperature and save the most energy when the facility is not in use. The key to the systems is that they are designed to help maintain a safe and comfortable facility. When any system goes down, the entire facility is affected. Facility users demand that systems work—for example, that lights work during an event and toilets flush properly—or that they be repaired very quickly. The next three chapters deal with facility operations and maintenance, which are critical for maintaining the building systems.

Discussion Questions and Activities

1. Give five reasons why an HVAC system is important for an arena.

2. What would be the best fire suppression system for an arena? For a health club?

3. Visit a large facility in your town or city and ask to examine the HVAC system. Write a report describing the system.

4. Visit a large facility and examine the types of lighting systems used, such as indirect lights, direct lights, and ambient lighting.

5. Examine the type of pest management system used in your dorm or classroom, and evaluate its effectiveness.

6. Visit your campus gym and examine the ductwork system used for the HVAC system. If you were to move the ductwork to generate additional space or reduce costs, where would you move it to?

7. Imagine that you are putting together your own arena. Where would you cut costs in your facility systems and operations, what systems would you spend extra money on, and what system operational strategies from the chapter would you use in the facility once it is fully operational?

8. What do you think is the most important system in a facility? Why?

Facility Operations

Chapter Objectives

- Appreciate some of the nuances associated with managing the operations of sport facilities.

- Understand the steps in the changeover process.

- Analyze the management requirements for key components of sport facilities such as weight rooms and gymnasiums.

- Appreciate how an attractive and playable grass field is created.

- Know the tasks involved in creating and maintaining proper soil and good ground appearance.

- Characterize the components of an effective field maintenance program.

- Appreciate some of the concerns unique to baseball and football fields.

Chapter 3 deals with effective managerial strategies for a facility. It is critical to understand how to apply theory and strategies to the day-to-day operations of a sport facility. Scheduling, for example, is one of the major tasks of a facility manager. Whether the goal is to attract events or simply accommodate current programs, scheduling can become difficult. Several groups may want to use a gym at the same time. Who will get priority? Will priority be based on politics or revenue generation? What are the goals and objectives for the facility? These are just a few of the questions that management needs to deal with in order to make operations decisions.

In indoor facilities, various concerns are associated with scheduling, cleaning, floor maintenance, and ancillary areas such as restrooms. Management also needs to analyze how to transform a facility from one event to another. **Changeover** management requires significant time, money, and energy. Numerous online videos show the process of changing over an arena from one sport to another or of turning the infield of a baseball stadium into a hockey rink for an outdoor hockey event. Outdoor facilities have their own unique issues, weather being among the most important. It is not uncommon to see a nationally televised football game being played in the mud. Could the mud have been prevented? What steps can be taken to make sure a facility is in reasonably playable condition? Much is involved in preparing a field for an event, from removing snow and painting lines to mowing the lawn in a uniform manner.

This chapter covers some of the basics of scheduling and changeover management and then considers traditional components of sport facilities such as weight rooms, locker rooms, and gymnasiums. Attention is given to specific aspects that need to be managed as well as issues such as general maintenance. The chapter also looks at outdoor facilities from a managerial perspective and outlines the steps required to produce a playable and safe outdoor surface. Important issues in this context are the types of grass used for playing fields and how to maintain them properly, from mowing and fertilizing to providing for proper field drainage. Significant attention is paid to developing a field maintenance program.

The chapter ends with an analysis of unique sport concerns such as grounds management and safety.

SPACE MANAGEMENT

Space management examines how a facility will be used. A facility that sits vacant wastes space as well as resources. On the other hand, a facility that is overused can deteriorate rapidly. Management has to balance between the extremes of overuse and underuse. Usage of facilities differs in various parts of the world. In China, for example, the sport facilities are considered public buildings and are therefore open for public use. Thus, whereas a publicly built National Football League (NFL) stadium is open only for major football games or concerts, a large stadium in China could be used for the Olympics one day and could be open for citizens to walk on the track the next day. Because such facilities are open for use that does not produce revenue, almost all government-owned buildings in China are losing money.

Most facilities have a reservation system whereby someone who wants to use the facility completes a reservation form indicating the desired date, time, and space. In a college, the physical education department often has first choice, followed by the athletic department, intramural and recreational sports, student groups, and finally community groups. Facility usage and scheduling are often dictated by political pressure or money. A particular group may have fewer facility users than other groups but receive the best time because of political pressure. Title IX is shifting the priorities and scheduling practices at many high schools and colleges. Whereas historically the men's football and basketball teams were given the best facilities and times, women's teams are now receiving more equal treatment. Recent government directives require colleges to give athletes who are disabled equal access to facilities, so facility managers need to properly schedule facility usage by all users, who often have competing needs and wants.

Whether using a reservation system or a computer management maintenance system, a manager needs to have access to information, and computers are the key to proper facility operations. Operations cannot be completed

Westfall: Prioritizing maintenance equals positive customer experiences

My name is Don Westfall. I am the general manager of the Connecticut Sportsplex in North Branford, Connecticut. I have been in my current position for over 10 years. I began my management career as house manager of a multiplex movie theater for Pacific Theatres in Northern California. I played and coached college baseball and earned a bachelor's degree in sport studies with emphasis on sport business. My first sport management job was as an account manager for the New Haven Knights. Within a short period I was promoted to the position of director of ticket sales for the minor league hockey team. After two seasons I was hired as the corporate sales manager for the New Haven Ninjas, an Arena Football 2 team. After one season with the Ninjas, I sold insurance for 1 year and then was hired as general manager of the Connecticut Sportsplex, which is a privately owned 70-acre indoor and outdoor sport and entertainment facility.

My daily responsibilities include but are not limited to the following:

- Oversee and direct the day-to-day operations including all concessions, amusements, and human resources
- Oversee and direct all repairs and maintenance
- Oversee and direct all sales and marketing
- Oversee all sports leagues and programs
- Oversee and direct baseball instruction and leagues
- Oversee and direct all customer relations

The Connecticut Sportsplex is unique because we are a privately owned facility and must pay for all our operations through our sales. The most difficult part of my job is balancing the expectations of our customers with our fiscal issues and policies. Many of our customers are accustomed to using tax-subsidized public facilities where there are fewer expectations and more freedoms. Because of the size and scope of our business, we are always affected by utility rate increases. Passing these increases to the customer is not always an option, so we must find creative ways to match revenues with expenses.

A large part of creating balance is keeping up with maintenance and repairs. Since the facility is privately owned we must either fix everything ourselves or hire outside contractors, which can get very expensive. Prioritizing repair jobs and keeping up with the daily maintenance have been challenges for me as I had very little prior experience in facility maintenance.

Along with managing maintenance issues, I spend a significant amount of time making sure our employees understand their roles in regard to their specific duties and to our customers. Although my love of sports got me into this business, I have found that the sport aspect is ancillary to the success of our business. The facility—and how it operates—demands constant attention. If the facility is not looking and running its best, our sport programs and customer relations deteriorate quickly and permanently.

effectively without using a computer system to provide insight, control, and coordination. **Insight** refers to being able to obtain real-time status of all activities, receive timely alerts when predetermined performance levels are not reached, have all relevant information readily available, and receive regular scheduled reports on time. **Control** refers to the ability to define, deploy, and apply best practices as required; establish and comply with performance levels; automatically interact with vendors; obtain warranty information; and manage a mix of demands with the same system. **Coordination** refers to being able to establish real-time communication between all constituents and leverage all various platforms to communicate effectively, whether in person, through phone, fax, e-mail, or the Internet.

Managing Multiple Venues

The management process is even more demanding when one is overseeing several facilities. Most colleges have several athletic or recreation facilities that require significant managerial oversight. Facilities can be located miles apart (e.g., the university boathouse, golf course, bowling alley, recreation center, stadium, arena, and fields). Because of tight budgets and in many cases neglected repairs, facility managers often have an uphill battle. A successful facility manager at the college level needs to be an expert in organizing and consolidating resources. Each day a number of events may be taking place in stadiums, arenas, gyms, and playing fields. The manager must be able to change gears at a moment's notice to handle a variety of events.

To effectively manage the space in multiple facilities, a senior manager needs to appoint a management team. A facility management team, typically reporting to one director, can help manage multiple facilities more effectively. In this case each facility may have its own manager, or there may be a manager for fields, for example, and managers for maintenance and other trades positions. It is often more effective to have team members who can apply their trades to a group of facilities than for each facility to have its own specialists. At a single facility, a repairperson might have to do plumbing, electrical, and maintenance work in order to justify her position. In contrast, a plumber who is a member of a team that manages multiple venues may take care of all the plumbing fixtures in the various facilities. Thus, the management team becomes more intimately involved with the overall functioning of the facilities, and this type of decentralized system helps ensure that the facilities are operating properly.

Managing Changeover

It can be interesting to watch the changeover process in a facility. Changeover refers to converting a facility from one activity to another. Changeover at a high school gym can be as simple as putting basketballs away and rolling out dodgeballs. More is involved in changing from badminton to volleyball because of the differing nets, standards, and equipment. It becomes important for a facility manager to explore all options when scheduling in order to group similar events together to reduce the time and costs associated with changeovers.

The process becomes more complicated when two events use completely different surfaces. In multisport facilities such as baseball and football stadiums it is necessary to move bleachers, remove pitching mounds, and extend fields to change over from baseball to football. However, since the seasons overlap for only a limited time period, the demand for changing over is limited. In contrast, the need to change over from ice hockey to basketball, or vice versa, occurs over an extended period of time because the seasons overlap significantly.

Changeover management is one of the more complex assignments for maintenance crews. The most complex version entails changing over from an event on ice to any other event. Some facilities can melt the ice so that the floor can be laid on the hard cement. However, this is a very expensive proposition. Madison Square Garden thaws and removes the ice only once during the entire New York Rangers' season—for the Westminster Kennel Club Dog Show, because the dogs are sensitive to the ice. Thus, when a basketball game is to be played, the court is normally installed over the ice.

A basketball floor cannot be placed right over ice without damaging both the floor and the ice. An intermediary surface is used to protect the ice; the different types of floor covers include plywood, pressed paper sheets, laminated wood with a foam core, polyethylene shell with a foam core, and thermo-formed urethane foam sheets with fiberglass to reduce expansion and contraction (Townsend, 2003).

The changeover process typically begins as soon as an event ends. Whereas changing over used to take all night, it now can take just a few hours. First Union Center in Philadelphia is managed by Global Spectrum, which introduced a quick-change process. The center is home to the Philadelphia Flyers, 76ers, and Wings (lacrosse) and hosts more than 400 events each year. Global Spectrum uses a 47-member crew that includes 25 to 30 changeover employees, six carpenters, six ice crew members, two Zamboni drivers, two electricians, and one telephone technician (Richman, 2001).

Changeovers require a great deal of planning, and facilities are being designed with changeovers in mind. For example, Staples Center in Los Angeles averages 130 changeovers each year. The fastest changeover from a hockey surface to a basketball surface was accomplished in 1 hour and 50 minutes. On average, most arenas use 35 to 60 staff members for a changeover, with the greatest amount of time being spent on removing seating areas (Bisson, 2001). In 2013, Staples Center hosted playoff games for the Clippers, Lakers, and Kings. Six games were held over 4 days (Thursday through Sunday) and included five changeovers because the Lakers and Clippers each have their own wood floor.

Although managing a changeover can be very time consuming, it is also exciting because every facility has its own unique character and spirit. Most facility managers get the changeover process down quickly, and after several months it can be similar to an orchestra where everyone knows their parts and the manager is simply the conductor. Although it is great to be involved in changeovers, a manager needs to delegate as much responsibility as possible in order to focus on higher-level tasks. Changeovers often occur late at night and early in the morning, and a manager who undertakes such work on a regular basis will be too tired the next day to manage effectively.

MANAGING SPECIALIZED COMPONENTS

Some sport facility components, such as locker rooms, do not need to be scheduled or changed; but they still need to be properly managed. Management still needs to schedule employees to work in these areas. Also, time needs to be spent getting areas ready for daily use, from basic cleaning to making sure that the weights in a weight room are in place. This section discusses areas that require additional managerial oversight: weight rooms, locker rooms, concession areas, gymnasiums, and ice hockey sheets.

Weight Rooms

Weight rooms are among the most difficult facility components to manage because of constant use and abuse. Weight rooms must be kept clean and safe because of liability concerns. Other issues for weight rooms include maintaining the equipment and developing a positive environment for users. Also, understanding and being able to work with technology is becoming a critical part of operating fitness equipment in a facility. It is easy to inspect weight plates; however, computer-based training systems, television monitors, and even virtual trainers on a screen require employees to be properly trained in monitoring and possibly fixing broken technology.

To maintain a proper level of safety and cleanliness, it is essential for the facility manager to create and implement a customized preventive maintenance program. An effective preventive maintenance program incorporates daily, weekly, monthly, and yearly cleanings and repairs (Dahlgren, 2000b). The majority of the daily chores involve cleaning of equipment. Odors and perspiration can accumulate quickly, so the walls, equipment, and sitting and resting areas should be cleaned daily with general household cleaning agents, the floors should be vacuumed daily, and facility users should be given access to cleaning wipes (soap solution or a mild antibacterial disinfectant on small wipes) to allow them to wipe down the equipment. Staph infection (from methicillin-resistant *Staphylococcus aureus*, or

MRSA) is a serious threat, and any bodily fluid should be cleaned off of equipment as soon as possible. Managers need to develop a culture of support in which employees look out for risk areas and proactively protect facility users.

For vinyl parts of exercise machines, it is best to use an antibacterial agent diluted to a 10% solution (Dahlgren, 2000b). It is also very important to lubricate all machine joints weekly using lightweight (30-weight) motor oil and to clean them first to avoid lubricant buildup (Dahlgren, 2000b).

Although employees can fix many simple maintenance problems, at least one employee should take certifying courses provided by machine manufacturers to learn how to fix the machines. Managers may also keep spare parts in the facility to avoid long delays waiting for parts. In some cases there are simple ways to head off repair problems, such as switching one bike for another when one is used more frequently than the other (Dahlgren, 2000b). If equipment is leased rather than purchased, the leasing company should be local so that an agent can quickly come to the facility to make any repairs needed.

Because of the abundance of odors and moisture in the air, the manager should change heating, ventilation, and air conditioning (HVAC) unit filters fairly often (every 1 or 2 months). Care should be taken to avoid moisture damage in weight rooms tucked in the middle of larger buildings. Fans, dehumidifiers, and air fresheners can help improve air quality and user enjoyment and can prevent rust, mildew, and bacteria buildup.

The weight room's location can affect the ability to provide proper supervision. With weights and machines blocking one's view, it is often difficult to supervise the weight room and monitor conduct. Supervision can be improved by moving employees around, reconfiguring the room setup, and installing ceiling-mounted mirrors or even a closed-circuit television system. A check-in desk is an effective tool for monitoring both who enters the weight room and the patrons using the room. Some health clubs have a security access point at the check-in desk, which helps make patrons think that the club is in some sense exclusive and is concerned about crime and inappropriate conduct.

Locker Rooms

Players of all ages and levels carry waves of emotions into the locker room after the game and can quickly create a hazardous environment for others. From spitting and regurgitating on the floor to letting their blood drip on various surfaces, athletes might not think about their actions when they are tired or upset. Athletes allow their skin to come in contact with many different surfaces in the locker room. Illnesses attributed to unclean surfaces, such as staph infections, are commonly contracted in locker rooms. Because of the moist conditions in this area, bacteria are easily bred and then spread to others (Turner and Hauser, 1994). Care should be taken to clean all surfaces in a locker room at least daily, depending on the use.

Of major concern is MRSA, which usually manifests as a skin infection, such as pimples or boils, and can occur in otherwise healthy people. Having an MRSA outbreak does not mean having a poor facility. Over the past 10 years there have been outbreaks in many facilities, from elementary school gyms to NFL locker rooms. In 2003, a Lycoming College football player died from a bloodstream infection linked to MRSA bacteria. In 2004, newspapers reported that some members of the Denver Broncos had come down with the virus, and Junior Seau allegedly caught it while playing for the Miami Dolphins. In 2007, a former college football player sued Iona College over an antibiotic-resistant staph infection that nearly cost him his leg. The player claimed that the team's locker room was an unsanitary environment in which players shared towels and equipment. Although the college disputed the allegations, it disinfected a weight room and reviewed hygiene advice after 10 members of an athletic team (including a coach) were diagnosed with MRSA. Most recently, Tampa Bay Buccaneers kicker Lawrence Tynes contracted MRSA, which caused him to miss the entire 2013 season. MRSA is not the only concern. In 2014 over 20 NHL players suffered from a mumps outbreak attributed by some to locker room conditions. The threat of serious injuries from MRSA has prompted the installation of MRSA-resistant flooring (in which the floor covering contains resistant chemicals) and regular cleanings with strong cleaners that kill most or all bacteria and infectious material. Existing surfaces can be treated on a regular basis to prevent MRSA, but flooring made with these chemicals does not require treatments or cleanings as frequently.

Another concern with locker rooms is multiple chemical sensitivity, which affects 15% to 30% of the general population. Individuals with multiple chemical sensitivity react in different degrees to the various chemicals and fragrances they encounter. A facility should be sensitive to user concerns with all the chemical cleaners and smells used around a locker room. Some locker rooms have designated areas that are spray free to minimize patrons' exposure to after-shower sprays.

Another critical concern is the threat of slipping on water in areas where there are sinks or showers and in changing areas. The following strategies can create a safer environment in the locker room:

- Control traffic flow in the locker room by creating both wet and dry areas.

- Reduce the moisture level with a strong HVAC system to help stop the spread of bacteria and keep the floor dry.

- Move outlets at least 6 feet (1.8 m) away from any water source, or install **ground fault circuit interrupters** (GFIs) to reduce the threat of electrocution.

- Kill bacteria using a quaternary ammonium solution once a week and a mild phosphoric acid solution once a month.

- Avoid placing full-length lockers in the middle of a room to keep sight lines open for supervision. Other options are slant-topped lockers or lockers that are flush with the wall (Turner and Hauser, 1994).

The floor will help determine the locker room's look, feel, and safety. Because slipping is such a major concern, the floor needs to be constructed with slip-resistant materials or painted with non-skid paint. The following are materials used for most locker room floors:

- Ceramic tile provides both durability and a clean look and is primarily used in the wet areas of locker rooms. However, tile can easily become very slippery, and the grout between tiles is hard to clean and can house bacteria.

- Carpet, although not common, is slip resistant and has a nice look; however, water-soaked carpeting can create a musty smell.

- Epoxy quartz floors are created when several layers of clear or colored epoxy are put down with a topcoat of sealer. This type of flooring is slip resistant and resilient, but is harder to maintain than other types of floors and is not very attractive.

- Coated concrete is basic concrete topped by paint or a thick sealer. It is fairly slip resistant but not very aesthetic.

- Similar to the rubber floors used in weight rooms, rubber shower floors are slip resistant but are harder to maintain than other types of flooring (Cohen, 1994a).

- To help prevent infections, MRSA-resistant surfaces (whether manufactured or just treated) should be installed and the locker room should be cleaned regularly with products specifically designed to prevent MRSA.

Concession Areas

One of the big concerns with operating a concession stand is complying with various health regulations. The potential for a surprise inspection at concession areas can raise numerous concerns and has resulted in numerous violations. In a study conducted in 2009, all 107 of the venues serving the four major professional leagues in the United States had some health inspection violations, including the following: food stored or served at improper temperatures, insect infestations in liquor bottles, lack of a sneeze guard over the buffet, lack of hand-washing stations, inadequately concentrated sanitation solutions, chemicals improperly stored near food, raw food stored near ready-to-eat items, unclean countertops, and expired food (Steinbach, 2010b). One newer stadium that underwent significant scrutiny is Lucas Oil Stadium, which opened in August 2008. Less than 2 years later, the facility had received more than 1,400 violations, including more than 500 critical violations (some were repeat violations). In November 2009, the stadium had received 42

FACILITY FOCUS

ARIZONA STATE UNIVERSITY'S LOCKER ROOM

The needs of a locker room can present unique challenges. A locker room is no longer simply a place to take a shower and change; it has become the sanctuary for a team. Dallas Maverick's owner Mark Cuban created a locker room that is the envy of the National Basketball Association and that helped attract new star players. A manager at the college level can take the same approach. Some locker rooms stand out in a crowd, and the locker room of Arizona State University's men's basketball is one such example. Designed in 2002, the renovated locker room is environmentally friendly while offering the latest in innovative technology. The goal was to give athletes and coaches a comfortable, user-friendly space specially designed for maximum productivity.

One of the most exciting elements of the locker room is the X Locker, a revolutionary personal storage system that looks more like a rental storage locker than a sport locker. The X Locker's features include the following:

■ Motorized door with a silent motor to help create an acoustically friendly environment

■ Personal lockable drawer at each station, ensuring two layers of security

■ Integrated ventilation system to eliminate odor and moisture from clothing

■ Computer control panel that allows a personalized touch-screen combination, a custom screen saver for each athlete, and computerized communication from coaches and staff

Every detail, from the flooring to the acoustic insulation, was carefully chosen to fit into the innovative, sustainable design. Following are some of the key features:

■ Recycled and sustainable materials, such as fabrics, carpet, and bamboo flooring

■ Energy-efficient lighting with dimmable fixtures as well as sensor light switches

■ Appropriately sized furniture and fixtures that meet the unique needs of larger basketball athletes

■ Recycled-cotton acoustic insulation instead of fiberglass

■ Low (to zero) VOC (volatile organic compound) paints

■ Low-flow water fixtures

■ Antibacterial and antimicrobial finishes

■ Recycle bins

Acoustics and sustainable design elements were incorporated throughout the project. Locker rooms are known for the constant loud noise associated with yelling, lockers slamming, and other sounds. Research has shown that noise negatively affects an athlete's ability to focus and can even be detrimental to health. Thus, a 100% recycled cotton product was used to deaden the sound. This product was safe for the installers (compared with fiberglass) and performs just as well as traditional acoustical products (ASU Basketball, 2003).

Not to be outdone, the University of Arizona also updated its locker room and installed a switch with six light settings, called scenes. The most unique scenes include the following:

■ The game-day scene shines inset ceiling lights on coaches and players.

■ The everyday lights are softer and more relaxed.

■ For recruiting tours, dramatic lights shine upward from the lockers and illuminate a University of Arizona jersey (Leung, 2011).

citations for repeat violations (almost one-third of all such violations for the entire county), and the stadium food operator had already been fined almost $4,000. Cleanup efforts continued through December 2009, but several reinspections resulted in more than 100 additional violations and more fines (Steinbach, 2010b). Although some of the concerns were associated with the facility or equipment, other concerns dealt with proper employee conduct or training, including the following: not washing hands, not changing gloves after handling raw meat, touching one's face or blowing one's nose, and drinking or eating in the food prep area (Steinbach, 2010b). Management needs to aggressively address concession concerns to prevent possible harm to fans and because the poor reputation of a concession operation can result in significant monetary loss.

TIPS FOR MAINTAINING A GYMNASIUM

- Small dents in the floor can be removed by covering the dent with a damp cloth and then pressing on the cloth with an electric iron.

- Any repairs should be discussed with the floor manufacturer before they are undertaken to make sure the repair will not void any warranty.

- Gum stuck to various surfaces can be removed by freezing the gum with dry ice and then removing the gum with a putty knife. Gum can also be removed by applying peanut butter to the area.

- Urethane floors can be repaired by pouring or painting a new layer of urethane over the entire floor.

- Masonite should be placed under the wheels of movable bleacher systems to avoid damage to the underlying floor.

From Cohen 2000.

Gymnasiums

Whether the facility is a 15,000-seat multisport arena or a high school gym used just for basketball, certain standard maintenance steps exist (see "Tips for Maintaining a Gymnasium"). A properly maintained gym not only reduces the risk of injury to athletes and spectators but also increases the aesthetic appeal and extends the building's life. Decent lights, a floor with some give, and the proper equipment may be all that is absolutely necessary. However, most gym users want more. Athletes want a well-finished surface free of defects, a good HVAC system so air can circulate, and appropriate lighting.

Key areas that should be examined when installing and maintaining a gym include the floor (hardwood or synthetic), bleachers, dividers, basketball goals, padding, dashers, and glass.

Flooring

The primary surfaces used in gymnasiums are wood and synthetic. Wood floors may be maple or other wood options in a variety of grades depending on the amount of money spent. Wood needs to be properly maintained.

The drive to create a floor finish that is able to bend without cracking has resulted in two types of finishes that have varied effects: oil based and water based. The floorboards must bend in order to withstand multipurpose usage and improper cleaning by janitorial staff (Cohen, 1998).

Oil-based wood-floor finishes utilize vegetable oils and are modified to create a urethane. The urethane is applied to the floor wet and can be damaged in the drying process (Cohen, 1998). As the urethane dries, chemicals are released into the air that are harmful to both humans and the environment. As the liquid portion of the urethane evaporates, it leaves a hard resin on the floor. These types of finishes tend to be higher gloss and not as wear resistant, but they are more flexible than other finishes (Cohen, 1998). Oil-based urethanes are the most common type of floor finish for gym floors.

Water-based finishes have a clear color (unlike the oil-based finishes, which are amber colored) and are generally not as thick or glossy (Cohen, 1998). This means that to achieve a higher gloss, more coats must be applied. Unlike oil-based products, water-based finishes do not give off harmful vapors as they dry. Also, water-based products act more like an adhesive when they are applied. This can be bad if there are separations between some of the floorboards. The finish can get between the boards and glue the boards together when it dries (Cohen, 1998). Using a simple surface-prep solution to fill the cracks before applying the finish can avert this problem.

Under normal circumstances a 0.75-inch-thick (1.9 cm) tongue-and-groove solid maple floor can last from 40 to 80 years (Brickman, 1997). The floor's life span is affected by

- the events held on the floor,
- the moisture level in the gym,
- how frequently the floor is cleaned,

- whether mats are used to wipe feet before people enter,
- the quality and frequency of finish recoating (completed every year or every other year),
- the quality and frequency of sanding and refinishing (complete sanding and refinishing needed every 10 to 20 years), and
- the frequency of minor and major catastrophes such as floods (Brickman, 1997).

The cost to completely sand and finish a typical gym floor is around $12,000 to $16,000, while the cost of a new gym floor averages around $60,000. Thus, it is a worthwhile investment to properly manage and maintain a wood floor.

Synthetic floors are often used for multisport facilities that offer basketball, tennis, in-line hockey, soccer, and track and field events. Synthetic materials include nylon turf, rubber, poured urethane, and ethylene propylene diene monomer granules in a urethane binder. Each floor system has unique issues that need to be addressed from a management perspective, such as seams, cleaning, and repairs. Exposed seams can present a tripping hazard. Also, some surfaces that have a granular finish are very hard to clean, making it necessary to use special machines or leaf blowers.

Bleachers

There are guidelines and standards for both indoor and outdoor bleachers, as well as various techniques used for repair and maintenance.

Most gyms are built with telescoping bleachers that are easily taken in and out when necessary. In contrast, arenas are normally built with fixed seating that may include mold-injected plastic seats. Access is a key concern for bleachers. Aisles placed in the middle of the bleachers are the most effective means of access (Scandrett, 1998). A double-loaded bleacher allows aisle access to all its sections. Rows should be spaced about 24 inches (61 cm) apart, although a 26- to 28-inch (66-71 cm) space is most desirable to make passage between rows easier (Scandrett, 1998). Usually bleachers rise between 11 and 16 inches (28 and 41 cm) from one row to the next to help create acceptable sight lines for the crowd (Scandrett, 1998).

BEHIND THE SCENES

MERCURY IN THE FLOORS

Although most schools replace only one gym at a time, sometimes a better deal can be made if several gyms are repaired at the same time. This scenario occurred when the Fairfax, Virginia, public school district replaced four gym floors. The gyms had various surfaces, such as poured urethane, wood, and vinyl tiles, that were all changed over to maple wood. The gyms are of various sizes ranging from 4,800 to 28,000 square feet (445-2,600 sq m) and are used daily by the students for classes and athletics; some are also open to the general public.

Fairfax County entered into a contract in 2000 with Southwest Recreational Industries to replace the gym floor at one of the county's secondary schools. Shortly before entering into the contract, the school board learned that the existing flooring material contained mercury in excess of the regulatory limit of 0.2 mg/L. Because of these test results, the contract required that the flooring material be handled as a hazardous waste requiring certified proof of disposal. Southwest acknowledged the requirements. Thereafter, Southwest entered into a subcontract agreement with Floor-Tec for the gym floor replacement project. There was finger-pointing between Southwest and Floor-Tec about whether the hazardous material was properly conveyed, but nonetheless, the material was improperly disposed. The dispute resulted in a consent order issued by the Virginia Waste Management Board against the county school board and Southwest (Virginia Waste Management Board Enforcement Action, 2002). The school board faced delays, safety concerns, and a poor reputation while waiting for the floor to be corrected.

One school installed Taraflex Sport M flooring, which is 0.25 inch (6.7 mm) thick and covered with a resistant stain to reduce friction burns, prevent bacteria growth, and minimize maintenance costs. The multilayered floor utilizes a 100% pure vinyl wear layer with reinforced fiberglass and a closed-cell foam backing underneath that helps reduce stress on athletes' joints when they jump ("Fairfax County School District," 2003).

Schools throughout the world are constantly installing or replacing gym floors. This example highlights that although it is exciting to get a new gym floor, care needs to be taken to avoid environmental or other hazards during the transition process.

Although some facilities require only 4 feet (1.2 m) of space between the face of the bleachers and the court, it is much safer to significantly exceed this minimum amount. If a scorer's table and player benches are in front of the bleachers as well, there should be a minimum of 10 feet (3 m) from the out-of-bounds line to the front of the bleachers to give 4 feet of circulation space for fans and 6 clear feet (1.8 m) for the athletes, coaches, and staff (Scandrett, 1998). Most diagrams for basketball courts show a buffer zone of at least 3 feet (from the sideline to any potential significant obstruction) on the sides and 6 feet (1.8 m) behind the baskets' end lines. Recently, a number of universities such as Duke University had issues with the proximity of the fan section to the court because the fans are almost at the end line and there is no margin of error for players to avoid running into fans.

It is imperative to refer to building codes before installing or modifying bleachers. Following are some of the regulations (whether by the International Building Code or the Consumer Product Safety Commission) that may apply:

- No more than 16 rows are allowed if they are accessible only from either the top or the bottom.

- Aisles are required only when the bleachers are more than 11 rows high.

- There should be no more than 20 seats between aisles.

- To accommodate wheelchairs, cutouts can be made in various spots along the first row of telescoping bleachers. Platforms can be built overlooking the top rows to provide seating that complies with the Americans with Disabilities Act. For a facility that seats more than 500 people, 6 wheelchair-accessible seats are required, with an additional wheelchair location required for every 100 spectators over the initial 500 (Scandrett, 1998).

Everyday bleacher maintenance can be as simple as sweeping the bleachers and underneath the structures before closing them. While walking underneath open bleachers, a worker can easily look for signs of structural damage such as bent metal cross-braces or chipped paint that indicates fatigue cracks (Steinbach, 2000). Small repairs may be as simple as bending parts back in shape by hand. Moving parts can be lubricated with a lithium-based grease that is dabbed onto the structure using a small paintbrush (Steinbach, 2000).

Gym Components

Several other components in a typical gym present legal, managerial, or maintenance challenges. The components covered here include gym dividers, basketball goals, wall padding, dasher boards, and glass panels.

Divider curtains are frequently found in gyms where multiple activities that require some separation will take place. The separation is needed to prevent people from tripping over balls or other objects that might travel from one activity area to another. The curtains can also create distinct areas so that multiple events can occur without the need to use more than one facility. A metal pole or weights at the bottom help keep the curtain straight and taut, but care needs to be taken to make sure that no one is hit by the curtain when it is going up or down. Hanging curtains tend to tear near the bottom. These tears can easily be remedied in place using a portable carpet-stitching machine or by resealing with a strong epoxy. Holes can also be patched by using epoxy to affix spare pieces of vinyl fabric to both sides of the hole (Steinbach, 2000).

Basketball goals can be fixed, dropped from the ceiling, or swung out from the walls. All nuts, bolts, wires, and gears need to be examined for wear and tear. Goals can be shattered and rims can be broken, and these items are hard to repair. Every facility with basketball goals should store an extra backboard and rim in case equipment breaks. Minor repairs and maintenance issues include welding of new net hooks to keep the net in place, repainting a chipped or peeling rim, and reattaching padding to the underside of the backboard.

Wall padding, used to protect players from injury when they run into walls or doors behind the basketball goals, can take significant punishment. Facilities often have torn, missing, or ripped pads. Damaged pads can be refurbished in-house. Pads can be removed from the wall, and the inside padding can be removed to patch the vinyl. After the padding (and maybe even the vinyl cover) is replaced and secured with contact cement, the vinyl can be rewrapped and stapled using industrial staples (Steinbach, 2000). Small tears can be repaired by using epoxy to glue a small piece of vinyl over the hole.

Dasher boards—used for events such as in-line hockey, indoor soccer, and arena football—need to be inspected to make sure they are not broken, splintering, or improperly secured. The majority of damage to these boards comes from the vehicles used in the arena (e.g., Zambonis, forklifts). Bad reinstallation can also damage the boards (Steinbach, 2000). Aluminum- or steel-backed dashers can be bent back into shape by heating the studs first to soften them. Scratches in glass dasher boards can be removed by applying light automotive polish, allowing it to dry, and then removing it with a buffer. When cleaning other marks off the glass, the recommendation is to use only products designed for Plexiglas, as other cleaners can weaken the glass (Steinbach, 2000). Several spare glass panels and plywood dasher boards should be kept in storage to be used if a board breaks.

The facility manager must make sure that all components in a gym or an internal facility are in good shape for the intended purpose. Pre-event inspections can help reduce the chance of injury and identify problems that can be fixed through routine maintenance. The same applies to external sport facilities.

Ice Hockey Sheets

It can take several days to create a sheet of ice to play hockey or to skate on. Building 1 inch (2.5 cm) of ice can take about 10,200 gallons (38,600 L) of water. The process starts by having a facility specifically built for an ice sheet. This requires a concrete slab with special coils built into it that can be chilled with a brine (salt water) solution that does not freeze at low temperatures. The coils are chilled with the goal of cooling the concrete to around 12 °F (–11 °C). This process takes several days to avoid cracking the concrete. A couple layers of specialized water (the water goes through a reverse osmosis system to remove impurities) are sprayed to create a good bond between the ice and the concrete. The frozen concrete freezes

the water sprayed on it. Several coats of white ice paint are sprayed, followed by several layers of plain water. Even after all these layers, the ice is still only an eighth of an inch (0.3 cm) thick. Lines and logos are then added before a crew floods the sheet several times a day for several days until the ice is around 1 inch thick. The ice surface is 21 °F (–6 °C), and 3 feet (0.9 m) above the ice the temperature is 50 °F (10 °C) ("Freeze Frame," 2008).

How does one freeze ice in warmer weather for an outdoor hockey rink? This question has become a big issue over the past decade with the National Hockey League Winter Classic and other outdoor hockey matches played in temporary rinks. Building a temporary outdoor rink requires 240 aluminum plates, almost 2 inches (5 cm) thick and embedded with piping for the glycol, to be pieced together. A total of 20,000 gallons (75,708 L) of water (almost double that required for an indoor rink) creates the ice surface. This process takes several days and can vary based on weather concerns such as higher temperatures or rain.

ESTABLISHING GRASS FIELDS

Although sod fields (rolls of pregrown grass) might take more quickly, seeding produces the best turf over the long run. Seeding, which entails preparing the soil and then manually spreading seeds, is the preferred method because of its relatively low cost and reduced labor requirements. Most grass fields need to grow for at least two growing seasons before they can be exposed to athletic competition. This can take from 9 months to a year, so if a field needs to be used sooner, the only good option is to use sod. It takes 6 to 10 weeks for sod's grass roots to grow 3 inches (7.6 cm) into the ground. A field comprising sod with aggressive hybrid Bermuda grass can often be football ready in 45 days (Steinbach, 2006).

A poor field can also be expensive. In 2002 and 2003, for example, Giants Stadium in East Rutherford, New Jersey, was in such poor condition that $120,000 had to be spent to put a new field down before the playoffs. This was the second field installed that season, which created a significant expense because another field was scheduled to be installed later that year. Because of the problems with the natural grass surface, the New Jersey Sports and Exposition Authority was considering synthetic turf ("Giants Stadium Resodded," 2002). The owners of the new MetLife Stadium installed an artificial turf field. Such fields can often last 10 years with significant use; however, the field was replaced after 3 years because the NFL required a new field when the stadium hosted the 2014 Super Bowl.

The process of establishing and maintaining an athletic playing field can be daunting. It is easy to avoid difficulties, however, with proper research regarding types of grass, species of grass, varieties of grass, seeding rates, and seed quality. The proper choice of **turfgrass**, either cool season or warm season, depends on the facility's location. Cool-season turfgrass, as the name suggests, is best suited for areas that are subject to low temperatures during the winter months. The optimal growing temperature is between 60 °F and 75 °F (15 °C-24 °C). Warm-season turfgrass, on the other hand, is less hearty and will die if exposed to freezing temperatures for an extended time.

The optimal growing temperature for warm-season turfgrass is 80 °F to 95 °F (27°C-35 °C) (Rogers and Stier, 1995). Not surprisingly, warm-season turfgrass is best suited for southern regions. The swath of land in the United States that begins in southern New Jersey and continues in a southwest direction to New Mexico is known as the transition zone because both warm-season and cool-season turfgrass can grow in this area, although neither is very well suited for the climate. Thus, facilities in the transition zone often experience trouble maintaining athletic fields.

Cool-Season Turfgrass

Three basic types of cool-season turfgrass are used for playing fields: Kentucky bluegrass (*Poa pratensis* L.), perennial ryegrass (*Lolium perenne* L.), and tall fescue (*Festuca arundinacea* Schreb) (Rogers and Stier, 1995). Kentucky bluegrass can reproduce itself because of its underground lateral stems called rhizomes, which allow it to spread over a large area. A drawback of Kentucky bluegrass, however, is its slow growth and thus its inability to provide facility managers with a quick fix.

Perennial ryegrass, on the other hand, germinates very quickly and is therefore an ideal turfgrass when facility managers require a quick fix. However, it is a bunch-type turfgrass and has trouble recuperating from excessive traffic. Perennial ryegrass and Kentucky bluegrass work well together in that their respective benefits and drawbacks complement each other.

Tall fescue, a turfgrass characterized by coarse wide-leaf blades, is by far the most wear tolerant of the three turfgrasses but is a slow-growing, bunch-type grass. Certain cool-season turfgrasses are not wear tolerant or are intolerant in relation to the cutting heights necessary for playing field maintenance and hence should not be used. These grasses include rough bluegrass, annual bluegrass, annual ryegrass, creeping bentgrass, colonial bentgrass, fine-leaf fescue, centipede grass, bahia grass, and St. Augustine grass (Rogers and Stier, 1995).

Warm-Season Turfgrass

Bermuda grass and zoysia grass are the most frequently used warm-season turfgrasses, with Bermuda grass most commonly used for fields where soccer and football are played. The seeds produced by these warm-season grasses are sterile, so the grass is established by sprigs or sod. Warm-season grasses grow both by rhizomes and by stolons, which are aboveground lateral stems, making them very wear tolerant and able to recuperate quickly.

The resilience of the warm-season turfgrasses, coupled with the various weaknesses of cool-season turfgrasses, makes warm-season grasses the preferred turfgrass for athletic fields. Because the warm-season grasses do not flourish in colder weather but instead lie dormant and then recuperate with warmer weather, facility managers often overseed a playing field with both types so that regardless of the conditions there is ample green grass on the field. Some universities, such as Michigan State University, have also begun experimenting with turfgrass in an attempt to breed a grass that will flourish in both cold and warm conditions (Rogers and Stier, 1995). Michigan State University has been a leader in turf science and helped develop the grass used at the Beijing Olympics.

A new type of grass called seashore paspalum may provide some strong benefits to golf courses. This grass, originally from South Africa, has deep roots and is salt-water tolerant. Because of the deep roots, it does not require as much water as other grasses. Furthermore, because this type of grass can thrive in salt water, salt—which can kill weeds without the use of any other chemicals—can be used as an herbicide. One golf course in the United States spent more than $300,000 a year on water but after switching to the new grass was able to cut water bills by more than 80% (Foust, 2002).

Seeding Rates

Once the facility manager has chosen the most appropriate species and varieties for the playing fields, it is imperative to order the proper amount of seeds. Seeds for various species differ in size. Table 8.1 provides the necessary information for determining how much of each type of seed is needed. Deviance from these guidelines will result in either a turf that is too thin or one that is too dense, making maintenance difficult.

Seeds should be spread at a rate of 6 to 12 seeds per square inch (6.4 sq cm) using a broadcast spreader. The broadcast spreader throws the seeds in all directions, resulting in uniform distribution.

Seed Quality

It is important to examine seed quality, including the percentage of each turfgrass and variety in the bag, the test date, and the purity percentage. The test date is important because germination declines with time. Therefore, a bag of seed with an old test date will yield less grass than will newer seed. The purity percentage gives the percentage of weed seed in the bag. A weed seed percentage of more than 0.5% is unacceptable.

Drainage

Whether they're playing Little League baseball or major league football, players want to use the field even after it has rained. A quality drainage system increases the chances that fields will be playable after rain. The key to proper drainage and a successful grass field is the couple inches of soil beneath the grass. The area where the grass roots are the strongest is called the **root zone**. If a person was to take a side cut of a typical field, the grass would be about 2 inches (5 cm) high, while the root zone just under the surface could be 3 to 4 inches (7.5-10 cm) thick. If the root zone is weak, the grass can come out very easily. Fields that take a lot of beating but are still in great shape have a strong root zone. A good field needs to have enough space in the root zone for optimal drainage and for water and minerals to penetrate and enrich the roots. Although the various drainage systems are similar (underground piping and catch basins), the way they are set up depends on which sports are played on the field. The facility manager must carefully plan the type of system that will be used before building the field. Changing or modifying a drainage system after construction is very costly (Watson, 1998).

Soil heavy in fine particles (e.g., silt, clay) compact more rapidly, which affects drainage. In contrast, coarse material (e.g., sand) does not inhibit drainage. When testing drainage rates (infiltration), the test should be conducted under normal compaction conditions and in various parts of the field. If the infiltration rate is low, the bulk of the drainage is handled at the surface through crowning and sloping the field to allow water to run off toward the sidelines. If the infiltration rate is high, there needs to be a

Table 8.1 Seeding Rates

Type of grass	Approximate number of seeds per pound	Seeding rate (lb/1,000 ft²)
Kentucky bluegrass	1,000,000-2,200,000	1-2
Perennial ryegrass	200,000	5-10
Tall fescue	200,000	5-10
Bermuda grass	2,000,000	1-2
Zoysia grass	1,000,000	2-3

From Roger and Stier 1995.

strong subsurface drainage system to help remove the water. In fields where grass rooting is not as aggressive, an ideal composition might be 70% sand, 15% native soil, and 15% compost.

Soils tests can be conducted with various devices such as a core sampler, augers, or splitspoon samplers. Tests conducted with these devices provide a cross-section of the soil strata and can be taken at various points of the filed. Some of these holes are small, whereas others can be several feet deep and wide to critically examine the field's foundation. Drainage pipes typically are laid 18 inches (46 cm) below the playing surface. They are covered with 6 to 12 inches (15-30 cm) of stone to allow water to filter to the pipes without the pipes getting clogged with dirt. Another approach is to create a 1-inch (2.5 cm) layer of open air about 11 inches (28 cm) below the surface using a plastic support grid. Irrigation piping is also placed 18 inches (46 cm) below the surface to avoid frost damage and damage from aeration tines. Pipes on the sidelines take the water away from the field.

Football Fields

There needs to be a crown at the top of the turf of a football field to help water run off to the sidelines and away from the playing surface. A laser level can help guide a tractor or other equipment in producing the correct grade. Fields that drain well need a grade ranging from 0.5° to 0.75° of slope per foot. From there, the slope might need to increase to 1° per foot for fields that drain adequately and 2° per foot for fields that drain poorly. Standard football field crowns are about 18 inches (46 cm) above the ground level at the sidelines. If the football field is a combination field for football and soccer (flat field), a more moderate approach of about 8 to 10 inches (20-25 cm) is needed (Watson, 1998). No field should be built completely flat, but if a crown cannot be used, the entire field should be angled to allow for better drainage.

Baseball Fields

For drainage of surface water from a baseball infield, the highest point is always the pitcher's mound. The infield should grade down 4 inches (10 cm) toward each base, and then from each base another 4 inches toward the outer edges of the infield. The highest point of the outfield should be where it meets the infield. From this point there is a 10-inch (25 cm) drop toward the fence at a 0% to 2% grade (Watson, 1998).

Water Removal

Several techniques can be used to remove standing water from a field. If the standing water is due to blocked drainage pipes, the drainage system needs to be cleaned. Simply cleaning clogged catch basins may be all that is needed. If the water still does not drain, the problem could be **compaction** (where the ground is so hard and the soil so tight that there is no room for water or minerals to seep down) or a faulty drainage system. In either case, the water must be removed if play is to begin or continue. Water can be removed by using Turface (a soil conditioner) or other compounds that absorb water and leave behind a granular residue that breaks up into the soil. Other techniques include using hand sponges, sponges attached to poles, sponges attached to feet, hand or motorized pumps, leaf blowers, and squeegees to move the water to another area.

Field drainage is just one component of a field maintenance program. Fields do not keep themselves in good condition; they require significant care and attention to make sure grass is growing correctly. The watering, weeding, fertilizing, mowing, painting, and aeration procedures must be carefully managed to avoid destroying the field.

MAINTAINING GRASS FIELDS

Every field is different and requires a customized maintenance program. Players and spectators notice when a field has holes, has not been mowed, or is lacking painted lines. These may be relatively minor issues when people are looking for any grassy area in which to play. However, when there is a choice of fields or when safety is a priority, a well-maintained field is critical. Factors to be analyzed when examining field maintenance concerns include financial and human resources, field layout (northeast versus south), types of soils and grasses, use of fields (intensity and frequency), and the sport or sports being played on the field. The first two variables are hard to control. If there

BEHIND THE SCENES

GRASS FIELDS AT THE OLYMPICS

GreenTech's natural grass sport-field system was installed at National Stadium in Beijing for the 2008 Olympic Games at an estimated cost of $1.5 million. The turf system, which uses interlocking trays, was also installed at Olympic Stadium in Athens, Greece. The GreenTech sod system is used at Virginia Tech's Lane Stadium, the old Giants Stadium in New Jersey, and a handful of other stadiums around the world such as Wimbledon and Luzhniki Stadium in Moscow.

The grass used in this system is initially grown inside 46-inch-square (297 cm sq) trays that are 1 foot (0.3 m) deep. The trays, called modules, are grown at an off-site location. The modules are then brought to the stadium and connected like tile floor pieces. The installation process takes several days. Once the field is set up, sections of a stadium that receive a lot of wear and tear can be replaced or moved. For the Beijing Olympics, the grass was grown in trays at a location about 15 minutes away. The playing field at Beijing National Stadium was made up of about 6,500 modules. The field has about 80,000 square feet (7,400 sq m) of grass (Gilligan, 2007). The grass system was designed to be installed after the opening ceremony. Thus, the wear and tear of concerts and thousands of performers would not damage the playing surface for track and soccer events.

Not every stadium uses such systems. Traditional grass fields are still the primary option for major events. In 2014, an Oregon company provided all the perennial ryegrass mixture used to overseed the 12 fields used during the World Cup.

is not enough money or time to maintain a field optimally, or if space is not sufficient, those who run the facility will be forced to make do.

Soil

Soil-based fields are constructed using native-type soil materials, which are able to hold higher water and nutrient levels. Unfortunately, soil-based fields are the most susceptible to compaction. Still, when they are well aerated they are very good for all root zone types (Depew and Guise, 1997).

Sand-modified fields are native-based fields to which sand has been added on-site through topdressing and aeration. As more sand is added, the resistance to compaction is also increased. A field is not considered sand modified until the amount of sand is in a 60% (sand) to 40% (native soil) ratio. Apart from the higher level of sand, there are not many noticeable changes in the root zone's properties until the sand volume is about 80% (Depew and Guise, 1997).

Fields with sand-based root zones are high-end fields as judged by cost and performance potential. Sand-based fields should have high drainage and aeration rates but low water retention rates (Depew and Guise, 1997). By building this type of field over a layer of coarse gravel, the facility can help slow water movement so the root zone has more time to retain draining water.

The latest trend in natural fields is to add artificial substances. The addition of synthetic materials to the root zones can enhance aeration and drainage properties and help stabilize the soil (Depew and Guise, 1997). However, if the roots do not bond or intertwine with the material, this approach is ineffective.

The three basic components of soils are sand, silt, and clay. The proportions of these components control the factors that constitute field playability: infiltration rate, percolation, and degree of compaction (Mrock, 1999). The **infiltration rate** of soil is the rate at which water is absorbed from the surface into the soil. **Percolation** is the amount of time it takes for water to pass through the soil and the turfgrass roots. Compaction, as highlighted earlier, refers to the way in which the individual particles in the soil fit together. In a good growing environment, particles are packed together loosely enough to create pore space for air and water. If air and water cannot pass through the soil, the roots will be deprived of two vital ingredients for growth and will die.

The faster the infiltration rate, the more quickly field surfaces will be ready to be played on, even in rainy weather (Mrock, 1999). On the other hand, a slow percolation rate can create the false impression of a dry field. Although the field surface may appear dry, the soil underneath the surface is still wet and in this softened state is more prone

A beautiful field is the goal of every groundskeeper, but the amount of time and money needed to accomplish a perfect look is significant.

to compaction. A facility manager can determine the percolation rate by taking core samples every half-hour from various sections of the field once infiltration has occurred (Mrock, 1999).

Both infiltration and percolation rates can be improved through processes known as aeration and topdressing. **Topdressing** is the spreading of new soil over the existing soil to create permanent pore space for the soil over time. Topdressing is often used in combination with aeration and overseeding to generate an effective environment for new grass growth.

Aeration and Aerators

Aeration is the process of opening channels in the soil so that air, water, and nutrients can flow through the soil and compaction is avoided (Landry, 1995). The areas that are subject to the most traffic (e.g., in front of soccer goals, between football hash marks) will suffer the greatest

amount of compaction (Landry, 1995). A soil probe or stick or even a shovel can be used to test the compaction level. The more difficult it is to sink the device into the ground, the greater the compaction level. Compaction can be reduced through three aeration techniques.

Core aerators are vertical-action aerators. Their piston-like action drives hollow metal tines into the ground. Upon entering the soil, the tine scoops out a hole, and as it exits the ground it deposits the soil core on the surface. The core can be broken up with field use or metal drag nets (Steinbach, 2001a). This is the most effective type of aerating but also the most time consuming.

Circular or drum aerators are simply rolling drums with spikes. The spikes penetrate the ground as the drum is rolled over the surface. This is a time-efficient method for aerating fields, but penetrating the soil this way can also cause damage. Unlike what happens with core aeration, nothing is removed from the ground, which makes circular aeration more common during playing seasons.

Slicer or slicing aerators provide the least compaction relief but also create the least amount of surface disruption (Steinbach, 2001a). Slicers use triangular-shaped knives to cut thin slits into the ground while traveling at relatively high speeds.

Turfgrass Maintenance

It is not enough to have good grass seed, perfect soil, and the proper blend of nutrients in the soil. A turf needs to be constantly maintained through such means as addition of chemical fertilizers, weed-killing treatments, and appropriate watering and mowing schedules. Mowing, fertilizing, and pest control account for the greatest amount of time and money spent on a lawn. Other steps involved in turfgrass maintenance include the following:

- Leaf removal
- Edging
- Weed control (pre-emergent, postemergent)
- Core aeration at least once a year
- Mechanical slit-seeding
- Lime (if necessary) for soil balance
- Dethatching dead grass (if necessary) (Lewis, 1999)
- Topdressing the field, which entails adding soil or sand to keep the surface level

Besides the various turf care steps highlighted above, a turf manager needs to carefully interact with the turf because it is a living part of the facility. If errors are made in turf care, the field can be killed and cost the facility several hundred thousand dollars to replant. Some guidelines that should be followed include:

- Excessive fertilizing can result in "burn" grass where the grass turns brown.
- Overwatering can be as bad as underwatering and can result in the growth of mushrooms and weeds.
- Scalping more than one-third of the grass height is the primary lawn care mistake because the grass will need to move energy away from the roots to replenish the grass blades.
- Lawnmower blades should be regularly sharpened to help minimize blade-related damage to grass.
- The key to mowing is mowing often and at shorter lengths.
- The native soil needs to be tested regularly to ensure that it has the proper pH level for optimal grass growth.

Mowing

Mowing is an important maintenance function that managers must perform to keep a field's appearance and playability at its best. An overzealous mowing schedule or a few shortcuts can have devastating effects on the field. A neglected field can quickly overgrow and can suffer significantly from extreme growth when mowing is too infrequent.

Two types of mowers are used on sport fields: reel mowers and rotary mowers. Both types come in the walk-behind, riding, and pull-behind varieties. A reel mower uses a rolling cylinder to scissor grass along a stationary bed knife (Steinbach, 2001a). The most popular form of reel mower is the triplex. This is a riding mower that offsets three reels (two in front of the tractor and one underneath) so that the reels always reach the grass before the tractor's wheels flatten it (Steinbach, 2001a). Reel mower blades should be sharpened at least twice a week, if not after every use.

Rotary mowers—the most common form of mower—are similar to home mowers. Rotary mowers are able to cut grass at much more varying lengths than reel mowers (Steinbach, 2001a). They are also more time efficient as they can cut well while traveling at higher speeds, and the blades do not need to be sharpened as frequently.

Proper mower maintenance requires checking and maintaining all fluid levels (oil, hydro fluid, and water), filters, belts, and tire pressure. Another key maintenance issue is cleaning the equipment when moving from one field or facility to another. Turf diseases can be carried from one field to another if infected grass clippings are not washed off the mower (Trotter, 1996).

Although cutting height varies from field to field depending on grass types and growing rates, a general cutting height for most fields can be determined. It is vital that the grass not be cut too short, as this can severely reduce its life span. When the blade is cut short, the plant tries to send stored food to the blade to regenerate growth. Once it has started feeding the leaf to create aboveground repair or growth, it tries to balance itself by feeding the roots to generate belowground growth (Trusty and Trusty, 1995). Since the effort is placed on strengthening the roots, the blades do not grow as well.

The cool-season grasses—bluegrass, perennial ryegrass, and turf-type tall fescue—have a suggested cutting range of 2 to 3 inches (5-7.6 cm) (Trusty and Trusty, 1995). Warm-season grasses have much lower cutting heights. A normal height for a warm-season field is anywhere from 0.75 to 1.5 inches (1.9-3.8 cm) (see tables 8.2 and 8.3).

Fertilizer

Television commercials often show beautiful lawns with families at play. Sport fans also relish the opportunity to see a freshly cut outfield. These images may make one wonder how such lawns are achieved. More lawns seem to have problems than not. For example, many fields in the South have fire-ant hills. The key to avoiding problems is proper care. Everything has to be analyzed, from the base soil composition to the fertilizer used to the techniques of cutting and chemically treating the grass.

Keys to a great lawn include applying the proper amount of fertilizer and mowing the lawn at the appropriate times with a sharp blade. Fertilizer can improve grass longevity by 40% to 50% when proper amounts are applied nine times a year rather than five. One study showed that longevity also improved by 20% to 40% when the lawn was mowed twice a week rather than once a week (Martin, 2002). Such statistics highlight that there is a science to quality field maintenance.

Pests

Most facility managers at one time or another face the problem of pests, although the species and the severity of the problem vary from region to region. The challenge is how to get rid of the pests while limiting the potential associated safety and

Table 8.2 Cool-Season Turf Care

January/February	If the ground is not frozen or covered with snow, this is the best time to repair drainage problems and low spots by adding more soil underneath the turf. Equipment can also be repaired for the upcoming season.
March/April	This is a good time to test the soil (test every 1-3 years). This is also the best time to aerate fields. In the North it is also the ideal time to start applying weed grass controls. If seeding, the pre-emergents should not be used until the seeds have germinated. At this point, the facility manager should be ready to apply the first fertilizer treatment for the year. A fertilizer should be selected that suits the field's needs based on prior soil-testing results.
May/June	Identifying broadleaf weeds and selecting an effective herbicide are very important. Late June is a good time to apply fertilizer with a higher potassium base. This helps get the grass ready for the summer months. As the summer months approach, it is useful to irrigate the fields frequently. Fields should once again be aerated.
July/August	If problems with diseases or insects occur, it may be wise to use fungicides and insecticides to help reduce the problems. If the field manager plans on using this time to overseed the fields, he or she should be ready to apply more fertilizer at a rate of 0.5 lb (0.2 kg) of nitrogen per 1,000 ft² (93 m²).
September	If financially feasible, another dose of fertilizer allows the field to continue growing and recover from the excessive usage.
October	In some areas there may be a need for more broadleaf weed controls as winter annuals start to germinate.
November/December	If the facility manager notices damage to the field at this time, it should be fixed immediately.

From Horman 1993.

Table 8.3 Warm-Season Turf Care

January	During this time, fields can be dethatched and drainage systems can be repaired. The soil should be tested and fertilizer applied to any areas that will be overseeded.
February/March	This is a period when turfgrasses begin to grow again, so it is important to fertilize the field with a balanced fertilizer (25-3-10). Insecticides should be applied to fields in the South. Once the turf is actively growing, it is time to aerate again.
April/May	Fertilizer and weed control need to be reapplied.
June-August	These months tend to require applying nitrogen at 1 lb (0.4 kg) per 1,000 ft².
September/October	Reduce the amount of fertilizer to 0.5 lb (0.2 kg) per 1,000 ft² while increasing the amount of potassium in the applications.
November/December	Fertilization and aerification are not recommended for turfgrass that is dormant.

From Horman 1993.

political hazards (Dahlgren, 2000a). In some areas, insects such as white grubs and mole crickets get in under the soil and eat the grass's root system. Even when pesticides are used, white grubs are usually responsible for destroying about 10% of fields each year (Dahlgren, 2000a). Turf managers have started to change the way they attack insects. Instead of using insecticides, managers are using pesticides that alter the insects' metabolism. If there still is an insect problem, then birds and other animals that feed on these types of insects will be attracted to the fields. Then the issue is no longer how to get rid of the insects, but how to get rid of the insects and the animals (Dahlgren, 2000a). Because individual pest control problems can vary, there is no one best approach to eliminating insects.

Another nuisance is geese, who leave their droppings all over a field and eat the grass. Various chemicals can be used to help repel geese, but one of the most effective techniques is to use fake wolves and foxes made of cardboard or foam. Some towns hire companies, such as Geese Police, that use trained dogs to scare geese away from golf courses and fields.

Field Preparation

If a field is being used for football, soccer, lacrosse, or similar sports, it needs to be lined. Painting lines on the grass using stakes and strings as a guide for the roller is usually the best method. The following are some tips for painting sidelines or logos:

■ Cut the area of the grass that will be painted a little lower than the other grass sections. Thus,

if the regular playing length is 2.5 to 3 inches (6.4-7.6 cm), the area that will be painted should be mowed to 1 to 1.25 inch (2.5-3 cm) high for best appearance.

■ The first field painting each year should be done slowly with diluted paint. The same line should be painted from the opposite direction with a less diluted paint mixture.

■ Subsequent paintings can be accomplished on one sweep with a two-head sprayer.

■ When painting multiple colors, it is best to paint the area white first, let it dry, and then paint other colors on top, as the white will serve as a good base.

■ These steps do not cover coloring dirt areas such as the batter's box or the first or third base lines, which is accomplished with a dry line marker using a white powder in a 2- or 4-inch (5 or 10 cm) band (Pioneer Athletics, 1998).

Other field preparation issues include weeding and spraying. Weeding is hard to undertake by hand but may be necessary if the field is to look its best. The process is more difficult when the weeds are intertwined with the grass. Some facilities utilize weed and feed granules that fertilize the grass and at the same time kill weeds. Spraying can be a good alternative if the proper chemicals are used.

A facility manager or employee without proper licensure cannot undertake the spraying of certain chemicals. For example, laws dictate what chemicals can be sprayed if certain trees are located even a mile (1.6 km) away from the field. Other rules indicate whether spraying can occur on a

EQUIPMENT NEEDS FOR MANAGING A FIELD

Field maintenance requires significant equipment. Many field groomers spend hundreds of thousands of dollars on the equipment needed to maintain a field. Such equipment also requires gas and maintenance, and employees must be trained to make sure the equipment is properly utilized. The following list highlights the basic equipment used to maintain a field. Synthetic turf also requires vehicles (utility vehicles and tractors), topdressing (for spreading infill), grooming equipment to help stand up synthetic fibers, and sanitation equipment to apply chemicals such as germicidals and antimicrobials that help prevent various diseases.

Vehicles
Most facilities use a variety of vehicles, including trucks, utility vehicles (often carts to transport people, equipment, or chemicals), and tractors.

Mowers
- Reel: The highest quality mower uses a cutting motion similar to scissors to cut grass.
- Rotary: A spinning mower blade hits and shears off the top portion of the leaf blade. These mowers are the most affordable. Blades on these mowers can range from around 20 inches (51 cm) to a gang of rotary blades on multiple platforms that can expand to a 15-foot (4.6 m) cutting area.
- Flail: Pivoting blades (flails) spin at a high speed around a horizontal axle and shear in a manner similar to rotary mowers.

Cultivation Equipment
- Hollow tine aerator: Hollow tines penetrate the soil to various depths (3-6 inches, or 7.6-15.2 cm) and diameters (0.25-0.75 inch, or 0.6-1.9 cm) to remove core samples. This is the most common aerator. Also available are aerators with deep tines (solid or hollow) that are 8 to 12 inches (20.3-30.4 cm) long.
- Solid tine aerator: Instead of taking out a core sample like hollow tine aerators, solid tines simply make holes in the turf.
- Spiker or slicer: Solid metal blades cut into the soil, allowing water and air to reach the grass roots.

Irrigation Equipment
- Traveling irrigator: A rotating sprinkler is attached to a hose and is self-propelled along a designated path.
- Quick coupler: Pipes underground lead to couplers that are flush with the ground. Hoses attached to the couplers bring water to designated areas. A coupler is often found right behind the pitcher's mound to help irrigate the mound and second base area.
- Various hoses and nozzles can be used for hand watering and for major watering needs.- An elevated large sprinkler, called a rain gun, can be used to irrigate large areas.

Seeding Equipment
- Slit seeder: Uses disks to cut into the soil, where a seed is then deposited.
- Rotary spreader: Slings seeds around in a broad pattern; can also be used for fertilizer.
- Drop spreader: Distributes seeds in a radius of only two-three feet away from the spreader and is used for precise seeding.
- Harrow: Drags metal disks, teeth, or sharp tines over plowed land to pulverize the clods of earth and level the soil; also used to uproot weeds, aerate the soil, and cover seeds.

Fertilizing Equipment
Rotary spreaders sling fertilizer and other products across a broad area in a wide pattern, whereas drop spreaders are much more precise using smaller and fewer distribution holes.

Pesticide Application Equipment
A backpack sprayer (carried on an employee's back; uses one precise nozzle) or boom sprayer attached to a tanker truck help spray chemicals on desired areas.

Hand Power Equipment
Various pieces such as chainsaws, string trimmers, backpack leaf blowers, and vacuums.

Hand Tools
Various pieces such as soil probes, shovels, rakes, edgers, post hole diggers, pruners, sledgehammers, pitchforks, picks, and tamps.

Topdressing Equipment
Used to level the field surface or apply more soil in a uniform manner. One of the most common topdressing pieces is a drag used to smooth the surface; it can be made with nails, mats, or mesh.

Painting Equipment
Paint application equipment such as compression-driven or airless sprayers can be attached to walk-behind or riding equipment. Stencils should be purchased for quality painting.

given day based on the weather conditions. For example, spraying must be postponed if it is raining or windy. Because of complex laws relating to when certain chemicals can be sprayed and where, some facilities outsource the chemical spraying and treatment to professional contractors.

Field preparation can also entail such activities as snow removal. How will snow be removed, and where will it be moved? How can snow be moved without damaging the turf? Will the vehicle used to move the snow damage the field? What will happen to the painted portion of the field, and can paint be applied in the wintertime? A facility manager needs to prepare for snow removal contingencies, including snowstorms, well before the weather changes; in fact, the best approach focuses on preparation. Having a snowblower does little good if there is no gas or electricity to operate it. Care should be taken not to remove snow too early, which may require additional rounds of snow removal when accumulations increase.

ADDITIONAL OUTDOOR CONCERNS

Grass fields are only one of the concerns with outdoor facilities. Other field-related issues have to do with synthetic surfaces, infield dirt areas, baseball and softball fields, outdoor bleachers, and safety.

Infield Dirt

Dirt playing areas need as much care as fields do. Baseball players do not want a bumpy infield, as it can cause a bad hop, irregular bounces, and a hazard for those sliding into bases. To minimize these problems, numerous techniques are used to make sure the infield is in proper shape (see "Primary Rules for Infield Care"). The starting point is analyzing the material that composes the infield. Infields can include lava rock, agricultural lime, Stabilizer Pro Red, stone dust, crushed brick, Turface blends, pumice, heavy clay, heavy sand, native soils, and infield blends (Perry, 2002a).

Whatever material is used for the infield, the surface will become hard over time, and different techniques need to be used to make the ground playable. This is especially true if there is too much clay in the field; with only a small amount of clay, the ground is easier to work with. Hardened clay can be as tough as rock when dried in the sun for an extended period. The typical technique used to make surfaces playable includes scoring and dragging. **Scoring** entails using various techniques to break up the ground. Heavy equipment or tools with nails or claws are often used to penetrate the field 3 to 6 inches (7.6-15 cm). The more common technique is to use smaller equipment that turns over only the top 1 or 2 inches (2.5-5 cm) ("scarifying"). **Dragging** involves using screens, rakes, or other devices to smooth the field. The techniques need to be frequently changed so that there is no rippling or any washboard effect from constant dragging in the same direction (Steinbach, 2002). Raking the buildup by the baseline back into the infield can also eliminate lips that can cause bad hops. After dragging the dirt, the field groomer should apply light moisture to the dirt to help keep dust down (Steinbach, 2002).

Baseball and Softball Fields

Baseball and softball fields provide some of the greatest challenges to field managers because of the multiple types of surfaces. Certain areas take more of a beating during games and require

---

PRIMARY RULES FOR INFIELD CARE

- Water the infield before working the dirt, as the water loosens the surface.
- The top 1 to 1.5 inches (2.5-3.8 cm) of the infield should be scarified (broken apart).
- The ground should be dragged, broomed, and leveled back to a clod-free, smooth surface.
- Rewater the field to prevent wind-blown dirt or erosion damage.

From Perry, 2002, "Tailor outdoor lighting to your facility," *Buildings* 16-17.

extensive attention on an almost daily basis. As with most fields, a regular routine should include daily as well as pre- and postgame maintenance.

The pitcher's mound and batter's boxes are the most seriously abused part of any baseball or softball field. Every play that occurs in the game is initiated from these locations. In addition, the motions and techniques that pitchers and batters use to throw and bat the ball are constantly digging up these areas. The first step in protecting the pitcher's safety is to construct a quality mound. The mound can be constructed in many ways, with new materials including mound blocks, packing clay, poly-blend soils, two-tiered pitching rubbers, and subsurface pads.

A regulation-size pitching mound in baseball is 18 feet (5.5 m) in diameter, with the rubber set 10 feet 6 inches (3.2 m) from the home plate side of the circle. Using a leveling device to determine the height, the top of the pitching mound should be 10 inches (25 cm) above the height of home plate (Perry, 1997). The pitching mound itself should be set 60 feet 6 inches (18.4 m) from the apex of home plate and should sit near the front of a level area that is 5 feet (1.5 m) by 34 inches (86 cm). From 6 inches (15 cm) in front of the rubber, the mound should slope toward home plate at a rate of 1 inch (2.5 cm) per foot. The underbelly of the mound should be made from hard-packed clay blocks to a height of 4 inches (10 cm) and then filled in with a mixture of soils that will help keep the clay moisture free (Perry, 1997). In contrast to baseball, the mound in softball is level, but the same basic underbelly should be developed.

The two areas that need the most attention around the plate are the right-handed batter's box and the catcher's area. Using clay blocks or a subsurface pad about 1 to 1.5 inches (2.5-3.8 cm) below the surface will help solidify the area. This lessens the amount of damage that occurs during a game. To prevent damage, artificial covering pads are now being used during pregame batting practice (Perry, 1997). Pads or mats help eliminate some of the damage done to the batter's box on a daily basis. When damage occurs, the fix is simply a matter of removing the covering dirt down to the clay blocks and repacking the area to the desired shape.

Facilities Trivia

Groundskeepers have their tricks, and these tricks can directly influence the outcome of a game. For example, if a home team is having problems fielding grounders, the groundskeeper can add more sand to help slow the ball down or let the grass grow higher by the baseline. A pitcher's mound can also be modified to help slow down a pitcher or alter their delivery. The grounds crew in Detroit at the turn of the 1900s watered the areas around home plate to help Ty Cobb's bunts stay in fair territory; this area came to be known as Cobb's lake. The San Francisco Giants used the same strategy in the 1960s to water the areas by first base to slow down opponents stealing bases, especially Los Angeles Dodgers' speedster Maury Wills. This led to so much diamond doctoring that umpires and coaches now regularly inspect the field before a game to prevent any unfair advantage (Leventhal, 2011).

The issues regarding baselines, base paths, and areas around the bases are similar. A broom or hose can help move infield dirt to prevent high lips. The dirt about 10 feet (3 m) around the base should be softened to help cushion the blow a player sustains when sliding into the base (Perry, 1997).

Outdoor Bleachers

The Consumer Product Safety Commission has issued guidelines on how to retrofit bleachers to increase spectator safety (LaRue, 2002). The standards were developed after it was reported that 19,000 people visit emergency rooms every year from bleacher- or grandstand-related injuries. Injuries occur when people slip or trip, fall off bleachers, or fall between boards. The primary concerns with bleachers are gaps between seat boards and footboards, guardrails that are not high enough, bleachers that are structurally unsafe, and aisles that are affected by weather conditions (LaRue, 2002).

Many of the same techniques used for maintaining indoor bleachers can be utilized for outdoor structures. The most important step is to set up a schedule of regular inspections. The Consumer Product Safety Commission guidelines suggest conducting inspections no fewer than four times per year, but if the bleachers are in constant use it

ROSE BOWL

In 1897 the city of Pasadena, California, purchased 10 acres of land. In 1921 the city decided to build a stadium with the south end left open. This gave the structure a horseshoe-like shape. The stadium was designed to fit as many people as possible as close to the action as possible. When first built, it sat 57,000 people. The stadium was given the name Rose Bowl by a police officer named Harlan W. Hall. The Rose Bowl was officially dedicated on January 1, 1923. The south end of the stadium was closed in 1929, giving the structure its now famous sight line-enhancing elliptical shape. The closing of the south end brought the seating capacity up to 76,000 people ("History," 2004b).

Today the seating capacity of the Rose Bowl is 92,542 people. The stadium has approximately 77 rows of seats. It measures 880 feet (268 m) from the north to south rims and 695 feet (212 m) from the east to west rims. The circumference of the rim is 2,430 feet (741 m), while the circumference inside at field level is approximately 1,350 feet (411 m). The turfed area inside the bowl measures 79,156 square feet (7,354 sq m). The fence around the Rose Bowl is 1 mile (1.6 km) in circumference. The dimensions of the playing field for football are 53.33 yards (48 m) by 100 yards (91 m) and for soccer are 70 yards (64 m) by 120 yards (110 m). The stadium itself is approximately 830 feet (253 m) above sea level. The Rose Bowl press box is the highest point of the stadium at 100 feet (30.5 m) above ground level. The first personal seat licenses ever sold were sold to build the Rose Bowl. A total of 210 individuals and corporations purchased what were then referred to as "seat subscriptions" to finance the $272,198 building cost of the stadium ("General Information," 2004).

The Rose Bowl is a longtime partner of the Toro Company, an internationally known lawn care company that produces specialty equipment for turf care. The turf professionals at the stadium have used Toro's mowing equipment, utility vehicles, turf cultivation solutions, spraying equipment, and irrigation control systems for both the playing field and the exterior landscaping and vegetation.

"Our expectations here are higher," said Will Schnell, the Rose Bowl's turf superintendent. "We want the best surface in the country, and we want it perfect every time. Even if we're not on national television that day, if it's just a Little League game, you always want the surface to be perfect. Toro's turf maintenance equipment and irrigation system meet our high standards" (Toro, 2004).

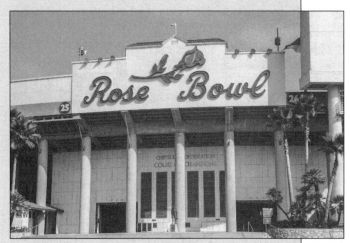

© Photoshot/ Eye Ubiquitous

may be wise to conduct more frequent inspections (LaRue, 2002). All manufacturers' guidelines for inspections need to be followed. Inspections also need to be documented (with date and signature) for the maintenance program as well as to help with litigation. If problems are found, the bleachers should be closed until a structural engineer or construction professional has remedied the problems (LaRue, 2002).

Safety Concerns

Outdoor facilities can be potential hazards, especially when children are involved. Playgrounds are notorious for hazards such as inadequate matting or fall protection, pinch points, and choking hazards. In a 1992 study, 31% of inspected playgrounds had surfaces made of cement, packed dirt, or asphalt. In 2002 the number was down to 4.5% (Popke, 2003). Some playgrounds have equipment too high off the ground, swinging hazards, and even wood-based products with possible carcinogens. Thus, playgrounds need to be vigilantly analyzed and maintained to ensure that they do not represent a threat to users. Between 1990 and 2000, more than 147 playground-related deaths were reported. The enhanced safety from utilizing appropriate surfaces can reduce injuries, but the surface is not the only concern: Patrons need to be educated. Thus, there has been significant effort to aggressively educate playground managers, parents, and children on how to be safer. Similar aggressive educational campaigns need to be undertaken for all other outdoor areas to prevent problems and injuries.

Another child-based concern is **attractive nuisance**—the concept of legal liability for a part of the facility that an operator knew or should have known was dangerous and that an operator knew or should have known a child would want to go to. An outdoor facility that has a pond, for example, has an attractive nuisance. Facility managers should know that children may want to play around a pond and can fall in and drown. Thus, any facility with a pond must properly secure it so that children cannot enter the area without authorization.

Summary

Indoor sport facilities present various unique concerns typically not found in facilities such as office buildings. A sport facility manager must deal with equipment that can cause significant injury, such as weights that could fall on a patron's foot. A general facility has moving parts such as photocopiers, fax machines, and people movers, but sport facility equipment can be much more dangerous, and appropriate precautions need to be taken. Sport facility components such as floors and bleachers need to be maintained more frequently than office flooring and seating areas.

Although a traditional office building probably has landscaping, the scope of the environment and the focus on grass turf with sport facilities make turf planting and maintenance one of the top priorities for a sport facility manager. Planting the right seeds, having the right soil, and mowing at the appropriate times are only part of the process of maintaining a well-manicured field. Facility managers must determine the amount of time and money they want to spend to make their fields look the best they can. The key is to develop a strategy and then to follow it.

Discussion Questions and Activities

1. What steps can be taken to make sure a field is in the best condition before an event?

2. What steps can be taken to make sure a gym or grandstands are in the best condition before an event?

3. What would be the best grass type to plant in your region?

4. Walk through a gym or physical education facility on your campus and examine what could have been built or installed better. What changes might you recommend to make the facility better?

5. Consider the concerns raised about artificial turf and possible pollution and lead contamination. Would you recommend using such a field? Why or why not?

6. Visit your school's athletic facilities. How do they allot equal time for all students and athletes?

7. Imagine that you are head of facility operations for a baseball team. Rain is on the way, and an extremely important game is scheduled. What field surface do you want to have? If problems arise with water runoff, how will you handle the situation?

9

Facility Maintenance

Chapter Objectives

- Describe various techniques used to present a safe, clean, and functional facility.

- Develop a maintenance plan for a facility and its components.

- Appreciate how benchmarking affects a maintenance program.

- Understand how to conduct a maintenance audit.

- Design a maintenance department and strategies for keeping a facility clean.

- Know the basics of facility repair management.

Think for a moment about a house. Once a house is built and all the amenities are in place, does a family live in the house forever without fixing or changing it? Of course the answer is no. They will constantly examine the house and work to make it their home. They may want to redo a bathroom after a couple years, add a deck, or convert a bedroom to an office. A home owner must purchase supplies such as light bulbs, toilet paper, and cleaning agents on a regular basis and constantly maintain the property. The exterior needs to be cleaned, plants need to be pruned, lawns need to be mowed, salt needs to be added to water softeners, and air filter screens need to be replaced or cleaned. In the living spaces, dishes need to be washed, toilets need to be plunged, walls need to be repainted, and other maintenance and repair concerns need to be addressed.

A large sport facility must also be constantly maintained and repaired. Some stadiums and arenas have hundreds of restroom stalls. Constant work is needed to keep locks operating, seats attached, paper seat-cover dispensers stocked, and toilet paper dispensers stocked and operating; it is an ongoing task to maintain sufficient water flow, keep toilets unclogged, and even remove graffiti. The maintenance issues can become even more complex in concession preparation areas and in boiler and chilling mechanical areas.

Maintenance does not have the same allure as building a large facility. Big donors might be interested in slapping their names on new college stadiums, but they rarely want to fund a maintenance program. An example of such a mindset can be found in a number of major park and recreation departments throughout the United States. Some large cities expend money on new parks because they look great and show that elected officials are taking action. However, these new parks often come at the expense of not maintaining existing parks. In 2013, Hartford, Connecticut, was looking at spending $500,000 on a new park, but existing parks were in a poor state of repair. Some fields had destroyed grass and others had big ruts, holes, and other concerns that affected the parks' ability even to host practices for local children. Maintenance increases the value of a field or facility investment in that it keeps the field or facility working and usable. Without dedicating significant resources to maintaining a facility, the facility will quickly fall apart.

Maintenance is the key to operating a safe and clean facility. Operation and maintenance activities normally account for 5% to 15% of a facility's total expenditure (Applied Management Engineering and Kaiser, 1991). However, the human resource time and effort are hard to calculate. The repair center at a major stadium can receive several hundred phone calls during a game for everything from spills to broken door handles. With everything going on in a facility, maintenance can often be pushed aside. The result can be an ugly and unsafe facility. The cost is even greater when routine maintenance is ignored and what could have been a minor repair becomes a major replacement costing thousands of dollars. Think about never changing the transmission fluid in a car. Although it might take 20 minutes and $40 to complete the fluid change, failure to change and monitor the fluid could lead to a $2,000 transmission replacement bill.

The hallmark of any maintenance effort is implementation of a comprehensive maintenance and repair (M&R) plan. Such a plan typically starts with an understanding of what needs to be maintained or repaired, and this can start with an **audit**. An audit can identify the biggest concerns and the areas needing the greatest amount of time or money. An audit might lead to the conclusion that a maintenance department should be developed. Of course, maintenance is not always the answer, since sometimes items need to be repaired or replaced. But whether the need is for maintenance or repair, any effort must be tracked through the process of **benchmarking**, which helps determine whether the M&R program is working correctly. Special care needs to be taken regarding certain sport-specific issues such as maintaining gym floors, as discussed in chapter 8. Last, the push for environmentally friendly buildings has put pressure on facility managers to maintain their facilities in a more responsible manner.

MAINTENANCE AND REPAIR PROGRAM

How critical is maintaining facilities? The answer can be seen when the existing national college infrastructure is examined. Through 2007, the

Schneider: Considerations for preparing unique maintenance plans

My name is Mike Schneider and I am the director of campus recreation for Centers LLC, an outsourcing company managing the recreation center at Moraine Valley Community College in Palos Hills, IL. Before that I was the director of campus recreation for the 57,000-square-foot (5,300 sq m) David A. Beckerman Recreation Center at the University of New Haven. Before my position at the University of New Haven, I was the facility manager of the 296,000-square-foot (27,500 sq m) Mizzou Student Recreation Complex in Columbia, Missouri. The facilities I've managed have been new or newly renovated, so I consider myself experienced in planning and preparing maintenance plans using today's industry standards. I've learned that people often lack appreciation for the unique maintenance needs of a sport and recreation facility. As an industry professional, it has been my job to communicate the considerations needed when designing a maintenance plan unique to a sport and recreation facility. Some of those considerations include the following:

- The overall use of the building and of each space (think of how the use of a weight room is different from the use of a gym floor)

- The facility use times (recreation centers are typically open for much longer periods than most buildings)

- The unique differences in flooring throughout a sport facility

- The effect cleaning and maintenance can have on the performance of sport spaces

- Special events and facility rentals that call for additional cleaning and maintenance

When the facility appears to be well maintained with minimal impact to the user, you know you've done a good job creating a plan. Critical components include daily cleaning, monthly and annual preventive maintenance, and a comprehensive communication plan ensuring that problems are addressed in a timely manner. One of the keys to ensuring these items is maintaining proper documentation. To date, the Beckerman Center is the only building on campus in which custodians are required to turn in a daily checklist of what has been performed. Of even greater importance is documentation during the warranty phase of a new facility. One example of that importance is a roof leak discovered late into the standard 1-year construction warranty. After several failed attempts were made to repair the leak, the warranty was soon void. Fortunately, detailed e-mails and punch-list documentation showed that the leak (and therefore any associated damage) was clearly discovered during the warranty phase. As a result, all costs of repairing the leak and the associated damages were covered by the building contractor even though the repairs were made well beyond the warranty phase.

There are many guidelines and standards that can and should be used when designing and implementing a maintenance plan. Keep in mind that every facility is unique, and being proactive and creative are important traits for any facility manager. While being mindful of the unique challenges each facility holds, I have found the following items to be critical before the implementation of any plan:

- Always develop performance factors that are agreed on by those charged with the actual cleaning and maintenance of the building. Without agreed-on standards, you will have no success in holding people accountable.

- Determine early on how communication will take place. Will you use e-mail, checklists, work orders? (Keep in mind how critical documentation is.)

- Be proactive in your budgeting approach. Unforeseen repairs are par for the course, and building appropriate contingencies in the maintenance and repair budget is a necessary evil.

Facility maintenance is boring, unglamorous, and sometimes just plain annoying. For those same reasons it is often overlooked and underappreciated. Remember that by doing the "dirty work" early and preparing effectively, you will save time, money, and most likely more than your fair share of headaches.

estimated bill to repair the problems on American campuses was close to $40 billion. That does not include the estimated $140 billion to fix public elementary and high schools (Porter, 2007). This represents the largest infrastructure repair bill in the nation. In 2013, the American Society of Civil Engineers gave the United States a grade of D+ for infrastructure repair and estimated that the total infrastructure repair bill across the country will be $3.6 trillion by 2020. Some repairs are minor, while other facilities might need to be torn down because of neglect. One sport-related example entails the University of Pittsburgh, which had to replace the roof on the $119 million Petersen Events Center only 3 years after the facility was built (Schackner, 2005). The university sued the architect (and the roof builder), claiming the roof had more than 200 holes; was missing roof fasteners; and caused heating, ventilation, and air conditioning (HVAC) problems. The architect countered that the university made numerous changes to the design and drove up the construction cost (Schackner, 2005). No matter who is to blame, a roof should last for 15 to 20 years with proper maintenance and should never last only a few years without a reason. A roof is just one of many facility systems that needs constant vigilance to prevent a facility from falling apart.

Although some facilities attempt to limit spending on maintenance, the financial effect of such a decision can be disastrous. Some expenses can be minimized, but other expenses that could have been reduced through normal maintenance can in fact increase significantly without regular maintenance. Maintaining a home HVAC system may cost $500 a year, but failing to maintain it and then having to replace it earlier than would otherwise be necessary could cost thousands of dollars. In a public assembly facility, the replacement cost could be in the millions of dollars.

Underfunding maintenance can also lead to building code violations, structural failure, safety and health failures, lower productivity, excessive repair costs, service failures, premature loss, higher absenteeism, and other social costs (e.g., poor morale, increased pollution, and harm to employee recruitment and retention efforts) (Cotts and Lee, 1992). Thus, proper maintenance department funding can produce both tangible and intangible benefits for a facility.

The specific keys to an effective M&R system are daily housekeeping, prompt response to needed repairs, installation and execution of a maintenance schedule to prevent premature failures, and completion of major repairs based on the lowest life-cycle costs. Other components include identifying improvement projects, lowering energy usage and costs, identifying ways to reduce operating costs, performing accurate cost estimates for future growth, accurately tracking maintenance work costs, properly scheduling necessary work, maintaining historical data, and monitoring the progress of all M&R efforts (Cotts and Lee, 1992).

An effective M&R system entails planning and programming, budgeting, staffing, supervising, and evaluating. This section discusses the components of an M&R system.

Planning and Programming

In planning and programming, a facility examines basic data, plans, existing policies, procedures, and standards to establish maintenance policies. This phase examines what equipment and systems currently exist and how to keep the various elements operating effectively. The facility management team analyzes the work that will be performed and the benchmarking standards or other criteria it wishes to meet. If a restroom stall can be cleaned in 10 minutes, then a goal might be for a janitor to clean at least five restroom stalls in an hour. Thus, goal setting is a major component in this phase.

Besides examining current equipment and facility needs, this phase examines future needs. Part of the planning process also entails tracking industry developments to determine whether more efficient equipment is available. For example, if a refrigerator is working fine but costs $2,000 a year just for electrical usage, the planning process may involve exploring more cost-effective machines. Although the evaluation phase deals with whether goals can be reached, the maintenance staff needs to know whether more cost-effective solutions exist. If $2,000 per year is a reasonable cost and newer machines do not save money, then the equipment should not be replaced.

STEPS IN A MAINTENANCE AND REPAIR PROGRAM

1. Planning and Programming
- Taking an inventory of the facility
- Categorizing work to be done
- Developing appropriate standards
- Analyzing the facility's deficiencies
- Reviewing owner manuals and warranties
- Prioritizing work by activity, class, or deficiencies
- Developing short- and long-term plans

2. Budgeting
- Setting the tone for all M&R work developed from the work plan
- Analyzing the effect of the capital budget on M&R
- Developing a comparison with prior budgets
- Developing an impact analysis if funds are cut
- Identifying and eliminating ways money is overspent on M&R
- Organizing all materials and inventory to save money
- Allocating budgeted funds to resolve problems
- Managing contracting strategies

3. Staffing
- Developing an organizational model of the M&R department
- Creating clear lines of responsibility and authority
- Hiring employees with technical competencies
- Training workers to accomplish tasks and improve skills
- Managing both in-house and outsourced workers
- Possibly outsourcing for specialized or less expensive workers

4. Supervising
- Providing leadership and monitoring workers
- Managing the work flow
- Providing rapid responses to crises
- Analyzing the condition of repaired equipment
- Controlling budgets and financing
- Managing the facility information system
- Ensuring accountability
- Ensuring that proper documentation is kept and managed
- Utilizing a quality control plan
- Administering a tenant relations program
- Coordinating activities with potential unions

5. Evaluating
- Evaluating prerepair and postrepair condition for quality
- Comparing results with historical data
- Examining customer and tenant feedback
- Evaluating employee performance against set standards

From Cotts and Lee 1992.

The planning process classifies work into six basic scheduling categories (Cotts and Lee, 1992):

- Inspection and repairs only when absolutely necessary

- **Cyclical repairs** (e.g., replacing the roof every 20 years)

- **Preventive maintenance**, which is maintaining the equipment or facility according to pre-established standards (e.g., oiling motors every 100 hours of use); preventive maintenance is referred to by some as routine maintenance if the equipment is regularly maintained on a set calendar to prevent problems

- **Breakdown maintenance** (e.g., when a light bulb burns out or a machine stops running)

- Repair projects, ranging from replacing a broken window to making major repairs

- General housekeeping and janitorial services

Preventive maintenance is the prebreakdown work performed on a facility's equipment and systems to eliminate problems, malfunctions, or breakdowns or to keep failures within predetermined limits (Lewis, 1999). Thus, preventive maintenance is undertaken after a cost–benefit analysis has shown that more money will be saved through prevention than through replacement of failed systems or equipment. For example, water needs to be moved through the plumbing system to make sure pipes do not become corroded or scaled (a buildup of minerals such as calcium carbonate that slows water movement in pipes and reduces water pressure). Thus, pipes need to be flushed and regularly cleared.

Routine maintenance refers to the day-to-day work required to make sure a facility stays open. For example, an employee must check that toilet paper dispensers are not broken, that toilets are flushing well, and that faucets are not dripping. Fixtures may need to be checked before, during, and after each game to identify anything that is not working.

Major repairs are hard to classify, as a $10,000 repair might be considered minor at one facility and a $100 repair considered major at another. As a general rule, however, any significant project outside the normally budgeted M&R scope would probably be considered major.

Maintenance plans can be supplemented with additional procedures such as alterations and janitorial care, which do not necessarily maintain the facility or equipment but enhance its operation. An **alteration** is a change that allows a facility, system, or piece of equipment to perform a function different from the one it was originally designed for. A restroom can be altered to include a changing table for a baby as a convenience to parents. An improvement increases the functional or productive performance of a facility, system, or piece of equipment (Lewis, 1999).

Janitorial care refers to cleanliness and to providing a facility with needed cleaning agents and supplies. The industry term used to describe this function is *housekeeping*, which entails various activities from sweeping and mopping floors and cleaning restrooms to replacing toilet paper or removing trash. Housekeeping includes janitorial, ground maintenance, and operating services. Janitorial services primarily refer to cleaning, dusting, waxing, and furnishing of expendable supplies.

When examining any maintenance program, special care must be given to unique issues that can disrupt the cleaning process. For example, if not properly vented, the moisture in a locker room or kitchen can lead to mold and mildew. Due to indoor air quality (IAQ) and allergy concerns, mold has become a major concern over the past 10 years. One concern with moisture in any facility is debonding, which occurs when a new floor fails due to moisture problems. A floor can start buckling, which creates a tripping hazard, results in an unsightly appearance, and can foster mold growth underneath. These concerns are often more prevalent with nonbreathable floor products such as vinyl tile or when water-based adhesives are used to bond the floor to the cement base. Special chemicals are often used to remove mold and mildew; however, these chemicals can also cause allergic reactions in those using them or exposed to them.

Budgeting

Maintenance is a critical component of the life-cycle cost of a system or component in a facility. The overall cost of ownership of a facility starts with a facility assessment. This assessment examines the physical plant (all the buildings and their components), the building's condition, and the condition of all the systems within and outside the facility. The actual cost of operation (based on the age of the facility or system) is compared against benchmark standards. This analysis also examines how well the system supports the facility's mission. Every facility is different, and the overall cost of ownership will vary based on usage, support, materials used, and weather conditions, among a host of other concerns.

The following represents a typical example of life-cycle costs for a building system. Assume that a 5,000-square-foot (464.5 sq m) floor might cost $4.50 per square foot installed. The initial investment would total $22,500. Assume that annual maintenance (e.g., daily sweeping, mopping) is $3,000, which includes both the hourly rate and cleaning supplies. The floor is expected to last 30 years, so the total cost of maintenance over the floor's life span is $90,000. Further assume that the floor will require two major repairs over the 30 years that will cost $3,000 each. The total life-cycle cost of the floor is $118,500. The initial investment in the floor represents less than 20% of its total life-cycle cost. Thus, the facility could examine a more expensive initial investment if the yearly maintenance costs are lower. If a floor costs $40,000 initially but has a yearly maintenance cost of $2,000 and requires only one repair for $4,000 over 30 years, the total cost would be $104,000. Therefore, spending an extra $17,500 initially would result in a savings of $30,000 on maintenance. Every system within a building can be examined using the life-cycle cost approach.

In the budgeting phase, policies are examined, prioritized, and then submitted for budgetary approval. If funds are insufficient, then all items that are delayed need to be prioritized so they can be completed at some later point. Ordinary, less costly alteration and construction projects are usually excluded. Managers utilize historical comparisons, benchmarking standards, past budgets, and other techniques to help establish an M&R budget. The budget needs to be realistic and needs to highlight the primary tasks that must be completed immediately. In one analysis of school repair needs in Florida, a school district had 7,100 backlogged safety repairs; 1,800 of the repairs had been on the list for more than 3 years, and 67 safety concerns had been on the list for more than a decade ("Repair Backlog," 2003). These projects either were very low priority or were too expensive and beyond the scope of any budget developed over the 10 years.

Budgeting is the primary reason why maintenance programs and plans are often not implemented. However, if senior executives can be shown the **return on investment** from effective maintenance programs, they are likely to be more receptive to allocating necessary funds to support an M&R program. Another approach to proper budgeting is the **life-cycle cost** analysis. Through identifying the lifetime cost of acquiring, installing, maintaining, and repairing a given system or piece of equipment, an executive can determine the life-cycle costs. Once these costs are known, the executive can appropriately budget and set aside funds for future repairs. For example, an HVAC system might cost $20,000 to install, but the lifetime cost might be $30,000 when the annual repair, maintenance, and new filter costs for the next 10 years (if that is how long the system should last) are added together. To cover the additional $10,000 lifetime cost, the manager can budget $1,000 a year for repairs, maintenance, and filters.

A life-cycle cost analysis gives a facility manager a chance to determine the best options for maintaining a roof over its intended life span. Assume that an existing 100,000-square-foot (9,290 sq m) roof is 15 years old and consists of two layers of modified bitumen and a base sheet over a wood roof deck. The field membrane, seams, and flashing are normally weathered but are usable. The roof management program costs $50,000 a year, preventive repairs cost around $60,000 a year, and leak repairs cost on average $40,000 a year. A life-cycle analysis can be done to determine whether the roof should be replaced, recovered, or coated. A new roof would last 20 years and cost $2.3 million, and the equivalent annual value would be $80,328. A roof recovery would last 15 years and cost $2.05 million, and the equivalent annual value would be $75,408. Finally, the coat would last 10 years and cost $1.85 million, and the equivalent annual value would be $66,506. The equivalent annual value takes into consideration the yearly maintenance costs and the average investment costs for the chosen roofing option. Based on life-cycle costs alone, the coat would be the most economical option (Hasselbusch, 2013). Such an approach can be taken with every major component of a facility.

Staffing

The M&R program should be overseen by a manager who will be in charge of all M&R activities, including tracking those activities to make sure that work is accomplished properly and in a timely manner. Staffing entails hiring and managing the right employees to perform the work required by the M&R program. One of the hurdles often encountered in this regard is unionized workforces. Conflict may arise if employees do not want to undertake any extra work not called for in the collective bargaining agreement.

The heart of staffing an M&R program is to have the right people doing the right job at the right time. This is much more difficult than it sounds. Although routine maintenance can be planned and is easy to organize with computer maintenance programs, the daily routine is often interrupted by emergencies. Thus, significant time is spent trying to organize workers to accomplish routine tasks as well as respond to emergencies.

One additional staffing option is outsourcing. Independent contractors and tradespeople can be hired to handle one-time issues such as unclogging a blocked sewer line, or a long-term commitment can be made with a company to provide services when needed. For example, a long-term contract can be secured with a landscaping company that plows the parking area whenever there is more than an inch (2.5 cm) of snow. The key to hiring the right independent contractors is to thoroughly educate them about the facility and its needs so they know the scope of work required, the quality of work expected, and the price to be paid for the work.

Supervision and Evaluation

In addition to appropriately budgeting and spending the department resources, supervising the M&R program requires the manager to prioritize projects, execute the work plan, and analyze the facility's general condition. The focus at this point is on the actual work. It is easy to schedule someone to work at a given spot or to perform a given task. It is much more difficult to make sure that the work is actually accomplished—and accomplished correctly. Supervision requires constant monitoring. Timing is also a major concern. Projects cannot be undertaken if they will conflict with ongoing events. Unless there is an emergency, repairs are not done on a basketball floor during a game. The repairs could be major, but it is preferable to attend to them before and after events. The goal is to minimize the need to shut down the facility or cancel an event. Two National Football League (NFL) games were cancelled in the 1990s because of exposed seams in the AstroTurf fields in Houston and Philadelphia.

Controlling is necessary in various contexts, from the budget to expenditures to crisis situations. It may be, for example, that a project is budgeted for $20,000, but after some initial work the contractor discovers the presence of a hidden problem such as dry rot that will double the cost. This type of situation is not unusual for those involved in facility repairs. In fact, most repair projects run over budget because it is often impossible to determine the true condition of a facility, system, or component without actually getting into it and examining it. This is one reason some contractors in the trade areas (e.g., electrical, plumbing, security) refuse to give a solid quote until they have examined a system after doing some initial work. Controlling can focus on choosing the right workers who will do the job at the least expensive rate while still providing quality work.

Successful controlling can often produce a budgetary windfall, which can free some funds for repairs on the prioritized list. This can be accomplished by close monitoring of time and expenses for various projects and tracking of activity to see how quickly the work can be done. For example, the time required to change a facility over from hockey to basketball can be tracked and the process modified to save time and money. After a number of changeovers and revisions, it might be possible to reduce the process from 4 hours to 3 hours; with 20 employees doing the job at night, this might save hundreds or even thousands of dollars.

Evaluation entails examining whether the M&R program has been successful. Work orders can be reviewed to determine the amount of time spent on various projects and where the greatest expenses occurred (Cotts and Lee, 1992). Another focus is evaluating the performance of employees. For example, a facility manager can plant trash in strategic places to see whether the cleaning crew will find and remove it. If the cleaning crew is doing a cursory cleaning rather than a complete cleaning, corrective steps need to be taken. Through utilizing a comprehensive M&R program, a facility can provide a clean and safe facility at the most reasonable cost.

MAINTENANCE AUDITS

Maintenance audits provide the framework and discipline to systematically review, analyze, and recommend performance-related improvements for facility mechanisms (Applied Management Engineering and Kaiser, 1991). Audits help provide the working plan that shows what areas need improvement, what corrective actions will rectify potential problems, and how to monitor the outcome of any given action.

As shown in "Audit Process," a maintenance audit starts with establishing priorities. Then an audit schedule is developed. After the schedule is developed, the audit parameters are defined and organized. Either before or after this step, an audit team needs to be established. Some argue that an audit team should be developed at the very beginning of the process to make sure that all issues are covered. Others argue for establishing the audit team after upper management has defined what it wants from the audit process. This could save time in that the audit team will not reach decisions that are contrary to the directive established by upper management.

The audit team sets some parameters but primarily performs the audit. The audit examines what occurred from a mainly objective point of view. Subjective issues such as how someone changed light bulbs are not as important as whether all the broken bulbs were replaced in a timely manner. After the audit is completed, a formal report needs to be presented to upper management. Upper management is then asked to take action. After the audit, actions such as corrective maintenance must be taken. Thereafter a follow-up report is made to re-examine the process and determine what additional steps may be required.

One of the key elements in any maintenance auditing system is measuring effectiveness. Effectiveness can be measured through productivity (how productive is time spent on given projects?), performance (do the employees work well?), work quality (is the work satisfactory?), and priority (is time being spent on the right projects?) (Applied Management Engineering and Kaiser, 1991). "Key Elements of a Maintenance Audit" outlines the elements that are fundamental in determining how efficiently and effectively a program is operating.

After a thorough facility audit, the maintenance department will need to handle all the various concerns identified in the audit. One person can take care of a small building, but a larger facility needs a large staff of tradespeople trained in such disciplines as plumbing, electricity, and carpentry.

The audit often focuses on specific key facility systems that must be constantly monitored in order to avoid potential fines and safety hazards. Critical systems to audit on a regular basis include the HVAC system, the structural integrity of the facility, and burglar alarms. A security system has little value if a sensor is disconnected or a

---

AUDIT PROCESS

1. Establish priorities. Do certain systems need to be analyzed first? Senior management may establish large priorities for a future audit review team.

2. Establish an audit schedule. A time frame has to be established to determine whether maintenance will be examined on an annual, monthly, or other basis, as this time frame dictates what resources are needed and when.

3. Organize and define the audit. Through acquiring and organizing the required data, the various affected units or managers will understand the audit's scope, and a proposed statement of scope can be developed.

4. Select an audit team. Those who will be affected by the process need to have input into and involvement in the process.

5. Perform the audit. Once the scope, parameters, and team are defined, the audit plan is developed with practicality in mind to ensure that it can be implemented.

6. Prepare the report. Once the audit is completed, a detailed report highlights the findings.

7. Take action. Management needs to critically analyze the audit report and institute plans and procedures for implementing the findings. One of the critical points is for management to allocate funds to help accomplish the desired results.

8. Follow up. Has the process been successful? Will the maintenance plan save money and extend the useful life of facility assets?

From Kaiser 1991.

KEY ELEMENTS OF A MAINTENANCE AUDIT

1. Organization. What policies, procedures, personnel, and organizational structure are being used to assist in implementing the maintenance goals and objectives?

2. Workload identification. What equipment is available in the facility's inventory, and what is the equipment's general condition? What maintenance system is currently being utilized, how are work requests processed, and how is inventory ordered? Is preventive maintenance undertaken, and how is routine and recurring work, as well as all resulting documentation, handled?

3. Work plan. What priority is given to which projects? For example, when will alterations and improvements be undertaken compared with emergency repairs or cyclical activities? Specific policies need to be developed for backlogged

work, and budgets need to be developed for all backlogged projects.

4. Work accomplishment. Have all the necessary supplies and parts been available for required maintenance work? Are the employees properly trained and equipped to perform necessary maintenance or repairs? Are employees properly supervised and provided with necessary resources such as transportation vehicles to quickly respond and reach their assigned locations?

5. Appraisal. Is a management information system, such as a computerized maintenance management system, in place? Are performance, productivity, priority, and work quality measured and analyzed? Are all records for the facility and all equipment properly stored and analyzed?

From Kaiser 1991.

---

door is left open and someone can sneak in undetected. The government mandates inspection of such elements as elevators, escalators, and food preparation equipment. Insurance companies and leagues might also inspect facilities. Finally, the facility itself can hire "secret shoppers" to spot maintenance and operational problems as well as successes.

Similarly, the fire prevention and extinguishing system needs to be inspected and maintained on a regular basis as mandated by law. To prepare the facility for a fire inspection, the facility manager needs to prepare by using a checklist to ensure that everything is reviewed. Because inspections can be unscheduled, a facility needs to keep current on maintaining fire-related equipment and have all the necessary inspection, testing, and maintenance (ITM) reports for the fire system. A normal fire panel is so complicated that internal personnel are normally not qualified to maintain it, so ITM evaluation is often undertaken by third-party entities specialized in such inspection. A strong ITM report is the most important proof that the facility is properly maintaining the fire system. Fire inspectors will also examine areas with heat-producing appliances, heaters, exit signs, emergency lights, fire extinguishers, smoke

alarms, carbon monoxide detectors, and locations of combustible materials and make sure that items such as empty boxes or trash are not blocking an exit path.

MAINTENANCE DEPARTMENT

Although not all facilities have a designated maintenance department, all facilities have at least one person responsible for maintenance-related issues. Typically a maintenance department is responsible for the following activities (Borsenik and Stutts, 1997).

- Performing preventive and routine (daily, weekly, monthly, quarterly, and yearly) maintenance

- Ordering, processing, storing, and utilizing parts, inventory, and supplies

- Maintaining appropriate records on everything from energy usage to requested and completed repairs

- Monitoring energy management programs

- Performing minor restorative work such as light painting or repairs

■ Assisting in purchasing large capital assets for facilities or making other major decisions

These categories could be supplemented by many additional activities. For example, the maintenance department at an ice rink may be responsible for securing goals, monitoring and repairing the ice surface, fixing dasher boards and replacing glass, and other specific activities associated with the ice-cooling system. Smaller facilities also need to utilize their maintenance departments differently, perhaps by having these employees work on construction, move management, janitorial functions, and administrative duties.

FACILITY REPAIR MANAGEMENT

Although the goal of maintenance is to keep systems and equipment running, repairs are inevitable. Repairs are immediate expenses that are necessary to make a system or piece of equipment operable, and they are done at the expense of previously scheduled maintenance. For example, a facility may have scheduled $10,000 to maintain a roof, but if the roof leaks too much it may be necessary to make a repair costing $20,000 that was not previously budgeted. This process is completely different from what happens in a marketing department, which can create a budget at the start of the year and then adhere to it since marketing involves few true emergencies. A facility maintenance department has to respond to emergencies daily. Since it is hard to determine when an emergency might occur, there is always a struggle to allocate money, time, personnel, and other resources.

Whatever the maintenance or repair, it involves a process, and that process must be managed. The process can be as simple as seeing a problem and fixing it or as complicated as having to go through a major bureaucratic exercise just to change a light bulb. "Repair Process" outlines a typical process for a repair project at a large facility and indicates in parentheses which division in the facility is responsible for the work.

The list illustrates that making repairs is a process. Any process can run into trouble or bottlenecks. If someone is absent, will the work orders

be dealt with or will they stay on the person's desk until she returns? As a process, the maintenance program can be managed so that work is completed more promptly and inexpensively. The process can be streamlined if the form passes directly from one person to the relevant worker or can be completed online. These are both ways in which an existing process can be modified. It is often possible to streamline processes through comparing an existing program with other programs by means of benchmarking and monitoring the repair process.

Early detection is the critical piece for an appropriate maintenance program. A building's facade is a great example. The brick wall might look great at first glance, but a number of problems on top of or underneath the brick can indicate possibly significant problems that need to be repaired. Some concerns include the following:

■ Cracks. Cracks are signs that the building wants to move. The most important ones to address are wide cracks, vertical cracks running up concrete columns, or cracks near the corners of a building.

■ Displacement. All building materials move in response to temperature or moisture issues. Constant vigilance is needed to address such concerns.

■ Leaks. All holes in buildings, whether windows, air vents, or chimneys, can foster an environment where leaks might occur. The key to adequately repairing the problem is to determine what is causing the leaks.

■ Material deterioration. No matter how well designed a facility is, building materials do not last forever. Deterioration eventually resorts in cracks, blistering, peeling, and other conditions.

■ Corrosion. The steel in buildings is often hidden under various protective layers, but water can still lead to corrosion. When steel corrodes, it expands and might cause buckling in surrounding areas.

To help identify these types of issues, a facility executive should check for stained ceiling tiles, stained interior finishes, water puddles, white efflorescence staining on masonry, and rust staining. She should also check all seals and sealants, cracks, transitions from one construction material to another, and corners; perform an infrared scan for moisture and temperature leaks; and examine the roof for any problems such as blocked drains on the roof.

Benchmarking

Maintenance can be a complicated issue for a facility; benchmarking makes it simpler. Benchmarking is the process of comparing what one facility does with an industry standard. It measures the performance of a facility's systems and components against their expected optimal performance. It is in essence a baseline comparison. For example, industry data may show that a motor used under given conditions typically lasts 10 years with utilization of a particular maintenance plan. If a facility buys that motor, management could expect it to last 10 years if the facility adheres to the maintenance plan. Thus, industry standards and best practices are used to help facilities maximize the return on their system investments.

The key to benchmarking is a critical physical analysis and review of the facility with respect to architectural, mechanical, electrical, plumbing, fire protection, energy usage, telephone, data, security, structural, environmental, facility operations, and related systems (Simons, 2002). There is a significant relationship between a facility's operation and the facility's physical condition. The operational plans need to be monitored to ensure that operations, policies, and preventive maintenance procedures are calibrated and working together to maximize system effectiveness.

Several surveys track benchmarking standards for maintenance and operations. American School and University conducts an annual survey of schools and universities. The results highlight that the yearly median maintenance and operations cost per square foot of school space was

---

REPAIR PROCESS

1. Someone sees a problem and calls it in to the repair department help desk.
2. Take the call. (help desk)
3. Create work order. (help desk)
4. Authorize work order. (management)
5. Define scope. (planning)
6. Obtain necessary documentation such as warranties or blueprints. (planning)
7. Determine which trades, parts, and materials are required. (planning)
8. Determine cost estimates. (planning)
9. Obtain approval. (accounting)
10. Schedule resources. (management)
11. Purchase parts and hire preapproved labor. (accounting)
12. Perform work. (maintenance)
13. Complete work and close work order. (help desk)
14. Close work order. (accounting)
15. Update all files, warranties, and blueprints. (help desk and planning)
16. Conduct quality assessment. (management)
17. Update benchmarking standards and measurements. (management)

From Noferi 2003.

$4.56, with $2.05 of that amount being dedicated to payroll and $1.52 dedicated to utilities (Agron, 2008). Broken down as a percentage, payroll consumed 43%, energy and utilities 34%, equipment and supplies 8%, and outside labor and other costs the remaining 15% (Agron, 2008). At the college level, an average custodial employee maintains 34,084 square feet (3,166 sq m) and an average maintenance employee maintains 69,873 square feet (6,491 sq m) (Agron, 2008). The median salary of a college custodian is $23,004, and the median college employed 15 employees in their custodial department (Agron, 2008). This and similar information can help a facility manager plan for the future and determine whether his maintenance department is meeting or exceeding industry standards.

Monitoring Repairs

Besides benchmarking, numerous facility monitoring programs exist to optimize facility maintenance. Some companies focus on providing better maintenance and janitorial services by offering computer analysis of current procedures. Thus, through benchmarking and using computers, a facility manager can more efficiently and effectively manage a facility's operations.

The systems used to manage maintenance and cleaning are referred to as **computerized maintenance management systems** (CMMS). These programs streamline the maintenance system by processing critical information and providing solutions to help maintain systems and decrease life-cycle costs. They can produce work order

---

BEHIND THE SCENES

BENCHMARKING STANDARDS

The average custodian can clean between 2,500 and 5,000 square feet (232.3 and 464.5 sq m) per hour when using a "zone" or "area" approach to cleaning, during which he focuses on cleaning a specific area. Custodians working as a team can clean 5,000 to 10,000 square feet per hour. This highlights how benchmarking affects the maintenance process. Benchmarking numbers help a facility determine how effective its maintenance is compared with that of other facilities. Following are some pertinent statistics from the International Facility Management Association (IFMA) benchmarking survey:

■ The mean cost per square foot (0.09 sq m) for cleaning restrooms, offices, work areas, and common areas is $1.29 per year.

■ On average, maintenance departments respond to emergencies in 6 minutes or less 14% of the time versus within 30 minutes 18% of the time.

■ The amount of space used per employee declined from 471 square feet (44 sq m) per person in 1997 to 407 square feet (38 sq m) in 2001 ("IFMA Surveys," 2001).

By 2005 these numbers had increased a bit in educational institutions to $1.62 per square foot per year ($0.135 per square foot per month) for educational institutions and $1.20 per square foot per year ($0.10 per square foot per month) for office buildings. On average, custodians are able to clean from 2,975 to 3,300 square feet (276-307 sq m) per hour (Hanson, 2005). However, customer satisfaction should be considered in this benchmarking standard as numerous studies have shown that the more area cleaned by a custodian, the more customer complaints are generated (Hanson, 2005). It is clear that a custodian cannot clean more space without sacrificing quality. Note that most of these numbers are for cleaning office buildings. Schools, for example, are often cleaned in shifts and might include both part-time and full-time custodians. Also, custodians who work during the day might have more responsibilities than those who work at night. In general, the rule of thumb is that a school needs one custodian for every 20,000 to 30,000 square feet (1,858-2,787 sq m).

When examining benchmarking standards, it is important to compare the right information. For example, some discrepancies could revolve around the following:

■ The measurements need to be comparable as there are numerous ways to calculate the area being cleaned such as gross square feet, cleanable square feet, and rentable square feet as well as how accurate the measurements are.

■ Cleanable square feet is normally calculated as building gross square feet minus walls (1.5% of gross) minus noncleanable square feet.

■ Are special tasks (e.g., extra attention to the president's office) and noncleaning activities (e.g., setting up events, changing lights, removing recycling) included in the analysis? These tasks take extra time and must be considered when trying to establish a benchmarking standard (Hanson, 2005).

printouts, maintenance histories, material inventories, and financial analyses; improve monitoring and inventory management systems; and track utility usage.

A CMMS catalogs all the assets in a facility and their maintenance or monitoring schedules. Utilizing this type of system, facility operations and maintenance staff know when a machine has reached 1,000 hours of service and when it may need to be serviced according to manufacturer specifications. Following these strict guidelines will make the piece of equipment or the facility itself last longer and will decrease the need for major repairs. Guidelines for maintaining automobiles are a familiar example. Cars purchased today come with manuals that indicate what services are needed at specific time or mileage intervals. At 3,000 miles (5,000 km), very little work—perhaps an oil change—may be required. At 50,000 miles (80,000 km), 20 items may need to be checked, repaired, replaced, or monitored. If the timeline or mileage milestones are not followed, problems may develop and the car may break down before it should, costing the car owner a significant amount of money.

As any car owner will tell you, one reason for not following the maintenance schedule is a lack of time. People may be too busy to bring the car to a repair shop. Another reason may be money. If a maintenance check costs $100 and the owner does not want to spend the money, the schedule becomes irrelevant. All facilities and their equipment have maintenance schedules, but the schedules are not followed for various reasons. Some facilities do not have enough employees to accomplish all the required work. In other cases, staff do not know in what order work should be done, so less important items may receive attention before more important items. A CMMS can provide appropriate reminders and develop calendars that maintenance staff can follow, thereby reducing future expenses and making the facility and equipment last longer.

Some companies are reluctant to spend money on a CMMS. These companies may be reluctant to change from the older card-based system for tracking maintenance projects. Others may not think that the benefits justify the cost of installing a CMMS. This mind-set has to do with the fact that these systems produce soft dollar savings; more executives are looking for hard dollar savings such as those achieved by terminating an employee. The soft dollar savings of a CMMS come from

- minimization of lost productivity,
- fewer operational interruptions,
- optimized labor costs,
- reduction in size of maintenance staff or their hours,
- reduction in number of emergencies that need to be handled,
- decreased overtime pay for off-hour nuisance alarm calls,
- decreased personnel time needed for manual machine inspections (called "rounds and readings"),
- reduction in time required to prepare management reports (which can be performed instantaneously), and
- reduction in costs for internal staff (Buckley, 2003).

Costs can be reduced by enlisting technical staff from external sources. Through a service contract, a third party can monitor the facility's CMMS and immediately dispatch repair persons when the program identifies a problem. This is similar to just-in-time inventory management systems in which a supplier and manufacturer know at the same time that a part is needed (Buckley, 2003). Hard dollar savings can result from eliminating costs by selling a facility or terminating an employee, meaning that remaining employees assume more work.

BASIC MAINTENANCE AND CLEANING

Imagine that you run a stadium and that both the home and visitor locker rooms started flooding with sewage during a game (see Facilities Trivia). In a 2011 survey of 1,053 restroom users, 91% indicated that they would perceive a business negatively if the bathrooms were not properly maintained. A whopping 37% of respondents indicated that they would never return to an establishment where they had a poor bathroom experience, and another 34% said they would think twice before returning. The major complaints included an overall unappealing appearance (71%), empty or jammed toilet paper dispensers (45%), partition doors that did not latch (41%), water puddles on the floor (39%), empty or malfunctioning soap dispensers (38%), empty or malfunctioning hand towel dispensers (34%), and lack of space to put belongings (30%) (Penny, Morton, and Tack, 2012).

One of the byproducts of an unclean facility can be pests. One strategy for dealing with pests in a facility is heat. Most pests can be killed by heating the facility to at least 120 °F (48.9 °C) for at least 1 hour. To be the most effective, the process should run for 24 hours. However, a facility cannot simply turn on the thermostat to reach 120 °F—special heaters must be brought in to heat the facility. Before the heating process can begin, all sprinkler units in the facility should be inspected to ensure they are rated for more than 248 °F so the units do not engage by accident. All equipment and fixtures in the facility need to be inspected to make sure they can handle the heat; for example, wax seals at the bottoms of toilets will often melt under these treatments. Although this might appear to be an extreme maintenance step, it might be the best way to ensure that pests are removed from food-related areas when conventional approaches fail (Mach, 2005).

Facility maintenance is not just about planning, budgeting, and auditing. Obviously at a certain point the work needs to be accomplished. Tradespeople, from carpenters to electricians, and general maintenance employees must be informed about the work to be done and given the resources (parts and tools). Maintenance work focuses primarily on floors and on equipment and surfaces that can pose a safety hazard, as well as on ensuring that procedures do not harm the environment.

Floor Maintenance

A shiny gym floor is probably a well-maintained floor. Workers in facilities spend significant time and energy mopping floors, using the right finishing materials, and regularly inspecting and maintaining floors. There is no one best way to take care of a flooring surface since there are so many different types of surfaces. For example, a locker room floor raises water-related slipping and mold concerns, and a poured urethane or tile gym floor must be treated differently than a wood floor.

If a floor's finish wears excessively and earlier than it should, the problem could be the result of improper maintenance, which can lead to an increased coefficient of friction (more slippery surface). Steps to help reduce this problem can include placing mats at entrances to reduce dust and regularly mopping the floor with an approved floor cleaner.

A peeling or bubbling finish on a maple wood floor typically means that the floor was not properly screened or cleaned between coats or that substances such as soap were not properly removed between coats. If the peeling problem is inherent in the topcoat, the topcoat can be screened and repainted. However, if the problem exists in lower layers, all coats need to be sanded and then refinished. Finish roughness is often due to contamination in the drying process and requires following the same procedures as for peeling (Cohen, 1998).

The typical maintenance requirements for daily cleaning of a wood gym floor include the following:

- Sweeping with a properly treated dust mop (possibly several times a day if there is excessive activity or if dirt and other objects are being brought into the gym)
- Immediately cleaning any spills
- Using an approved floor cleaner to remove marks such as heel marks
- Checking the HVAC system to make sure it is functioning properly, as too much humidity can cause wood warp and other problems
- Inspecting the floor for any tightening or shrinkage and making sure expansion voids are clear so that the wood can expand ("MFMA Maintenance Tips," 2003)

Besides wear and tear and other conditions necessitating maintenance, floors can suffer water damage. Overexposure to water can cause wood flooring to swell or buckle, creating a possible tripping hazard. Problems can become acute when liquid leaks are not detected for an extended period. Wood flooring that has been exposed to liquids for several days normally cannot be saved. If the exposure has been shorter, the maintenance staff should try to dry the wood as quickly as possible. This could involve pulling up some of the boards, using a wet–dry vacuum to suction any remaining water, and placing fans or heaters on the floor to help speed drying (Hamm, 1998).

The following lists the steps required to renovate a gym floor.

1. Any colored court marking lines are removed with a paint peeler.

2. Stripping of the floor begins at one end using polyurethane peeler, which will cause the old finish to blister. After it blisters, the old finish is scraped away with a putty knife.

3. After the finish has been removed from a large section of the floor, stripping begins. Stripping is done with a single-brush floor machine utilizing a steel-wire brush.

4. After the entire floor has been stripped, all the old finish needs to be appropriately disposed of according to EPA guidelines.

5. The floor is thoroughly swept or vacuumed.

6. An 80-grit steel-wool pad is put under the wire brush, and the entire floor is disked (sanded) in the direction opposite to the way the floorboards run. This process normally utilizes several steel-wool disks.

7. The floor is swept in the same direction the floorboards run to remove all sanding dust.

8. The floor is redisked using 100-grit disks in the same direction the floorboards run. This step entails light sanding and removes any swirls created by the 80-grit disks.

9. The floor is swept and then a dry vacuum is used to remove any last dust particles. Care should be taken to make sure that dust is removed from cracks and joints. Before any final cleaning of the floor, all raised areas such as window sills and bleachers need to be dusted. The floor should then be mopped several times with a damp mop containing cleanup solvent.

10. The floor should dry for 24 to 48 hours before the first coat of sealant is applied.

11. Sealant is poured into an application pan, and a lamb's wool applicator is dipped into the pan. Care should be taken to make sure that the sealant is not dripping. The sealant is applied across the wood grain in a U-shaped motion. One person applies the sealant while another person feathers it (smoothes it out). The feathering process follows the grain of the wood.

12. The seal should dry overnight, and then a number 2 steel-wool pad is attached to the single-brush floor machine. The machine is worked with the grain over the entire floor, and the floor is then mopped with damp towels dipped in solvent. The floor should dry for 30 minutes before the second sealant coat is added.

13. After the second coat dries, game lines can be added before application of the final finish.

14. After the lines are added, the floor is wiped with the solvent at least 30 minutes before the finish is applied. The finish is applied in the same manner as the sealant: cross-grain application, with-grain smoothing, and sanding between the first and second coats of finish. The final coat should be allowed to dry for 72 hours, and the floor should not be subjected to heavy wear for at least 1 week ("Basics," 1980).

Many wood floor finishers rely on the time-honored approach of treating bare wood flooring with several coats of oil-based sealers, adding court lines and game lines, and finishing with several coats of oil-modified polyurethane finish (Brown, 2009b). However, this process has come under fire in recent years. At least 18 states have placed significant limitations on the amount of volatile organic compounds (VOCs) allowed in wood floor sealers, stains, and finishes. VOCs combine with nitrogen oxide and ultraviolet light to produce ground-level ozone, which can cause health concerns in some people. VOCs are produced by oil-based finishes and sealers but not by water-based finishes. However, oil-based solvents often cost $20 to $25 per gallon, whereas water-based products cost around $60 per gallon. One gallon can cover about 700 to 750 square feet (65-69.7 sq m); a typical floor of a small gym is at least 6,000 square feet (557.4 sq m). Thus, to comply with these mandates, facility designers have to balance cost, quality, and legal concerns when choosing finishes for a facility.

FACILITY FOCUS

NEW ORLEANS SUPERDOME AFTER KATRINA

Most facilities take time to prepare for typical maintenance and supply issues. There might be a stock of extra toilet paper or food in case more people need them on any given event date. There also might be an emergency generator in case the power goes out. However, what happens if a natural disaster strikes a sport facility? Will the facility be able to handle all the people and issues that might arise in such a disaster?

This exact scenario was faced by the New Orleans Superdome after Hurricane Katrina. Despite the planned use of the Superdome as a potential evacuation center, government officials at the local, state, and federal levels came under criticism for poor planning and preparation. On August 25, 2005, in anticipation of the storm, many citizens fled to the Superdome. Hurricane Katrina hit on August 28, causing significant damage to New Orleans as well as the Superdome. That day the Louisiana National Guard delivered three truckloads of water and seven truckloads of ready-to-eat meals, enough to supply 15,000 people for 3 days. There was no water purification equipment on site, no chemical toilets, no antibiotics, and no antidiarrheals stored for a crisis. As a result of the storm there was no power, water, sanitation service, waste removal, or other critical life necessities, so the sanitation conditions were horrible. This, combined with a 70% failure of the roof system, led to more than 2 inches (5 cm) of water at field level, and human waste and trash filled the facility (Turner, 2005). When evacuations started in early September, many of the residents in the Superdome had not been allowed to leave or to have showers for more than a week. As the evacuation continued, the number of people in the Superdome swelled to 30,000 as people waited around the facility for a ride to Houston. After the hurricane, it took more than a year to repair the facility so it could be used again.

The concern associated with proper maintenance budgets is that no facility knows when a major disaster might arise. A fire, earthquake, hurricane, tornado, or terrorist attack can have a major effect on a facility if the occupants need to shelter in place, meaning that no one can leave the facility. To best deal with these circumstances and prevent the need to respond on the fly, a plan of action must be developed before a disaster strikes. Does the facility have enough drinking water, food, blankets (especially during winter), fuel for generators, and so on? A budget also needs to be established for future repairs. This sinking fund can be critical for any major maintenance or repair needs. For example, after Katrina, the federal government had to kick in more than $100 million to repair the Superdome. The NFL contributed $15 million for the $185 million repair project. The total repair cost was $17 million more than how much the dome cost when it was built in the 1970s (Simmelkjaer, 2006).

© Everett Collection/age fotostock

Maintenance and Safety

Maintenance concerns can be prompted by reports from athletes or patrons of conditions such as poor lighting or slippery surfaces. Someone who has been injured may inform a facility manager that she slipped on a puddle caused by a leaking faucet, which will start the maintenance or repair process. The failure to properly maintain a drinking fountain can lead to spilled water, which can create a slipping hazard—the same goes for a leaking ketchup or mustard dispenser.

Leaking showerheads or sinks in a locker room also create a dangerous environment.

Failing to replace light bulbs can lead to various problems. A parking garage or lot with low lighting or broken bulbs may be an ideal environment for criminal misconduct. This is why lights need to be constantly monitored. Nonfunctioning lights in a gym or inadequate lighting on a playing field can contribute to player injury.

Other safety concerns include rough edges on bleachers, broken cement in walkways, loose floorboards, missing floor tiles, and a host of other problems that must be addressed. It is also important to take special care in maintaining safety equipment.

Improper maintenance and cleaning can also lead to health issues. If a facility does not properly clean food preparation equipment, there could be both health code violations and potential harm to food consumers. Imagine buying a hot dog that had not been cooked at the right temperature because a cooking machine was broken or one that was dirty because the counter was not properly cleaned. This is not far-fetched based on the number of health code citations at ballparks.

In one survey of health code violations at 11 stadiums, the Los Angeles Dodgers had the highest number of violations with 732. Other teams with significant violations include the Oakland A's with 493 and the Houston Astros with 107. Most of the teams in the survey had between 30 and 60 violations. The Colorado Rockies had only 16 health code violations (Liebman, 2008). It is impossible to eliminate all health code concerns, but a strong janitorial program in a comprehensive maintenance program can significantly reduce health-related issues.

BEHIND THE SCENES

DEVELOPING A CLEANING SCHEDULE

The following is a typical breakdown of daily duties for a janitorial or cleaning crew. Most crews work on three shifts: 8:00 a.m. to 4:30 p.m., 4:30 p.m. to 10:00 p.m., and 10:30 p.m. to 7:00 a.m.

- Pick up all trash on the floor.
- Spot clean carpets and floors.
- Empty waste and recycling receptacles.
- Spot clean glass windows and doors.
- Dry mop lobbies, foyers, and hallways.
- Mop locker room floor and pour disinfectants down floor drain.
- Make sure runners or mats at entrances are dry and in place. Last shift should shake out mats outside building to remove debris.
- Dust furniture in common areas and rearrange any moved furniture.
- Make sure all HVAC vents, grilles, and diffusers are clean and dust free.

- Mop up any spills.
- Remove any gum or other sticky substances.
- Remove any graffiti.
- Wipe down water fountains and make sure they are not clogged.
- Test all toilets and sinks to make sure they are working and clean (and disinfected).
- Make sure there is enough toilet paper, paper toweling, and soap in their respective containers.
- Sweep outside all building entranceways so dirt is not brought into the building.
- Respond to emergency situations.
- On a weekly basis, polish furniture, scrub and buff floors, and undertake more aggressive cleaning such as removing scuff marks from walls.

Summary

A clean facility is like a clean home: an inviting place to be. It takes time, energy, and resources to keep a house clean and functioning well, and the scale is much greater for a sport facility. (Imagine thousands of people using your bathroom every day.) A well-developed and well-funded maintenance program enables a facility to keep sufficient supplies to remain attractive to users and patrons.

However, a facility that looks good but does not have a good maintenance program will not survive. Equipment and structures that are not taken care of will stop functioning. To prevent this, a facility needs to allocate appropriate funds, develop and staff a maintenance department and program, and evaluate the results. An audit can help determine what needs to be done and then serve as a tool for evaluating the maintenance program's success, especially against well-established benchmarks. Special care should be taken in maintaining floors and specialty equipment and devices as well as in striving for an ecological focus.

Discussion Questions and Activities

1. Why is maintenance so important?

2. What are some of the key issues that a manager needs to examine when implementing a facility maintenance program?

3. Interview a maintenance department worker and a custodian at your university or college to see what they do on the job and how they do it. Also ask them what the best and worst aspects of their jobs are.

4. If you had to develop a schedule for cleaning a gym, what activities would be included in that schedule?

5. Imagine that you run a facility in the northeastern United States that houses a football team that operates throughout cold winter months. You decide to hire an independent contractor to plow the parking lots when it snows. What details might you share with the contractor to ensure they can properly handle the job and tasks required?

6. What area of a facility is vital to maintain and keep clean at all times? (Hint: In a survey, 91% of users indicated that they would view a business negatively if this area was not maintained.)

7. Explain the importance of benchmarking.

8. What would you look for when inspecting the roof of a gym?

10

Green Facility Management

Chapter Objectives

- Understand why green facilities are so important.

- Appreciate different strategies that can reduce the carbon footprint of a sport facility.

- Calculate the most effective strategies for saving money while operating a sport facility.

- Understand how to create a green, sustainable culture with all constituents.

Green buildings, or environmentally-conscious construction and management of buildings, which are (should this be were) briefly covered in chapter 6, require special care. For example, a trend in Europe is to plant grass on rooftops to help insulate buildings. This raises the issue of how to maintain the grass. It may be impossible to bring a mower onto a slanted roof, but goats can be put on the roof to eat the grass and keep it short. This type of approach is often referred to as **sustainability.**

The word *sustainability* is not new to the field of facility management, but it is one that many managers still do not use when designing facilities. Sustainability is a holistic approach to protecting the environment by incorporating design practices and materials that use energy most efficiently (Heikkinen, 2001). The theory is that the less energy we use, the less damage we cause to the environment while producing energy. In the past, facility managers have been nervous about taking this approach to their buildings because the upfront building costs are greater. As this practice has gained more momentum, costs have been reduced, and a properly designed sustainable building does not have to cost more. Although green facilities are best planned for when a building is being designed, many conservation projects are being launched to modify and maintain existing facilities as green buildings.

Three main factors help create a more sustainable environment: the design or layout of the building, the materials used in the construction, and the materials used to keep the facility clean. A maintenance program can be combined with any remodeling or rebuilding efforts to design new or existing facilities so that they use better materials and are more efficient. For example, an old wood fence may need to be replaced. The wood may have been treated with arsenic to prevent decay and insect infestation, but such wood is bad for the environment. A green approach would be to use treated wood that minimizes the impact on nature.

When looking into building or renovating a green arena, a facility manager should consider many issues before choosing to go forward. Considerations include not only the cost but also safety factors, the life cycle of the materials in the building, operating costs, and the effects of the manufacturing processes behind the products being used. An arena can become more sustainable through use of the following:

- *Gray water.* Water that has been previously used to wash hands, clothes, or dishes or for bathing, as well as collected rain water, is called gray water. Through creation of a system that not only collects the water but also filters and redistributes it, water can be reused in restrooms, for irrigation of the grounds, and for fire extinguishing (Yaeger, 1998).

- *Natural light.* Using windows in certain areas of the facility will reduce the amount of energy needed to light those areas. One must be careful when using an abundance of natural light so that it does not hinder the ability of the arena to host functions such as concerts and televised games.

- *Lighting.* Using fluorescent or high-intensity discharge lighting to light a facility is the most cost- and energy-efficient option. Another effective tool for reducing lighting costs is to analyze every event separately to determine how much lighting is actually needed; this will prevent wasting electricity (Yaeger, 1998).

Through a maintenance program, many of these steps can be developed and implemented. For example, the maintenance department can be supplied with fluorescent bulbs instead of standard light bulbs. Instead of draining fluid into a sewer system, hazardous liquids need to be properly disposed of, not just to protect the environment but also to avoid breaking the law. Similarly, cleaning agents used to maintain the facility need to be properly disposed of and monitored.

Green custodial and maintenance operations involve investigating current practices and eliminating those that can hurt the environment. For example, if light bulbs and old batteries are just thrown away, then the facility should develop a hazardous waste removal program. All cleaning chemicals need to be carefully examined. Some cleaners contain toxic chemicals that can cause significant bodily and environmental harm. Cleaners should be carefully examined, and environmentally friendly cleaners should be used whenever possible.

Abernathy: Sustainability practices for efficient facilities

Photo courtesy of Joe Abernathy.

My name is Joseph A. Abernathy, and I am the vice president of stadium operations for the St. Louis Cardinals. I have worked with the Cards for more than 19 years, and before my current position track I was on the engineering and construction side of the old Busch Stadium. I have served as a member of the board of directors of the Green Sports Alliance, a member of the board of directors and the past president of the Stadium Mangers Association, and cochairman of the Sustainable Stadium Operations Committee of Major League Baseball.

When managing a sport facility, a manager needs to remember that he or she is a facility manager and that the facility just happens to host sporting events. So many times in sport facility management we focus on the sport rather than the facility. One of the most important factors in managing a facility is managing it as efficiently as possible. In the constant evolution of efficient facility management, *green facility management* has become a popular term. This has become synonymous with sustainable facility management. Mike Richter, USA Hockey Hall of Fame goaltender and founding partner of Healthy Planet Partners, simply defines sustainable management as the efficient use of resources. This efficient use of resources has long been an important objective for facility managers. Today, using the terms *green* or *sustainable* brings an additional focus on how we can use resources with sensitivity and how our actions affect our environment. Efficient use of energy, water, paper, food, and all our natural resources is good for the environment. We must understand that these natural resources are limited.

We began our green programs at Busch Stadium in 2008, and by the end of the 2014 season we've diverted more than 2,400 tons of recycling and more than 800 tons of yard waste from local landfills—a diversion rate of 29%. We reached this level by placing more than 500 recycling bins in the stadium, and we have a team of volunteers go down the aisles collecting recyclables. Our volunteers get to watch the game from the standing section, as they perform their duties only between innings and during pitching changes. Waste has also been reduced by the partnership with Operation Food Search; food donations worth more than $159,000 have been directed to St. Louis food banks. During the month of April the St. Louis Cardinals host their annual Green Series, with special activities that publicize reusing, recycling, and solar power at Busch Stadium. Fans at Busch Stadium also enjoy food, beverage, and retail shops powered by 106 solar panels, producing approximately 32,000 kilowatt-hours of solar energy per year. This is a modest portion of the facility's energy needs, but it is projected to accumulate significant savings during the system's life.

Whether the issue is conserving energy or recycling building products, conservation has become a major concern for new facilities. A key for new facilities is their ability to minimize waste. From reducing the amount of wasted energy to building with sustainable materials, constructing more efficient facilities is a sound and correct decision. When Qualcomm Stadium hosted Super Bowl XXXII, the 68,000 fans in attendance generated approximately 70 tons of trash. The numerous games, tailgate parties, and other activities associated with major sporting events generate an enormous amount of waste each year. American buildings consume 30% of the nation's total energy such as electricity, coal, and natural gas and 60% of all electricity used

(McCarron, 2001). The remaining amounts are used for manufacturing, transportation, communication, and numerous other uses. The process of creating energy-efficient buildings is called green design. Green design should be analyzed in the facility planning and design processes (discussed in chapters 4 and 5, respectively). However, even if a building is designed with conservation in mind, the facility may not accomplish this goal if it is not constructed properly. To help address the divide that might exist between developing a green facility and actually running such a facility, facility managers need to implement proactive programs that make it easier for everyone to be green. As an example, the New York Giants now distribute garbage bags to tailgaters in the parking lots before games. The fans can fill and then leave the bags outside their cars when they go into the game, and the trash is collected during the game.

The best-designed building will not work well if the materials are not efficient or not properly connected to reduce air loss. Green design considers the building's design, site, region, building envelope, construction materials, building systems, and other variables. Using life-cycle costing of materials or initial costs, maintenance costs, and replacement costs, a facility or its components can be examined to determine whether they are operating efficiently and conserving energy. Green facilities typically cost more to build, but in the long run their maintenance and energy usage costs more than make up for the higher starting price (McCarron, 2001). Facilities built to comply with **Leadership in Energy and Environmental Design** (LEED) criteria cost 5% to 10% more than other buildings. LEED certification takes into consideration a facility's site and its usage of water, energy, air, and materials. It is hoped that LEED-compliant facilities will be environmentally friendly and, in the long run, reduce facility operational costs.

All the LEED variables affect the construction process. For example, the site criterion is affected by local environmental conditions. If care is to be taken to avoid harming adjoining land, the construction process may need to be significantly altered. Chapter 7 highlights the money-saving options in various lighting systems. If energy-efficient lighting systems are installed from the beginning, subsequent costs of converting a system can be eliminated and energy efficiency can be reached right away. Additional building considerations include cogeneration. Cogeneration involves analyzing the combined heat and power produced at a power plant. Most power plants convert only 35% of the fuel into electrical energy; an additional 8% of the electricity is lost during transmission, and the remaining 57% is used by the end users. The rest of the energy produced during the conversion process is heat energy that is released into the environment (McCarron, 2001). A green facility would be designed so that the power plant is near a pool or other area that could use the heat energy to reduce heating costs. If the plant is closer to the area that will use the electricity, less electricity will be lost in the transmission process.

Building materials play a major role in energy conservation. Insulation and vapor barriers help reduce heating, ventilation, and air conditioning (HVAC) needs but do not address air circulation because air is trapped in a building. Exterior color can also have a significant effect. Facilities in the South are often built with light-colored or reflective materials to reflect heat, which reduces cooling demands during the summer. Walls can be designed to collect sunlight during the winter and then radiate the heat throughout a facility. The roof can even be used as either a recreation area or a rooftop garden. Although numerous materials are available for constructing a building, and many are now made with recycled products, potential health concerns exist. Chapter 7 highlights some of the air quality issues that can occur with any facility, including green facilities. Green-related sport efforts are gaining in popularity. Every facility manager needs to seriously examine the issues, from gray (reclaimed) water usage to the facility's carbon footprint, because customers and government officials will start demanding accountability.

One key component of green building is reducing trash during the construction process. The average new construction project generates 3.9 pounds (1.8 kg) of waste for every square foot (0.09 sq m) built. Thus, if a 50,000-square-foot (4,645 sq m) building is being considered, the builder can expect to generate 97.5 tons of waste (Monroe, 2008). Because plastic, aluminum, and tires take on average 300 years to decompose, it is critical to reduce the waste generated during the construction process. The owner, architect, contractors, and construction manager need to be on the same page before a project starts and follow a detailed waste reduction plan to minimize construction waste.

This chapter discusses why going green is so important and examines some of the possible strategies for a manager to make their building greener. The chapter also explores the actions that several sport facilities have taken to reduce their carbon footprint in terms of both facility designs and facility operations.

THE NEED FOR GREEN STRATEGIES

Why do we need to develop green strategies for facility management? It is easy to say that it is the right thing to do. However, green strategies also represent the natural evolution of sport facility management. Facilities will be built and run, and programs therein will need to be green to meet government, tenant, and customer mandates as well as financial benchmarks.

Sporting events can produce vast amounts of waste. A significant amount of trash can be collected during the 6 hours after a major college football game. Before the major shift to greening games, a Big Ten football game could produce around 400 cubic yards (305.8 cu m) of trash, which translated to 2,400 cubic yards (1,835 cu

m) in a season. It cost the athletic department more than $10 a cubic yard to compress the trash and $8,000 a season to dispose of it. Of the total amount of trash collected during games, only 11% was actually trash; the rest was recyclable or compostable. The stadiums could have generated money from selling recyclables because plastic and paper can be sold for around $10 per cubic yard. A large percentage of the trash collected after a game consisted of plastic water bottles and souvenir cups. During the 2004 college football season, Michigan State University sold 66,000 souvenir cups and 57,000 bottles of water. About one-third of the trash that made it to landfills was recyclable or compostable paper (Mallett, 2009). In comparison, an average Super Bowl can generate around 70 tons of trash. Special events can also generate significant amounts of trash. For example, the group carbonfund.org calculated the **carbon footprint** of the 2008 Daytona 500 to be 14,163 tons (Ryan, 2009).

The following are some key facts about the waste American society produces and the need for green thinking.

- The average American uses 650 pounds (294.8 kg) of paper each year.
- Each day Americans throw away enough trash to fill 63,000 garbage trucks.
- In 1995, 27% of the U.S. food supply—48 million tons of food—spoiled or went unused.
- Americans throw away 570 diapers per second, which translates to 49 million diapers a day. The average child uses 8,000 to 10,000 diapers before being potty trained.

ECOLOGICAL FOOTPRINT

Greenhouse gases are the carbon dioxide (CO_2), nitrous oxide, and methane emitted into the atmosphere through which a facility or event has direct control as well as emissions from those using the facility and from power providers or other suppliers. For example, a sport facility (such as Madison Square Garden) built on top of a subway station cannot be held responsible for an increased carbon or greenhouse footprint created by the subway station that is beneath it. Some laws require greenhouse gases to be measured and offset, whereas other laws require facilities to reduce their overall ecological footprint (i.e., the amount of land or resources needed to generate the resources consumed and to absorb the waste created), including greenhouse gases. Whatever the requirement, to effectively reduce greenhouse gases a facility needs to measure the amount of gases produced, develop strategies for reducing gas usage, and then measure whether the mitigation efforts really worked.

- Americans throw away 2.5 million plastic bottles every hour.

- Recycling an aluminum soda can saves 96% of the energy used to make the can from metal ore.

- Paper takes up 40% of the space in landfills. Recycling 1 ton (907.2 kg) of cardboard saves more than 9 cubic yards (6.8 cu m) of landfill space.

- Americans make 750,000 photocopies every minute and a total of 400 billion copies a year.

- One ton (907.2 kg) of paper from recycled pulp saves 17 trees, 3 cubic yards (2.3 cu m) of landfill space, 7,000 gallons (26,498 L) of water, 4,200 kilowatt-hours (enough to heat a home for 6 months), and 390 gallons (1,476.3 L) of oil and prevents 60 pounds (27.2 kg) of air pollution.

- More than 100 million tons of wood could be saved each year if all the paper used in the United States were recycled. If every American recycled just one-tenth of their newspapers it would save around 25 million trees.

- About 80% of what Americans throw away can be recycled, yet only 28% of all trash is recycled by Americans.

- The average American home produces 300 pounds (136.1 kg) of green trimmings and brush, 200 pounds (90.7 kg) of leaves, and 1,000 pounds (453.6 kg) of grass clippings a year.

- Americans produce an estimated 4 million pounds (1.8 million kg) of hazardous waste (e.g., paint, batteries, chemicals) every day.

- Of the 17,000 petrochemicals available for home use, only 30% have been tested for human health or environmental impact.

- The institutional cleaning industry uses 5 billion pounds (2.7 billion kg) of cleaning chemicals each year.

- The average janitor uses 23 gallons (87 L) of chemicals each year; 25% are considered hazardous (Burns-DeMelo, 2008).

- In the United States, buildings are responsible for 48% of CO_2 emissions, whereas transportation produces only 27% of CO_2 emissions.

Buildings in the United States consume 72% of all electricity available for consumption, 14% of potable water, and 40% of all produced energy. There is a difference between electricity generated by coal burning plants, trash burning plants, solar collectors, and nuclear power plants as examples, and all other energy produced such as natural gas, oil, and electricity. In comparison, sustainably designed buildings are able to reduce energy usage by 24% to 50%, CO_2 emissions by around 35%, water consumption by 40%, and the amount of solid waste going to landfills by 70%. Sustainable design can also reduce operating costs by around 8%, increase the building's value by around 7%, and increase the return on investment by 6.6% (Sherrard and Boyer, 2009).

Some products that humans manufacture have a long shelf life. Items that take a long time to decompose include the following:

- Carpet fiber: 10+ years
- Plastic: 300-500 years
- Aluminum: 200-500 years
- Tires: 500+ years
- Glass: lasts forever

One of the biggest green issues involves water. Water is a key asset that has led to—and will continue to lead to—wars throughout the world. Americans waste water at a much greater rate than any other country. The average American uses 70 gallons (265 L) of water every day. Toilets use an average of 18.5 gallons (70 L), which accounts for approximately 26.7% of daily water use. This is followed by clothes washing (15 gallons, or 56.8 L) and then showers (11.6 gallons, or 43.9 L). One of the largest uses of water comes from the manufacture of products and food: 70% of global freshwater use is devoted to irrigation (including countless lawns and grass playing fields). It takes 30 gallons (113.5 L) of water to produce one slice of bread, 528 gallons (1,998 L) a day to produce a day's worth of food for one person, 1,680 gallons (6,359.5 L) to create 1 pound (0.45 kg) of grain-fed beef, and 10 gallons (37.9 L) to produce 1 gallon (3.8 L) of gasoline. In addition, 4.4 billion pounds (2 billion kg) of human waste enters freshwater around the world every day, and developing countries will increase their water usage by 50% by the year 2025. Water usage has grown twice as fast as the population over the past century. Although water is precious, humans have a way of wasting large amounts of it. In fact, 1 trillion gallons (3.8 trillion L) of water is used each day to produce food that ends up wasted.

Another major concern entails energy availability and usage. The amount of gas, coal, and electricity used on a daily basis is staggering. Sport facilities use a large amount of energy. Electricity is used for cooking food, chilling beer, powering video equipment and air conditioning fans, and numerous other needs. One of the biggest electrical demands comes from lights. For example, powering the 560 2,000-watt lights at Safeco Field in Seattle costs around $250 an hour. A 3-hour game and 2 hours of batting practice result in an electrical bill of $1,250 per game and more than $100,000 for an 81-game schedule (Steinbach, 2010c). Any opportunity to reduce these costs saves the team hard cash.

U.S. organizations squander roughly $2.8 billion and emit 20 million tons of CO_2 (equivalent to 4 million cars) by leaving on office equipment that is not in use. A large company with 10,000 personal computers could save more than $260,000 a year if all computers were turned off at night (Swartz, 2009). Other ways energy is lost include the following:

- Not cleaning windows (internal lighting is required to compensate for low natural lighting when windows are dirty) or HVAC filters (dirty filters are less efficient)

- Not fixing dripping faucets [a hot-water faucet that leaks 1 gallon (3.8 L) per hour wastes $30-$120 in energy per year]

- Unnecessarily leaving vending machines on all night

- Cleaning at night rather than slow times during the day

- Improperly scheduling when devices turn on (e.g., having the coffee heater turn on hours before employees arrive at work)

- Mounting thermostats in the wrong areas

- Running exhaust fans at the wrong times

- Blocking grills and vents with other equipment or furniture (this reduces their efficiency)

- Using incandescent exit lights (Garris, 2008)

GREEN SOLUTIONS

Numerous possible solutions exist for reversing the harm sport facilities and their operations can cause. Some solutions are developed by individual facilities, some are developed by an industry, and others might be mandated by a government entity. The Energy Policy Act set benchmarks for water consumption and prohibited the manufacture or import of plumbing fixtures that did not meet these benchmarks. A commercial toilet has to use less than 1.6 gallons (6 L) per flush. High-efficiency toilets consume around 1.28 gallons (4.8 L) per flush, whereas foam-flush toilets use 0.05 gallons (0.2 L) per flush and waterless toilets use no water. The benchmark for faucets is 2.2 gallons (8.3 L) per minute, but LEED mandates an even stricter 0.5 gallons (1.9 L) per minute, which can be met with aerators and timed units that minimize the total amount of water used. Showerheads and faucets should use less than 2.5 gallons (9.5 L) per minute (Jahrling, 2007). It should be noted that some energy conservation ideas cannot be implemented. For example, the water temperature in dishwashing units cannot be reduced below the minimum temperature to ensure that germs are killed. These standards are set by government health agencies.

Whatever the reason for adopting a green strategy, it needs to make financial sense. Savings can be substantial for certain renovation projects, but long-term financial analysis needs to be performed. Some modifications can reduce energy consumption by $1,000 annually; however, if it costs $100,000 to make the modification, the project should not be undertaken. The following example highlights a successful renovation project that saved significant energy consumption and costs. The parking lot at Bryant College in Rhode Island used 32 mercury vapor fixtures (400 watts each) mounted on eight 30-foot (9 m) poles. Because of the poor lighting in the location, five auto accidents and a dozen break-ins occurred each year. The school replaced the lights with eight 1,000-watt high-pressure sodium fixtures. The new fixtures cut the operating and maintenance costs by 45%, which saved the college $3,000 annually. Just as important, the parking lot became safer; this saved the college $6,000 annually in

A GREEN METLIFE STADIUM

The $1.6 billion MetLife Stadium, which houses two National Football League (NFL) teams, was built by the contractor Skanska USA. The stadium's primary architect (called architect of record) was EwingCole, and the design architect was 360 Architects. The stadium footprint is 55 acres (222,577 sq m), and the stadium itself is a total of 2.1 million square feet (195,096 sq m). There are two 15,000-square-foot (1,393.5 sq m) home team locker rooms and two visitor locker rooms. There are more than 200 suites on four levels; each suite can hold between 16 and 24 fans. The seating capacity of the stadium can range from 82,500 to 90,000. There are more than 10,000 seats in the club seating area. To help move all these fans there are 20 elevators and 38 escalators. Fans can use one of the 28,000 parking spaces around the stadium. The 10,000-square-foot (929 sq m) team store has specially designed displays that allow the merchandise to be quickly changed from the Jets to the Giants and back again. A 350,000-square-foot (32,516 sq m) outdoor plaza includes several playing areas and a mini FieldTurf field. The stadium is lit by 624 2,000-watt sport lights. Videos are displayed on four 30- by 118-foot (9.1 by 36 m) 12-mm high-definition light-emitting diode video display boards. A video display ribbon wraps the inner bowl of the entire stadium and measures 4 feet (1.2 m) high by more than 1,800 feet (548.6 m) wide. Twenty video display boards are positioned outside the stadium.

The new stadium was designed to be as energy efficient as possible. The goal was to reduce air pollution, conserve water and energy, improve waste management, and reduce the environmental impact of construction. The building was designed to reduce annual water usage by 25%, reduce energy usage (compared with the old Giants Stadium) by 35%, increase in-event recycling by 25%, and recycle 80% of the construction waste. These goals were reached, and the green efforts stand to save the equivalent of 1.68 million metric tons of CO_2 annually—the equivalent of taking 30,000 cars off the road for a year. Some green efforts include the following:

- Using 40,000 tons of recycled steel in building the stadium and recycling 20,000 tons of steel when the old Giants Stadium was demolished

- Using recycled plastic and scrap iron in the production of the seating

- Building the stadium on a former brownfield site (a construction site reclaimed for other purposes after normal remediation of the site for any chemical or toxic residue)

- Reducing the amount of air pollution produced by construction vehicles by using cleaner diesel fuel and minimizing vehicle idle time

- Using environmentally friendly concrete in construction

- Replacing traditional concession plates, cups, and carriers with compostable alternatives

- Salvaging concrete foundation piles from the old stadium

- Spending and hiring locally (more than $700 million of the $1 billion in hard construction costs was spent locally, and 85% of subcontractors were hired locally) ("Beacon on Environmental Issues," 2010)

---

claims payouts. Thus, a $12,000 investment in new fixtures paid for itself in about 16 months (Sanders, 1998).

New technologies are also furthering energy conservation. Computerized maintenance management systems (CMMSs), discussed in chapter 9, are now being developed with very unique features that save money and energy. Besides shutting down lights or turning off systems, new CMMSs can respond to external weather conditions by switching off certain systems or reducing the amount of resources utilized. For example,

if lawn sprinklers are on a timer, the CMMS can automatically override the timers when it is raining so that water is not wasted.

Waste Reduction

Waste reduction is both an environmental concern and a potential cost reduction strategy. The first step in implementing a waste reduction program is obtaining administrator approval. For example, in a survey of fans at a professional tennis event, one of the potential improvements most frequently cited was the use of recycling containers for soda and beer cans. Management did not think of recycling as a marketing tool, but patrons have applauded the new effort on recycling. In many facilities, if management has not undertaken a recycling effort, patrons can become very upset.

Certain recyclable materials may frequently be seen in the trash, but if separating them is too difficult, they may not be the best materials to recycle. For example, food scraps are regularly thrown in the trash with plastics and paper, all of which can be recycled through separate processes. It may be possible to eliminate this problem by developing user-friendly storage and collection locations (Hennesey, 2001).

Food is the number one material sent to landfills each year. The only real solution to not wasting food is to make less of it. However, a stadium or arena cannot afford to make less food and have fans waiting for a long time or refusing to buy due to the time required to prepare food. Thus, these facilities need to make enough food in advance to deal with anticipated demand. Demand can be estimated by tracking the number of units sold at prior similar events. For example, how many hot dogs are sold at a typical game: 18,000 or 30,000? With these data, a facility will know in rough terms how much food to make. However, if a game is rained out or finished quickly, the number of units sold can decrease significantly, resulting in a large amount of leftover food. In the past this food would have been thrown away. However, over the past several years stadiums and arenas have been donating leftover food to a variety of charities. The wrapped, edible food is frozen and then given to charities the next day. Such a practice looks good to the general public and can save a facility money. Between 2009 and 2012, TD Garden donated an average of 15.5 tons of food each season to the Boston Rescue Mission (Broughton, 2012). Similarly, between 2010 and 2012, 30 National Hockey League (NHL) clubs combined to donate 205,000 pounds (92,986 kg) of leftover food per year. The NHL developed an online spreadsheet to help teams enter game-day donations, recycling, composting, and landfill data. In 2007, CenturyLink Field, home of the Seattle Seahawks and Sounders FC, sent 81% of its trash to the dump, recycled 16%, and composted

3%. By 2011, only 24% of trash went to landfills, whereas 55% was recycled and 21% was composted. This represents three-fourths of the 1.5 million tons of trash the facility produces annually.

This "trash" was actually a valuable asset. Through recycling and composting, facilities can significantly improve their bottom line. Selling cardboard can be a lucrative source of additional income. Furthermore, reducing the amount of debris reduces the amount a facility has to pay for trash removal. Sportservice, which runs concessions for Cleveland's Progressive Field, witnessed an increase of 22% in events from 2007 to 2011. Even with more events, the facility reduced landfill hauls by 46% (down to only 682 tons of waste) and saved more than $250,000 during that time period. The waste haulers came to Progressive 99 times in 2011 compared with 254 times in 2007. Each visit from the garbage collectors costs the

A bottle-shaped recycling container at PPL Park gives patrons a way to quickly identify a recycling location.

team $550, but the cost to haul away compost (where no dumping fees apply) was only $7 a load. Through these efforts, the average visitor generated less than 1 pound (0.45 kg) of landfill trash (Broughton, 2012).

Composting is one strategy for recycling food, but composting does not produce as much cash. Thus, leftover food can also be used to create energy. Food waste can be converted to a methane-rich gas when eaten by bacteria in a process called anaerobic digestion. It is estimated that such a process can produce energy equivalent to around 10% of a small country's power needs.

Recycling efforts are popping up all over the place. Recycling efforts are designed to divert trash from landfills and incinerators and instead reuse as much of the material as possible. Reusing materials saves money but also reduces trash hauling expenses. It also can serve as a revenue source: Some facilities sell old oil, paper, cardboard, and other materials that formerly were considered trash. For example, the Boston Red Sox sold surprise bags to fans that included everything from old bricks from Fenway to jerseys and promotional giveaways. Instead of throwing such items away, the team turned them into cash.

Typical trash around a house can be broken down as follows:

- Organic: 32.1%
- Paper: 25.2%
- Plastic: 12.9%
- Construction and demolition debris: 10.5%
- Other waste: 10.1%
- Metals: 4.6%

- Glass: 2.2%
- Electronics: 2.0%
- Hazardous waste: 0.4% (Schoeffler, 2013)

Almost all of these items can be recycled in one way or another. Similarly, a typical stadium or arena generates significant amounts of recyclable materials such as paper, plastics, and cardboard.

Almost anything can be recycled. At the 2010 Vancouver Olympic Games, waste heat from sewage was recovered to help provide space heat and domestic hot water for the Olympic Village. The sewage went through a treatment process and then was sent through a heat pump that transferred thermal energy to hot water. This does not mean that people were drinking untreated sewage; rather, instead of being wasted on its way to the treatment center, the heat was processed and used for other purposes—a form of recycling.

Energy Conservation

Energy inefficiency is the single largest impediment affecting energy conservation. Although industry is the single largest user of energy in the United States (at 19.5%, followed by residential use at 9.2%), 57% of energy usage is actually lost energy. This occurs because the U.S. has an old and inefficient energy infrastructure and other inefficiencies such as light-duty vehicles that convert only 20% of the fuel they consume into usable energy ("The Power Plan," 2010). Other inefficiencies include motors running at full speed when not necessary, losing power when transforming power from AC to DC (12% of energy loss), improper grid management (e.g., storage on

STRATEGIES FOR CONSERVING ENERGY

- Leave appliances and electronics off and unplugged when not in use.
- Clean dirty air filters.
- Fix dripping faucets and other leaks.
- Clean during the day to minimize lighting at night.
- Place thermostats in the right area (i.e., not next to a vent, which can register one reading while the rest of the facility is much

hotter or cooler), and try to use zone cooling and heating.
- Keep windows and skylights clean to let in more light and heat.
- Make sure vent and air returns are not blocked and are operating efficiently.
- Switch to energy-efficient models, appliances, and lights.
- Switch to waterless toilets and urinals.

From various sources including Garris 2008.

energy created but not used at night), exhaust heat from manufacturing equipment, and transmission losses due to copper wiring (7% of energy loss).

Alternative Energy Sources

Energy solutions can come from either finding new sources of energy or undertaking new strategies to conserve energy. New energy sources can range from solar power to water power and several other options. No matter what alternative energy source is pursued, a facility should utilize a web-connected and/or smart thermostat to help reduce electrical and total energy consumption. Some alternative energy strategies include:

- Solar energy: Instead of large, expensive solar panels, new technology is creating thin-film solar, solar thermal, and solar heating panels that can be installed almost anywhere and on any surface.. The expense associated with solar projects often results in a return on investment over 15 years.

- Hydro power: Harnessing waves, rivers, and tides (especially in the oceans) can create a reliable energy source.

- Biofuels: Ethanol (an alcohol-based fuel made by fermenting and distilling starch crops, such as corn, and which can also be made from cellulosic biomass, such as trees and grasses) is just one source of biofuel and ethanol can be developed through other organic material such as switch-grass, sugarcane, algae, sewage, and even medical waste.

- Wind power: Wind farms are not only on land—they are moving out to sea, where not as many people object that they clutter the view.

- Nuclear: Nuclear energy reactors are getting smaller and safer.

- Geothermal heat pumps: By drilling holes in the ground a facility can tap into the trapped cooler temperatures deep in the ground that can help warm a building during the winter and cool a building during the summer. Geothermal heat pumps consume 70% less energy than an electric HVAC system.

- Cleaner fossil fuels: Carbon-capturing technology helps clean the dirty emissions from coal-burning plants and helps reduce the CO_2 produced by burning natural gas.

- Fuel cell technology: A device converts the chemical energy from a fuel (usually hydrogen) into electricity through a chemical reaction with oxygen or another oxidizing agent. It is anticipated that the size of these units will keep shrinking as technology improves. In the future, a box the size of a loaf of bread could power an entire house.

All operations at Lincoln Financial Field are powered by the sun and wind. This means that the Philadelphia Eagles' electricity needs come from two nonpolluting, renewable energy sources and that the organization is effectively "off the grid." The environmental benefit of the green energy the Eagles generated and purchased in 2010 is equivalent to the following:

- Removing 2,189 cars from the road for a year
- Sequestering enough CO_2 annually to deflect 2,380 acres (9.6 sq m) of forest
- Offsetting the CO_2 emissions created by the annual electricity use of 1,392 homes
- Offsetting the CO_2 emissions created by using 1,251,604 gallons (4.7 million L) of gasoline

Wind turbines on top of Lincoln Financial Field in Philadelphia contribute to running the facility entirely on green energy.

Even though the solar panels at the Eagles' corporate headquarters and training facility (Nova-Care Complex) are a small part of the team's green energy program, they produce enough energy from the sun to power more than 400 homes for 1 day ("Go Green," 2013).

Facility tenants are also following the trend. NASCAR has launched its own NASCAR Green program, which recycles tires and fuels and plants trees to offset carbon emissions. Of the 126 teams in five major professional leagues in 2013, 38% used renewable energy for at least some of their needs, 68 had adopted energy efficiency programs, and 15 venues housing these teams had received LEED certification (Mihoces, 2013). Every league has launched some type of conservation program for its teams to follow. Thus, even if a sport facility does not undertake a conservation program on its own, the tenants might require the facility to develop such programs.

Water Conservation

Water conservation is designed to reduce the amount of water used because the amount of water in the world is limited. Saving water can reduce future water bills, reduce energy bills, help a facility withstand possible future droughts, and help improve a facility's reputation and community engagement.

Similar to other green efforts, water conservation starts with management setting a goal, prioritizing actions, and providing resources. Management's commitment is the key, and managers can make the decision easy by obtaining current usage rates and setting specific and measurable goals for reduction. This should work its way down to the staff because they will be the ones charged with implementing the program. In between management and the staff are the facility and system or product levels, where both staff and management need to develop techniques that help reduce water usage, such as limiting the watering time for a field, inspecting for leaks, and minimizing water usage in concession areas (e.g., using low-water-use dishwashers, not running a dishwasher that is not full). Local energy or water districts will work with facilities to help them reduce their usage and might even give some financial assistance for implementing green initiatives.

Water conservation is even more critical during times of drought. Much of the United States suffered through droughts between 2011 and 2013. In Denver the water authority called a stage 2 drought, which required a reduction in usage and mandated a maximum of 2 days a week for external water usage (except for major facilities such as a stadium, where the water authority demanded a reduction) but allowed businesses to water more frequently to prevent failure. Denver's Sports Authority Field upgraded the water irrigation control system, used central controls, broke the field up into 230 watering zones, and replaced more than 140 regular toilets with low-flow toilets. The water authority paid $60,000 based on actual performance and gave the facility $18,000 in rebates. The stadium reduced its watering to Tuesdays and Fridays only and shut off nonessential restrooms. The team was losing almost 1,000 gallons (3,785.4 L) a day, primarily through a leak in a catch basin; through repairs this water loss was reduced 85%. Urinals were programmed for reduced flush and to flush only every third user. The stadium used fire hoses to help clean up after a game, but that practice used almost 1 million gallons (3.8 million L) of water after each event. The facility switched to electric pressure washers to reduce the amount of water used. The facility utilized precision turf management to determine the right time to get the right resources to where they were most needed. The electronic system uses a variety of sensors, some fixed at 2-inch (5 cm) and others at 6-inch (15.2 cm) levels, to measure turf water, temperature, and salinity levels. Some mobile sensors can be inserted at various points in the turf and can be synced to create a map of where the field has too much or too little water. This information can then be entered into computer programs that allow the information and sprinkler control to be accessed by all employees, even from home. In 2008, the facility paid $28,000 for water conservation equipment just for landscaping. This resulted in a $60,000 rebate, an equipment rebate of $7,000, and water savings of $51,000 ($17,000 a year) for a total savings of $90,000 over 4.5 years. Also, from 2005 to 2007 the facility used around 19 million gallons (71.9 million L) of water. The goal was to reduce this use to around 15 million gallons. However, through aggressive efforts from 2009 to 2011, the usage was closer to 10 million gallons (37.8 million L).

Reclaiming (collecting and reusing) water from rooftops, leaching ponds, and parking lot runoff is a solution to reclaiming the countless gallons of potable water that end up in storm drains and sewer systems. The problem with such efforts is that significant energy is required to pump water from storage areas to where it is really needed.

Rooftop Gardens

Rooftop gardens are a way to grow food or add an attractive element to a facility. These gardens can provide insulation for a building and can help prevent water leaks. A facility cannot simply put dirt on a roof and create a garden. The typical green roof has the following elements:

- The roof panel on top of the roof is about 1 foot (30.5 cm) thick and made of recycled expanded polystyrene, which can support up to 70 pounds (31.8 kg) per square foot.
- A sheet of insulation is installed on top of the roof panel at a slight pitch to help drain excess water.
- The insulation is covered with a sticky foam adhesive to help secure the roof board to the insulation.
- The roof board, which is made of fiberglass, serves as a hard surface and helps prevent mold and wayward roots.
- On top of the fiberglass is a sheet of thermal polymer that protects against temperature extremes and ultraviolet damage.
- The top layer is a 4-inch (10.2 cm) bed of lightweight dirt.

Transportation Solutions

Transportation strategies can significantly affect the total amount of energy used by those traveling to a sport facility. Although the facility might not save a lot of money by fans commuting to the facility, the fans who attend games can significantly reduce their energy usage, which results in the facility reducing its total carbon footprint. Some facilities are built near subway, train, or other public transportation areas, and some sta-diums have started offering bicycle parking areas to encourage people to bike to games. However, many stadiums or arenas are built in the suburbs to take advantage of cheaper land and more open areas for building larger facilities. Such facilities need to pursue alternative transportation strategies. Special carpool parking, buses, and other shared transportation options can help reduce the carbon footprint of these facilities.

Technological Aids

Technology is helping drive green changes in sport facilities. Some green technology strategies include the following:

- Submetering devices can help more effectively allocate and monitor electrical usage.
- Windows and doors can become more effective with high-performance glazing. Such glazing is easy to install, can help prevent ultraviolet damage to furniture and floors, and can reduce energy loss by up to 5%.
- SkinzWraps created a low-wind-resistance vinyl sticker that has been used by NASCAR as well as regular cars and trucks. The dimple pattern (similar to that on a golf ball) can help cut fuel bills by 20%.
- Precast building panels are made with light-gauge metal studs and a special polystyrene called Neopor, which is nontoxic and fully recyclable and blocks out heat, moisture, and mold. The panels lock together to create a wall that already includes channels for plumbing.
- Roofing tiles that double as solar panels are just one solar option. Solar panels can also be incorporated into parking lots (either in the ground or on canopies covering parking areas) so energy is generated when cars are not parked.
- EC02 created a waterless recycling process using a corn-based biodegradable liquid solvent to replace the 100,000 gallons (378,541 L) of water used on a daily basis in many recycling plants.
- PoolNaturally uses peat moss from New Zealand (in pouches similar to large tea packets) to clarify water in pools and spas. The moss helps eliminate the need for daily pool cleaning, reduces the need for chemicals, and reduces water consumption due to a decreased need for backwashing.

- Wysips has produced a see-through solar film that can turn plastic and glass into solar power generating panels.

- ThermalCore wall panels use microscopic capsules that are filled with wax, which changes from solid to liquid when the outside temperature reaches 73 °F. As the wax melts it absorbs heat and cools a room. At night when the temperature drops below 73 °F, the wax hardens and releases heat back into the room.

GREEN BUILDING DESIGN

This chapter has identified the need for going green and various green solutions, and it is critical for the industry to apply these solutions. This part of the chapter explores design and operational strategies that have been implemented in the industry. Pocono Raceway built a 3-megawatt solar farm to power the track and some of the surrounding homes. That is an example of a green building strategy. In contrast, some strategies are purely operational and focus on the programs run in the facility. Go Green Fitness in Orange, Connecticut, has attached generators to the spinning bicycles. A typical group spinning class (with around 20 bikes) has the potential to produce up to 3.6 megawatts (3.6 million watts) of renewable energy per year. This is enough energy to light 72 homes for a month while also reducing carbon emissions by more than 5,000 pounds (2,268 kg).

The 1.1-million-square-foot (102,193 sq m) Nationals Park, which earned an LEED silver rating, was the first Major League Baseball stadium to receive LEED certification. The facility was constructed on a previous brownfield site and is located next to transportation hubs to reduce the need for cars. Bicycle parking also was made available, including a bike valet service. Low-flow toilets and air-cooled rather than water-cooled air chillers were supposed to save almost 10 million gallons (37.8 million L) of water a year. Efficient lighting was also expected to save $440,000 over 25 years. One of the biggest savings came from the construction process. A nice percentage (35%) of the extracted, processed, and manufactured elements of the facility came from within 500 miles of the construction site. In addition, 83% of the construction waste was diverted from the landfill

(U.S. Green Building Council, 2008). One unique feature that fans will never see at Nationals Park is the sump pit system. Several hundred thousand gallons of water can be used to clean a stadium after a game. A sand filter system, located in six areas around the stadium, screens the water before it enters the storm water system and the nearby Anacostia River. The water enters one chamber that removes all debris, such as peanut shells. The second chamber reduces the water flow. The third chamber—a sand filter that the water flows through—removes small particles. The water then goes through the last chamber, an outfall chamber, before it enters the storm water system (Murphy, 2008).

Other green examples include FedEx Field which created a multiuse structure by covering the parking area with 7,542 solar panels. The panels provide cover for those parking in the area, and the $12.5 million project (finished in 2011) can provide up to 20% of the game-day power needs and 100% of the non-game-day power needs. Home Depot Center installed 280 waterless urinals, which save approximately 10,000 gallons (37,854 L) of water every game.

GREEN BUILDING OPERATIONS

Coca-Cola has brought an educational trailer to various auto races and placed 2,600 recycling bins at a dozen tracks; in 1 year these bins collected 65,000 pounds (29,483.5 kg) of recyclable materials (Ryan, 2009). Safety-Kleen, an oil recycling and waste clean-up company, collects 125,000 gallons (473,176.5 L) of used oil at racetracks each year. In 2008 the Michigan International Raceway recycled more than 153.5 tons of materials such as cardboard, concrete, plastic, and steel.

In 2009 the St. Louis Cardinals spent roughly $2 million on electricity and $200,000 on water. By changing to more efficient lights they were able to reduce electricity expenses by $10,000 per year. Over a 3-year period ending in 2013, Busch Stadium reduced its energy usage by 24% (Mihoces, 2013).

The Philadelphia Eagles purchased 14,000 kilowatt-hours from renewable sources in 2008, becoming the first NFL team to switch to renew-

BEHIND THE SCENES

SYDNEY, THE FIRST GREEN OLYMPICS

The Sydney Olympic Games set a standard for future Olympic Games by approaching facility construction and operations from a green perspective. The critical areas they analyzed included gray water, natural lighting, solar power, recycling, trash removal, energy-efficient lighting, and more effective mechanical, electrical, and plumbing systems.

Gray water (recycled water) was used in Sydney for flushing toilets, site irrigation, and the fire suppression system. A central cleaning system collected, filtered, and redistributed the gray water.

Natural light was considered for everything from concourses to the seating bowl. The use of louvers on the roofs of some buildings was proposed to let in light and allow for natural ventilation. Operable windows were also considered for the same reasons. However, louvers were deleted from the plans because of fire-related concerns. In several studies, louvers were shown to force smoke downward rather than allow smoke to exit the building. Also, although organizers hoped to have as many windows as possible to allow for natural light, many events such as concerts need blackout conditions, and more windows can make such efforts problematic. Thus, natural lighting was considered, but few efforts were successful.

Solar power was considered but was felt to be too ineffective. Although some solar panels were installed on the roof of the warm-up court, the major investment was the purchase of green power.

Various issues (e.g., cost, regeneration of each resource, energy used to manufacture each product, life expectancy, and recycling costs) were analyzed before final materials were chosen. Some items such as heavy timber, which could have been a good choice, were cancelled and replaced with steel due to the safety issue associated with wood and fires. Polyvinyl chloride (PVC) piping was not used because it is not recyclable, it is caustic when burned, and the manufacturing process is environmentally unfriendly. Thus, copper piping (even though it has its own issues, such as the impact associated with mining copper) was used as an alternative.

To assist with trash removal, three trash chutes were used to separate paper, plastic, and nonrecyclable items. The bins, which are now common, were not as common back in the late 1990s.

Lighting has evolved significantly, but in the late 1990s the options were not as diverse. The Sydney Olympics utilized no incandescent lights and used more effective fluorescent or high-intensity discharge lights.

To more effectively distribute air, vents were located under each seat in the bowl of the stadium. The mechanical air conditioning system was broken down into 6 zones on each level for a total of 18 zones. Only certain zones were turned on depending on the type or configuration of the event (Yaeger, 1998)

---

able energy. Since then the team has gone to great efforts to promote their green efforts, including almost 100% diversion of trash from landfills (through recycling and composting) and a website (with a sponsor) focused on their green efforts.

The San Francisco Giants partnered with their food service partner, Bon Appétit Management Company, to install a 4,320-square-foot (401.3 sq m) vegetable garden at AT&T Park. Named The Garden, it supplies fresh fruits and vegetables for ballpark menu items and serves as an outdoor classroom. The Garden also features a bar, dining tables, benches, and fire pits. The Garden is sponsored by Peet's Coffee and Tea and provides coffee grounds to fertilize the planter beds. It is hoped that The Garden will be in production year round, producing items such as blueberries, avocados, peppers, kale, lettuce, and tomatoes ("San Francisco Giants," 2014).

RESEARCHING WISE INVESTMENTS

True greenness can be seen through the entire process of a facility or event. Building a green facility is not enough; the facility also needs to be maintained in a green manner. This is akin to life-cycle costing of a system. The entire process of creating or running a green facility needs to be evaluated. Some organizations provide certification that helps communicate the result of a product's life-cycle assessment. The life-cycle assessment is based on information such as the source of raw material, how the raw material is transported, the manufacturing process, construction and installation of the product on site, how the product is used, and how the product is disposed of or repurposed.

Facilities Trivia

The solar-powered trash compactors that have appeared on various street corners, including those in Philadelphia, can go four times as long as trash cans before needing to be emptied. These trash compactors, which have a payback period of around 5 years, can save municipalities millions of dollars. The high-tech trashcans can send alerts when they're full, making pickup much more efficient. As a result, Philadelphia has reduced the size of its trash-collection crews by 73%. The device is made by Big Belly Solar, which is also targeting parks and beaches as ideal locations for the trash devices.

LEED certification should not be the primary pursuit. Although such certification is important, it is an end result of planning, preparation, and execution. Most of the work required in preparing for LEED review is nothing more than good design work. Good architectural and design work will help any facility achieve significant points toward LEED certification. However, poor design work or poor execution can doom any LEED effort. One key component of any LEED review is the installation of renewable energy options, and the price for such efforts has been decreasing over the years.

Energy conservation works. However, companies need to focus on outcomes because if they do not succeed they can actually waste more than they save. A consulting group called Aberdeen (http://www.aberdeen.com/) surveyed 6,300 businesses, and the most efficient businesses were able to generate a 9% reduction in electricity usage. The average business was able to realize a 2% reduction in electricity usage. Surprisingly, those who did the worst actually increased their electricity usage by 19%.

Although some technologies can prove their value quickly, the value of others is not as provable. For example, various types of fitness equipment (e.g., treadmills, exercise bikes) can be retrofitted to generate energy through use. The problem with this approach is that the current cost of doing so makes such efforts a nice novelty but not a valuable investment. In 2009, one California fitness facility installed electricity capturers on 13 machines. Assuming these machines were operated 10 hours a day, they would generate around $183 worth of electricity a year, which means that it would take 82 years to recapture the initial $15,000 investment (Cohen, 2009). The average bike rider can generate 100 to 130 watts per hour (enough to light four compact fluorescent lamp bulbs for 1 hour), whereas an elite athlete can generate up to 300 watts per hour and a group of 20 in a spinning class can generate 2.5 to 3 kilowatts an hour (enough to light 100 compact fluorescent lamp bulbs for 1 hour) (Koch, 2010).

The results of a 2009 study of 2,000 tenants in 154 buildings (all either Energy Star or LEED certified) showed that employees in these greener buildings took on average 2.9 fewer sick days each year. This represented a cost savings of roughly $1,200 per worker. In addition, 50% of respondents indicated that employees were more productive; this 5% increase in productivity could be valued at around $5,000 a year (Palmeri, 2009).

Going green saves more than just sick days. Sustainable buildings can reduce energy usage by 24% to 50%, CO_2 emissions by around 35%, water consumption by around 40%, and the amount of solid waste going to landfills by 70% (Sherrard, 2009). Thus, going green can provide significant monetary savings and promote a healthier work environment.

Not everything is green in green facilities. Although low-flow toilets and recycling programs are simple and easy to implement green strategies, solar panels are not a proven saver. This concern might change as the cost of panels declines, but in the past the investment in solar panels was normally not a value proposition. Placing solar panels on the roof of a sport facility can reduce the opportunity to place revenue-generating logos or names on the building's roof. The 1,300 square feet (120.7 sq m) of solar panels installed at Progressive Field in Cleveland cost $180,000 in 2007. These panels provided 29,000 kilowatt-hours over the initial 3 years—a fraction of the 17 million kilowatt-hours used each year by the stadium (Boudway, 2010). In 2008, Staples Center paid $2.3 million for a 25,000-square-foot (2,322.6 sq m) solar array that supplies 456,000 kilowatt-hours per year. At 12 cents per kilowatt-hour, the facility saves $55,000 a year with the solar panels.

The payback period for the solar panels is more than 40 years; by that time the panels will be obsolete. Thus, a facility needs to carefully determine why they are investing in green efforts. It might be that the facility is doing it for the right reasons, but not all investments provide the same payback.

Summary

There is no question that the future of sport facilities—whether building new facilities, renovating existing facilities, or launching innovative programs—is green. Going green is a mind-set that includes developing and launching green initiatives across a facility (e.g., organic, locally grown food and green advocates among the fan base). Everyone involved in a facility—architects, designers, builders, operators, managers, frontline staff, and even facility users—needs to have a green focus. The best strategies and equipment will have less of an effect if people do not properly operate equipment or if fans refuse to throw trash in appropriate bins.

Discussion Questions and Activities

1. Using the green facility management strategies discussed in this chapter, list some of the ways you can avoid waste and loss of revenue.

2. What does green mean to you and how do you implement it in your personal life?

3. Visit a local facility to see how they address sustainability and green strategies. Do they have a strategy for recycling or dealing with waste? Does the building use power efficiently? Are postings of green or environmentally friendly strategies placed around the building?

4. Think about how you would design a facility. Would it be green, where would you build it, how would you finance it, and what sports would you build it for? Conversely, if you believe that sport facilities should not be built, explain why (e.g., because they are a waste of resources, because they harm the environment).

PART IV

Facility Administration

Once a facility is up and running, managers need to run the business side of the operation. A facility manager needs to market the facility to numerous constituents, operate within a budget, and follow the law to avoid litigation. Part IV covers these key areas.

Chapter 11 focuses on marketing and sales, first examining the basic elements associated with marketing and the various methods used to promote an event or facility. The chapter then analyzes the marketing process, which starts with identifying the customers, positioning the product, and selling the product, then switches to marketing new facilities and attracting tenants and events to a facility. The chapter ends with an analysis of the sales process and securing naming and sponsorship rights.

After securing sales, a facility manager needs to document and analyze the money generated and spent at the facility. Chapter 12 highlights the finance and budgeting process. Although this topic is not as exciting for many compared with marketing a facility, finance is just as important and possibly more important. The chapter starts by analyzing the revenue and expenses generated by a facility and then explores financial analysis through some key financial documents, such as an income statement and a balance sheet. The chapter then discusses the budgeting process and how critical it is for a facility to develop and follow a budget. Next, the chapter examines capital cost considerations for funding a new or renovated facility. Through establishing a specific standard for success, a facility manager can calculate and apply various financing strategies to make a sound decision. The chapter ends with an analysis of how to pay for building a new facility, focusing primarily on various bonds that have been used in the past.

Finally, chapter 13 examines a broad array of legal concerns a facility manager might face. Some of the topics covered include negligence, risk management, contract law, property law, constitutional law, and various government statutes such as the Americans with Disabilities Act. This chapter uses a sample facility concession contract to highlight the language used in facility rental contracts.

11

Marketing and Sales

Chapter Objectives

- Appreciate how the four Ps interact to help market a facility.
- Understand how to effectively market facility and sport experiences.
- Know how to sell products, from signage to sponsorship packages.
- Appreciate the effect that marketing has on a facility's profitability and long-term viability.

A facility should be designed for marketing success and be able to sell itself. A major trend over the past decade is the concept of destination locations. A destination location is a place where everyone wants to go to be seen and to experience the festivities. Patriot Place, as discussed earlier in the text, is an example of a destination location attracting fans for more than just a game. How can a facility become such a destination? Through marketing, of course. **Marketing** is the concept of packaging a product and services in the right way, at the right price, and in the right environment to encourage individuals to buy.

Every facility needs to have a unique marketing approach to sell what goes on within the facility. If there are several health clubs in the same general area, why would a person want to join one versus another? Would there be a difference in price, quality, perceived value, ancillary services, or accommodations? These types of issues need to be analyzed in developing a facility to take advantage of marketing opportunities. If a health club is going to cater to affluent clientele, it must be located close to that demographic segment; must be built to the highest quality level with materials such as marble and other fine finishings; and must offer exclusive services such as a day spa, manicures, and massages.

Whether a facility is engaged in public relations (free publicity) or advertising (paid publicity), the focus is always to encourage people to buy a product. Although a sales effort is required to get elected officials to support and "buy into" building a facility, most facility sales efforts focus on selling various products (which could be called assets), from tickets to naming rights.

This chapter examines the marketing elements critical for a successful sport facility, starting with the four Ps and then turning to marketing strategies, the marketing process, the ways in which a facility sells itself, and the selling of assets such as naming rights.

MARKETING CONCEPTS

Marketing focuses on getting a customer to purchase goods or services. Goods can be food, novelty items, or a parking space at a facility. A service can include the game, personal treatment such as an usher walking someone to her seat, and the nostalgic feel of being in an old stadium or arena.

Marketing includes numerous functions such as advertising and selling, but these activities do not define marketing. It may be defined as a process of planning and executing the development, pricing, promotion, and distribution of ideas, goods, and services to create exchanges that will satisfy the objectives of everyone involved in the transaction (Zikmund and d'Amico, 1996). Thus, marketing attempts to bring buyers and sellers together so that they can conclude a transaction and both parties will leave the exchange satisfied. Marketing is not successful if a customer buys a ticket to a game and then has a horrible time and vows to never return. This is referred to as buyer's remorse.

One marketing challenge for stadiums, arenas, and teams is the availability of game tickets on secondary markets. Many people avoid buying tickets from the facility or team in hopes of buying tickets at a lower price through online and other ticket brokers. Some teams have partnered with these brokers. The problem with such a relationship is that those who pay full price for a ticket can possibly get upset when they see the market flooded by tickets, thus reducing the price, and might either not renew ticket packages or wait for tickets to be sold on the secondary market. This secondary ticket market example helps demonstrate the sensitivity that needs to be examined when making marketing decisions.

Marketing a facility starts with examining what the facility has to sell. A facility has two types of products to sell—experiences and goods—referred to here as products or assets. Although the term *assets* is used in the financial realm, the same term can be applied in marketing since an empty seat is a potential financial asset that could generate revenue, and a marketer needs to be able to market that asset. The experience is the joy of attending a game or working out at a magnificent facility. It is hard to place a price on these experiences, but they are nonetheless very valuable to some. Goods can include foam cheese heads, hot dogs, game programs, and the facility itself.

The New York Mets opened a new stadium, Citi Field, in 2009 with an expectation to increase revenue more than 30% (Massey, 2008). Such a

Mahoney: All personnel support marketing efforts

Photo courtesy of Kim Mahoney.

My name is Kim Mahoney, and before my move to academia I spent more than 20 years in the sport and entertainment industry, primarily in the areas of facility and event management. I previously served as the director of communications and program development with Columbus Arena Sports and Entertainment and as an assistant commissioner with the Ohio High School Athletic Association. In addition, I have worked with the Jerome Schottenstein Center, Nationwide Arena, Show Pros Entertainment Services, Charlotte Convention Center, Charlotte Coliseum, Independence Arena, and the Georgia Dome.

My journey into the world of sport management began with an internship at the Charlotte Coliseum, at the time the home of the National Basketball Association (NBA) Charlotte Hornets. Just like professional sport or intercollegiate athletics, facility management provides opportunities to work in finance, ticketing, operations, event management, sales, and marketing, among others. However, unlike professional or college sport, facility management offers a great variety of experiences. In addition to working sporting events a manager may be involved with concerts, family shows, conventions, trade shows, and many other types of events. One of many things I learned during my time in the industry is the importance of marketing. You may have an efficient and effective organization, but it will not succeed if no one knows about it.

Marketing efforts affect all aspects of the organization, and everyone on the staff—regardless of their position—plays a part in the marketing efforts. For example, the general manager is the liaison to the ownership or governing board. The receptionist greets customers and answers their inquiries. The housekeeping staff helps provide a clean, comfortable environment for customers and clients. The actions of each individual affect the public image of the organization. In addition, the marketing manager often needs the support of other facility personnel to carry out marketing activities.

The successful marketing manager is skilled in the development of mutually beneficial relationships with local media, facility tenants, facility users, industry professionals, and other stakeholders. For example, strong working relationships with local media may enable the marketing manager to more effectively market an event for an organization renting the facility. If the event's marketing budget is more effectively used, resulting in increased ticket sales, then the client is happy and more likely to bring business to the facility in the future.

The successful marketing manager knows the market and knows their audience. Existing information may include data regarding the local or regional market, demographics of the target market, insight from industry colleagues, and past history of the facility and its operations. Direct customer research may include customer surveys and focus groups. The industry is constantly evolving and the marketing manager who simply does what has always been done will quickly fall behind. Social media is a perfect example of a continually changing marketing medium. Not only must marketing managers track constantly emerging social media channels, they must also determine which is the most effective for reaching their target audience. The successful marketing manager continually searches for creative methods for maximizing resources and attracting attention for their facility, tenants, or services. The creative use of social media and the creation of additional sales and marketing opportunities through existing partnerships can generate meaningful results for those willing to think outside the box.

Competition is tremendous for customers' discretionary income, program participants, clients, fans, sponsors, and events. Every organization is looking for an edge and, as a result, there will always be a demand for a creative facility marketing professional who can support the mission of the organization while helping to achieve its goals.

revenue increase was anticipated even though the seating capacity was reduced from 57,000-plus to 45,000. The lowest ticket price was increased from $5 to $12, and the highest ticket price jumped from $117 per game to $495 per game. Although the number of luxury suites increased by only a few (from 45 to 54), the price increased considerably to close to $500,000 for some suites. The main reason is that the suites were moved from the outfield to right above the action. Other major revenue streams included expanding restaurant seating capacity from 500 to 3,100, doubling the size of the stadium store, and building more concession points of sale—all in an effort to generate additional revenue (Massey, 2008).

Before undertaking the process of developing a marketing program, a facility needs to conduct a marketing inventory, which is an examination of all the various experiences and goods the facility can sell or give away. A facility also needs to know what is involved in marketing. Marketing is often examined in terms of positioning a product or service according to the **four Ps**: product, place, price, and promotion. Some marketing experts add a fifth P to the list: public relations (Mullin, Hardy, and Sutton, 1993). Other Ps that are used include publicity, people, position, payback, policy, partnership, and professional connections. Thus, some marketing executives reference the five P's or even more Ps. Although this text focuses on the four Ps, it is important to note that new strategies are being articulated on a regular basis,

such as partnerships in which companies work together to promote strategies. Companies might have been engaged in this approach for years, but only recently have academicians and practitioners started exploring these relationships to best leverage how partnerships can help both sides.

Product

Product is what the facility has to offer to its prospective customers, users, clients, or constituents. A product can be an idea, a service, or goods (e.g., the goods that are sold in facility concession stands or a health bar). Products can also include the facility itself, the teams that play in the facility, and the events held by and within the facility. For example, a stadium can be a product, but when several stadiums join together they can become an even stronger product. That is what happened when several National Football League (NFL) stadiums formed the Gridiron Stadium Network. The network was created to entice the promoters of major music events and other opportunities to negotiate with multiple possible stops rather than negotiate with each stadium individually.

Unlike consumer goods such as soap, soft drinks, or motor oil, the products offered by sport facilities can change daily. Most sport facility customers are not comparing two products (e.g., two bars of soap) that may differ only in the packaging (e.g., the box and price). Sport facility customers are often comparing significantly different products. A New York Mets game is different each night, whether in outcome, opponent, or atmosphere. Furthermore, many Mets fans are very loyal and would not go to a Yankees game even though the facilities are not that far apart. This refers to brand or team loyalty, which exists in sports as well as other consumer products such as beers and cars. One health club may offer swimming and racquetball, while another club is more socially oriented or emphasizes weights and machines. Each club would market itself differently depending on the **target market** for the service or goods offered. A target market is the group of potential customers the advertiser is trying to reach, as they will be more inclined to purchase the product. The target market is determined through the market segmentation process discussed later, in the marketing process section.

Facilities Trivia

Every facility wants raving fans. However, not all fans are created equal, and some can be a bigger problem than they are worth. On November 6, 1993, James Miller, who calls himself "the fan man," used a paraglider with a fan attached to hover over a heavyweight title bout between Riddick Bowe and Evander Holyfield at Caesars Palace outdoor pavilion in Las Vegas. Miller flew overhead at 800 feet (243.8 m) for around 20 minutes before he dove into the ring. His entrance delayed the fight 21 minutes while security took him away and removed the parachute that entangled a number of fans. Several months later he was arrested again after circling the Los Angeles Memorial Coliseum during a Raiders versus Broncos playoff game (Bathroom Readers' Institute, 2009).

Once the consumers are identified, the product can be grown through product extensions that make it more desirable. Product extensions are additions that enhance or improve a product. Extensions in sport marketing include additions that do not change the basic nature of the product but make it more appealing. This concept is often referred to as the sizzle, whereas the product itself is the steak (the **steak and sizzle**). For example, some people go to a football game to watch the game (the steak), whereas others may attend to enjoy the sizzle, which could include cheerleaders, dogs catching flying disks, drunk fans, mascots in the stands, and countless other sights and activities. Thus, someone who may not be as interested in the game could enjoy other activities and still have a good time.

Place

Place refers to where the product or service is sold or distributed. It also refers to how the product reaches customers, how quickly it reaches them, and the condition the product is in when it finally reaches the customers. In the facility context, place can refer to how convenient the facility is for customers. A facility that is located next to several freeway on- and off-ramps is more convenient for fans and users than one that is not. If convenience is a major motivator for the given fans and users, the marketing effort can emphasize this aspect.

Another example of place marketing is concession sales. If all fans have to go to permanent concession stands, it may become difficult to sell items if the lines are very long. This has prompted facilities to utilize multiple sale points and roving hawkers. Providing a more convenient place to purchase items generates more sales. With recent technological advances, more patrons are able to order their food and other services right from their seats through cell phones and other personal communication devices. Since many patrons want convenience, the facility can increase sales by making the place where the product is sold more convenient.

Price

Price can include numerous variables. For example, there may be admission, reservation, rental, program, or concession fees. There are also numerous pricing points, such as per day usage, membership rates, equipment rental fees, and family versus individual rates. Because it can be considered too high or too low at different times, price is always on trial in every marketplace. If a ticket price is too high, people may not purchase a ticket. If a ticket is too cheap, then customers may perceive the ticket as lacking in value. Thus, price is a major concern from a marketing perspective. It should be noted that sport and other recreation facilities are competing against other entertainment venues, from theaters to bowling alleys to bars. If someone regards the ticket price for a sport event as high or has limited funds, he may decide to forgo a game and instead go with friends to a bar where beers are $1.00 versus $6.00 at a game. For others the price is not a concern since they want to attend a game almost regardless of the cost. All this being said, marketing demands are not the only factors affecting price. It is also dictated by contract provisions setting a minimum price, by laws that specify taxes or charges, and most important by financing. If a facility makes its money exclusively from ticket sales, then the ticket price has to cover the cost of opening the doors and putting on the show.

The cost of doing business in sport facilities has soared over the past 20 years. In the late 1980s the Miami Arena was built for $89 million. In the late 1990s the Staples Center in Los Angeles and the American Airlines Center in Dallas were built for more than $450 million each. More recently, several stadiums were built in New York (Mets, Yankees, and joint Giants and Jets) and Dallas, with price tags around $1 billion each. But stadiums and arenas are not the only facilities facing higher costs. All facilities face higher costs, from construction to payroll to insurance. All these costs lead to increased prices for customers. However, if costs decrease, very few facilities or teams pass the savings on to the ultimate purchaser.

Price is affected by the concept of supply and demand. Supply and demand can create a higher value for a product if there is a small amount of the product and significant demand for it. This situation is often called a seller's market since sellers can ask what they want. The market for Super Bowl tickets is typically a seller's market. Since the supply is limited (only one game), scalpers can ask what they want for tickets. Because tickets to some championship events are scarce, the ticket may sell at the box office for one amount but be worth five times that amount the minute it is bought. Scalpers often engage in the supply side of the demand equation by purchasing tickets any way they can and then selling them at the market rate. But scalpers are not alone in their willingness to test the marketplace. Many professional and collegiate teams are now selling tickets on a per game basis according to the opponent, game date, or significance of a given game. Such a strategy maximizes the demand for key games, with increased prices helping to generate additional revenue for the team instead of allowing the scalpers to benefit. This process is being further refined as teams develop their own secondary market where fans can sell their unused tickets on a team's auction website. This service is in direct competition with second-party online ticket auctions.

Each pricing strategy needs to be specifically formulated to maximize revenue while minimizing potential backlash. The law of diminishing returns states that as prices increase, more customers may shy away from purchasing. It may be that customers want tickets and that the supply is sufficient but the price is too high, which can cause regular ticket buyers to pass on buying the more expensive tickets. Thus, while the revenue per customer increases, the total revenue will at some point decline because fewer customers will purchase the product.

One of the major advances in ticket pricing is dynamic ticket pricing. This approach moves away from the "one size fits all" pricing model and uses numerous variables to determine the best price for a given game ticket. Many teams and colleges have adopted this dynamic pricing model, including the St. Louis Cardinals. Using advanced computer programming linked to the team's ticketing system, the Cardinals adjust ticket prices up or down on a daily basis based on changing factors such as team performance, pitching matchups, weather, and ticket demand. The structure applies to the sale of individual-game tickets only and does not apply to the sale of season tickets. The dynamic pricing model proved to be a great benefit for fans. In 2012, 77%

of games had tickets available for $10 or less; 37% of games had tickets available for only $5 (St. Louis Cardinals, 2013).

Promotion

Promotion refers to the process of informing people about the product, price, and place. If a wonderful product is available at the right price and the right place, will it sell? What if the customers do not know about the quality of the item or its selling price? What if they want the product but cannot find it? These types of questions affect whether or not an item will sell. Promotion involves the effort required to market a product or service. The primary vehicles used to promote a service or product are advertising, publicity, and public relations.

Advertising

Advertising is a paid message designed to inform customers. It can include television, radio, newspaper, magazine, and countless other media. Internet advertising has gained popularity over the past decade, but sometimes the ultimate customers do not get the message because of clutter or noise in the communication channel. For example, do people really read or respond to pop-up ads, or do they feel violated by the unwelcome intrusion and purposely avoid doing business with the companies?

Advertising can also incorporate such methods as point-of-purchase displays that place a product at the end of a grocery store aisle for extra visibility. Thus, a display shaped like a race car, paid for by the product seller, can be positioned at the front of a store to maximize visibility and drive sales before a major race. Advertising can appear anywhere someone thinks a potential customer may be located. Elevators and urinals are two advertising locations that have been used more recently; the idea is that since people often spend close to a minute in these locations and are attempting not to make contact with others, these are great places for an advertising message.

Advertising traditionally has two objectives: to push a product, which encourages consumers to purchase a product, and to pull a product, where consumers are encouraged to ask retailers to stock a given product. Although some advertisements

FAN COST INDEX

It can be very expensive to take a family to an event. Team Marketing Report of Chicago produces a Fan Cost Index, which analyzes the cost for a family of four to attend games played by professional teams. The index showed that the average price for a family of four to attend a Major League Baseball (MLB) game in 2003 was $148.66. By 2008 the total had reached $191.92, and in 2013 the average cost was $210.46—a 41.5% increase in 10 years. However, this is significantly less than the average cost of attending an NFL game, which was $396.36 in 2008 and $443.80 in 2012—around a 12% increase in 4 years. The high price of NFL tickets might price many families out of the market. Also, advancing television technology has NFL teams concerned that many fans would rather stay home to watch a game. Comparisons in a given market could also be made. For example, in the Baltimore and Washington area, the average price for a family of four to go to various events (including game tickets, parking, concessions, a program, and a souvenir item) was as follows (Carter, 2003; "Fan Cost Index," 2008, 2013; Merda, 2013):

Team	Price in 2003	Price in 2008	Price in 2013
Washington Capitals (NHL)	$320	$245	$393
Washington Wizards (NBA)	$375	$195	$186
Baltimore Ravens (NFL)	$350	$426	$548
Washington Redskins (NFL)	$372	$441	$486
Baltimore Orioles (MLB)	$175	$165	$176
Washington Nationals (MLB)	Did not play	$196	$198

The highest-priced teams in North American professional sports according to the 2008 Fan Cost Index and the change in average price from 2008 to 2013 are as follows:

Team	Price in 2008	Price in 2013
Dallas Cowboys (NFL)	$759	$635
Montreal Canadiens (NHL)	$411	$616
New York Knicks (NBA)	$506	$660
Los Angeles Lakers (NBA)	$454	$489
Boston Red Sox (MLB)	$321	$337
New England Patriots (NFL)	$595	$292

Note that in 2008 the Dallas Cowboys had the highest Fan Cost Index in the NFL. They have since reduced some of their prices in their new stadium.

are designed specifically to inform people or promote what a company is doing, the ultimate goal of such advertisements is to promote the advertiser in a good light to help sell additional products in the future.

Publicity

Publicity is a facility's window to the public. It is referred to as "earned media" since it is unpaid and is disseminated based on its newsworthiness. Publicity is often derived through word of mouth, news releases, press conferences, editorial comments, and public service announcements (see "Potential Marketing Tools for a Sport Facility"). Each of these techniques is an added benefit that supports the marketing effort and does not cost any money. Word of mouth, for example, is invaluable. Happy customers tell others that they had a great experience, and this can often be the best promotion possible. On the other hand, if customers had a bad experience they will communicate their dissatisfaction. It is estimated that those who are happy with an experience will tell 2 people about it; if they are not happy, they will tell 10 people how bad the service or product was.

Publicity works by providing additional coverage. Some say it does not matter whether publicity is good or bad as long as it is publicity. This is not true. Positive publicity is great and can increase awareness and possibly patronage. Negative

FACILITY FOCUS

DODGER STADIUM ALL-YOU-CAN-EAT PAVILION

The right-field pavilion at Dodger Stadium used to be a barren wasteland with very little fan interest. In 2007 the Dodgers converted the area into a special section, giving around 3,000 fans unlimited hot dogs, peanuts, popcorn, nachos, and sodas. Tickets the first season were sold for $35 in advance and $40 on game day. Not every item is free: Beer, ice cream, and candy are sold separately at regular prices. The all-you-can-eat concept is rapidly spreading throughout baseball, allowing fans to buy a ticket and then eat as much food as they want. The ticket includes a buffet-style self-service area for some items. There are some limitations (e.g., the booth opens only 90 minutes before the first pitch and closes 2 hours after the game begins) (Los Angeles Dodgers, 2009).

For the 2009 season, the team dropped the ticket price down to $25 per game and obtained a sponsorship deal with AM/PM markets to sponsor the pavilion. Several games were not available in the plan, including games against top teams such as the Los Angeles Angels or Chicago Cubs and games with special promotional giveaways. In 2014 the Dodgers sold season tickets (83 games) to the all-you-can-eat section for $2,050, or about $25 per game; VIP tickets for the section were $3 more per game.

The team uses two concession counters below the bleachers. Shelves are stacked four high with nacho containers, ready to be whisked to fans' cardboard trays. At the touch of a red button, melted cheese comes oozing out. Because there is no cash exchange and fans are limited to four food items per visit, lines move very quickly.

Eating a lot is not relegated just to these all-you-can-eat locations. At Tropicana Field, the concessionaire

Centerplate offers a meal fit for a king . . . if you can eat it. In a takeoff of the show *Man v. Food,* the facility now sells an item called Fan v. Food. Florida fans can try to consume a 4.5-pound (2 kg) hamburger that includes four slices of cheese, half a pound (0.2 kg) of bacon, and 1 pound (0.4 kg) of french fries. The $30 dish is a bargain for those who complete it because they receive two free tickets to a future game, a T-shirt, and their picture on the wall. After 30 games in the 2009 season, only four fans had been able to successfully pass the gastronomical challenge (Muret, 2009a). Tropicana Field also offers a unique culinary experience and focus on freshness. Rather than concession stands it has 45 mini restaurants, each with a kitchen, so that every hamburger is prepared individually when a fan orders it.

publicity can destroy a facility. If a news story documents health concerns at a facility, a person concerned about unsatisfactory conditions will likely stay away from the facility. That is why "spin control" is such an important part of any promotion campaign. Everyone working in the facility is an ambassador and spokesperson for the facility as it relates to all interactions with fans and constituents. Most facilities designate a specific person who can talk about facility issues with the media, but everyone can help a facility engage in damage control, often through a simple smile or saying "I'm sorry." Every facility should cultivate a culture in which customer service is the priority

because it is much easier to grow a relationship with an existing fan than to generate new fans.

The press will either help or harm a facility, so mastering the press is critical. For example, numerous facility spokespersons say, "No comment," to a question by the press. This type of response can appear to be an admission of guilt, even if the facility did nothing wrong. If spokespersons say instead that they are looking into the matter and will contact the media immediately upon learning what happened, this type of response is not newsworthy and will probably not lead to a negative story. Some of the other "secrets" for dealing with the media include understanding publishing deadlines, knowing how to contact key reporters, meeting with reporters before any problems arise so that reporters know the facility and facility management, being brief with the media, never trying to sell the media tickets to an event, and creating a contact list with the names and numbers of all the facility officials (Wilkinson, 1988).

If a facility plans to close one entrance gate for an event, it is a good idea to communicate this decision to the general public to avoid any confusion. The facility may want to produce and post closing signs as well as purchase advertisements in newspapers, on radio, or on television. Another approach is to ask radio stations to play a public service announcement about the gate closure. Advertising and publicity, in other words, can communicate this information.

Public Relations

A blend of advertising and publicity, **public relations** entails trying to reach out to the public with a positive message. A health club may advertise that it is giving away memberships for free to the elderly to encourage their physical activity. Through television, radio, or newspaper advertising, and by trying to get a story printed in the paper, the health club is engaging in public relations. If seniors do come, they may bring others who are not qualified for the free membership and encourage them to join also. The purpose is to put forward a good public image and hopefully grow the customer base.

THE MARKETING PROCESS

Everyone has heard the saying that the customer is always right. Customers are the primary focus of any facility, so it is crucial to know who they are. Without members, a gym or health club would have a hard time staying open. A stadium or arena needs fans to generate income. Thus, facility managers need to focus on attracting fans or customers to their facilities. Some facilities—sportsplexes, for example—have multiple customers, such as spectators and participants. A sportsplex manager needs to develop multiple marketing approaches to attract these two different types of customers. No matter who is being courted as a customer, a facility manager needs to develop a strategy to reach the right people and get them to the facility. The right customers will hopefully be reached through the marketing process.

Identifying Customers

The key to a facility's marketing efforts is identifying and communicating with a target market. There are numerous potential customers, but

---

POTENTIAL MARKETING TOOLS FOR A SPORT FACILITY

- Publication of the marketing vision (using a slogan such as "Let's sell out the joint!")
- Business cards and company letterhead
- Brochures
- Newsletters
- Published surveys
- Press packets with media credentials, a media guide, pictures, statistics, and so on
- Signage, including logos
- Personal history endorsements from athletes, coaches, or fans indicating why they love the facility
- Coupons
- Bumper and other stickers
- Websites
- Customer awards
- Attempted world records
- Employee-of-the-month awards that introduce fans to marquee employees, such as vendors who use tricks or devices to get the crowd involved
- Newspaper, television, and radio advertisements
- Fliers
- Posters
- Bulletin boards
- Word of mouth
- Public service announcements
- Press releases

there are fewer potential customers interested in a given sport facility. A facility needs to find the customers who are the most likely to attend an event at the facility and can afford to attend. Market segmentation is the process of examining who will want to use or purchase a given product. Once the people who may want to purchase the product are identified, marketing efforts can focus on advertising or promoting the product to that group. This process is called positioning the product. All products need to be positioned in the mind of the consumer who will use or purchase the product. Sport is normally not a necessity. This creates a challenge for the marketer; it is not as easy to market sport as it is to market a necessity. For example, gas stations rarely advertise to encourage people to buy their primary product, gas, because just about everyone needs gas. Instead, gas stations advertise to encourage people to pick one gas station over another based on service attributes or lower prices. Since sport is not a necessity, a sport organization or facility has to position itself to fill a customer need in order to encourage participation or purchase.

Sport can fill the need for art, relaxation, recreation, entertainment, pleasure, loyalty, and companionship. For example, Fenway Park in Boston is positioned as a sport experience. The field is historic. "The Green Monster" is very well known and has an aura all its own. The Boston Red Sox can market to out-of-towners the fact that they are engulfed in history when attending a game. However, this same positioning strategy cannot be used for season ticket holders since they are more interested in enjoyment or in seeing the team win. Thus, in sport facility marketing, numerous positioning efforts need to be undertaken simultaneously. Once a facility determines how it wants to position itself (i.e., its product), it can examine the potential individuals who may fit the newly positioned product. For a smaller facility such as a health club, if the product is a relaxing exercise environment that prohibits skimpy workout clothing, the product is ideally positioned to reach senior or less active segments of the market who might be turned off by revealing or seeing too much skin. This process can be accomplished through market segmentation.

Research

One of the keys to successful marketing is research. To successfully market a facility or event, both the event or facility and the intended market need to be analyzed. Thus, the first step requires the facility to examine itself—its strengths, weaknesses, opportunities, and threats (SWOT analysis). The first two elements, strengths and weaknesses, are internal issues; the last two, opportunities and threats, are external. Strengths can include a great facility, good employees, strong events or tenants, a supportive political environment, and possibly good access to transportation. Weaknesses could include the lack of good seating, poor tenant contracts, lack of star athletes on tenant teams, poor sight lines, and few advertisers. Opportunities can include the prospects of attracting new events, community growth, lower potential taxes, and a possible bond to finance building a new stadium. Threats could include a new facility opening in the area, an economic downturn, a players' strike, or sponsors leaving a facility because of changed marketing strategies.

Although used for planning purposes, the SWOT analysis is just as important for marketing purposes. A facility needs to market its strengths, attack its weaknesses, seize opportunities, and anticipate threats. Concerns and opportunities are identified through research. There are two types of data: primary and secondary. Primary data are obtained by the facility itself through surveys or other means. Secondary data are obtained through research and publications produced by second parties. Both primary and secondary data can help shape how a facility will market itself. Assume that a college is going to build a new fitness center for its students. The athletic director could possibly decide herself what should be in the facility, but involvement of students, especially if they have to pay the bill, is critical. Thus, the primary data could come from surveys of students in the cafeteria and in the current athletic facility to see what they want. It may be determined after conducting several hundred interviews that the students primarily want swimming, basketball, aerobics, weights, and a climbing wall. The college conducts some additional research (secondary research) and discovers that a recent study reviewed the problems with climbing walls. Based on both the primary and secondary information and the allowed budget, the facility is designed to meet all the major preferences of the students except for the climbing wall.

Research has become the key for stadium marketing efforts. Many people feel that marketing is all about developing fancy advertising campaigns. In reality, top marketing officials now focus on data. "Big data," the analysis of a large amount of data such as all concession sales at a stadium, is driving all marketing decisions. For example, social media allows advertisers to determine who is looking at their advertisements, where they are from, what else they have viewed online, and so on, and this information can help pinpoint more appropriate marketing investments to target the right people. This helps position the product to those who are most likely to purchase it.

Positioning

A **market** is a group of actual or potential customers for a given product. These people have various attributes; the primary attributes are the ability to purchase a product such as a ticket to a game, willingness to buy the ticket, and the authority to make the purchase decision. Children may not fit into the ticket purchasing market segment because they do not have the money or authority to purchase a ticket. Nonetheless, children can have a major influence on someone who is in the market segment, such as a mother or father interested in taking a child to an event or facility. People who fit into the market segment need to be identifiable, significant in number, likely to respond to a marketing campaign, accessible, and measurable.

Methods of segmenting the market include demographic, psychographic, benefit, and geodemographic segmentation. **Demographics** refers to variables associated with people who may want to purchase the product such as age, sex, race, nationality, residency (area the person lives in), and income level. Location, for instance, is a major concern for health clubs. Most health clubs do not anticipate drawing people who live 100 miles (160 km) away, so marketing efforts should not be directed toward those people. Any market segment needs to have a certain size and have the

ability to purchase the product. Some companies market exclusively to women with the idea that they may make more purchasing decisions in the house than men. A product that is marketed to children may be difficult to sell if children do not have a say in the purchase decision.

Psychographics refers to people's actions and thought processes. It attempts to get into the customers' heads to determine how they make decisions. These decision factors can be used in marketing to motivate similar consumers to buy the product or service in the future. Why does someone buy beer at a stadium—to get drunk, to enjoy time with friends, or because he is succumbing to social pressure? These questions and their answers are very important. If the answers show that fans are drinking because it is considered the appropriate activity to engage in during an event, then the product marketing effort will be significantly different from marketing to those who just want to party. The latter group may purchase beer regardless of the cost. When profits from beer sales can reach 400% at a stadium, the marketing decision can be significant.

Benefit segmentation analyzes what benefit someone wants to receive from the product or service. If women want to work out without having men around, then they may want a health club for women only. An exclusive all-women's health club has a benefit that would be attractive to these consumers. If consumers express interest in a given benefit, marketers will find a way to reach and sell to these individuals if they represent a large enough group willing and eager to spend money.

Geodemographic segmentation looks at customers and potential customers based on where they live or do business. A team that wants to sell tickets to the wealthiest people in a community can identify the wealthiest neighborhoods, look up the zip codes, buy a mailing list that covers those zip codes, and then send the marketing materials to those people.

Regardless of the segment targeted, the marketing strategy needs to communicate a message that appeals to the potential buyer. In sport the buyer typically does not look for a single result such as a win or not having to spend too much time in the parking lot when trying to get home. In sport a buyer is often looking for an experience.

FACILITY FOCUS

MARKETING AND SALES FOR WORK OUT WORLD

Work Out World (WOW) is a family-owned and -operated chain of fitness centers. WOW is always looking for ways to increase membership and keep current members. In October 2001, a WOW center opened in Freehold, New Jersey. The 25,000-square-foot (2,320 sq m) center opened in a location that had previously housed a movie theater. WOW Freehold offers fitness services including group fitness classes, strength and cardio equipment, one-on-one personal training, fitness testing, chiropractic services, free child care, and many others. By 2014 there were 10 WOW facilities in New Jersey.

A unique feature of WOW Freehold—one that has increased female membership—is a private, ladies-only fitness area. Female members can access the ladies-only area directly from the locker room. There are also two private doors that lead into the regular fitness center. Two other special features that have attracted members to WOW Freehold are the physical therapy center and the cardiac fitness rehab center (McDonnell, 2004).

"WOWing" potential members is part of WOW's marketing strategy. The marketing plan includes a monthly direct mail program with a 7-day free pass. Internet users can receive a guest pass when they register online. Also, WOW markets itself with in-person promotions at local businesses, community events, corporate health fairs, and other events. Some of the marketing items WOW Freehold uses are coins, glasses, pizza boxes, and dollar bills. When you become a WOW member you are granted, among other benefits, access to all WOW fitness centers in New Jersey, four free personal training sessions, and ongoing monthly fitness evaluations and assessments. WOW also offers many programs to keep members happy and coming back. When members sign up they are given a guidebook about the facility called *WOW Discovery*. They are also given e-mail coaching, which provides fitness information to help members reach their fitness goals. A monthly newsletter, *WOW Squeeze*, informs members about club happenings and contests (McDonnell, 2004).

WOW's success led to the formation of the WOW Foundation, which focuses on helping the local community, giving opportunities to school-age students and teachers, and writing a health and fitness newsletter for kids throughout New Jersey (WOW, 2009). However, with success comes competition. In 2014, WOW offered memberships for no money down and $19.95 a month and allowing members to use any WOW facility in New Jersey. Planet Fitness, as an example, had in 2014 a no-contract rate of $10 per month covering several clubs in New Jersey.

Selling Experiences

Statistics show that the average family saves for 2 to 3 years for a trip to Disney World. The reason people save for so long is that the trip is a memorable experience, and they want to have enough money to derive the utmost enjoyment from it (Coleman, 2000). Experience can include passive participation—just sitting in a seat—or active participation through involvement in a total experience. By marketing toward an active participant, a facility increases its chances of attracting new customers interested in receiving an enhanced experience. A total experience consists of a number of components—aesthetic, educational, escapist, and entertainment.

Aesthetic experiences have to do with immersing fans in an environment full of sights, sounds, smells, touch, and tastes. The focus is on the sensory thrill of being at an event (Coleman, 2000). The smell of popcorn or hot dogs is an excellent example, as people remember a facility by the smells and tastes they associate with the facility.

Food is only one element in the experience of a facility, game, or event. Everything from highbrow business meeting facilities to Internet access, cigar humidors, unusually comfortable seats, and hard-core cheering sections enhances the facility experience. These elements are offered because the facility is no longer just selling a team or event but is providing an experience.

Sporting events also include an educational element. Fans can see a memorabilia display and learn about the team or how the facility was built. This gives the fans a better feel for the facility in that it allows them to appreciate the hard work that went into building it.

The escapist realm involves immersing fans in the aesthetic and educational components. An escapist effect is achieved when fans participate in activities such as in-game promotions, go into batting cages, meet players, and do similar activities that involve them physically in the experience. The last component of the total experience is entertainment, which focuses on making the facility or event the most personal experience possible. To successfully sell an experience, each experience needs to be customized. For example, themed restaurants such as Hard Rock Cafe or Dan Marino's use the experience they offer to highlight a theme and a feeling that resonates through the activity of dining (Coleman, 2000). Other strategies include harmonizing impressions with positive cues (cleanliness, friendliness, fun), eliminating negative cues (dirt, bad smells), mixing in memorabilia, engaging a fan's senses, and training employees to support the impressions.

Food

Although a sporting event in a facility is the main attraction, almost all fans will say that their food experience also influences the quality of the event. In the past, fans were often content with a hot dog and beer. However, as times have changed, the palates of fans have also changed. Product evolution has been growing to match the growing fan sophistication. Fans' food preferences also vary by region (see "Culinary Treats Around the United States"). People want the food service to be clean and friendly, and they want their food fast but also of the highest quality. Fans do not want long lines, untrained staff, inadequate numbers of staff behind the counter, confusing or misleading signs, and an insufficient number of service points (Galloway, 2001).

The outfield in AT&T Park in San Francisco was designed so kids could reach the counters, sold packages that resembled McDonald's Happy Meals with small entrees, fries, a soda, and a small toy (Finken, 2001). The baseball fans in St. Louis and Kansas City used to be able to buy a ticket behind home plate for $15, but now the cost is $120. However, people sitting in these seats get unlimited food and drinks. The craze for unlimited food quickly spread to other clubs and teams, who were able to sell previously hard-to-sell seats at a steep profit by offering all-you-can-eat opportunities. (See the Facility Focus for Dodger Stadium as an example.) Research has helped highlight how much a typical fan can eat, and even with an all-you-can-eat menu the teams have priced the tickets at a point where they are making a significant profit.

Food and other concession items are closely analyzed by facility managers because of the high profit margin from these items. New items are constantly being added at different price points (i.e., $3.99, $4.50, $4.99, and so on) to see what the market will bear. A facility marketer needs to closely monitor food trends to maximize the potential food sales. Thus, if the population switches to special diets such as vegetarian or kosher cuisine, the facility needs to quickly adapt to the changes or face significant lost sales. For example, many concession stands now sell vegetarian food at a significant premium and have added numerous healthy options such as salads, fresh fruit, and skinless chicken. However, although appetites may change, there is a constant need for liquid refreshments such as beer, soda, and water.

CULINARY TREATS AT STADIUMS AROUND THE UNITED STATES

- Baltimore Orioles Birdland Dog: a hot dog covered with charcoal-grilled beef, hash potatoes, pepperoni, onion rings, and tomato relish
- Cincinnati Reds Cheese Coney: a hot dog covered in chili, cheddar cheese, onions, and mustard
- Colorado Rockies Rocky Mountain Oysters: breaded and deep-fried bull testicles
- Detroit Lions Victory Knot: a 2-pound (0.9 km) soft pretzel with three sauces (beer cheese, spicy mustard, and sweet cream cheese)

- Philadelphia Phillies Schmitter: a sandwich with fried salami, steak, three slices of cheese, fried onions, tomatoes, and a special sauce.
- New York Mets "Shack-cago" Dog: a hot dog with Rick's Picks Shake Shack relish, onion, cucumber, pickle, tomato, pepper, and celery salt
- Texas Rangers: a 2-foot-long (0.6 m) taco that sells for $26

Incentives and Giveaways

Fans can also have their experience enhanced through incentive programs. Several companies currently produce swipe cards that allow a facility or team to provide added benefits to frequent fans. When fans enter the facility, they can swipe their membership cards and receive coupons or other discounts based on the number of games they have attended. These programs are often part of a **customer relationship management (CRM)** program (McGlynn, 2001). The systems build fan support but also serve to obtain valuable information about fans such as when they visit, what they purchase, and other psychographic elements. More and more facilities are combining customer relationship management programs with discounts and even global positioning system tracking. For example, when a fan walks by a concession stand, she might receive a text stating that she can get a discount if she buys something right now at the concession stand.

The potential giveaways are limitless. Examples include baseballs, T-shirts, autographed items, bobblehead dolls, beanbag toys, collectible cards, free drinks and food, free tickets, school supplies, and countless other personal or household items. The Birmingham Barons, a minor league baseball team, worked with Roto-Rooter to give away special bathroom plungers that bore the Barons and Roto-Rooter logos and phone numbers. This innovative giveaway provided 1,500 homes with plungers and a phone number if the plunger was not able to clear the line (Vertical Alliance's Sports Marketing Newsletter, 2004). Some options leave the fans scratching their heads. For example, in 2013 the Mariners gave away beard hats, the Cubs gave away toiletry sets, and the Dodgers gave away Hello Kitty bobblehead dolls. These unique giveaways might attract new customers, but also could possibly turn-off die-hard fans.

FACILITY MARKETING

In addition to selling and marketing an event, a sport facility must sell itself in order to grow. A facility must market its tangible and intangible products and assets. Tangible assets can include its floor space, location, and seating configuration. Intangibles can include affiliation with an anchor tenant, being the only large facility in a location, and satisfying a city's need to have a big-time sport facility.

Significant effort needs to be devoted to marketing a facility, not just for the end users or fans but also for those who will support the facility. Supporters can range from politicians to anchor tenants. Through aggressive marketing campaigns, several cities have been able to win an anchor team even though they may not have had the largest potential market. Such was the case with Tampa Bay, which spent years marketing its almost vacant stadium to various MLB teams.

GIVEAWAYS AND SAFETY

Although it is important to entertain the crowd, care has to be taken to make sure fans are not injured. There are documented cases of people engaging in the dizzy bat promotions and getting injured when they later stumble to reach the finish line. Fans can also be injured in promotional events; a peanut vendor may throw a bag of nuts that hits someone in the head, and people can be injured when hot dogs or T-shirts are shot through air-pressurized cannons. Billy the Marlin, the Florida Marlins' mascot, along with the team, was sued by a fan who was hit in the eye by a fired rolled-up T-shirt. The fan sued the team for $250,000, and the jury, after deliberating for nearly 2 days, ruled in favor of the team ("Billy the Marlin," 2003). In 2009, a Kansas City Royals fan was hit in the eye by a foil-wrapped hot dog that the team mascot passed behind its back to a different fan. The injured fan, who suffered a detached retina, sued the team for his injuries, which included two eye surgeries. As of this writing, the case was still winding its way through the courts. The case was initially dismissed by a lower court, but in 2014 the Missouri Supreme Court sent the case back to be tried in court.

In a promotion at Bank One Ballpark, some anti-tobacco-campaign squeezable balls were tossed from the broadcasting booth during the seventh inning stretch. Some landed next to an older fan, and in an effort to obtain the balls the woman was knocked over by a zealous fan.

The woman needed surgery on her knees, and the team learned a valuable lesson. Although a promotion might be for a good cause, if there is a chance of injury the promotion should be cancelled or redesigned to eliminate the potential risks.

Additionally, all special events should be carefully analyzed to examine their potential effect on safety. A ball giveaway can possibly arm an entire stadium with projectiles that people can throw at each other or the players. One of the craziest promotions—and one that went far out of control—was the Cleveland Indians' 10-Cent Beer Night in 1974. More than 25,000 fans showed up for the game, and many were drunk before they even reached the stadium. The team made money selling an estimated 60,000 cups of beer (10 ounces [0.3 L] each). As early as the first inning, an explosion was heard in the stands. In the fourth inning, a nude man slid into second base. In the fifth inning, a father and son team jumped onto the field and mooned the crowd. With the game tied in the ninth inning, fans rushed the field and surrounded Texas Rangers slugger Jeff Burroughs, and punches were exchanged. Thousands of drunken fans poured onto the field and battled with police, players, and one another. Ultimately the game was called by the umpire, who himself was hit in the head with a chair (Hruby, 2002).

Finally, after an aggressive marketing campaign, the city won the rights to a new MLB franchise that was awarded in 1995 and started playing in Tropicana Field in 1998. An enormous effort was made by many in trying to land the future baseball team for the new stadium. Everyone from the mayor to lay civic leaders had a role in marketing the city and community to anyone who could possibly influence the decision to help attract a professional baseball team to Tampa Bay.

Marketing New Facilities

In the case of a new sport facility, facility managers must undertake significant marketing efforts to win over those who will be crucial for the project's success. In the earliest stages, this type of marketing targets existing and potential investors. Investors need to be informed about any changes that could affect the project and their investment. Once a facility is planned or under construction, however, the marketing emphasis switches to those who will use and surround the facility. For

example, local residents need to know what is going on and how the facility will affect them. Facility managers do not want to surprise residents with a completed plan, as this will almost always lead to backlash rather than support. Through press conferences, mailers, open houses, and other techniques, the local community can be educated about the facility.

Local politicians also need to be kept abreast of the facility's progress and plans. Marketing in this regard can include taking politicians on a tour of the facility. Although this is common and is a useful tool for marketing a facility and generating support, it can also border on unethical behavior. If politicians are influenced by such activity and support a project purely for their own gain, there could be potential legal and political problems. Ethical marketing goes beyond just trying to build a facility and determining whether the decision makers can be bribed to build a certain facility in one county versus another. Ethical issues also affect who may get the facility naming rights, construction contract, and management contract as well as whether beer or cigarette advertisements will be allowed in the facility. Any ethics breach can quickly lead to customer backlashes and voter distrust.

A central focus of a new facility's marketing campaign is developing the facility's identity. For example, the Toronto Blue Jays launched a contest to name their new facility. Numerous fans suggested the name SkyDome, so these contestants' names were put into a drawing and the winner received two season tickets for life. A facility's identity goes beyond just a name, however, often focusing on its image and reputation. How should the community and external entities perceive the facility? Will the facility be known as a health club for serious weightlifters or one for older people interested in cardiovascular rehabilitation? No marketing effort can be undertaken until the facility can establish or remake its identity. A facility can use market segmentation to position itself within the intended target market. This can be seen with Gold's Gym, which has heavily promoted shirts that show big muscles to highlight their emphasis on free weights and on helping people pump up their muscle mass. This strategy contrasts significantly with that of other gyms such as 24 Hour Fitness or LA Fitness, which highlight sexy people working on toned bodies with interval and machine workouts.

Attracting Anchor Tenants

Facilities also need to constantly market themselves to attract major tenants. A sport team at a stadium or arena is an anchor tenant. Anchor tenants can leave, or threaten to leave, and this pressure becomes a bargaining chip for better contractual terms. A facility can strengthen its position by constantly exploring potential tenant options. Facilities learn about potential new tenants from new owners, those wishing to relocate a team, or leagues interested in expanding into new markets. For example, in 2000 New Haven and Bridgeport, Connecticut, were battling to win a new Arena Football League 2 (AFL2) franchise. The AFL had awarded a franchise to the area, and both markets were actively pursuing the team. New Haven won the bidding battle in part by offering to pay all the marketing expenses for the team. Bridgeport lost the bidding war but designed the arena it was building without a center scoreboard anyway in case the team ever decided to move from New Haven to Bridgeport, about 15 miles (24 km) away. After only two seasons the New Haven Coliseum closed. The AFL2 team, having lost its home, attempted to negotiate with Bridgeport to move the team. Those negotiations broke down, and the team folded. With no prospect for an arena football league team, the arena installed a center-hung scoreboard in 2012. That scoreboard allowed existing tenants such as the AHL's Bridgeport Sound Tigers to generate more revenue from scoreboard-related advertising.

Current tenants can be kept happy if they are provided with lucrative contractual terms such as controlling a facility schedule or being allowed to keep all the revenue from parking or naming rights. There is no one method to keeping a tenant or event promoter happy. However, complying with the contractual terms and keeping the facility in good condition are keys to keeping both parties satisfied with the contractual relationship.

It is not enough just to land a major tenant for a sport facility. The facility needs to keep promoting and marketing itself to its current and future tenants or events. Once a primary tenant is landed, it is usually easier to attract other events and tenants, especially if the primary tenant is successful. Some markets are not strong sport markets. For example, minor league baseball and hockey have traditionally had a tough time succeeding in New Haven. A new team would be reluctant to consider coming to New Haven unless an established team or facility had already proven that the market can support the entity. That is why community support is so critical to a facility project.

Attracting Events

A facility can make money only if activities are going on in the facility. With a large stadium or arena, revenue can be generated by attracting shows, concerts, conventions, theatrical productions, and sporting events. Small facilities may not be able to draw such events but can hold special events such as fund-raisers, recitals, community plays, and other smaller events that generate revenue and increase exposure without incurring significant cost.

The first step is determining what events should be brought in and what events should be excluded. An arena may be very interested in attracting a circus, for example, but may find the demographics or security concerns associated with a rock or rap concert undesirable. Other events may be rejected because of political pressure, among other factors. A facility on the campus of a religious school would probably be marketed to a significantly different group of potential events than a public facility. Once an acceptable event has been identified, the event needs to be booked.

Booking is the actual contracting of an act or event in the facility. The booking process secures specific space for a specific date and time for an agreed amount of compensation. Booking can occur only if the facility is available, but it entails more than just checking availability. A facility needs to assess an event's quality, the terms of the contract, a promoter's reputation, and other variables. A facility can also co-promote an event, but unless the show is very well known and has strong ticket sales, such a relationship is unusual.

Scheduling refers to identifying and securing the specific dates and times for the event. All marketing efforts to attract additional events revolve around the scheduling needs of the anchor tenant. No matter how much a facility and event want to work together, if the space is being used by an anchor tenant such as a professional team, the event cannot proceed. Typically, facilities utilize diverse scheduling to provide the best mix of events. A facility will have a hard time marketing 15 concerts in a 2-week period compared with different events that attract different crowds each night. Different events bring different spectators. A family event may generate more food sales, while a hockey game could generate more beer sales. Booking leverages the scheduling process to maximize revenue.

A facility manager needs to identify the facility's goals and objectives to make sure that the marketing and booking efforts comply with those goals and objectives. If a facility is in charge of bringing nightlife to a city, then more night events may be scheduled. However, the tenant often makes such decisions, especially if it is a professional sport team with a broadcasting agreement to air games at night. Competitive seasons and touring schedules also affect a facility manager's ability to attract certain events. Regardless of what it is, once the event is set, the facility manager and the marketing staff, along with the event's marketing staff, must coordinate their efforts to maximize ticket sales. These efforts will be directed at individual ticket buyers and often at groups, who represent the greatest opportunity to sell more tickets with the least amount of effort.

Developing Relationships

Part of the selling process entails developing relationships. Relationships need to be developed both with teams or acts and with promoters. A promotions company such as Live Nation manages numerous facilities and events and can help determine what events (e.g., concerts) will play in what cities based on booking patterns and dates. This does not mean that a facility will be excluded from potential dates, but if a relationship is developed, event dates can be coordinated to help benefit all facilities. By developing strong relationships, facility management can schedule competing events such as circuses, which may play at different times of the year and appeal to different patrons (e.g., Cirque du Soleil versus Ringling Bros.).

Often smaller facilities also need to attract new members and retain existing members. In health clubs, especially, customer turnover is a constant concern. Some larger clubs are constantly advertising to attract new members but are not marketing enough to existing customers. This creates a revolving door of clients and promotes little goodwill or loyalty. Facilities can minimize loss of patrons by developing relationships through surveying and interviewing fans or patrons to determine what they want from the facility and then providing it, within limits. Thus, making patrons part of the process helps create a bond that can make them believe they are respected, which can lead to very loyal customers.

Facility managers need to cultivate numerous relationships. Having an event sign a long-term contract is one of the primary goals for a booking specialist. If events sign only short-term contracts, the facility is constantly working to attract new events. This is much less desirable than knowing that particular events will be coming back every

One of the prime marketing locations for promoting a sponsor is the scoreboard.

year. Some acts enter into a long-term contract to obtain a better price. A facility may charge an event 10% of the gross receipts if it is a one-time show. In contrast, if a well-known event signs a 15-year agreement, the facility may charge only 5% of the gross receipts.

SALES

The purpose of facility marketing efforts typically focuses on selling items or experiences. It is not enough that people know about a facility; the goal is for them to go to the facility as customers. This process involves identifying potential purchasers, communicating the value of going to the facility, and then closing the deal by having them buy tickets. The sales process aims at completing the marketing process by having the customer decide that the price and timing are right to make a purchase. Many variables enter into closing the marketing process with a sale. Timing, standings, special events, giveaways, price options, and other variables can help finalize the sale.

Whether through the Internet, mass mailings, or personal selling, sales is the primary entry point for many people working in the industry. Those who can sell, especially in person, will always have a job selling sport related assets.

When research indicates who is the ideal customer, a relationship can be developed with that customer and numbers might finalize a deal. However, a relationship can also finalize a contract with otherwise uninterested or unconvinced customers.

For many, the marketing process ends with selling a ticket, product, or membership, but most executives would disagree and would argue that the marketing process is only partially completed with the sale. After the sale, the marketing effort needs to continue to make sure that the customer has a good experience, as cognitive dissonance (buyer's remorse) can kill future buying from the same customer. For example, a fan could have a miserable time at a facility. That fan might never return. However, if management knows the fan had a bad time, management can take a proactive step to win back the fan. Maybe the fan can be offered a free ticket to a future game or some other incentive. One minor league baseball team executive carries around the stadium numerous single dollar bills. Whenever he hears someone complain about parking, he offers to refund the several dollars it cost to park at the stadium. Even though the city receives the parking revenue, he believes it is more important to make the fans happy so they will come back to another game regardless of the parking hassle. In fact, most fans who receive such funds spend them at the facility and tell others about how the team executive was looking out for their best interests. Such a small act can create intense customer loyalty.

Commercial rights, such as sponsorship and signage, or naming and pouring rights, which are both discussed later in this chapter, are all assets that can be sold by the facility to generate funds. Most facilities built in the past 25 years for professional or collegiate teams (and even some high schools) have sold naming rights, luxury suites, or other assets. Some assets, such as the naming rights for a facility or a sponsorship designation, are intangible. Other assets are real, such as tickets, luxury boxes, or even the old basketball floor at a famous arena.

Ticketing

Professional and collegiate sport teams generate revenue primarily from broadcast rights and ticket sales. Tickets are a consistent revenue source when a team has a die-hard following. Teams with a weak fan base have a harder time generating revenue from ticket sales. This has led to mini season ticket and specialty game packages designed to attract infrequent fans. No matter how many tickets or what types of tickets are sold, facilities need to develop a ticket inventory and then sell the inventory. This requires computer-based systems that can communicate between various ticket-selling locations such as team stores and ticket outlets. With computer-based systems, each ticket seller knows what tickets are available (ticket inventory) and can print tickets.

Ticket sales have changed with new marketing techniques. For example, years ago the only means to buy a ticket was to obtain a hard copy of a single game ticket. Now fans can buy tickets online (as discussed later), purchase luxury suites that often require tickets, or obtain personal seat licenses. With a broad range of seating options available, a facility has to carefully examine pricing strategies and ticket delivery options.

Seat Pricing

Tickets have increased significantly in cost over the past 50 years. A seat at Dodger Stadium cost $3.50 per game in 1962 and had increased to $31.00 per game by 2000—a 785.7% increase. However, by 2013 the average price had declined to $22.37 as many fans were being priced out of buying tickets and attendance started declining. Figure 11.1 illustrates the pricing trends for basketball (NBA), football (NFL), hockey (NHL), and baseball (MLB) from 1991 through 2013. Baseball has been relatively inexpensive compared with other sports because of a larger ticket inventory based on more seats in a facility and a large number of games. In the NFL there are only a few games each year, and every game has potential playoff ramifications. The concept of supply and demand and the law of diminishing returns both affect the price for tickets.

Pricing, though, should not be examined in a vacuum. Many collegiate football programs charge significantly less for student tickets. This is designed to accomplish two primary missions. One is to reward the students who are helping to underwrite the athletic programs through increased tuition or fees. The second is to develop a strong following so that when the students become alumni they will remain dedicated fans willing to pay a higher price for tickets and hopefully donate back to the program at a later date. Similarly, professional teams often give free tickets to fans they want to attract to buy season packages, personal seat licenses, or luxury seats.

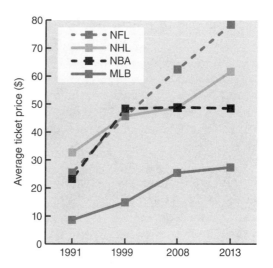

Figure 11.1 Average league ticket prices from 1991 through 2013.

Data from *NBA Ticket Prices* 1999; *Team Marketing Report* 2009, and various articles over the years.

A small investment in free tickets can generate goodwill and larger future sales. It should be noted that free tickets to events may not necessarily be free if the tickets are taxed and the facility or team needs to pay a set tax per ticket.

Other parties can also dictate ticket prices. If the team or facility sets the ticket price, the process is called house scale. If a promoter indicates that tickets have to be sold at a given face value, this is called performance scale. Either option is usable at the box office, but ticket prices also must take into account any surcharges for Ticketron or other outlets and the various taxes that may need to be charged.

Ticketing Methods

The technological advancements of the Internet provide venues and ticket-selling organizations an innovative way to sell tickets. The goal is to make ticket purchasing fast and easy for consumers. Selling online has created a new opportunity to reach consumers and establish relationships. Similar to airline tickets, many stadiums and arenas are now making paperless tickets an option, purchased and sent electronically to a specific phone number or email address. Once at the facility the phone is placed next to a scanner to open the turnstile.

Veritix, a company owned by Cleveland Cavaliers owner Dan Gilbert, and other companies such as Ticketmaster and Tickets.com have significantly promoted paperless ticketing, which allows teams and events to cut ticketing costs, provides new revenue streams from coupons and loyalty programs, and generates valuable sales lead data. A Veritix subsidiary created a process in which a person buying a digital ticket registers a form of identification that is used in lieu of a ticket to enter games. This means that secondary sales must occur via a medium controlled by a team, which eliminates ticket scalping. Similar technology is used internationally by soccer clubs to monitor who is buying tickets and to eliminate some possible concerns associated with hooligans.

Tickets can be sold in various forms. However, the regular paper ticket is still the primary means by which many people attend an event or facility. Thus, one of the important managerial components for any facility with a ticketing revenue source is box office management. The box office represents the connection between the facility and the fans and needs to be managed appropriately to avoid upset clients, disappointed fans, and lost revenue. The box office is responsible for helping to determine what types of tickets will be sold for an event. Will there be general admission, along with all the problems associated with people pushing for the best seat they can find, or will the event have reserved seating? Can tickets be ordered over the phone and picked up at the will-call window? How will entry passes be distributed to the media? Are the box office attendants trained to answer questions beyond those about tickets? How many ticket booths will be used, and where will they be located to ease congestion and reduce lines? Who will establish the appropriate ticket prices and the taxes charged on the tickets?

The San Francisco Giants developed a resale system whereby their season ticket holders can resell tickets on the Internet. A season ticket holder can post unwanted tickets on the Giants' website, and people wishing to purchase tickets can buy them online. At the end of the year, season ticket holders will have fewer unused and unsold tickets and hopefully renew for the next season. Other teams have developed similar systems to help cut out the middleman or scalper.

New techniques and strategies are being developed around dynamic pricing, including the "purple pricing" strategy used by Northwestern University for the 2013-2014 season. Under this strategy, the tickets for the Ohio State and Penn State games (the final two home games of the year) would not have a set price but rather would start at a certain amount at the beginning of the ticket sale season and then change according to demand as the dates of the games approached. Anyone who bought a ticket at a price that was later reduced would be refunded the difference of the final price offered for the game. Conversely, fans who delayed purchasing a ticket could end up paying significantly more than early purchasers and would not be compensated for the price increase. For example, if the price for a 200-level ticket started at $25 and was later reduced to $20, the buyer would be refunded the $5 difference (Rossman-Reich, 2013). If the demand for the event was high, that same ticket could increase in price to $100 or more if purchased closer to the event date. The ticket cost of the Northwestern versus Ohio State basketball game decreased to $38 by game day, which means that those who bought tickets for $70 received a refund of $32 the following day. Such an approach reduces the hard feeling of those who buy tickets at a higher price and then see low-price tickets flood the market. And, if someone buys tickets at the initial price and the demand for tickets skyrockets, they would get the benefit of the bargain.

Although scalpers are a reality, in most cases numerous laws restrict their activities. Some laws limit the premium that can be charged over the issue price; other laws limit where scalpers can sell tickets. A facility manager needs to work with local law enforcement to enforce the law but still allow legitimate fans the opportunity to sell extra tickets. The online exchanges developed by teams such as the Giants allow ticket holders to sell tickets without risking arrest or losing the right to buy future tickets. One of the most powerful ticket resellers is StubHub.com, which is owned by eBay. StubHub has created numerous strategic relationships, but many teams have established their own reselling networks and bar fans from selling with anyone else.

Luxury Seating

Luxury boxes and suites are often several hundred square feet of paradise. Offering scaled-down furniture to make the suites look larger, these mini high-tech centers provide luxury for those who can afford it. Besides containing normally 12 to 16 seats, the suites or boxes also offer televisions, fireplaces, pool tables, video games, and premier food services (Dorsey, 2001). Part of the appeal associated with the luxury suites is that they are a place to be and to be seen. With corporate America playing a major role in sport facilities, the amount of money spent on luxury suites and seating areas is one of the cash cows for sport facilities. Spectators at an arena or stadium may spend on average $7 to $8 per capita (per person) on food; the per capita average for those in a luxury suite is around $30 (Dorsey, 1999). The cost associated with a luxury suite can range from $50,000 to more than $500,000 annually. The 146 suites at the American Airlines Center in

Dallas range in price from $150,000 to $250,000 for 5-, 7-, or 9-year leases. The suites come with touch-screen monitors, television monitors with live feed, wet bars, exclusive restrooms, private concourses, VIP parking, and concierge service (Dorsey, 2001). The suites were an integral component of financing the facility. The initial construction price was projected at $230 million but increased to $335 million due in part to major changes such as expanding the facility by 100,000 square feet (9,290 sq m), which increased the cost by $17.5 million. Dallas was obligated to pay $125 million of the total construction costs from hotel and car rental taxes ("American Airlines Center," 2001). The cost for a luxury suit in Dallas is a bargain as the new Yankee Stadium was selling suites for as much as $850,000 a year.

Personal seat licenses (PSLs) were first introduced in the 1980s at the Palace of Auburn Hills, Detroit; the facility was built with more than 100 suites and a number of club seats. It is estimated that PSLs helped raise more than $500 million for building stadiums and arenas in the 1990s (Hall, 2001). PSLs are designated seats for which a fan pays a premium and they are often in the most desirable locations of the facility. Fans often have to pay for the right to use the PSL (usually in long term leases for 5-10 years) and then also have to buy a game ticket for every game. PSLs are sold for basically all new facilities since the 1990s. On average, a new facility is built such that about 16% of the seats are premium seats (Dorsey, 1999).

The major difference in luxury seating is not just the seat location but also how much each seat can earn. Assume that a typical premium seat can generate ticket revenue of $75 versus $25 for an average ticket. The ticket income appears to be three times higher, but the actual number is much greater with the $30 expenditure on food and beverages. This is only the tip of the proverbial iceberg, as the holder of a $75 ticket will probably also pay for a seat license and is more likely to renew ticket contracts, spend more on merchandise, and have a business relationship with the team or facility. The change in the economy has decreased the demand for PSLs, however. The New York Jets auctioned their PSLs online before their new stadium opened. Although the team sold 620 PSLs for a total of $16 million, it had hoped to sell

2,000 ("Jets Earn," 2008). In 2014, several websites were offering Jets' PSLs for resale. The market for Jets' PSLs might have been tough, due in part to a saturated New York sport market, but for many other teams their PSL seats have sold very well.

One concern with PSLs is that a seat is in fact an asset for the PSL holder. Several major court battles have been fought over the right to control PSLs during divorce cases, and at least one court held that a collegiate PSL was owned by the team, even though the couple had paid thousands of dollars to purchase the rights to buy the PSL seats. Similarly, what happens if the PSL holder runs into financial hardship? Does a team or facility have any mechanism to help sell the PSL for the fan, or will the fan stop paying and the seat go empty? The Denver Broncos actually sued some of their PSL holders for not paying their contractual obligations. Although such a strategy may not be endearing to fans, the team gave the fans several chances to correct the problem, to no avail ("Broncos Sue," 2002).

Commercial Rights

Some of the primary intangible benefits for a facility include the right to put a name on the facility, the right to conduct activities there, and the right to sell drinks. Although commercial rights are primarily associated with large facilities at the collegiate and professional levels, a storm of controversy has erupted over the selling of rights at the high school level to put corporate names on buildings or sell only one brand of soda. Because of financial demands, state and federal government units have tested the market for selling naming rights to national monuments, state parks, and airports.

Naming Rights

Naming rights are somewhat controversial. A city or municipality may pay the bulk of the construction expense, and citizens should be recognized for their contributions. That is why so many older stadiums and arenas were named after people from the community as a tribute to their participation in a war. With the building boom of the 1990s, anchor tenants at large stadiums and arenas were asked to contribute funds to the building process. Many municipalities allowed the teams to sell the naming rights and use those funds as part of their contribution to the construction effort. The name was an asset the municipality could have sold to reduce the public obligation; however, in order to entice teams to stay, the municipalities were willing to transfer the asset to the teams. However, some facilities such as historic Lambeau Field in Green Bay and Soldier Field in Chicago have kept their names. Other teams believe their stadium name is an asset in itself, such as Fenway Park and Yankee Stadium.

Another controversy associated with naming rights has to do with the strength of the sponsor. The Houston Astros' field was named after Enron, which became a disadvantage when the company collapsed. At the same time, other companies faced similar scandals, and these controversies significantly affected several facilities. Enron had agreed to a deal worth $100 million for 30 years. PSINet Stadium in Baltimore was part of a $105.5 million, 20-year deal before PSINet collapsed. Adelphia Coliseum in Nashville did not last long before the company went bankrupt. Mergers and bankruptcies can also affect naming rights. The TWA Dome in St. Louis was changed to Edward Jones Dome after TWA filed for bankruptcy; TWA had agreed to a 20-year, $36.7 million naming rights contract (Sieger and Patel, 2001).

Selling naming rights is a form of corporate sponsorship. North American companies were expected to spend $8.7 billion on sponsorship in 2000. Before the economic collapse in late 2008, total sponsorship spending in North America was expected to be $16.78 billion (Klayman, 2008). Although deals after the collapse were not as common, some major facilities found sponsors before they were even built. Farmers Field in Los Angeles was named and had a sponsor before an NFL team was even awarded to or moved to Los Angeles. Farmers Insurance purchased the naming rights in a 30-year deal worth $700 million, and they received significant publicity before a stadium was finalized or approved. Sponsors provide either cash or an in-kind asset such as advertising in an effort to improve the fortune of the company or product sponsoring the facility. Sponsorship is not philanthropy. The company doing the sponsorship is expecting something in return, whereas philanthropy is a one-way gift without any expectation. Because there exists an expectation of receiving something of value in exchange for the sponsorship, the process is more like a business transaction than a gift. Thus, there are numerous tax implications associated with sponsorship.

Naming rights can range from several hundred thousand to millions of dollars (see table 11.1). The value of such deals is based on multiple variables, including the following:

- The length of the contract, which normally runs for 20 to 30 years
- The type of facility, events, anchor tenants, or teams
- Whether the deal involves only cash or also a trade-out of services
- What tie-in marketing strategies and campaigns will be used (Sieger and Patel, 2001)

Some of the newer naming rights deals are Levi-Strauss's agreement with the 49ers for 20 years at a total of $220 million and AT&T's deal with the Dallas Cowboys, which is estimated to be between $17 and $19 million a year. Minnesota Vikings owner Zygi Wilf is reportedly looking for $10 to $15 million a year for the new stadium's naming rights. The Seattle Seahawks' CenturyLink Field (formerly Qwest Field) penned a deal for between 15 and 20 years for $60 to $100 million, depending on the length.

Some deals have focused just on local businesses in an effort to be civic minded. For example, the Heinz Company paid $57 million to name the new stadium in Pittsburgh, where Heinz is headquartered. The amount of $57 million was appropriate because Heinz is known for its company slogan "57 varieties." The ownership of the FleetCenter's sponsoring bank changed in 2008, and while the center was without a name, it auctioned off online daily naming rights. Thus, a fan could bid (starting at $25) to put his name on the scoreboard, the website, and the facility's automated phone system. This gave fans an opportunity to more meaningfully engage with the facility and the teams playing in it.

The key to valuing any asset is usually what the market will bear, and the market is often very fickle. During good economic times, naming

rights and other assets are often easy to sell. However, during tough economic times they can be almost impossible to sell. Thus, the $57 million may seem gimmicky or appear to be an overpayment, but the facility and Heinz had specific strategies that justified assigning that value to the rights deal.

No matter what the strategy is, rights raise some serious financial issues. For example, an important commercial rights issue involves how the Internal Revenue Service (IRS) will classify the sponsorship or advertising revenue. If the facility provides significant benefit to the sponsor, the money received from the sponsor may be taxed as unrelated business income. The unrelated business income tax is currently around 28%. Ohio State University received more than $1 million from advertisements on its football stadium goalposts from various sponsors. The IRS concluded that the activity of promoting the sponsors on the scoreboard did not support the university's educational mission and was not related to the nonprofit purpose of the university, so the university had to pay 28% of the $1 million as unrelated business income tax (Fried, Deshriver, and Mondello, 2013).

One needs to evaluate many other issues when determining the price of sponsorship. For example, will the sponsor be a name sponsor for the facility or just have its name on several billboards? The price is often based on the number of impressions that can be expected. Table 11.2 lists some of the industry norms for costs associated with each impression received. An impression refers to how many people may be exposed to the message. If there are 1,000 people at a game, it is assumed that everyone would see an outfield sign at least once, which means there would be at least 1,000 impressions. It is assumed that through these impressions a fan may form an opinion to purchase a product.

Pouring Rights

Assets can also include the right to conduct business in the facility such as selling concessions or pouring rights, or facility management rights. Pouring rights are often paid by beer and soft drink companies to gain the exclusive right to sell their product in the facility. Dallas Cowboys

Table 11.1 Some of the Largest Stadium Naming Rights Deals

Facility	Location	Deal value (millions of dollars)	Deal length (yr)
Citi Field	New York	$400	20
Barclays Center	New York	$400	20
Reliant Park	Houston	$300	30
Levi's Stadium	San Francisco	$220	20
FedEx Field	Virginia (D.C.)	$205	27
American Airlines Center	Dallas	$195	30
Philips Arena	Atlanta	$168	20
University of Phoenix Stadium	Phoenix	$154.5	20
Lincoln Financial Field	Philadelphia	$139.7	20
Lucas Oil Stadium	Indianapolis	$121.5	20
Invesco Field at Mile High	Denver	$120	20
Sports Authority Field at Mile High	Denver	$120	20
PSINet Stadium	Baltimore	$105.5	20
Minute Maid Park	Houston	$100	30
Staples Center	Los Angeles	$100	20
Gillette Stadium	Boston	$95	15
Gaylord Entertainment Center	Nashville	$80	20
PNC Center	Raleigh	$80	20
M&T Bank Stadium	Baltimore	$75	15
Xcel Energy Center	St. Paul	$75	25
Compaq Center at San Jose	San Jose	$72	18
Savvis Center*	St. Louis	$70	20
Pepsi Center	Denver	$68	20
Chase Field	Phoenix	$66.4	30
Bank One Ballpark	Phoenix	$66	30
Comerica Park	Detroit	$66	30
Edison International Field	Anaheim	$50	20
AT&T Park**	San Francisco	$50	24
Tropicana Field	St. Petersburg	$46	30
Air Canada Centre	Toronto	$45 (Canadian dollars)	15
MCI Center	Washington, D.C.	$44	13
American Airlines Arena	Miami	$42	20
Miller Park	Milwaukee	$41.2	20
Bankers Life Fieldhouse***	Indianapolis	$40	20
CoreStates Center	Philadelphia	$40	29
First Union Center	Philadelphia	$40	31
Ford Stadium	Detroit	$40	40
Safeco Field	Seattle	$40	20
Wells Fargo Center	Philadelphia	$40	21
AT&T Stadium	Dallas	$17-20/yr	20-30
Bridgestone Arena	Nashville	$2.5/yr	5

*Savvis paid $5.5 million to end the deal in 2005. **Originally Pac Bell Park before SBC purchased Pac Bell. The stadium was renamed under same deal after the SBC–AT&T merger created AT&T Incorporated. ***Deal retained, but the original company name (Conseco) was phased out after Conseco's filing for bankruptcy.

From *Stadium & arena sponsorship* 2002.

Table 11.2 Industry Cost Norms per Impression

Activity	Cost per impression ($)
Public service announcements	0.0025-0.05
Banners	0.0025-0.05
Name on ticket	0.05
Logo on brochure	0.0025-0.05
Sponsor ad	Varies
Coupon	0.05-0.10
Sample products	0.075-0.15

From Moler 2001.

owner Jerry Jones created a controversy when he signed Pepsi as the official soft drink for Texas Stadium, even though Coca-Cola was the official sponsor of the NFL. Because of this deal the NFL–Coca-Cola contract was not renewed, and some teams lost significant money when teams or facilities had entered into individual contracts with various soda companies (Sullivan, 1995). Companies are willing to purchase assets in the hope of selling more products. Ogden Facility Management helped build the Arrowhead Pond in Anaheim for the Mighty Ducks. The concession company was interested in being part of the facility since it had a contract giving it exclusive rights to manage the facility and sell concessions for 30 years (Fried, Shapiro, and Deshriver, 2003). After Ogden changed its name, went bankrupt, and was purchased by a venture capital company, a new sponsor (Honda) was found and a new facility management company came in.

Since the number of drinks sold at an NFL stadium or other major facility is immense, it is worthwhile for the sponsor to buy pouring rights to generate a perceived sales volume and to gain valuable marketing exposure from involvement with a professional team. Because of the success associated with pouring rights, a number of other rights have been sold; for example, a company may be the official hot dog or pretzel provider.

FACILITY FOCUS

GIANTS STADIUM NAMING FIASCO

Allianz is a German financial services corporation that was the front-runner to secure naming rights to the new Giants and Jets football stadium in the Meadowlands. Allianz acknowledges its historic ties to Nazi Germany, so when the news broke that the insurance and finance company was possibly acquiring the naming rights to the stadium, a public outcry erupted in New York, where there exists a large Jewish community. Even though Allianz was willing to pay $30 million a year, and there was no other potential naming rights deal in the same financial neighborhood, the teams declined the offer.

To reduce sticker shock for some potential sponsors (Citi bought the naming rights for the Mets' stadium for $20 million a year), the Jets and Giants sold the stadium's corners to four "cornerstone partners" (SAP, Pepsi, Verizon, and Anheuser-Busch) and sold the right to name the entire facility to a "naming partner" (MetLife Insurance). The four cornerstone partners receive advertising on each of the 5,000-square-foot (465 sq m) corner scoreboards and in the stadium from the field to the parking lot (Kuriloff, 2007).

The Cleveland Browns followed the same strategy but instead sold the name for each of the four main gates. Tickets to a Browns game direct fans to the Cleveland Clinic gate, National City Bank gate, CoreComm gate, or Steris Corp. gate.

Advertising Sales

Selling advertising rights can be a major marketing hurdle. Advertising is easy to sell when the facility can prove a direct correlation between the advertisement and sales. If a given advertising campaign at the facility helps generate sales, there may be a possible direct correlation that can be measured. If the effect can be measured and is greater than the advertising investment, then the advertising buy was worthwhile on a cost–benefit basis. For example, advertisements in a facility promoting a specific hot dog can be valued based on the number of those hot dogs sold at the facility. However, advertising is often purchased for strategic reasons, unrelated to cost–benefit analysis. If a company wants to preclude a competitor from advertising at a venue, it will pay more than the advertisement is really worth just to preempt the competitor.

Advertising is typically priced on the basis of the anticipated exposure. If a baseball team will bring in 2 million fans and will have 20 games broadcast on national television, the team can estimate what the perceived value of an outfield sign may be on a per exposure basis. Using such an analysis, a team that draws more fans or more broadcasts will typically charge more for signs, and signs will be more expensive based on where they are located. For example, left field signs are seen more on television when a primarily right-handed team is batting since more balls will be hit to left than to right.

Facilities are always developing new means to generate advertising revenue. Some facilities are starting to use virtual advertising to increase revenue. This advertising can appear in the outfield or behind home plate at a baseball stadium. To those in the stadium the blue background is plain, but an advertisement can be imposed on the background during the broadcast. The same technology has been used in other sports such as football and tennis.

Summary

Some think that if they open a sport facility, people will come—as with the fictional baseball diamond in a cornfield. However, an imaginary baseball field does not correlate with the reality of a competitive entertainment marketplace. To start the marketing process, a facility needs to determine what assets or products it has to sell. The four Ps help define the product and its attributes. The facility then needs to determine who the customers are and how to reach them. By developing a unique sport experience, a facility can more easily market itself, whether it is a new facility or a facility trying to attract new tenants, acts, or customers.

The marketing process moves to the sales area in which tickets, memberships, naming rights, luxury seats, and other assets need to be sold. The marketing process is not about selling a ticket or a single facility use—it is about an experience. This requires the marketing effort to constantly enhance and modify the product to encourage additional consumption of the facility experience.

Discussion Questions and Activities

1. How would you market a health club in the south versus the east coast or west coast?
2. What additional assets (both tangible and intangible) can a facility sell?
3. What can a small stadium do to market itself without spending a lot of money?
4. Develop a marketing plan for a local sport team (high school, college, professional). The class should divide into groups. Half of the groups should choose a team with a winning record, and the other half of the groups should choose a team with a losing record.

5. Interview the owner or manager of a sport facility who has had to close the facility, and analyze the reasons given for closing the facility.

6. Explain some of the positive and negative effects a secondary ticket market can have on a facility.

12

Finance and Budgeting

Chapter Objectives

- Understand the basics of sport facility finance.
- Know how to prepare and follow a budget.
- Understand how new stadiums and arenas are funded.
- Apply the concepts of basic time value of money and capital project analysis to various building options.

Facilities cannot function without money. Money is needed to plan, build, open, operate, and maintain facilities. The problem is that there is often no guarantee that money will be available to keep a facility operating. Some facilities, such as government facilities, may appear to have deep public pockets. However, that appearance is misleading, as most public facilities have tighter budgets than private facilities. The major emphasis in this chapter is on determining what money is available for a facility and how to establish what funds are needed through the budgeting process.

The chapter starts by examining basic financial concepts, such as revenue and expenses, used to determine where money comes from and what the primary expenses for a facility are. Financial analysis is then covered in terms of measuring financial progress through income statements, balance sheets, cash flow analysis, and reconciliation statements. The chapter then turns to the basics of budgeting, with a focus on reducing expenditures and increasing revenue generation in accordance with pre-established criteria. A key area in the budgeting process is the capital budget and deciding which new facility option makes the most financial sense. The chapter then examines how to finance building a facility and the various sources of such funds. The final section covers what is often unthinkable—what if the facility fails and has to be sold?

FINANCIAL CONCEPTS

Finance can be considered a language unto itself. There are very specific financial terms that are not well known. This section presents some specific terms that are important to know to grasp the rest of the chapter.

It should be noted that accounting and finance are completely different fields. Accounting is the process of calculating how much money a facility may have. **Revenue**, money obtained by the facility from selling assets (see chapter 11), and **expenses**, payments made by the facility, need to be calculated to see if the facility has made money. This calculation process is very rigid. Generally accepted accounting principles categorize all revenues and expenses. Finance, on the other hand, utilizes the numbers obtained by the accountants to determine the facility's future direction. The analyses conducted by financial analysts focus on developing a roadmap for the future based on past financial information and projected financial performance. This process is called budgeting. Thus, a budget is a roadmap that helps the facility executives reach the facility's goals.

A budget is not the only document produced by financial analysts. Various types of financial statements tell the story of the facility. An **income statement** highlights the profit earned from all sales minus the cost of producing the events, taxes, and other expenses. A **balance sheet** explains how much a facility is worth and is based on two primary terms: **assets** and **liabilities.** An asset is something of value such as land, naming rights, and concession items. The greater the assets, the more a facility is worth. Liabilities are debts that are owed to others. A facility may owe money to lenders who purchased bonds to help build the facility or to the gas company for gas used to heat water in the building. If a facility's debts are worth more than the facility's assets, then the facility has a negative cash value.

Assets and liabilities are further classified as current or long term. Current assets and liabilities are assets that can be redeemed within a year and liabilities that need to be repaid within a year. Current assets include cash, stocks, and money market notes. Current liabilities include monthly bills and salary obligations. Long-term assets are assets that will be held for more than year. Long-term assets include a building, which has value and could be sold within a year but normally will not be sold within the year. Long-term liabilities are debts and obligations that would normally take more than year to repay. Long-term liabilities include bond and mortgage debts.

Other financial statements examine the flow of cash in a facility or can be used to calculate how much money was made or lost during a given event through the process of reconciliation. These various documents are not analyzed in a vacuum. The documents are compared with information for prior years to determine if the budget was met, if the facility grew monetarily, or if the facility can be compared favorably with other similar facilities.

Wajda: Evaluating and reporting financial performance

Photo courtesy of Ken Wajda.

My name is Ken Wajda, and I am the vice president of finance for Global Spectrum, a public assembly facility management company. Our company is based in Philadelphia, and today we manage more than 100 public assembly facilities around the world, primarily arenas, stadiums, and convention centers. I have been in the sport and building management business for the past 15 years. After graduating with a degree in accounting, I started my professional career in public accounting, where I earned my CPA designation. Then, I accepted a position with Global Spectrum's parent company, Comcast-Spectacor, which allowed me to apply my accounting skills in the sport and entertainment field. I spent my first several years doing tax work for each of Comcast-Spectacor's divisions, including professional teams, arenas, television production, facility management, food and beverage, ticketing, and commercial rights sales. I then entered my current position with Global Spectrum, where I oversee all financial matters of our company.

My responsibilities include the following:

- Oversee financial reporting for the facilities Global Spectrum manages.
- Hire and direct on-site facility finance departments.
- Set financial policy for the facilities Global Spectrum manages.
- Review and approve budgets.

As a facility management company, Global Spectrum manages financial reporting for multiple venues. This allows us to benchmark certain financial data and use the data as a basis for expectations for other similar facilities. These data may be useful for evaluating the success of an event in an existing venue, or they may be used to predict the results for a venue that has yet to be built. When someone is looking to build a new facility, the forecasted operating cash flow plays a key role in the financing plan and may, in some cases, ultimately determine whether or not the facility is ever built. A facility represents an extremely large investment of capital, and a facility owner is rightfully seeking some financial return on the investment or the ability to use cash flow from operations for debt service.

Evaluating the financial performance of any operation is certainly critical to its success. Financial performance is among the top goals of any facility owner, and that is why budgeting plays such an important role in a facility. The budget serves as a roadmap for where you want to go financially. If things start to stray from budgeted expectations, the facility operators must be quick to react.

As finance professionals, we play a very important role in the management of a facility. We touch every aspect of the business in some way. We work with all departments—from operations to box office to marketing—and ensure fiscal responsibility among all disciplines. We are not just counting dollars. We are business advisors, and it is our financial reporting that drives business decisions. Our reporting may indicate that we need to tighten the belt on expenses, or it may dictate a need for expansion. That's the importance of the role of finance.

One of the important points to remember about financial analysis is that it is difficult to examine numbers from a single point in time. If a facility charged $10 for a ticket in 2010 and charges $10 for a ticket in 2014, the facility is in fact not getting $10 worth of value in 2014. According to the concept of the time value of money, money does not maintain its value over time. A dollar tomorrow is not worth as much as a dollar today. Because of inflation and the demands for money, to get the same dollar value as this year a fan might have to pay $1.05 next year. On the basis of this concept, budgets typically increase every year because the cost to accomplish what was undertaken this year is going to be greater next year.

When a temporary event comes to a large facility, the facility needs to make space for vendors to set up displays and sell merchandise in order to justify their sponsorship dollar expenditure. It is hoped that through selling items at the event the sponsor will recoup some or all of the money they paid to help sponsor the event and obtain the vending location.

REVENUE AND EXPENSES

Revenue represents funds coming into a facility, and expenses are funds leaving the facility (i.e., to pay bills). Revenue and expenses are listed on financial statements, such as the income statement, and can tell a story such as what it cost to open the facility for an event. If an arena cannot open without guaranteeing at least $5,000 in revenue to cover expenses, any event generating less than that amount will not break even and should not be booked unless profit is not a motive. For some events, the facility management may not have a choice; the expenses for a graduation ceremony at a college facility will obviously exceed the revenue, but the event needs to be run anyway.

A facility can generate revenue from numerous sources. Some sources, such as ticket sales, parking revenue, concession sales, sponsorship revenue, advertising revenue, and naming rights revenue, are discussed in chapter 11. Other revenue sources can be unique for each facility. A facility that has extra cash can put that money into a bank account or invest in securities. Extra cash can also be invested in buying additional assets that can generate more revenue. A health club could use extra cash to buy another club; the combination of the two clubs can then generate even more revenue.

One of the first steps in understanding revenue and expenses is to identify what they are used for at a given facility. Revenue and expenses for a typical facility are highlighted in "Public Stadium Revenue and Expenses."

Revenue streams at various facilities can be enhanced through unique marketing efforts and innovations; a health club, for example, may add game rooms, babysitting, a juice bar, and a pro shop. However, all new revenue-generating ideas also entail new expenses. The expenses can include construction work, inventory, new employees, and even the cost of time for planning and developing a new revenue stream. A budget can help indicate how the proposed revenue-generating idea will affect the facility's bottom line.

One concern in this process is how to define certain revenues and expenses. For example, tickets can be defined differently from one facility to another, and such differences can have major ramifications. For instance, luxury suite revenue was not counted as part of the revenue-sharing agreement between the National Football League

(NFL) and its players' association, but regular ticket sales were included. When the collective bargaining agreement was negotiated and signed in 2006, the two parties extended the revenue definition to include most luxury suites but not super suites. To increase revenue, teams charge a significant amount for the suites and then charge people sitting in the suites for individual tickets as well. In addition, *rent* is a vague term because it can be a flat fee or a percentage of gross ticket sales. However revenue and expenses are defined, a complete picture of revenue and expenses is needed to properly budget for the future.

As described in chapter 9, benchmarking is the process of comparing one facility or business with another. It is often hard to determine what the primary revenues and expenses are for facilities. Most facilities or teams do not disclose their revenue and expenses. However, several publicly owned facilities are required to publish these numbers. "Metrodome Revenue and Expenses" highlights the 2005 and 2011 revenue and expenses for the Metrodome in Minneapolis. The Metrodome is possibly the most dynamic stadium in the United States, hosting in its storied history an NFL team, a Major League Baseball (MLB) team, a National Basketball Association (NBA) team (for the Timberwolves' inaugural season), college football, and college baseball, to name a few.

FINANCIAL ANALYSIS

All facilities require financial planning. Will the facility generate enough revenue to pay all the salaries, cover debt service, and turn a profit to justify staying open? How much should it charge for tickets or memberships? These are the types of questions facility managers face. The questions and the answers lie in financial statements. The two primary types of financial statements are the income statement and the balance sheet.

The income statement and balance sheet are used for various managerial activities. First, they help show a facility's financial health. Income statements show how much money a facility generated. The balance sheet highlights how much the facility is worth when all the assets are added together and the liabilities are subtracted from the total. The numbers can also be compared with industry ratios to examine how the facility is doing financially relative to other facilities. This process of benchmarking is used as well in specific areas such as maintenance, marketing, and

---

PUBLIC STADIUM REVENUE AND EXPENSES

Revenue	Expenses
Ticket revenue	Capital replacement fund (sinking fund)
Concession revenue	Contractual expenses
Naming rights	Salaries
Premium seating	Janitorial
Personal seat licenses	Equipment
Advertising	Supplies
Parking revenue	Maintenance
Novelty revenue	Insurance
Tenant rent	Taxes
Facility rental	Utilities
Special events income	Debt service
Government subsidies	Professional expenses (legal)
Various bonds	
Ticket surcharges	

METRODOME REVENUE AND EXPENSES

The following are the actual revenue and expenses as highlighted on the Metrodome's financial statement for 2005 and 2011. Note that the Minnesota Twins played their home games at the Metrodome until the end of the 2009 season. Thereafter, only the Minnesota Vikings played at the stadium. The Vikings are currently scheduled to move into a new stadium for the 2016 season, which will drastically change the financial viability of the Metrodome.

Category	2005	2011
Revenue		
Concessions	$22,172,245	$6,992,064
Admission tax	$7,547,144	$3,773,441
Rent payment	$4,465,850	$3,979,614
Charges for services	$3,146,331	$1,208,276
Advertising revenue	$2,396,461	$64,800
Novelty sales	$156,625	$0
Parking revenue	$144,630	$75,000
Other revenue	$347,528	$254,058
Investment earnings	$523,089	$390,018
Total revenue	$40,899,903	$16,737,271
Expenses		
Concession costs	$12,276,504	$4,022,076
Tenant's share of concession revenue	$6,572,428	$1,047,471
Facility cost credit	$7,116,138	$3,438,185
Personnel costs	$3,453,431	$2,142,063
Professional services	$474,359	$541,845
Contractual services	$3,965,868	$2,226,220
Audiovisual costs	$234,594	$170,875
Travel and meetings	$44,238	$11,910
Repair maintenance and supplies	$1,113,391	$678,656
Utilities	$3,237,338	$3,131,637
Insurance	$539,870	$694,354
Communication	$75,092	$73,399
Facility planning and research	$4,865	$644,601
Event costs	$472,767	$431,367
Marketing and advertising	$484,334	$81,850
Miscellaneous	$163,011	$78,733
Depreciation	$5,198,157	$4,092,146
Loss of disposable capital asset	$753	$1,920
Roof restoration	$0	$1,150,565
Total expenses	$45,427,138	$24,659,873
Total loss	$4,527,235	$7,922,602

From *Comprehensive annual financial report* 2006 and 2011.

The largest changes that occurred over the 6 years include the significant decrease in revenue from the Twins moving to a new facility and the loss of concession, rent, taxes, services, and all other revenue sources. Expenses normally decreased, but facility planning and research costs increased as the facility researched ways to keep the Vikings or explored building a new facility. Insurance costs also increased, in part due to the roof collapse caused by too much snow, which cost a lot to repair. However, the repair costs were significantly offset by the value of the new roof (paid for mainly by the insurance company), which increased the facility's value by almost $23 million. Metrodome revenues in 2011 decreased by $3,881,459 from 2010 totals due to the cancellation of several events after the roof collapse, which was widely shown on television and the Internet. The commission's operating revenues decreased by $3,548,648 over six years. The largest decreases from 2005 to 2011 were in concession sales, which decreased by $1,219,288, followed by admission taxes and rent, which decreased about $1 million each (Comprehensive Annual Financial Report, 2012).

Various publicly funded studies of the Metrodome showed that the tax revenue collected by the state from professional sport teams between 1961 and 2009 amounted to more than $458 million on a public investment of around $191 million to fund building and operating the facility. The greatest amount of tax revenue ($170 million) came from the Vikings, and $266 million was associated with payroll taxes on athletes (RSM McGladrey, 2009).

© Matthew Hintz/Bloomberg via Getty Images

the legal area. For example, if a facility earns $10 per fan from concession sales but other facilities are averaging $15 per fan, the facility is failing to meet industry standards. Finally, the numbers can be used to educate stakeholders, including elected officials, investment advisors, stockholders, the public, and tenants or customers, to help budget for the future.

Income Statements

An income statement highlights the revenue and expenses generated over a given period of time, normally 1 year (see "Sample Income Statement"). Through accounting, all revenue and expenses are calculated and then inserted into the income statement to show whether the facility generated any profit. Assume, for example, that a concession company operates a single drink stand at a facility. The stand sells 1,000 drinks at $5.00 each at an event. After the event, the accounting process adds up all the money the stand took in and then calculates all the expenses to determine if there was a profit or loss. The cost associated with selling the

drinks included 50 cents for each drink for the cup, ice, water, syrup, and lid. Another cost was 25 cents for the time to process each order. These are the costs of the goods sold. In this example, the sales would total $5,000, and after subtracting the cost for the drinks ($500) and labor ($250), the gross profit is $4,250. Other expenses include depreciation, which is an accounting term referring to decreasing the value of equipment and property over a fixed period of time (allowing a company to reinvest future money to buy new equipment). Such an expense is normally calculated at the end of the year on all the equipment and property the government allows to be depreciated. Selling expenses are associated with overall marketing efforts such as the thousands of dollars the concession company spent to gain the right to operate the stand. The last major expense faced by the concession company is taxes that need to be paid to the government. Other expenses that could be included on an income statement are interest owed on money borrowed to build a facility or to use as operational funds. The sample income statement shows the concession stand made a profit of $2,800 after all costs, depreciation, and taxes were accounted for.

Balance Sheets

A balance sheet lists the facility's assets and liabilities on a given day (see "Sample Balance Sheet"). The balance sheet changes every day because the amount of money owed to the facility and the amounts owed by the facility are constantly changing. A balance sheet contains three categories: assets, liabilities, and owner's equity. Assets range from the land and building itself (real property) to any personal property such as televisions, computer systems, and ticketing machines. Assets also include money owed to the facility such as membership fees or refunds. Liabilities are all the financial obligations that the facility has on the given date. These could include such obligations as repayment of a bond used to finance the building of the facility and salary obligations that have yet to be paid. Owner's equity refers to the amount owed to investors from their investment in the facility. The assets for our concession example could include cash, inventory (cups, ice, lids,

syrup, and so on), and serving carts. The liabilities could be accounts payable (what the concession company owes vendors for supplies) and salaries payable. Owner's equity is the value the owner has in the business. The sample balance sheet shows that the amount of money the owners owe others is relatively small; the owners have significant value in the business since they possess the assets rather than owing money to others for them. In a balance sheet the assets always have to equal the liabilities and owner's equity.

Using Financial Analysis

Table 12.1 presents a comparison of two sport events held several years ago at a now demolished arena. The table indicates how financial numbers can be compared to examine revenue and expenses over various events and suggests the importance of the data in the income statement for future planning. For example, the concession per cap (per cap refers to the average per person expenditure on a given item) was $2.37 and did not change over the analyzed period. However, since there were approximately 1,200 more fans in the first year, the total gross concession revenue

SAMPLE INCOME STATEMENT

Sales	$5,000	Selling expenses	$300
Material costs	$500	Profit before taxes	$3,800
Labor costs	$250	Taxes	$1,000
Gross profit	$4,250	Profit after taxes	$2,800
Depreciation	$150		

SAMPLE BALANCE SHEET

Assets		Liabilities	
Cash	$10,000	Accounts payable	$5,000
Inventory	$4,000	Salaries owed	$4,000
Carts	$30,000	Current liabilities	$9,000
Total current assets	$44,000		
Depreciation	$4,000	Owner's equity	$39,000
Total assets	$48,000	Total liability	$48,000

was significantly higher that year. Since the average ticket price increased $2.40, though, the total gross ticket revenue did not decrease as much as it might have. However, the data may also indicate that the increased ticket price scared a significant number of patrons away from attending the event.

The financial analysis after an event is important for both the team or act and the facility to ensure that all parties know the correct numbers. The process of determining the final numbers, often called **reconciliation**, brings a promoter or team representative together with the facility's financial parties to determine the exact expenses and revenue for an event. A sample football game report from a major university shows how the financial analysis for an event is completed (see "Postevent Financial Analysis"). A postevent financial analysis is conducted for most single events such as a game, an event, or a concert. Typically the promoter and the facility finance director review the revenue and expenses to determine the final amounts owed under the contract. Accuracy is critical during this analysis; if a contract

requires revenue to be split 60%/40%, for example, any unaccounted-for revenue or expenses can significantly affect either party.

The information developed through the reconciliation process can also be utilized in budgeting

Table 12.1 Sport Event Comparison

Category	Year 1	Year 2
Attendance	4,437	3,219
Average ticket price	$13.38	$15.78
Gross ticket revenue	$59,346	$50,806
Rental income	$2,578	$9,715
Concession per cap	$2.37	$2.37
Concession gross	$10,525	$7,635
Concession income	$6,244	$–1,454
Novelty per cap	$3.10	$2.81
Novelty gross	$13,738	$9,050
Novelty income	$3,426	$2,489
Parking gross	$3,141	$2,013
Parking income	$2,826	$1,751
Total event income	**$21,060**	**$15,084**

POSTEVENT FINANCIAL ANALYSIS

Tickets available for selling

78,484	Reserved seats	@ $15.00
0	General admission	@ $7.00 or $3.00 (none available for this game)

Ticket distribution

5,589	Returned or unsold		
5,334	Sold by opponents	@$11.00 =	$58,674.00
32	Issued to press		
360	Issued comp to opponent's staff	@$5.50 =	$1,980.00
16,834	Issued to students	@$2.75 =	$46,293.50
690	Sold to faculty and staff	@$5.50 =	$3,795.00
49,645	Sold by host school	@$11.00 =	$546,095.00
78,484	Gross sales		$656,837.50
Less cost of officials			($3,298.00)
Subtotal			$653,539.50
Less 15% for game expenses			($98,030.93)
Net sales to be shared			$555,508.57
50% of net sales to opponents			$277,754.28
Less cash retained by opponents 5,334 × $15.00			($80,010.00)
Amount due opponents			$197,744.29

for future events. However, before examining budgets, it is important to understand that there is a lot of cash in most sport facilities. Accountants cannot provide accurate numbers to base decisions on if all the cash is not accounted for.

Tracking Cash

One of the primary daily concerns associated with financial management for a facility is cash management. Facilities are often overflowing with cash. If 50,000 people spend $10 cash each on various concession and souvenir items, the total is half a million dollars. There is also cash from ticket sales and parking revenue. At the end of an event, there can easily be more than $1 million in cash. Obviously this does not include all the credit card transactions, checks, or electronic fund transfers that might be used.

All cash transactions need to be properly recorded and verified to make sure that money is not lost from the time it is used to purchase an item until it is deposited in the bank. Numerous checks and balances are used to make sure cash is not lost. For example, a facility may have two people at each parking lot entrance. The attendants wear aprons that cover their pants pockets to prevent them from sliding cash into their pockets. One attendant processes transactions, and the other counts the cars with a counter. At the end of the event, management attempts to reconcile the ending balances. Thus, if each car had to pay $5 to park and there is a total of $5,000 in cash, the counter should have tallied 1,000 cars. If the numbers do not match, the reason for the discrepancy has to be determined. Some major stadiums also use a loop system under the pavement that counts each car so they can compare the electronic count with the hand count as an additional way to prevent fraud and ensure accuracy. More important over the long run, if the numbers do not match, the facility will never be able to develop accurate forecasts and budgets.

BUDGETING

Revenue and expenses from a prior year can be used as the starting point of developing a budget. A budget is a roadmap for the future of a facility.

Just as people look at a map to figure out how to get where they want to go, a facility manager looks at the budget as a way to reach financial success. After examining a map, people sometimes take a route different from the one they had planned to take and get lost. After examining a budget, a facility manager may try to follow the proposed plan but find that numerous distractions make it difficult to achieve the intended financial goals. The results can be either negative or positive. Through financial analysis a facility manager can see how close the facility is to the budget. Such regular analysis can help the facility determine if it is necessary to cut costs, generate additional revenue, or even cancel events.

The budget is a tool management uses to utilize resources effectively in order to reach a predetermined goal. If a wealthy investor offers to pay $200,000 to develop an initial site and feasibility study, the budget will work around that sum. If no other money is available, then $200,000 is the maximum amount of money available for the study, and total expenses have to come to less than $200,000. If the feasibility study will cost $75,000, then all other elements need to be accomplished for under $125,000 or additional funds will need to be found.

People follow this same process when they buy a car, house, or any other major item. A person would not buy a car requiring $400 a month in payments if she earns $2,000 a month and already spends $1,800 a month on food, rent, and so on. The process of making this determination is guided by a budget. Budgets help guide the financial decisions of most facilities. A facility cannot buy a $1 million heating, ventilation, and air conditioning (HVAC) unit if the machine is not in the budget. If the existing HVAC system breaks, the maintenance and repair budget may have to be tapped, or the capital improvement component of the budget will need to be examined. If there are not enough funds in the budget, management will need to consider inserting a line item in the next year's budget or authorizing an emergency expenditure that will possibly throw the entire budget out of sync. Similar to the way in which a major medical emergency can destroy a person's finances, an emergency can destroy the financial position of a facility.

Budgets are roadmaps, but like all maps they can contain mistakes. Because budgets are estimates and best guesses for the future, they can contain a number of problems:

- Overlooked revenue and expenses
- Items that were added to the budget without adjusting the budget (e.g., incurring a new cost without reviewing total expenses)
- Using "wish list" management where someone hopes that a sale will occur or that an expense will decrease when in reality such occurrences are not very likely
- Incomplete documentation
- Unforeseen issues
- Unrealistic estimates
- Inaccurate estimates of costs or revenue
- Unreasonable goals
- Incompetent oversight or management

Knowing all the revenue and expense items is critical for a budget. Imagine developing a home budget and forgetting to include utilities, which could be one of the biggest expenses. Such a mistake can throw an entire budget into chaos. Different types of budgets exist, and in any facility different departments might have their own budgets. An operating budget shows a facility's forecasted revenue and expenses, typically over at least a year. As an example, the basic expense elements in an operational budget could include the following:

- Cash budget: Represents an estimate of the facility's cash position at a particular point in time. This budget can help estimate current cash inflows (sales) and outflows (expenses).
- Personnel budget: Examines all the employees and their expected hourly rate and number of hours worked. This represents the total labor cost, including benefits, taxes, unemployment insurance, and so on.
- Sales budget: Estimates the anticipated future sales so the facility knows how many items to order or stock, how many tickets to sell to break even, and so on.
- Production budget: Represents the cost of producing the goods that will be sold, such as concession items. Using the sales budget, a facility might anticipate that 10,000 fans will attend an event. If data show that 8,000 hot dogs will be sold with a crowd of 10,000 fans, then the production budget would include all the buns, hot dogs, and so on necessary to make those hot dogs.
- Planning budget: Considers expenses that the facility may face in the future. These include items such as a new roof, new scoreboard, a major renovation, or even a new addition.
- Expense budget: Examines the regular expenses the team will face. These include:
    - Utility expenses such as gas, water, and electricity
    - Rental expenses such as lease obligations and landlord-related expenses
    - Planning and design expenses such as consultation fees, computer-assisted design and drafting expenses, photography, printing, and advertising expenses
    - Maintenance and repair expenses such as preventive maintenance (grounds, roof, electrical, HVAC, and so on), custodial, and repairs and alterations
    - Borrowing expenses
    - Moving expenses such as direct support for moving from one facility to another
    - Management expenses (Cotts and Lee, 1992)

A budget is only a start. Once the budget is developed and the event is held, a facility manager (and/or the finance department) needs to analyze whether the budget was close to being accurate. The evaluation process, called **variance analysis**, examines how accurate the budget was. If the budget was very accurate, then it might be used as a model for the future. If the true results are significantly different than predicted, then the budget would need to be altered in the future.

Forecasting

The revenues and expenses a facility might face cannot be examined only after they have been earned or spent. A facility manager needs to know past numbers and the potential future numbers to properly forecast revenues and expenses and thus to build an accurate budget.

The **financial forecast** is a bridge to help move the financial plan to the budget. There is no one correct way to forecast the future. Some facilities utilize their sales staff to analyze future conditions, based on which customers have entered into long-term contracts, for example. If research shows that customers are not interested in a facility, then such data need to be analyzed in the financial planning process. A facility manager can plan more effectively when he knows that for the next 20 years a given team will play its home games at the facility or that a college or high school is a member of a given athletic conference. If a circus or other event is booked for only 2 years, the facility manager knows that the third year is not as certain. Other techniques for forecasting are more complicated, such as regression analysis, econometric modeling, the Delphi method, and moving averages, and are not covered in this text (Cotts and Lee, 1992).

The starting point for a budget is typically any prior budgets. If the facility anticipates that revenue and expenses will increase 10% next year, a rough budget can be developed by just adding 10% to this year's budget. But this simplistic approach rarely works because the numbers are never cut and dry. Any revised budgets need to focus on accurate information being communicated to the right people. If the ticket sales force is having trouble selling tickets, they need to quickly provide such information to those involved in the budgetary process so they can help modify budgetary projections.

Another option is called zero-based budgeting, which requires a budget to be based on a competitive internal battle. All divisions in the facility prepare their budgets as if they had never had a budget before and base their monetary requests on what they perceive they can do to benefit the facility's goals and objectives. The divisions that management feels will enhance the facility's goals the most will receive the greatest proportions of the budget.

One technique entails developing an annual work plan highlighting capital costs (construction, repairs, equipment purchases, and so on), nondiscretionary annual costs (utilities, opera-tions, custodial, moving, and maintenance), discretionary annual costs (alterations, repairs, maintenance), lease costs, overhead costs (salaries, office equipment, and so on), and the cost of space needed for future projects (Cotts and Lee, 1992). These figures are used for both mid- and long-range plans. A facility can establish what anticipated repairs may be forthcoming in various ways, ranging from facility inspections to comput-erized systems indicating that a given component is past its useful life. Thus, if a roof has a 20-year life and has been in place for 24 years, the facility should be budgeting for a new roof. The roof can fail at any time; it has lasted this long because of luck or exceptional maintenance.

The greatest cost in any facility is upkeep. Over the life of a facility, the salaries of those who work in the facility account for 92% of the life-cycle costs. The operating and maintenance costs account for 6%, and the actual design and construction account for only 2% of the life-cycle costs of a facility (Cotts and Lee, 1992).

Paying the Daily Bills

Budgeting and financial analysis occur on a daily basis. If a given event does not generate the expected revenue and that revenue was going to pay certain bills, then other revenue sources need to be tapped to pay those bills. Managers frequently have to juggle between current needs, such as bills that are currently due, and future revenue such as that from future events. Managers also have to balance cash flow and streams. If there is $1 million in the bank, should it be put into long-term investments, put into lower-paying short-term investments, or used for capital improvements that will pay bigger dividends down the road? Similarly, with bills, should they be paid immediately, should they be paid after 30 days, or should they be ignored? Although it might be illegal to ignore a bill, some businesses follow this strategy and might pay only when threatened with a lawsuit.

Bill tracking is a critical skill for any facility manager. How much did the facility spend on energy last year versus this year? Is there any reason for the change, such as cooler weather or an increased cost for fuel? Similarly, are repair and maintenance costs increasing? Would outsourcing facility management save money, or would there be a potential problem with union employees if such a step were taken?

Although bill tracking and analysis help determine if the budget is on track, the process is significantly different for the day-to-day management of a facility, as discussed so far, versus the situation in which a facility is being built. The operational budget can be fairly consistent, with the expenses such as payroll and inventory remaining relatively constant. In contrast, building a new facility requires a capital budget that will face numerous changes almost daily. The next section focuses on finances related to building new facilities, including capital cost considerations and capital budgeting decision making to help determine which construction option may be the best for a proposed facility.

Capital Cost Considerations

Capital costs are costs associated with long-term investments such as buildings or equipment that may last more than 10 years. Capital expenditures in the sport facility area relate primarily to building the sport facility. Since facilities are extremely expensive, most entities building sport facilities utilize capital budgeting to fund construction.

Capital budgeting starts with determining the needed space for any given planned activity and determining whether existing facilities can fill those needs. It is not worthwhile to build a facility when other facilities exist that could serve the needs and are not fully utilized. After determining whether existing facilities can serve the planned needs, the capital budgeting process requires management to examine additional options for acquiring any additional needed space, whether by leasing, building, or redistributing space in existing facilities (Cotts and Lee, 1992). If management decides to renovate or construct a new facility, then capital funds will be needed. The decision is influenced by several factors, including the prevailing tax codes and the effect associated with depreciating assets. The budgeting process is also affected by the financial market, how easily cash can be raised, and the cost associated with raising the funds (interest rates, bond issuance costs, and so on).

One of the primary capital budgeting concerns faced by those trying to decide whether to build is the choice between building a new facility and leasing an existing facility. When leasing land, a developer signs a contract indicating that she will pay the agreed-on amount over a certain time period. At the end of the time period, the landowner has the option of renewing the lease. If the lease is not renewed, the facility must relocate, and the cost of relocation can be very high. In addition to this expense, leasing does not generate any equity for the facility developer. Thus, no money is being saved for the next facility through equity enhancement. On the other hand, advantages of leasing are that it allows a developer to limit the amount of commitment to the project and to write off lease payments as a business expense.

The major advantage of purchasing a facility is the ability to build equity and control the facility. In the future, when the facility wants to expand or relocate, the funds will be much easier to obtain because of the company's equity. There are two major difficulties with buying land. First, the up-front payment for the land can be so high that the developer may not be able to afford building according to the original plans. Another problem is the long-term loan. If the facility should incur financial difficulty, the owner may be forced to sell the land and building.

The capital budgeting process starts with acquiring appropriate information. The next step entails prioritizing projects. Prioritization occurs through various predetermined methods such as average rate of return, average payback period, annual return on investments, cash payback methods, discounted cash flow, net present value, internal rate of return, and the benefit–cost ratio (Cotts and Lee, 1992). Table 12.2 shows projected profits and cash flows for three different projects. Based on this financial planning analysis, different capital budgeting options are available (see table 12.3). A discussion of these options follows.

Using the **average rate of return** (ARR) method, project C would be the best choice since it produces the highest rate of return—115% versus 107% or 80%. Utilizing the **average payback period** (APP) method, project C is once again the best choice since it repays the initial investment in the shortest time period. However, with

Table 12.2 Financial Planning Analysis

	PROJECT A		PROJECT B		PROJECT C	
Net investment	$240,000		$150,000		$150,000	
Year	Profit	Cash flow	Profit	Cash flow	Profit	Cash flow
1	$40,000	$88,000	$60,000	$90,000	$20,000	$50,000
2	$60,000	$108,000	$60,000	$90,000	$40,000	$70,000
3	$140,000	$188,000	$60,000	$90,000	$80,000	$110,000
4	$200,000	$248,000	$60,000	$90,000	$120,000	$150,000
5	$200,000	$248,000	$60,000	$90,000	$170,000	$200,000
Totals	$640,000	$880,000	$300,000	$450,000	$430,000	$580,000
Averages	$128,000	$176,000	$60,000	$90,000	$86,000	$116,000

Adapted from Cotts and Lee 1992.

Table 12.3 Capital Budgeting Options

Prioritization technique	Project A	Project B	Project C
Average rate of return (%)	106.6	80	114.5
Average payback period (yr)	1.44	1.67	1.29
Actual payback analysis (yr)	2.23	1.67	2.27
Net present value × 2 ($)	306,892	141,694	203,934
Internal rate of return (%)	50.9	52.8	51.0

Adapted from Cotts and Lee 1992.

the **actual payback analysis,** project B would be the best choice because it actually pays back the initial investment in 1.67 years (note that profits are consistent throughout the 5 years) versus 2.23 years for project A and 2.27 years for project C. The **net present value** (NPV) analysis is based on a current cost of capital of 15%. Using the NPV approach, project A has the highest present value and should be chosen. Using **internal rate of return,** project B has the best return.

The ARR helps determine the rate of return in a percentage so that various projects can be compared with one another. Rate of return is calculated by dividing the net income (after taxes), commonly called profit, by the average cost of the investment. The average investment cost is calculated by subtracting the facility's salvage value from the construction cost and then dividing by 2. This formula is easy to use, is well known and respected, and considers the full time frame for the capital investment decision. Problems with ARR are that it is difficult to calculate profit, the method ignores the time value of money, and

arbitrary time frames for a facility's existence may be required (Cotts and Lee, 1992). The formula is as follows:

ARR (%) = profit/average investment cost

Using project A, this is found by first calculating the average investment cost:

average investment cost = (construction cost – salvage value)/2

Assuming no salvage value, this is as follows:

average investment cost = ($240,000 – 0)/2 = $120,000

Using that value in the ARR formula results in the following:

ARR = $128,000/$120,000 = 106.6%

The APP analyzes a capital decision based on how long on average it will take to repay the initial investment assuming an average cash flow rather than possibly a more specific rate of cash flow (e.g., the actual payback period). The net investment is divided by the average annual cash inflow to get the APP. The APP method is easy to use, analyzes cash flows, and can analyze risk. The drawbacks are that it does not consider time value of money, cash flows can be very subjective, and APP does not consider subsequent cash flows (which could decrease or increase significantly) (Cotts and Lee, 1992). Many utilize the APP approach because it analyzes the actual time it takes to cover the initial investment in building the facility. The next method discussed, NPV, is similar to the APP but also considers the timing of cash flows.

NPV determines the dollar value of some future series of cash flows, discounted by the facility's cost of capital. This process examines the time value of money, which means that a dollar tomorrow is not worth as much as a dollar today. Thus, the initial capital investment is subtracted from the NPV of future cash flows to get the NPV. This process requires the use of time value of money tables and considers relevant cash flows. Thus, it is a well understood calculation, but it is also difficult for most people without some financial experience to use.

The internal rate of return is the discount rate assuming an NPV of zero. The initial investment and future cash flows are analyzed to determine a project's value. This process analyzes cash flows and the time value of money, but it is very difficult to calculate and hard for people to understand. A last evaluation technique for capital investments is the **benefit–cost ratio**. This calculation divides the value of a project by the cost. The cost may be fairly easy to calculate, but the benefits are both economic and subjective so they are harder to calculate. That is why the benefit–cost ratio is used only when an experienced staff of economists can help with the calculations.

Although there are numerous tools for comparing various projects, these tools are not accurate unless they all utilize the same basic numbers. If two separate formulas use different data for the same project, it will be impossible to compare the numbers. Thus, the capital budgeting process often utilizes a worksheet (see "Budget Worksheet for a New Facility") that highlights the basic costs anticipated with the capital project.

Once the analysis is complete and the numbers are finalized, management needs to choose which project meets the planned needs. Some projects will provide appropriate payback in a set number of years and will be chosen over other projects that might take a longer time to repay the initial investment. This process is referred to as the cost justification process, used when costs are the overriding concern. However, numerous projects do not meet the predefined criteria. Some projects are accepted because they produce the greatest reward regardless of price, limit or minimize risks, or rank higher on the priority list.

One of the key concerns associated with capital budgeting is that many managers stop at that point. They determine that a facility will cost $200 million to construct and realize that they can raise that amount of money, so they move forward with the project. However, as described earlier, the greatest cost in a facility is upkeep. If the capital budget is not integrated into the operational budget from day one, the facility will probably face some financial hardships. If the operational budget is established while the facility is being built and enough funds are set aside to help operate at least for the first year, the facility should be in a strong financial position.

After the decision has been made to build or lease a particular facility, the construction funds need to be secured. The next section highlights the various financing options available to build a new facility.

NEW FACILITY FINANCING

With costs escalating every fiscal year, it is becoming increasingly difficult to finance a major sport facility or complex using funds from only one person or group, including public taxes. There are three major financing options: private financing, public (government) financing, and miscellaneous methods. Each option has distinct advantages and disadvantages.

Private Financing

Private financing can come from different sources, from stock and bonds issued by private companies to private funds. For example, the Miami Dolphins used to play in Joe Robbie Stadium (now Dolphin Stadium), which was built with private funds from the Robbie family. The Green Bay Packers are a

BUDGET WORKSHEET FOR A NEW FACILITY

Preproject Expenses

Temporary offices: _____

Utilities: _____

Insurance: _____

Moving costs: _____

Temporary furnishings: _____

Consulting Expenses

Feasibility studies: _____

Legal fees: _____

Design fees: _____

Site investigations: _____

Marketing expenses: _____

Site-Related Expenses

Land location expenses: _____

Title search: _____

Site appraisals: _____

Site surveys: _____

Boring tests/soil tests: _____

Zoning compliance: _____

Land costs: _____

Closing fees: _____

Finance fees: _____

Utilities to site: _____

Demolition expenses: _____

Development fees: _____

Miscellaneous assessment: _____

Professional fees: _____

Preconstruction Expenses

Architectural/engineering fees: _____

Models and drawings: _____

Interior design costs: _____

Consulting fees: _____

Copying expenses: _____

Bidding-related expenses: _____

Construction Expenses

Construction contract: _____

Contingency fund: _____

Project manager for owner: _____

Insurance: _____

Furniture, fixtures, and equipment: _____

Site development: _____

Landscaping: _____

Excavation: _____

Parking: _____

Access roads: _____

Signage: _____

Security: _____

Lighting: _____

Irrigation: _____

Storage facility: _____

Miscellaneous fees: _____

Miscellaneous Expenses

Bidding expenses: _____

Interest on construction loans: _____

Construction contingency: _____

Moving expenses: _____

Utility expenses: _____

Start-up staff: _____

Staff training: _____

Operating expenses: _____

Maintenance expenses: _____

Sinking funds: _____

Total Project Costs

Preproject expenses: _____

Consulting expenses: _____

Site-related expenses: _____

Preconstruction expenses: _____

Construction expenses: _____

Miscellaneous expenses: _____

Grand total: _____

Adapted from Wiggins 1993.

publicly traded company that issued approximately $24 million worth of shares to help finance renovations to Lambeau Field in 1997 and 1998 and then issued more shares several years later to finance an additional expansion of the stadium. In total, the Green Bay Packers have had five separate stock offerings. More than 269,000 shares were sold during the offering that began December 6, 2011. All proceeds from that offering went toward the expansion of Lambeau Field, a $143 million project (Packers, 2014). Other facilities, especially smaller ones, are often built with private funds, whether obtained from savings, bank loans, or inheritances. Other facilities have private backers or may be part of a business partnership. Still others are built with corporate funds—corporate gyms, for example.

Collateral Financing

New and developing enterprises sometimes face the uncertain and difficult process of obtaining capital to build or grow their business, and lenders will require some **collateral** or **equity**. Private equity can come from various sources. Equity represents the total value of personal money, stocks, and property (both real and personal). Money can include the actual cash that someone has on hand, stocks, bonds, and anything else that has value. Property is divided into two categories: real and personal. Real property is land and anything secured to the ground, including buildings and houses. Personal property is anything that can be lifted and moved. This can include teams, businesses, equipment, and automobiles. The problem with collateral-based borrowing is that if the borrower fails to pay the loan he can lose the collateral. Houses are a familiar example. A house serves as the collateral for a home loan. If the borrower defaults, the lender can foreclose and sell the house to get its money back.

Private Investors

Strategic investors are established companies with similar products that are looking for growth and expansion opportunities. Because strategic investors may lack the experience and ability to expand their own company, investing in another company gives them a low-cost alternative that will improve their company's value. For example, a large consumer product company may enter into a strategic alliance with a small fitness equipment company. The larger company can provide facilities to manufacture a new product, while the small company can lend its fitness product expertise without having to rent facilities or buy equipment.

Another source of private financing is wealthy individual investors or venture capital groups. These investors have dedicated a certain amount of their investment toward private investment opportunities. Most people have heard about **venture capital** investors, especially in connection with the "dot com" boom and bust. A venture capital investor supplies significant cash at the start of a business (or possibly at times of crisis) in exchange for a large percentage of the business. Venture capital investment is a form of private equity investing. Private equity investing can have significant benefits, such as financial flexibility, stable costs, and managerial expertise from investors. On the other hand, venture capitalists demand a high rate of return (often more than 40% profit per year) and often a seat on the board of directors.

Corporate Bonds

Corporate bonds are bonds that are issued and backed by the issuing corporations. Unlike most government bonds, corporate bonds are not tax exempt. Tax-exempt bonds provide income protection for investors in that the interest payments made by the bond issuer are not taxed when paid to the investor. Otherwise, investors would not receive the total expected return since between 20% and 40% of the interest payment would have to be paid as taxes. However, the downside of tax-exempt bonds is that they pay less interest than corporate or private bonds.

Corporate bonds are issued when a corporation believes it can obtain a lower interest rate than if it borrowed from a bank and wants a longer repayment period. If a facility builder approaches a bank and is offered a loan of $100 million at 9% but could issue a bond paying 8%, the 1% difference could be worth tens of millions of dollars over the bond's life. The one major caveat is that there must be bond buyers interested in purchasing corporate bonds. This problem makes bond issuance an option only for the biggest corporations or for prominent professional teams.

Partnerships

Money can also come from other people or organizations working together to build a facility. For example, two or more people can join together to build or finance a facility, or two or more government entities such as a school district and a parks department can join together to build playing fields to be used by both entities. In limited partnerships, partners put predetermined amounts of money or assets into the project. The obvious downfall is the great amount of risk that this type of arrangement involves. If a partnership fails, everyone involved in the partnership loses money. On the other hand, profits made by the facility are split among partners.

A strategic partnership occurs when a developer forms an alliance with another company that has congruent goals. This goes beyond a transfer of cash and entails strategic cooperation. A strategic partnership may be pursued when it promotes an effective means to enter the market. Another benefit with partners is geographic location. Partners can operate in several different areas and start franchises with facilities in the various areas. Health club owners in different areas have used partnerships as a means to merge their clubs into a larger entity and then attempt to expand. While such an option may appear attractive, the numerous financial and legal concerns that can arise make strategic alliances less common in the realm of sport.

Partnerships are practical solutions to financial problems, but they are not advised when it appears that the relationship is going to be very one-sided or when the partners do not have a good working relationship. It is also very important to be able to trust partners. One concern with partnerships is the liability of each partner for the actions of other partners. Thus, if one partner makes a mistake and subjects the partnership to liability, then all partners can be personally liable.

Public Offerings

Public offerings involve selling corporate shares to the public in the form of stock. Corporations can raise significant funds in this manner. A number of examples exist in the sport industry, primarily in horse racing, auto racing, and health clubs. Facilities and corporations need money to grow, and a public offering may represent the best way to grow and acquire or build additional facilities. But although a public offering might be a good way to raise a lot of money, it opens the facility to intense scrutiny, first from the Securities and Exchange Commission and state regulators and then from entities in the financing community such as brokerage houses. Another concern is that corporate financial records become public records through annual reports and various government filings. Corporations have another major concern: double taxation of revenue—first when earned and then when paid to stockholders as dividends. However, there are significant benefits to a facility going public, such as access to more capital, prestige, and the ability to limit the shareholders' liability for action taken by the corporation.

Public Financing

Whether the money is their own or has come from others, facility developers need enough cash to buy land, build a facility, and then operate the facility. These same funds are needed if a government entity builds a sport facility. The major difference is that government entities can raise money by other means. For example, as highlighted in chapter 5, government entities can acquire land through eminent domain. Even though this process costs money, it is often easier than other ways of acquiring property. The question becomes one of how the government entity will pay for the land. Funds can come from increased tax revenue, bonds, certificates of participation, or a combination of these. Increasing taxes has been used as a means to finance facilities such as the Alamodome. Even though a bond was issued for the Alamodome, the bond was secured by an increased sales tax. Lenders were eager to purchase the bonds since they were backed by a steady revenue stream that would guarantee repayment.

Over the past two decades, most sport facilities have been financed through tax-exempt bonds. **Bonds** are, in a manner of speaking, a promise that in a specific period of time the borrower will pay back the lender the amount of money borrowed along with a specific amount of interest. Government entities often issue bonds to pay for schools, roads, and other construction projects. Most municipalities and school districts, subject to certain restrictions and limitations, have the right to raise capital by issuing bonds. To issue a bond there must be legal authorization from either the voters or a legislative body. Obtaining authorization can prove to be difficult, and at times impossible, because project opponents are more likely to show up for the vote than supporters are (Howard and Crompton, 1995).

In 2002 there were 111 major professional sport franchises in America, and 91.9% (102) had moved into new or significantly renovated stadiums in the 1990s. The total taxpayers' price tag for stadiums or arenas built from 1995 through 2000 has been estimated at more than $9 billion (Fried, Shapiro, and Deshriver, 2013). That number increased dramatically when four new stadiums, each costing more than $1 billion, opened in 2009 and 2010. Although these stadiums were built using significant private funds, public funds are still the backbone for most major facility construction projects, and the economic downturn of 2008 and 2009 put a significant squeeze on public contributions. Municipalities interested in luring a new team or keeping an existing team argue that tax dollars should help finance facility construction because entertainment dollars are brought in from outside the community, thus infusing "new" money into the local economy. Even in tough economic times, municipalities usually find a way to keep a team. Examples include the proposed Minnesota Vikings' stadium, which is to be financed with $462 million in stadium bonds that will go toward financing the state's and the city of Minneapolis' contributions to the project, and Barclays Center, which received the right to sell $511 million in tax-exempt bonds in 2009 to help finance the building and convince the Nets to move to New York. The city of Newark paid $211 million in 2007 for the Prudential Center to keep the Devils and Nets in New Jersey. The investment failed to retain the Nets, but it got the Devils to move from the Izod Center in East Rutherford to Newark.

Teams also help cover building expenses. The average level of team contribution to a new NFL stadium increased in the early part of the 20th century to 29%, or $82 million of the typical construction cost for a football stadium. The percentage of owner contribution to stadium projects increased significantly with Cowboys Stadium (now called AT&T Stadium) and MetLife Stadium, which was primarily financed publicly. Although the stadium was built with private funds, public funds were used for numerous infrastructure projects around the stadium, which can often cost several hundred million dollars. Even without any team contributions, some municipalities are willing to foot the entire price of a facility to become a big-league city. Besides increased economic activity and increased sales, income, and employment tax revenues from those attending games and working at the facilities, proponents argue that the facilities help promote community image (Fried, Shapiro, and Deshriver, 2013). Making the "big leagues" can be expensive and can subject the citizens to paying debt service on bonds for years to come, without the facility ever generating a profit. One major study concluded that older arenas with little debt and numerous scheduled events (NBA, National Hockey League, Ice Capades, family shows, circuses) tended to make the highest profit, while new stadiums for outdoor sports were less profitable (Fried, Shapiro, and Deshriver, 2013).

Bonds

As highlighted by the examples presented in this chapter, the thrust of any government financing, whether complete or partial, is on issuing bonds. Unless the government or team has significant cash reserves, it will be necessary to borrow. A bond is a detailed IOU. While a stock certificate is proof of ownership and can be given to a facility owner, a bond does not represent ownership. A bond represents a debt owed by the facility builder, whether private or governmental. The money obtained from issuing the bonds is used to pay for facility acquisition and construction costs. Bonds are a debt instrument that requires repayment of principal and interest over many years. Most bonds are for 10, 20, or 30 years; if a facility

FACILITY FOCUS

PNC PARK

In early 1999, an $803 million package was funded to build PNC Park (home of the MLB Pittsburgh Pirates); build Heinz Field (home of the NFL Pittsburgh Steelers), retire the debt on Three Rivers Stadium; and destroy the stadium, expand the convention center, and construct a new Pittsburgh Development Center. The projects totaled more than $1 billion in financing. Out of necessity, the $1 billion was raised through a strategy that tapped into the existing 1% county sales tax. The Regional Asset District contributes $13.4 million annually to finance $170 million in bonds for the project. The county hotel tax contributes $8 million annually to finance $99 million in bonds. A 5% surcharge on Pirates and Steelers tickets raises $3 million annually to finance $22 million in bonds. A 1% wage tax is levied on players who do not live in the city and contributed $7 million to the project. The state of Pennsylvania contributed $300 million in matching funds. Funds totaling $36 million of the project came from interest earnings; $28 million was tapped from a fund for federal infrastructure improvements; $11 million came from parking revenues for leasing the convention center garage; $45 million was given to the project from a Pittsburgh Investment Capital fund. The Pirates and the Steelers contributed $85 million combined. The Pirates are also expected to cover operating costs (utilities and maintenance) as long as the team receives the revenues from concessions and advertising. Last, on August 6, 1998, Pittsburgh-based PNC Bank Corporation announced that it had purchased the right to name the new Pirates ballpark PNC Park when it opened in 2001. Under the deal, PNC Bank, a financial services company, will pay approximately $1.5 million a year through the 2020 baseball season for the naming rights (Gearhard and Schuler, 2001).

The citizens of Pittsburgh received a reprieve in terms of having to pay for their NHL team's arena. Consol Energy Center, where the Pittsburgh Penguins play, was built with funds from Isle of Capri Casinos, which agreed to fully fund the new arena if they were awarded a state gambling license. The arena was built in 2010 at a cost of $310 million.

© Talking Sport/Photoshot

is built with $100 million worth of bonds to be repaid over 30 years at 10% interest, the facility will eventually have paid the bondholders in the neighborhood of $300 million.

Bonds are rated based on the strength of the issuing company or municipality and on whether the entity has ever defaulted on prior bonds. General obligation bonds and other bonds are rated by independent companies such as Moody's and Standard and Poor's based on the issuer's ability to repay the loan. General obligation bonds are often highly rated since currently existing and future tax revenue sources can be tapped for bond repayment. Bond ratings can be influenced by a multitude of factors, including

- the ability to repay the loan with existing revenue streams;
- the strength, breadth, and reliability of the tax base;
- the historical performance of the revenue stream;

- the risk associated with the project;
- the underlying economic strength of the stadium or arena or the community;
- political volatility; and
- whether or not the project is economically viable (Fried, Shapiro, and Deshriver, 2003).

The higher the quality rating, the more likely the bond is to be issued and the lower the interest rate will be. To enhance the marketability of a bond issue, a government entity may purchase bond insurance to guarantee repayment. The strength of the tax base to repay the bond is one of the most important criteria for general obliga-

BEHIND THE SCENES

ANATOMY OF VARIOUS STADIUM DEALS

■ The Colorado Rockies built their stadium with a 1% six-county-area sales tax, with the team contributing $53 million and Coors Brewing scheduled to pay $1.5 million a year for naming rights. Under the 17-year lease, the city receives 20% of parking revenue on game days and 3% of the revenue from a brew pub. The team receives 100% of net concession revenue.

■ The United Center in Chicago was built in 1994 at a cost of $175 million; 80% of the financing was with funds from private bank loans, and 20% was with funds from the building owners. United Center Joint Venture privately funded the entire project. United Airlines currently pays approximately $1.8 million a year in naming rights.

■ The Baltimore Ravens have a financially lucrative stadium deal, with the team receiving revenue from seat licenses and 100% of the revenue from concessions, ads, suites, club seats, and naming rights—and the team pays no rent. Ticket, novelty, parking, sponsorship, and advertising revenues are split between the team and government.

■ Portland's Rose Garden was built using a complex blend of private and public funding, including a $46 million cash contribution from Portland Trailblazers owner Paul Allen. Three major banks loaned a total of $16 million to the pot. Last, nine insurance companies purchased $155 million in privately placed bonds paying 8.99% interest over 27 years. The city of Portland paid $34.5 million for street, parking, and related improvements. These city-funded projects will be paid for by a ticket tax of 6.5%, which will pay off the city's contribution in 6 years and thereafter provide the city with a perpetual return on its investment.

■ The Gateway project in Cleveland was financed through a tax-exempt county bond offering that raised 45% of the $152 million needed to build the Gund Arena, which is now named the Quicken Loans Arena. Liquor and cigarette taxes (sin taxes) covered another 42%, and private naming rights covered the remaining 13%. Bonds were sold to various investors, and the income stream used to repay the bonds came from state capital improvement funds and a countywide sin tax of $3 per gallon of liquor, 16 cents per gallon of beer, and 4.5 cents per pack of cigarettes. These taxes were to be in place for 15 years (Fried, Shapiro, and Deshriver, 2013).

■ Tourism and sin taxes (alcohol and cigarettes) also have been widely used to fund recent stadium projects such as Marlins Park, which received $347 million in tourism taxes, and the University of Phoenix Stadium, where the Cardinals contributed $109 million and the rest was covered by hotel and rental car taxes.

■ The Florida Marlins' plan for a new stadium moved forward in 2009 after receiving 9 of 13 votes from the Miami-Dade County Commissioners in support of building a new stadium. The stadium's price tag is $634 million, with Miami-Dade County on the hook for $297 million from tourist taxes, another $50 million from a separate bond referendum, and $12 million for road and utility repairs. The City of Miami pledged to spend $94 million on the parking structures, $13 million toward stadium construction, and $12 million for other improvements. The city was also going to operate the garage and pay the yearly debt payment. The Marlins agreed to buy most of the expected 6,000 parking spaces at between $10 and $12 over the 35-year stadium contract. The Marlins would then keep any profits made from selling those spots to their fans (Rabin and Haggman, 2009). The public share of the tab would total $480 million, most coming from tourist tax dollars. The team spent $120 million on constructing Marlins Park and repaid a $35 million county loan for the 37,000-seat retractable-roof stadium that opened in 2012 (Rabin, 2009). The county share of the funds was to be secured through hotel taxes, but they had decreased 17% the month before the vote, and in a down economy those taxes might not be enough to secure a bond. Another major concern was whether the government would be able to raise sufficient funds with acceptable terms since the bond market was very weak. As of this writing the Florida Marlins Park financing deal is under investigation by the Securities and Exchange Commission for possible fraud. The primary claim raised by the SEC was the floating (selling) of tax-free bonds totaling some $500 million for the stadium construction as well as additional loans, leaving the taxpayers and bondholders on the hook for billions of dollars over almost 40 years.

tion bonds. A small city with a low tax base may suffer significantly if property values decrease or sales drop markedly. In contrast, a large city with thousands of properties can experience downturns in the economy and still have a large enough tax base that the damage can be minimal.

Municipal entities frequently issue various bonds to fund such buildings as schools, police stations, and sport facilities. The various types of municipal bonds include general obligation, special tax, revenue, and lease-backed financing bonds, as well as certificates of participation. Each bond type is typically distinguished based on what revenue source is being used to repay the bond.

Certificates of participation allow a municipality to form a corporation to purchase land or build a facility. The corporation then issues certificates of participation to pay for the land or building. The government then leases the building back from the corporation, and the lease payments are used to repay the bonds. Since the bonds are issued by a corporation rather than the municipality, they are not backed by the full faith and credit of the municipality. Thus, they carry a greater risk than traditional bonds. However, during tough times when a municipality may not otherwise be able to borrow money, the certificates of participation may be the only way to build a facility.

General obligation bonds are among the instruments most commonly used to fund public facilities. These bonds are often called full faith and credit obligations as the city, county, municipality, state, or other government unit pledges to repay the obligation with existing tax revenues or by levying new taxes (Fried, Shapiro, and Deshriver, 2013).

With a **revenue bond**, the tax revenue to support repayment may come from the project itself. For example, an entrance tax of $1.50 per ticket could be charged, and all revenues from this tax would first be allocated to repaying the revenue bond. These bonds traditionally have a lower credit rating than other bonds because there are significant financial risks associated with limiting repayment requirements to one specific tax or revenue source. The repayment concern arose in the 1998 NBA strike, for example. If games were canceled and admission revenue was lost,

some bond issuers might not have had any of their anticipated revenue sources to repay bonds secured by attendance taxes. This left the option available for a bondholder to declare an arena builder (team or municipality) in default and possibly foreclose on the property and have it sold to repay the bonds.

A public entity can also target a specific tax to finance a bond, termed tax-backed bonds. Cleveland utilized a sin tax on alcohol and tobacco sales to help finance Jacobs Field and Quicken Loans Arena. San Antonio utilized a sales tax-based bond issue to help finance building the Alamodome. Special tax bonds are repayable from a specific pledged source and are not backed by the full faith and credit of the issuing entity. Thus, if the specific revenue source is inadequate, there may not be enough tax revenue to repay the bondholders. Examples of specific funding sources include the following (Greenberg and Gray, 1996):

- Utility taxes. A utility tax is added to an electricity, water, or gas bill to help pay for the bond's debt service. In the 1990s, the San Francisco Giants were considering a move to San Jose, California. The proposed stadium was to be partially financed by a utility tax. Opponents of the stadium distributed light-switch covers to communicate the idea that every time people turned on the lights they would be paying for the proposed stadium. The stadium ballot measure was defeated.

- Car rental taxes or tourist development taxes. These taxes are designed primarily to tax out-of-towners who visit the city. This is a popular technique because it is easy to tell a voting population that out-of-towners will pay for the facility even if local residents are really the most frequent users of rental cars.

- Ticket surcharges. A ticket surcharge is an additional amount, such as $0.50 or $1.00 per ticket, that increases the ticket price. The funds go directly to repaying the bonds. This option is popular with voters since the people who go to the event pay a larger share than others.

- Real estate taxes. All property owners pay real estate taxes unless they have a special dispensation authorizing them not to pay such taxes. A municipality may increase the real estate tax obligations to help fund building a new facility. The concept is that the facility can help increase property values, so property owners should help support the facility.

■ Possessory interest taxes. A possessory interest tax is charged to whoever possesses control of the facility and is designed to tax the primary facility user. This type of tax is very popular with taxpayers.

■ Excise tax. Excise taxes are a general tax added to various products and are often initiated in periods of financial need such as times of war or economic downturn.

■ Nontax fees such as permits. Nontax fees are special expenses passed on to particular parties. For example, the permit costs for other developers in the city can be raised. Other city expenses that are normally charged to vendors and citizens can be raised, with the extra funds going to pay for the facility.

■ Lottery and gaming revenue. A municipality can dedicate funds received from special lotteries or games to fund civic growth projects such as roads, schools, and stadiums. Some states have received significant windfalls from Native American-owned casinos opening in the state.

■ General appropriations. General appropriations are funds that are set aside for various purposes. Through political dealing, a municipality may convince the state legislature or federal government to give a "gift" appropriation to help pay facility construction expenses or to fund bond repayments. The San Antonio Alamodome was built as a bus stop in order to help secure a federal appropriation for interstate transportation. Thus, there are few parking spaces next to the facility, but there are numerous bus stops.

Repayment Sources

Whichever type of bond is issued, repayment will always be the key concern for investors. Other factors can also be important to a potential investor, such as whether the bond is tax exempt, whether the government entity purchased bond repayment insurance, and whether **contractually obligated revenue** or **contractually obligated income** is sufficient to repay the bond. Even with these variables, investors look toward a stable repay-

ment source as an additional assurance that the bond will be paid.

Although these revenue sources or payment guarantees can often support significant repayment obligations, contractually obligated revenue can also provide a strong guarantee that a debt will be repaid. Contractually obligated revenues are any contract whereby a party agrees to pay a specific sum for a guaranteed number of years. Typical long-term contracts that form the basis of contractually obligated revenue backing include premium seating, luxury boxes, naming rights, pouring rights, signage rights, and parking rights (Fried, Deshriver, and Mondello, 2013). Contractually obligated revenues have two primary functions. They can be used as a source of revenue to guarantee repayment of bonds or other loans. They also can be utilized as an independent funding source. If the bonds are all covered through other revenue streams, the team or facility may be able to sell the naming rights and use those funds to enhance its bottom line.

Contractually obligated revenue from prepaid membership can help secure a loan to build a facility. Similarly, when anchor tenants are found who are willing to sign a long-term lease, then the contractually obligated revenue associated with that lease can help fund the borrowing required to build a facility.

Miscellaneous Funding

In addition to the standard funding options such as loans, bonds, or contractually obligated revenues, there are numerous unique strategies for financing a facility. One of the easiest is to have someone donate a facility. Sometimes a facility can be built with a gift. Some colleges, universities, communities, and schools will not even entertain the idea of building a facility unless funds have been donated for that purpose. North Dakota received a $50 million gift from a wealthy alumnus to fund a $100 million arena. The University of Houston had a wealthy alumnus donate the athletic and alumni center and baseball field. Especially at the collegiate level, numerous sport facilities have been funded by private donors, who often receive a tax deduction for their gift. Other unique funding options include grants and user funding.

Facilities Trivia

Investing in a sport facility is supposed to be a financial boon for a region, but it does not always turn out as planned. The City of Allen, Texas, built a $60 million stadium to seat 18,000 fans and was ridiculed by the media as the epitome of overexpenditure in sport. The facility was the most expensive high school football stadium built in the United States. Voters approved the stadium in 2009, with 63% of the voters approving a $119 million bond for the stadium and other facilities. The new stadium replaced a 35-year-old, still-used stadium with 4,000 fewer seats. However, 18 months after the facility opened, it was shut down due to extensive cracking along the concrete concourse. The negative fallout from this facility fiasco, which has yet to be resolved, has affected other potential stadium projects in Texas. In 2013, about 55% of voters in Katy, near Houston, rejected a $99 million bond measure that would have paid for a $69.5 million football stadium (Dave, 2014).

Grants

In a strategy that is similar to individual giving, organizations and people can also grant money for projects. Many foundations have large sums of money that they need to give away. Eli Lilly and Company is a large drug manufacturer based in Indianapolis. The Lilly Endowment has granted a significant amount of money to the city to build sport facilities. The process typically starts when the foundation provides nonprofit organizations that are interested in receiving funds with some rough parameters for proposals to be submitted by a specified date. All the proposals are analyzed, and the foundation's board selects the ones they wish to fund entirely or partially. Most foundations receive numerous requests, so the grant process is highly competitive. However, if a nonprofit organization or school has an innovative idea that the board likes, it may award significant cash to help build a facility.

Nonprofit Funding

Some facilities such as YMCAs, JCCs, high schools, and even college facilities can receive gifts to help finance their construction. These gifts can range from major naming rights gifts (i.e., naming a building after someone) to individual donations of a couple dollars. A number of political and legal battles have occurred over the years between tax-exempt YMCAs and for-profit (i.e., taxed) private fitness clubs. The clubs complained that they had to pay taxes on membership dues and had to pay the going rate to buy or rent a facility, whereas the nonprofit facilities did not have to pay taxes on membership dues (thus pocketing more money or reducing dues) and could get the facility constructed through donations.

User Funding

There are numerous ways in which facility users can help finance a facility. One of the most frequently seen forms of user support is student fees. A university with 10,000 students may charge an activity fee of $100 per semester to fund a new recreation center. This would represent a $2 million contribution to the facility and could possibly fund debt repayment and operating expenses, depending on the facility's size. The hazards with such a strategy are that students can resent the fee, especially if they do not use the recreation center, and that revenue is hurt if enrollment declines.

SELLING A FACILITY

One financial consideration that is often overlooked with a facility is the financial repercussions of selling or otherwise disposing of the property. At a certain point a facility may outlive its usefulness. There are various methods for disposing of a facility, including the following:

- Transfer the facility from one operating division to another at full book value.
- Put the facility on the market as a sport facility, and see if someone will pay the value of the facility based on its current usage.
- Sell all the equipment and then put the building on the market for any potential use.
- Sell the facility to whoever will buy it for any use.
- Sell the facility to a lender or financial institution and then lease it back.
- Demolish the facility and rebuild a new structure on the same site.
- Donate the facility to charity (Cotts and Lee, 1992).

The **sales–lease-back strategy** is gaining popularity with many facility and equipment owners. Someone who owns a building that is worth $100,000 and has $50,000 in equity could sell the building to a lender for $100,000. After paying the $50,000 owed, the former facility owner would have $50,000 to expand or grow the business. He would then make a lease payment of possibly $1,000 a month for 10 years and then could either repurchase the facility or enter into a new lease. This option allows the former facility owner to gain valuable cash and reduce income by paying tax-deductible rent.

Summary

Many people do not like to talk about finance because they may not understand some of the numerous terms and formulas. However, for facility managers to have any credibility, they need to have a strong grasp of finance and how to run a facility under a budget. A facility has identifiable revenues and expenses that the manager needs to determine in order to learn how to make more money or reduce costs. Once the dollar value of income and expenses, along with assets and liabilities, is calculated, management can plug these numbers into various financial tools such as income statements and balance sheets to determine how well the facility is doing financially.

Financial analysis is used to forecast the future and develop an operating budget that will help the facility reach its goals. If the forecasts or budgets are wrong, it is almost impossible for a facility to reach its goals. The budget process does not focus only on day-to-day concerns; it may also include developing a capital project to renovate an existing facility or build a new one. Once a strategy has been chosen and a building type identified, the money needs to be raised from private, public, or other sources. However, the financial analysis should not end when a building is built but rather should continue as long as the facility is operating. Financial analysis is also needed when the time comes to dispose of a facility.

Discussion Questions and Activities

1. What should be the primary financial concerns for a large stadium versus a small fitness facility?

2. What bills relating to a facility are the most time sensitive and require fast repayment?

3. How would you handle a major financial surge or slump that might affect your facility?

4. Research a major sport construction project in a city such as Dallas, New York, Brooklyn, or Santa Clara. Was the project a financial success? Include your criteria for measuring financial success.

5. Develop a budget for yourself for the rest of the semester. Then build one for next year. What additional information would you need to make sure the budget for next year is as accurate as possible?

6. Research a publicly traded sport company that owns stadiums or race tracks. Examine its balance sheet or income statement and read its annual or other report. Is the company in a strong financial position?

7. Should colleges use student activity fees to finance building a new student recreation center on campus?

8. Look up the stadium or arena of your favorite team. How did they finance the site purchase and construction process?

13

Legal Responsibilities

Chapter Objectives

- Understand the breadth of legal issues affecting sport facilities.
- Apply basic principles of tort and contract law to daily facility operations.
- Appreciate how constitutional law and government regulations affect stadiums and arenas.
- Learn how to apply risk management techniques to make facilities safer.

The law is one of the more difficult topics to cover appropriately, and it is hard to do justice to the topic in one chapter. Thus, this chapter highlights some of the most important legal concerns facility managers face, primarily tort- and contract-related issues. These two issues are emphasized over others because facility managers face these concerns on a daily basis. Issues regarding constitutional and property law are seen less frequently, although their effect can be just as important as that of tort or contract disputes.

This chapter focuses on the main legal issues facing sport facilities. It starts with an overview of the law and then examines several key concerns that all facility managers should understand. Besides tort and contract law, special attention is given to property law issues such as zoning and eminent domain. Next the chapter looks at constitutional law, including First and Fourteenth Amendment freedoms related to management of public assembly facilities. Finally, government regulations such as the **Americans with Disabilities Act** (ADA) and smoking and alcohol regulations are discussed. Employment law also affects all facets of facility management; see chapter 3 for a discussion of employment issues.

BASIC LAW

The law is an abstract concept. It is designed to provide guidance and direction for individuals and businesses. The law is designed to benefit society but can also hamper and confuse businesses. For example, some municipalities have outlawed scalping of tickets (selling tickets above the listed face value of the ticket), while other municipalities allow scalping to be conducted outside the facility, on public property, or only on private property or allow resale without any ticket price increase. Thus, what is legal in one area may be illegal elsewhere.

Numerous legal issues apply to sport facilities. Some laws are developed by legislative bodies and are called statutory laws. Tax laws, Occupational Safety and Health Administration (OSHA) legislation, health code regulations affecting concession operations, and legislation related to the tax deductibility of donations to athletic programs

and the tax-free status of construction bonds are just some of the statutory concerns at the local, state, and federal levels. Laws developed outside the legislative process can originate from administrative actions such as hearings and legislation or from federal and state constitutions; the latter may cover free speech, freedom of religion, due process rights, and the inspection of property such as locker rooms.

Laws are also developed through the court systems. These laws are called **common law.** For example, someone who is hit by a foul ball may file a claim of negligence (see next section), which is a claim that the team or facility deviated from a duty to protect the fans. Courts have refined this concept over the years. The courts have also developed another concept called assumption of risk, which is a defense that a team or facility can raise to counter a negligence claim.

Among the various types of laws that can affect a facility, the legal issues most frequently seen in these settings involve tort and contract law.

TORT LAW

Tort law refers to a broad variety of claims based on damage to a person or property. There are both intentional and unintentional torts. An intentional tort against property includes theft of personal property. An intentional tort against a person can include assault, battery, false imprisonment, and defamation. If someone throws a punch that injures another person, the injured person can sue in civil court. Similarly, if someone makes a false statement about another person, the person with the injured reputation can bring a defamation claim.

Unintentional torts can occur to property through such instances as nuisance (e.g., when the noise or lights from a facility travel into a neighbor's house and cause the neighbor to lose the value or enjoyment of the property). This is in essence taking someone's property without compensation. Another unintentional tort is negligence, which refers to unintentional bodily or mental injury through failure to act in a reasonably prudent manner.

Varriale: Crafting the best management practices for safe venues

Photo courtesy of Carla Varriale.

My name is Carla Varriale. I am a partner in Havkins, Rosenfeld, Ritzert, and Varriale, LLP, in New York. I have represented Major League Baseball (MLB) teams and players, minor league teams, and other entities in the recreation and sport industries. I also teach a course in sports law and ethics at Columbia University School of Continuing Education's sports management program. I have worked with my clients in the sport and entertainment industries to develop successful risk management practices and litigation strategies. Increasingly, our focus is turning to security measures, both within and outside the venue. Although I am a litigator who thrives in the courtroom, one of the most challenging aspects of my job is to keep my clients on the field or in the boardroom—and out of the courtroom.

In many ways, sport and entertainment venues are microcosms of the outside world, and there are risks of injury to participants and spectators alike. Venues do, however, confront unique risks and challenges when seeking to control the action both on and off the field. To maintain reasonably safe premises, the modern venue operator must address, among other challenges, those relating to alcohol management, emergency preparedness, and the conduct of spectators as well as the liability that can arise from each. Moreover, as the line between entertainment and sport blurs, venue owners and operators are also confronting the changing nature of the modern spectator experience. This often results in enhanced liability and underscores the importance of understanding the nature and extent of potential liability and obtaining sound counsel regarding ways to minimize or avoid such liability.

An owner, operator, or manager of a sport and entertainment venue should possess a fundamental understanding of the legal elements of potential claims and defenses, particularly with respect to tort actions. Once armed with that knowledge, he or she can craft best practices and risk management strategies in order to avoid liability. Consequently, from counsel's perspective, a well-informed and responsive owner, operator, or manager is a critical asset.

Negligence

There are four elements necessary for any **negligence** claim:

- Duty. Some of a facility manager's duties are to provide a safe facility, inspect the facility on a frequent basis, repair any dangerous conditions, provide proper supervision, and provide appropriate matching of opponents. One of the primary duties is to act as a reasonably prudent facility administrator would, which requires the manager to act similarly to the way other managers with the same amount of training, education, and experience would act in similar circumstances. There also is a duty to take steps to protect facility users when there is a known risk or threat to others that makes an injury foreseeable.

- Breach of duty. Facility managers are required to act on their duty and exercise reasonable judgment to prevent a dangerous situation. If a facility manager has a duty to provide a safe facility but does not comply with appropriate fire code requirements, then the manager has breached his duty. The requirement to have a 4-foot-high (1.2 m) fence around a pool's perimeter to keep children out might be a duty. If the fence is not present, the pool owner has breached a duty. When a breached duty is a statutory duty such

---

FALL FACTS

More than 12,000 people die annually from slip-and-fall accidents. In addition, 17% of all disabling workplace injuries are caused by falls, and 26% of all deaths in public places are attributable to falls (Roderick and Quintana, 1996). In 2008, there were an estimated 2.2 million emergency room visits from falls in businesses and residences. By 2012 that number had reached 8.6 million; percentages of reasons why individuals fell stayed roughly the same. The following lists the reasons for the slips, trips, and falls (National Floor Safety Institute, 2011):

Reason	%
Walking-surface issue	55
Footwear problems	24
Lack of warning or signs	10
Lack of employee training	8
Fraudulent claims	3

---

as a required fence, the violation is considered negligence as a matter of law, or negligence per se in Latin.

- Proximate cause. Even if a duty was breached, that breach of duty may not be the direct cause of someone's injury. **Proximate cause** implies that an injury was the direct result of someone's breach of duty. For example, if a facility owes a duty to provide a safe environment but fails to clean the floor and remove a slipping hazard, the facility has breached a duty. If someone is injured on the slipping hazard, the facility may be found not guilty if there was an intervening act that broke the chain of causation. For example, if the person was injured not as a result of the slippery surface but as a consequence of being pushed by someone else, then the person who did the pushing would probably be considered the direct cause of the injury. In one famous case, a person was drowning in a pool. During the rescue attempt, the person was being pulled out of the water when his head slipped and slammed into the side of the pool. The court concluded that the proximate cause of the death was not drowning but rather the botched rescue attempt since the swimmer died from his head trauma (Fried, 1999).

- Injury or damages. Any negligence claim will require someone to have been injured, whether physically or emotionally.

When examining duty, the first step is to analyze what a reasonable person would have done in a similar circumstance. The definition of *reasonable* is based on what others in the same field or position with a similar background and level of experience would do in a similar situation. For example, a first-year athletic director would not be compared with one that had held the position for 30 years. If an established athletic director or several similar athletic directors would have cancelled an event due to poor field conditions, then the reasonable person with similar experience probably also should have cancelled the event. If a danger exists, then a duty to minimize or eliminate that danger exists. For example, if a sport facility is located on a roof, what steps (e.g., netting) are taken to keep balls and equipment from leaving the roof? In one actual case an older woman was walking on the street below a soccer field, which was on the third floor of a school's parking deck, and was hit in the head by a soccer ball that had been kicked off the roof. Allegedly, no netting was in place to prevent the ball from leaving the playing area, and the injured woman sued the school in Tennessee as a result of her injuries (Allyn, 2013).

All four elements need to be present for a valid negligence claim. If one element is missing, then there cannot be a valid negligence claim. Other defenses include contributory or comparative negligence, assumption of risk, and immunity. Depending on the state, either comparative or contributory negligence can be raised as a defense. Such a defense basically claims that the injured party was somewhat or wholly responsible for injuring herself. In a comparative negligence state, the court examines each party's respective actions and can allocate damages accordingly. If the plaintiff contributed 40% to her own injuries and receives a $1 million verdict, then she would recover only $600,000. In contrast, a contributory negligence state allows the plaintiff's own negligence to act as a complete bar. Thus, in this example, the plaintiff who was 40% at fault would recover nothing.

Assumption of Risk

Assumption of risk is a defense that a facility can use against the injured party. Assumption of risk means that the plaintiff knew about the risk of participating in a given activity, voluntarily assumed that risk, and then was injured. Under these conditions, the injured party should not recover any damages. One of the classic examples of assumption of risk entails foul balls at a baseball game. In numerous sports, the participants know the risks involved. If a person willingly participates while knowing all the risks and is subsequently injured, the courts might bar the injured participant's claim. For example, it is well known that players can be elbowed going up for a rebound while playing basketball. If a player gets elbowed in the normal course of the game, his claim would likely be dismissed. However, if he was pushed into an unpadded wall that was 3 feet (0.9 m) from the end line under the basket, he might not have known about the risk or the facility might have created such a dangerous condition [at least 6 feet (1.8 m) of unobstructed space behind the basket end line is normally required] that the assumption of risk defense would be minimized or not used.

Immunity

Immunity is another major defense that can be used by government entities and some nonprofit agencies. For example, the state of Alabama has in its constitution a provision that the state cannot be sued for negligence. Thus, someone who is injured in a public high school gym cannot sue the school. In other states, the immunity protection is more limited and basically protects government entities from simple acts of negligence but allows suit if that entity acted in a willful, wanton, or reckless manner. Thus, a public facility could be liable if its staff knew about a very hazardous condition but did nothing to eliminate the hazard. Furthermore, some states allow the immunity

BEHIND THE SCENES

FOUL BALLS

One concern with stadiums and arenas is projectiles, such as foul balls and hockey pucks, leaving the playing area. The death of a young Columbus Blue Jackets hockey fan in 2003 started a new trend in examining safety at sport facilities. That trend was expanded with the death of a Tulsa Drillers base coach from a foul ball in 2007. Stadiums normally have a screen behind home plate to protect fans. But how wide and tall should the screen be? Is the most dangerous part of the stands protected? Can additional protection be provided, such as the new screens being placed in front of dugouts to protect players? Can safety be incorporated throughout stadiums similar to the way Japanese parks screen the entire lower bowl to protect fans?

How much protection is needed for those sitting in picnic areas, where fixed benches might put their backs to the action on the field? What about multiple balls in play at the same time, such as during batting practice or when multiple balls are hit in succession? Is the warning on the back of a ticket enough or do fans need more information to protect themselves? These are just some of the questions about a topic that many people feel is easy to analyze but that facts might prove otherwise. For example, many of the initial limited duty cases (which traditionally limited a facility's liability if it screened the most dangerous part of the ballpark and provided screened seats for those who wanted such protection) in baseball were decided in the 1920s, when ballparks were significantly different and when spectators attentively watched the game (compared with today's viewers, who are distracted by wireless devices, flashy scoreboards, and numerous entertainment options). Thus, the law is trying to catch up with all the changes that have occurred over the years. For example, whereas in the past the area right behind home plate was considered the most dangerous area in a ballpark, recent research has shown that the areas down the first and third base lines can be equally or more dangerous.

Some fans need more protection than others. In a rare case from 1957, Richie Ashburn, a slugger with the Philadelphia Phillies, fouled a ball into the stands and hit a female fan. The fan was being treated and was put on a stretcher to exit the stands. As she was being moved, play resumed. On the very next pitch, Ashburn fouled the ball again, and guess who was hit by the ball? That's right: the woman on the stretcher. Thus, on two pitches, Ashburn hit the same fan twice (Nash and Zullo, 1992).

defense to apply to public employees if they are acting in a discretionary manner. This refers to activities such as planning an event at a facility or scheduling security personnel. The states do not want public employees to be sued for every decision they make, so they are given immunity protection. However, even in these states, the courts are clear that immunity protection is not provided when the employee is engaged in ministerial conduct. Ministerial conduct refers to mechanical execution of a directive. For example, it is a discretionary act when a supervisor develops a facility inspection and maintenance schedule. It is a ministerial act when the custodian follows the schedule. The supervisor can have immunity in the planning process, but the custodians will not have immunity for their ministerial act of failing to follow the schedule and inspect the facility in a timely manner. If someone is injured and the facility has breached a duty to provide a safe environment, the supervisor will probably be immune from liability, while the facility (as the employer) can still be liable for the custodian's conduct since the employee did not follow set regulations.

RISK MANAGEMENT AND INSURANCE

Although injuries and accidents are always going to occur, various risk management strategies can be used to minimize the potential for injuries and litigation.

Risk management focuses on two major issues: identifying risks and then eliminating or reducing those risks. Identifying risks involves a significant effort to examine current operations and then to systematically generate new strategies and techniques to reduce potential lawsuits. The **ECT approach** is one strategy for implementing a risk management system. The ECT approach is so named because every element ends with the letters *ect*.

- Reflect. A facility manager needs to determine why he is interested in implementing a risk management program. Is the purpose to save money, reduce insurance obligation, run a safer facility, or a combination of these? Another part of the reflect stage is to rank potential concerns

BEHIND THE SCENES

ACKLER V. ODESSA-MONTOUR CENTRAL SCHOOL DISTRICT

Risk management can involve simple details such as tape on a floor that may be a tripping hazard or more complex issues such as insurance. The following case highlights a problem that may occur when temporary measures are taken in a facility and are not implemented properly.

A high school student in New York was injured when he fell on a gym floor. The student was trying out for the school's basketball team. He claimed that during a particular drill his foot hit a sticky substance, causing him to fall and injure his knee. The student sued the school, claiming that the school was negligent for creating a dangerous and defective condition. The dangerous condition had been created when a piece of tape placed on the floor to mark a volleyball boundary line had been improperly removed. After removal of the tape, a sticky residue remained, and the student tripped at the point where the residue would have been. The school district filed for summary judgment, which is an attempt to have the court rule on a case before it gets to a potential jury. But the court concluded that there were sufficient facts to warrant proceeding with the

case, as the facts appeared to demonstrate that the school had acted negligently in handling and removing the tape (Ackler v. Odessa-Montour Central School District, 1997). This particular concern also arises in facilities where electrical cords are taped down to prevent a tripping hazard.

This case raises an important issue associated with risk management, in that putting tape on a floor is not a negligent act in and of itself. The liability concern is the negligent maintenance, application, or removal of any flooring tape. Once a facility manager begins to make a facility safer, she has to implement the safety plan in a reasonable manner. Safety-conscious administrators sometimes place nonslip tape on a stair lip to provide extra traction, but over the years the tape can wear down or peel. It is common to see staircases with poor or missing nonslip tape. Customers do not necessarily notice the tape's condition, but they expect it to be there. If they fall on an area where tape is missing, they may sue. To improve safety related to traction and vision, some facilities have installed permanent tread lips that illuminate in the dark.

in order of magnitude and effect. For example, an earthquake is not a major concern on the east coast but could be one of the bigger concerns on the west coast.

- Deflect. A facility can possibly improve risk management efforts by deflecting liability onto others. This can be accomplished through purchasing insurance that will pay attorney fees and any damages if a claim is filed; inserting clauses in rental contracts that require the renter to have insurance, assume liability, and hold the facility harmless from any claims; and having participants (possibly parents) sign a waiver indicating that they understand the risks of participating in the activity and will not sue the facility if they are injured while participating.

- Detect. A facility manager needs to learn how to identify potential concerns or retain people who are knowledgeable in risk management. For example, the National Fire Protection Association requires larger facilities to conduct annual life safety inspections. Such inspections identify numerous potential concerns.

- Inspect. It is not enough to identify risks and dangerous conditions; someone has to physically examine the facility and its policies to see whether any hazards exist or whether any area needs to be repaired.

- Correct. Once an area, object, or situation has been identified as hazardous, someone has to repair the hazard. This may require completing a work order or other means of communicating the needed repair to the appropriate individuals.

- Reinspect. The mere fact that a work order has been completed does not mean that the repairs or required actions were undertaken or were undertaken correctly to resolve the hazard. Thus, the area needs to be reinspected to make sure it is safe.

- Reflect. After a set time, such as a year or after an event, the entire risk management process needs to be reevaluated to determine whether it was effective and what steps can be taken to make it more effective in the future (Fried, 1999).

Risk management entails more than just following specific elements from an easy-to-remember slogan such as "ECT." Risk management also entails training employees to appreciate and apply risk management principles on a daily basis. Employees need to live risk management. When a napkin is on the floor, a well-trained employee will pick it up even if trash collection is not part of her job, since someone can slip on the napkin if it is not picked up. Thus, risk management flows throughout a facility and its staff and needs to be internalized in order for it to be effective.

One risk management strategy is the layering approach to reducing the risk of injury. Going back to the example of foul balls, it is easy to create a risk management environment that can significantly reduce the chances an injury will occur. The following are layers (the reason it is called the layering approach) a baseball stadium could use to ensure that fans are in the best position to protect themselves and understand the risk associated with attending a game:

1. Print a warning on the back of tickets. Put the warning in type that is larger and bolder than the rest of the print so that it is easily visible.

2. On all websites and stadium maps, mention the areas that are most dangerous or where foul balls are more likely to land.

3. Have ticket sellers mention whether a seat is an unprotected area.

4. Post signs (including visual signs and signs in different languages) warning patrons about the risk of bats and balls leaving the field during both games and batting practice.

5. Mention on both the stadium public address system and the scoreboard the risk of being hit by balls and bats. Play the warning several times before and during the game.

6. Have ushers and security personnel warn people when they take their seats that objects are more likely to enter the area and that they need to be alert.

7. Have ushers and security personnel remind fans to stay vigilant for their own safety.

A stadium does not need to undertake every one of these layers. However, the more layers taken and documented, the easier it is to defend against a suit brought by an injured fan to show that reasonable steps were taken.

In addition to risk management strategies, a facility manager needs to consider numerous types of insurance policies besides the traditional comprehensive general liability policies that cover basic business losses such as fire or liability for injuries on premises. Other necessary policies may include the following:

- Workers' compensation
- Automobile
- Business interruption
- Alcohol sales
- Employment practices liability insurance

There are also unique policies that can be purchased for a single event or for rare occurrences. Recent policies have been written to protect against such losses as natural disasters that in the past may not have been covered. For example, snow-removal insurance policies protect businesses if a snowstorm makes a business inaccessible for more than a set number of days (Yarborough, 1998). In 1995 to 1996, Logan International Airport purchased snow-removal insurance; the policy was written to activate after 44 inches (1 m) of snow had fallen. The policy provided a $50,000 payment to the airport for every inch over 44 inches up to 84 inches (2 m). More than 100 inches (2.5 m) of snow fell that winter, and the administrators at Logan were considered geniuses since their $400,000 investment in the snow-removal insurance brought a $2 million return from the insurer. The insurance was necessary to help cover the costs associated with snow removal, lost parking, and lost concession revenue due to fewer passengers.

Such narrowly focused policies can be crafted to address or exclude specific circumstances. In the case of snow-removal insurance, the policy can specify what lost business will be covered, during which dates, whether snow removal is covered versus just lost business income, and which days will be specifically addressed as key business loss dates. For example, a football stadium may want snow-removal insurance only for Sundays when home games are played against opponents with a win–loss record over 70%. Any terms can be included in an insurance policy if it is negotiated and accepted as a valid contract.

A simple warning sign is the start of a risk management program.

CONTRACTS

Most **contracts** do not need to be in writing to be effective. Numerous transactions occur in a facility without a written contract, such as when a patron pays $5.00 for a beer. When the money and the beer are exchanged, a contract is completed. A written contract merely provides evidence of what the contractual terms were. Some contracts, such as a contract for the sale of real estate or a contract that cannot be fulfilled within 1 year, need to be in writing. Although it may not be necessary for a contract to be in writing to be legal, every contract needs to have four basic elements to be valid:

1. An agreement includes an offer and acceptance. If Mr. A offers to paint Ms. B's house for

$1,000, there is an offer. If Ms. B says yes, there is an acceptance and the potential for a valid agreement. However, if Ms. B says she will pay only $800, the first offer is terminated, and Ms. B has just made a counteroffer. The contractual terms in the agreement should be as specific as possible to avoid confusion. This can be very difficult in application. Sometimes people or entities enter into a memorandum of understanding. These simple contracts may provide basic terms, with a more detailed contract to follow. Memos of understanding have been used between a professional team and a city to build a stadium or arena. The memo is used to start the construction project, and then the complex and detailed contract can be completed at a later date.

2. **Consideration** is an exchange of value or promises. There is no requirement that any consideration have a minimum value as long as one party believes there is value. This point is important because without an exchange of value there cannot be a contract. Assume that a woman promises her grandson that she will give him $1 million. This is a gift that can be withdrawn without any repercussion, since there was not a contract. However, if the woman promises her grandson $1 million if he graduates from college, then a contract exists. The grandson does not have to stay in college or even go; in such a case, the woman would not be obliged to give him the money. However, if he chooses to attend college and graduates, she owes the money. His staying in college was consideration for her promise to pay a certain sum.

3. Capacity represents the ability to enter into a contract. Some people cannot be legally bound to a contract because of their age, mental status, or mental state. Those under age 18 cannot be bound to a contract because it is presumed that they do not understand what they are agreeing to, no matter how mature they may be. Thus, although a facility should still ask minors (those under age 18) to sign a waiver to participate, the parents should also sign the waiver to make the contract legally binding. This does not mean that the minor cannot back out of the contract. It also does not necessarily mean that the parents have waived the minor's right to sue, because in certain states

> ### Facilities Trivia
>
> Some fans just have no sense. Frank Martinez, a New York Mets fan, was evicted from his apartment for running down the hallways shouting "M-E-T-S!!!" after his team won. He was also evicted from the old Shea Stadium in 2007 for bringing a high-beam flashlight to a game against the Atlanta Braves. From his seat behind home plate, Martinez shined the light into the pitcher's and fielders' eyes until the team complained and security apprehended him (Bathroom Readers' Institute, 2009).

parents can waive their own rights but not those of a minor. Persons who are insane or mentally deficient also cannot bind themselves through a contract, and any contract they enter into can be voidable. Last, those who are impaired through drugs or alcohol also do not have the capacity to enter into a contract.

4. Legality is the last element of a valid contract. Contracts must have a legal purpose. Thus, a court would not intervene to enforce a contract for selling or buying illegal drugs. Since the drugs are illegal, any contract regarding them is void from the outset and cannot be enforced in any court.

As already mentioned, all four elements of a contract need to be present. However, having a valid contract is not the end of contract law. The contract has to be performed. If all parties perform their contractual obligations, the transaction is completed. A party that does not comply with its contractual obligations has breached the contract. For example, if a corporation signs a 20-year naming rights contract for a facility and cannot pay the required amount in a given year, the company has breached its contractual obligation. The facility can ignore the breach and try to settle the dispute, terminate the contract and look for another sponsor, assess damages under the contract, sue to enforce the contract, or take these actions in combination. If a contract is breached, the aggrieved party can sue to recover actual losses and possibly other damages.

There are numerous facility-related contracts, from simple ticket purchases or concession sales contracts (see "Sample Facility Concession Contract") to complex lease agreements and bond

SAMPLE FACILITY CONCESSION CONTRACT

THIS AGREEMENT made this _____ day of _____, _____ by and between _____, a municipal corporation, having its main office _____, (hereinafter "Facility"), and Facility Operator, Inc., whose mailing address will be _____ (hereinafter "Operator").

WITNESSETH:

WHEREAS, the Facility is a multiuse sport facility; and,

WHEREAS, Operator is qualified and knowledgeable in the field of concession operation; and,

WHEREAS, the Facility desires that Operator provide concession service at the Facility during sporting events.

NOW, THEREFORE, the parties agree as follows:

1. Service to Be Provided. Operator shall, during the term of this Agreement and for and during the hours of operation herein below provided, provide concession items as mutually agreed upon by both parties.

2. Fees.

    Occupancy Fee. Operator agrees to pay a concession fee of $ _____ for permission to sell concessions at the Facility. This payment of $ _____ must be received by _____ to be valid.

3. Term. This Agreement shall apply from the date hereof through December 31, _____. The Facility and Operator may by mutual agreement extend this Agreement for two successive 1-year options, with modifications to this Agreement subject to the approval of both parties. Such renewal shall be in writing and signed by both parties.

4. Permits. Operator shall be responsible for obtaining all appropriate and necessary licenses and permits for the sale of its products. Appropriate and necessary permits and certificates for food service and from County Health Department must be obtained and exhibited prior to serving customers. Repeated health code violations or other poor performance leading to Health Department citation(s) shall result in this contract's termination.

5. Insurance. During the term hereof, Operator shall maintain in full force and effect bodily injury, property damage, and comprehensive public liability insurance of not less than $1,000,000. Operator shall deliver to the Facility a certificate issued by the insurance carrier naming the Facility as an additional insured.

6. Indemnification. Each party shall indemnify and hold harmless the other and their respective successors, assigns, officers, directors, agents, affiliates, and employees from and against all costs, liabilities, damages, expenses, claims, and demands whatsoever, including reasonable attorneys' fees, suffered by or asserted against the other party, that result directly or indirectly from any negligent, willful, reckless, or wrongful act or omission of the other party, its employees, representatives, or agents, under this Agreement, or from any breach of its representations and warranties herein. If a claim arises, upon receiving notice or knowledge of any claim, event, or loss for which indemnity is sought hereunder, the indemnified party shall tender the matter to the defending party and cooperate with its defense as that party may reasonably request, and permit the defending party to defend, try, settle, arbitrate, or appeal such matter as the defending party shall determine. After tender and acceptance of defense have occurred, the indemnitor shall not be responsible for further defense costs or further attorneys' fees.

7. Trash Removal. The Facility shall provide trash receptacles for Operator's operation at no additional cost or expense to Operator. It shall be Operator's responsibility to empty trash receptacles at the end of each day, located inside each concession and eating area, and place trash outside the Facility for final removal.

8. Uniforms. Operator's employees will use Operator's standard uniform designating them in a manner that sets them apart from security personnel.

9. Conduct. Courteous and polite behavior is required and expected of Operator's employees.

10. Applicable Laws. Operator shall observe all laws, ordinances, and regulations applicable to its operation hereunder and shall promptly pay when due all sales, employment, income, and other required taxes.

11. Acts of God and Force Majeure. Neither party shall be liable for damages for its failure to perform due to contingencies beyond its reasonable control, including, but not limited to, war, fire, strikes, riots, storm, flood, earthquake, explosion, accidents, sabotage, public insurrection, public disorders, lockouts, labor disputes, labor shortages, or any other acts of God.

12. Attorneys' Fees. In any action to construe or enforce the terms and conditions of the Agreement, the prevailing party (as determined by a court of competent jurisdiction, if necessary) in such action and in any appeals taken therefrom shall be entitled to recover all reasonable attorneys' fees and costs.

13. Waiver. Failure or delay on the part of either party to exercise any right, power, privilege, or remedy under this Agreement shall not constitute a waiver thereof.

14. Severability. The provisions of this Agreement shall be severable, and the invalidity of any provision, or portion thereof, shall not affect the enforceability of the remaining provisions.

15. Authorized Signatures/Effectiveness. The persons signing this Agreement shall have all legal authority and power to bind Operator and Facility.

16. Entire Agreement. This Agreement constitutes the entire understanding between the parties and supersedes all previous agreements or negotiations, whether written or oral, and shall not be modified or amended except by written agreement duly executed by the parties.

17. Binding Agreement. This Agreement shall be binding upon and inure to the benefit of the parties, their heirs, successors, and assigns.

18. Pricing and Signs. All display signage and advertising and promotion located in the Facility must be approved by the Facility prior to display and shall not conflict with current Facility sponsors.

19. No Competition. During the term of this Agreement, the Facility agrees that it will not enter into an Agreement with any other entity permitting any concession operation at the Facility.

20. Security. The management staff at the Facility and the local police shall have keys to each concession location. The Facility is responsible for hiring, training, and managing the activity of all Facility security personnel. Security personnel should make regularly scheduled visits to Operator's sites and help with securing money deposits after each event.

21. Default. In the event Operator shall fail to comply with all the terms contained herein or fails to remain open for business at the times provided, or fails to abide by any of the terms and conditions thereof, the Facility may at its sole discretion provide written notice of any such breach or default.

22. Notice: In the event the Facility gives written notice of any claimed breach or default, Operator shall be allowed 72 hours after hand-delivery receipt of such notice within which to cure the breach or breaches specified therein. If the breach(es) take longer than 24 hours to correct, Operator will keep the facility manager informed of the daily progress being made to correct the breach(es). No breach(es) will take longer than five (5) days to cure, and if the breach(es) cannot be cured the Agreement will automatically terminate.

IN WITNESS THEREOF, the parties hereto sign this Agreement on the date below and hereby acknowledge acceptance of all the terms and conditions set forth herein.

_____

Title

_____

Title

Reprinted, by permission, from G. Fried, 1999, *Safe at first* (Durham, NC: Carolina Academic Press).

issuance contracts. Lease provisions need to be carefully crafted. During the 2002 football season, county commissioners in Cincinnati sued the Bengals for breaching their lease obligations. The Bengals had lost six straight games at the start of the season, were 10-28 since moving into the newly built stadium, and had sold out only 7 of 19 home games. A sentence in the lease stated that the sales tax increase used to fund the stadium was needed to "keep competitive and viable major league football and baseball teams in Cincinnati." Since the commissioners did not perceive the team as competitive, they were examining the option of suing the team for breach of contract for failing to field a competitive team ("County Probes," 2002). The case was later dismissed by the courts for being filed in an untimely manner (too many years after the contract was supposedly breached).

One of the important concerns associated with contracts is keeping them current. This is especially important for leases, as provisions written 20 years ago may no longer be applicable. Significant bargaining and renegotiating often need to be undertaken when contracts such as leases expire. For example, extending a lease may not be worthwhile if more favorable terms can be found. If numerous buildings are vacant, some landlords may go into a reverse bidding war to offer the lowest price and best amenities to attract a tenant. Some of the strategies used when renegotiating a lease include the following:

- Finding a "walk-away" alternative facility that could serve the same purpose and would not be difficult to move to (if a landlord knows the facility cannot be replicated, then the landlord has all the bargaining power)

- Avoiding unfair escalation clauses that can significantly increase rent obligations

- Obtaining the right to audit the books to calculate operating expenses

- Changing the base year for future increases to the current year to avoid unfair increases

- Avoiding holdover clauses that charge large sums for staying just several days over the former lease ending date

- Eliminating any personal guarantees that will secure the lease obligations (Perry, 2002b)

PROPERTY LAW

Sport facilities are affected by **property law** in various ways. A sport facility represents real property. Real property is any property attached to land. Personal property, in contrast, such as a car or lawnmower, can be moved. Numerous laws, regulations, and ordinances affect real property. For example, as discussed in chapter 4, zoning is a major consideration for any proposed facility. Local officials want to protect a neighborhood's integrity and may allow only residential property in a given area. However, if a community benefit can be derived from the facility, the zoning laws may be bent to allow a JCC or YMCA, for example, to be built in the neighborhood even though the existing zoning does not allow such a facility.

Other property issues previously discussed include the use of eminent domain by a municipality to take land for a public use. In one circumstance the city of Baltimore attempted to use eminent domain to try to keep a professional team from moving. The Baltimore Colts were interested in moving, and the city council voted to use eminent domain to keep the team. However, the team packed up its bags in the middle of the night and moved in its entirety in several trailers to Indianapolis. If the team was not in the city, it could not be touched. Some legal authorities also believed that eminent domain would not work on a team since a team is not real property. However, the Colts did not want to stick around to see how the potential legal battle would end.

One concern often overlooked is criminal law claims based on property damage. Although facility managers are aware of the potential for criminal conduct against people, it is just as likely that criminal acts against the property will occur. The most common type of crime against a property is vandalism. Vandalism can be a minor nuisance, such as graffiti on a trash can, or can cause major damage, such as that caused by a truck driving onto a wet grass field, creating major ruts. In one case of sport vandalism, in 2011 an upset University of Alabama fan poisoned trees at Auburn University's Toomer's Corner using a strong herbicide. The trees had to be removed.

One of the biggest legal concerns associated with property law is the concept of nuisance.

NEGOTIATING THE BEST CONTRACT

When negotiating a contract, especially a construction contract, a facility manager should make sure the contract does the following:

- Specifically defines the work to be completed, including the quality of material, time to complete the job, insurance coverage, government requirements, and so on

- Awards the contract to a builder or contractor who has been properly vetted (e.g., credit, insurance, and references have been checked)

- Protects the project from the contractor making a lowball bid to get the contract and then flooding the project with numerous small extras to make a profit

- Defines deduction clauses for instances in which the contractor might lose pay (e.g., failing to remove debris, having an inadequate crew size, or missing firm completion dates)

- Includes a cancellation clause that allows the facility manager to cancel the contract for lack of performance or any other negotiated reason

- Specifies responsibilities and who is responsible for what. This can include site rules (e.g., how the site should look at the end of the day), who supplies what material, who pays for materials, and who needs to obtain necessary permits and variances

- Requires an insurance policy covering both the construction site and off-site issues (e.g., if the builder damages a neighbor's property)

- Specifies what constitutes doing a good job (e.g., complying with all codes or completing all work in a professional manner)

- Specifies when payments will be made and the amount of each payment. The contract should also specify who can authorize payment and who needs to approve payment to avoid any confusion

In order to get the right contract, a facility manager needs to negotiate the right terms from the very beginning. Weak negotiations will not make a contract any stronger, and any attempt to correct weak negotiations by changing or contradicting the terms in a contract will cause a facility manager to lose the trust of not just the contracting party but the entire industry. Thus, a facility manager needs to have a plan before negotiating, do his homework so he knows what he wants (and, more importantly, know what the other side might want from the deal), be patient because time can be a great negotiating tool (some sides might be under extreme pressure to finalize a deal and this could actually harm them in the negotiation process), know that almost everything is negotiable, know what the deal breakers are for each side, and know when to walk away if the deal is not good.

The leases negotiated between MLB teams and spring training sites are a great example of how the contract negotiation process can vary greatly. Palm Beach County is the spring training home for both the St. Louis Cardinals and the Miami Marlins. The county entered into a lease in 1998 that runs through 2027. Under the lease the county does not receive any revenue from the two teams but also does not have to pay any expenses generated during the time the facility is run in spring training. However, the net cost to the municipality of operating the facility was more than $2.5 million in 2011. In contrast, Osceola County entered into a lease agreement with the Houston Astros that ran from 2001 through 2016. Under that contract the county receives 25% of ticket revenue, 75% of concession revenue, 25% of merchandise and novelty revenue, 20% of scoreboard ads, and 85% of parking revenue. In 2011, the county received $427,196 in revenue from the facility but also had to assume all ballpark operating expenses. Thus, the county had a net cost of just under $1.5 million for operating the facility in 2011 (Broughton, 2012).

Nuisance is a type of tort in which a party's use of land interferes with others' uses. For example, if a facility has outdoor lighting or a sound system that allows light or sound to spill over into adjoining property, the property owners can ask that the lights and sound be reduced. If the facility does not act, the homeowners can bring a nuisance suit to force the lights and sound to be turned down. Thus, a facility that has its own property does not have unfettered use of the property if it violates a law or interferes with other property.

CONSTITUTIONAL LAW

Constitutional law exists at the federal level and in all 50 states. Constitutional law applies only to state and federal actors, not to private facilities. The first question to ask when dealing with any constitutional law issue is whether or not a state or federal actor is involved. However, even in a private facility, state action can occur if a public entity, such as a college team, is using the facility for an official event. If a state employee (e.g., the coach) is forcing players to pray before a game with an opponent from a private university, there could be constitutional issues associated with the First Amendment's free exercise clause. This section covers several key constitutional issues associated with sport facilities.

First Amendment Freedoms

The First Amendment concerns rights such as freedom of religion, free exercise of religion, and freedom of speech. Issues related to freedom of religion and free exercise can arise when religious material is played over loudspeakers, a religious invocation is allowed before an event at a facility, or prayer is allowed in a locker room. In all these cases it may be argued that the state is providing support to or hindering a religion.

Freedom of speech issues occur more frequently in sport facilities but can be intertwined with religion-related issues. In one case, a fan brought a religiously oriented sign to a stadium and was expelled. This type of incident may be a blend of free speech and freedom of religion issues. The fan ended up settling the suit with the team, with no admission of any guilt or wrongdoing. Other cases involve free speech only (e.g., if a facility does not allow people to picket at the front entrance). Several cases have been raised by persons selling unofficial programs in front of stadiums and arenas. Courts are reluctant to impose a total ban against such activities and often impose what are referred to as reasonable time, place, and manner restrictions. Such restrictions allow a facility or municipality to regulate speech, not based on content but on other standard criteria. Thus, such restrictions are typically content neutral. Examples include noise ordinances that do not allow amplified sound after a certain time at night, requirements to obtain permits to assemble on public property, and rules precluding people from assembling at given areas or certain times. Such regulations are designed to prevent disruption to cities or facilities, but they need to be enforced in such a way that they apply to all speech so that content is not an issue.

Although the concept of content-neutral regulations is often used, other laws can override these regulations. For example, certain no-assembly rules may need to be enforced in front of a facility but may be relaxed if a union is calling a strike. This example suggests the complexity associated with free speech issues and the reason an attorney needs to be contacted before any attempt is made to regulate any speech. This is especially important if a facility is being leased to outside organizations. It is legal to lease a public facility to a religious organization, but if the facility is open to one group it must be made available to other groups regardless of their agenda or ideology. For example, if a facility is leased to a church group one week and a neo-Nazi group wishes to rent it the next week, the neo-Nazi group must be allowed to rent unless the facility is already booked or is unavailable for some other legitimate reason.

Fourteenth Amendment Protections

Equal protection is another major constitutional concern. Publicly owned sport facilities are state actors (act as agents of the state) pursuant to the Fourteenth Amendment and as such must provide equal protection under the law to all persons working in the facility. This can apply not just to the players and field workers but also to the press. One case highlighting this point was brought by a female reporter against the Yankees. The reporter was not allowed into the locker room and sued, claiming that the Yankees played in a public facility and thus she was owed equal protection under the law to be treated the same as male reporters (Ludtke v. Kuhn, 1978). On the basis of such cases, men's sports often allow both male and female reporters into the locker room to provide both sexes with the same access opportunity. To avoid the issue, women's sports do not let any reporters into the locker room. Often the press is allowed

FACILITY FOCUS

RAYMOND JAMES STADIUM

The Tampa Bay Buccaneers were following a 2005 National Football League (NFL) mandate to conduct searches of all fans entering Raymond James Stadium. The policy was designed to prevent a potential terrorist attack and prevent banned items from entering the stands. One season ticket holder objected to the searches, claiming they violated his constitutional rights to be free from unreasonable searches.

The fan argued that pat-downs were an unreasonable invasion of privacy that did little to make fans safer. In fact, he claimed that the lines outside the stadium exposed game patrons to greater danger. A lower court agreed. But a panel of the 11th Circuit Court of Appeals overturned that decision in June 2007, saying the fan had consented to the searches by purchasing tickets. Pat-downs at Raymond James were on hold during the legal battle but resumed October 12, 2007, after the appellate court lifted a stay. Until that point, Raymond James remained the last NFL stadium where the pat-downs did not occur.

The appellate court concluded that there is no constitutional right to watch football games and that his rights were not violated solely by the fact that the stadium is a publicly owned facility. Normally the constitution applies in public facilities, but the court concluded that the fan was given sufficient warning about the search and that if the ticket holder did not want to be searched he did not have to go to the football game (Stacey, 2007).

The case went all the way to the United States Supreme Court, which agreed with the appellate court and allowed the stadium to resume the pat-downs (Varian, 2009). The following is the specific language on the stadium's website relating to its policy for searches (Raymond James Stadium, 2009):

PAT-DOWNS

To ensure the highest level of safety and security, all guests will be subject to a courteous pat-down screening upon entry into Raymond James Stadium. The pat-down procedure entails an unobtrusive head-to-waist inspection for persons of all ages. Pat-downs will be done expeditiously by highly trained individuals of the same gender, done with the back of the hand; women will search women and men will search men. Fans that refuse pat-downs will not be admitted into Raymond James Stadium. THERE ARE NO EXCEPTIONS. We ask for everyone's cooperation as we continue to improve upon the safety at Raymond James Stadium. By tendering your ticket, you consent to such searches and waive any related claims that you might have against the stadium landlord, the NFL, the Buccaneers, or their respective agents.

in only after everyone has showered, or athletes are interviewed in a separate pressroom.

GOVERNMENT REGULATIONS

Sometimes laws are imposed on sport facilities based on perceived needs, new technologies, or even a tragedy. For example, in 2013 the state of Connecticut adopted new rules relating to swimming pool safety after two high school students died during swim classes. It was later discovered that no consistent standards for high school swimming pools existed and that the hodgepodge of rules or standards was inadequate (Griffin, 2013). The new rules identified various safety requirements and required both instructors and lifeguards to be present at each swim class.

This is just one example of how government regulations can affect a facility. Bleacher safety received a significant boost in 2002 when the Minnesota legislature passed legislation that conforms to the Uniform Building Code 2000. The regulations require bleachers over 55 inches (1.4 m) high to have no more than 4 inches (10 cm) of spacing between the floor and seat boards. Telescoping grandstands in gymnasiums can have a spacing of up to 9 inches (23 cm). Guardrails also must have less than 4-inch spacing at the openings and must not be climbable. Guardrails can be protected using chain-link fencing. The mesh of the chain-link fencing must have a maximum 1.75-inch (4.4 cm) opening if it is reinforced with plastic or wooden slats, or otherwise a maximum 1.25-inch (3.2 cm) opening, to make the fence more difficult to climb. Guardrails should also be installed with vertical spacing bars every 4 inches to prevent children from falling through. Last, the regulations require that a building official or design professional certify that the bleachers meet the safety requirements ("Minnesota Leading," 2003). Other potential code concerns for grandstands and bleachers include aisle width, access to exits, and structural soundness.

Other government regulations affecting facilities include OSHA regulations and taxes. The OSHA regulations affect the work environment and make facilities as safe as possible for workers. Injuries happen frequently in sport facilities. For example, in the first 3 years the Bridgeport Arena at Harbor Yard (now Webster Bank Arena) was open, at least three employees were injured and lost fingertips while working with glass dasher boards used for hockey. All serious injuries need to be reported to either federal or state OSHA offices.

Tax-related issues can include income taxes for employees, collection of taxes on various items sold, collection of a ticket-related surcharge tax, and possibly property-related taxes. The New Haven Ravens approached the city of West Haven in 2002 to reduce the team's property tax obligation. The Ravens were the only team of the 130 teams in minor league baseball that had to pay property taxes. They paid $25,000 a year in property taxes for using the field (Zaretsky, 2002). The tax obligation was only one of the team's obligations. They also owed almost $80,000 for back overtime pay for police officers who worked games. The Ravens were required to have three or four officers work the street in front of the stadium for every game, regardless of the number of spectators.

Clearly, government involvement in sport facilities has many facets. From zoning regulations to federal legislation affecting the environment, sport facilities constantly have to be aware of new regulations that can affect operations. Some important government regulations are discussed at the end of this section, but the most important law affecting sport facilities is addressed first. The ADA has had and will continue to have a greater effect on sport facilities than possibly any other law ever passed by the federal government.

Compliance With the ADA

In a watershed event for millions of Americans, the ADA was signed into law on January 26, 1992. The new law promised millions of Americans (more than 50 million according to some estimates) the opportunity to obtain equality in facility usage and employment opportunities (Fried, 1999).

Nowhere can the ADA's effect be seen more prominently than in facilities. Sport and recreation facilities are especially prominent in relation to ADA coverage because of the publicity generated by such facilities and the number of people who attend events or engage in activities at facilities. Sport facilities have become the target for organizations such as Paralyzed Veterans of America, which has engaged in concerted efforts on behalf of its 17,000 members to challenge new sport facilities that do not meet ADA requirements. The group filed suit against several arenas claiming that although spaces were available for wheelchairs, the seating did not offer a clear view of the action when surrounding fans stood up. Regulations under the ADA require all wheelchair seats to be designed so that the wheelchair-using patron is not isolated and has the choice of various seats and ticket prices, and, in places where fans are expected to stand, facilities must provide a line of sight comparable with the view from seats provided to other spectators.

ADA Requirements for Sport Facilities

Title III of the ADA covers places of public accommodations and commercial facilities such as establishments serving food and drinks, entertainment facilities (movie theaters, concert halls), public gathering places (auditoriums, convention centers, stadiums, arenas), public transportation centers, places of recreation (parks, zoos, bowling alleys), places of education (private schools), and places of exercise or recreation (gymnasiums, golf courses). The only exceptions from Title III coverage are private clubs and religious organizations.

Under the ADA, a place of public accommoda-

DO YOU HAVE A LEAD LIABILITY?

Although installing a field is not normally considered a liability issue, mixed messages can create a legal quandary for field owners. In May 2008, a front-page article in *USA Today* raised the concern about the potential for AstroTurf to be contaminated with lead after a number of older artificial turf fields in New York and New Jersey were shut down. Some opponents against artificial turf fields had suggested that the fields were problematic because the green coloring used lead, that the crumb rubber infield could cause health concerns, that gases can be released in hot weather, and that the rubber can be exposed to sewer runoff that might pollute the water stream (McCarthy and Berkowitz, 2008). Shortly thereafter, the United States Consumer Product Safety Commission issued a finding that the fields are not a risk for children. That finding did not prevent the California Attorney General's office from filing suit against a number of artificial turf manufacturers for allegedly failing to disclose the use of toxic substances as mandated by California law. The manufactures countered that no one had ever reported an injury or illness caused by the field and that California standards were stricter than federal standards (Perez, 2008). The case was settled in 2010 when the manufactures agreed to limit the amount of lead in future products.

---

tion must remove all **architectural barriers** to access if such removal is readily achievable. When an architectural barrier cannot be removed, the facility must provide alternative services. However, any new construction or facility alteration must comply with all ADA accessibility standards. New construction is required to be readily accessible and usable unless this is structurally impracticable.

The primary focus in analyzing sport facilities relates to the **public accommodation** requirements. Public accommodations may not discriminate against persons with disabilities. Persons with disabilities cannot be denied full and equal enjoyment of the "goods, services, facilities, privileges, advantages, or accommodations" offered by all covered facilities (**Americans with Disabilities Act, 1990**). The ADA applies to covered facilities regardless of whether they are owned by the private, nonprofit, or government sectors.

Disabilities Covered by ADA

The ADA employment provisions clarify what constitutes a disability under the ADA. Persons covered by the ADA include those with significant physical or mental impairments, those with a record of an impairment, and those regarded as having an impairment. Persons with a record of disability are protected even though they may not currently suffer any impairment. Thus a cancer patient in remission is covered by the ADA. Furthermore, persons regarded by any other person as having an impairment are protected even if they have never had any impairment. For example, even though people with dwarfism might not consider themselves disabled, they are protected because other people might think they are. A person has a disability if he has a significant condition that substantially limits one or more major life activities. Major life activities as defined by Department of Justice regulations include "functions such as caring for one's self, performing manual tasks, walking, seeing, hearing, speaking, breathing, learning, and working" (28 CFR Section 41.31, 2010). To help determine significance, the following factors are examined: the length of time the condition has existed, the number and types of life activities affected, the extent to which the disability limits opportunities, and whether the condition is medically diagnosable.

Common examples of protected disabilities include acquired immune deficiency syndrome (AIDS), paralysis, diabetes, arthritis, cancer, epilepsy, asthma, vision impairments, hearing impairments, speech impairments, learning disabilities, muscular dystrophy, heart disease, and manic depressive disorder. Conditions commonly regarded as impairments include dwarfism, albinism, cosmetic deformities, controlled diabetes, and visible burn injuries. The ADA specifically excludes a host of conditions or traits such as sexual orientation, pyromaniacs, kleptomaniacs, and compulsive gamblers. Other conditions that are not covered by the ADA include colds, broken bones, appendicitis, hair color, hair type, and left-handedness (Fried and Miller, 1998).

Persons with disabilities are not the only people protected by the ADA. The ADA prohibits discrimination against any individual or entity because the person has a known relationship or association with a person who is disabled. Thus, the roommate of a disabled participant cannot be excluded from attending. This does not mean the roommate can get into a stadium for free. But if the roommate and the disabled patron both have tickets, they should be allowed to sit together. These seats are often called companion seats.

Reasonable Accommodation

Reasonable accommodation refers to correcting both architectural and program-related barriers. An architectural barrier is a physical element of a building that impedes access for disabled individuals. Examples of architectural barriers include the following:

- Steps and curbs (rather than ramps)
- Unpaved parking areas
- Conventional doors (rather than automatic doors)
- Office layouts that do not allow a wheelchair to move through the space
- Deep-pile carpeting, which is difficult for wheelchairs to traverse
- Mirrors, paper towel dispensers, and sinks that are positioned too high on a restroom wall

All covered facilities must reasonably modify their policies, practices, and procedures to avoid discrimination. Modifications do not need to be undertaken if they would fundamentally alter the nature of the goods, services, facilities, privileges, advantages, or accommodations.

When faced with possible access barriers, facility operators often have to struggle with a prioritization process. To provide guidance, the Department of Justice has established priority suggestions for removing barriers, as follows:

- Removal of any and all barriers that would prevent a disabled person from entering the facility
- Providing access to areas where goods and services are made available to the general public

- Providing access to restrooms
- Removing all barriers to using the facility

Reasonable accommodation for ensuring equal communication can include a multitude of auxiliary communication aids such as qualified interpreters, transcription services, audio recordings, speech synthesizers, telecommunication devices for the deaf, telephone handset amplifiers, video text displays, written material (including large print), note takers, assistive listening devices, closed caption decoders, and Braille materials. Besides purchasing needed equipment, facilities must keep all equipment in accessible locations and in working condition.

Public accommodations are required to remove barriers only when such removal is readily achievable [ADA Section 302(b)(2)(A)(iv)]. "Readily achievable" means that the repairs or modifications can be made without significant difficulty or expense [301(9)]. Several factors influence the expense associated with barrier removal, including the nature and cost of needed remedial action, the financial strength of the facility or organization that is required to provide the accommodation, and the relationship of the facility to the overall financial picture of the parent company.

Traditionally, landlords are responsible for facility repairs and modifications. Thus, landlords are typically responsible for financing required renovations or repairs. If a lease agreement specifically allows a tenant to renovate a facility, it will be the tenant's responsibility to pay for ADA-required modifications. If a lease is silent concerning responsibility for required repairs, the Department of Justice could force both the landlord and tenant to pay.

Penalty for Noncompliance

The ADA is enforced through several means. Private citizens can file their own ADA claim in federal court. Private claims are entitled only to injunctive relief and attorney fees. Thus, if a bowling alley does not provide reasonable accommodation, a patron can sue to force the facility to build a ramp so a wheelchair user could reach the lanes.

A private citizen can also file a claim with the attorney general. After receiving a complaint, the attorney general can then sue the facility owner and seek injunctive relief. The attorney general can also recover monetary damages and civil penalties.

Practical and Inexpensive ADA Solutions

Numerous ADA solutions can be implemented at little or no cost. Although facility renovation costs and repairs are hard to reduce, it is much easier to implement program-wide attitude changes, which can significantly reduce the chance of incurring an ADA complaint.

To discover what potential ADA problems exist, a facility manager should perform a complete facility and program review. This involves six steps.

1. Designate one employee as the ADA expert. This person will have to review literature in the field, become familiar with ADA regulations and specifications, and listen to the needs of employees and customers.

2. Conduct a comprehensive facility audit. All facility components should be analyzed and evaluated for accessibility. A written evaluation should be prepared to track needed repairs, facility evaluation dates, repair dates, repair costs, priorities, and so on. Such documentation is critical when facing an ADA investigation.

3. Evaluate policies, procedures, and facility practices. All policies, procedures, or practices that may affect persons with disabilities need to be addressed. Servers can be instructed to ask each party being served how she can accommodate any special needs that any patron may have. The key to any such effort is co-opting all employees into the process, with the idea that they should not be afraid to ask how they can help or what they can do. For example, a sporting goods store's normal practice may be to require a driver's license when accepting a personal check. If someone does not have a license, the sales clerk should not automatically reject the check. The sales clerk could ask for other pieces of identification or find another reasonable accommodation to help meet the person's needs.

4. Acquire and maintain in readily usable fashion any necessary auxiliary aids such as interpreters, taped text, Braille text, and assistive listening devices.

5. Follow up to make sure the plans are acted on.

6. Always check with the accountant to determine whether accommodations the facility makes can be used to receive a tax break.

Cigarettes and Alcohol

Government regulations affect facilities and patrons. Numerous cities throughout the United States have adopted rules banning smoking in restaurants, in office buildings, on beaches, and in numerous other locations. Stadiums and arenas have not escaped the scope of these regulations. For example, Chapter V of the San Francisco Municipal Health Code was amended by adding Article 19E, which prohibited smoking in places of employment and certain publicly owned sport arenas. A pertinent part of the ordinance is the following:

> No owner, manager, or operator of a sport arena or stadium shall knowingly or intentionally permit, and no person on the premises shall engage in, the smoking of tobacco products in any enclosed or open space at a sport arena or stadium except in
>
> 1. concourses and ramps outside seating areas,
> 2. private suites and corridors to private suites, and
> 3. areas designated for parking.
>
> Any portion of a sport arena or stadium used as a bar or restaurant shall be subject to the provisions of this article governing bars and restaurants as places of employment.

The only way a facility could be found innocent of knowingly or intentionally allowing others to smoke would be if steps had been taken to prevent smoking. These steps include posting clear and prominent "No Smoking" signs at each entrance to the premises and requesting, when appropriate, that a person refrain from smoking in an enclosed area. Reasonable actions do not include the physical ejection of a person.

If a facility owner or manager fails to take these reasonable steps, she could be served with a notice from the director of public health. The failure to comply with the notice within the specified time period could result in an action being filed by the city attorney to enjoin or enforce the provisions of the article and to assess and recover civil penalties. The article also authorizes damages up to $500 a day for each day a violation occurs or is permitted to continue.

Alcohol regulations also need to be considered. The most universal regulations deal with the minimum age to purchase alcohol. However, regulations also affect alcohol advertising. Like their tobacco counterparts, alcoholic beverage manufacturers and advertisers are regulated in numerous states. One such law in California regulates the type of advertising (signs, billboards, and so on) that can be purchased from on-site retail licensees. An on-site licensee is defined as the owner of either an outdoor stadium or a fully enclosed arena with a fixed seating capacity in excess of 10,000 seats. The regulation (Business and Professional Code section 25503.6) limits advertising space and advertising time purchased for events at the stadium or arena. Alcoholic beverage manufacturers who participate in inducing a breach of the statute can face jail terms, a fine of an amount equal to the entire value of the advertising space or time involved in the contract plus $10,000, or both.

The regulatory provisions dictate what signs may be used in a stadium or arena. Signs cannot exceed 630 square inches (0.4 sq m) for interior use in premises where alcoholic beverages are sold for consumption on the premises. Facility owners need to be cognizant of this regulation, especially during special promotions where inflatable beer bottles or other such items are prominently displayed. The regulation (in section 25611.1) limits pictorial advertising—illuminated or mechanized—including, but not limited to, posters, placards, stickers, decals, shelf strips, wall panels, plaques, shadow boxes, mobiles, dummy bottles, bottle toppers, case wrappers, brand-identifying statuettes, tap markers, and table tents, which are not deemed to have "intrinsic or utilitarian value." Similar laws exist in other states and in Canada. Great Britain passed a law in 2002 that outlawed tobacco advertising and made it illegal for even race cars to have tobacco advertising.

To help prevent problems with new laws affecting tobacco and alcohol usage, sales, and advertising, a facility manager can utilize a two-step contractual approach to minimize the potential effect of changing laws.

1. Every sponsorship contract should contain a clause requiring compliance with all applicable laws. The contract should specifically designate which party is responsible for ensuring that all signage complies with local, state, and federal regulations.

2. To further protect a facility's sponsorship and advertising income stream, all sponsorship contracts with tobacco- and alcohol-related manufacturers and distributors should contain escape clauses providing either party with the option of terminating the agreement based on the passage of new regulations or laws. Such an escape clause would allow facilities to attract tobacco and alcohol advertisers and at the same time limit their exposure to potential liability.

OSHA

One concern that should be addressed in a discussion of government regulations is OSHA and code compliance. Risk management also applies to employees, and employee safety is a major concern for any facility manager. When Lambeau Field was being renovated in 2013 (a $146 million expansion), 2,000 employees worked a total of 625,000 hours. Various government officials conducted 400 site inspections and audits, which identified approximately 1,700 hazards that needed to be addressed. All workers attended a 30-hour OSHA course on site, and the course proved to be effective, as no lost-time injuries occurred. This means that although some employees might have received minor injuries, no deaths or major injuries requiring hospitalizations or missed work time occurred ("Lambeau Renovation," 2013).

Summary

Sport facilities can be dangerous according to the activities that occur within them. Even if a facility such as a gym is very safe, someone can still get injured in a freak basketball accident. It does not matter how safe the facility is if the injured person decides to sue to recover some of his losses. Thus, facility risk management may seem to be a losing battle in that no matter what managers may do, they always will have some legal exposure. Nonetheless, it is important to realize that through solid legal planning such as analyzing contracts, property law, and constitutional law and following government regulations, the potential for being sued or penalized is dramatically reduced.

Discussion Questions and Activities

1. Walk through a sport facility and develop a list of the top 20 safety concerns you see in the facility. Give specific steps and suggestions for eliminating or reducing the risks.

2. In pairs (with one student the seller and the other the buyer), write up a contract to sell and buy a pen or some other small item. The idea is to see how detailed the contract can be and what elements each pair of students will insert into their contract.

3. Research a facility that was constructed in the past 10 years to find out what legal battles arose when the facility was being planned and what tax levy was being voted on, as well as any suits that arose when the facility was being built. (For any project, normally a number of suits are filed by parties such as disgruntled voters, land rights advocates, and eminent domain opponents.)

4. What is negligence, and how can it affect a sport facility?

5. Why is it important to have a written contract?

6. What are the most important clauses to include in a lease contract and why?

7. Research criminal law issues that might exist in a sport facility in your town/ city. You should examine possible federal, state, and local criminal issues, which may range from drug issues to fights. Categorize them based on the types of laws you find (i.e. federal, state, or local).

8. Since intoxicated fans can cause numerous negligence claims, facilities often develop different policies to minimize alcohol-related concerns. Numerous situations may arise at pregame tailgate parties, where drinking is a common occurrence. What tailgating policies would you adopt for a college football facility to minimize alcohol related concerns?

PART V

Event and Activity Management

After a facility is built, all the systems are operating effectively, and all the administrative components are in place, the facility needs to actually host an event. Part V examines two specific areas for managers: security and running an event.

Since 9/11, security has become a large concern for sport facilities. Sport facilities need to protect all fans, players, employees, and other constituents, and planning for their safety does not happen in a haphazard manner. Through reaching out to all constituents, a manager can prepare the facility to host an event as safely as possible. Chapter 14 provides suggestions for both novice and experienced facility managers for implementing a security plan.

Chapter 15 examines how to prepare a facility to host an event. The first step is bidding for or contracting to host an event. Once an event is secured, the facility needs to secure proper personnel, arrange the finances, examine legal concerns, implement a risk management plan, purchase insurance, and implement a comprehensive marketing plan. Management needs to examine every detail, and having appropriate checklists can help a manager determine whether the facility is ready to host an event. The chapter examines various issues that might occur before an event and examines how a facility manager might deal with these issues both during and after an event.

14

Implementing a Security Plan

Chapter Objectives

- Appreciate that fans need a safe facility but often contribute to making the facility dangerous.

- Apply specific security management strategies to make facilities and events safer.

- Understand how crowd mentality can affect a person's judgment about engaging in inappropriate conduct.

- Describe the steps involved in implementing a crowd management program.

- Understand how alcohol affects individuals and crowds.

- Understand the steps that need to be followed in order to respond to a crisis.

In the 1970s, fans entered the field to congratulate Hank Aaron after he hit his 715th home run. Morganna the Kissing Bandit tantalized audiences with her on-field shenanigans. Eventually such activities became less benign as fans rushed onto fields or courts to tear down goalposts or steal a memory such as a towel or chair. In the 21st century, the antics became more sinister as fans actually attacked players, coaches, and referees.

As noted in chapter 2, the primary directive for any public assembly facility manager is safety. Safety applies to employees, participants, guests, and spectators. Employee safety is covered by requirements such as Occupational Safety and Health Administration (OSHA) regulations or provisions in a collective bargaining agreement. Participants are informed of concerns and asked to sign waivers and consent forms, and coaches, players, and officials are often provided significant protection by uniformed officers. Guests and spectators often require the greatest safety effort because they are the most unpredictable. No facility manager can anticipate how anyone or everyone will react. All it takes is one person to possibly set off a mob. This chapter addresses these types of concerns and provides solutions for dealing with crowd-related issues.

Through engaging in specific actions or developing appropriate plans and strategies for particular situations, a facility can prepare for the worst, so people know that if the worst occurs they are ready. The key topics covered in this chapter include the nature of security, the elements of a security program, entry and exit management, fan education, alcohol management, and responding to crisis situations.

WHAT IS SECURITY?

Security is the process of safeguarding an item, person, or place. A facility may have many valuable items that are needed to operate effectively. A typical larger spectator facility may have 200 to 500 televisions. People also need to be secured. Every large crowd presents different security concerns, from pickpockets to drunken brawlers. Smaller facilities have the same problems. How does a facility react to a fight in the parking lot over a parking space? How would a facility

respond if a health club member stole something from someone else's locker? Numerous crowd-related problems have arisen in stadiums or arenas when jubilant or distraught fans got out of control:

- Detroit witnessed significant criminal activities after major games in the 1980s involving baseball fans.

- Hooligan activities both in and around soccer stadiums are common in Europe and South America.

- After the 1986 World Series, rioting fans left 1 dead, 80 injured, 41 arrested, and more than $100,000 in damages.

- After the Cleveland Browns' last home game in 1995, the infamous "Dawg Pound" erupted as fans vandalized the facility by destroying bleachers to bring home as souvenirs (Fried 2004a).

- A street reveler was killed at a Boston Red Sox celebration in 2004 when she was hit in the eye by a projectile filled with pepper spray that was designed to be a nonlethal weapon.

- In 2004, Ron "Metta World Peace" Artest of the Indiana Pacers went into the stands after fans threw beer on him and an all-out brawl ensued.

The final category of security needs entails the facility itself. Closed-circuit televisions (CCTVs) are frequently used in sport facilities to deter vandalism and graffiti. These cameras can also pick up criminal conduct on the part of employees. Other techniques that can help secure a facility and its users include the use of security guards, bomb-sniffing dogs, turnstiles, pre-event screening, and metal detectors.

Facility managers are not doing their jobs if they prevent security problems inside the facility but fail to prevent violence in the areas outside the facility, such as the street or parking lot, where the results could be more serious. Through proper planning, many of the security and safety problems that have arisen over the years could have been prevented.

Security Management

The key to proper security management is **foreseeability.** Cases brought against facilities often allege claims such as poor lighting, missing or broken light bulbs, weak locks, no access control, poorly

Zito: Formatting comprehensive safety plans

My name is Steve Zito, and I joined Andy Frain Services in June 2010 to become president of the sports and entertainment division. Andy Frain Services started in 1924 and is the true pioneer of crowd engineering. Before joining Andy Frain Services, I managed many types of facilities, including stadiums and arenas, for 26 years. I opened and oversaw the design, construction, and operations of such facilities as the FedExForum for the Memphis Grizzlies, the AT&T Center for the San Antonio Spurs, and the Alamodome in San Antonio. I am a certified facility executive (CFE), a graduate of the Oglebay Graduate Public Assembly Facility Management School programs, the Leadership Masters Academy, and am a longtime member of the International Association of Venue Managers. I majored in sport management at the University of Massachusetts at Amherst.

In the sport and entertainment business there are the sacrifices of working days, nights, holidays, and weekends, but the rewards are meeting new people and seeing the fruits of our labor when the crowd leaves our venues safe and with smiling faces, wanting to return. If the day comes that I don't have goose bumps when looking at the excited crowd as the national anthem is being sung, that will be the day I need to look for a new career.

It is our job as facility managers to expect the unexpected. With the constant threat of terrorism at our doorsteps, we can never become complacent. We must always be proactive, look to improve our processes, and make some of our practices more transparent than others. The "bad guys" are always going to be out there, internationally as well as locally. It can be difficult to compromise customer service with life safety practices, but that is the price of trying to provide an environment that is as safe as possible for our customers.

We all can and must keep learning. It is important to study the design and architecture of our facilities, the technologies utilized in facility design and operations, the intelligence learned from past events, the lessons learned by networking with others across the industry, and the facility security training.

Those in the facility management industry need to capitalize on the experiences of not only the law enforcement agencies but also the "operational" veterans in these facilities and the industry: facility designers, facility operators, production professionals, promoters, artists, and the fans. The design of these facilities to operate in the safest and most efficient manner possible, constant proper planning and communications, ongoing training, the ability to execute the plan, the ability to expect and react to the unexpected, the ability to successfully screen, and ultimately to succeed in selling tickets is the ultimate game plan for a successful event.

The content that this chapter covers is critical to the success and safety of any event. Facility safety encompasses proper planning, determining staffing levels, dealing and communicating with all stakeholders, having and communicating established crisis management plans (including plans for medical, structural, terrorist, or environmental emergencies; event postponement; or even event cancellation), and having established and practiced policies and procedures (e.g., ingress and egress, evacuations, event command center, crowd management and pedestrian movement, and permitted items).

The evolution of an event is a very comprehensive undertaking that involves a tremendous amount of thought, experience, resources, due diligence, and communication. As the saying goes, "Proper planning prevents poor performance." In facility security it could the difference between life and death.

If you recall some of your favorite memories, at least one likely involves going to a ticketed event. These are the memories we try to create each and every day! I wish each of you all the best in your quest for a successful, rewarding, and exciting career.

trained guards, or poor management policies (Gordon and Brill, 1996). The civil cases reported to date primarily relate to crowd management and crowd supervision matters. One key case involving the failure to prevent a fan stampede was the 1983 case of *Bowes v. Cincinnati Riverfront Stadium*, which was brought after 11 fans were trampled to death at a The Who concert. The court concluded that the facility was liable under negligence and other theories because it was foreseeable that injuries would occur with the chosen seating arrangement. The facility had utilized a **general admission** arrangement in which the first people into the facility had the first choice of seats.

Almost every facility will have some foreseeable security concerns. These can be as mundane as kids stuffing toilets with paper to flood a floor or as serious as union members sabotaging a facility during a strike. Proper security planning entails appropriately trained security personnel, an appropriately sized security force, understanding building safety requirements, utilizing the most appropriate security equipment, and security planning strategies.

Security Staff Training

The best way to obtain appropriate security personnel is to hire people with security training. Some states require security personnel to be trained and even licensed. Many larger facilities need to have police or off-duty police on the premises. Other facilities utilize private security companies and incorporate in the contract a requirement that all security personnel be appropriately trained.

Regardless of who is providing the facility security, all security personnel should be properly trained to accomplish their specific tasks. There is no one correct method of training security personnel. Regardless of the training material used, the training program should include theory, experiential education, real-world shadowing, and testing to make sure employees have internalized the information. Although 2-hour training programs exist, they are often inadequate. Some of the best training programs are conducted over a full day and focus on real skill development, not just fan relations or a facility tour. Training should be regularly refreshed, and new employees need

to go through training before a facility can entrust them with the safety of fans. Security personnel should have significant training in interpersonal communication and dispute resolution. They also need to be trained in the facility's policies and procedures. Such training can include how to monitor intoxicated fans and how to prevent or resolve fights. In baseball, for example, ushers and security personnel are trained in how to monitor fans by conducting a "roving T," where they descend to the bottom of an aisle, turn in both directions if there is space to walk, and then walk back up the center aisle. The visible presence of these personnel can help set the tone of conduct for the fans, and troublemakers will often change their actions when they see an official or police officer in uniform.

The need for training applies also to non-security personnel. In fact, every employee or volunteer is in essence a security person. Receptionists are normally not considered security persons, but they represent the first line of defense and therefore also need to be properly trained. Maintenance staff may be a valuable source of information as they are often in a position to observe unusual activity (e.g., someone casing the facility). Thus, all employees and others such as volunteers working at the facility need training.

Training is often undertaken on the job. Security personnel frequently have a minimal amount of formal training but might have real-life experience. Nevertheless, a facility cannot rely on random life experiences but rather needs to have a formal education program for security personnel. Thus, most facilities offer some type of training, whether it involves reading, classes, or hands-on learning. The four phases of training that security personnel should receive are orientation, site-specific, ongoing, and advanced training (Morris, 2004).

Orientation training occurs when a security person or any other employee is hired. The material covered can include administrative issues such as break times, clock-in and clock-out procedures, overtime schedules, and change of shifts. Orientation training that relates to security can cover workplace violence, the use of pepper spray, protective services policies, and assertiveness training.

Site-specific training focuses on how to handle specific security protocols, with detailed examples showing how forms are completed. This phase also includes on-the-job training. This phase can include stints working at security gates, entrances, command posts, and other strategic positions.

Ongoing training includes refresher training. Such training may focus on new technology or techniques. Many facilities have weekly meetings at which employees are updated on security concerns. Weekly training can be very informal, with people reviewing recent industry articles or news stories about upcoming events and security issues raised at other facilities. Part of the training can also include pre-game meetings with all security personnel (often broken down by coverage areas) to cover any issues specific to that day's event.

Advanced training may include managerial courses and other programs that may lead to certification. Certification categories include certified facility manager (CFM), crime prevention specialist (CPS), and certified protection professional (CPP), among many others. These certificates are offered by various trade associations such as the International Association of Venue Managers. Other training options include team-building exercises, **tabletop exercises** (which analyze how team members would respond in a crisis), functional exercises that test equipment systems such as the emergency backup generator, and simulation exercises where an attack or disaster is simulated in real time or at half speed and the results are analyzed to improve execution for the next time the test is run or for when an emergency actually occurs.

Security Staff Size

The number of security personnel or police must be adequate to secure the facility. The force must match the needs of the event and the type of crowd that will be present. The Los Angeles Police Department put 4,000 officers on the streets during the 1984 Summer Olympic Games. The 1996 Summer Olympic Games utilized Atlanta's 1,550-member police force, volunteer security professionals from around the world, and more than 11,000 soldiers to complete the security staff numbering nearly 20,000 (Fried, 2004a). The 2012 London Olympic Games had a security crew of more than 23,700 professionals, and the security detail at the 2014 Winter Olympics in Sochi comprised more than 30,000 police and military troops.

Having enough security personnel is critical for resolving any disturbance in a large crowd. The Riddick Bowe versus Andrew Golota fight at Madison Square Garden provides an example. The postfight melee, which started in the ring before spreading into the stands, resulted in 22 injuries and 16 arrests (McShane, 1996). Eighteen New York City police officers were assigned to patrol outside the arena; however, the Garden and event promoter were responsible for internal security, which consisted of 70 security officers and 50 ushers. Some commentators claimed that the melee could have been prevented or would have been less serious if additional security forces comprising uniformed police officers had been used inside the arena.

There is no clear-cut standard for the number of security personnel needed to staff any event or

AN UNEXPECTED SECURITY BREACH

It is not every day that a competition is affected by, of all things, a shoe-wielding mom. That is exactly what happened in September 1989 when 29-year-old British lightweight boxer Tony Wilson was helped in the ring. Wilson was losing in the third round and was in trouble after taking an eight count when his 62-year-old mother somehow bypassed spectators and security and entered the ring. She removed her high-heeled shoe and attacked her son's opponent, opening a wound in his scalp. The referee tried to restart the fight but Wilson's opponent, bleeding profusely from his head, refused. Thus, the referee disqualified the opponent and awarded the fight to Wilson—with the help of his mother (Sports people: Boxing; Victory is upheld, 1989). This illustrates that no "typical" troublemaker exists and that facility managers must be as vigilant as possible and critically review all attendees.

facility. Among the purported industry standards for fire prevention and safety developed by the National Fire Protection Association (NFPA) is one that applies to a number of crowd management professionals. According to the NFPA's *Life Safety Code Handbook* (Cote and Harrington, 2003), there should be one trained crowd management professional for every 250 fans in any facility that accommodates more than 250 people. Note that this is not necessarily the law (even though 32 states have adopted the NFPA code) or a standard that is commonly followed but rather a recommendation that was developed in England after several major soccer tragedies occurred. The ratio is simply a base guideline, as fewer trained crowd managers might be needed at an opera compared with a game between bitter rivals.

Some of those who commented on the incident in Madison Square Garden pointed to poor training on the part of the security force, arguing that if the security personnel had known their roles the dispute would not have gotten out of hand and would not have lasted as long. Clearly the number of security personnel and the amount and quality of training are both critical. A trained crowd management professional must understand crowd management issues and concepts, which are discussed later in the chapter.

Technology

Proper training and adequate personnel are complemented by high-tech security mechanisms. The 1996 Summer Olympic Games utilized more than 1,000 video cameras, technology that scanned handprints of people who wanted to access residential areas, and radio frequency fields that were programmed to scan an employee's identification card and allow access to an area only if the identification card was approved for that area.

Video security is increasingly deployed to monitor student sections as well as police arrest procedures (Fried, 2004a). Closed-circuit television systems are so refined that they can take pictures from any part of the stadium and zoom in on any particular fan. This technology is changing rapidly; the photophone, for example, combines CCTV technology with the ability to transfer images anywhere for immediate access and assistance. A photo can be taken in a command center and sent digitally to an usher or security person.

In the future, these systems might be expanded to include smell, hearing, and touch (Goss, 2003).

Technological advancements have also resulted in new products that would not have been considered years ago. **Biometric scanning** (scanning a person's hand or retina) and facial recognition systems are being deployed more frequently at large stadiums and events such as the Super Bowl. One doctor developed a scent-based defensive mechanism that uses manufactured foul scents (including Stench Soup, Burned Hair, and Bathroom Malodor) to help dispel an unruly crowd ("Give 'em a Stench," 2003).

Other Security Strategies

Animals are being utilized more frequently in crowd management. The animals most commonly used are horses and dogs. Horse-mounted security details can quickly respond to incidents throughout a facility. Second, horses position officers above the crowd so it is easier for the officers to see. Last, when horses are backed into a crowd, fans start moving. It is one thing for a drunk fan to argue with a security officer; it is another thing for the fan to see the derriere of a large horse approaching. There is no way to negotiate with a horse, and if horses kick they can cause significant injury. This is why officers turn horses around in a crowd: It is a highly effective way to get people to move.

Dogs can be utilized for inspecting illegal or unauthorized items. Dogs can intimidate people, so the animals need to be on tight leashes. However, as with horses, it is hard to argue with a dog, and people tend to think twice about their actions with a dog around. This is true for untrained as well as trained dogs. Thus, facilities may want to let people know that bomb-sniffing dogs are being used for an event. People who see a dog with a handler will automatically assume that the dog is sniffing for bombs when in reality the dog has been trained only for working with the disabled.

To ensure adequate security, the facility administrators must also effectively coordinate the applied technology for all security matters with the local police, sheriff, or other law enforcement entities. Pre-event cooperative meetings with all uniformed and nonuniformed security and law enforcement personnel are critical for event safety.

BEHIND THE SCENES

SOCCER HOOLIGANISM

Hooliganism in sport facilities emerged during the 1960s in Britain. It initially was an outgrowth of social, class, religious, regional, or racial antagonism. However, this flame was also fueled by poorly designed stadiums, inadequate fan segregation, insufficient crowd management policies and practices, and poor ticketing allocation and distribution systems (Goss, 2003). Some researchers think that hooliganism is simply a form of patriotism or loyalty taken to an extreme, whereas others believe it is a portrayal of a class struggle and allows the poor and disenfranchised a means to act out as a group and have safety in numbers. The following quote highlights the typical view of those who track hooliganism:

> The behaviour of the hooligans seems to be aimed at gaining prestige. The ability to fight, group solidarity and loyalty, plus the aggressive defence of culturally defined areas, are all elements of a satisfying masculine identity. Fighting at football is largely about young males testing out their own reputations for manliness against those of other similarly motivated young men. (Adang, 1999)

Because of a fear of such fans, hosts of major soccer tournaments are extra vigilant to deter such bad behavior. At the 2006 World Cup, German authorities set up check points on national borders, which are normally open, to check for hooligans. They welcomed 500 police from 13 countries, including about 80 from Britain and 50 from Poland who had the power to arrest their own nationals. British authorities confiscated passports of known troublemakers ("World Cup," 2006). Finally, holding pens were erected near stadiums to jail potential troublemakers on the spot. Such measures have become common at the World Cup. In 2014, Brazil put a 10,000-strong elite security force on standby at the World Cup to prevent a repeat of the disorder that marred the 2012 Confederations Cup. Protesters had vowed to target the tournament, when an estimated 600,000 foreign fans and about 3 million Brazilians would be traveling between the 12 venues. The special forces group, which comprised military, civil police, firefighters, and logistics experts, trained for 2 years to prepare for the games, and the World Cup went off with few problems. The number of protests was minimal. In fact, the people who were most upset were Brazilian fans, whose team performed poorly in the semifinal and consolation games.

Security Planning

Security management cannot be successfully implemented without proper planning. Facility managers need to critically examine the risks they anticipate, as well as those they think can never happen, and then provide a secure environment in which the event can go forward. Planning focuses on identifying the various risks and types of incidents that are most likely to occur and that can cause the greatest harm to the facility. Examining the most likely risks is a key issue. It is impossible to address every single possible risk. A facility manager should focus on likely and foreseeable concerns that can produce the greatest amount of harm rather than focusing on the most unlikely risks, such as a comet hitting the facility. Because there are so many potential risks, it is important for the facility manager to develop a comprehensive list to help identify them. (See "Emergency Action Plan Checklist" for a sample security and crowd control checklist.) Planning strategies that provide a more secure environment include the following:

- Provide additional security.
- Provide refresher training courses (e.g., handling bomb threats, fire response, response procedures, baggage inspection).

Security at a stadium entrance may include bag checks, stadium security officers, and the presence of local and national law enforcement officers.

- Check all employees to make sure they are in the proper location.

- Coordinate with all appropriate government agencies.

- Work with facility users to make sure that plans are in place and everyone knows who is responsible for what security issues.

- Distribute keys appropriately to those who require access to critical areas.

- Require ushers to watch the crowd rather than the game or event.

- Require all security officials to wear appropriate identification markings such as badges or coats.

- Track people who are photographing the facility or wandering around in a possibly inappropriate manner.

- Develop internal communication through meetings, newsletters, and memos addressing security protocols and procedures.

- Check the emergency response manual to ensure that it is accurate and up to date.

- Conduct on-site mock drills to test response time and accuracy ("San Diego," 2001).

The key to safety preparedness is to have a plan in place to deal with any contingency that may arise. For example, various lists (from emergency phone numbers to asset lists) could be available to all pertinent officials, including insurance representatives. **Contingency planning** and business continuity planning refer to the need for plans to be developed and followed by all employees when a disaster occurs (Leibowitz, 2001).

The first step in properly managing inappropriate conduct entails developing, communicating, and enforcing written guidelines that set forth specific prohibited behaviors and the measures that can be taken when someone engages in these behaviors (Farmer, Mulrooney, and Ammon, 1996). Additional concerns that the security guidelines should address include developing proper seating arrangements, screening possible projectiles, reducing alcohol consumption, educating people about possible repercussions of illegal acts, and increasing police and security presence in and around sport facilities.

Miscellaneous Security Concerns

Facilities should refrain from using general seating whenever possible. General seating was the problem at a The Who concert in Cincinnati in 1979, where 11 fans were crushed to death, and has been the problem at numerous international soccer matches. Stampedes at various soccer matches around the world led to the banning of standing-room-only seating at some World Cup events. Eliminating general seating can reduce the concentration of fans in certain areas, and fixed seating normally prevents the problem of fans fighting over seating assignments.

Projectiles such as snowballs and bottles need to be considered. Major League Baseball (MLB) faced significant scrutiny when ball giveaways resulted in fans pelting the field and players. Similarly, bat giveaways represent a significant concern. Any hard item meant as a giveaway promotion should be handed out after a game, or fans can be given a coupon to redeem for the item at a later date (Fried, 2004a). Special attention has to be paid to checking people entering a facility to prevent the entry of bottles, cans, and fruit. Even something as seemingly innocuous as marshmallows can pose a problem. At the University of Wisconsin, the university president wanted to stop students from throwing batteries, coins, CO_2 cartridges, and other items at opposing players, so he suggested using marshmallows, which resulted in a huge cleanup problem (Fried, 2004b). Students were resourceful and inserted coins in the marshmallows to throw them further. In addition to preventing projectiles from entering a facility and not distributing any projectiles, managers must take special care to ensure that the facility is free of certain natural elements such as accumulated snow, which can lead to snowball fights.

CROWD MANAGEMENT

One of the biggest risks that any facility or event faces is patrons getting out of hand. A crowd can become violent for various reasons, such as a controversial call or a close game. In another scenario, crowds are passive throughout the event but quickly get out of hand when an incident

EMERGENCY ACTION PLAN CHECKLIST

The following items should be completed when preparing for any event that a crowd might attend.

Event date: _____ Event time: _____

Primary facility used: _____ Secondary facility used: _____

Police department contact: _____ Fire department contact: _____

Ambulance provider contact: _____ External security contact: _____

Anticipated number of spectators: _____ Anticipated number of security personnel: _____

Anticipated spectator profile: _____

Number and type of associated events: _____

Spectator history from prior events: _____

Anticipated or known rivalries: _____

Competing events affecting the crowd: _____

The following items should be analyzed for each event. Make a note in the space provided if any strategies or protocols will differ from the facility's documented operating procedures, and attach a copy of any updated document(s).

❏ Facility's policies and procedure statement for security: _____

❏ Facility security protocols (e.g., door access, perimeter patrols, camera policy, pat-down procedures): _____

❏ Steps taken before people arrive at the facility: _____

❏ Communication system to be used: _____

❏ Signage communication protocol: _____

❏ Audiovisual communication protocol: _____

❏ Communication of exit routes to patrons: _____

❏ Steps to establish and man the command post: _____

❏ Policies and procedures to be used by those in the command post: _____

❏ Policies for handling lost people (primarily children) or property: _____

❏ Available first aid assistance: _____

❏ Required first aid training for each type of employee: _____

❏ Parking configuration: _____

❏ Protection strategies for VIPs, athletes, and officials: _____

❏ Protection strategies for employees and spectators: _____

❏ Special circumstances affecting protection strategies: _____

❏ Specific steps taken to reduce criminal activity _____

❏ Strategies to use if a crowd rushes the field or court: _____

❏ Strategies to use if a fight breaks out in the stands: _____

❏ Strategies to use if a fight breaks out in other areas: _____

❏ Strategies to use if a fight breaks out outside the facility: _____

❏ Strategies for handling intoxicated fans: _____

❏ Strategies to use if spectators need to be evacuated: _____

❏ Strategies to use if a fire occurs: _____

❏ Strategies to use if a bomb threat is reported or a bomb is found: _____

❏ Strategies to use if a terrorist situation arises: _____

❏ Strategies to use if hazardous materials are found: _____

❏ Strategies to use if a tornado warning or watch is issued: _____

❏ Strategies to use if a winter or lightning storm warning is issued: _____

❏ Strategies to use if the facility is picketed by demonstrators: _____

❏ Strategies for complying with all applicable fire code regulations: _____

❏ Strategies for complying with all applicable National Fire Protection Association (NFPA) regulations: _____

❏ Strategies for complying with all applicable constitutional and legal rights: _____

❏ Strategies for complying with all applicable OSHA code regulations: _____

❏ Strategies implemented to reduce risks: _____

❏ Strategies for documenting incidents and retaining evidence: _____

❏ Attach a copy of the panic statement to be used by the public address announcer and others.

❏ Attach a copy of the insurance policy.

❏ Attach copies of the contracts with independent vendors (e.g., security).

❏ Attach a phone list for all emergency personnel.

occurs or when a small group decides to rush the field. Once the crowd starts moving, it may be impossible to break up without causing serious injury. **Crowd management** is the process of taking proactive steps before a crowd gets out of hand. Crowd control is what happens once the crowd has become unmanageable and police, dogs, sprays, or other solutions need to be used.

Movement Theory

A facility manager needs to know how and why people move—questions that are addressed by **movement theory**. There are three basic movement characteristics: density, speed, and flow. Density refers to the number of people in a given space. Speed refers to the distance covered by moving people in a given unit of time. Flow refers to the number of people that pass a given reference point in a given time frame. These elements come together in a formula to determine how quickly people can exit a facility:

flow = speed × density × width

For example, flow will be minimal if the exitway width is minimal or the density is high. Speed is also dependent on density. If there is a lot of space between people, they can move very quickly. However, if there is very little space between people, then no one can move quickly. This analysis can be expressed quantitatively. When the people density is 21 square feet (2 sq m) per person, people can move freely at the rate of 4.1 feet (1.2 m) per second. If the people density level increases from more people compacting into an area, the movement rate decreases to a standstill of 2.1 to 2.6 feet (0.20-0.24 m) per second (Society of Fire Protection Engineers [SFPE], 2002). Speed is significantly reduced on stairs, where even a fit person in low-density situations can average only 3.3 feet (1 m) per second. This leads to an optimal flow condition in a 44-inch-wide (1 m) stairway of descending one floor every 15 seconds (SFPE, 2002).

Critical density for pedestrians is less than 1.5 square feet (0.14 sq m) per person, which leaves basically no room between individuals. In such a situation, the crowd can involuntarily move a person as much as 10 feet (3 m) laterally. The force can be so strong that it can be impossible to resist the combined force of people pushing in a given direction. This force can cause asphyxia or the collapse of steel support structures or railings. In fact, the pressure in several crowd-rush disasters was so severe that it could bend steel railing with a diameter of 2 inches (5 cm), which requires 1,100 pounds (500 kg) of pressure per square inch (SFPE, 2002). However, these numbers are never absolutes because they are dependent on such variables as age, disabilities, clothing, and family groupings. Thus, in every facility the event staff must examine all exitways, impediments to travel, and fan characteristics to help determine crowd movement concerns.

Scottish scientist Keith Still concluded, based on the science of complexity, that crowd movement is not random, but more like a pattern similar to how birds fly (Connor, 1998). Using computer models he developed, Still was able to show that fans exhibit a self-organizing movement pattern. The analysis was tested using an entryway with no barriers and then an entryway with a handrail in the middle. The first entryway had a flow rate of 150 fans per minute. Each patron had her own programming for reading and reacting to others and the environment. The second group, using the entryway with the railing, moved through an opening of the same size, but the number of people who were able to move through increased almost 30% to 190 per minute (Connor, 1998). It was assumed that the difference was due in part to how people think and interact rather than the

Crowd management focuses on safely and efficiently moving people in and out of sport facilities.

physical barriers. One of Still's conclusions was that in a crowd, a person loses his freedom of movement, and the geometry of the location has a greater effect than the fan's individual psychology.

Ingress and Egress

Once it is understood how people move, the facility can establish specific steps to make it safer for patrons to move into (ingress) and out of (egress) a facility. The reason it is important to analyze movement in and out is that when patrons are in their seats they do not pose as great a threat of surging as a crowd. However, when people are anxious to get into a facility or eager to exit, they can push and shove. This can lead to a struggle or to people being pushed down and possibly trampled, as in the Camp Randall Stadium occurrence (see "Camp Randall Stadium").

To get patrons into a facility, the facility needs to monitor and manipulate their movement in relation to the parking area. When people are parked far away from the entrance, it takes them longer to reach the facility, which can slow the rush toward the gate. Entrance areas need to be designed with screening locations, will-call windows, ticket-taking locations, accessible entryways for the disabled, VIP and media entrances, and group entrances. Entrances can be spread out over several gates so everyone is not congregating in front of one entry point. It may be impossible to move structural impediments to ease traffic flow, so these structures need to be incorporated into the movement plan to serve as barriers that block access to areas or help slow pedestrian movement. No matter what function particular structures have, they need to be integrated into the crowd management plan.

In addition to knowing how people get in, managers need to calculate how people will leave. Not every patron knows where the nearest exit is located. Unlike the situation in an airplane, where the cabin crew points out the locations of all exits, most facilities do not have a communication and education effort pertaining to exitways. Most people enter a large stadium or arena at the entrance closest to their car and leave at the exit closest to their seat. Fans often do not look at all the exiting options and locations. After a 2003 night club tragedy in Rhode Island that killed more than 100 people, Connecticut passed a law requiring all assemblies of more than 100 people to be stopped at the beginning of an event for instruction on exiting the facility.

Evacuation Process

Evacuation time involves two major components: the delay time until the beginning of the start of the evacuation, and the time needed to travel to a place away from danger. Both of these elements focus on patron reaction and education. A sequence of events occurs in a disaster, and education helps patrons exit safely. Education is critical to address patron delay relative to starting an evacuation.

The delay refers to the time span from when a device or person detects the problem until movement begins. If the perception is that a disaster is imminent, crowd-related problems greatly increase. Thus, all efforts should be undertaken to ensure that the delay time is minimized through education of both patrons and event personnel. This can be accomplished by educating people about warning signs, sounds, sights, and symbols. Fire drills allow employees and patrons to hear a siren and put their knowledge to the test. However, facilities can also play sample siren sounds over the public address system to help teach patrons about the emergency communication system.

Exiting a facility should be a process rather than a series of random acts. Some observations not yet mentioned that relate to the evacuation process include the following:

- Panic is very infrequent even during fires, as normal behavior patterns and route choices stay constant.

- People's behavior tends to be reasonable.

- People often ignore initial warning signals.

- When faced with little time to respond, people tend to exit by the most familiar route.

- People tend to evacuate as a group and with people they have emotional ties to.

- If a problem such as communication or wayfinding difficulties exists before an emergency, that problem will be exacerbated during an emergency (SFPE, 2002).

CAMP RANDALL STADIUM

Camp Randall Stadium is home to the University of Wisconsin Badgers football team. The stadium was built in1895 and modified numerous times with a major renovation in 1967.In 1993, the stadium had a seating capacity of 77,745 fans. There were 11,800 fans in the student section on October 30, 1993, when tragedy occurred. A crowd surged to the field at the end of the Michigan versus Wisconsin game, pinning a number of students against railings and fences, which collapsed under all the weight and resulted in numerous injuries. The following highlights some key security facts:

■ On average, 65 security personnel worked each football game.

■ On average, 125 to 180 ushers worked each game, and the security contract required 100.

■ The security company provided 175 to 250 employees per game, with 200 employees for the Michigan game.

■ The security company provided 19 security personnel for the student section (a ratio of 1 to 621).

■ University regulations required 4 walking patrols (8 people), 45 beverage and container duty personnel, and 29 portal guards.

■ The Madison police assigned 9 supervisors to the event, 4 officers to the command booth, 67 officers at posts, 5 vehicular patrols, 5 squads, and a mounted patrol for the game.

■ The police assigned 16 officers to work the area in and around the student section.

■ The university conducted only physical inspection of fans; no pat-downs were conducted to prevent people from sneaking alcohol in.

■ Track access near the student section was fenced in to allow athletes to leave the field.

Some very specific factors influenced the crowd behavior that fall day, including the following:

■ There had been past incidents of fan misconduct (e.g., drinking, throwing batteries, fan passing, fan surfing, scalping).

■ The fans were celebrating Halloween.

■ It was daylight savings day—the time to change clocks.

■ It was Parents' Day on campus.

■ The weather was cold and dry.

■ Wisconsin and Michigan were rival schools.

■ The game had a morning start time, 11:30 a.m.

■ The game was nationally televised.

■ The student newspaper had run a full-page advertisement earlier in the week encouraging students to rush the field.

On the day of the game, the gates opened 90 minutes before game time, and by 10:30 a.m. the student section was completely full. During the game, between 800 and 2,000 fans migrated to the student section. Security and police attempted to clear the filled aisles but were unsuccessful. The following timeline highlights the activities surrounding the crowd surge toward the field.

Time	Comments
10:30 a.m.	An hour before kickoff, student section appears full.
12:51 p.m.	Aisles in student section are still visible.
12:54 p.m.	Student section is packed, and students are throwing marshmallows.
12:55 p.m.	Students in costumes are seen celebrating a touchdown by throwing beach balls and toilet paper.
12:57 p.m.	Students point at field, shouting, "Rush the field!"
1:00 p.m.	Everything looks fine at field level.
1:02 p.m.	Michigan players start returning to locker room for halftime.
1:04 p.m.	Band plays during halftime.
1:36 p.m.	Students can still get through aisles to portals.
1:39 p.m.	View of aisles in part of student section is clear.
2:00 p.m.	Fans seen climbing up and down side of vomitory entrance.
2:02 p.m.	Commotion occurs in stands when students try to impress cameraman.
2:05 p.m.	Police are seen on the field; the field fence and padding are visible, and fans are moving freely in the area between the stands and the field fence.
2:08 p.m.	Band members start moving toward field.
2:12 p.m.	Fans are moving freely between field fence and first row.
2:17 p.m.	Body passing is seen in student section.
2:26 p.m.	Fourteen minutes before game ends, aisles in student section start to fill.
2:29 p.m.	Students chant, "Rush the field!"
2:31 p.m.	Camera shows ecstatic fans.
2:32 p.m.	Security personnel are seen freely opening and closing gate to allow people through.

2:36 p.m.	Fans start crowding around field fence.
2:37 p.m.	Fans start descending the bleachers.
2:38 p.m.	Police start forming ring around field, and band starts moving to field.
2:39 p.m.	Badgers mascot and cameraman near students are encouraging them. However, no movement is seen in student section.
2:40:50 p.m.	Fans from upper row start pushing with force, and fans are being pushed against red safety railing. Students count down final seconds on clock and yell, "Rush the field!" and "Storm the field!"
2:40:52 p.m.	Red safety railing in student setion collapses.
2:41:05 p.m.	With 6 seconds remaining, UW team takes a knee to end the game.
2:41:11 p.m.	Gates are closed as Michigan players start exiting the field.
2:41:50 p.m.	The top of the student section is almost completely empty as fans descend.
2:42:26 p.m.	Chain-link fence in student section comes down.
2:42:50 p.m.	Additional fencing collapses, and students stream across people underneath for another 50 seconds before they realize that people are being trampled.

As a result of the collapse and the crowd surge, 70 fans required hospitalization and 4 required extended hospitalization. Five hours after the rush, the university police established a command post, which operated until November 4, 1993. As a result of the injuries, 51 notices of claims were filed with the state, and 18 injured parties filed 15 lawsuits against the university and other defendants. The university and its employees were removed from the suits several years later based on sovereign immunity. This case shows that accidents and tragedies can occur even if numerous steps are taken to make a facility safer for patrons, and the results can be devastating (Fried, 2004b).

Fan Education

The best-trained and best-equipped security staff has very little value if fans do not know how to respond and care for their own safety. Education often focuses on ways to exit buildings, as just discussed, with facilities communicating information about exit procedures and about warning sounds that patrons should listen for. Fans can also be asked to actively participate in the safety process by being proactive in identifying potential problems. As of 2013, 29 of the 32 National Football League (NFL) teams had either text messaging or phone systems where fans could anonymously report inappropriate fan behavior. Although this technology is great, it does not relieve a facility from its obligation to effectively monitor a crowd, as anecdotal evidence has shown that few fans use these systems for their intended purpose. Command centers obtain complaints about fan behavior but also prank calls, complaints about plays on the field, and miscellaneous customer service questions.

Fan education should address other areas as well, such as crime prevention and general safety.

The National Crime Prevention Council produced and distributed more than 50,000 brochures and posters on crime prevention and general safety procedures for visitors and athletes at the 1996 Summer Olympic Games. People need to be told that their conduct could lead to criminal liability and, often more importantly, that continued unacceptable conduct could force a team or program to cease operations (Fried, 2004a). Some people might change their behavior only if they know that failure to do so might force their team to forfeit the game. Coaches and referees have used this type of information effectively by announcing that the home team will forfeit a game if inappropriate conduct continues.

Another key aspect of fan education is alcohol awareness. Arrests at sport events often have to do with alcohol abuse or intoxication. Fans under the influence of alcohol sometimes throw items on the field, which is disruptive as well as dangerous. Special precautions need to be deployed whenever alcohol is being served or consumed. Various sport facilities have designated certain areas as alcohol-free family areas or have eliminated alcohol sales after a specified time. Also, alcohol servers are trained to refuse service to those who are visibly intoxicated.

Alcohol Policy

Sport events are unique in that the infusion of alcohol into the event can generate significant revenue but also significant risks. This is not true for most other types of events. A night at the symphony is usually not marred by brawls among drunken attendees. In contrast, people often expect to see several drunk and obnoxious fans when they attend sport events. Why is there such a difference in perceptions? It might be based on numerous issues, from the social status of attendees to the fact that alcohol seems to be an integral part of the sport experience but not of the symphony experience. In any case, the two primary problems related to alcohol at sporting events are aggression and impaired driving.

A 1982 study concluded that between 4% and 7% of fans at a sporting event consumed enough alcohol to be legally impaired. Another study from 2011 of both MLB and NFL fans in one market showed that 8% of fans were above the legal limit. At a large stadium or arena, this could represent more than a thousand people. The authors of the study also concluded that the severity of the problem was directly related to the length of the sporting event. If the event was relatively short, there was less likelihood that fans would be drunk, whereas at a doubleheader in baseball, the likelihood was much greater that fans would drink more (Single and McKenzie, 1991). Canada has taken some specific steps to address this concern and reduce the risk of alcohol-related problems. Effective alcohol management techniques include the following:

- Developing alcohol-related regulations for specific sports representing the greatest likelihood of problems
- Providing "dry" areas where alcohol is not served or allowed
- Ensuring compliance with all age limits and laws to prevent underage alcohol sales
- Limiting each person to a maximum of two alcoholic beverages at any given purchase time

- Starting alcohol sales no more than 1 hour before the beginning of the event, and stopping at a specific time before the end of the event to give people less time to buy alcohol and some time to possibly sober up before leaving the facility and driving
- Developing and promoting designated driver and other fan education programs with input from staff, fans, and local authorities
- Requiring all servers and managers to undertake TEAM (Techniques for Effective Alcohol Management) or SIP (Server Intervention Program) training, which has been successful in reducing alcohol-related problems and increasing overall income (these training programs focus on teaching servers how to identify appropriate identification cards (IDs) to prevent underage drinking, already-intoxicated fans, and other danger signs)
- Requiring each facility to have an adequate security staff, post informational signs, provide alternative beverage options (e.g., reduced-alcohol and nonalcoholic beverages), and develop safe transportation strategies such as taxis and public transportation (Single and McKenzie, 1991)
- Separating alcohol sales from food sales so customers have to wait in two different lines
- Posting signage indicating when alcohol sales stop and how many drinks each patron can buy at one time
- Not selling bottles or cans
- Preventing alcohol sales in family areas
- Placing signage to indicate where beer cannot be consumed
- Having security patrol the facility and look for alcohol-related concerns
- Monitoring service areas and consumption areas with CCTV

Alcohol has played a significant role in fan-related violence. Drunken fans at a Chicago Cubs game stole a hat from a Los Angeles Dodgers pitcher, and the ensuing altercation brought 16 Dodgers into the stands. The players were suspended for 84 games and fined $72,000 for their part in the incident, but the fans were primarily to blame. In response to the incident, Wrigley Field changed its policy on when to stop selling beer to the middle of the sixth inning rather than the top of the seventh inning ("Touched," 2000). The New York Yankees are even more strict: They have cut off all beer sales to the bleacher area.

Some of the policies and procedures applicable to alcohol management have originated in Europe. In Scotland there has been a complete ban on alcohol sales at rugby and soccer matches since 1980 (Frosdick, 1998). Fédération Internationale de Football Association (FIFA) rules also prohibit both selling and possessing alcohol at the World Cup and other FIFA-sponsored events.

OTHER SAFETY CONCERNS

Safety should not be analyzed only in terms of the spectators or facility users. The annual cost of violence in the workplace was estimated at $3 billion, stemming from 2 million physical attacks in 2000 ("Safeguarding Employees," 2001). The cost of workplace violence skyrocketed over the next 13 years when in 2013 the estimated cost was around $36 billion. In fact, in a nationwide study of security threats in the United States, many of the top 10 risks involved crime or violence in the workplace:

1. Workplace violence
2. Business interruption or disaster recovery
3. Terrorism
4. Computer crime
5. Employee selection or screening concerns
6. Fraud or white-collar crime
7. Unethical business conduct
8. General employee theft
9. Property crime (vandalism)
10. Drugs or alcohol in the workplace ("Top Security Threats," 2002)

Although times change, this list is basically the same several years later. Some risks are more common to sport facilities. Vandalism often occurs at unsecured areas such as parks and high school athletic facilities. A car driven on a wet field can cause thousands of dollars in damage or even destroy the field.

Facilities Trivia

Attending a sport facility can be an almost religious experience, and many people claim they would die to get into a game. However, for one fan that request backfired. The last wish of a deceased Seattle Mariners fan was to have his ashes spread around Safeco Field. A plane was hired to drop the ashes. However, the retractable roof was closed when the pilot dropped the ashes over the field, and the bag of ashes burst into a puff of gray smoke as it hit the roof. A startled eyewitness called 911, which resulted in the evacuation of the stadium. It took the sheriff's office more than an hour to trace the tail numbers on the airplane and determine that the mysterious substance on the stadium roof was the ashes of a fan rather than anthrax from a terrorist attack (Barber, 2002).

CRISIS MANAGEMENT

Management needs to know how to deal with a crisis. This concern is the foundation for the discipline of **crisis management**. A crisis is any event that threatens people, tangible assets, or intangible assets. Crisis management refers to how to return to normal as soon as possible after a crisis occurs. If someone drowns at a pool, for example, how long will it take for the facility to investigate the situation, for the authorities to conduct an investigation, for any corrective actions to be taken, and then for users to be allowed to return?

Since 9/11, the need for security has grown at all large sport facilities. So has the cost, including everything from specialty security personnel and off-duty police officers to insurance. For example, in 2001 the Milwaukee Brewers paid $225,000 for property and liability insurance. The next year, after the 9/11 attacks, they purchased the same insurance policy for $2.25 million. The price had increased because sport facilities are among the prime potential spots for terrorist attacks given the large number of people in a small area (Ryan, 2002).

Crisis management focuses on identifying the multitude of concerns that can affect a facility. When analyzing the concerns, the facility manager should focus not just on attacks but also on other activities that can result in damage. Having an event that offends community leaders or releasing sensitive data to the media exemplifies a crisis that can destroy a facility without an attack or natural disaster. Some of the areas managers should review to prevent a crisis include many that relate to communication:

- Press releases
- Marketing information
- Web-based materials
- Community outreach programs
- Public emergency response plans
- Sensitive material not destroyed through shredding
- Facility signage
- Building plans filed with public agencies
- Information provided to vendors, contractors, consultants, and the like
- Information produced in litigation or by expert witnesses, consultants, and so on (Baybutt, 2003)

Any one of these communication vehicles can backfire and turn a good idea into a disaster. All these items can be important tools for a facility, but sensitivity dictates that not all information should be disclosed. For example, a press release should never indicate the number of security personnel at a given site or all the techniques being employed to secure a site. When some information is withheld, it is more difficult for anyone planning to circumvent security to gain knowledge about how the event will be protected.

Crisis Planning

Facilities often start the crisis management process by building a crisis team that may include politicians, authorities, lawyers, the media, and others who can provide assistance. The crisis management team needs to examine and rank potential threats to prioritize response options. A threat matrix weighs the probability of a risk against the potential magnitude of the results that would occur if the risk indeed happened. The facility needs to develop specific plans of action through such means as defining the role of various departments, preparing training schedules to rehearse appropriate response strategies, and developing a proactive crisis response culture (Trest, 2003).

The number and types of crises that can occur are almost limitless. Numerous crises are man-made, such as terror attacks, legal disputes, employee misdeeds, and patron sabotage. Other potential crisis situations are natural—tornados, hurricanes, floods, lightning, earthquakes, and so on. Such crises can also be classified as internal, external, and even computer-based threats.

Management can plan for each of these events or situations. Emergency plans need to be developed before a facility is ever open to the general public. Such a plan is as important as a budget or insurance policy. No fans or customers should be allowed into a facility that has not developed and written plans for, and trained employees in, proper crisis response. One of the typical emergencies that will occur at almost any facility is a heart attack. No matter how much time is spent in preventing other crises, heart attacks will happen. The question is how the facility will respond. If the facility has developed appropriate plans for handling medical emergencies, required employees to read the plan, and taught employees what to do, then employees should be able to provide appropriate assistance to prevent the attack from turning into a death.

Employees also need to be trained on the location and use of equipment such as **automatic external defibrillators**. Employees also should receive hands-on first aid training with mock drills to see how they would handle an emergency. Even if someone has CPR certification, it does not mean they would feel comfortable providing CPR during an emergency. That is why mock drills are critical.

Emergency Action Plan

The International Association of Venue Managers established the Center for Venue Management Studies, which produced a guide called *Safety and Security Protocols: Best Practices Planning Guide for Security at Arenas, Stadiums, and Amphitheaters.* The protocols address concerns such as fire, medical, power, bomb, and terrorist emergencies (Fried, 2004a). These protocols describe specific elements in an emergency action plan. The first component of the plan entails choosing a team that will handle the emergency. The team members can range from police and fire personnel to facility managers, security providers, and state officials. These persons should have a vested interest in the project so that they are fully committed to it and can help attract personal and institutional support.

Management can help the team by undertaking a **vulnerability analysis** to identify what events are most likely to occur. Vulnerability can encompass historical incidents (fires, earthquakes, tornados); geographic, technological, and human conditions; physical elements; and regulatory requirements. The various vulnerabilities need to be ranked based on probability after an analysis of the potential human, property, or business impact.

The team should first identify the plan components, which are traditionally broken down into the categories of regulatory, human, building, and business components. The regulatory component applies to the governmental agencies that may dictate how emergencies need to be handled. From a local fire department to OSHA officials or the Department of Homeland Security, the facility needs to know what emergency prevention, response, and recovery concerns must be addressed.

Regarding the human component, the facility must examine the staff, tenants, artists or athletes, patrons, sponsors, media, and anyone else that may be in the facility and how they may respond to an emergency. Based on the populations using the facility, the emergency plan may need to be customized. The building component of the plan examines how the building would respond in an emergency, specifically with respect to the following elements:

- Building structure (resistance to fire, wind, water, and so on)
- Fire element (detection, containment, and suppression systems)
- Notification systems (alarm, power, and public address systems)
- Ingress and egress points (opening width, load capacity, signage, lighting, traction, and so on)
- Building security (access control, surveillance equipment, alarms, and so on)
- Transportation systems (vehicles, elevators, escalators, and so on)

- Emergency systems (smoke control, emergency power, fire control room, and so on)
- Heating, ventilation, and air conditioning (secure intake, zone controls, quality management, and so on) (Fried, 2004a)

The business component examines the potential effect an emergency may have on a business' ability to keep functioning. This requires analysis of financial implications, marketing implications, communication concerns and techniques, inventory control, records management, insurance assessment, and potential contract or legal ramifications. Plans also need to be made in case an emergency occurs and the event needs to utilize a different facility.

Once the planning team has studied the basic components, each component should be critically analyzed to determine what steps can be taken to prevent a disaster.

- Some actions may prevent the risk from occurring; what are they?
- Early detection of risks in their infancy can prevent a small incident from becoming a major issue.
- Once an emergency has been identified, appropriate officials and key constituents need to be contacted.
- Strategies must be developed for possibly evacuating or relocating patrons, if such action is the most appropriate step to take.
- Control and mitigation systems are designed to identify and eliminate the cause of an emergency and help protect against the effects of the emergency.
- Documenting emergency efforts before, during, and after an emergency is critical for litigation and for management's use to change policies and procedures in light of results.
- After an emergency, the facility must try to return to normal.
- Especially with sport facilities, perception can become reality. If patrons think a facility is not safe, they will avoid it.

With this knowledge base, an **emergency response management team** (ERMT) can be formed. The team members should have the authority, knowledge, and decision-making capabilities to implement the emergency plan. Following are some of the key elements the plan should address:

- Emergency power for lighting and public address systems
- Distribution of the emergency plan to personnel
- The ability to contact ERMT members at all hours
- Proper firefighting equipment such as fire extinguishers and sprinkler systems
- Proper signage
- Adequate doorways and corridors for ingress and egress
- Prepared and recorded evacuation messages
- Ability to record phone calls when a bomb threat is made
- Public address systems that broadcast inside and outside a facility
- Cellular phones to communicate with other employees and ERMT members

Once the analysis is performed, the next step is coming up with a plan. Part of this plan should include securing necessary documentation and equipment in the event of a crisis. Documentation that would be critical in preparing for or responding to a crisis includes property contracts, operational records, accounting and tax records, current personnel records, client records, critical reports, necessary manuals, and any specially developed software that cannot be easily reproduced (Carlisle, 2003).

Finally, implementing a crisis management plan requires funding. Senior managers often do not find the dollar value in crisis management to warrant significant expenditures on a possibly remote occurrence. In fact, 24% of companies do not initiate a crisis management program because of a lack of funds, while 37% of those who have a plan need more money to effectively implement it ("Gartner: Businesses Can't Pay," 2003). Clearly a plan will not be successful unless the facility can find the funds to implement it. Often the best way to obtain the funds is to garner support from government officials and facility owners through an aggressive educational campaign.

Continuity Management

One of the often overlooked components of any crisis management plan is continuity management. In any business, **continuity management** focuses on how to keep the business operating even if a disaster occurs. For example, if the roof of an arena collapses, facility managers cannot just pack their bags and leave because there may be valid contractual obligations. The facility manager can establish a relationship with another venue such that if an emergency occurs at either facility, the other facility is made available, if possible, to assist in continuity. Thus, if a roof collapses, the facility manager could call the other facility and shift events there.

Some of the elements inherent in a continuity management program include risk management, disaster recovery, supply chain management (with vendors), health and safety management, knowledge management, emergency management, security protocols, and crisis communication and public relations (Smith, 2003). All these elements need to be integrated so that when an emergency happens, the facility is prepared to keep going. No one element is more important than another, but without money a facility will have a difficult time staying open. Although it is often difficult to put money away for an emergency, a "rainy day" fund is critical even if the facility has insurance because bills will need to be paid now and not several months down the road when the insurance issues are settled.

Summary

Safety is the most important element for any facility. No one wants to go to an event or a facility if there is the threat of a terrorist attack or even the risk of serious injury. However, there are so many potential safety concerns that patrons and employees are constantly exposed to risks. The extent to which such risks may in fact become a hazard is controlled by the facility management. Even if there is a possibility of a crowd surge that could injure fans, facility management can take specific steps such as redesigning seating arrangements and using more security personnel to reduce the risk of serious injuries. Through appropriate safety planning, most facilities can be reasonably safe and can survive most serious incidents.

Discussion Questions and Activities

1. How would you deal with a hostile crowd at your facility?

2. What should a facility do when an event is cancelled several hours before it is to be held and a huge crowd is starting to descend upon the facility?

3. Research a major crowd management problem that occurred in the United States and determine what was done right and wrong in handling the problem.

4. Research a major sport facility disaster that occurred anywhere in the world and determine what was done right and wrong in handling the problem.

5. Complete the following threat matrix based on the likelihood that the incident or situation would occur and the magnitude or seriousness of the potential damage.

Seriousness of injury or damage		RISK OF OCCURRENCE		
		Likely	Possible	Unlikely
	Minor			
	Medium			
	Significant			

Place each of the following threats on the matrix in the area where you think it should go:

A: A bad case of athlete's foot is reported in the locker room.

B: A player has been stealing from other players.

C: A hailstorm hits during a tournament.

D: Cars are broken into in the parking lot during an event.

E: A person breaks her leg during an event.

F: A spectator slips on the sidewalk and is injured.

6. How can a facility better handle fans storming the court or field in order to prevent tragic events like the one that occurred at Camp Randall Stadium?

15

Facility Preparation and Event Management

Chapter Objectives

- Understand the various steps involved in obtaining an event for a facility.
- Know the specific steps required to prepare a facility for an event.
- Appreciate the multitude of issues that go into planning to prevent major disasters.
- Recognize how quickly something can go wrong at an event and how to come up with solutions.
- Develop strategies for making even unhappy patrons into future customers by providing quality service.
- Understand the importance of concessions to a facility's bottom line.
- Appreciate how even the small details included in or missing from the planning process can affect the event.
- Learn what is involved in analyzing an event after it is over.
- Understand survey techniques to determine what is needed to improve an event or facility.
- Understand why the planning process for future events starts immediately after an event ends.

The text so far has reviewed numerous issues and topics related to facility management. This chapter gathers all the previously discussed information together so that the reader can see what is really involved in facility management—taking the reader through an actual planning process to bring an event to a facility. Since public assembly facilities (PAFs) exist to put on events for the public commensurate with their mission and goals, this chapter deals with the heart and soul of PAFs.

The process of developing and attracting events is one of the most important components of any facility's marketing efforts. Numerous facilities compete to get the same event because of the potential effect a large event can have on the local tourism market. Once an event is secured for a facility, the real planning begins for everything from marketing to securing enough parking attendants to work the event.

Elements followed to help attract events include the bid and selection process, facility scheduling, developing policies and procedures, checking the facility for safety, and marketing the event. An inattentive employee or a careless fan can disrupt all these steps in minutes. For example, the facility can develop risk management protocols and train employees to pick up trash or clean spills as soon as they happen, but these procedures and training are worthless when an employee fails to act as instructed. Frequently employees know what they are supposed to do but procrastinate or become caught up in other tasks. As an example, suppose that to save time and money a facility has switched from pump-dispensed condiments to little plastic packets. A fan takes several packets of ketchup and drops one on the floor. No one picks it up, and before long there's a mess. This may generate the feeling among fans that the facility is not well kept up and can represent a slipping hazard. It is not that the facility is irresponsible or has failed to plan. Rather, facilities need to re-evaluate themselves constantly according to what happens during use. A facility may believe, based on this scenario, that the condiment area is the riskiest slip location and use nonskid paint or install metal grates to make it safer and more attractive.

Everything learned and considered in the planning process needs to be acted on. The hot dogs ordered in anticipation of the event need to be located in a convenient storage and cooking location, cooked, stored, served, and then reordered. The topics this chapter covers include event analysis, postevent surveys, marketing for the future, and facility analysis. These topics are covered in relation to what occurs during an event, immediately after the event, and at some later time.

After an event, most people go home and do not think about the event. A facility manager does not have this option. The facility manager needs to prepare for the next event, which could be several hours away. He must again be ready to deal with issues such as trash removal, changing merchandise in the concession areas, or changing over a floor from basketball to hockey. The issues are the same after an event as they are during the planning and running of an event.

For example, during the planning process, all insurance options need to be examined. During the event, the event must be monitored to make sure nothing violates the terms of the insurance agreement. After the event, management needs to determine if any claims were raised—and later, whether the insurance company handled the claims, how the claims were handled, and if the policy provided appropriate coverage.

REVISITING PLANNING

A facility manager needs to develop a business plan to provide direction for the facility. The plan should outline the challenges for the coming year and ways to meet those challenges while reflecting on performance and achievement for the previous year. The following key elements should be included in the business plan:

- Vision and values. This aspect relates to how the facility sees itself and how it wants to be perceived by others. It provides the framework for goals and expectations.

- Last year's accomplishments. Reviewing the previous year's business plan tells the facility manager what has been accomplished and how the new objectives should be formulated to repeat the successes or avoid the failures.

- Lessons learned. Understanding where mistakes were made in the previous year helps avoid

Beardsley: Responsibility from start to finish

Photo courtesy of Shane Beardsley.

My name is Shane Beardsley, and I am the senior director of operations and events at the 10,000-seat Webster Bank Arena in Bridgeport, Connecticut. My career in facility operations has progressed from my initial internship with the Boston Red Sox to my current position in Bridgeport. I spent three seasons with the New York Mets after my internship working in the group sales department, was able to see a World Series, and decided it was time to move on. During my time at Shea Stadium, I met several members of the staff of Steiner Sports Marketing and Memorabilia and procured a position working with charitable foundations and not-for-profit companies selling hand-signed memorabilia as fundraising items. After 4 years with Steiner Sports Marketing and Memorabilia I moved to the Islanders organization, helping to rebuild the team's American Hockey League affiliate in Bridgeport. Four years later we had righted the ship and in turn created Harbor Yard Sports and Entertainment and assumed day-to-day responsibility for the Webster Bank Arena.

Over the past 3 years we have hosted more than 125 events a year, with concerts including Elton John, Carrie Underwood, The American Idol tour, and Neil Young. Included in our event calendar are several visits from Feld Entertainment, which includes monster trucks, the Barnum and Bailey Circus, and several Disney-themed shows. Our main two tenants are the Bridgeport Sound Tigers and Fairfield University Athletics, and we have developed a relationship with multiple institutions such as University of Connecticut basketball, Yale hockey, and many trade and convention outlets. The most enjoyable part of my position is the fact that every day—and often twice in one day—we host a completely different event and the look of our facility is always changing.

With those changes, a well-defined facility preparation plan is a requirement. In any given week an arena of our size can go from a midweek concert to a high school basketball game to a second concert on Friday night to a weekend of two hockey games. All of this takes a toll on staff,

the facility, equipment, and the budget. The booking process for a facility begins more than a year in advance, and the job of a facility manager is to plan out items such as changeovers and possible scheduling overlaps. The facility also has ongoing projects that require time and space within the footprint (walls of the arena), which all requires a high level of planning and forethought.

Three years ago in Bridgeport we took over a facility that was outdated well in advance of its years and invested millions in infrastructure upgrades. We took care of the visual entertainment factor by installing 800 linear feet (243.8 m) of light-emitting diode (LED) digital fascia boards—the largest scoreboard on the East Coast for a facility of our size. In addition, we installed a state-of-the-art LED lighting system in both the seating area and the concourse to maximize the visual aspects of attending an event. We also installed an updated digital infrastructure that allows patrons to order food and merchandise from their seats and to receive full cellular service throughout the arena.

We built three public-access commons areas to maximize floor space in the concourse. We also completely upgraded nearly all of our 39 suites and created the Fairfield University Stags Club as a 120-seat supersuite, which is a tremendous asset for the arena. Our projects are continuous. Upcoming projects including a complete overhaul of the heating, ventilation, and air conditioning (HVAC) and security systems and the completion of a barbeque restaurant to be located off the concourse.

In the end, all of these upgrades are only as important as the events that are brought in and the management of these events. We emphasize to our staff that we are responsible for a patron from the moment they leave their house to the moment they return. The planning and management of an arena—from traffic outside the arena all the way to concession delivery speed and clean restrooms—is a 24-hour-a-day, 365-day-a-year endeavor that I truly enjoy. A line in the Jackson Browne song "The Load Out" always makes me smile: "But I can hear the sound of slamming doors and folding chairs, and that's a sound they'll never know." The quiet before and after a great event of any kind is what carries an operations guy from one event to the next all year long.

the same errors and shows whether the expectations are too high or too low.

- Overall objective. This is the main goal the facility will focus on for the coming year or event.

- Key strategies. Five or six strategies are selected that will help the facility achieve the overall objective.

- Tactics. The strategies are broken down to outline ways to complete each key strategy (i.e., specify how the work will get done).

- Performance measurements. Measurements are used to rate the facility's performance to ensure that the goals are being met successfully. Measurements should be both quantitative and qualitative (Hunter, 2001).

These goals and objectives should be monitored throughout the year and updated as needed. This process gives staff a clear picture of the business objectives and provides an understanding of what is expected from each employee to help accomplish the facility's goals.

Business plans can be developed for the long term (years out) or for the short term (monthly plans). The business plan should be reviewed at least quarterly to account for any unanticipated market changes. The plan should not exceed 20 pages because then it becomes too complex. Also, all levels of the organization should be involved in creating the plan so that employees feel that their thoughts and ideas are being heard.

Although many textbooks highlight the need for goals and objectives, most larger companies utilize more concrete policies and procedures rather than vague and abstract goals and objectives. Policies and procedures highlight what activities the facility approves and the steps needed to reach the intended outcomes. Thus, if the policy is to schedule three events per week, the procedures will include specific activities that help attract or create the events. Regardless of whether goals and objectives or policies and procedures are used, the key is for the facility to incorporate the business plan into an actionable strategy. Existing tenants and future event promoters under contract need to be involved in the planning process to make sure they are willing to work toward the same goals.

ATTRACTING EVENTS

A facility exists to host events. A vacant building serves no purpose and costs money in terms of upkeep, insurance, and even opportunity costs. Thus, facilities need to explore hosting events and teams that will help them achieve their goals. Some facilities with permanent tenants do not need to attract events. Other facilities must constantly compete with others to attract the best events, since the best events hopefully produce the greatest financial return on a facility's investment. Madison Square Garden, one of the most respected arenas in the world, hosts numerous events every year (e.g., Knicks and Rangers games) that will undoubtedly continue to be held. This limits the number of potentially available event dates. If dates are available, a large number of events are probably willing to play at the Garden because this would show that the event is in the big time. Madison Square Garden management is swamped with proposals for events and can choose which events to take based on the potential financial return or other variables.

In contrast, many smaller facilities are fighting for traveling acts such as the Ice Capades, circuses, or the Harlem Globetrotters. Facilities are often trying to win the rights to host such events as National Collegiate Athletic Association (NCAA) events and Amateur Athletic Union youth championships. Other small facilities such as health clubs also hold events. The primary tenants at a health club are the members who work out at the club. The club may host an event such as a weightlifting tournament or a community-wide fund-raiser. Any such event should not conflict with existing usage unless the users are told in advance or are participants. Even if most existing users agree, there will always be some members who will object to losing their workout time.

The process of trying to win larger events is very competitive. Local chambers of commerce or convention and visitors bureaus often aggressively compete to win these events to increase the number of people staying in the host city and spending money to stimulate the local economy.

FACILITY FOCUS

DISNEY'S WIDE WORLD OF SPORTS COMPLEX

In 1997, Disney opened a sports complex designed to help attract more families to Disney World. Components of the sports complex include the following:

- A field house
- A baseball stadium
- A baseball quadraplex
- Two youth baseball fields
- A track and field complex
- A softball quadraplex
- An 11-court tennis complex
- Four sport fields

The entire facility was designed for comfort and enjoyment; for example, the seats for the baseball stadium are 21 inches (53 cm) wide versus an average of 18 to 19 inches (46-48 cm) for most other stadiums in the United States. The facility is so nice that it has attracted several major events. Pop Warner Little Scholars moved its football championships to Disney, which brought thousands of families and kids to Disney-owned hotels and the theme park ("Disney's Wide World," 1998). Since its opening, the complex has grown to encompass 40 square miles (104 sq km) of land. It has served more than 1.7 million fans and in 2008 hosted 170 events. An admission fee of $12.75 for adults and $10.00 for children is charged just to get into the facility. A strong list of clients utilize the facility, such as the aforementioned Pop Warner Little Scholars, the Amateur Athletic Union, National Football League (NFL) Youth Football, the Metro Atlantic Athletic Conference, the Atlanta Braves, and the Tampa Bay Buccaneers. By developing these relationships, Disney can grow its revenue stream because it already owns the entire destination location around the sport facility. Thus, through hosting sport events, Disney can generate additional revenue for its hotel and theme park industry.

Organizational Structure

One of the first questions asked by a facility manager is who is sponsoring, underwriting, or bringing the event to the facility. This might seem like a simple question, but the answer can be highly political. The politics can stem from factors such as the desire to raise money and the prestige of hosting the event. For example, a major NCAA championship would be a feather in the cap of anyone involved. Perhaps a large university has an arena and the city has a larger facility, and the two fight over who should back the event and be the primary host.

No matter who takes the lead, some person or institution must resolve the political issues early on to prevent scandals or disruptions. At times it is impossible to prevent political fighting, while at other times a political leader such as a mayor or university president may step in to prevent the fighting and secure an event. Whoever facilitates bringing an event to a facility, the facility needs to have at least one person or a group to serve as the point person(s) to finalize the event's coming to the facility.

Some large facilities are able to dedicate one individual to attracting and booking events, while other facilities have a department that manages the process. Smaller facilities often rely on the manager to attract events. Others, especially public or nonprofit facilities, may have to utilize either a paid or a volunteer group called a planning committee. In these cases the planning committee addresses any needs of the event, from the types of trophies to be awarded to how to attract potential volunteers. Just as it may be desirable for a building planning committee to involve opponents in the design process, it is often worthwhile to bring marginal persons or opponents into the event planning process to win their political support. It is especially important to obtain support if there are controversial regulations that could affect the event. For example, the Marlboro Grand Prix of New York, which was scheduled for 1993, was canceled because of opposition, including lawsuits alleging that New York City failed to follow the required environmental reviews. There also was significant opposition to having a major tobacco company sponsor the event (Haven, 1992).

Bid Process

The **bid process** starts with either a mass mailing or an advertisement in publications such as *Sports Travel*, *NCAA News*, or *Athletic Business*. The announcement indicates that one or more facilities are needed for a given event on specified dates. The process normally occurs several years in advance, so bids may be solicited in 2015 for an event in 2018. The bid process for the Olympic Games usually starts more than 12 years in advance since there is a 6- to 8-year time lag from when a city is selected until the Games are held. A typical bid request asks for detailed information such as the following:

- A facility's size, such as seating capacity and parking capabilities
- The number of hotel rooms in the immediate area
- What other events have been held in the facility or the region
- The experience of employees and volunteers
- How the event will be integrated with other activities in the area

The bidding process may be dictated by a formal bid package. Assume that the United States Badminton Association (USBA) is searching for a host site for the national championships in 3 years. The USBA may send those who inquire about the event a package with forms that need to be completed. The forms may request the following types of information:

- Facility dimensions, locker rooms, spectator seating, lighting configuration, and so on
- Past events hosted at the site
- Transportation issues such as the closest airport and available public transportation
- Skills and background of the people who will manage the event
- Experience working with the media sources in the area
- Accommodations for fans and athletes
- Proposed budget for the event

The package also usually contains numerous specifications such as the playing court size, broadcasting requirements, number of seats that will be needed, and number of free passes that will need to be given to USBA board members.

A facility manager interested in bidding for the USBA event will review the submission guidelines, research the local community to find facilities and housing that comply with the bid, and complete the bid response. Time is also spent contacting the USBA for clarification, aligning political support, and finding sponsors. It can take weeks to months to gather all the necessary materials and information.

Bidding for an event can be a major undertaking requiring significant time and energy. It is not uncommon to spend months on a bid. The process also costs a considerable amount of money. For example, the bids to host an Olympic Games can cost millions and require numerous meetings, facility tours, site visits, attendance at conferences, advertising campaigns, and significant travel to meet with officials and sell the city. The process is more informal for other events when the planners know which facility they want to go to; they simply call to see if the date is available. If the date is available, the parties merely need to agree on contractual terms.

Before the expense of bidding is undertaken, it is critical for the bid committee to examine its existing schedule and the process of booking dates and times to avoid conflicts. However, even if there is a conflict, some events are just so attractive that the facility is willing to face the conflict in order to possibly win the bid. This could occur with a major event such as an NCAA championship—a facility might bump an existing event if it wins the bid. Of course, if a facility moves another event there may be some contractual penalties, but this is a concern that should be examined when submitting the bid.

For purposes of this discussion, assume that there is no conflict between the proposed date for an event and the currently booked events. The facility manager will need to book or reserve the date for the event she is bidding on in case the bid is successful.

Personnel

An important aspect that needs to be covered is the key people backing the event. Have they hosted similar events? Do they have the political clout and experience to make things work when there may be a large number of bureaucratic land mines?

With any bid, there are numerous people who will need to have their names lent to the process. It is always important for the facility to gather some big-name supporters, especially if the bid is very competitive.

The facility also must have enough people to work on the bid. An Olympic bid may require 5 to 10 people working for several years. Most bids for smaller events are completed by one person, such as a facility manager, with the help of some volunteers or a combination of employees and volunteers. Even if only one person is writing the bid response, he needs to show that there will be appropriate support if the bid is won.

Administrative

Bid committees often put several city officials, local civic or business leaders, and former or current star athletes on the committee. For example, when Houston was trying to secure the 2012 Olympic Games, the committee included a city employee who worked full time on the bid for more than 3 years, a city council member noted for his work in sport, and several athletes in sports from basketball to track and field.

Besides big names backing the bid, the bid reviewers also like to know the names of the support staff that will be used, from secretaries to lawyers, accountants, and even mechanical and structural engineers. Sometimes someone associated with the event wants to contact the accountant or another administrator, and providing these contact names, along with their phone numbers and e-mail addresses, is a helpful gesture.

Before holding an event it is vital to consider all possible employment and volunteer needs (Farmer, Mulrooney, and Ammon, 1996). It is imperative that facilities employ enough people to adequately serve patrons, whether they are full-time employees, part-time employees, volunteers, or a combination of these. Employees could be required for the following duties:

- Ushers
- Food service
- Novelties
- Ticket sales
- First aid
- Security
- Event staff
- Housekeeping
- Management

One of the often-overlooked concerns with running an event is the use of booster clubs or nonprofit groups for working concession stands. Volunteers need to be properly trained in all aspects of food service, health regulations, and alcohol sales. A newer concern is healthy foods. School districts across the country are mandating healthier foods, and this mandate is reverberating down to concession stands at athletic events. Some schools now require all food served during the school day to meet the Gold Award standard established by the United States Department of Agriculture's HealthierUS School Challenge. This requires keeping total fat less than 35% per serving, minimizing sodium, and reducing portion sizes. Some of the healthier recommendations include whole-grain soft pretzels, fruit cups, sunflower seeds, baked potato chips, granola bars, air-popped popcorn, and Lipton Cup-A-Soup (Popke, 2012a).

Youths and families typically require more attention—looking for lost or separated children, being alert to mischievous adolescents, and performing continuous housekeeping are just a few of the extra activities involved when young people are present. Also, events that families and children attend are often high-energy, action-packed events (e.g., the circus, Disney on Ice, rock concerts), so the staff should be physically and mentally able to handle a high-energy crowd. Employees should be properly trained in people management—how to politely answer questions, give directions, and provide immediate assistance, as well as how to ensure a positive experience at the facility.

Management

Management policies, procedures, and protocols need to be in place to make sure the event and facility will run smoothly if a bid is won. For example, how will purchasing be completed? Is the process complex? Who signs the form, and where are the forms located? What needs to be signed when the item is received? The answers are fairly simple for a small facility. However, a large public facility may have numerous bureaucratic levels that need to be understood and streamlined by management to make sure that the bid and the event planning processes are as smooth as possible.

One example of the ability to smooth the bureaucratic process is the film and movie divisions in some city halls. These units are responsible for working with movie and film producers interested in shooting films in the city. The staff help navigate potential problems relating to matters such as permits and the use of police to block traffic. If a producer who plans to do filming has to devote a lot of time, energy, and money to making the arrangements, the city may not appear as attractive. It becomes more attractive if one or more people are designated to streamline the process. Management can provide the same assistance to a potential event at a facility by des-ignating one person who can make arrangements for such issues as security and crowd management and finalizing the menu from the concessionaire.

Financial

The financial component of a bid involves everything from what price to charge for renting the facility to how much revenue the event could generate. A financial analysis for a college basketball game at a 2,000-seat local gymnasium might reveal these costs:

Cost for bringing teams:	$3,000
Marketing costs:	$1,500
Total costs:	$4,500

Financial analysis also indicates these revenues based on past experience:

Ticket price:	$4.00
Average spent on food per person:	$3.00
Average revenue from parking per car:	$3.00

Note that for parking there are normally three or four people in each car.

Financial projections associated with the rough budgets and expected income are affected by numerous variables. Thus, most events have multiple budgets that rely on a best-case, a most likely, and a worst-case planning scenario (table 15.1). This is a very simplistic model that shows what a smaller facility might take into consideration. Larger facilities often use complex modeling, algorithms, and computer programs to crunch numbers and develop appropriate projections.

On the basis of these numbers, it appears that the basketball game is a good event to bring to the gym because there is a most likely projection

Table 15.1 Best- Through Worst-Case Scenario Analysis

Category	Best case	Most likely	Worst case
Tickets	1,800	1,500	1,000
Ticket revenue	$7,200	$6,000	$4,000
Food	$5,400	$4,500	$3,000
Parking	$1,800	$1,500	$750
Total revenue	$14,400	$12,000	$7,750

of $7,500 profit ($12,000 – $ 4,500 in expenses). Even in the worst-case scenario, the event will still make a profit of $3,250.

Legal

During the bid-writing process, the facility must address specific legal concerns. The pre-event legal concerns can be significant. The primary legal aspects that affect events include contract issues, potential government or industry concerns, risk management, and purchasing insurance.

Contracts

As discussed in chapter 13, a valid contract has four elements: agreement, consideration, capacity to enter into a contract, and the contract must be for a legal purpose. Thus, if the facility is bidding for an event but does not win, there is no contract. In fact, the bid is an invitation to make an offer, and if the offer is rejected, a contract never existed since there was no acceptance.

Additional contract concerns that should be examined include **waivers** (especially waivers signed by children), renewable contracts, and future consideration. Children often sign waivers, or parents sign waivers to allow children to participate in an event. For example, a youth marathon would have a waiver requirement, and the event organizers would want the facility to get all the participants and their parents to sign waivers agreeing not to sue if injured. It is essential to examine the law in the state where the event will be held to make sure that the waiver will be valid and to determine who has to sign the waiver.

Some contracts are entered into in a particular year and then kept open. These **open-term contracts** often allow an event to return to the same facility in the future. Frequently such contracts are forgotten and the terms are not fulfilled. In one case, a gym let a basketball league use the facility every year. During the first several years under the contract, the league complied with the contract and provided proof of insurance coverage. The contract was renewed on a regular basis without the league being asked for proof of insurance. Several years after the league had stopped providing proof of insurance, someone was seriously injured at the gym during league play. That person sued, and during the litigation process it was discovered that since the league had not been asked for proof of insurance for several years, it had stopped purchasing insurance. Thus the gym was the only deep pocket, and the protection that the gym had intended to obtain via the contractual requirement for insurance did not exist.

Consideration is required for new or revised contracts. The pre-event preparation process involves numerous changes to the initial contract terms as new issues arise. For example, the number of reserved seats or personnel needed to work an event can change quickly. It is imperative to specify who is authorized to modify the contract and whether any new consideration is required. If new consideration is required, then any modification will in fact become a new contract, and this can become cumbersome. To prevent this problem, most contracts provide for modification, in writing, signed by both parties.

Government and Industry Regulations

Many governmental concerns need to be addressed before an event. Permits are a major issue, as some activities may not be allowed in certain facilities or certain parts of the city. The police, fire, and emergency units in the local, regional, state, or federal government units that may have jurisdiction, or may have a say in the event or facility, need to be contacted. Some events not only require contact with a government agency but also require personnel to be at an event. For example, the Webster Bank Arena in Bridgeport, Connecticut, has a special room with double cement walls to store fireworks for indoor shows. The state fire marshal sends someone to the facility on the event day to do a test run. Thus, each time fireworks are used, they are fired twice: once in the morning and then at the event itself, with specified fire and safety officials present both times.

Risk Management

Risks abound during an event. People can fall, run into others, get hit by projectiles (e.g., foul balls, pucks), and sustain numerous other injuries. Many injuries can be prevented if risk management principles are adopted and practiced before an event. Ultimate responsibility for event safety needs to be determined from the very beginning of the contractual process. The facility needs to have a precontract or pre-event walk-through to make sure the facility is safe. Special care needs to be taken to check playing surfaces, bleachers, equipment, and other components to ensure that they do not represent a risk to potential users. Once the facility has been examined, photographs can be taken to document the facility's true condition before the event started.

Insurance

Insurance must be examined from several perspectives. A facility that is leasing space out to other users or to a tenant must make sure that a current policy for at least $1 million in liability protection has been purchased. The insurance contracts should be examined on a yearly basis to make sure they are still current and that there have not been any major changes in the coverage. The event or team using the facility needs to purchase an appropriate insurance policy regardless of whether the facility requires one. The failure to purchase insurance coverage leaves the event or team owner or promoter open to so much potential liability that it does not make sense to run the event without insurance. Nevertheless, countless events and games occur each year without insurance coverage, and countless facilities run events without coverage. Although many will never face a suit, the few that do are devastated financially.

Marketing

As covered in chapter 11, a facility or event needs to identify the target audience for a potential event and determine whether there are enough people in the greater demographic area who may wish to attend. A circus draws a family type of crowd, whereas a wrestling event draws a different type of crowd. Are there enough families in the area? Do the families have available time—for example, is the event during the school year or over a 3-day weekend? Do the families have enough money to afford the event? What could be the potential per cap sales for concession items? These are the types of issues a marketer needs to examine to determine whether or not to hold an event.

A protective screen needs to be wide enough and high enough to protect the most dangerous parts of the ballpark.

Numerous ancillary activities can be offered by a facility to market an event. These activities are offered to make the bid more attractive but can be so diverse that grouping services, perks, and attractions together can make the package more appealing. Family-oriented facilities are one example. Some facilities have family restrooms that several people can enter together. Other facilities separate the rowdy fans from the family groups and tell families when they are buying tickets that they are being offered seats in areas that prohibit swearing. Other special services or amenities include the following:

- Nursery or day care
- Picnic areas
- Swimming pools and hot tubs
- Special dining areas accommodating children
- Slides, playgrounds, inflatables, and other play structures
- Preferred family parking

- Special Americans with Disabilities Act (ADA) facilities that do more than what is required by law
- Special facility tours
- On-site banking, dry cleaners, and other such services
- Specified autograph areas
- Special post offices for events to get stamps canceled
- Latest communication technology (e.g., Wi-Fi, video on demand)

Advertising and Promotion

The primary marketing concern is typically bringing people to the facility as users or spectators. How will the event be communicated to these people? Is there an advertising or promotions budget? Will that budget allow for television, newspaper, Internet, or radio advertising? Will word of mouth be successful? Is there a sponsor or promoter who can help draw a large crowd? There are numerous techniques for selling tickets. An event can use trade-outs whereby a newspaper may give $10,000 worth of advertising space for $13,000 worth of tickets. Although this does not necessarily translate to ticket sales, it does put people in the seats and generates significant exposure through contests and giveaways.

Sponsorship

One of the critical elements of any marketing effort is obtaining sponsorship. Sponsors can range from name sponsors to minor sponsors who provide trade-outs or a minor cash payment. Name sponsors, as the term implies, pay a certain sum to be the primary sponsor of the event, and their name is used to promote the event. This exchange of value provides the sponsor with visible recognition or community support. Examples include companies that have put their names on stadiums or arenas and on events such as bowl games or major golf tournaments. The focus is on whether someone will receive simply a promotional plug or rights. Commercial rights refer to options such as naming rights. Owning a right gives someone control. In contrast, a sponsor may not have as much in the way of rights and may be relegated to secondary status unless granted exclusivity.

Booking and Scheduling

Once all the pieces for the bid are in place, the bid is submitted. After the bid is submitted, it may be weeks to months—or in the case of the Olympics, years—before a decision is reached. Most cities and facilities do not bid on only one event; rather, they are constantly bidding on various events, and they win some and lose most of the events they are trying to win. However, if they do win an event, they need to book it into their schedule to avoid any disruptions. Booking is the process of contractually finalizing an event on the schedule. When all the forms or contracts are completed, the event is recorded in such a way that all parties know the who, what, where, when, and why. The process requires more than simply completing paperwork. The facility or the event may have to contact the media, local hotels, local attractions, the police, security companies, concessionaires, and a host of other parties to make sure everyone is ready for the event.

Scheduling requires examining how events interact with one another to avoid potential conflicts. The term *booking and scheduling* is often used in the industry, but the scheduling should always come first, as an event should not be booked if there is a scheduling conflict that cannot be corrected. In fact, the booking process may uncover some symmetry between existing events and the proposed event that may enhance the value of the event and the credibility of the bid. On a college campus, for example, if Parents' Day and Homecoming Day occur on the same date as a night event that has been bid on, there may be a natural audience for the night event.

EVENT PREPARATION

Once the event is scheduled, contracted for, and planned, the process of preparation begins. The facility must be ready for every event. For example, if a pool will be used, the chemicals must be checked, the water temperature needs to be adjusted (which means that all the heaters must be functioning), the filters must be operating, all safety equipment needs

---

USING A DETAILED SCRIPT

Most events utilize a script so that all employees know what is going on and so that everyone is on the same page. These scripts can be developed for everything from lights to music to pyrotechnics. The following is a script written for game-day operations personnel for game 1 of the 2000 World Series between the New York Yankees and the New York Mets.

Time	Activity
5:25-6:30 p.m.	Yankees hit
6:30-7:10 p.m.	Mets hit
7:10-7:20 p.m.	Yankees infield
7:20-7:30 p.m.	Mets infield
7:30-7:40 p.m.	Jersey All-Star Marching Band
7:40-7:50 p.m.	Video highlights
7:50:30 p.m.	Introduce Mets reserves
7:51-7:54 p.m.	Introduce Mets manager and starting lineup
7:54-7:54:30 p.m.	Introduce Yankees reserves
7:54:30-7:57:30 p.m.	Introduce Yankees manager and starting lineup
7:57:30-7:59 p.m.	United States Navy Color Guard; Billy Joel sings national anthem; American bald eagle soars into stadium when national anthem ends
7:59 p.m.	Ceremonial first pitch: Don Larsen and Yogi Berra
8:04 p.m.	Umpires and managers to home plate
8:07 p.m.	Yankees take the field
8:09 p.m.	First pitch

The script needs to be developed and closely followed because a nationally televised event cannot be delayed when the television cameras are running. The key to running any successful event is proper planning.

---

to be in place, all lifeguards need to be trained and ready, and the facility must be clean. Similar concerns apply to all facilities, regardless of the size or the event. Are there enough supplies such as toilet paper? Are all building systems functioning properly? Is the equipment properly maintained? Is the field or playing surface in good shape? These types of issues must be examined during pre-event operations and addressed before and during the event.

Facilities

The facility must be examined on a regular basis, but especially before a major event. Will the structural integrity of the facility be compromised by the addition of the weight of thousands of fans? Can the facility process enough air to be at an appropriate temperature and humidity level while allowing enough air exchanges per hour? Getting a facility ready can be as simple as cleaning the floor or much more complex, involving activities such as mowing lawns, painting lines, and preparing the infield.

No matter what elements are required to prepare a facility for an event, the process needs to be carefully planned. At one track and field competition in the Midwest, it appeared that all the issues had been covered. However, when participants arrived, it was discovered that the long jump pit had not been loosened; after several rainstorms and compaction, the pit was hard as rock. The event had to be delayed while a rototiller was rented to loosen the sand. Although these types of problems may appear minor, they are a major concern for participants who have paid money and want the best available facility. How can preparation of a portion of a facility fall through the cracks? Without checklists identifying everything needed to get the facility ready, it is very easy to make a mistake. In fact, for the event in question, the jumping pits had been forgotten because the event administrator had

EVENT SAFETY CHECKLIST

Date: _____ Name: _____ Title: _____ Number: _____

Pre-event Protocol

Who is responsible for providing security measures? _____

❏ Y ❏ N If security is outsourced, are there indemnity and hold-harmless provisions in the contract to protect the facility?

❏ Y ❏ N Have an adequate number of security personnel been reserved for the event?

❏ Y ❏ N Is all safety equipment in place, such as padding behind basketball baskets?

❏ Y ❏ N Are the playing surfaces ready for their intended usage?

❏ Y ❏ N Are ancillary facilities (restrooms, locker rooms, parking lots, concession areas, and so on) inspected before the event to detect problems?

❏ Y ❏ N Do you have a regularly updated security plan?

❏ Y ❏ N Do you modify the security plan for different types of events?

❏ Y ❏ N Do you have any emergency communication procedures in place?

❏ Y ❏ N Will staff members and volunteers need CPR certification?

❏ Y ❏ N Will an on-site defibrillator be used?

Who is trained to use the defibrillator? _____

❏ Y ❏ N Are there enough trash receptacles and recycling containers?

❏ Y ❏ N Are trash cans emptied properly and in a timely fashion?

❏ Y ❏ N Are pictures taken of the facility before an event (both general areas and key problematic areas)?

Event Protocol

❏ Y ❏ N Is a command center established for larger events?

❏ Y ❏ N Is the command center staffed during larger events?

❏ Y ❏ N Are weather conditions tracked, especially if inclement weather or lightning is expected or reported in the vicinity?

❏ Y ❏ N Is adequate supervision provided throughout the event (before, during, and after)?

❏ Y ❏ N Is adequate supervision provided for participants, including officials?

❏ Y ❏ N Is adequate supervision provided for spectators?

❏ Y ❏ N Is there a system in place to track keys?

❏ Y ❏ N Is there a system in place to prevent theft of office equipment and other property?

❏ Y ❏ N Will identification systems (e.g., photo IDs) be used at the event?

❏ Y ❏ N Will doors be monitored (by individuals or technology)?

❏ Y ❏ N Will some doors have limited access?

❏ Y ❏ N Will event staff wear identifiable clothing or hats?

❏ Y ❏ N Will there also be plainclothes event staff members circulating among the crowd?

Postevent Protocol

❏ Y ❏ N Do you hold postevent safety meetings to discuss what occurred?

❏ Y ❏ N Do you have a relatively injury-free record concerning reported patron injuries?

❏ Y ❏ N Do you respond to patron complaints about safety concerns in a timely manner?

❏ Y ❏ N Do you take pictures of the facility after the event?

❏ Y ❏ N Do you analyze all incident and injury reports after an event?

❏ Y ❏ N Do you properly store and preserve reports after an event?

(continued)

Parking Lot Safety

❏ Y ❏ N Is there a parking lot attendant for lots greater than 300 spaces?

❏ Y ❏ N Do you utilize video monitoring of the parking area?

❏ Y ❏ N Do you regularly change the angles of the cameras to avoid creating identifiable patterns?

❏ Y ❏ N Do you record images in a storable and retrievable manner?

❏ Y ❏ N Are fake cameras also used (but not too many)?

❏ Y ❏ N Is the parking lot attendant(s) trained in risk management?

❏ Y ❏ N Is there adequate line of sight for any attendant to see the lot?

❏ Y ❏ N Does the attendant regularly patrol the lot?

How frequently is the parking lot patrolled before an event? _____

How frequently is the parking lot patrolled during an event? _____

How frequently is the parking lot patrolled after an event? _____

❏ Y ❏ N Are lighting concerns addressed by having the light strength (in foot-candles) measured on a regular basis?

❏ Y ❏ N Are there police and emergency contact boxes at the far reaches of lots (if applicable)?

❏ Y ❏ N Is there adequate signage directing people to the facility and other locations?

❏ Y ❏ N Is there adequate safety signage and "park at your own risk" signage?

❏ Y ❏ N Is external access limited by fences or other means?

❏ Y ❏ N Is additional security provided when the parking lot is in a neighborhood with a high crime rate?

❏ Y ❏ N Do you track crime in the parking lot?

❏ Y ❏ N Do you track accidents in the parking lot?

❏ Y ❏ N Do you respond and make any program changes in response to increased crime or accidents?

❏ Y ❏ N Do you monitor intoxicated fans heading to their cars?

❏ Y ❏ N Do you provide assistance if someone has car trouble?

❏ Y ❏ N Are there adequate accessible parking areas and clear travel routes for people with disabilities?

❏ Y ❏ N Are there adequate bus parking and safe movement areas for those leaving buses or waiting for buses?

Comments

_____

_____

_____

_____

_____

_____

I attest to the fact that the completed checklist is true and correct and signed by me on this _____ day of _____.

_____

Signature

PREGAME CHECKLIST

❏ Y ❏ N Is parking available for VIPs, athletes, officials, entertainers, and spectators?

❏ Y ❏ N Are security personnel in place both inside and outside the facility?

❏ Y ❏ N Are restrooms clean and well stocked?

❏ Y ❏ N Are locker rooms well equipped and clean, with all team supplies properly secured to prevent theft?

❏ Y ❏ N Are the will-call windows and other ticketing operations staffed and opened in a timely manner?

❏ Y ❏ N Are all entrances properly marked, staffed, and conveniently located?

❏ Y ❏ N Are special accommodations made available to those who might need them, and are employees trained to recognize when someone might need assistance?

❏ Y ❏ N Is there an appropriate amount of change for ticketing, parking, and concession operators?

❏ Y ❏ N Is the field or floor cleared from the last event?

❏ Y ❏ N Has all the trash been removed so the facility does not look like a dump?

❏ Y ❏ N Did the grounds crew arrive on time and complete all their tasks?

❏ Y ❏ N Are all the security personnel accounted for and properly positioned?

❏ Y ❏ N Is the press box clean, equipped with phone and data lines, and monitored by security to prevent unauthorized access?

❏ Y ❏ N Has food been ordered and delivered to the pressroom or designated area for the press and officials?

❏ Y ❏ N Have the scoreboard and public address system been tested to make sure they are operating correctly?

❏ Y ❏ N Are all concession stands (food, novelties, programs) properly stocked and situated to maximize revenue?

❏ Y ❏ N Are service trays for roving vendors prepared and ready to circulate?

❏ Y ❏ N Are enough garbage cans in place?

❏ Y ❏ N Are flags raised, and is all ceremonial material ready for activities such as the first pitch or national anthem?

❏ Y ❏ N Have lights been turned on with enough time to reach maximum efficiency when needed?

been busy with five other facilities where ancillary events were going on and did not realize that the pits were in such poor condition. A checklist could have reminded the event administrator about the small details. "Event Safety Checklist" lists some critical details a facility manager should be aware of and attend to before, during, and after an event. Every facility and event is different and checklists need to be customized to insure they are relevant and appropriate.

Sanitation

Every event produces waste in the form of water, sanitation, or garbage. The facility should be examined to determine if there are any problems with drains or the septic system. A typical exercise involves bringing as many volunteers or employees as possible together and having them simultaneously flush the toilets. This exercise tests the water pressure and simulates what will occur during a major event, especially during intermissions.

An interesting exercise is to go to a facility and count the trash cans. In stadiums and arenas, the fans produce tons of trash. Preparation needs to be made to address the trash receptacle needs, recycling needs, and postevent trash needs. A significant amount of trash will not make it into the trash cans. Thus, the event planning process must include making sure there are enough trash cans, enough cleaning people, and enough sanitation supplies such as trash bags and brooms.

Ancillary Accommodations

Ancillary accommodations can range from additional office space to dorm rooms for participants. These facilities need to be secured, managed, and monitored to make sure they are functioning correctly. Ancillary facilities include living quarters, parking areas, dining areas, medical and first aid stations, outdoor restrooms, and postal facilities.

Each facility that will be used needs to be examined to make sure it is functional, clean, and not dangerous. Security may be an issue in some areas, whereas other areas may require greater vehicular access for emergency vehicles or mail trucks. All facility areas used in an event must meet the event requirements.

Emergency Planning

At any facility, an emergency action plan must be researched and developed before a disaster occurs. Since no one knows when a disaster may occur, a disaster plan must be developed before every event. Managers must look into all potential threats and plan what actions would happen if they were to occur. A risk evaluation matrix can help establish this. The risk evaluation matrix is a chart that identifies the most realistic threats to a business and helps prioritize a response and backup plans. A group of emergency coordinators including management, human resources, information technology staff, and security should be appointed or assigned to develop the matrix. After the coordinators and matrix are in place, a recovery plan can be developed. A backup plan with backup personnel needs to be created in case any emergencies arise that alter the primary plan. The plans should be documented. After the local fire and police personnel are informed about the emergency action plan, it should be tested as a means to appropriately train personnel (Bassett, 2002).

Equipment and Warehousing

One of the often overlooked components of an event is making sure there are enough supplies and that the supplies are stored in an easily accessible location. It is difficult to store several thousand rolls of toilet paper in a convenient location. Thus, space needs to be set aside for storing supplies that will be used during the event and for items that need to be placed out of the way. For example, in an arena, significant storage space is required for extra chairs, dasher boards, portable floors, forklifts, trucks, carts, tractors, refrigeration units, mechanical equipment, spare parts, and a host of other items. If you ask most facility managers what they would like more of in any facility, the invariable answer is additional storage space.

Communication and Technology Systems

Although a significant amount of wiring is now included in buildings as they are being built, many smaller or older facilities are not properly wired for communication or technology needs. If a facility is wired, then all the connectors and junction boxes need to be examined to make sure that outlets and phone lines are working. Although the bid process for larger events may require proper wiring, most facilities wait to install any such wiring, if needed, until after they have won the bid because then they can justify the expenditure. Wi-Fi can address some wireless communication needs, but cables are still needed for many video and broadcasting applications.

The sound system and scoreboard need to be tested before an event. Are any lights burned out? Are all speakers properly aligned? Does the public address announcer have a prewritten script for announcing emergencies? Can the system become overloaded? What backup system is in place if power is lost or there is an emergency? These are the types of questions that need to be researched and answered before an event.

Media

One of the primary concerns with the media is making sure they have access to the facility. Media kits and credentials should be developed for the invited press. Uninvited press also need to be considered, along with the steps that will be taken if uninvited media representatives attend the event. Every event should expect both invited and uninvited press.

A pressroom needs to be developed with appropriate communication outlets and computer hookup stations. There also should be an area for serving food, since providing food for the press is an industry standard. There should be refrigeration, outlets for coffee makers, and possibly a sink to help serve the food and allow for easier cleanup.

Another pre-event concern is appropriate lighting. Lighting for still photographs is not too critical because of flash cameras. However, television broadcasts require very specific lighting that sometimes means it is necessary to purchase or rent additional lights. Also, some seats need to be "killed," or kept empty, because of camera platforms and line-of-sight requirements to get the best shots.

Box Office and Ticketing

Tickets can be distributed through phone sales, ticket windows, the Internet, ticket brokers, mail orders, or even kiosks or sales buses. Although pre-event ticket sales are often part of the event marketing efforts, the facility also needs to be aware of various concerns affecting ticket distribution and sales on the day of the event. For example, what rules regulate scalping in and around the facility? Is there to be a will-call window, and which tickets will be placed there? What identification or other procedures are used to monitor ticket distribution at will-call windows? Will event-day tickets be sold, and how? Will there be ticket lines in front of the ticket windows, and will these lines interfere with people entering the facility? These are the types of questions about ticket operations that arise before an event.

The answers to these questions depend on the municipality and the facility. For example, if there are numerous will-call tickets, it may be necessary to set up several will-call windows, perhaps outside the entrance gate to avoid overcrowding near the entrance. Screening that slows people down at the front gate may minimize lines at ticket windows since all patrons have to wait in line to be searched before entering the facility.

One pre-event concern that needs to be addressed with significant care is seat relocation, which may occur when a new facility is built, a facility is renovated, or a season ticket holder needs to be moved. Seat relocation can potentially affect many fans, and the results could be disastrous if the process is not clear and well communicated. For example, fans need to know that if a new facility is built, will they lose their PSL, would they have priority compared to other season ticket holders, and how much the new seats will cost. Proposed or renovated facilities often send out mailers, hold invitation only events for season ticket holders, and might develop a mock seating area to educate fans on seating options. A 2013 study showed that 7% of sport fans bought 24% of game or event tickets throughout the United States. These fans are for major professional/collegiate sporting events and concerts/shows at major arenas. When a few major buyers purchase a large percentage of tickets facility managers need to make sure these frequent fans are treated well. Thus, if the fans that spend the most money are moved, negative backlash can be significant.

Security

The need to protect assets, money, participants, and fans is paramount for any event. A successful security plan must be developed months or years before an event. The threat of terrorist activities at the Olympics forces organizers to spend years developing security systems and a security force. Pre-event security issues are primarily associated with crowd management and can include the following:

- When will the event start? Crowds do not have as much time to drink before early events, whereas an evening weekend event can lead to more problems resulting from pre-event drinking.

- Will traffic patterns affect how crowds arrive?

- Will the event be on a holiday such as Easter, when a different crowd can be expected?

- Have there been prior problems with the event? Is the event a touring event that had problems at a prior stop?

- Are event participants known for getting a crowd riled, such as a rock band that encourages mosh-pit activity and crowd surfing, even if such activities are not allowed in the facility?

- Will the crowd be large, and will it exceed the facility's capacity?

- What experience does the event administrator or facility manager have?

- What experience does the security company have?

- What are the weather conditions, and what will happen if rain forces fans to scurry for cover?

- Can the will-call and press areas be moved away from the front entrance to avoid crowding?

- How will alcohol sales affect the audience?

Parking and Transportation

Before an event is scheduled, all parking options must be examined. For example, will patrons park on surface streets or in a garage? Will there be an effect on local traffic or neighborhoods? Some neighbors do not mind a major event since it is an opportunity to sell parking spaces in front of their houses or on their property. Other residents may be annoyed about the traffic and complain to local officials.

Is the parking lot area fenced in? Is there a significant amount of crime in the neighborhood that may spill into the parking area? Will there be tailgate parties in the parking lot? When will people show up for tailgate parties? How many accessible parking spaces are there, and how many will be needed? Parking attendants will need to be hired and in place several hours before the event begins. Since traffic-related concerns frequently lead to disgruntled fans, a facility should emphasize proper signage and ease of movement to accelerate parking and exit strategies.

Buses and shuttles are often used to transfer spectators and participants from one area to another, particularly to help people get from large or remote parking lots to the facility. Buses and shuttles are also used to transport participants and officials from their hotels to a facility. At Ohio State University, buses transporting both the home team and the opponents for football games drove down a fraternity- and sorority-lined street where the fans could cheer and boo the players. This created an event within an event and a significant amount of tradition. The trip also was a logistical challenge, since all cars had to be moved from the street, police escorts had to be in place, and crowd management strategies had to be implemented.

Concessions and Food Service

Numerous regulations must be followed in order for food to be served. Health and safety regulations are dictated by local, state, and federal governments; if these regulations are violated, there are significant penalties. All food vendors need to have proper licensing from all pertinent regulatory agencies. For example, municipal health departments need to be contacted to make sure the concession areas comply with all local regulations. This may require compliance with fire, plumbing, electrical, and health-related codes and compliance protocols. For instance, sinks are required whenever raw food is being handled, and local codes can dictate how far away the sink can be from the preparation area. Private businesses and venues are also governed by the Occupational Safety and Health Administration (OSHA) regulations and rules concerning children working with sharp objects and dangerous equipment pursuant to the Fair Labor Standards Act.

Issues that affect operating a concession area include the location of the stand, the spatial dimensions, the equipment being used, and the type of food served (Sherman, 1998). The location of a concession stand can be anything from a table to a permanent location in a venue. A table or temporary stand may be used in high schools, community centers, colleges, and even small venues. Tables and stands can be used to serve bottled drinks, prepackaged foods, and in some cases prepared sandwiches. On the other hand, venues that have built concessions into the physical structure have the opportunity to sell fresh and hot food more conveniently through the ability to utilize electrical outlets rather than the generators required for mobile carts. Technology is also affecting food delivery. Aramark has deployed tablets at Soldier Field to help process customer orders, replace cash registers, and track items. The system updates every 15 minutes with inventory reports so managers know in real time if some items are running low rather than running into a situation where a stand runs out of food.

Spatial dimensions of concession areas help determine the food served at a venue. Concession stands should have a sanitary prep area, a cooking area, and a warming area. Also, if there is any raw food preparation, there must be a sink for hand washing. In the larger stands, fire codes and the amount of power allocated to the area define the safe level of equipment usage. If the equipment that will be used requires a greater electrical load, different equipment or new wiring or transformers may be needed.

Planners should remember that concessions can make or break an event depending on the organization, location, and foods served (Sherman, 1998). Every organization has its own unique food-related issues. Whether regarding menus or training of employees, policies and procedures must be developed. Is the primary focus revenue generation or service? Is the organization more interested in ease and convenience or in complicated, expensive items that generate more income? For example, the revenue from food in luxury suites is much greater on a per person basis than that from spending by average fans. Thus, the facility needs to determine where the emphasis will be for its concession program.

Additional concession policy concerns include training employees to use hairnets, gloves, slicers, and other equipment. Alcohol management, from knowing when to cut off beer sales to how to spot fake IDs, also requires significant employee training.

Most employers do not promote the fact that they use inexperienced or cheap labor. Facilities often have numerous young employees who are eager to work at certain events. However, experts suggest asking employees under age 15 to work a maximum of 20 hours a week to avoid high turnover numbers (Emmons, 2001). There also are a number of state and federal laws that limit how many hours teenagers can work, how late they can work on school nights, and what types of jobs they can undertake.

Food-related concerns can also become policy-related concerns. For example, should condiments be provided in pumps, which are cheaper to purchase than other types of containers but are messy and hard to clean? In contrast, packets, which are more expensive, are easier to store and manage but are often wasted when people take too many, and they can be a hazard when people drop them on the ground. Similarly, although it may be more

convenient to offer only two drink sizes, statistics show that having four drink sizes generates the greatest profit level (Emmons, 2001).

The food preparation and service areas should be built based on the proposed menu (Emmons, 2001). When buying the equipment for a concession area, the facility manager should ask the salesperson for 50% off the list price. The facility should ask for references to see who else uses the equipment in order to find out if others have any trouble with the equipment. Care should be taken to make sure that the reference is not getting a kickback from the equipment seller (Emmons, 2001).

Food service locations should be designed for speed and flexibility. The more quickly food gets from the preparation area to the service and sales area, the lower the chances of having problems. Outdoor locations present unique challenges such as rodents and bugs. Therefore, outdoor food areas are inspected more frequently than indoor food areas. Food kept outdoors needs to be covered, and the refrigerator has to be cold enough and the heater hot enough to comply with all applicable health codes.

Food-related concerns before an event often center around what food to sell. Every facility has a unique menu based on the type of facility, the region, the local fans, and even the event itself. A health club, for example, typically offers a health-oriented menu because of its clientele. A ballpark in New York may have to offer more variety to handle the broad array of fans than a park in Kansas City or Pittsburgh, which may have more traditional fare. "Concession Trends" lists interesting recent food and concession trends in North America.

Before an event, the facility marketing staff needs to survey what foods may bring the best sales results with the least amount of work. All food items should be either packaged or interchangeable. Packaged products reduce preparation time, and items such as nachos can now be purchased in individual packets requiring only that the cheese be microwaved. Even if convenience food is used, the process should be examined to make sure that food is not wasted. For example, not every 50-pound bag of popcorn is the same; some types of kernels pop more thoroughly, which generates

CONCESSION TRENDS

Food concessionaire Centerplate conducted research on the similarities and differences between U.S. and English fans in terms of food purchases. Some of the findings are startling ("Catering Solutions," 2013).

Category	United States	England
Average number of games fans attended each year	2.6	5.4
Average number of attendees at games who are male	62%	77%
Number of people in a group going to games	3	2
Average amount spent on food per person	$15.50	£2.00 (US$4.50)
Likelihood of paying for purchases with cash	82%	97%
Number of food runs during a game	2.2	1.5
Percentage of fans who eat before a game	36% tailgate	27% go to a pub
Percentage of fans who eat during a game	92%	65%
Most popular food during a game	Hot dogs	Chicken balti pie
Second most popular food during a game	Chicken fingers	Beef and ale pie

Some concession stands offer unique food items or services, such as the following:

- Offering fans craft beers (e.g., $30 beer at Cleveland's Progressive Field) and old-school beers (e.g., $4.50 cans of Blatz, Schlitz, and Pabst Blue Ribbon) to meet the tastes of a wide group of beer fans.
- Bringing local popular restaurants into the stands (e.g., Petco Park in San Diego added one hamburger joint and two Mexican restaurants) to enhance the destination location feel where fans can attend a game and eat at a well-known restaurant rather than a concession stand.
- Companies buy specific naming rights to help sell their products. For example, Malibu Rum converted a storage area into the Malibu Rooftop Deck, which is a bar at Yankee Stadium.
- The Texas Rangers' Globe Life Park offers a 1 pound, 2-foot-long (0.45 kg, 0.6 m long) hot dog for $26 (about 500 are sold each game) and a 1.5-pound (0.7 kg) pretzel for $12.50.
- Nationals Park has offered an 8-pound (3.6 kg) StrasBurger (named after pitcher Stephen Strasburg) made with round brisket, chuck, and short ribs for $59.00 (Muret, 2012).

Some of the top food trends include the following:

- Fresh food: Fans want fresh food (e.g., sushi, sandwiches) and often prefer for it to be prepared in front of them and made to order rather than wrapped and held for hours in a cooler or on a heater.
- Going local: Fans like to think they are supporting the environment, so they appreciate locally grown produce.
- Specials: Fans want specials, such as a price point combination (e.g., a drink, hot dog, and chips for slightly more than two items by themselves) or event-driven offerings (e.g., kosher food for Jewish Heritage Night).
- Digital menu boards: The sizzle of beautiful pictures and a flashy display can help drive concession sales.
- Local brands: Consumers like to support local businesses, such as local makers of craft beers or specialty foods.
- Feeding the need: If fans are clamoring for gluten-free or vegetarian options, a facility should provide such offerings and test the market.
- Technology: Leverage existing and future technology from energy efficient kitchen equipment to fans ordering and paying for concession items without leaving their seats.

- Loyalty: Some facilities reward loyal fans who use fan cards or websites with extra products or discounts (Bigelow, 2013).
- Gluten-free choices: In 2013, Citizens Bank Park debuted a gluten-free food stand that offers hot dogs, pizza, cheesesteaks, chicken tenders, Bull's barbeque pork sandwiches, and snacks such as cookies and brownies.
- Popcorn: Savory popcorn options, including spicy and sweet options, are gaining in popularity.
- Snow cones: New sugar-free syrups are making snow cones a little healthier.
- Smoothies: Although soda and beer are still king, healthier options such as seltzer and smoothies are gaining in popularity.

additional revenue (Cohen, 1994b). Interchangeable foods are crossover foods that can be used in several dishes. Ingredients become expensive and hard to store if they are not used for several different dishes. Thus, if lettuce cannot be used for multiple dishes served at the event, it should not be used at all since it is expensive and does not have a long shelf life.

Alcohol

If liquor will be served, proper procedures must be in place, including obtaining a liquor license. Employees need to be trained on how to know when a customer is visibly intoxicated and how to spot underage drinking; they should also be able to tell when spectators bring in their own beverages and should be familiar with ejection policies. Two nationally recognized alcohol training organizations are Training for Intervention Procedures (TIPS) and Techniques for Effective Alcohol Management (TEAM). Having either of these organizations train alcohol servers and management will help create a more successful alcohol strategy and serve as a useful risk management tool for all events. Beer distributors can be a good source of additional help in developing an alcohol sales program. Their clout in the area can be used to help the facility through proper training, advertising, sponsoring designated driver programs, their knowledge of government regulations, and their extensive political contacts.

The issues associated with food concessions also apply to beer and alcohol sales. A facility needs to determine whether they want to sell alcohol (which might be banned at college facilities) and, if they do, what they will sell, whether they will allow fans to bring in drinks, and when

alcohol sales will end. One big recent trend is craft beers, which can often sell for several dollars more per cup than regular beers.

What do the Phoenix Suns and the New York Knicks have in common? They both charge $9.00 for a beer, highest in the NBA. Washington Wizards, Miami Heat, and Boston Celtics each charge $8.00 per beer. Major-market teams are used to charging more for concession items because the market can bear the higher cost. Lower-priced beers are sold in markets where price sensitivity appears to be much greater. Teams that charge between $6.50 and $5.00 per beer are (in descending order of cost) Milwaukee Bucks, Charlotte Hornets, Denver Nuggets, Indiana Pacers, Dallas Mavericks, Orlando Magic, San Antonio Spurs, and Oklahoma City Thunder. (Dwyer, 2013). During the 2011 NFL season, the lowest cost for a beer was $5.00 at a Cleveland Browns game and the highest cost was $9.00 at a St. Louis Rams game. During the 2012 Major League Baseball (MLB) season, the lowest cost for a beer was $4.00 (14 ounces, or 414 ml) at an Arizona Diamondbacks game and the highest cost was $7.50 (12 ounces, or 355 ml) at a Boston Red Sox game. During the 2013 National Hockey League season, the cheapest beer was $5 (12 ounces) at a Pittsburgh Penguins game and the most expensive was $9.50 (16 ounces, or 473 ml) at a New York Islanders' game.

Beer has not always been a staple at baseball games. In the 1870s a dispute arose about whether beer should be served at games. In the 1880s, the Cincinnati Red Stockings were kicked out of the National League for allowing beer to be sold at their stadium. Thereafter, some of the major beer brewers in the Midwest founded a new major league called the American Association, which was referred to as the Beer Ball League. These teams willingly allowed the sale of beer and promoted the close relationship among beer sponsors, baseball stadiums, and concession stands (Leventhal, 2011).

Emergency Services

A facility cannot respond to an emergency if it does not have enough of the necessary emergency response equipment. A facility also needs to have properly trained employees capable of implementing the emergency plan.

Before an event, the facility should examine local fire and police departments as well as ambulance companies to evaluate response times and the medical attention they can provide. Local emergency crews should be familiar with the venue in order to make an efficient response. Often an **emergency medical technician** (EMT) crew visits a site before an event to familiarize themselves with the location and to become knowledgeable about the quickest routes around the facility and to local hospitals, as some roads may be blocked for the event. Major injuries that require transportation to a hospital should be taken to the closest hospital. All medical situations, regardless of their severity, should be recorded in either the security log or a medical log. There is the possibility of lawsuits with any medical injury, and documentation will be crucial to help defend against such claims. The documentation should focus on the injury, facts about the incident, witness statements, and the actions taken.

In the event of a major injury, communication is the key to getting a quick response. Facility staff and security need to be able to communicate by two-way radios, walkie-talkies, Nextel systems, or cell phones. Instructions for medical personnel and patrons should be posted to indicate medical stations, emergency phones, and emergency exits.

Medical Services

Before an event, a medical response team must be in place. All levels of medical response should be included in the development of an emergency action plan. Starting with first responders, facility staff should be certified in first aid, cardiopulmo-nary resuscitation (CPR), and use of defibrillators. A medical station should be set up in a commons location, possibly next to the security command post. With some basic first aid materials, first responders, and a triage program in place, an event is ready for basic cuts, bruises, and minor injuries.

MIDEVENT CONCERNS

Many issues can occur during an event. Soccer facilities throughout the world have had to deal with fans throwing lit flares, and such actions have led to the evacuation of several events. In 2011 a major windstorm occurred during a Sugarland concert at the Indiana State Fair, causing 7 deaths and 58 injuries. These are just a couple examples of midevent concerns that can throw facility management into chaos.

One concern not usually anticipated is cancelling an event right at the start or while it is in progress. Disgruntled fans have in the past filed lawsuits when an artist cancelled a show and fans were upset with the show's cancellation. The band Guns N' Roses cancelled concerts several times at the last minute or when fans were already in the stands. In one instance a fan was injured while trying to exit the Spectrum Arena during riotous behavior after the show was cancelled and sued the facility (Heenan v. Comcast Spectacor, 2006). In another instance, a 2013 performance of the children's show "How to Train Your Dragon" at the HP Pavilion in San Jose, California, was cancelled right after intermission because a dragon got stuck in the air and was in danger of falling. Management dealt with multiple issues, including ineffective communication (between the facility and the promoter, the facility and the fans, and so on), management being unable to communicate with all staff members at once, management needed to make sure event cancellation policy existed before load in, and management should not have tried to solve problems such as booking the guests for a later show. Booking fans for a later show can be a complicated procedure and the best strategy would have been to give everyone a refund and then let the customer decide afterwards what they wanted to do (Kirsner, 2013).

Policies and procedures developed before an event must be monitored during the event to ensure that they are being followed. The checklists presented earlier in this chapter contain items relating to security, concessions, parking, scoreboards, and other concerns. During the event, all these items need to be revisited. Although concessionaires might have had enough cash and change before the event started, they may run out of small bills and must be able to communicate with someone that they need change. They probably cannot leave their stations, so a manager or other employee will need to bring the change to them. Financial analysis is needed to track where the change is going and to make sure all money movement is properly recorded so that final settlements can be calculated at the end of the event.

It is during an event that management has the best opportunity to praise or note the performance of employees. Although an employee responsible for acquiring sponsorship revenue will be judged before an event begins, concessionaires and ushers, as well as security, operations, and mechanical workers—among numerous others—can be evaluated in their work environments to determine if they are performing their duties.

Thus, managers cannot just sit back when the event begins and think the worst is behind them. The event or facility manager must ensure that all the right steps are being taken by subordinates and front-line personnel. For example, a disaster plan has been developed, but how would everyone act if a disaster really occurred? Would people move as rehearsed? At such times, managers earn their stripes by being able to lead effectively given the information, resources, and time available.

POSTEVENT ANALYSIS

Checking the contract is not a task that's wrapped up before an event, but one that should be reviewed during and after every event as well. This section highlights those tasks, as well as the evaluations of employees, finances, and liabilities.

Checking the Contract

One of the issues that must be carefully analyzed during and after an event is compliance with any contract, lease, or rental terms and conditions. For example, a facility rental agreement may require a tenant to comply with all applicable local laws and regulations. What happens if the municipality where the facility is located has a noise ordinance that prohibits a facility from generating loud noise after 9:00 p.m.? Hopefully management would have known about the law, but sometimes managers are unaware of laws that could affect the event. If management does not know about the law and problems arise during the event, they have two options: comply with the contract terms or violate the ordinance and risk problems with government, the landlord, and possibly the public.

Another contractual concern is the number of employees. Lease and event contracts often require a minimum number of employees to work in areas such as concessions, entry management, security, and box offices. Numbers can also be established based on management research in areas such as ticket sales, type of event, anticipated crowd, the day of the week, the time the event begins, and whether other events are being run on the same date. If the contract calls for 700 ushers, how can management ensure that a sufficient number of ushers are present and doing what they are supposed to do? What if too many ushers show up for the event? What if only 600 show up? Under such conditions, managers have a difficult choice to make. They can cancel the event and violate the contract, or they can proceed with the event—knowing in this case also that they are violating the contract—and try to use other managers and concession workers as an ad hoc staff. If too many ushers show up, they can be placed around the facility for training purposes and be paid for their time.

This concern has significant ramifications in terms of liability, but it also can show whether or not management can accomplish the job. If the manager has trouble meeting contractual requirements, this can lead to trouble renegotiating the contract or lease at a later date.

If there is a dispute between the facility and the event and the parties cannot resolve issues in the contract, both parties should first try alternative dispute resolution such as mediation or arbitration. The contract should have a mediation or arbitration clause or both. Mediation can allow the parties to work out the dispute and hopefully come to a conclusion that will be mutually beneficial and then allow the relationship to grow. If mediation is not successful, the parties can go to arbitration to resolve the dispute. If the dispute is more adversarial and cannot be resolved through arbitration, litigation is the next option.

Evaluating the Employees

A performance appraisal for employees and subcontractors is one of the most important postevent activities. Did the employees do what they were supposed to do? Did they provide quality services? Did the salespeople sell tickets or merchandise aggressively? Did the ushers perform their job well and with a positive attitude? It is difficult to evaluate an employee unless there are objective criteria, such as the number of tickets sold or the number of complaints handled during a given event. Most positions have only subjective performance criteria such as whether the usher acted appropriately and watched the crowd rather than the event. But even if evaluating employees is difficult, it has to be done. The most effective method is to have their immediate supervisors evaluate them based on pre-established criteria discussed with the employees when they are hired or promoted.

Another employment evaluation concern is liability for acts of others who are not directly employed by the facility. If third-party vendors provide ushers, security, and concessionaire services, can the facility be liable for their conduct? The answer may be yes. A facility can be liable if the vendor discriminates in hiring, since the facility should have examined the employment practices of the vendor before assigning that vendor the contract (Fried and Miller, 1998). Thus, if a vendor terminates an employee for the wrong reason, the facility can be sued after the event for the wrongful termination. This type of issue can be resolved through including appropriate language in the contract indemnifying the facility from all acts by the vendor.

Evaluating the Financial Success

After an event, the facility manager must evaluate the financial success of the event. Rental and lease contracts often require payment of a given amount before an event to guarantee that the facility owner will be able to cover expenses. A facility knows in advance the cost of opening the facility to the public and will charge at least that amount as a pre-event payment in case gate receipts are low. Thus, if it costs $5,000 to open the facility, the facility owner would ask for at least this amount.

Management must carefully examine the financial viability of an event as it is going on. If concession sales are not doing well because of low turnout or bad weather, can the manager change prices or offer a new item to generate revenue? For example, on hot days, facilities often sell more bottled water than traditional drinks. In the hot opening weekend of the 2001 pro football season, stadiums posted significant sales for bottled water—40,000 units were sold at the Buffalo Bills' Ralph Wilson Stadium, and 20,000 bottles were sold at the Baltimore Ravens' PSINet Stadium (Muret, 2001). By vigilantly monitoring sales throughout an event and over a season, a facility manager can identify new strategies to help increase sales.

If the rental agreement calls for revenues to be shared, are there any problems with calculating the revenue after the event? For example, would press passes count against the attendance totals? Although the agreement may cover such issues, the postevent evaluation is designed to determine whether the agreement can even be enforced or whether provisions need to be changed for the future.

The postevent evaluation may show that an event should not be allowed back in the facility even if it was financially successful. Some events might generate significant media and public outrage, even if the event generates revenue. These reactions need to be critically reviewed to determine whether an event should be accepted again.

The major task in postevent financial analysis is balancing the books. For each employee responsible for generating revenue, are all revenues accounted for? A ticket booth attendant might have been given 1,000 tickets to sell at $5 each. If the attendant has 400 tickets remaining after the event, then she sold 600 tickets and should have $3,000. If the person has only $2,500, then management needs to investigate why there is a $500 discrepancy.

Facility lease agreements often contain provisions for allocating income derived from ticket sales and concession revenue. Since the facility normally collects the money, the event producer or team relies on the facility to provide accurate and detailed records. Chapter 12 includes a sample reconciliation from a major football game. If a promoter collects the money, the facility should be careful to obtain all money owed before the event leaves town to avoid a possible collection problem. Facilities have lost significant amounts of money when a promoter left without paying bills; in cases like this, the facility may never see its share. Similarly, a problem arises when the facility, after paying all the suppliers, vendors, and employees, does not have enough money to pay the amount it owes the event. If this occurs, the facility may have to borrow money, try to renegotiate the debt, or, in extreme cases, file for bankruptcy.

If an event or facility is not successful, the final decision for management may be to close. Closing may generate contractual issues such as breach of contract. Many new facilities are constructed with provisions that the anchor tenant or team must use the facility for 20 to 30 years. If the team leaves earlier, it must pay a penalty. Similarly, if a fitness center located in a shopping mall has a 10-year lease and decides to terminate the lease after 5 years, it will be responsible for another 5 years' rent. Normally it is incumbent on the landlord to find another tenant, if possible, to mitigate the damages. However, if the landlord tries and does not find another tenant, then the original tenant will be responsible for all the owed rent.

Evaluating Liability

After an event, management needs to review all incident reports to determine if there is a likelihood of litigation. Most insurance policies require notification within 24 hours after an event of any incident that could possibly lead to a claim. Thus, any injury resulting in an ambulance ride or a visit to a hospital should be documented and the information shared with the insurance company. All facts should be documented, the area where the injury occurred should be photographed, and everyone in the area should be interviewed. The insurance company may want to be involved in this process. Furthermore, depending on the type of injury and who was injured, government officials such as OSHA investigators may want to review the accident scene.

Risk management issues covered in the lease contract need to be analyzed before the event. For example, was the proper **certificate of insurance** issued with the requisite amount of coverage? Was the facility named as an **additional insured**? Does

Facilities Trivia

Baseball stadiums often host intriguing events to keep fans entertained. One such event involves pitting costumed characters against each other in fun races. Some well-known races include the following:

- The Milwaukee Brewers showed an animated race on their video scoreboard from 1994 until 2000, when they began holding live races. In 2006 they added Cinco, a chorizo sausage that wears a sombrero.
- The Pittsburgh Pirates have held the Great Pierogi Race, which includes Cheese Chester, Jalapeño Hannah, Sauerkraut Saul, and Oliver Onion, since 1999.
- Three costumed hot dogs race against each other at every Friday-night home game for the Kansas City Royals. The hot dogs look the same but wear caps corresponding to their favorite condiment (red for ketchup, yellow for mustard, and green for relish).
- Red, yellow, and green chili peppers race each other at Toronto's Rogers Centre.
- Hot dog buns, ketchup bottles, and mustard bottles race in Baltimore; boats race in Seattle; subways race in New York; and the four presidential heads depicted on Mt. Rushmore race in Washington.
- Possibly the most exciting race of all time occurred in 2003 at a Milwaukee game against the Pittsburgh Pirates. While Guido, the Italian sausage wearing a chef's hat, was chasing after Frankie Furter, Brett Wurst, and Stosh the Polish Sausage, Pittsburg's first baseman Randall Simon intervened and hit the 7-foot-tall costumed Guido in the back of the head with his bat. The person inside the outfit, 19-year-old Mandy Block, who stood only 5 feet 3 inches, was knocked down but was not out of the race, as the mascots stopped and helped her up to finish the race. Simon apologized but was arrested for assault. Block did not press charges, but Simon was fined $432 and suspended for three games ("Police Report: Sausagegate," 2003).

the policy cover attorney fees and costs? Although a contract may require these provisions, the policy needs to be examined to make sure the proper coverage was purchased and is in place for the event. Also, are waiver forms available for participants, and are all necessary signs in place to educate spectators? These simple steps are regularly discussed before an event but sometimes forgotten when the event is held. Thus, all employees need to make sure all risk management strategies are implemented during and after the event.

Another insurance-related task after the event is reviewing the number of claims associated with a particular type of event or facility. If there are very few injuries, then the claims experience would be low, and the premium cost should decrease in the future. However, above a certain number of claims, the insurance rates will increase.

During and after the event, management should also look at the relationship with the insurance company. Some insurance companies provide personnel to work events as risk managers. If an insurance company takes proactive steps to make an event and facility safer, this is a strong indication that the company is dedicated to protecting its investment and maximizing safety.

POSTEVENT SURVEYS

Postevent evaluation is another key management task. Did all the strategies work? Were employees successful at their assigned tasks? Did the mechanical systems work as intended? Did the marketing campaign bring enough sponsors or ticket sales? Did the event make or lose money? Did the event generate goodwill in the community? These types of questions are paramount for any manager. If the facility did not live up to expectations, tenants can be upset, owners can be furious, and patrons can decide to not attend again. One bad facility experience is often enough to dissuade people from attending a future event at that facility. If a patron spends several hours in the parking lot trying to leave after an event, can that patron be persuaded to attend another event? If the parking issue is not corrected, the patron will be hesitant to come back or will want there to be other options for reaching the venue, such as a shuttle service.

If a facility is having a problem with parking but management does not know about it, management cannot do anything to make the facility experience better. Management needs to know about problems and then take action. If there is a problem, management needs to be upfront. It is essential to let people know that the postevent surveying process has uncovered a problem and then to indicate what specific steps are being taken to solve the problem.

Customer Satisfaction

Postevent surveying is often undertaken to determine the degree of customer satisfaction. But even during an event, management often is forced to examine the little things. For example, if a ball lands in the stands, was anyone hit? If so, what condition is the person in? Did a kid get stomped on during the battle for the ball? Did an elderly fan get pushed by a drunken fan who was trying to get the ball? Was someone's food or beverage spilled in the process? Is the ball a memorable ball that should be retrieved? By paying attention to these small but often overlooked issues, management can take advantage of opportunities to develop relationships. Relationship building is just as important for spectators and facility users as it is for employees. If a fan loses his food or otherwise is not having a good experience, can management do anything to make it better? The fan can be offered other food, a coupon for a free ticket, or possibly even an opportunity to meet a player. People who receive this kind of attention can become lifelong supporters and will communicate their positive feelings to others.

In an MLB game in 2004, a 4-year-old boy was about to catch his first foul ball when a man sitting behind him took the ball away after it landed on the ground. While the man jumped up with ecstasy, the little boy was crying. The scoreboard showed both the man and the boy, and fans started shouting at the man to give the boy the ball. The man refused to give the ball to the child. Team officials went out of their way to comfort the child, and a star player gave the boy a game-used bat. At the end of the day the youngster received significant media attention, several pieces of memorabilia, and some free game tickets ("Boy Will Get Foul Ball," 2004). Such reactions turned a very negative experience into a lifelong memory that might make the boy a loyal future baseball fan.

Every effort should be made to discover what people are thinking. It is well documented that happy customers will tell 1 or 2 others about their good experience. In contrast, dissatisfied customers will tell 8 to 10 others about their poor experience (Zikmund and d'Amico, 1996). However, many dissatisfied customers never mention their feelings to the facility management for fear of retribution, a perceived lack of interest on management's part, or a lack of time. Management has to remove obstacles to allow customers to freely indicate their concerns as well as their satisfaction.

A critical task for management is surveying spectators and facility users. Information is most easily obtained from written, phone, or focus group questioning or from surveys. Surveying is undertaken to plan for the future. It is impossible to plan without proper information. One common strategy is to survey season ticket holders since their names are already in a database and they represent the most frequent facility users. Fans are often sent a survey and offered a discount or premium item for responding. A suggestion box is another way to allow people to give positive and negative feedback.

There is no one correct survey instrument. The key is to determine what information the facility wants from the survey before writing the questions. The facility also needs to determine how to distribute the survey to obtain a well-rounded sample representing the broad array of patrons who may be at the facility. (See "Customer Satisfaction Survey" for a sample survey.)

On-Site Surveys

Another way to obtain valuable information is for facility managers to shop the facility themselves. The manager should drive to the facility from different directions to see firsthand what traffic issues exist. The manager should also be a "regular" fan and buy a ticket, go through the parking lot, enter through the front gate after waiting in the crowd, observe security and directional signage, obtain directions to the seat, buy concessions, use the restrooms, try to com-

plain about service, fake an injury, pretend to be intoxicated, get lost in the parking lot after an event, and engage in countless other activities to test the employees. Since many employees will recognize the facility manager, a "secret shopper" can be more effective in the information retrieval process during an event.

Once an evaluation is completed, it should be documented and shared with others in order to gain their perspective. If action needs to be taken, management needs to see what changes are necessary and what can be done to accomplish those changes. Some changes may be easy to make with a minimal financial expenditure or with minor modifications to policies and procedures. Other changes can be very costly or will take a significant amount of time to complete. Thus, the facility manager needs to know his budget and time restrictions before undertaking any renovations or repairs.

MARKETING FOR THE FUTURE

The postevent time is not just for evaluating the planning and execution of the event; it should also be used to market the next event. If a sponsor provided money or services, how was the sponsor acknowledged? Was there an official thank-you in a publication? Was someone in the sponsor company personally thanked? Significant value can come from postevent recognition and marketing. It is recommended that a thank-you note be sent to each sponsor and all major participants in the event. Following up with sponsors communicates to them that the event or facility is genuinely appreciative.

If information about the event's success is included, the relationship can be strengthened for the following year. For example, if attendance increased 20% over the past year, this information could be critical to a sponsor and should be communicated. Other items that can be sent include newspaper clippings, event photos, signed photos of a star athlete standing next to the sponsor's sign, a thank-you plaque, sample tickets, and video of the event showing signage location and appearances on broadcasts. These and a host of other items can help show sponsors that they

CUSTOMER SATISFACTION SURVEY

What is your zip code? _____

❏ Y ❏ N Is this the first event you have attended at this facility?

How did you hear about the event? _____

❏ Y ❏ N Did you enjoy the event?

Did you purchase tickets?

Where did you get the tickets from? _____

❏ Y ❏ N Did you drive to the facility?

How was the traffic coming to the facility?   Good   Bad   Okay

How was parking?   Good   Bad   Okay

❏ Y ❏ N Did you use the restrooms?

❏ Y ❏ N Were the restrooms clean?

❏ Y ❏ N Were there enough supplies such as toilet paper and towels?

❏ Y ❏ N Did you purchase any food?

❏ Y ❏ N Was the food served quickly?

❏ Y ❏ N Was the food tasty?

How much do you think you spent on food at the event? _____

❏ Y ❏ N Did you purchase any concession items?

What did you buy? _____

❏ Y ❏ N Were you satisfied with the quality of the item you purchased?

How much did you spend in total on concession items? _____

What could the facility have done to make the event better? _____

_____

_____

_____

_____

Other suggestions or comments: _____

_____

_____

_____

If you would like to be added to our mailing list, please write your name, address, phone number, and e-mail address below.

_____

_____

_____

made a wise decision. Such information should also be sent to organizations that were solicited for sponsorship and that appeared somewhat interested but declined sponsorship. A potential sponsor who realizes that the event or facility was a good investment may try to set aside funds to become a sponsor the next year.

MARKETING EFFORTS AND COSTS

Facilities need to examine how they have marketed the game experience. If the experience is wonderful, the patron will become a valuable customer and move up the **marketing escalator** to become a more frequent purchaser. The marketing escalator represents a spectrum of facility users, from nonusers to frequent users. Most facilities focus their efforts on converting the casual users to frequent users.

After an event, managers need to analyze the entire marketing effort to determine what worked and what needs to be changed. Such an analysis can be complicated. If an event used only word of mouth to generate interest, it would be easy to determine whether or not the marketing effort worked. However, most events and facilities utilize multiple campaigns at the same time, and it is often difficult to determine which campaign worked. For example, a circus may utilize billboards, newspaper advertisements, supermarket giveaways, radio, and even televised commercials. It is not easy to decide which communication medium was most successful and should be used in the future or whether to continue using all the mediums.

Television and other media coverage, which can be publicity, need to be monitored to ensure that no negative publicity is aired. Management should be careful with all media relations, but this concern is much greater after an accident or tragedy. The facility should designate a person to handle press-related matters. Only one person should speak to the press on behalf of the facility, and that person should be trained in how to deal with media inquiries.

FACILITY ANALYSIS

Operational issues abound during an event. What if the facility is too hot? Can the HVAC system be modified, and if yes, how? What happens if the lights go out, and how long will it take to bring them back to their required illumination level? What happens if the rink ice begins to thaw? These situations are all related to the facility operations side of running an event or facility.

Operational issues inherent in any facility can range from sanitation problems to HVAC breakdowns. A facility and its management team will be judged by how they respond and how quickly they respond to a problem. It is anticipated that problems will occur at every facility and at every event. Facility users will understand if the lights go out or if there is a problem with the blowers. However, if the problem is not corrected quickly, even understanding people can become irate. In order to ensure continuous operations with the fewest problems, the facility manager needs to have a maintenance staff in place that includes the various tradespeople who may be needed. In a smaller facility, the manager should have appropriate independent contractors available to come within a 1-hour period. Normally a facility senior engineer helps direct several tradespeople—in plumbing, electric, crafts, and other areas—who are responsible for maintaining and repairing systems during an event.

To avoid a major tragedy, such as the stands collapsing, the facility structure itself is the first concern. Thus, the facility structure needs to be reviewed not just before the event but also during and after. Systems may be monitored for sounds, heat, pressure, or related potential clues that a problem may exist. Most larger facilities have a call center or an electronic monitoring system or both. A call center can receive several hundred phone calls during an event for problems such as a broken toilet seat or a malfunctioning refrigerator at a concession stand. The call center dispatches appropriate personnel to make necessary inspections and corrections, if possible. An electronic monitoring system identifies when a problem occurs and automatically indicates where the problem is located and what steps could be taken to correct it. Some systems are so thorough that they can identify whether the facility tradespeople can complete the work, and a system may even contact outside vendors if the work needs to be outsourced to a third party.

A facility needs to be carefully examined after each event to make sure that no structural damage was caused by the event or the crowd. For example, a bleacher could have been broken or come unbolted. Structural problems could arise, such as weakening of cement from years of use or possible misuse. A roof does not collapse after most events, but if it does, the results can be disastrous if anyone is in the facility. Some of the components that need to be inspected include the following:

- Light bulbs (change as needed)
- Emergency generators (weekly inspection of all gauges, connections, batteries, fluid levels, and so on; monthly load testing)
- Elevators (weekly inspection)
- Burglar alarm system (monthly inspection)
- Trash chutes (quarterly inspection)
- Site drains (quarterly inspection)
- Sprinkler system and sensors (quarterly inspection)
- Smoke detectors (semiannual inspection)
- Irrigation system (semiannual inspection)
- Facility envelope (annual inspection)
- Roof (annual inspection)
- Fire alarm system (annual inspection)

- Water heaters (annual inspection) (Lewis, 1999)

All aisles, restrooms, stairwells, walkways, and food counters and related areas need to be cleaned immediately after an event. Cleaning of the food preparation area needs to be carefully reviewed. Failure to properly clean kitchen equipment can lead to numerous health code violations and can make future cleanup jobs more difficult.

Where does all the garbage go after everyone leaves? With recent innovations and technology, sport venues are integrating recycling into concession sales. Recycling containers for cups, paper, and bottles are appearing more and more often. Even though the costs of a recycling program are greater than those for traditional garbage removal, society has changed and facilities need to become more environmentally concerned. For a recycling program to work, employees and signage should be placed near the containers to remind people, and announcements about the recycling program should be made throughout the game. Sport venues are also using recycled materials to make napkins, cups, and towels for use at a later time (Berg, 1992). Special attention also should be given to general maintenance for things such as broken seats, clogged drains, dripping faucets, and broken dispensers (both soap and condiments).

The lighting system should be checked to make sure all the lights work well and to determine whether any lights need to be replaced or redirected. The HVAC system should be checked to make sure the heating and cooling units work effectively and whether any oiling, screen cleaning, or other services are required.

BEHIND THE SCENES

AN OPENING TO REMEMBER

Although you might assume that an experienced facility manager knows how to run a facility, screwups occur on a regular basis. On April 9, 1913, the Brooklyn Dodgers opened Ebbets Field—or at least they tried to. The owners forgot the keys to the front door, and fans had to wait in line for more than an hour while an employee went home to get a spare key. Since the builders had forgotten to build a press box, the press had to watch the game from the grandstands. The owners even forgot the American flag that was supposed to be raised during the opening ceremonies (Nash and Zullo, 1992).

The playing surface should be examined. For example, muddy outdoor areas may need to be drained or resodded, or indoor gym floors may be peeling. Checking the playing surface is especially important in cases in which the facility will be changed over from one event to another in minimal time. Skipping a problem because of time constraints can lead to bigger problems later on.

Equipment and Warehousing

All equipment not being used for the event needs to be properly stored so it does not get damaged. Seats, barricades, extra concession booths, and other similar items need to be moved before an event and properly stored to avoid getting damaged or creating a hazard. A potentially dangerous item such as a trampoline can be an attractive nuisance and needs to be properly secured so that children cannot use it. If necessary, doors should be locked or a security person should be stationed in the area. Most storage areas can be properly monitored with a closed-circuit television (CCTV) system, which saves the cost of a security person. Regardless of the strategy used, the storage area should be secured.

Special attention is usually warranted at championship-related events. Some events have a final awards ceremony that may require a platform. Platforms normally need to be stored away from the competition and then put in place at the end of the competition. There should be a clear and direct path for moving the platform. Trophies also represent a potential concern during an event. Steps must be taken to prevent damage and theft. Additionally, someone must be designated to present the trophies, and arrangements must be made to deliver them. If a team does not win a game, it may be necessary to make arrangements to send the trophies to another site.

After an event ends, the items utilized for that event may need to be stored until they are required for a future event. Madison Square Garden has numerous overlapping events. If the New York Rangers are playing on Friday night, the facility must find storage for all the novelty items, nets, dasher boards, and even the Zamboni so that the floor can be converted to a basketball surface and the concession stands stocked with primarily Knicks gear. This process is repeated the next day if a collegiate competition is scheduled. After an event it is also necessary to clean storage areas. Fire hazards can be created when storage areas are not properly cleaned. The accumulation of debris can be a tripping hazard as well.

Storage areas are typically built into facilities, but they often are full or difficult to manage. Significant storage room is needed to ensure proper access to needed supplies. A regular spring cleaning can help get rid of clutter that may reduce the amount of storage space in a facility.

Box Office and Ticketing

Most larger facilities utilize computer-based ticketing systems that streamline the purchasing process, but numerous ticketing concerns can occur during the event. For example, multiple tickets might have been sold for the same seat, or ticket takers might have accepted forged tickets. Other issues typically dealt with by the box office include providing armbands for people who can purchase alcohol and giving out special discount vouchers to buy items in the facility.

Another concern is the amount of cash that may be stored at the box office. Precautions need to be taken to make sure the money is secured. Some facilities regularly collect money from the concession areas, parking lot attendants, and others and then bring these funds to the ticket office to be counted and processed, either through a safe drop or an armored car pickup.

The box office's books need to be examined to determine if anyone is skimming money or failing to report all sales. The computer system needs to be reviewed to determine if there were any glitches such as double printing of tickets for the same seats. If the computer malfunctioned, then the program needs to be examined for programming glitches or hardware problems. Speed is of the essence since tickets often must be printed for the next day, and the system cannot be down too long without causing major difficulties.

The event and facility also need to examine the relationship with ticket brokers to determine how tickets sales are going. Are third-party vendors succeeding in selling tickets? Is the phone-based sales system working well? How many tickets are sold over the Internet, and how are those sales managed? Is the facility ready to handle people buying e-tickets? Those are just some of the questions that need to be examined both after an event and during the long-term planning process.

Event Security

Command posts must be staffed with properly trained personnel. Almost every larger facility faces security problems at each event. A facility must be prepared to handle security problems, from pickpockets to auto thefts to lost children. Chapter 14 discusses numerous security concerns that should be addressed to provide a safer facility. However, the proof is in the execution. No matter how well trained the personnel may be, facing a live emergency is different from any textbook analysis. Although tabletop exercises and live drills help educate and train the staff, only a real disaster can provide the most comprehensive training.

Staff members should continuously monitor the CCTV system and scan the crowds to see what activities are occurring and whether it is necessary to send ushers or security personnel into any given area. If there is no CCTV system, security personnel rely on their own observations. Security needs to be provided to monitor areas both inside and outside the facility (e.g., in parking areas or adjoining city streets where some fans may be celebrating).

After an event ends, the security personnel and ushers cannot leave the facility until all patrons have left. In one case during the 1990s, it was raining as an event ended. While fans remained in the stands awaiting the award ceremony, the security personnel were nowhere to be found. They had probably moved to out-of-the-way places in order to stay dry. This resulted in a situation in which several fans were injured. If the security personnel had been at their assigned stations, the incident probably would never have happened.

Besides protecting fans, the security personnel protect players, officials, administrators, the media, mascots, cheerleaders, and others who are involved in producing the event. There are numerous examples of fans chasing after officials to challenge a call. Security companies have gone so far as to clothe police officers in officials' uniforms to serve as decoys while the real officials are leaving the facility.

Parking and Transportation

During an event, the parking area must be monitored for criminal behavior. Break-ins are the primary concern, but sometimes cars are stolen from lots. Other concerns include tailgate parties that are continuing and hot or burning areas where barbeque grills have been used. Monitors also keep an eye on the parking lot in winter to see when it needs to be plowed so that people do not have difficulty leaving.

Another situation in lots is drunken fans trying to get to their vehicles. Sometimes intoxicated fans leave a game early because they are not feeling well. These fans can represent a concern to others. Several suits have been brought by patrons who were injured when a drunk fan fell on them while walking in the parking lot (Fried, 1999).

After an event, the action moves to the parking area. Upset fans can take out their frustration on opposing fans or their vehicles. Intoxicated fans can cause problems by urinating on people or property, crashing vehicles, or falling down in the middle of a lot and disrupting traffic. Security personnel should be redeployed to the exit gates and parking areas while fans are exiting the facility.

After most of the cars are gone, there are normally several cars left in the lot with mechanical problems. There is usually a significant amount of trash in the lot as well. Management has to have personnel or third-party providers clean the lot and examine the area for problems such as potholes, broken lights, and holes in security fences.

Concessions and Food Services

Concessions is one of the largest activities going on behind the scenes during an event. One reason is that concessions is sometimes the biggest single profit center. Concessionaires strive to receive about 80% profit to cover their expenses. Thus, if an item costs $0.20, the goal is to sell it for $1.00 (Cohen, 1994b). Profit margins on specific foods are listed in table 15.2.

Drinks can be sold either in cans or as a mixture based on a syrup. A syrup-based soda generates

Table 15.2 Concession Profit Margins

Food	Bulk cost	Sales price	Profit margin
Hot dogs	$0.61	$1.50–$2.50	59%–75%
Popcorn	$0.23	$1.00–$1.50	77%–84%
Nachos	$1.15	$3.00–$5.00	61%–77%
Soda, syrup	$0.25	$3.00–$4.00	120%–150%
Soda, bottle	$0.50	$4.00–$5.00	80%–100%
Beer	$0.40	$5.00–$6.00	125%–150%

MEG Concession Supply. (2015) Guide to fun foods profits. Retrieved February 18, 2015 from www.concession-supply.com/Guide-to-Fun-Foods-Profits_ep_108-1.html.

more profit than cans or bottles. A 5-gallon (19 L) bag-in-the-box of fountain syrup should deliver 3,800 fluid ounces (112 L) of soft drink and costs around $40. About 15 ounces (0.44 L) of liquid is poured into a 20-ounce (0.6 L) cup on top of ice. Including the cost of the cup, ice, straw, and lid, the total cost should be approximately $0.25. If the drink is sold for $4.00, then the profit is $3.75 per drink. In contrast, if a distributor sells cans or bottles to the facility for $0.50 each, and the facility sells the drink to a fan for $4.00, the profit margin is reduced to $3.50 per drink (Holtzman, 2001).

Other profits can be derived from premium food and novelty items. For example, the 2002 MLB All-Star Game generated $40 per head in revenue from concession and merchandising sales. The breakdown was $18 in retail sales, $13 from concessions, and $9 from premium dining ("All-Star Fans," 2002). A significant chunk of the revenue came from anything that bore the word *All-Star*, such as caps, shirts, and balls. These financial results need to be constantly monitored during and after an event to ensure that the right products are being offered at the right prices.

Since management has to focus on profits, anything occurring during an event that can harm profits needs to be remedied. Long lines, warm beer, few options, dirty conditions, and poorly prepared products can all hurt profits for years to come. Management has to focus on providing customer satisfaction in the quickest time possible and at a relatively inexpensive price. Fans are accustomed to paying more for food at a ballpark or stadium than they would in other settings, but they demand high quality and quick service. Thus, consultants are

often retained to show how the menu can be enhanced, how employees can be trained to be more effective, and how the facility can be laid out to maximize speed in placing and processing orders. Management should monitor when, where, how, and how often fans purchase foods. For example, because most sales occur early in an event rather than close to the end, more sales staff are needed earlier in an event.

After an event, the concession area needs to be thoroughly cleaned. Various government regulations cover the temperature required to clean certain food preparation equipment. Utensils normally need to be cleaned in extremely hot water. Employees must be trained on using cleaning equipment and avoiding injuries. Management should check that the equipment is working properly so that the concession area will be in working order at the beginning of the next event.

Food needs to be properly stored. Some foods can be refrigerated and some can be frozen; others cannot be stored for use at a later date and must be discarded. Leftover food can be eaten by employees, thrown out, or donated to a charity. Many soup kitchens are willing to take leftover food, and this is an option worth pursuing since it can result in a tax deduction for charitable giving and help develop positive public relations.

The concessions inventory is another postevent concern. A complete inventory needs to be made at each concession area to determine what drinks, snacks, and food items must be ordered. Is there enough room in the freezer? How long will it take to order more food? Is there enough room in the storage area to store all the necessary drinks, cups, plastic utensils, and condiments?

Medical Services

Medical issues can be delegated in part to external providers such as EMTs and the local fire department. However, not every medical issue is an emergency. Athletic trainers or other qualified persons are needed to operate a triage unit at a facility. Does a bee sting require medical care? What if a fan is hit by a foul ball or hockey puck? What if someone is injured slipping on a walkway? Each injury and the effect on the person are different, and the event or facility must respond appropriately. The issues may be more difficult when participants or employees are injured.

- Will the team physician take over?

- What will the media say?

- Will the injured party sue?

- If an employee is injured, will there be an OSHA investigation? Is the facility safe?

Bloodborne pathogens are among the medical issues that must be addressed during an event. If someone has been injured and is bleeding, facility employees cannot just wipe up the blood and put it in the trash. Because of the threat of methicillin-resistant *Staphylococcus aureus* (MRSA), hepatitis B, human immunodeficiency virus (HIV), and other bloodborne illnesses, OSHA mandates that facilities implement a risk management plan to deal with blood spills (Vivian, Daugherty, and Dunn, 1994).

All facilities should have a designated OSHA compliance representative (either a manager or an employee). This representative needs to implement the following medical-related rules:

- Develop a written exposure-control plan.

- Develop a comprehensive precaution policy.

- Properly train and educate employees.

- Keep appropriate records.

- Examine engineering- and work-related practices.

- Purchase appropriate protective kits and equipment.

- Purchase vaccines and exposure follow-up protocols.

- Utilize appropriate labels and signs.

- Develop and implement appropriate housekeeping practices and procedures (Vivian, Daugherty, and Dunn, 1994).

Besides having kits to handle spilled blood, a facility must have a standard first aid kit with splints, bandages, and wound cleaners. The kit should be replenished each time material is used. In addition, some states are starting to require sport facilities and even high schools to have defibrillators.

Numerous insurance-related concerns arise with medical services and require careful attention. One that is crucial is proper documentation of every injury, all treatment received, and all ambulance usage. All photographs and incident reports should be immediately submitted to insurance companies to prevent rejection of a claim.

When someone has been injured, the management staff needs to show compassion and concern. If a patron went to the hospital, did the facility send someone along to make sure he was all right? Did the facility cover the medical bills? Was the insurance company notified? Was an autographed item given to the fan in order to create positive feelings? Small gestures such as these may make someone think twice about suing.

Inventory of medical supplies must be checked in case small adhesive bandages, ice packs, Ace bandages, and so on were used during an event. Management should also evaluate how the athletic trainers, fire department personnel, and EMTs coordinated their services. Sometimes medical service providers do not cooperate with one another, and management needs to evaluate personnel to make sure that all those involved in medical care work as a team.

Summary

The process of competing to bring events to a facility can be cutthroat. Facilities with existing tenants and a solid reputation do not need to struggle the way smaller facilities do. The battle to land events is not unique to sport facilities; convention centers have to fight the same battles. Facilities can reduce the time and cost associated with the bidding process if they develop a template that responds to most information requested in typical bid packets.

Once a bid is pursued, a facility needs to garner all the appropriate personnel, resources, and strategies to help win the bid. Once the bid is won, a facility needs to deliver on everything that was promised, from having appropriate personnel to ensuring marketing and financial success. A facility manager spends a majority of her time finalizing all the details before an event. The most important area that cannot be left to last-minute planning is security.

The planning process for hosting an event and then preparing the facility for the event is time intensive, but the event itself can raise various concerns. Has the facility complied with all its contractual requirements? Are the employees doing their jobs? Will the event be a financial success? Will the event raise legal issues? These are just some of the questions the facility manager needs to ask and answer when evaluating an event. The facility manager's job is not completed when the event starts. Although planning can take months or years and many problems are resolved before the event starts, numerous issues can arise during an event. Facility managers need to be as proactive as possible in addressing potential concerns during an event.

The facility manager also needs to spend a significant amount of time analyzing future marketing opportunities based on the event's success and the patrons' experience. Through surveying, the facility should understand what patrons liked and did not like about a facility. The facility manager then needs to turn his focus toward the facility and evaluate whether or not the facility performed as it was supposed to. This review includes not only the facility structure but also specific elements such as ticket operations, transportation, and concessions.

Discussion Questions and Activities

1. What would be the key steps to consider if you are thinking about renting your facility to a potential user for an event?

2. What would you recommend as a potential new concession item that might be the next big rage?

3. What steps would you take to prepare a facility for an event?

4. What steps would you take to attract fans to a new event you are about to host at your facility?

5. Develop a sample bid package specifying what you would want a gym or arena to offer in order to host a boxing competition.

6. Examine the bid process undertaken by the Salt Lake City Olympic Organizing Committee. What steps did they have to take to win the event? What ethical concerns arose from the event?

7. What are some of the key concerns that need to be analyzed during an event?

8. What is management's role during an event?

9. Contact a facility manager and follow the person during an event to see what he or she does as the event proceeds. Note in percentage form how the person's time is spent (e.g., 40% of the time spent is on personnel matters).

10. After an event, stay in the parking lot to see how people leave and how long it takes various people (families, elderly, groups, or the disabled) to leave. This exercise will help you learn how to be a secret shopper and identify good and bad policies, procedures, and execution.

11. What do you think are the biggest concerns that need to be examined after an event?

12. Attend an event and note how pre- and postgame activities are scheduled. Were they executed well and did transitions appear seamless, or were they poorly pieced together? What would you have done differently?

Glossary

actual payback analysis—How long it actually takes to pay back the initial investment.

additional insured—Another person or entity who will be covered by an insurance policy.

advertising—The use of paid sources to generate interest in a product or service.

aeration—Cutting or punching holes in the soil to help air, water, and nutrients filter down to the roots.

airborne sound—Sound made by people's activities (e.g., yelling or stomping on the floor) that travels through the air.

air exchange—Circulating air into a building from the outside and exhausting air from the building.

alteration—A change in a facility, system, or equipment that makes it better or more responsive to people's needs.

ambient light—Naturally occurring light, such as sunlight coming through a window.

ambient sound—Naturally occurring sound.

Americans with Disabilities Act (ADA)—Law that ensures equality for Americans with disabilities and includes equal rights to employment and access to facilities.

architectural barrier—Design barriers that prevent someone from fully enjoying a facility; such barriers need to be modified, if feasible, to comply with the ADA.

arena—An enclosed playing area with fixed seating capacity.

asset—Something that has value and can be converted quickly to cash.

assumption of risk—Defense to a negligence claim based on the injured person knowing the risk of injury and voluntarily continuing even though doing so is dangerous.

attractive nuisance—A hazard that can attract and then injure a child.

audit—A detailed study that identifies problems such as lost cash or poor management.

automatic external defibrillator (AED)—A device used to help resuscitate a person having a heart attack; can be operated by someone without significant training.

average payback period—Analyzes a capital decision based on how long on average it will take to repay the initial investment, assuming an average cash flow.

average rate of return—Helps determine the rate of return as a percentage so that various projects can be compared with one another.

balance sheet—Highlights how much a facility or company is worth at a specific time by examining its assets, liabilities, and shareholder's equity (ownership value).

benchmarking—The process of establishing industry norms or standards by which a facility can compare its operations to make sure it is efficient; can be undertaken to review everything from ticket sales and concession revenue to maintenance standards.

benefit–cost ratio—Used to evaluate a project by comparing the costs with the benefits; also called a cost–benefit analysis.

benefit segmentation—Examines what benefit someone wants to receive from the product or service.

bid process—Used by public entities to evaluate different vendors and determine which company can perform the required work at the best cost.

biometric scanning—References body parts (e.g., eyes, handprints) to authenticate known individuals and to allow them to access the facility.

bloodborne pathogens—Diseases passed by blood.

blueprint—A technical drawing showing how a facility will be built.

bond—A promissory note stating that the issuer (whether a government organization or private corporation) will repay a loan with interest.

booking—The process of entering into a contract to secure a date and event for a facility.

breakdown maintenance—Maintenance undertaken as soon as an item breaks.

building area—The area 5 feet (1.5 m) around the proposed building's exterior walls that provides enough room for building the facility.

building load capacity—How much weight the roof or rigging can support.

business plan—The road map for any facility that helps identify the product and market as well as the legal and financial outlook.

capital budgeting—Evaluating and determining long-term needs of the facility and whether new facilities need to be built or leased.

capital costs—Costs associated with long-term investments over many years.

capital planning—Examining and implementing programs that will help a facility and equipment last longer.

carbon footprint—The total amount of waste (e.g., trash, carbon dioxide emissions) generated by a facility and the people who use the facility.

certificate of insurance—A form that shows that insurance coverage has been purchased.

certificate of participation—Allows a municipality to form a corporation to purchase land or build a facility.

changeover—The process of transforming a facility from one event surface, such as basketball, to another event surface, such as ice hockey.

Civil Rights Act of 1964—Act that provided the framework for many key employment rights laws, such as protection against sexual harassment and discrimination under Title VII or gender equity under Title IX.

closed-circuit television—Self-contained video systems that record conduct to use as evidence or to investigate crimes.

collateral—Funds or assets used for securing a loan.

collective bargaining agreement—The contractual agreement developed between an employer and a union that sets terms and conditions associated with the work environment.

commercial rights—Assets owned by a facility that can be sold, leased, or borrowed by others for a price; includes naming rights and pouring rights.

common law—Law developed and interpreted by the courts.

common space—Hallways, foyers, concourses, and general open areas for people to move around in.

compaction—Pressure on the soil that pushes sand and soil together.

composting—The process or reusing or repurposing food and other resources (such as yard scraps, paper, cardboard, etc.) in order to convert it into other uses (such as fertilizer) and divert waste from landfills.

computer-aided drafting—Designing buildings on a computer for ease of operation and making changes.

computer-aided facility management (CAFM)—A software system that allows a facility manager to monitor needed repairs and adjust temperature and humidity controls.

computerized maintenance management system (CMMS)—Monitors a facility and the equipment and systems in it to optimize their performance and minimize repair and replacement costs.

consideration—An exchange of value; required for a valid contract.

constituents—The people (e.g., patrons, athletes, and employees) who use a facility.

contingency planning—Alternative plans used in response to the closing of a facility or the cancellation of a show.

continuity management—How a facility can continue operating after a disaster occurs.

contract—An agreement between at least two parties to complete a transaction.

contractually obligated revenue or income—Money guaranteed by a contract that can be used in obtaining a loan.

control—The ability to define, deploy, and apply best practices as required by a CMMS system.

coordination—The ability to establish real-time communication between all constituents and to leverage phone, fax, e-mail, or the internet to make sure everyone knows their respective responsibilities/obligations .

core drilling—Drilling to see what lies underneath land such as rocks or water tables.

corporate bonds—Loans undertaken by a corporation for long-term purchases such as a new stadium; the new facility is used as collateral to secure repayment.

crime prevention through environmental design (CPTED)—Using architecture and landscaping to provide added protection against crime.

crisis management—How to respond to and prepare for a potential crisis.

crowd management—Specific steps or strategies taken to prevent a tragedy involving patrons; can include structural, signage, and personnel strategies.

customer—A person who purchases or receives services at a facility.

customer relationship management (CRM)—A program that analyzes as much information about customers as possible and uses this information to more effectively sell to those customers.

cyclical repairs—Repairs conducted at predetermined times, such as yearly or monthly.

demographics—Data about a given population, such as age, sex, or income level.

design–build contract—Allows the future owner to provide the land and some control over the construction process, but the developer designs and builds the facility.

diffuse lighting—Lighting that is directed all over the facility so that light is spread throughout the facility.

direct costs—Costs of building the facility; includes material and equipment costs and workers' fees.

direct lighting—Lighting that shoots directly down from a fixture onto the area where light is intended to go.

displacement—The fact that some hotel rooms would be booked and diners would be present in the area regardless of whether a facility is holding an event, which reduces the total economic impact of an event.

dragging—Going over the infield dirt with a screen to make sure it is smooth and without rocks and clumps of dirt.

economic impact—The net economic change in a community based on hosting an event.

ECT approach—Technique used to help reduce the chance of injuries and lawsuits.

emergency medical technicians (EMT)—Emergency first aid and transportation personnel who help injured patrons or athletes.

emergency response management team—Persons dedicated to responding immediately to an emergency at a facility.

eminent domain—Ability of a government entity to purchase private land and convert it for public use.

end-product units method—Method used when enough historical data are available to compare the proposed building with previously built facilities. For example, if other gyms were recently built in a given region for $1.5 to $3 million, the builder could assume that a new gym would fall into the same range.

energy audit—An attempt to find all uses of energy and help eliminate any waste.

equity—The total value of personal money, stocks, and property.

evacuation—The process of removing people from a facility in a safe manner.

expenses—Obligations that need to be paid, such as bills and salaries.

external constituents—A group of individuals who have an interest in the facility, such as stakeholders, lenders, and government entities.

facility management—The art and science of managing a facility to help meet the facility's objectives, goals, and mission.

Fair Labor Standards Act (FLSA)—Federal regulations for the workplace, such as minimum wage and overtime regulations.

feasibility study—Helps determine whether a project is worth pursuing from a marketing, legal, and community perspective.

financial forecast—An attempt to plan for future financial needs based on expected revenues and expenses.

foreseeability—The process of utilizing all the facts to know whether a specific event is likely to occur.

four Ps—The four key elements of marketing, which are product, place, price, and promotion; some include an additional P, public relations.

front-of-the-house—An activity taking place in front of the audience, such as the game itself, versus back of the house, which refers to areas used for staging and running the facility.

functional plan—A plan that helps define what the operational plan will try to accomplish; includes marketing or safety plans.

furniture, fixtures, and equipment (FFE)—Chairs, tables, televisions, paint on the walls, pictures hung on the walls, and other such items in a facility that help complete it.

general admission—An event where there are no reserved seats and the first people into the facility have the first choice of where they will sit or stand.

general obligation bonds—Bonds backed by the full faith and credit of the issuing (borrowing) municipality, which promises to repay the bonds with general tax revenue.

geodemographic segmentation—Looks at customers and potential customers based on where they live or do business.

glare—A point of light that affects a person's eyes.

grading—The process of smoothing over the land to build the foundation of a building.

gray water—Reused or repurposed water, such as that from gutters or washrooms, that is diverted for watering plants.

green building—A facility that is built or operated to be as energy efficient as possible and reduce waste; can lead to LEED certification.

ground fault circuit interrupter (GFI)—Helps interrupt the flow of current to electrical outlets to prevent electrocution when water is in contact with an electrical appliance.

growth space—Unused space attached to the existing facility that could be used for future expansion needs.

grubbing—The process of removing brush, trees, and underbrush to clear the site to start building.

heat load—The number of people, the types of equipment in a facility, and the amount of heat they generate, such as heat from people running and sweating.

heating, ventilation, and air conditioning (HVAC)—Allows cold and warm air to circulate in a facility.

horizontal space dividers—Components that separate areas in a building horizontally, such as floors, ceilings, and floor heating systems.

hostile or offensive work environment—Sexual talk, actions, or photos that materially affect someone's ability to work.

immunity—Defendants will not be responsible, even if they would otherwise be liable, because they are protected by the government or some other legal or statutory protection.

income statement—Highlights the revenue and expenses for the prior year and factors in taxes and interest payment to determine whether the facility earned a profit or a loss.

independent contractor—A person who performs work for a facility but is not an employee of the facility; a facility cannot control a contractor's activities, resources, and assignments, whereas a facility can control these aspects of an employee.

indirect costs—Costs incurred during building a facility, but not direct building costs (i.e. not concrete, steel, construction labor). Examples include: printing costs, attorney fees, and permits.

indirect lighting—Lighting that is directed toward other objects, such as a wall or ceiling, so the light does not go directly into people's eyes.

induced effect—The ripple effect throughout an economy based on additional expenditures (rooms, meals, transportation, etc.) from an event that filter throughout an economy and expand the direct economic impact.

infiltration rate—Rate water is absorbed into the soil.

insight—The ability to obtain real-time status of all activities from a CMMS system.

internal constituents—Persons inside the facility, such as employees, patrons, owners, and athletes, who could have an effect on the facility.

internal rate of return (IRR)—The IRR is the facility-created return on investment that would need to be achieved to undertake a project. Using IRR, the initial investment and future cash flows are analyzed to determine a project's value.

job analysis—Determining what activities need to be accomplished to reach a specific goal.

job description—Specific skills required for accomplishing the goals set forth in the job analysis.

landscaping—Using plants, dirt, water, and rocks to make the exterior of a facility more attractive.

Leadership in Energy and Environmental Design (LEED)—Certification of "green" (environmentally friendly) buildings.

liability—A financial obligation to pay someone; current liabilities are debts owed now, such as salaries and utility bills, whereas long-term liabilities typically refer to bonds or other borrowing instruments.

life-cycle costing—The total cost of a building or equipment over its life; includes initial construction, energy costs, maintenance, and repairs.

light intensity—How bright a light is; measured in foot-candles.

luxury boxes and suites—Sold to those wishing to attend games or events in the best environment or location.

management—The art of getting people and resources to work together efficiently to achieve the goals of the facility.

management by objective—Managers and employees work together to develop realistic and achievable objectives that make both parties happy.

market—A group of actual or potential customers who will be interested in the product.

marketing—The process of packaging a product or service and setting the right price, manner, and strategy for selling it.

marketing escalator—Theory that some people will not use a product while others will use it frequently. The more often a person purchases the product, the faster that person moves up the escalator to become a frequent user.

Maslow's hierarchy of needs—Helps a manager identify what possibly will motivate an employee to perform better.

millwork—Customized finishes, such as wood, plastic, or metal.

mission—The overall ideal the facility wants to achieve; focuses on general terms such as *profitability*, *quality service*, and *workplace*.

move management—Focuses on how a company can plan for and execute a full or partial move from one area or facility to another.

movement theory—The science of crowd movement; focuses on density, speed, and flow.

multiuse facility—Facility that can be used for different events.

naming rights—Allows a company to put its name on a building for a specific contractual amount.

needs assessment—Focuses on whether a community really needs a proposed facility.

negligence—The failure to act in a reasonable manner; that action is the proximate cause of someone's injuries.

net present value (NPV)—Determines the dollar value of some future series of cash flows, discounted by the facility's cost of capital.

objectives—A specific result that a person or facility aims to achieve within a defined time frame and with available resources. Objectives help people focus on reaching specific goals.

occupancy permit—A form completed by a government building inspector indicating that the finished building can be occupied and meets applicable building code requirements.

Occupational Safety and Health Administration (OSHA)—Establishes rules for workplace safety and investigates workplace accidents and hazards.

open-term contract—A contract that has no specific ending period and keeps renewing unless terminated by one of the parties.

operational plan—Highlights what specific steps are required for accomplishing either a strategic or a functional plan.

organizational flowchart—Highlights the line of command in a facility and indicates who reports to whom for direct supervisory responsibility.

outsourcing—The act of hiring an external party to manage the entire facility or parts thereof, such as security, cleaning, or maintenance.

owner's representative—Acts on the owner's behalf to monitor the construction process and protect the owner's investment.

percolation—The amount of time it takes for water to pass through the soil to reach the roots.

personal seat license—A contractual right a person acquires for a fee that allows the person to purchase tickets for a specific seat; others cannot acquire tickets for that seat as long as the PSL contract is in effect.

personal transportation system—Vertical transportation, such as elevators and escalators, and horizontal transportation, such as people movers.

personnel management—The process of managing or inspiring people to work together to achieve the goals of the facility.

physical dimensions method—Examines the square foot values of a facility's major components and systems to determine a potential construction price.

place—The location in which a product is being sold or enjoyed.

planned approach—Forces a facility developer to examine what is needed and then to develop a facility pursuant to some predetermined guidelines.

planning—The strategic process of identifying what the facility wants.

preventive maintenance—Undertaken on a predetermined basis to help prevent equipment and systems from breaking and to increase their longevity.

price—How much someone is charging for a given product.

product—The item (whether a service or goods) that is being marketed.

progressive disciplinary approach—The progression from a warning to written warning, formal complaint, and then termination; a manager can be more confident in terminating an employee knowing that the employee was given a chance to correct behavior on several occasions.

promotion—The activity being used to help sell a product.

property law—A variety of laws that affect the use of property, from buying and selling property to how the property can be used.

proximate cause—Refers to the fact that a facility manager's actions are the direct cause of an injury rather than an intervening incident that led to the injury.

psychographics—The reason behind people's actions; determines how or why people decided to purchase or not purchase a given product.

public accommodation—Facilities in which people congregate or attend events, such as theaters, arenas, and stadiums.

public assembly facility (PAF)—Any facility in which the public can enjoy an event, such as stadiums, arenas, theaters, convention centers, and performing arts centers.

public offering—Occurs when a stock is sold to the general public.

public relations—Uses free sources such as newspapers and word of mouth to help sell a product or service.

publicity—Earned media; publicity is unpaid and is disseminated based on its newsworthiness.

punch list—Itemizes all the repairs required for finishing the construction process of a new building.

ratio method—A method used for facilities with extensive equipment needs; high equipment costs are multiplied by a ratio based on historical data to help determine the potential cost of the completed facility.

reasonable accommodation—Repairs or reconstructions that need to be done in order to comply with the ADA.

reconciliation—The process of calculating the total revenue and expenses for a given event.

redirected spending—Money that would have been spent on other activities (e.g., movies or bowling) in a community if the money had not been spent at a sport facility.

renovation—Modernizing an old facility.

request for bids (RFB)—A completed proposal in which the purchaser receives fixed bids in order to choose the most experienced company that has submitted the lowest bid to perform the proposed job.

request for proposals (RFP)—A request for external companies to suggest strategies for resolving a problem or developing a new program.

request for qualifications (RFQ)—A request for different companies to prove that they have the skill or experience required to complete the proposed job.

restoration—Refurbishing a facility to its former appearance and replacing deteriorating and broken elements in a manner that is consistent with historical accuracy.

return on investment (ROI)—The financial return an investment generates.

revenue—Money received primarily from selling goods or services.

revenue bond—Utilizes revenue from specific sources (e.g., sales taxes or ticket surcharges) to repay the bond.

rigging—Trusses and beams that support items such as scoreboards and ropes from the ceiling and walls.

ripple effect—Similar to how water spreads in a ripple throughout a lake when a stone is thrown into the water, a dollar spent in a community will likewise have an effect throughout the community.

risk management—The art of reducing the potential of someone being injured by a hazard that could have been avoided or minimized.

root zone—The area around grass roots that needs to have the proper amount of water and minerals to keep the grass strong.

sales–lease-back strategy—Allows someone to sell an asset (equipment or building) to an investor who receives lease payments from the seller, and the seller obtains a cash infusion.

sand-modified fields—Fields that use native soil combined with sand to help prevent compaction. To qualify as sand modified, the field needs to be at least 60% sand and 40% native soil.

scale model—A miniature model of the facility built to scale.

scoring—The process of breaking up the infield soil so that it is not hard or bumpy.

security—The safeguarding of an item, person, or place.

seeding—The process of spreading grass seeds to start a lawn instead of rolling out pregrown grass, which is called sodding.

site plan—A rendering of the facility with various subplans, such as the master plan, grading plan, landscaping plan, and traffic plan.

sky glow—Light that is directed or reflected upward and is wasted in space; it is seen as an orange haze over a city when one is flying in a plane at night.

soil testing—Testing to ensure that soil is not contaminated.

soil-based fields—Fields that use native soils and materials that have a high water retention level.

space management—A focus on effectively organizing the space in a facility; scheduling, maintenance, and related concerns are often part of the process.

sport complex—A facility or group of facilities centrally located for ease of access and use.

sport facility—A facility in which sport activities are played or viewed.

sportsplex—A multiuse facility combining different activities on various fields or courts.

stadium—A large bowl or square- or rectangular-shaped playing area with spectator seating that can have either a sideline or a full concrete grandstand.

stakeholder—Anyone who has an interest in the facility, such as neighbors, fans, or government officials.

steak and sizzle—The steak is the primary feature of a product, such as a football game, whereas the sizzle entails ancillary features of the product, such as cheerleaders or a halftime show.

strategic goal—Goal set by the highest-level managers to help run a facility and determine its future direction.

strategic plan—Plan that outlines the steps needed to achieve the facility's strategic goals; often called the master plan.

structural load—The weight of the building and all the items in it.

structure-borne sound—Sounds made by the facility, such as exhaust fans or squeaky floors.

substructure—The entire building from the ground to the foundation, including the basement or underground parking structure.

superstructure—The entire building above ground level, such as beams, frame, and structure.

support—The outside of the building, which helps support the building and protect it from the elements.

sustainability—Developing and running a facility that minimizes the impact on the environment and uses energy more efficiently.

swing space—Any space available to be used during renovations or alterations to an existing facility.

SWOT analysis—A focus on a facility's strengths, weaknesses, opportunities, and threats in order to plan for the future.

tabletop exercises—Safety training using models or maps indicating where trainees would go and what they would do during a real emergency.

tactical goals—Goals developed by midlevel managers for reaching a strategic goal of a facility.

target market—The intended group of people (market) that an advertiser is trying to reach.

topdressing—Spreading additional soil over the existing soil.

tort law—A variety of claims against people for their actions (whether intentional or unintentional) toward another person or a person's property.

trespass—Light that spills over beyond the area intended, such as on neighboring businesses or homes.

turfgrass—Grass on a playing field that is planted specifically to hold up to excessive use.

turnkey contract—A situation in which a construction company builds a facility with very little input from the owner and then turns the complete facility over to the new owner.

unintentional tort—Harm that might occur to someone that resulted from an unintended act with the primary example being a negligence claim.

value-based engineering—Forces a developer to examine shortcuts that could save money but not compromise the appearance or safety of a facility.

variance—A document from building inspectors or other government officials that states that a facility can be built in violation of established regulations.

variance analysis—Reviewing a budget against the actual costs to determine whether the budget was accurate.

venture capital—Initial funding from investors for a facility or company; investors demand a significant return on the investment. The investment is risky because most new facilities and businesses normally do not generate enough funds to interest most investors.

vertical space dividers—Components that separate areas in a building vertically, such as walls and columns.

vulnerability analysis—Examines situations in which the facility is most vulnerable; can include economic, natural, and manmade disasters.

waiver—A contract whereby someone agrees not to sue for a future claim the person might have if he or she were to be injured at a facility or event.

workers' compensation insurance—A no-fault system that provides coverage for any employee injured at work, regardless of who is responsible for causing the injury.

zoning—Laws that prevent unsightly or unorthodox buildings in a given neighborhood.

References

A smarter roof. (2013, Summer). *Pan Stadia and Arena Management, 38.*

Abbott, J., and Fried, G. (1998). Asphalt jungle. *Cornell Hotel and Restaurant Administration Quarterly, 40*(2), 46-60.

Ackler v. Odessa-Montour Central School District, 663 N.Y.S.2d 352 (A.D. 1997).

Adang, O. (1999, September 30). Football hooliganism. Committee on Culture and Education, Council of Europe. Retrieved December 10, 2000 from http://policestudies.homestead.com/hooliganism.html.

Agron, J. (2008, April). 37th annual maintenance and operations cost study. *American School and University,* 21-38.

All-star fans post $40 per cap. (2002, July 16). *Venues Today* (e-mail newsletter).

Allyn, B. (2013, June 7). Woman sues Montgomery Bell Academy after being knocked unconscious by wayward soccer ball. *The Tennessean.* Retrieved July 21, 2014 from www.tennessean.com/article/20130607/NEWS/306070115/Woman-sues-Montgomery-BellAcademy-after-being-knocked-unconscious-by-wayward-soccer-ball?gcheck=1.

American Airlines Center costs rise. (2001, July). *Stadia,* 5.

American College of Sports Medicine. (1992). *ACSM's health/fitness facility standards and guidelines.* Champaign, IL: Human Kinetics.

Americans with Disabilities Act, Public Law 101-336 July 26, 1990 104 Stat. 327, 42 USC 12132, Sec. 203. Enforcement.

Americans with Disability Act (ADA). 28 CFR Sec. 41.31. (2010, July 1 revision). ADA compliance under Part 41. Implementation of Executive Order 12250, nondiscrimination on the basis of handicap in federally assisted programs.

Ammon, R., Jr. (1993). Risk and game management practices in selected municipal football facilities. Dissertation, University of Northern Colorado.

Amphitheater. (2002). Retrieved September 29, 2004 from http://depthome.brooklyn.cuny.edu/classics/gladiatr/amphthtr.htm.

Andelman, W. (1992, Winter). Profile: The economics of sports in the Tampa Bay area. Retrieved November 15, 2004 from www.andelman.com/articles/sportseconomics.html.

Antonen, K. (2006, October 19). Tiger Stadium will be history. *USA Today,* 1C.

Antonen, M. (2009, June 2). Homer inflation pumps debate. *USA Today,* C1.

Applied Management Engineering, PC, and Kaiser, H. (1991). *Maintenance management audit.* Kingston, MA: RSMeans.

Arndt, R. (2013, March). City of tomorrow. *Popular Mechanics, 190*(3), 20.

Astor, M. (2007, November 26). Collapse shows Brazil's stadium woes. ABC News. Retrieved September 29, 2008 from http://abcnews.go.com/International/wireStory?id=3915646.

ASU Basketball. (2003). ASU men's basketball: Pioneering excellence in collegiate facilities. Arizona State University. Retrieved July 28, 2009 from http://asubasketball.com/index.html.

Athens 2004. (2004). Retrieved November 9, 2004 from www.athens2004.com.

Athens' challenge. (2001, May). *Stadia,* 17-18.

Athletic field turf committee. (2004, December 21). Chappaqua Board of Education. Retrieved June 10, 2009 from sau70.org/spotlight/athletic_fields/Supporting_documents/ChappaquaSchoolTurf.pdf.

Athletic fields. (2009, July). *American School and University, 81*(12), 38.

Aurandt, A. (2002). Games—in all seriousness. Retrieved September 29, 2004 from www.zianet.com/desertx/june98/game.html.

Bagli, C. (2013, January 1). Problem with weak bolts has complicated the Barclays Center's early days. *The New York Times.* Retrieved July 21, 2014 from www.nytimes.com/2013/01/02/nyregion/weak-bolts-have-complicated-the-barclays-centers-early-days.html?_r=0.

Ballard, K., and King, J. (2002). Avoiding public recreation center planning pitfalls. Presentation at the Athletic Business Conference, Orlando, Florida.

Barber, M. (2002, May 24). Mariners fan's ashes fly, fly away, causing scare at Safeco. *Seattle Post-Intelligencer.* Retrieved November 25, 2014 from http://www.seattlepi.com/news/article/Mariners-fan-s-ashes-fly-fly-away-causing-scare-1088032.php

Basics of wood gym floor maintenance, the. (1980). St. Joseph, MO: Hillyard Floor Treatments.

Bassett, M. (2002, February 19). Emergency plans vital to cope with disasters. *Connecticut Post,* D1.

Bathroom Readers' Institute. (2009). *Uncle John's bathroom reader sports spectacular.* Ashland, OR: Bathroom Readers' Press.

Baybutt, P. (2003, March). A real threat. *Contingency Planning and Management,* 10.

Beacon on environmental issues. (2010, September 6-12). *SportsBusiness Journal, 13*(19), 18A.

Beasley, K. (1997). *The Paralympic village: A barrier free city.* Lausanne, Switzerland: International Olympic Committee.

Beijing to spend 3.4 billion US dollars on Olympic facilities. (2002, March 29). *People Daily.* Retrieved December 19, 2002 from www.peopledaily.com.cn/200203/28/eng20020328_93035.shtml.

Benazzi, R. (2010, July). Strategies for stormwater. *Buildings, 104*(7), 36-38.

Bentil, K. (1989). *Fundamentals of the construction process.* Kingston, MA: RSMeans.

Berg, R. (1992, September). Concessions going green. *Athletic Business,* 49-52.

Better ventilation could save billions, studies say. (2012, January). *Buildings, 107*(1), 12.

Bigelow, C. (2013, February/March). The trends in 2013. *Facility Manager, 29*(1), 30.

Billy the Marlin wiggles off hook. (2003, January/February). *Facility Manager,* 6.

Bishop v. Fair Lanes Georgia Bowling, Inc., 803 F.2d 1548 (11th Cir. 1986).

Bisson, M. (2001, July). Turn it around. *Stadia,* 82.

Blickstein, S. (1995). *Bowls of glory, fields of dreams: Great stadiums and ballparks of North America.* Encino, CA: Cherbo.

Bogar, C. (2008, Fall). Trends in collegiate recreational sport facilities. *The Sport Journal.* Retrieved July 28, 2009 from www.thesportjournal.org/article/trends-collegiaterecreational-sports-facilities.

Borsenik, F., and Stutts, A. (1997). *The management of maintenance and engineering systems in the hospitality industry* (4th ed.). New York: Wiley.

Boudway, I. (2010, October 25-October 31). The sun doesn't shine on green stadiums. *Bloomberg Businessweek,* 24-26.

Boulianne, C. (2008, September 28). Artificial field turf vs. natural grass injuries. Retrieved July 21, 2014 from https://suite.io/carla-marie-boulianne/11r6278.

Bowes v. Cincinnati Riverfront Stadium, Inc., 465 N.E.2d 904, 911 (Ohio Ct. App. 1983).

Boy will get foul ball from man who knocked him aside. (2004, June 16). Retrieved November 22, 2004 from www.cbs.sportsline.com/mlb/story/7425822.

Brailsford, P, and Noyes, B. (2000). Top ten project pitfalls. Presentation at the Athletic Business Conference, Orlando, Florida.

Breath of not-so-fresh air, a. (1999, March). *Athletic Business,* 10.

Brickman, H. (1997, November). Helping hardwood perform. *Athletic Business,* 67-72.

Bridges, F., and Roquemore, L. (2004). *Management for athletic/sport administration. 4th Edition* Decatur, GA: ESM Books.

Broncos sue 40 season-ticket holders. (2002, June 24). Retrieved September 16, 2003 from http://benmaller.com/archives/benstakes/2002_06_23_benstakesarch.shtml#85194215.

Brooks, J., and Martinez, A. (2002, May). Direct, indirect costs. *Athletic Business,* 54.

Broughton, D. (2012, February 27-March 4). Clubs give winter homes a branding boost. *SportsBusiness Journal, 14*(43), 26-30.

Brown, D. (2013, June 17). Raw sewage at Coliseum forces Athletics and Mariners to share Oakland Raiders clubhouse. Retrieved July 21, 2014 from http://sports.yahoo.com/blogs/mlb-big-league-stew/raw-sewage-coliseum-forces-athletics-mariners-share-oakland-065912101.html.

Brown, N. (2007, November). Fundraising—Tiger Stadium relics sold at auction. *Athletic Business.* Retrieved July 21, 2014 from www.athleticbusiness.com/articles/article.aspx?articleid=1651&zoneid=35.

Brown, N. (2009a, January). Love and money. *Athletic Business, 33*(1), 56-62.

Brown, N. (2009b, August). Finish lines. *Athletic Business, 33*(8), 36-42.

Brown, N. (2010, January). Post-games. *Athletic Business, 34*(1), 23-26.

Brown, T., and Haines, D. (2009). *Space planning guidelines for campus recreational sport facilities.* Champaign, IL; Human Kinetics.

Buckley, J. (2003, January). Calculating the true ROI of facility monitoring. *Contingency Planning and Management.* Retrieved March 12, 2003 from www.contingencyplanning.com/article_index.cfm?article=532.

Burns-DeMelo, H. (2008, Spring). Green, healthy cleaning. Allgreen Magazine, Connecticut Edition. P. 14.

Carey, B. (2012, August). Change of venue. *Popular Science,* 54-55.

Carlisle, V. (2003, March). All records are not created equal. *Contingency Planning and Management,* 20-24.

Carlson, R., and DiGiandomenico, R. (1992). *Understanding building automation systems.* Kingston, MA: RSMeans.

Carlson, S. (2013, September 26). Official: Drop golf course manager. *Hartford Courant,* 1B.

Carter, D. (2003). How much are you paying? *Baltimore Chronicle.* Retrieved August 4, 2004 from www.baltimore-chronicle.com_sports_aug01.html.

Carving up the concessions business. (2013, May 13-19). *SportsBusiness Journal, 15*(22), 12.

Catering solutions. (2013, Summer). *Panstadia and Arena Management,* 80-86.

Certified ice technician designation. (2001, September). *Stadia,* 38.

Charlotte Motor Speedway, estimated economic impact. AutoFair: September 15-18, 1994. (1994, November 3). Internal document.

Chelladurai, P. (1985). *Sport management: Macro perspectives.* London, Ontario: Sports Dynamics.

Chetwynd, J. (2011). *The secret history of balls: The story behind the things we love to catch, whack, throw, kick, bounce, and bat.* New York: Perigee.

Circus Maximus, the. (2002). The Circus Maximus. Retrieved September 29, 2004 from www.romeguide.it/MONUM/ARCHEOL/ccircus_maximus/circus.htm.

City of Lewiston. (1995). Arena definition schedule. Unpublished.

Cohen, A. (1994a, October). Don't give 'em the slip. *Athletic Business,* 53-56.

Cohen, A. (1994b, November). Food fight. *Athletic Business,* 45-48.

Cohen, A. (1998, November). The finish line. *Athletic Business,* 67-74.

Cohen, A. (2000, July). Feet first. *Athletic Business,* 54.

Cohen, A. (2001, November). Fabric fact and fiction. *Athletic Business,* 55-61.

Cohen, A. (2009, July). Running in place. *Athletic Business, 33*(7), 18-20.

Cohen, A. (2012, August). Billion dollar babies. *Athletic Business, 36*(8), 21-26.

Coleman, W. (2000, March/April). Let's go again! *Facility Manager,* 14-20.

Comastro v. Village of Rosemont, 461 N.E.2d 616 (1st. Dist. 1984).

Comprehensive annual financial report for fiscal year 2005. (2006, June 8). Metropolitan Sports Facilities Commissions, Minneapolis, Minnesota. Retrieved March 28, 2008 from www.msfc.com/images/dynImages/#1MERGED FINANCIAL REPORT 2005.pdf.

Comprehensive annual financial report for fiscal year 2011. (2012, June 22). Metropolitan Sports Facilities Commissions, Minneapolis, Minnesota. Retrieved July 21, 2014 from www.msfc.com/content/doc/MERGED%202011%20 FINANCIAL%20REPORT1.pdf.

Connor, P. (1998, August). Designer space. *International Magazine of Arena Construction and Management,* 26-30.

Conrad, C. (2000). Power meetings. Presentation at the Athletic Business Conference, Orlando, Florida.

Context of the Games and the Olympic spirit, the. (2002). Retrieved June 13, 2002 from www.persus.tufts.edu/Olympics/spirit.html.

Cote, R., and Harrington, G. (Eds.). (2003). *Life safety code handbook.* Quincy, MA: National Fire Protection Association.

Cotts, D., and Lee, M. (1992). *The facility management handbook.* New York: American Management Association.

County probes Bengals lease. (2002, October 17). Retrieved September 29, 2004 from www.findlaw.com/ap/s/2002/10-17-2002/20021017144506_077.html.

Curtland, C. (2012, July). Three factors make the case for trash compactors. *Buildings,* 18.

Dahlgren, S. (2000a, January). Fowl play. *Athletic Business,* 63-73.

Dahlgren, S. (2000b, July). Pumped-up prevention. *Athletic Business,* 71-78.

Daktronics. (2009, June 9). Oklahoma City Thunder's new Daktronics scoreboard to feature 10 video displays. Retrieved June 9, 2009 from www.daktronics.com/Company/NewsReleases/Pages/FordCenter.aspx.

Dave, P. (2014, March 1). "Extensive cracking" shuts Texas high school's $60-million stadium. *Los Angeles Times,* Retrieved July 21, 2014 from www.latimes.com/nation/nationnow/la-na-nn-texas-high-school-stadium-closed-for-cracks-20140228-story.html.

Davis, C. (2009, December 25). Dryer? 25 cents a load; TV 2 cents an hour. *Hartford Courant,* D1.

Davis, K. (1994). *Sport management: Successful private sector business strategies.* Dubuque, IA: Brown.

Day, D. (1992, October/December). Feasibility studies. *Facility Manager,* 10-21.

Depew, M., and Guise, S. (1997, May). In the root zone. *Athletic Business,* 67-71.

Details, details. (1985, July). *Athletic Business,* 32-36.

Dillon, D. (2002). About AA: Retrofit. DallasNews.com. Retrieved June 9, 2009 from www.dallasnews.com/s/dws/spe/2002/aacenter/architecture.html.

Dillow, L. (2013, October 2). The St. Louis Rams partner with ScentAir for an innovative way to boost secondary revenue streams. Retrieved July 21, 2014 from www.scentair.com/why-scentairnews-press/st-louis-rams-boost-concession-sales-with-scentair-national-sports-forum/.

Disney's Wide World of Sports Complex emerging as leading facility. (1998, October). *Facilities,* 15.

Dodd, M. (2009, April 3-5). Baseball's new palaces. *USA Today,* 1A-2A.

Domed stadiums of the world. (2002). Retrieved September 29, 2004 from www.ballparks.com/baseball/general/facts/domes.htm.

Donovan, H. (1994, January/February). Rigging the gig. *Facility Manager,* 16-18.

Dorsey, B. (1999, April/May). The premium-seat market: Reaching critical mass. *Facilities and Event Management,* 20.

Dorsey, B. (2001, May). In the lap of luxury. *Stadia,* 87-90.

Drexel, P. (2008, August 13). Rooftop football. *New Jersey Monthly.* Retrieved July 21, 2014 from http://njmonthly.com/articles/towns_and_schools/union-city-high-school-new-footballstadium.html.

Dwyer, K. (2013, February 27). The Phoenix Suns have the most expensive beer in the NBA, weirdly, while Spurs and Thunder brew the cheapest. Yahoo Sports. Retrieved July 21, 2014 from http://sports.yahoo.com/blogs/nba-ball-dont-lie/phoenix-suns-most-expensive-beer-nba-weirdly-while-203537122--nba.html.

Education laws and regulations. (2002). 606 CMR 38:00 School Construction. Retrieved September 29, 2004 from www.doe.mass.edu/lawsregs/603cmr38/603cmr38_1.html.

Ellis, M. (2002). Can't tell the stadium without a scorecard. Retrieved September 29, 2004 from www.footballproject.com/story.php?storyid=102.

Elsberry, C. (2001, October 21). Arena by the numbers. *Connecticut Post,* 7.

Emmons, N. (2001, October 22). Holtzman tells attendees to develop concept, design around the menu. *Amusement Business,* 1.

Energy efficient lighting. (2009). Eartheasy.com. Retrieved January 3, 2009 from www.eartheasy.com/live_energyeff_lighting.htm.

Environment News Service. (2008). Washington Nationals open first green U.S. ballpark. Retrieved May 12, 2014 from www.ens-newswire.com/ens/mar2008/2008-03-29-091.asp.

Epidauro. (2002). Retrieved September 29, 2004 from www.arcaro.org/epidauro.

Esposito v. New Britain Baseball Club, Inc., 895 A. 2d 291 - Conn: Superior Court, 2005

Fairfax County School District upgrades gym floors with Taraflex by Gerflor. (2003). Retrieved June 2, 2004 from www.gerflortaraflex.com/press/20030210.htm.

Fan Cost Index, 2008. (2008). Team Marketing Report. Retrieved January 9, 2009 from http://teammarketing.com/fancost.

Fan Cost Index, 2013. (2013). Team Marketing Report. Retrieved October 1, 2014 from http://teammarketing.com/fancost.

Farmer, P., Mulrooney, A., and Ammon, R. (1996). *Sport facility planning and management.* Morgantown, WV: Fitness Information Technology.

Finken, Z. (2001, September). It's not all peanuts and cracker jack. *Recreation Management,* 20-23.

Fisher, J., and Martin, R. (1994). *Income property valuation.* Dearborn, MI: Dearborn Financial.

Foust, D. (2002, December 9). Even the greens will like these greens. *Business Week,* 84.

Freeze frame. (2008, October 8). *The Hartford Courant,* B1.

Fried, G. (1999). *Safe at first.* Durham, NC: Carolina Academic Press.

Fried, G. (2004a). *Academy for Venue Safety and Security (AVSS) manual.* Dallas: International Association of Assembly Managers.

Fried, G. (2004b). Case study: Camp Randall. Proceedings from the Sport and Recreation Law Association (SRLA) Conference in Las Vegas, Nevada.

Fried, G., Deshriver, T., and Mondello, M. (2013). *Sport finance* (3rd ed.). Champaign, IL: Human Kinetics.

Fried, G., and Miller, L. (1998). *Employment law.* Durham, NC: Carolina Academic Press.

Frosdick, S. (1998, August). Drink or dry. *International Magazine of Arena Construction and Management,* 20-24.

Gabrielsen, A., and Miles, C., eds. (1958). *Sports and recreation facilities for school and community.* Englewood Cliffs, NJ: Prentice-Hall, 43.

Galloway, D. (2001, November). Are fans being served? *Stadia,* 154-157.

Ganim goes to trial on corruption charges. (2003, January 6). Retrieved May 2, 2004 from www.nbc30.com/1871463/detail.html.

Gannon, M. (2002, February 1). Cheshire says pool builder in default. *New Haven Register,* B2.

Garris, L. (2006, August). Putting best practices into action. *Buildings,* 38-42.

Garris, L. (2008, February). 11 surprising ways that your building wastes energy. *Buildings,* 48-52.

Gartner: Businesses can't pay for disaster planning. (2003). Retrieved March 26, 2003 from www.contingencyplanning.com/Information/NewsAlert/News-Alert-3.cfm.

Gearhard, G., and Schuler, R. (2001, August). Retrieved March 15, 2004 from www.ballparks.com/baseball/index.htm.

General information. (2004). Retrieved September 29, 2004 from www.rosebowlstadium.com/stadium/gen_info/gen_info.html.

Giants Stadium resodded. (2002, December 31). *New York Times,* D4.

Gilligan, G. (2007, November 18). GreenTech grass is as good as gold. *Times Disptach.* Retrieved June 14, 2009 from www.greentechitm.com/project/default.asp?fpID=077FA6F7-99E7-4753-8587-9079B8677F9A.

Give 'em a stench and they'll take afoot. (2003, January/February). *Facility Manager,* 7.

Go green. (2013). Philadelphia Eagles. Retrieved July 21, 2014 from www.philadelphiaeagles.com/community/gogreen/renewable-energy.html.

Gordon, C., and Brill, W. (1996, April). Crime prevention through environmental design in premises liability. National Institute of Justice research brief.

Goss, B. (2003, January/February). Hooliganism moves across the pond. *Facility Manager,* 32-35.

Gosselin, K. (2013, February 8). Global chosen to run The XL. *Hartford Courant,* A1, A5.

Greek theater. (2002). Retrieved June 14, 2002 from www.ebicom.net/~tct/ancient.htm.

Green, A. (2013, April). A brief history of the skyscraper. *Popular Mechanics,* 190(4), 88.

Greenberg, M., and Gray, J. (1996). *The stadium game.* Milwaukee, WI: National Sports Law Institute of the Marquette University Law School.

Gregerson, J. (2010, September). Cool pavement generates hot debate. *Buildings,* 54.

Greusel, D. (1992, August). Building a shared vision. *Athletic Business,* 32-36.

Griffin, A. (2013, January 4). Lawmakers pushing for safety in pools. *Hartford Courant,* 144(4), A1.

Hall, B. (2001, November). Trading places. *Stadia,* 111-113.

Hamm, M.M. (1998, November 7). How to deal with damage after flood water leaves. *Houston Chronicle,* D5.

Hanson, S. (2005). Benchmarking for cleaning businesses. *Cleaning Articles.* Retrieved June 14, 2009 from www.cleaningarticles.com/Article/Benchmarking-for-Cleaning-Businesses/96.

Hasselbusch, E. (2013, September). Maximize roof service life. *Buildings,* 107(9), 54-58.

Haven, R. (1992, October 23). Cancellation of Marlboro Grand Prix of New York. New York: New York Public Interest Research Group.

Heenan v. Comcast Spectacor, Phila. Ct. Com. Pl. Lexis 138, 2006

Heikkinen, R. (2001, August). Sustainability in the building industry. *ASTM Standardization News,* 22-25.

Henig, S. (2010, September 24). The changing of the stadium. *The New Yorker.* Retrieved July 21, 2014 from www.newyorker.com/online/blogs/sportingscene/2010/09/the-changing-of-the-stadium.html#slide_ss_0=1.

Hennesey, K. (2001, May/June). It makes cents to recycle. *Facility Manager,* 40-45.

Hewitt, S. (1998, September 3). Ballpark, college tie-in supported. *The Columbian,* 1.

Heyman, B. (2003, December 10). Jets' stadium plan shows progress. *Journal News*. Retrieved September 29, 2004 from www.thejournalnews.com/newsroom/121003/c0110stadiumco.html.

History. (2004a). Retrieved September 29, 2004 from www.athens2004.com/athens2004/page/legacy?lang=en&cid=ec480812f7c39f00VgnVCMServer28130b0aRCRD.

History. (2004b). Retrieved September 29, 2004 from www.rosebowlstadium.com/stadium/history/history.html.

History of the Colosseum and Forum Romanum. (2002). Retrieved June 13, 2002 from www.iei.net/~tryan/h-colfer.htm.

Holtzman, M. (2001, December). Liquid cash. *Athletic Business*, 99-103.

Horman, W. (1993, January). A turf timetable. *Athletic Business*, 51-54.

Howard, D., and Crompton, J. (1995). *Financing sports*. Morgantown, WV: Fitness Information Technology.

Hruby, P. (2002, April 25). The 50 worst sports ideas ever. *Washington Times*. Retrieved April 26, 2002 from www.washtimes.com/sports/20020424-71647378.htm.

Hunter, B. (2001, July/August). The need for an annual business plan. *Facility Manager*, 42-43.

iceSheffield. (2009). Energy policy. Sheffield International Venues. Retrieved June 12, 2009 from www.icesheffield.com/energy_policy.

ICRI 2005 project award winners. (2005). International Concrete Restoration Institute. Retrieved June 9, 2009 from www.icri.org/awards/2005/soldier_field_stadium.asp.

IFMA surveys reveal security is top priority and office space is still shrinking. (2001, May). *Facilities Design and Management*, 9-10.

Immig, J., and Rish, S. (1997, March). Indoor air quality guidelines for Sydney Olympic facilities. Bondi Junction, Sydney, Australia: Green Games Watch 2000.

Imray, G. (2010, August 19). Little use for stadiums in South Africa. *The Sentinel*, B2.

International Facility Management Association. (2007). Exploring the current trends and future outlook for facility management professionals. Retrieved October 7, 2008 from www.ifma.org/tools/research/forecast_rpts/2007.pdf.

Introducing the TD Banknorth Sports Center at Quinnipiac University (2014). Quinnipiac University. Retrieved November 20, 2014. http://www.quinnipiacbobcats.com/information/facilities/tdsports_center/TDBanknorthFactSheet.pdf

Jackson, B., and Menser, N. (2000). Olympic sporting facilities await athletes and spectators. *Engineers Australia, 72*(1).

Jahrling, P. (2007, June). Water ways. *American School and University*, 32-36.

Jets earn over $16 million in online PSL auction. (2008, October 28). NBC Sports. Retrieved January 11, 2009 from http://nbcsports.msnbc.com/id/27421535.

Johnson, A., and Sack, A. (1996, November). Assessing the value of sports facilities: The importance of noneconomic factors. *Economic Development Quarterly*, 369-381.

Johnson, H., and Maki, J. (2009, August). Color sense. *American School and University, 81*(11), 143-145.

Jorgensen, P. (2001, December). Generation XXXL. *Stadia*, 18-20.

Joyner, C., and Copeland, K. (2008, March 28). Lights out for some gaining arenas. *USA Today*, 3A.

Kaplan, D. (2007). Giants and Jets to borrow $650 M each. *SportsBusiness Journal*. Retrieved October 20, 2008 from http://sportsbusinessjournal.com/index.cfm?fuseaction=article.main&articleId=54208&requestTimeout=900.

Kasper Group, Inc. (2001). Bridgeport Regional Sports and Entertainment Complex. Conference handout at University of New Haven, May 2001.

Kebric, R. (2000). *Roman people*. New York: McGraw-Hill.

Kellogg, S., and Pettigrew, S. (2008). *Toolbox for sustainable city living*. Brooklyn: South End Press.

Kick-off for 2002. (2001, January). *Stadia*, 15-16.

Kirsner, S. (2013, August/September). Exit the dragon. *Facility Manager, 29*(4), 38-39.

Klayman, B. (2008, January 22). North American sponsorship spending up in 2008. IEG Sponsorship. Retrieved January 11, 2009 from www.sponsorship.com/About-IEG/IEG-In-The-News/North-American-Sponsorship-Spending-Seen-Up-in--08.aspx.

Koch, W. (2010, August 31). Exercise converted to electricity. *USA Today*, 3A.

Kocher, E. (2007, January). Building understanding. *Athletic Business*, 43-47.

Korcek, M. (2001, September). Grass with class. *Recreation Management*, 48-50.

Kronish, E. (2002, May/June). Watch your step. *Recreation Management*, 20-25.

Kuriloff, A. (2007, March 22). Giants, Jets to split stadium naming rights 5 ways, Cross says. Bloomberg.com. Retrieved June 17, 2009 from www.bloomberg.com/apps/news?pid=20601079&sid=a2rPsEthOqvU&refer=amsports.

Lambeau renovation work fun facts. (2013, September 2-8). *SportsBusiness Journal, 16*(20), 8A.

Landry, G. (1995, March). Aeration strategies to reduce compaction. *Sports Turf Managers Association*, 4-7.

LaRue, R. (2002, August/September). Safe in their seats. *Athletic Management*, 61-63.

Lawler, R. (2008, April 16). Full specs on the Dallas Cowboys world's largest 1080p LED scoreboards. EngagedHD. Retrieved June 12, 2009 from www.engagethd.com/2008/04/16/full-specs-on-the-dallas-cowboys-worlds-largest-1080p-led-scor.

Leibowitz, J. (2001, July). When disaster strikes. *Facilities Design and Management*, 34-36.

Leonard, J.N. (1974). *Ancient America*. New York: Time-Life Books.

Leung, D. (2011, February 9). Arizona's locker room has mood lighting. ESPN.com. Retrieved July 21, 2014 from http://espn.go.com/blog/collegebasketballnation/post/_/id/22866/arizonas-locker-room-has-mood-lighting.

Leventhal, J. (2011). *Take Me Out to the Ballpark Revised and Updated: An Illustrated Tour of Baseball Parks Past and Present Featuring Every Major League Park, Plus Minor League and Negro League Parks*. New York: Black Dog & Leventhal Publishers.

Lewis, B. (1999). *Facility manager's operation and maintenance handbook*. New York: McGraw-Hill.

Liebman, J. (2008, June). Foul ballpark. Condé Nast Portfolio.com. Retrieved June 23, 2008 from www.portfolio.com/culture-lifestyle/culture-inc/sports/2008/05/12/health-code-violation.

Lindstrom, C. (1993, September). Light up the night. *Athletic Business*, 47-51.

London 2012. (2013). International Olympic Committee. Retrieved July 21, 2014 from www.olympic.org/london-2012-summer-olympics.

London Sports Council. (1975). *Film and broadcasting requirements in sports facilities*. London: Sports Council.

Los Angeles Dodgers. (2009). AM/PM All-You-Can-Eat Pavilion. Retrieved June 15, 2009 from http://losangeles.dodgers.mlb.com/la/ticketing/allyoucaneat_pavilion.jsp.

Ludtke v. Kuhn, 461 F. Supp. 86 (1978, USDC, New York).

Mach, K. (2005, September). Got pests? Kill them with heat! *Today's Facility Manager*, 24.

Madison Square Garden. (2008, April 3). Madison Square Garden unveils plans for renovations. Retrieved May 22, 2009 from www.msg.com//media/global/msg-renovations.pdf.

Make no small plans. . . . (2003). Retrieved September 15, 2003 from www.soldierfield.net/history.html.

Mallett, P. (2009). MSU fans leave big mess. Retrieved July 21, 2014 from http://environmental.jrn.msu.edu/football/talkingtrash.html.

Manchester, H. (1931). *Four centuries of sport in America: 1490-1890*. New York: Benjamin Bloom.

Mancia, D. (2003, January). Taking cover. *Stadia*, 27.

Maple Leaf Gardens history. (2002). Retrieved September 29, 2004 from www.angelfire.com/md/MattDurnford/gardens.html.

Martin, M. (2002, November). Good groundskeeping. *Recreation Management*, 23-27.

Massey, D. (2008, August 4). Mets' new base completes return to respectability. *Crain's New York Business*, 13-15.

McCarron, C. (2001, April). Reuse, recycle, rebuild. *Athletic Business*, 55-62.

McCarthy, M., and Berkowitz, S. (2008, May 8). Concern about lead prompts further question. *USA Today*, C1.

McDonnell, A. (2004, February). Wowing members with service and offerings. *Fitness Management*, 66.

McGlynn, J. (2001, November). Good relations. *Stadia*, 166-169.

McShane, L. (1996, July 13). Bowe's entourage blamed for brawl. *SouthCoast Today*. Retrieved November 22, 2004 from www.southcoasttoday.com/daily/07-96/07-13-96/c03sp077.htm.

Megan, K. (2013, April 25). Grad students oppose paying up to $400 more in fees. *Hartford Courant*, B1.

Merda, C. (2013, November 13). Fan Cost Index: The steep price of attending an NHL game. *Sun-Times*. Retrieved July 21, 2014 from http://voices.suntimes.com/sports/fan-cost-index-the-steep-price-of-attending-an-nhl-game/.

Meyer, M. (2009, August 3). One world, one dream, one year later. *Sports Illustrated*, 68-72.

MFMA maintenance tips. (2003, April). *Recreational Sports and Fitness*, 21.

Mihoces, G. (2013, April 23). Go green! Stadiums find victory in saving energy. *USA Today*, 6B.

Miniature golf on the roof at lunchtime a possibility with green roofing. (2002, January). *ASTM Standardization News*, 12.

Minnesota leading the way for bleacher safety standards. (2003, February). *Recreational Sports and Fitness*, 36.

Moler, C. (2001). Corporate sponsorship a golden opportunity. Presentation at the Athletic Business Conference, Orlando, Florida.

Monikowski, F., and Victor, T. (2005, December). Advanced fire sprinkler systems. *Buildings*, 58-59.

Monroe, L. (2008, March). Diverting construction waste. *Buildings*, 24.

Mooradian, D. (2001, July 23). American Airlines Center facts. *Amusement Business*, 23.

More than just a gym floor. (n.d.). Advertising piece from Sport-Tred, Sport Floors, Inc., Cartersville, Georgia.

Morris, R. (2004, February). Training your team. *Security Management*, 30-33.

Mrock, K. (1999, March). Turf wars. *Athletic Business*, 56-62.

MSG's lease limited to 10 years. (2013, June 15). ESPN.com. Retrieved July 21, 2014 from http://espn.go.com/new-york/nba/story/_/id/9507646/madison-square-garden-lease-limited-10-years-penn-station-renovated.

Mueller, T. (2011, January). Unearthing the Coliseum's secrets. *Smithsonian*, 41(1), 26-35.

Mullin, B., Hardy, J., and Sutton, B. (1993). *Sports marketing*. Champaign, IL: Human Kinetics.

Mundt, D. (1997, May). Laundry quandary. *Athletic Business*, 53-56.

Munsey, P., and Suppes, C. (2009). Air Canada Center. Ballparks.com. Retrieved June 2, 2009 from http://hockey.ballparks.com/NHL/TorontoMapleLeafs/newindex.htm.

Muret, D. (2001, September 17). Liquid flows freely during NFL openers. *Amusement Business*, 1, 13.

Muret, D. (2009a, June 8-14). Sampling the menu. *SportsBusiness Journal*, 16.

Muret, D. (2009b, September 28-October 4). Star power. *SportsBusiness Journal*, 12(21), 34-35.

Muret, D. (2012, May 7-13). Menu board. *SportsBusiness Journal*, 15(6) 19.

Muret, D. (2013, August 5-11). Can facilities keep up with wireless? *SportsBusiness Journal*, 16(16), 16-21.

Murphy, J. (2008, March 27). Baseball's newest field of green. *USA Today*, 9C.

Murphy, J. (2009, May 15). A cover-up at Wimbledon's renowned Centre Court. *USA Today*, 12C.

Murphy, J. (2011, November 9). College basketball lands on the USS Carl Vinson. *USA Today*, 6C.

Nash, B., and Zullo, A. (1992). *Funtastic trivia and sticker book*. New York: Little Simon.

National Floor Safety Institute. (2011). *Slips and falls*. Retrieved July 21, 2014 from www.lmcc.com/concrete_news/1108/slip-and-fall.asp.

NBA ticket prices skyrocket. (1999, November 12). *Connecticut Post*, D9.

New York landmarks. (2002). Retrieved September 29, 2004 from www.new-york-new-york.com/madison-square-garden-new-york.htm.

NFPA. (2002). *NFPA 101: Code for safety to life from fire in buildings and structures*. Quincy, MA: National Fire Protection Association. It was written by the National Fire Protection Assoc.

Nightengale, B. (2013, May 9). Wrigley rehab no wild pitch. *USA Today*, 1C.

Noferi, C. (2003, February). Setting the eCRE standards. *Facilities Design and Management*, 16-19.

Nokia Theater at L.A. Live. (2009). L.A. Live. Retrieved June 3, 2009 from www.nokiatheatrelalive.com/content.php?section=about&page=introduction.

Office temperature can affect productivity, survey finds. (2010, January 3). *Hartford Courant*, K1.

Ortiz, J. (2013, October 4). Sewage and all, A's embrace O.co Coliseum. *USA Today*, 14C.

Outside the arena, parking is the name of the game. (1997, October). *Parking Today*, 17-18.

Packers. (2014). Shareholders. Retrieved July 21, 2014 from www.packers.com/community/shareholders.html.

Padres' park back on track. (2001, March). *Stadia*, 13.

Palmeri, C. (2009, December 7). The dividends from green offices. *Businessweek*, 15.

Panja, T. (2013, November 26). Soccer World Cup stadium costs soar by $435 million in Brazil. Bloomberg.com. Retrieved July 21, 2014 from www.bloomberg.com/news/2013-11-26/soccer-world-cup-stadium-costs-soar-by-435-million-in-brazil.html.

Park, B., and Murphy, J. (2009, March). Skin surface selection and management for baseball and softball infields. Fact Sheet 1096. Rutgers University Cooperative Extension, a unit of the Rutgers New Jersey Agricultural Experiment Station.

Patton, J. (1999, April). Fitness in flux. *Athletic Business*, 51-56.

Penny, J. (2012, December). Tailor outdoor lighting to your facility. *Buildings*, 16-17.

Penny, J., Morton, J., and Tack, D. (2011, November). Survey: Unclean restrooms impact public perception. *Buildings*, 8.

Perez, A.J. (2008, September 3). California backs mandatory lead removal from field turf. *USA Today*, 11C.

Perkins, O. (2013, August 18). Fast-food workers more often adults than teens, analysis shows. *The Plain Dealer*. Retrieved July 21, 2014 from www.cleveland.com/business/index.ssf/2013/08/fast-food_workers_more_often_a.html.

Perry, F. (1997, January). Smooth operators. *Athletic Business*, 55-61.

Perry, F. (2002a, March/April). Infield care requires a variety of techniques. *SODAsite*, 11.

Perry, P. (2002b, October). Renewal time. *Athletic Business*, 52-56.

Pihos, P. (2001, January). Past and present. *Stadia*, 71-72.

Pioneer Athletics. (1998). *Designer fields: Stadium maintenance handbook*. Cleveland: Pioneer Athletics.

Pitzl, M. (1996, March 10). Tax protest a tea party: Stadium-levy foes rally support for petition drive. *Arizona Republic*, B1.

Police report: Sausagegate. (2003, July 9). From ESPN.com. Retrieved July 21, 2014 from http://espn.go.com/page2/s/sausagegate/030710.html.

Popke, M. (2000, September). Taking root. *Athletic Business*, 53-62.

Popke, M. (2001, May). Mixing it up. *Athletic Business*, 45-52.

Popke, M. (2003, January). Playground confidential. *Athletic Business*, 9-10.

Popke, M. (2009, November). The unforgiving. *Athletic Business*, 33(11), 34-35.

Popke, M. (2012a, October). Making concessions. *Athletic Business*, 36(10), 67-68.

Popke, M. (2012b, October). Moving water. *Athletic Business*, 36(10), 23-30.

Porter, J. (2007, July 23). Halls of ivy—and crumbling plaster. *Business Week*, 32.

Quinnipiac University. (n.d.). Introducing the TD Banknorth Sports Center at Quinnipiac University. Retrieved July 21, 2014 from www.quinnipiac.edu/prebuilt/pdf/TDBanknorthFactSheet.pdf?SPSID=88001&DB_OEM_ID=17500.

Rabin, C. (2009, March 25). Florida Marlins stadium won approval with one-two punch. *Miami Herald*. Retrieved June 17, 2009 from www.marlinsnewballpark.com/news/03-25-09_approval_with_one-two_punch.php.

Rabin, C., and Haggman, M. (2009, March 24). Miami-Dade agrees to pay share of Florida Marlins stadium. *Miami Herald*. Retrieved June 17, 2009 from www.marlinsnewballpark.com/news/03-24-09_miami-dade_to_pay_share.php.

Raymond James Stadium. (2009). Policies/security. Retrieved June 17, 2009 from www.raymondjames.com/stadium/policies_security.htm.

Read, D. (2013, February/March). Indoor innovations. *Athletic Management*, 25(2), 55-61.

Real story of the ancient Olympic Games, the. (2002). Retrieved June 13, 2002 from www.museum.upenn.edu/new/olympics/olympicintro.shtml.

Remigino-Knapp, E. (2008, April 10). Letter from William H. Hall High School athletic director to neighbors (personal communication).

Repair backlog in Broward County. (2003, September, 23). *Schoolhouse Beat* (e-mail newsletter).

Richman, I. (2001, November/December). Quick change artist. *Facility Manager*, 32-34.

Roderick, L., and Quintana, R. (1996, May). *Safety and ergonomics manual*. El Paso: University of Texas at El Paso.

Rogers, J. (1994, December). Bright prospects. *Athletic Business*, 52-56.

Rogers, J., III, and Stier, J. (1995, May). Sowing seeds. *Athletic Business*, 49-56.

Rogers, M. (2008, August 24). Beijing trumps Athens . . . and then some. Yahoo Sports. Retrieved August 26, 2008 from http://sports.yahoo.com/olympics/news?slug=ro-beijinglegacy082408.

Rossman-Reich, P. (2013, February 22). Northwestern's purple pricing experiment. *Lake the Post*. Retrieved July 21, 2014 from www.laketheposts.com/2013/02/22/north-westerns-purple-pricing-experiment-022213/.

RSM McGladrey. (2009, December). Analysis of the estimated historical tax revenue benefit to state, county and local governmental agencies from activities associated with major professional sports facilities in Minnesota. Retrieved July 21, 2014 from http://prod.static.vikings.clubs.nfl.com/assets/docs/download-rsm-study-021511.pdf.

Ryan, K. (2004, March). A stadium in the park. *Recreation Management*, 52-53.

Ryan, N. (2009, October 29). NASCAR, rooted in fossil fuels, turns over new, green leaf. *USA Today*, C1.

Ryan, P. (2002, July). Ready for anything. *Stadia*, 17-20.

Sadler, D. (2013, April/May). 34 minutes: The inside story of what was going on behind the scenes during the Super Bowl power failure. *Facility Manager*, 29(2), 48-53.

Safeguarding employees from workplace violence. (2001, July). *Facilities Design and Management*, 11.

San Diego Convention Center adopts safety measures. (2001, November/December). *Facility Manager*, 12.

San Francisco Giants press release. (2014, June 24). San Francisco Giants and Bon Appétit Management Company open The Garden at AT&T Park. Retrieved July 21, 2014 from http://sanfrancisco.giants.mlb.com/news/article.jsp?ymd=20140624&content_id=81371866&vkey=pr_sf&c_id=sf.

San Francisco Municipal Health Code (Article 19 A through E), Smoking Pollution Control Ordinance. (Added by Proposition P, November 8, 1983).

Sanders, P. (1998, April). The real cost of lighting. *Parking Today*, 14-17.

Sartori, A. (2011). European stadium insight 2011. KPMG. http://www.kpmg.com/US/en/Pages/default.aspx.

Scandrett, D. (1998, December). Bleachers. *Athletic Business*, 86-91.

Schackner, B. (2005, June 16). Pitt replacing Petersen Center roof already. *Post-Gazette*. Retrieved June 20, 2005 from www.post-gazette.com/pg/05167/522439.stm.

Schlossberg, D. (1983). *The baseball catalog*. Middle Village, NY: Jonathan David.

Schoeffler, N. (2013, December 15). Your scraps, her compost. *Hartford Courant*, 1D.

Schoenberg, D. (2001). Madison Square Garden turns 30. Retrieved October 16, 2001 from http://thegarden.com/cgi-bin2/msg?function=loadTemplate&file=about.html.

Schumacher, D. (2001, January). Keeping the score. *Stadia*, 29-31.

Shenker, J. (2002). Staff retention. Presentation at the Athletic Business Conference, Orlando, Florida.

Sherman, R. (1997, October). Strengthening weight rooms. *Athletic Business*, 74-80.

Sherman, R. (1998, April). Concessions and codes. *Athletic Business*, 63-67.

Sherrard, T. (2009, November). Green at the forefront. *American Schools and University*, 232-233.

Sherrard, T., and Boyer, S. (2009, March). Sustainability is a team sport. *Recreation Management*, 10(3), 10-11.

Sibold, S. (2002). The Olympic legacy. Retrieved December 19, 2002 from www.oval.ucalgary.ca/oval_olympics/oly_olylegacy.asp.

Sieger, S., and Patel, J. (2001, July). Striking a deal. *Stadia*, 62-65.

Simmelkjaer, M. (2006, September 25). Reporter's notebook: The Saints come marching in. *ABC News*. Retrieved June 16, 2009 from http://abcnews.go.com/US/story?id=2487491&page=1.

Simons, R. (2002, July). Chartered territory. *Stadia*, 44-46.

Single, E., and McKenzie, D. (1991, December). The regulation of alcohol in sports events. Retrieved February 6, 2003 from www.ccsa.ca/docs/alcsports.htm.

Slash water use with free resources. (2013, November). *Buildings*, 11.

Smith, D. (2003, March). BC culture shock. *Contingency Planning and Management*, 40-41.

Society of Fire Protection Engineers. (2002). *The SFPE handbook of fire protection engineering* (3rd ed.). Quincy, MA: National Fire Protection Association.

SODA. (1993). Member survey conducted by Sportsplex Operators and Developers Association, unpublished.

Sport disasters. (2003). Retrieved September 29, 2004 from http://print.factmonster.com/ipka/A0001453.html.

Sport England. (2010). Corby International Pool: Facility case study. London: Sport England.

Sports people: Boxing; Victory is upheld (1989, October 13). The New York Times. Retrieved November 22, 2014 from: http://www.nytimes.com/1989/10/13/sports/sports-people-boxing-victory-is-upheld.html.

St. Louis Cardinals. (2013). Dynamic pricing. Retrieved July 21, 2014 from http://stlouis.cardinals.mlb.com/stl/ticketing/dynamic.jsp.

Stacey, M. (2007, June 27). Court OKs searches at football games. USAToday.com. Retrieved June 17, 2009 from www.usatoday.com/sports/football/2007-06-27-2194225452_x.htm.

Stadium and arena sponsorship. (1998, June). *Facilities,* 46.

Stadium suit still alive. (1996, May 18). *Washington Post,* HO2.

Staples Center by the numbers. (2000, July/August). *Facility Manager,* 27.

Steinbach, P. (2000, May). Romper rooms. *Athletic Business,* 84-92.

Steinbach, P. (2001a, April). Ground control. *Athletic Business,* 89-97.

Steinbach, P. (2001b, May). Night games. *Athletic Business,* 61.

Steinbach, P. (2002, March). Dirty works. *Athletic Business,* 72-79.

Steinbach, P. (2006, April). The ground up. *Athletic Business,* 30(4), 88-99.

Steinbach, P. (2008, June). The rise and falls of the stadium escalator. *Athletic Business,* 14-16.

Steinbach, P. (2010a, January). Fire and mice. *Athletic Business,* 34(1), 10-12.

Steinbach, P. (2010b, September). Unappetizing operations. *Athletic Business,* 34(9), 12-14.

Steinbach, P. (2010c, October). Safeco savings. *Athletic Business,* 34(10), 33-38.

Steinbach, P. (2012, January). Court decisions. *Athletic Business,* 36(1), 23-28.

Steinbach, P. (2013, November). Switched on. *Athletic Business,* 37(11), 44-49.

Stewart, M. (2009). *The management myth: Why the "experts" keep getting it wrong.* New York: Norton.

Suddath, C. (2013, September 5). Last call. *Bloomberg's BusinessWeek,* 63-65.

Sullivan, B. (1995, September 15). Dallas maverick. *Houston Chronicle,* B1.

Sullivan, B. (1996, July 25). In Atlanta, the bus stops here—or there. *Houston Chronicle,* A1.

Swartz, J. (2009, March 25). Leaving PCs on overnight costs companies $2.8B a year. *USA Today,* 4B.

Swimming pool guidelines. (1997). Alaska Department of Education.

Table: SNR01. Highest rates for total cases—injuries and illnesses: 2007 (2008). OSHA. Retrieved November 26, 2008 from www.bls.gov/iif/oshwc/osh/os/ostb1905.txt.

Team Marketing Report. (2009). Fan cost index. Retrieved August 19, 2009 from http://teammarketing.com/fancost/.

Tech puts $45 million face lift on Olympic legacy. (2004, August 12). Georgia Institute of Technology. Retrieved April 16, 2008 from www.gatech.edu/newsroom/release.htm?id=276.

Teicholz, E., and Noferi, C. (2002, January). Higher ED integrates CAFM better. *Facilities Design and Management,* 13-14.

Tepfer, D. (1999, November 7). 4 neighbors sue Fairfield U. to halt use of athletic fields. *Connecticut Post,* A21.

The power plan. (2010, June). *Discover Magazine,* 47-51.

The score. (2012, December). *Athletic Business,* 36(12), 11.

Top security threats. (2002). Springfield, VA: Pinkerton Service Corporation.

Toro. (2004, December 22). Toro to prepare football field for the 2005 Rose Bowl. Retrieved June 14, 2009 from www.thetorocompany.com/companyinfo/pressrel/rose_bowl_12222004.pdf.

Touched by an Angeles. (2000, July/August). *Facility Manager,* 12.

Townsend, B. (2003, January/February). On dasher! *Facility Manager,* 18-21.

Trest, G. (2003, February). Effective crisis management. *Today's Facility Manager,* 26-28, 41.

Tridium. (2009). Case study. Retrieved June 12, 2009 from www.tridium.com/galleries/case-studies-gallery/CS-ICEsheffield.pdf.

Trotter, B. (1996, January). The cutting edge. *Athletic Business,* 61-64.

Trusty, B., and Trusty, S. (1995, February). Mowing tips: Cutting heights, frequencies, and patterns. *Sports Turf Managers Association,* 1-3.

Turner, D. (2005, September 7). Estimated cost of repairing Superdome: $100 million. *USA Today.* Retrieved June 16, 2009 from www.usatoday.com/sports/2005-09-07-superdome-future_x.htm.

Turner, E., and Hauser, D. (1994, May). Safe and sanitary. *Athletic Business,* 61-64.

Understanding the hazard. (2000). New York: Factory Mutual Insurance Company.

U.S. Green Building Council. (2008). A grand slam for Washington, DC. Retrieved November 25, 2014 from www.usgbc.org.

Varian, B. (2009, January 22). High court rejects a Tampa lawsuit aimed at ending searches of fans at NFL games. *St. Petersburg Times.* Retrieved June 17, 2009 from www.tampabay.com/news/humaninterest/article969580.ece.

Varouhakis, M. (2004, November 12). Final cost of Olympics soars to $11.6B. Retrieved November 12, 2004 from http://news.yahoo.com/news?tmpl+story&u=/ap/20041112/ap_on_sp_ol/oly_athens_cost.

Vekshin, A. (2012, April 16-22). The building boom that's sinking Stockton. *Bloomberg's BusinessWeek,* 45-46.

VenueDataSource. (2013, February/March). *Facility Manager,* 29(1), 14.

Vertical Alliance's Sports Marketing Newsletter. (2004, July 29). Vol. 3, Issue 30.

Victory Park. (2009). VictoryPark.com Retrieved July 28, 2009 from www.victorypark.com.

Viklund, R. (1995, July). High-performance floors. *Athletic Business,* 41-44.

Virginia Waste Management Board Enforcement Action. (2002). Consent order. Retrieved June 14, 2009 from www.deq.state.va.us/enforcement/finalorders/robinson.pdf.

Vivian, J., Daugherty, D., and Dunn, R. (1994, March/April). Bloodborne pathogens. *Facility Manager,* 17-19.

Walinski, G. (2012, June/July). Can you afford not to evaluate? *Facility Manager, 28*(3), 40-41.

Walker, M., and Stotlar, D. (1997). *Sport facility management.* Sudbury, MA: Jones and Bartlett.

Watson, J. (1998, January). Waterworks. *Athletic Business,* 59-64.

What fans want—Arup survey. (2012, June). *Stadium and Arena Management,* 4.

Whelan, M. (2001, March). Down to the wire. *Stadia,* 85-87.

Whitney, T., and Foulkes, T. (1994, December). Keep the noise down. *Athletic Business,* 57-60.

Wiedeman, R. (2013, July 22-28). Making the stadium more like your couch. *Bloomberg's BusinessWeek,* 30-31.

Wiggins, J. (1993, August). Building a budget. *Athletic Business,* 61-66.

Wilkinson, D. (1988). *The event management and marketing institute.* Toronto. The Wilkinson Group

World Cup security plan appears to be working. (2006, June 18). Dawn, the Internet Edition. Retrieved June 17, 2009 from www.dawn.com/2006/06/18/spt14.htm.

WOW. (2009). The WOW Foundation. Retrieved June 16, 2009 from www.workoutworld.com/aboutus_foundation.php.

Wrightson, Johnson, Haddon, and Williams. (2004). Stadia. Retrieved April 12, 2004 from www.wjhw.com/aac.html.

Yaffa, J. (2014, January 2). The waste and corruption of Vladimir Putin's 2014 Winter Olympics. *Business Week.* Retrieved July 21, 2014 from www.businessweek.com/articles/2014-01-02/the-2014-winter-olympics-in-sochi-cost-51-billion.

Yaeger, C. (1998, November/December). Sydney 2000: The first green Olympics. *Facility Manager,* 17-21.

Yarborough, J. (1998, October 15). Let it snow. *American Way,* 78.

Zaretsky, M. (2002, October 2). Ravens seeking property tax break. *New Haven Register,* B3.

Zikmund, W., and d'Amico, M. (1996). *Basic marketing.* St. Paul: West.

Index

Note: Page numbers followed by an italicized *t* indicate a table.

About the Author

Gil B. Fried, JD, is a professor at the University of New Haven in Connecticut. He has taught sport facility management for more than 20 years and has written numerous articles, books, and book chapters on sport facility management issues. Fried speaks throughout the United States on issues such as building and financing facilities and dealing with risk management concerns.

He was the director of risk management for OR&L Facility Management, which manages several million square feet of space. He has also worked with the International Association of Venue Managers (IAVM) and developed the curriculum and materials for the IAVM's Academy for Venue Safety & Security.

Besides taking pictures of numerous sport facilities to include in future versions of this text, Fried enjoys playing badminton, farming, being with his wife and kids, and traveling.

*You'll find
other outstanding
sport management resources at*

www.HumanKinetics.com

In the U.S. call

1-800-747-4457

Australia...08 8372 0999
Canada 1-800-465-7301
Europe....................................... +44 (0) 113 255 5665
New Zealand...0800 222 062

HUMAN KINETICS
The Information Leader in Physical Activity & Health
P.O. Box 5076 • Champaign, IL 61825-5076 USA